# 3-D Surface Geometry and Reconstruction:

## Developing Concepts and Applications

Umesh Chandra Pati
*National Institute of Technology Rourkela, India*

| | |
|---|---|
| Managing Director: | Lindsay Johnston |
| Senior Editorial Director: | Heather A. Probst |
| Book Production Manager: | Sean Woznicki |
| Development Manager: | Joel Gamon |
| Acquisitions Editor: | Erika Gallagher |
| Typesetter: | Jennifer Romanchak |
| Cover Design: | Nick Newcomer, Lisandro Gonzalez |

Published in the United States of America by
Information Science Reference (an imprint of IGI Global)
701 E. Chocolate Avenue
Hershey PA 17033
Tel: 717-533-8845
Fax: 717-533-8661
E-mail: cust@igi-global.com
Web site: http://www.igi-global.com

Library of Congress Cataloging-in-Publication Data

3-D surface geometry and reconstruction: developing concepts and applications / Umesh Chandra Pati, editor.
    p. cm.
  Includes bibliographical references and index.
  Summary: "This book provides developers and scholars with an extensive collection of research articles in the expanding field of 3D reconstruction, investigating the concepts, methodologies, applications and recent developments in the field of 3D reconstruction"-- Provided by publisher.
  ISBN 978-1-4666-0113-0 (hardcover) -- ISBN 978-1-4666-0114-7 (ebook) -- ISBN 978-1-4666-0115-4 (print & perpetual access) 1. Geometry, Descriptive. 2. Three-dimensional imaging. 3. Surfaces, Models of. 4. Surfaces--Areas and volume. I. Pati, Umesh Chandra, 1966-
  QA521.A155 2012
  516'.1--dc23
                                    2011042022

British Cataloguing in Publication Data
A Cataloguing in Publication record for this book is available from the British Library.

All work contributed to this book is new, previously-unpublished material. The views expressed in this book are those of the authors, but not necessarily of the publisher.

# Table of Contents

**Foreword**.................................................................................................................................xii

**Preface**....................................................................................................................................xv

**Acknowledgment**.................................................................................................................. xx

### Section 1
### Introductory Chapters

**Chapter 1**
Methods of 3D Object Shape Acquisition .................................................................................... 1
> *Pavel Zemcik, Brno University of Technology, Czech Republic*
> *Michal Spanel, Brno University of Technology, Czech Republic*
> *Premysl Krsek, Brno University of Technology, Czech Republic*
> *Miloslav Richter, Brno University of Technology, Czech Republic*

**Chapter 2**
Projective Geometry for 3D Modeling of Objects........................................................................ 28
> *Rimon Elias. German University in Cairo, Egypt*

**Chapter 3**
PDE-Based Image Processing: Image Restoration ...................................................................... 49
> *Rajeev Srivastava, Institute of Technology, Banaras Hindu University (ITBHU), India*

### Section 2
### 3D Reconstruction

**Chapter 4**
Hybrid GPU Local Delaunay Triangulation through Points Consolidation ..................................... 91
> *Carlos Buchart, CEIT, Spain & TECNUN (University of Navarra), Spain*
> *Aiert Amundarain, CEIT, Spain*
> *Diego Borro, CEIT, Spain & TECNUN (University of Navarra), Spain*

**Chapter 5**
3D Reconstruction of Underwater Natural Scenes and Objects Using Stereo Vision ........................ 114
    *C.J. Prabhakar, Kuvempu University, India*
    *P.U. Praveen Kumar, Kuvempu University, India*
    *P.S. Hiremath, Gulbarga University, India*

**Chapter 6**
3D Reconstruction of Graph Objects, Scenes, and Environments .......................................................... 137
    *Suhana Chikatla, Wallace State, USA*
    *Ukaiko Bitrus-Ojiambo, St. Paul's University, Kenya*

**Chapter 7**
Depth Estimation for HDR Images ........................................................................................................ 165
    *S. Manikandan, Electronics and Radar Development Establishment, Defense Research*
      *and Development Organization, India*

**Chapter 8**
Monocular-Cues Based 3-D Reconstruction: A Comparative Review ..................................................... 181
    *Sudheer Tumu, State University of New York-Albany, USA*
    *Viswanath Avasarala, GE Global Research, USA*
    *Sai Tejaswi Jonnalagadda, Hetero Med Solutions, India*
    *Prasad Wadekar, Mahindra Satyam, USA*

**Chapter 9**
Image Based 3D Modeling and Rendering from Single View Perspective Images ............................. 197
    *S. Mohan, Dr.N.G.P Institute of Technology, India*
    *S. Murali, Maharaja Institute of Technology, India*

**Section 3**
**Real-World Applications**

**Chapter 10**
Surface Modelling Using Discrete Basis Functions for Real-Time Automatic Inspection ................ 216
    *Paul O'Leary, Institute for Automation, University of Leoben, Austria*
    *Matthew Harker, Institute for Automation, University of Leoben, Austria*

**Chapter 11**
Application of Red, Green, and Blue Color Channels in 3D Shape Measurement ............................ 265
    *Zonghua Zhang, Hebei University of Technology, China*

**Chapter 12**
Widely-Separated Stereo Views Turn into 3D Objects: An Application ............................................. 284
    *Rimon Elias, German University in Cairo, Egypt*

**Chapter 13**
Complementary Part Detection and Reassembly of 3D Fragments........................................................314
    *Vandana Dixit Kaushik, Harcourt Butler Technological Institute, India*
    *Phalguni Gupta, Indian Institute of Technology Kanpur, India*

**Chapter 14**
3D Surface Reconstruction from Multiviews for Prosthetic Design ......................................................338
    *Nasrul Humaimi Bin Mahmood, Universiti Teknologi Malaysia, Malaysia*

**Compilation of References** ................................................................................................................352

**About the Contributors** ....................................................................................................................375

**Index**...................................................................................................................................................381

# Detailed Table of Contents

Foreword.................................................................................................................................xii

Preface..................................................................................................................................xv

Acknowledgment...................................................................................................................xx

### Section 1
### Introductory Chapters

**Chapter 1**

Methods of 3D Object Shape Acquisition ................................................................................. 1

*Pavel Zemcik, Brno University of Technology, Czech Republic*
*Michal Spanel, Brno University of Technology, Czech Republic*
*Premysl Krsek, Brno University of Technology, Czech Republic*
*Miloslav Richter, Brno University of Technology, Czech Republic*

This chapter describes the methods for acquisition of 3D data from surface as well as internal structure of the existing objects. The acquisition methods of interest are optical methods based on objects surface image processing and CT/NMR sensors that explore the object volume structure. The focus is on 3D surface shape acquisition methods based on multiple views, methods using single view video sequences, and methods that use a single view with a controlled light source. A set of algorithms suitable for the acquired 3D data processing and simplification are shown to demonstrate how the models data can be processed.

**Chapter 2**

Projective Geometry for 3D Modeling of Objects.................................................................... 28

*Rimon Elias. German University in Cairo, Egypt*

This chapter discusses the basic elements of projective geometry that are needed to reconstruct objects in 3D space. In particular, it discusses the role of this branch of geometry in reconstructing basic entities (e.g. 3D points, 3D lines and planes) in 3D space from multiple images. It investigates the geometrical relationships when one or two cameras are observing the scene creating single-view and two-view geometry. Finally, different approaches to deal with the existence of noise or inaccuracy in general are presented.

**Chapter 3**

PDE-Based Image Processing: Image Restoration ............................................................................ 49

*Rajeev Srivastava, Institute of Technology, Banaras Hindu University (ITBHU), India*

This chapter explains partial differential equation (PDE) based approaches for image modelling and processing for image restoration task. The general basic concepts of partial differential equation based image modelling and processing techniques are discussed. As a case study, the topic in consideration is oriented towards image restoration using PDEs formalism since image restoration is considered to be an important pre-processing task for 3D surface geometry and reconstruction and many other applications. An image may be subjected to various types of noises during its acquisition leading to degraded quality of the image. Here, the PDE-based models for removal of these noises are discussed.

**Section 2**
**3D Reconstruction**

**Chapter 4**

Hybrid GPU Local Delaunay Triangulation through Points Consolidation ......................................... 91

*Carlos Buchart, CEIT, Spain & TECNUN (University of Navarra), Spain*

*Aiert Amundarain, CEIT, Spain*

*Diego Borro, CEIT, Spain & TECNUN (University of Navarra), Spain*

This chapter presents a hybrid reconstruction method by combining interpolating and approximating features together in order to be implemented efficiently in parallel architectures. Hybrid methods are useful in areas such sculpting, medicine, and cultural heritage, where details must be preserved. The proposed method makes use of a point projection operator to create a regular distributed and noise free set of points, which is reconstructed using local Delaunay triangulations. Both points projection and triangulation methods are studied in its the basic serial version, but aiming to design parallel versions (more specifically GPU implementations) that increase their performance. The adaptations required for the parallel reconstruction are discussed, as well asand several implementation details are given.

**Chapter 5**

3D Reconstruction of Underwater Natural Scenes and Objects Using Stereo Vision ....................... 114

*C.J. Prabhakar, Kuvempu University, India*

*P.U. Praveen Kumar, Kuvempu University, India*

*P.S. Hiremath, Gulbarga University, India*

3D reconstruction for underwater applications is a relatively recent research area with higher complexity than the 3D reconstruction for general applications. 3D reconstruction of underwater natural scenes and objects is a challenging problem due to light propagation in underwater. In contrast to light propagation in the air, the light rays are attenuated and scattered, having a great effect on image quality. This chapter proposes a preprocessing technique to enhance degraded underwater images as well as a stereo vision based 3D reconstruction technique to reconstruct 3D surface of underwater objects. The developed reconstruction technique is expected to be robust enough to reconstruct objects or scenes in a realistic manner. The system is robust, which means that it should be able to reconstruct the object or scene which that is far away and captured in turbid water.

**Chapter 6**

3D Reconstruction of Graph Objects, Scenes, and Environments.........................................................137

*Suhana Chikatla, Wallace State, USA*

*Ukaiko Bitrus-Ojiambo, St. Paul's University, Kenya*

This chapter focuses on the theoretical background, pedagogical practice, usability, and applicability of using 3D surface charts. It seeks to discuss the importance of surface objects, scenes, and environments reconstructed to enhance the interpretation of charts. Different types of 3D charts available: bar, line, and pie charts are described. The chapter also provides enlightenment about two new concepts i.e. "3D actual" and "3D obvious" charts. Indeed, the visual communication theory provides a relevant framework from which educators can design and develop a tool to aid learners who need visually representative data via charts, graphs, and pictures to enhance learning.

**Chapter 7**

Depth Estimation for HDR Images.................................................................................................165

*S. Manikandan, Electronics and Radar Development Establishment, Defense Research*
*and Development Organization, India*

This chapter introduces a stereo matching algorithm that analyses grayscale or color images to estimate the disparity map for 3D scene reconstruction. The proposed algorithm consists of two major techniques namely conversion of High Dynamic Range (HDR) images to Low Dynamic Range (LDR) images or Standard Dynamic Range (SDR) images and estimating the depth from the converted LDR / SDR stereo images. Local based tone mapping technique is used for the conversion of the HDR images to SDR images. Depth estimation is done based on the corner features of the stereo pair images and block matching algorithm.

**Chapter 8**

Monocular-Cues Based 3-D Reconstruction: A Comparative Review ...............................................181

*Sudheer Tumu, State University of New York-Albany, USA*

*Viswanath Avasarala, GE Global Research, USA*

*Sai Tejaswi Jonnalagadda, Hetero Med Solutions, India*

*Prasad Wadekar, Mahindra Satyam, USA*

In recent years, some interesting breakthroughs have been made in constructing depth maps of images using monocular cues. This chapter provides a brief review on 3D reconstruction, with a particular emphasis on monocular-cues based reconstruction. Two recent 3D reconstruction techniques that use machine-learning algorithms trained by monocular cues are explained. The success of these algorithms is their ability to not only use local features of image regions but also their global context in relation to the entire image. The fusion approach improves the 3-D estimation accuracy significantly as compared to the original approaches.

**Chapter 9**

Image Based 3D Modeling and Rendering from Single View Perspective Images........................... 197
S. Mohan, Dr.N.G.P Institute of Technology, India

S. Murali, Maharaja Institute of Technology, India

In computer vision, 3D modeling refers to the process of developing 3D representation of the real world objects with systematic procedure. The 3D models can be built based on geometric information about the object or scene to be modeled using CAD/CAM software. This chapter addresses a method to construct 3D wireframes from single view perspective image based on edge length. A method for rectifying the perspective distortion has been discussed. An application of touring into picture has also been explained.

## Section 3
## Real-World Applications

**Chapter 10**

Surface Modelling Using Discrete Basis Functions for Real-Time Automatic Inspection ................ 216
Paul O'Leary, Institute for Automation, University of Leoben, Austria

Matthew Harker, Institute for Automation, University of Leoben, Austria

The chapter focuses on the applications of discrete basis functions in surface modelling and automatic inspection. Emphasis is placed on a formal and stringent mathematical background, which enables an analytical a- priori estimation of the performance of the methods for specific applications. A completely new approach to synthesizing constrained basis functions is presented. The resulting constrained basis functions form a unitary matrix, i.e. are optimal with respect to numerical error propagation and have many applications, e.g. as admissible functions in Galerkin methods for solution of boundary value and initial value problems. A number of case studies are presented, which show the applicability of the methods in real applications.

**Chapter 11**

Application of Red, Green, and Blue Color Channels in 3D Shape Measurement ........................... 265
Zonghua Zhang, Hebei University of Technology, China

Optical full-field measurement techniques have been widely studied in academia and applied to many actual fields of automated inspection, reverse engineering, cosmetic surgery, and so on. This chapter presents the application of red, green, and blue channels as a carrier in measuring 3D shape of objects surface. Since three fringe patterns can be simultaneously projected and captured through a single composite RGB image, the acquisition time reduces to 1/3 of the value by the gray fringe pattern projection. Two kinds of application methods of red, green, and blue as a carrier are discussed. The testing results confirm that red, green, and blue channels can be used as a carrier to reduce the acquisition time.

**Chapter 12**

Widely-Separated Stereo Views Turn into 3D Objects: An Application ........................................... 284
Rimon Elias, German University in Cairo, Egypt

This chapter describes different steps proposed to perform scene modelling through wide baseline set of images. The camera parameters are assumed to be known approximately within some range according to the error margins of the sensors used such as inertial devices. The proposed technique is based on detecting junctions in all images using the so-called JUDOCA operator and through homographic transformation; correlation is applied to achieve point correspondences. The match set is triangulated to obtain a set of 3D points, and point clustering is then performed to achieve a bounding box for each obstacle, which may be used for localization purposes by itself. Finally, a voxelization scheme is applied to determine a volumetric representation for each obstacle.

## Chapter 13

Complementary Part Detection and Reassembly of 3D Fragments......................................................314

*Vandana Dixit Kaushik, Harcourt Butler Technological Institute, India*

*Phalguni Gupta, Indian Institute of Technology Kanpur, India*

This chapter has explored a problem for determining the complementary part of a fragment of an object and of reassembling them to form the object. It has proposed an efficient surface inspection algorithm which detects the corresponding cleavage sites of fragments and registers them so that the object can be formed from the given fragments. For a given 3D scanned image of broken objects, the algorithm identifies the rough sites of the broken object, transforms the object to a suitable alignment, registers it with its complementary part, which belongs to the same object, and finds the local correspondence among the fragmented parts. The algorithm is found to be very effective on objects of ceramic material and archeological artifacts.

## Chapter 14

3D Surface Reconstruction from Multiviews for Prosthetic Design .....................................................338

*Nasrul Humaimi Bin Mahmood, Universiti Teknologi Malaysia, Malaysia*

Existing methods that use a fringe projection technique for prosthetic designs produce good results for the trunk and lower limbs; however, the devices used for this purpose are expensive. This chapter suggests an alternative approach to design prosthetic devices using multiviews reconstruction method and offers a significant advance for orthotic as well as prosthetic design by using an image processing technique. The design and evaluation methodology, consisting of a number of techniques suitable for prosthetic design, is developed. The 3D model is obtained by a computer program, while the 3D data uses the shape-from-silhouette technique in an approximately circular motion. The methodology developed is shown to be useful for prosthetic designers as an alternative to manual impression during the design.

**Compilation of References** ........................................................................................................352

**About the Contributors** ..........................................................................................................375

**Index** .................................................................................................................................381

# Foreword

3D reconstruction has been an important area in computer vision research since the mid-80s. The real-world is inherently three-dimensional; consequently, visual reconstruction provides an essential interface for digital technologies. This leads to numerous potential applications of 3D reconstruction from industrial inspection to clinical analysis and entertainment production.

Computer vision research has investigated approaches to reconstruction using both active illumination and natural images. Early approaches using laser stripe projection achieved highly accurate surface measurement, but require controlled surface and capture conditions, limiting their use to applications such as industrial inspection and reverse engineering. Structured light pattern projection systems allow area based surface measurement reducing acquisition time and making possible the 3D reconstruction of dynamic objects. Recent introduction of low-cost active measurement technologies, using infra-red illumination patterns, have enabled 3D surface reconstruction in the home as an interface for interactive entertainment.

Advances in the understanding of visual geometry over the past two decades together with the introduction of robust reconstruction algorithms have achieved accurate reconstruction from passive image and video acquisition. This has opened up the potential for visual reconstruction in real-world scenes with complex illumination, dynamic objects such as people, and complex geometry. Recent progress has seen the introduction of systems for image-based reconstruction of historic monuments and large-scale urban environments to create highly detailed models. Video-based 3D reconstruction allows the acquisition of dynamic scenes such as people enabling real-time acquisition of detailed non-rigid surface deformation. Recent advances in robust 3D reconstruction in natural real-world scenes are enabling widespread application of computer vision for human-computer interfaces, biometrics, security, automotive, medical, and entertainment applications.

In this book, the editor has assembled contributions covering the foundations, recent advances, and applications of 3D reconstruction. The book is divided into three sections covering introductory material, 3D reconstruction, and applications. This provides both an introduction to methods of 3D reconstruction and a state-of-the-art review of reconstruction techniques and applications.

The first section comprises three chapters giving an introduction to the field. The first chapter reviews methods of 3D shape reconstruction including both surface and volume measurement technologies (CT/NMR). Methods for 3D shape analysis together with single and multiple view reconstruction are reviewed. The second chapter introduces visual or projective geometry which provides the theoretical foundation for reconstruction from images. Practical considerations in visual reconstruction are also discussed. The third chapter of this section focuses on partial-differential equation (PDE) based methods for visual analysis. PDE based methods are an important class of techniques for both image processing xiii

(restoration, enhancement, segmentation) and computer vision (optic flow, stereo reconstruction). This chapter provides an introduction to this class of methods together with a comparison between PDE and alternative approaches.

The second book section focuses on the central topic of 3D reconstruction with six chapters covering state-of-the-art topics from fast GPU based reconstruction to image-based 3D reconstruction and rendering. This section provides a review of the state-of-the-art in a number of topics related to visual reconstruction. The first chapter in this section details a method for surface reconstruction from point features, which are connected using a local Delaunay triangulation. GPU implementation of the approach is also considered giving efficient parallel reconstruction. Due to their parallel computational performance, GPU implementation of computer vision algorithms, including 3D reconstruction, has recently received considerable interest. The second chapter in this section considers the problem of reconstruction in natural underwater scenes. This is an important practical problem for submarine navigation and underwater inspection. A review of existing approaches to underwater 3D reconstruction is presented together with a system based on reconstruction from stereo cameras. This presents a challenging problem due to the potential rapid attenuation of light propagation through water. The third chapter considers the use of information in 3D for use in education to enhance understanding. The chapter reviews the use of 3D information for presentation and provides insight into how 3D objects, scenes, and environments should be used. The fourth chapter considers depth estimation from high-dynamic range images. Over the past few years, high-dynamic range images and video have become available through techniques such as multiple exposure acquisition. This chapter introduced an approach for stereo matching and reconstruction from HDR images. The fifth chapter reviews recent research in reconstruction from monocular single image cues and shows how fusion of multiple monocular reconstructions can achieve improved results. The final contribution to this section continues this theme presenting a method to extract 3D models from single images which exploits cues such as symmetry. Image-based rendering is employed to achieve realistic rendering allowing the generation of virtual views within the image based on the recovered 3D structure.

The final section of this book focuses on real-world applications of 3D reconstruction. Five chapters are presented relating to applications in inspection, measurement, and object modelling. The first chapter presents a method for real-time surface inspection using a discrete basis function representation. This representation lends itself to the task of surface inspection and is demonstrated in a number of case studies. The second chapter considers surface measurement exploiting the colour channels of a digital light projector (DLP) which allows simultaneous projection of fringe patterns. This reduces the acquisition time for gray-code structured light to 1/3 and is tested on applications for surface measurement. The third chapter considers the reconstruction of 3D object locations from widely spaced views for remote vehicle navigation. Such an approach is applicable to use of mobile vehicles for inspection in hazardous environments. The fourth chapter considers the problem of assembly of 3D part fragments, which is highly relevant in cultural heritage applications. A well-known example of this problem is the assembly of the Forma Urbis Romae ancient stone map of Rome from the hundreds of 3D scanned fragments. The final chapter considers a contemporary application of 3D reconstruction for personalised prosthetic design. The use of multiple view video-based reconstruction as a low-cost tool for acquisition of limb shape is investigated. Results demonstrate that the passive image-based reconstruction approach is potentially a useful alternative to existing active measurement technologies.

The three sections of this edited book provide an overview of the field of visual reconstruction and its applications. This provides the reader with a review of many current topics together with a snap-shot of the state-of-the-art. Progress in visual reconstruction from images and videos in complex natural scenes continues to open-up new applications. This volume demonstrates the considerable advances made over the past decade and motivates continued research in this area to develop robust algorithms for reconstruction and analysis from natural images.

*Adrian Hilton*
*University of Surrey, UK*
*July 2011*

**Adrian Hilton** *(BSc(hons), DPhil, CEng) is Professor of Computer Vision and Graphics at the University of Surrey, UK. His research interest is robust computer vision to model and understand real world scenes. Contributions include technologies for the first hand-held 3D scanner, modelling of people from images, and 3D video for games, broadcast, and film. He currently leads research investigating the use of computer vision for applications in entertainment content production, visual interaction, and clinical analysis.*

# Preface

The methods used to digitize and reconstruct the shapes of complex 3D objects have evolved rapidly in recent years due to attention from many industrial as well as research groups. To capture complete shape of an object, many thousands of samples must be acquired. The resulting mass of data requires algorithms that can efficiently and reliably generate computer models from these samples. Earlier, 3D models were used primarily in robotics and computer vision applications. The models for such applications require only salient geometric features so that the objects can be recognized. Therefore, it was unnecessary in these applications to faithfully capture every detail on the surface of the object. However, more recently, there has been considerable interest in the construction of 3D models for applications where the focus is more on visualization by humans. Obviously, the 3D models constructed must capture, to the maximum extent possible, the shape and the surface-texture information of real-world objects.

3D surface reconstruction from images is common to several research domains and there have been a number of attempts to model the 3D geometry of objects and scenes from images. These attempts provide a complete geometrical 3D description from a sequence of 2D images. The demand for constructing 3D models has been steadily growing, and it will continue to grow in the future due to its wide-ranging applications in various domains like reverse engineering, collaborative design, inspection, entertainment, virtual museums, medicine, geology, and home shopping.

This book aims to provide relevant theoretical frameworks and the latest empirical research findings in this expanding field. It is important for the readers to understand this technology and its benefits. This publication aims to provide developers and scholars with an extensive collection of research articles from the expanding field of 3D reconstruction. It deals with the concepts, methodologies, applications, and recent developments in this emerging field. An outstanding collection of latest research associated with advancements in 3D surface reconstruction is presented in this book. It is written for students, researchers, academics, professionals and industry practitioners working in this area who want to improve their understanding of the inter-related topics.

The prime intended audience of the book corresponds to educators, students, practitioners, professionals, and researchers working in the field of 3D surface reconstruction in various disciplines, e.g. computer science, electrical engineering, electronics engineering, systems science, and Information Technology. Moreover, the book will be a valuable and multifaceted resource that will provide insights about where the technology is going and will give a sample of some of the most interesting applications, critical issues, and emerging trends. This publication will be invaluable to all those required to use theoretical analysis, algorithms, and practical applications of 3D surface reconstruction technologies. It is also for those who want to gain a complete understanding of all pertinent aspects of 3D surface reconstruction. Finally, this book will be a welcome addition to academic, research, governmental, and public administration libraries' research collections.

The book presents a selection of 14 high-quality chapters, written by 27 authors from 9 different countries. The book is organized into three sections: Introductory Chapters, 3D Reconstruction, and Real-World Applications, each of which is described briefly below.

**Section 1** contains three chapters that describe fundamental aspects and give an overview of different methods applied in 3D reconstruction. The first chapter contains an overview of methods for a 3D shape from both the surface and the internal structure of the objects. The second chapter surveys many fundamental aspects of projective geometry that have been used extensively in computer vision, and the third chapter describes the basic concepts of partial differential equations based image modelling.

*Chapter 1*, entitled "Methods of 3D Object Shape Acquisition" by Pavel Zemcik, Michal Spanel, Premysl Krsek, and Miloslav Richter, describes the methods for acquisition of 3D data from surface as well as internal structure of the existing objects. The acquisition methods of interest are optical methods based on objects surface image processing and CT/NMR sensors that explore the object volume structure. The focus is on 3D surface shape acquisition methods based on multiple views, methods using single view video sequences, and methods that use a single view with a controlled light source. A set of algorithms suitable for the acquired 3D data processing and simplification are shown to demonstrate how the models data can be processed.

*Chapter 2*, entitled "Projective Geometry for 3D Modeling of Objects" by Rimon Elias, discusses the basic elements of projective geometry that is needed to reconstruct objects in 3D space. In particular, it discusses the role of this branch of geometry in reconstructing basic entities (e.g. 3D points, 3D lines and planes) in 3D space from multiple images. It investigates the geometrical relationships when one or two cameras are observing the scene creating single-view and two-view geometry. Finally, different approaches to deal with the existence of noise or inaccuracy in general are presented.

*Chapter 3*, entitled "PDE-based Image Processing: Image Restoration" by Rajeev Srivastava, explains partial differential equation (PDE) based approaches for image modelling and processing for image restoration task. The general basic concepts of partial differential equation based image modelling and processing techniques are discussed. As a case study, the topic in consideration is oriented towards image restoration using PDEs formalism since image restoration is considered to be an important pre-processing task for 3D surface geometry and reconstruction and many other applications. An image may be subjected to various types of noises during its acquisition leading to degraded quality of the image. Here, the PDE-based models for removal of these noises are discussed.

**Section 2** contains six chapters, dealing with different areas of 3D reconstruction of objects, scenes, and environments. The first chapter of this section describes a surface reconstruction method which mixes interpolating as well as approximating features and its implementation in graphics hardware. The second chapter explores 3D reconstruction of underwater natural scenes and objects based on stereo vision, whereas the next chapter provides a basic understanding of how 3D statistical visual displays aid in education. The fourth chapter proposes depth estimation for stereo pair of high dynamic range images. The fifth chapter presents fusion of 3D reconstructions generated by two seminal monocular-cue based reconstruction algorithms. and the last chapter proposes a method to extract 3D models from single view perspective images.

*Chapter 4*, entitled "Hybrid GPU Local Delaunay Triangulation through Points Consolidation" by Carlos Buchart, Aiert Amundarain, and Diego Borro, presents a hybrid reconstruction method by combining interpolating and approximating features together in order to be implemented efficiently in parallel architectures. Hybrid methods are useful in areas such sculpting, medicine, and cultural heritage, where details must be preserved. The proposed method makes use of a point projection operator to create a regular distributed and noise free set of points, which is reconstructed using local Delaunay triangulations. Both points projection and triangulation methods are studied in its basic serial version, but aiming to design parallel versions (more specifically GPU implementations) that increase their performance. The adaptations required for the parallel reconstruction are discussed, and several implementation details are given.

*Chapter 5*, entitled "3D Reconstruction of Underwater Natural Scenes and Objects using Stereo Vision" by Prabhakar C.J., Praveen Kumar P.U., and Hiremath P.S., proposes a preprocessing technique to enhance degraded underwater images as well as a stereo vision based 3D reconstruction technique to reconstruct 3D surface of underwater objects. 3D reconstruction for underwater applications is a relatively recent research area with higher complexity than the 3D reconstruction for general applications. 3D reconstruction of underwater natural scenes and objects is a challenging problem due to light propagation in underwater. In contrast to light propagation in the air, the light rays are attenuated and scattered, having a great effect on image quality. The developed reconstruction technique is expected to be robust enough to reconstruct objects or scenes in a realistic manner. The system is robust, which means that it should be able to reconstruct the object or scene which is far away and captured in turbid water.

*Chapter 6*, entitled "3D Reconstruction of Graph Objects, Scenes and Environments" by Suhana Chikatla and Ukaiko Bitrus-Oijambo, focuses on the theoretical background, pedagogical practice, usability, and applicability of using 3D surface charts. It seeks to discuss the importance of surface objects, scenes, and environments reconstructed to enhance the interpretation of charts. Different types of 3D charts available: bar, line, and pie charts are described. The chapter also provides enlightenment about two new concepts, i.e. "3D actual" and "3D obvious" charts. Indeed, the visual communication theory provides a relevant framework from which educators can design and develop a tool to aid learners who need visually representative data via charts, graphs, and pictures to enhance learning.

*Chapter 7*, entitled "Depth Estimation for HDR Images" by S. Manikandan, introduces a stereo matching algorithm that analyses grayscale or color images to estimate the disparity map for 3D scene reconstruction. The proposed algorithm consists of two major techniques, namely conversion of High Dynamic Range (HDR) images to Low Dynamic Range (LDR) images or Standard Dynamic Range (SDR) images, and estimating the depth from the converted LDR / SDR stereo images. Local based tone mapping technique is used for the conversion of the HDR images to SDR images. Depth estimation is done based on the corner features of the stereo pair images and block matching algorithm.

*Chapter 8*, entitled "Monocular-Cues Based 3-D Reconstruction: A Comparative Review" by Sudheer Tumu, Viswanath Avasarala, Sai Tejaswi Jonnalagadda, and Prasad Wadekar, provides a brief review on 3D reconstruction, with a particular emphasis on monocular-cues based reconstruction. In recent years, some interesting breakthroughs have been made in constructing depth maps of images using monocular cues. Two recent 3D reconstruction techniques that use machine-learning algorithms trained by monocular cues are explained here. The success of these algorithms is their ability to not only use local features of image regions but also their global context in relation to the entire image. The fusion approach improves the 3-D estimation accuracy significantly as compared to the original approaches.

*Chapter 9*, entitled "Image Based 3D Modeling & Rendering from Single View Perspective Images" by Mohan S., and Murali S., addresses a method to construct 3D wireframes from single view perspective image based on edge length. In computer vision, 3D modeling refers to the process of developing 3D representation of the real world objects with systematic procedure. The 3D models can be built based on geometric information about the object or scene to be modeled using CAD/CAM software. A method for rectifying the perspective distortion is discussed. An application of touring into picture is also explained.

**Section 3** consists of five chapters, describing the application of 3D reconstruction in various domains. The first chapter presents the use of discrete basis functions in surface modelling and its application to real-time automatic surface inspection. The second chapter introduces two kinds of applications of red, green and blue as a carrier and their testing by measuring the shape of objects' surface. The next chapter discusses the representation of obstacles in an environment with planar ground through wide baseline set of images in the context of teleoperation, whereas the fourth chapter presents an algorithm for identifying complementary site of objects broken into two parts, and subsequently, reassembly of 3D fragments. The last chapter explains the use of an inexpensive passive method involving 3D surface reconstruction from video images taken at multiple views and the utility of the developed methodology for prosthetic designers.

*Chapter 10,* entitled "Surface Modelling Using Discrete Basis Functions for Real-Time Automatic Inspection" by Paul O'Leary and Matthew Harker, focuses on the applications of discrete basis functions in surface modelling and automatic inspection. Emphasis is placed on a formal and stringent mathematical background, which enables an analytical a-priori estimation of the performance of the methods for specific applications. A completely new approach to synthesizing constrained basis functions is presented. The resulting constrained basis functions form a unitary matrix, i.e. are optimal with respect to numerical error propagation and have many applications, e.g. as admissible functions in Galerkin methods for solution of boundary value and initial value problems. A number of case studies are presented that show the applicability of the methods in real applications.

*Chapter 11,* entitled "Application of Red, Green and Blue Color Channels in 3D Shape Measurement" by Zonghua Zhang, presents the application of red, green, and blue channels as a carrier in measuring 3D shape of objects surface. Since three fringe patterns can be simultaneously projected and captured through a single composite RGB image, the acquisition time reduces to 1/3 of the value by the gray fringe pattern projection. Two kinds of application methods of red, green and blue as a carrier are discussed. The testing results confirm that red, green and blue channels can be used as a carrier to reduce the acquisition time. Optical full-field measurement techniques have been widely studied in academia and applied to many actual fields of automated inspection, reverse engineering, cosmetic surgery, and so on.

*Chapter 12,* entitled "Widely-Separated Stereo Views Turn into 3D Objects: An Application" by Rimon Elias, describes different steps proposed to perform scene modelling through wide baseline set of images. The camera parameters are assumed to be known approximately within some range according to the error margins of the sensors used such as inertial devices. The proposed technique is based on detecting junctions in all images using the so-called JUDOCA operator and through homographic transformation; correlation is applied to achieve point correspondences. The match set is triangulated to obtain a set of 3D points and point clustering is then performed to achieve a bounding box for each obstacle, which may be used for localization purposes by itself. Finally, a voxelization scheme is applied to determine a volumetric representation for each obstacle.

*Chapter 13,* entitled "Complementary Part Detection and Reassembly of 3D Fragments" by Vandana D. Kaushik and Phalguni Gupta, has explored a problem for determining the complementary part of a fragment of an object and of reassembling them to form the object. It has proposed an efficient surface inspection algorithm, which detects the corresponding cleavage sites of fragments and registers them so that the object can be formed from the given fragments. For a given 3D scanned image of broken objects, the algorithm identifies the rough sites of the broken object, transforms the object to a suitable alignment, registers it with its complementary part which belongs to the same object, and finds the local correspondence among the fragmented parts. The algorithm is found to be very effective on objects of ceramic material and archeological artifacts.

*Chapter 14,* entitled "3D Surface Reconstruction from Multiviews for Prosthetic Design" by Nasrul H. B. Mahmood, suggests an alternative approach to design prosthetic devices using multiviews reconstruction method and offers a significant advance for orthotic as well as prosthetic design by using an image processing technique. Existing methods that use a fringe projection technique for prosthetic designs produce good results for the trunk and lower limbs; however, the devices used for this purpose are expensive. The design and evaluation methodology, consisting of a number of techniques suitable for prosthetic design, is developed. The 3D model is obtained by a computer program, while the 3D data uses the shape-from-silhouette technique in an approximately circular motion. The methodology developed is shown to be useful for prosthetic designers as an alternative to manual impression during the design.

This book, thus, gathers contributions from various research domains that address 3D surface geometry and reconstruction from different perspectives, including both theoretical and experimental points of view. Putting together a diverse set of contributions to constitute a coherent whole is a challenging task. But also it is an enriching and rewarding experience. As is true of most writing efforts of this nature, progress continues after work on the manuscript stops. For this reason, significant effort has been devoted to the selection of material that is fundamental and whose value is likely to remain applicable in a rapidly evolving body of knowledge. I am really grateful to the contributors, not only because of their outstanding work, but because of all the new and interesting things I learned from them. The variety of points of view is one of the key features of this book, making it a precious guide for researchers, students and practitioners. I trust that readers of this book will benefit from this effort and thus find the material timely and useful in their work.

*Umesh C. Pati*
*National Institute of Technology Rourkela, India*

# Acknowledgment

I would like to dedicate this book to my parents, late Dr. Kshirod C. Pati and Mrs. Sulochana Pati, my wife, Mita, and little daughter, Isha, all for their constant support, encouragement, patience, and understanding. Their cooperation, inspiration, and enthusiasm helped me in completion of this book. My father would have been very happy to see the book published in its final form.

*Umesh C. Pati*
*National Institute of Technology Rourkela, India*

# Section 1
# Introductory Chapters

*Three-dimensional (3D) reconstruction refers to rebuilding of a 3D model from the acquired images for better visualization. This section contains three chapters, and describes fundamental aspects as well as overview of different methods applied in 3D reconstruction. The first chapter contains an overview of methods for a 3D shape from both the surface and the internal structure of the objects. The second chapter surveys many fundamental aspects of projective geometry that have been used extensively in computer vision where as the third chapter describes the basic concepts of partial differential equations based image modelling.*

# Chapter 1
# Methods of 3D Object Shape Acquisition

**Pavel Zemcik**
*Brno University of Technology, Czech Republic*

**Michal Spanel**
*Brno University of Technology, Czech Republic*

**Premysl Krsek**
*Brno University of Technology, Czech Republic*

**Miloslav Richter**
*Brno University of Technology, Czech Republic*

## ABSTRACT

*This chapter contains an overview of methods for a 3D object shape from both the surface and the internal structure of the objects. The acquisition methods of interest are optical methods based on objects surface image processing and CT/NMR sensors that explore the object volume structure. The chapter also describes some methods for 3D shape processing. The focus is on 3D surface shape acquisition methods based on multiple views, methods using single view video sequences, and methods that use a single view with a controlled light source. In addition, the volume methods represented by CT/NMR are covered as well. A set of algorithms suitable for the acquired 3D data processing and simplification are shown to demonstrate how the models data can be processed. Finally, the chapter discusses future directions and then draws conclusions.*

## INTRODUCTION

3D object construction is one of the key issues of computer graphics and its applications both historically and at the present time. 3D object model representation in computers is the key information in 3D computer graphics, computer vision, and other fields of applications. The 3D models can be obtained through one of the two fundamentally different processes – creation of synthetic models and acquisition through measurement of real existing models. Also, combination of the processes is possible. While the first of the processes, creation of synthetic models, is addressed through many 3D editors, CAD systems, etc. and can be seen as relatively mature (Computer-aided design,

DOI: 10.4018/978-1-4666-0113-0.ch001

2010; Farin et al., 2002), this chapter focuses on the second approach – acquisition of the models through measurement of real existing models or structures.

The importance of 3D models for computer graphics is given by its fundamental purpose – manipulation and rendering of the models. The importance for other fields of computer science and applications can be different but often includes validation of hypotheses (e.g. in computer vision), planning (e.g. in robotics), representation of knowledge (e.g. in machine learning), etc.

Many definitions of the data structures for the 3D model representation exist and are being used. These definitions can generally be categorized as volume representations, surface representations, and point cloud representations (Foley et al., 1995). At the present time, the most frequently used for rendering purposes are surface representations and point cloud representations that share the property of consisting of a set of precisely positioned points in 3D space, possibly defining the position and shape of planar or non-planar surface elements. The acquisition process often leads in different data structures and in many cases, the acquired data model must be processed for further exploitation. Such processing typically includes conversion into another 3D model representation and simplification.

## BACKGROUND

The recognition of 3D shapes through measurement of the existing scenes and through processing of sensory information is a complex task. Description of all the approaches used and attempted would be beyond the scope of this text. The main approaches used today are overviewed and explained here. Nowadays, the main approaches include:

- Getting 3D coordinates from images or video of the scene – this approach is interesting as it is intended for acquisition of 3D scenes based on image and video information only without any other source of (sensory) information. Therefore, it can also be seen as means of acquisition of the 3D scene from image data sensors that are generally available and that exploit arbitrary data (Kraus, 2000; Koch, 1995; Pollefeys et al., 1998).

- Obtaining 3D data from specialized image sensors – the approach based on images but using specialized light sources. While this approach requires specialized sensor setups, it might be simpler, less expensive and also more precise compared to the above methods (Zhang, 2005).

- Processing other than image sensors to get 3D data – a typical example of such an approach can be seen in medical imaging where 3D models of tissues are obtained through CT and/or NMR data that are in their nature not image data but still can carry information about the 3D scene (Vivodtzev et al., 2003; Du & Wang, 2003; Labelle & Shewchuk, 2007).

- Other methods of getting 3D data - such as measurement of the scenes through various distance measurement devices, fusion of the information from different types of sensors, etc. These approaches are beyond the scope of this text.

The data obtained through the methods mentioned above do not necessarily fulfill the requirements of the application for which it is intended. Therefore, postprocessing of the data often needs to be done. The postprocessing can include conversion of the data representation, reduction of data size, ensuring integrity of the data, etc. This text outlines an overview of the approaches in order to give the reader further insight in this area.

# 3D COORDINATES ACQUISITION FROM MULTIPLE VIEWS

Localization of points in 3D space may be accomplished by finding correspondences between images obtained from either multiple cameras or a single camera while a viewpoint is changing. By knowing such correspondences and the geometry between cameras (or views), 3D co-ordinates of the points can be estimated. Many searching techniques for finding correspondences were presented by trying to reduce the complexity of this computationally expensive task. These techniques are closely related to a concrete setup because knowledge of the system geometry helps to reduce the search space. Typical examples of the setups include:

- **Stereo vision:** with a couple of calibrated synchronized cameras with known parameters and a fixed mutual position whose purpose is to obtain 3D location from a couple of images;
- **Multiple images setup:** where images are typically taken sequentially with a single camera arbitrarily positioned and oriented but generally with known projection parameters;

- **Video setup:** where images are frames of a single video sequence with the camera and scene changing their mutual position – camera or scene in motion.

## Stereopsis and Epipolar Geometry

The stereo vision setup for 3D co-ordinates acquisition is the closest to the human perception of 3D reality. The typical setup contains multiple cameras (projection planes) oriented in the same direction with (almost) the same axis system and projection (scale). Let us assume that the typical setup is used and the distance between the projection centers is called the base and it should be greater than zero (the system is described in Figure 1). The center of the first camera is located in point $O$, the second one lies in the distance $b$ (base) on $x$ axis. The camera constant describing the idealized camera parameters is $f$ (resp. $f'$). The 3D point in space has coordinates $(x,y,z)$, and $x'$ $(x'')$ is the projection of the point on the left (right) camera.

The systems that contain two cameras can be further categorized into three different categories. The first one has an exactly parallel axis and base in the direction of one axis. The second one has an almost parallel axis and base in the direction of one axis (it can be seen as a slightly imperfect

*Figure 1. Basic stereo imaging schema*

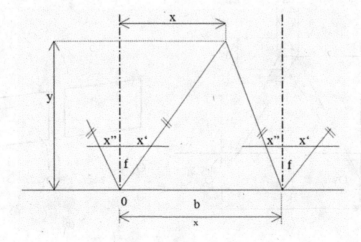

first case). The third one, the most general one, is characterized by almost arbitrary mutual positions of the cameras and the only constraint is that the camera views should cover roughly the same area.

If precise results are required, the most general form of algorithms for an arbitrary position of cameras must be used which calculates/calibrates the inner coordinates, rotation and translation matrices, and then calculates the position of points. For systems that are intended for preparation of images to be perceived by humans, a scale (of projection) must be preserved. For computer vision algorithms, the general form of algorithms is often simplified to assume a parallel coordinate system axis. In such cases, constrained (simplified) algorithms can be used especially if a precise HW setup is used.

The formulas for calculation of the 3D position are very simple. The important value in this case is the *disparity* (paralax) $p$, defined as $p = x'-x''$. The disparity is the shift of the same 3D point projection caused by camera offset. It is calculated as a subtraction of $x$ coordinates of projected points. The points in the same distance have the same disparity. From the mutual position (shift) of points, it is possible to create a

so-called disparity/distance map corresponding to the picture.

The 3D coordinates of a calculated point based on a pinhole camera model and perspective projection (Kraus, 2000) are:

$$
\begin{aligned}
x &= x'\frac{b}{p}, \\
y &= y'\frac{b}{p}, \\
z &= f\frac{b}{p} = f\frac{b}{x'-x''}.
\end{aligned}
\tag{1}
$$

Due to the non-zero pixel dimension that causes uncertainty in the localization of points, an error in the result occurs. Explanation of the error is described in Figure 2 (a). Every pixel represents a space and the intersection is also not a clear point, but an area.

It can be shown that it is advantageous to use a wider base or $f;$ however, a wider base also results in a lower number of corresponding points (the shared image space covered by both of the cameras). It can also be shown that the error is a quadratic function of the distance while along other axes the error is almost linear (but more

*Figure 2. Explanation of errors in stereo imaging setup (a); and epipolar geometry (b)*

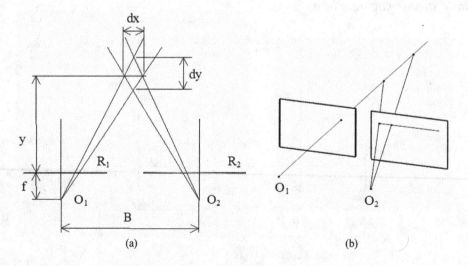

accurate close to the centre of image). The results are graphics depicted in Figure 3. For stereo vision, the most adverse source of error is the error caused by the distance. This error can be informally implied by the fact that we search for an intersection of almost parallel rays.

For image processing applications exploiting the stereo imaging, speed and robustness are very important factors. The main part of computational power is spent on finding the corresponding points. Fortunately, in stereopsis, it is possible to exploit the fact that the corresponding points lie on the so-called *epipolar line* (in the common case it should be a curve). Solution of the epipolar line is very simple and can be used to find the corresponding points or for obtaining an a priori knowledge of an area where the matching point lies.

*Epipolar geometry*, in general, describes relations between two pictures. It results from the idea that projection of a 3D point gives a 2D point. The 2D projection of the point together with the projection center gives a 3D line. And the image of this 3D line creates another line on the second image (Figure 2 (b)). It is called an *epipolar line*. The matching projected point always lies on that line. The epipolar line is a part of an *epipolar plane* that contains projection centers for both of the cameras, the original 3D point and both of the projection points. If the cameras are in an ideal position, the epipolar lines are parallel. The worse

the stereo setup is, the greater the angle occurs between the epipolar lines.

If the epipolar line-like area is used for corresponding key point search, correlation techniques can be used to obtain similarity of areas, linear programming for sorting and coupling points around lines or similar methods. Some problems, however, persist: similar textures around the epipolar line, big distance discontinuity, occluded objects, etc.

The stereo vision estimates the 3D co-ordinates of corresponding key points from multiple images. When several partially occluded objects are observed, it may be difficult to distinguish between them correctly. In such cases, additional information provided by motion detection can improve the precision of the 3D reconstruction (Wedel et al., 2008). It helps to perceive the scene in a right manner. This combination of the classical stereo imaging and motion detection (e.g. optical flow estimation) is called *6D-vision* because it processes the information about the spatial position as well as temporal changes of the position (Franke et al., 2005). One of the typical applications of the 6D-vision systems is the human gesture recognition.

Overall, stereo imaging can be seen as a robust, reliable and a relatively precise method. However, for the accurate 3D co-ordinates acquisition, it is crucial to have calibrated cameras. Un-calibrated cameras lead in distorted results (lens distortion, etc.) meaning that the resulting values contain errors in the form of nonlinear shifted estimates.

*Figure 3. Error in distance (a); and error in image plane (b)*

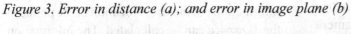

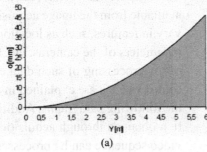

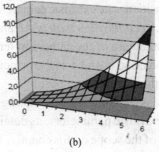

(a)       (b)

## Camera Calibration

A simple model of how the scene is perceived is the *pinhole camera model* (Hartley & Zisserman, 2004). The pinhole model declares that point $P$ in the scene is related to its image co-ordinates by the perspective projection in the camera co-ordinates system. In practice, there are two different co-ordinates systems: the world co-ordinate system and the camera's one. These co-ordinate systems are related by a set of *intrinsic* and *extrinsic* parameters (focal length $f$, position and orientation of the camera, etc.). The intrinsic parameters describe the camera co-ordinate system itself, while the extrinsic ones specify the camera position and orientation in the world co-ordinates system. The relationship can be expressed as:

$$q' = K \begin{bmatrix} R & t \end{bmatrix} Q,$$

$$K = \begin{bmatrix} f_x & & c_x \\ & f_y & c_y \\ & & 1 \end{bmatrix},$$

$$Q = \begin{bmatrix} X_{world} \\ Y_{world} \\ Z_{world} \\ 1 \end{bmatrix}, \qquad (2)$$

$$q' = \begin{bmatrix} x_{cam} \\ y_{cam} \\ 1 \end{bmatrix},$$

where $Q$ is a point in the word space and $q'$ is its projection on the image plane. The rotation matrix $R$ and the translation vector $t$ represent the camera orientation and position – the extrinsic parameters, and $K$ is the *camera calibration matrix* – $f_x$ and $f_y$ represent the focal length of the camera in terms of pixel dimensions, and $c_x$ and $c_y$ is the principal point (usually at the image center).

There are various techniques for estimating the intrinsic and the extrinsic parameters, its detailed description is out of the scope of this chapter. The most common techniques use a special *calibration object* (e.g. a chessboard) whose dimensions are known. Each correspondence between the 3D scene and 2D image point provides one linear equation, thus a system of linear equations must be solved. Because of the over-determined system, the parameters can be established by through the process of minimization of differences between set and computed values (i.e. *least squares* method).

Tsai presented a method (Tsai, 1987) that recovers both the intrinsic and the extrinsic parameters as well as power series coefficients that models a geometric distortion of the camera (real lenses mostly have some radial and tangential distortion), and an image scale factor that best fit the measured image coordinates corresponding to the known calibration object. A flexible new technique to easily calibrate a camera proposed by Zhang requires the camera to observe a planar pattern shown at a few different orientations. Either the camera or the planar pattern can be freely moved (Zhang, 2000). The proposed technique is easy to use and flexible.

## Key Points Localization in Images

Key points (sometimes called interest points) are points in images obtained through photographing or similar processes that are located on the surface of objects in scenes. The important feature of such points is that they are reproducibly detectable in different photographs of the same scenes.

The location of the key points in different images can be matched (Figure 4). Based on the information obtained, the location of the points in the 3D space can be calculated. The information available from the image acquisition process can vary in features, such as location of the cameras, parameters of the cameras, etc. Several versions of the processing of such data can be exploited, some of which are explained in further details in the following paragraphs. Additionally, information obtained through acquisition of frames of a video sequence can be processes similarly.

In order to be invariant to affine transformations (i.e. changes of the viewpoint), *Harris-Affine* and *Hessian-Affine* feature detectors were presented (Mikolajczyk & Schmid, 2002). The Harris-Affine detector combines the traditional *2D Harris corner detector* with the idea of a *Gaussian scale-space* representation (Gaussian kernels of various sizes convolved with the original image) and an iterative shape normalization algorithm that computes the affine transformation for each key point. Another well known affine-invariant detector is the *Hessian-Affine* detector. Unlike the previous one, it uses the multi-scale image representation to select scale and localize affine invariant points. However, the Hessian-Affine detector chooses interest points based on the *Hessian matrix* centered at that point rather than the *second moment matrix* that is typical for the Harris detector (Mikolajczyk & Schmid, 2004). These matrices encode changes of the intensity in the local window.

Both detectors respond well to textured or structured scenes, like buildings, while the Hessian-affine detector typically identifies more reliable regions than the Harris-Affine detector. A detailed analysis of several affine invariant region detectors has been presented by Mikolajczyk et al. (2005).

## 3D Reconstruction from Multiple Images Using Key Points

The multiple images setup is a more general case compared to the previously described stereo imaging setup. While the problem generally remains the same, additional undefined parameters of the setup occur due to the fact that in this setup the camera positioning and orientation is not known. This fact does not affect the mathematical complexity of the task too adversely but introduces an additional problem of key point matching in multiple views.

An important part of the point matching problem is the estimation of *fundamental matrix* that relates corresponding points in stereo images by means of the epipolar geometry. A summary of classical and the latest methods of the fundamental matrix estimation, including experimental results analyzing their accuracy in synthetic and real images, can be found in (Armangué & Salvi, 2003; Choi et al., 2009).

In the general multi view setup, the task of the search for the corresponding points is often addressed using the RANSAC (RANdom SAmple Concensus) approach (Chum, 2005). The principle of such an approach is the estimation that any form of "targeted search" for points in one image that would correspond to given key points found in another image would be too complicated and probably unsuccessful. Instead, some small

*Figure 4. Key points detected in different images of the same scene (a); and results of the matching (b)*

(a)                                        (b)

number of $n$ random couples of key points is taken from a couple of images and a hypothesis is tested whether they are corresponding points (which is, of course, in most cases not true). Based on the hypothesis, the parameters of projection that would be defined through the $n$ random couples are calculated.

The $n$ is selected so that the $n$ couples of points fully define the projection and based on the degree of freedom of camera location and the projection parameters, $n$ usually ranges between 3 and 7. This approach is repeated many times and the parameters of the projection are recorded as a multi-dimensional vector (whose number of elements again depends on the degree of freedom of the camera parameters). The key idea of the RANSAC approach is that the true projection parameters (true vectors resulting from the randomly selected couple of points being really the matching ones) will occur with a statistically much higher probability than the vectors resulting from the non-matching points (that would be distributed thought the multi-dimensional space as a noise). Therefore, it is sufficient to search for a dense cluster of parameter vectors, and when a cluster is found, it is likely that it corresponds to the true projection parameters.

Obviously (Choi et al., 2009), while the RANSAC approach is successful, it is a computationally expensive task because of the time consuming searching for the matching points. Therefore, any source of speedup is welcome and often it can be found in the key point features. If the randomly selected $n$ couples of key points are known not to possibly contain the corresponding points, it is not necessary to calculate the projection parameters and they can be eliminated. Such information can be obtained, for example, through an evaluation of color (points having different color parameters cannot be corresponding points); similarly, simple known geometrical features of the key points/relationships between the key points can be exploited.

Once the corresponding key points are found, the projection parameters can be recalculated through methods that generally reduce the residual error – it can be assumed that the task always leads in an over-defined set of equations. Overall, while the task is quite complicated, the results can lead to a relatively precise localization of points in the 3D space.

## Key Point Localization in Video Sequences

Processing of video sequences, while being similar to the stereo and the multiple view approaches, is different in two principal features. First of all is the assumption that can be made about the consequent frames of video sequences – they cannot be made from too different locations as the motion of the camera and the objects can be assumed to have a limited speed. Therefore, the search for the corresponding points in the consequent frames is not as complex task as in the general multiple image case mentioned above. The second important fact is that in its nature, the video sequence can be seen as unlimited in time and it is also often required that the video sequence is processed in real-time.

Tracking techniques (Tomasi & Kanade, 1991; Isard & Blake, 1998; Comaniciu et al., 2003) can be used to find the correspondence between the frames as the task of search of matching points can be seen also as a task of recognition of the motion of objects.

As for the computational methods intended for processing of the continuous stream of video data in order to get positioning information, *SLAM* (Montemerlo et al., 2002; Davison et al., 2007) methods are often used rather than the traditional approaches. The Simultaneous Localization and Mapping (SLAM) is a technique used to build up and update a geometrical map within an unknown environment without a priori knowledge while keeping <u>track</u> of the current location within the map at the same time.

Video sequence processing is one of the very perspective approaches of 3D shape reconstruction from video as the video cameras provide a large amount of information about the scene. However, contemporary video cameras still have relatively low resolution compared to the photographic cameras and so 3D reconstruction from the stereoscopic and the multiple camera setup can, at this moment, achieve better results.

## 3D COORDINATES ACQUISITION USING LIGHTS AND CAMERAS

The above paragraphs addressed the problem of 3D localization based on "passive" acquisition of images. An alternative to such an approach is to replace the information obtained through one of the cameras with the information projected through a controlled source of light. Most of the systems in use are based on a single light source, usually laser or projector, and a single camera or set of cameras, all in fixed positions.

## 3D Reconstruction Using Structured Light

In standard projective imaging, one dimension (usually the depth or distance information) from 3D scenes is lost. That is the reason why other principles of computer vision have to be used. In this section, the optical methods of shape acquisition based on a combination of different light sources and cameras will be introduced. The merits of optical methods are that they are usually very fast, non-contact and non-destructive.

For its simplicity and robustness, the active triangulation method is the most often one applied in practice. This method is based on photogrammetric reconstruction of a measured object by illumination its surface and contemporaneous scanning by a CCD sensor. The principle of this technique is shown in Figure 5. The light source, the detector and the illuminated part of the mea-

sured object form a triangle. The joining $b$ of the light source and detector is called the triangulation optical basis. The light source ray angle $\alpha$ is fixed whereas the angle on the detector side $\beta$ changes and it is defined by the variable illuminated point on CCD chip. Based on the knowledge of two angles, one side of the triangle and the intrinsic parameters of cameras and lenses (chip size, focal length, etc.), the distance then can be determined. Based on the light source type, three versions exist: 1D triangulation (light point), 2D triangulation (light stripe) and 3D triangulation (light volume).

If the reflected ray of light is projected to the $n^{th}$ pixel from the total number $N$ of pixels, then the size of the corresponding projection $a$ (in millimeters) can be calculated by Formula (4) (Kalová & Lisztwan, 2005), where $c$ is the chip size [mm].

$$a = \frac{c \cdot n}{N} \tag{4}$$

The projection $a$ can be used to compute the angle $\beta$:

$$\beta = actg\left(\frac{c/2 - a}{f}\right) + 90^\circ, \tag{5}$$

where $f$ is the focal length in millimeters. The distance $l$ can be determined due to angles $\alpha$, $\beta$ and the size of the base $b$:

$$l = \frac{b \cdot \sin \alpha \cdot \sin \beta}{\sin(180^\circ - (\alpha + \beta))} \tag{6}$$

Mathematical descriptions for the 2D and 3D triangulation techniques are, of course, more complicated but their principle is the same. If the investigated object is situated closer to the camera and light source, the angle is bigger and thus projection $a$ is bigger too. This means that a reflected light ray is projected to the pixel more

*Figure 5. Principle of the triangulation method*

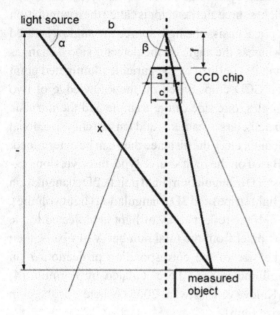

to the right (according to Figure 5). In this way, the distance of the object can be obtained just from the position of the light point in the image from the camera.

The formulas are very sensitive to the accuracy of the inserted data. Small shortcoming on the input side can lead to a big imperfection of the output. For this reason, camera calibration is necessary in most cases, together with compensation of camera and lens distortions. Both intrinsic and extrinsic parameters obtained during the calibration can be expressed as a single transformation matrix that has in general 4x3 dimensions. Each constituent member of the matrix represents a mutual relation between image coordinates and the object space. The dimension of the matrix for simpler variants is lower (3x3 for 2D case and only 2x2 for 1D triangulation).

The measurement accuracy along with the usability of this method depend on several parameters. The better resolution (smaller difference of measured distances of two neighboring pixels – the lesser discretization error) can be obtained by increasing the size of base $b$, the camera resolution $N$, the focal length $f$ and; on the other

hand, by decreasing the chip size $c$. Fine accuracy is achieved in shorter measuring distance $l$ too. Angle $\alpha$ is also important. The disadvantage of the triangulation method is that due to the concavities on object the projected point, a stripe or volume is not always visible so nothing can be said about object surface in these areas (Figure 6).

## Laser and Camera Based Systems

A laser is used with merit with 1D and 2D (the laser beam is expanded by a cylindrical lens to a plane) techniques thanks to its directionality and high shine intensity. The aim of the illumination is to mark part of the object surface. It is convenient to obtain an image on which just this opposed mark is visible. If there is some other light in the scene (other light sources or sunlight), it is necessary to reduce it. A thin band filter can be used according to source wavelength for this purpose. The wavelength of the used light source can be chosen in order to reduce representation of this wavelength in secondary light spectrum. For difference magnification between productive and useless light, a laser stripe can be substituted by a series of laser beams (lighting intensity on illuminated surface will be major).

If the 1D/2D techniques are used, the object has to be measured step by step, only one point or profile can be measured at a time. Gauging of whole object requires several separated measurements with a changed position of object or beam of light. On the other side, 1D or 2D techniques are usually faster (they use fast linear cameras or other faster image sensors). These methods are also advantageously used when some complementary linear or rotary movement of the objects occurs (for example on a production line where the objects being measured are moved along the production line).

In the situation shown in Figure 6, the light plane is created by laser and the scene is taken by camera. Gray color on the picture indicates the area that is not visible by camera. The lower

*Figure 6. Disadvantage of the laser scanning method*

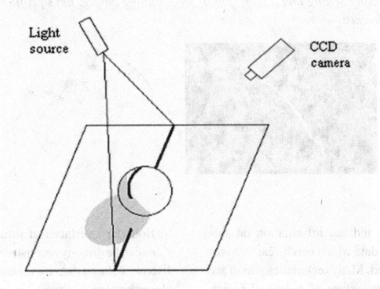

part of globe is also not illuminated by the laser. The surfaces that are almost tangential to laser will not be sharp on camera images. The quality of measurement depends on surface reflectivity of measured objects. For example, some granular materials, textile, or transparent materials that reflect less light can be measured with difficulties. Problems also arise with glossy materials because of reflections and "dancing fairies".

## Fixed Pattern Projector and Camera Based Systems

The 3D scanning technique works with different types of *structured light* according to a selected variant (moiré, color code, light pattern or phase shift). If the light volume is used, the whole object can be marked on the block so that no scanning is required. This is a big advantage against the 1D and 2D techniques.

Honec et al. (2001) projected a structured light through striped grating to inspect the volume of a viscose glue droplet applied to a flat base in production of tantalic capacitors. Volume measuring can be done through reconstruction of the surface (height of the droplet $h(x,y)$ over the base). The

volume is determined by a double integral (summation) over the area of the base. Just one image taken with one camera is required. A known pattern (several stripes) is projected onto the investigated object. The pattern is deformed on the image by an object surface (due to angle between camera and projector) so that the function $h(x,y)$ can be determined (Figure 8).

## 3D RECONSTRUCTION FROM CT/MRI

An increasing number of different imaging techniques have been introduced in the last few years. Nowadays, volumetric images can be obtained from different acquisition devices, including Computed Tomography (CT) and Magnetic Resonance Imaging (MRI). Each of them produces data in a planar 2D form as series of slices (i.e. images) through an examined object. The key advantage of the volume representation is that it details the interior structure of the object. In the case of medical imaging, this kind of information is crucial for an accurate medical diagnosis.

*Figure 7. Image of a hat form with laser stripe (a), hat's wire model (b). The measured hat form is set on a rotary table. After setting and calibration of the scanning device, hat's profiles are taken around the whole circumference.*

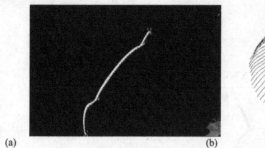

(a)

(b)

However, only indirect information on surfaces exists in the data which can be easily visualized and analyzed. Many techniques which are able to reconstruct surface of a desired region from the volumetric data have been proposed in the past. The main goal of such techniques is to extract meaningful information from the large volumetric data while providing reasonable and more effective representation of the data. These methods can be divided into two fundamental groups according to the type of model they produce:

- Plain surface reconstruction typically produces polygonal surfaces (e.g. triangular meshes),
- Volume meshing approaches aim at tessellation of the volumetric data by means of tetrahedral/hexahedral meshes.

Boundary surfaces of three-dimensional regions can be directly reconstructed from the given discrete volume data by means of an *iso-surface algorithm*. Iso-surfaces (Vivodtzev et al., 2003) are defined by connecting voxels with intensities equal to a given *iso-value* (intensity). Iso-surfaces can be extracted using an algorithm similar to the well known *Marching Cubes* algorithm (Lorensen & Cline, 1987).

The Marching Cubes (MC) algorithm creates a polygonal representation of predefined surfaces from a discrete volumetric data. It uses the divide–and–conquer approach to locate the surface in a logical cube created from eight adjacent voxels. The algorithm determines how the surface intersects this cube, then moves (*or marchs*) to the next cube. Unfortunately, a significant noise in the data causes artifacts to appear in the result. In order to deal with this problem, a

*Figure 8. Droplet image (a) and height map h(x,y) (b)*

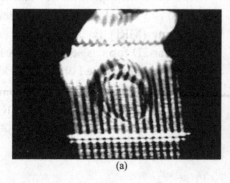

(a)

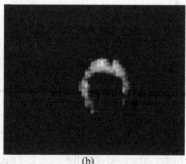

(b)

*Figure 9. Volume representation (a) versus surface representation (b)*

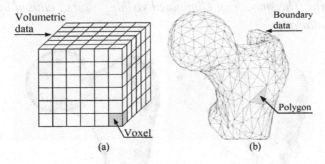

three-dimensional smoothing filter can be applied to the original data, or certain surface smoothing algorithms were introduced. The enhanced distance field representation and the extended MC algorithm (Kobbelt et al., 2001) were proposed to extract feature sensitive iso-surfaces from the volume data.

Three main families of algorithms for unstructured 3D mesh generation have been intensively studied over the last few years:

- Octree methods (Zhang et al., 2003),
- Advancing front methods (Ito et al., 2004),
- Delaunay-based methods (Alliez et al., 2005; Cavalcanti & Mello, 1999; Dardenne et al., 2009; Li, 2000).

Zhang et al. (2003) presented an algorithm to extract adaptive and quality 3D meshes directly from volumetric imaging data. In order to extract tetrahedral (or hexahedral) meshes, their approach combines bilateral and anisotropic diffusion filtering of the original data, with contour spectrum, iso-surface and interval volume selection. A top-down octree subdivision coupled with the dual contouring method is used to rapidly extract adaptive 3D finite element meshes from volumetric imaging data.

In 2007, the iso-surface stuffing algorithm (Labelle & Shewchuk, 2007) was presented that fills an iso-surface with a uniformly sized tetra-

hedral mesh whose dihedral angles are bounded. The algorithm is fast, numerically robust, and easy to implement because, like the Marching Cubes, it generates tetrahedra from a small set of pre-computed stencils. A variant of the algorithm creates a mesh with internal grading: on the boundary, where a high resolution is generally desired, the elements are fine and uniformly sized, and in the interior they may be coarser and vary in size.

Variation approaches relying on energy minimization have been presented as a powerful and robust tool in meshing. These methods basically define energies that they minimize through vertex displacements and/or connectivity changes in the current mesh. Du and Wang (2003) propose to generate meshes that are dual to optimal Voronoi diagrams. The centroidal Voronoi tessellation (Du et al., 1999) based on Delaunay triangulation provides an optimal distribution of generating points with respect to a given density function and generates a high-quality mesh.

Following Du and Wang, another tetrahedral mesh generation algorithm based on centroidal Voronoi tessellation, which takes volumetric segmented data as an input, has been presented (Dardenne et al., 2009). The algorithm performs clustering of the original voxels. A vertex replaces each cluster and the set of created vertices is triangulated in order to obtain a tetrahedral mesh, taking into account both the accuracy of the representation and the elements quality. The medial

*Figure 10. Femur surface extracted from CT data using the marching cubes algorithm (a) and the same model after smoothing (b). The smoothing eliminated visible "stairs" caused by dissimilar resolution of the CT data in particular axes.*

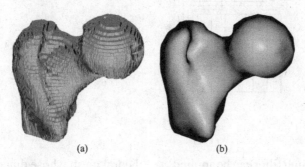

(a)                              (b)

axis of the original shape is used to generate a vertex density function in order to mesh more densely certain complex regions of the domain.

The resulting meshes exhibit good element's quality with respect to a minimal dihedral angle.

Alliez et al. (2005) presented a new variational tetrahedral meshing technique that uses a simple quadratic energy and allows for global changes in mesh connectivity during energy minimization. This meshing algorithm allows for the creation of graded meshes, and defines a sizing field prescribing the desired tetrahedra sizes within the domain. This technique produces a nicely shaped tetrahedra throughout the domain; however, "slivers (i.e. degenerate elements) could appear near the domain boundary, as the boundary vertices are unaffected by the 3D optimization" (Tournois et al., 2009).

## Basic Processing of CT/MRI Data

Two different groups of approaches were presented that model structures which appear in the volumetric data. The first group produces surface models – only the shape is represented. Methods in the second group deal with the interior structure of the model while trying to reduce the complexity of the original image data. These methods produce tetrahedral, or hexahedral, meshes which are suitable not only for surface reconstruction or visualization but also for more complex tasks such as the *FEM* (*Finite Element Methods*) simulation.

One of the most important steps in the analysis of CT/MRI data is the image segmentation. The image segmentation can be formally defined (Shapiro & Stockman, 2001) as "the process of partitioning a digital image into multiple segments. The goal of segmentation is to simplify and/or change the

*Figure 11. Tetrahedral meshes constructed directly from CT data using the variational tetrahedral meshing approach (Spanel, 2010).*

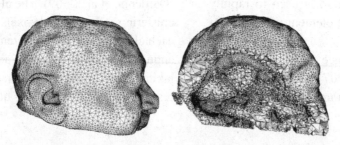

representation of an image into something that is more meaningful and easier to analyze".

The image segmentation is typically used to locate objects and boundaries in images. More precisely, the image segmentation is the process of labeling each voxel in an image to indicate structures that share certain characteristics (i.e. anatomical structures or tissue type in terms of medical imaging). The precise segmentation is crucial for the subsequent 3D modeling of examined structures.

There are many aspects that make the segmentation a difficult task, especially in the case of CT/MRI medical data (O'Donnell, 2001; Worth, 1996):

- The imaging process itself,
- Variability of the human anatomy,
- Imaging a moving patient,
- Artifacts that appear in the data,
- MRI inhomogeneity.

The first of the aspects is the imaging process itself. The scans obtained from different machines using different imaging parameters produce different absolute intensities and contrast may vary too. Moreover, the chosen imaging method provides relevant information about the tissue of interest, but this does not mean that individual tissues will be separable. Strong edges may not be present around the borders.

Another aspect is that the CT scanners usually require the patient to remain extremely still for several minutes. This is often difficult and in the case of involuntary movement, such as breathing, it becomes impossible. Moreover, the conventional CT produces artifacts when metallic objects are present in the patient's body.

In medical imaging, different tissues can appear very similarly. In order to highlight the relevant anatomy, the image can be adjusted through a wide variety of post-processing methods for

- Contrast enhancement,
- Noise filtering,
- Intensity inhomogeneity correction, etc.

A comprehensive survey of these enhancement methods applicable in the medical imaging can be found in (Bankman, 2000). Here, a brief overview of selected methods is given with reference to the literature.

Most of the contrast enhancement techniques (Gonzales & Woods, 2006) can be classified into two groups. Enhancement in spatial domain manipulates image pixels directly, while frequency domain approaches modify the Fourier transform of an image. Many spatial domain methods have been applied in the past:

- Gray level transformations – linear, logarithmic, power-law and piecewise-linear transformation functions,
- Histogram equalization and matching,
- Linear and non-linear spatial smoothing filters – mean and median filtering,
- Sharpening smoothing filters – unsharp masking, etc.

Filtering can be also done in the frequency domain (Forsyth & Ponce, 2003). Low frequencies in the Fourier transform give the gray-level appearance of a smooth image. High frequencies show detail, such as edges and noise. The commonly used *Butterworth* high-pass and low-pass filters were presented as good contrast enhancing filters (Bankman, 2000).

Multi-scale methods can decompose an image into components that can be used to improve contrast in the image. The *Laplacian Pyramid* (Forsyth & Ponce, 2003) and the *Fast Wavelet Transform (FWT)* (Koren et al., 1996; Bankman, 2000) are both typical multi-scale methods. Dippel et al. (2002) states that "enhancement based on the FWT suffers from one serious drawback, the introduction of visible artifacts when large structures are enhanced strongly. The Laplacian Pyramid allows a smooth enhancement of large structures, so that visible artifacts can be avoided".

In order to reduce noise in the data, image filtering techniques based on popular bilateral or anisotropic filters were presented (Gerig et al., 1992; Paris & Durand, 2009). Anisotropic filtering (Perona & Malik, 1990) performs piecewise smoothing of the original image. Its strength lies in the fact that it deals with local image structures which can be preserved and their positions will not be affected. Similar to the anisotropic filter, the bilateral filter (Tomasi & Manduchi, 1998) is also able to remove noise while not only preserving important features like edges in the image, but also enhancing them.

## Automatic and Semi-Automatic Segmentation

The segmentation is one of the most important steps in the analysis of medical image data. The precise segmentation is crucial for 3D modeling of tissues and anatomical structures for diagnosis, surgery planning, surgery simulation, etc.

An important feature of segmentation is automation. Performing automated segmentation still remains one of the most difficult problems. Due to the nature and complexity of the segmentation problem, there is no generic algorithm which can perform automatic segmentation on any given data set. Most of the algorithms are specific to particular problems such as cardiac MRI segmentation, brain image segmentation, lesion segmentation, etc.

In this section, a brief overview of the most important automatic and semi-automatic segmentation techniques which are, in a certain manner, general is given. In principle, the discussed techniques are not aimed at concrete treatment, tissue type or situation.

One natural view of segmentation (Forsyth & Ponce, 2003) is that "we are attempting to determine which components of a data set naturally belong together". This problem is known as clustering. A choice of literature is available (Bankman, 2000; Gonzales & Woods, 2006) discussing clustering for image segmentation. Many segmentation techniques built upon the idea of grouping items, like the *Fuzzy c-Means (FCM)* algorithm (Pham & Prince, 1999) or the *Gaussian Mixture Models (GMM)* (Ng & McLachlan, 2003) have received much attention in the past.

Other works are based on a partitioning scheme when a large dataset is decomposed into pieces. Typically, the dataset is described as a graph which is pruned according to a chosen criterion. The graph-based segmentation technique presented by Boykov and Kolmogorov (2004) belongs to the group of min-cut/max-flow algorithms building search trees for detecting augmenting paths in the graph in order to cut the graph. One should follow the given reference of the literature for further details.

The most widely used medical image segmentation methods are based on deformable models

*Figure 12. Anisotropic filtering of the CT data: original image (a); and filtered image (b).*

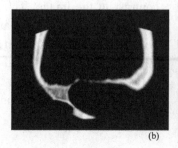 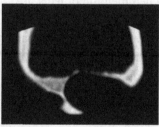

(a)                    (b)

(Zhang, 1999; Williams & Shah, 1992). The deformable models, sometimes called *Active Contour Models* (McInerney & Terzopoulos, 1997), are curves, surfaces, or solids defined within an image or volume domain, and they deform under the influence of external and internal forces derived from image characteristics. This type of active contour models is called parametric models – *Snakes* (Derraz et al., 2004).

The deformable models are robust with respect to the noise and boundary gaps. These models are also capable of adjusting themselves to significant variability of the human anatomy. The main disadvantage of the models is that they require manual initialization and interaction during segmentation. In more automatic methods, the initial model must usually be placed close to the region boundaries in order to guarantee good performance.

Extension of the deformable models into the 3D space is not a trivial task. Numerous researchers have explored application of deformable surface models to volumetric medical images (Bredno, 2003; Lachaud & Montanvert, 1996; Miller et al., 1991). A deformable surface model

capable of segmenting complex internal organs such as the cortex of the brain has been proposed (McInerney, 1996). The model is represented as a closed triangulated surface. This representation is more efficient, and is much less sensitive to initialization and spurious image features.

A second type of active contours exists as well – the geometric models (Droske et al., 2001), the best known being the *Level–Set* method. In this approach, a curve is embedded as a zero level set of a higher dimensional surface. The entire surface is evolved to minimize a metric defined by the curvature and image gradient.

Leventon et al. (2000) presented a level-set method that incorporates prior information about the intensity and curvature profile of the structure from a training set of images and boundaries. The intensity distribution as a function of signed distance from the object boundary is modeled. In general, level-set methods are used for highly convex shapes. These approaches achieve shape recognition requiring a little knowledge about the surface. In addition, initialization must be done

*Figure 13. Boundary surfaces extracted at two different levels of MR volume image pyramid (Adapted from Park et al. 2001)*

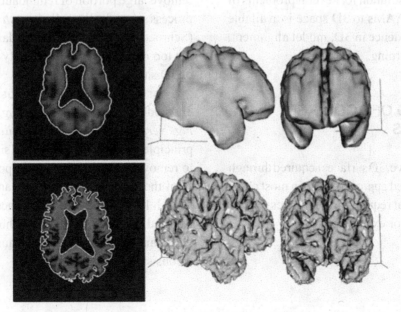

close to the desired boundary, and it often requires user interaction for initial starting.

In recent years, the *Active Appearance Models (AAMs)* (Cootes et al., 1998; Stegmann, 2000) have achieved much success in medical applications. This knowledge-based method uses a prior model of what is expected in the image. It typically attempts to find the best match of the model to a new image. A statistical approach based on the *Principal Component Analysis (PCA)* (Duda et al., 2001) is used to build the model analyzing the appearance of a set of training samples, while the model parameters can be adjusted to fit unseen images and hence perform image registration.

The main drawback of AAMs, much like any knowledge-based method, is the anatomical variability. Accurate segmentation of complex structures is very difficult. Hence, these approaches are best suited for segmenting structures which are, in some way, stable over the population of study. Objects such as blood vessels are not suitable. Due to the design of the AAMs, occlusions may cause the model fitting to fail. Finally, AAMs are dependent on a good, mostly manual, initialization.

Mitchell et al. (2002) presented an extension of AAMs to 3D space for three-dimensional segmentation of cardiac MR and ultrasound images. In that approach, solution for several problems of the extension of AAMs to 3D space is available – point correspondence in 3D, model alignment, and 3D image warping.

## PROCESSING OF ACQUIRED 3D SURFACES

As mentioned above, 3D surfaces acquired through the above described approaches are in most cases "raw surfaces" that require further processing for various reasons, for example:

- Reduction of mesh size – surface simplification, must be done in case the data produced by the 3D acquisition are too large for the application; this procedure might also be seen as optimization of the precision/size ratio.
- Ensuring the mesh integrity – in some cases, the 3D acquisition process can lead to inconsistent data (e.g. surfaces with holes, non-connected patches of surfaces, singularities, etc.).

Surface simplification (i.e. reduction of the mesh size) is described below in more detail as it presents the principal method nearly always used for the acquired models.

## Simplification of 3D Surface Meshes

The 3D polygonal meshes acquired by 3D scanning, or by the reconstruction from CT/MRI data, consist of a lot of small triangles. The size of the triangles depends on the scanning resolution (typically *0.1 – 1 mm*). Most of the triangles are redundant. Important features and details of a scanned 3D model are much bigger than the size of triangles. Therefore, it is very useful to remove large portion of redundant triangles. This process is typically called *mesh simplification* (Schroeder et al., 1992). Redundant triangles are not too important for high quality representation of 3D shape and geometry.

Four basic principles on how to simplify surface 3D models exist: *vertex removing*, *edge collapsing*, *vertex clustering* and *re-tiling*. The basic principle of the vertex removing simplification is to remove redundant (not so important) vertices from the 3D model. Removing any vertex from a mesh leaves a hole in the surface which has to be filled. Such filling of created holes is the main disadvantage of this method because it may cause inconsistency in the model.

*Figure 14. 3D surface model reconstructed from medical CT data: before simplification (a); and after simplification (b)*

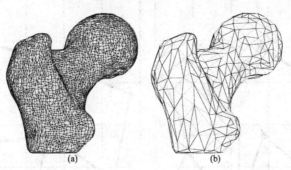

The vertex removing simplification consists of four traditional steps:

- Evaluation of all vertices according to their distance from the middle plane (~error measure),
- Sorting vertices against the error measure (the assigned value),
- Removing vertices with the minimal error and filling created holes (see Figure 16),
- Errors caused by vertex removing are distributed into neighboring vertices.

The vertex removing method is historically the first of all simplification methods. The final quality of simplified meshes is low in comparison with other techniques. Therefore, this method is rarely used in practical applications nowadays.

Edge collapsing (Lindstrom & Turk, 1998) is similar to the vertex removing method. The only difference is that this method is based on removing redundant edges from the mesh. An edge can be removed by collapsing it into a single vertex. Such an edge collapsing process produces no holes, hence, there is no problem with any inconsistency of the new surface.

Similarly, the edge collapsing can be briefly formulated in four steps:

*Figure 15. Scheme of the vertex removing principle (a); and the edge collapsing principle (b)*

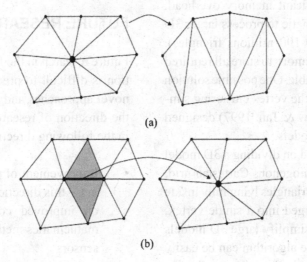

*Figure 16. Scheme of the vertex clustering principle*

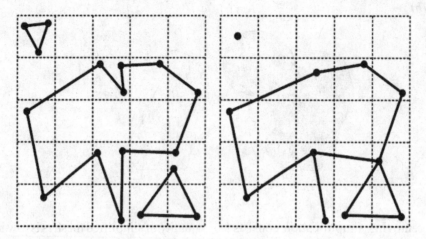

- Evaluation of all edges according to a chosen error measure,
- Sorting edges against the error,
- Edge collapsing of minimal edges,
- The error propagation from collapsed edges into neighboring edges.

Edges can be evaluated by using a number of different techniques. A good criterion was introduced by Garland (1999). The proposed *Quadric-Based Polygonal Surface Simplification* method computes an optimal vertex position, but it has large memory requirements and is computationally very intensive.

Both of the previously described simplification methods have a significant memory overhead. Therefore, it is problematic to process larger 3D models (more than 10-100 millions triangles). Basically, sufficient memory to store all required data would not be available. One possible solution to this problem can be the vertex clustering simplification method (Low & Tan, 1997) designed to simplify large 3D models.

The solution is based on dividing a 3D model bounding box on a homogenous Cartesian grid. All vertices, edges and triangles lying fully inside a one grid cell are merged into a single vertex. Thus, it is possible to simplify large 3D models very fast. Moreover, the algorithm can be easily parallelized. However, this algorithm may lead to

a distortion of the mesh geometry and topology. It depends on the cell size and concrete application.

The basic principle of the *re-tiling simplification* (Turk, 1992) does not lie in the modification of the original mesh; but it is based on the creation of a new simplified mesh. The new mesh is constructed on a set of newly created vertices distributed (randomly, poison disk) over the original surface. Then, the new vertices are connected using a triangular mesh with respect to the original model topology. The vertices can be uniformly distributed over the original surface, or the distribution can vary according to the curvature of the original surface.

## FUTURE RESEARCH DIRECTIONS

Future research in the field of 3D model acquisition is difficult to predict as the field is full of novel approaches and ideas. However, some of the direction of research will most probably be in the following directions:

- Improvement of precision of 3D positioning – this direction will probably be based on improved computational power and mathematics methods as well as improved sensors.

- Improved methods in the fusion of data from different sensors, specifically video and Lidar (Bileschi, 2009; Streach et al. 2007), video and Radar (Roy et al., 2009), and possibly other combinations.
- For some tasks, increased exploitation of consumer peripheral devices, such as Kinect (Kinect – Xbox.com, 2010), can be expected as well as increased presence of such devices directly in computer equipment.
- Novel methods of reconstruction based on video can be expected with increased precision and robustness.
- Perhaps the biggest opportunity and space for improvement is in the methods of creating a surface of the models based on the scene understanding.

## CONCLUSION

The methods for acquisition of 3D data based on the measurement of existing objects by using both the surface and volume were described in this chapter. While the methods shown in the document work relatively well, a lot of room for improvement remains. The complexity of the task lies in the need to combine sensors, optical elements, complex mathematics, and an understanding of the scene contents. This text brought only a brief overview of the methods used along with their principles. The extent of the text did not permit an in-depth analysis of all the methods, so the reader can find recommended further reading materials below. In any case, even given the contemporary imperfections, the 3D shape acquisition has a very strong application potential available today and it can be expected that in the future the application potential will continue to grow very quickly.

## REFERENCES

Alliez, P., Cohen-Steiner, D., Yvinec, M., & Desbrun, M. (2005). Variational tetrahedral meshing. *ACM Transactions on Graphics*, *24*(3), 617–625. doi:10.1145/1073204.1073238

Armangué, X., & Salvi, J. (2003). Overall view regarding fundamental matrix estimation. *Image and Vision Computing*, *21*(2), 205–220. doi:10.1016/S0262-8856(02)00154-3

Bankman, I. N. (Ed.). (2000). *Handbook of medical imaging: Processing and analysis*. Orlando, FL: Academic Press, Inc.

Bileschi, S. (2009). Fully automatic calibration of LIDAR and video streams from a vehicle. *IEEE 12th International Conference on Computer Vision Workshops (ICCV Workshops)* (pp. 1457-1464). Institute of Electrical and Electronics Engineers.

Boykov, Y., & Kolmogorov, V. (2004). An experimental comparison of min-cut/max-flow algorithms for energy minimization in vision. *IEEE Transactions on Pattern Analysis and Machine Intelligence*, *26*(9), 1124–1137. doi:10.1109/TPAMI.2004.60

Bredno, J., Lehmann, T. M., & Spitzer, K. A. (2003). General discrete contour model in two, three, and four dimensions for topology-adaptive multichannel segmentation. *IEEE Transactions on Pattern Analysis and Machine Intelligence*, *25*(5), 550–563. doi:10.1109/TPAMI.2003.1195990

Cavalcanti, P. R., & Mello, U. T. (1999). Three-dimensional constrained delaunay triangulation: A minimalist approach. In *Proceedings of the 8th International Meshing Roundtable* (pp. 119–129), Lake Tahoe, CA: Sandia National Laboratories.

Choi, S., Kim, T., & Yu, W. (2009). Performance evaluation of RANSAC family. In *Proceedings of the British Machine Vision Conference (BMVC)*.

Chum, O. (2005). *Two-view geometry estimation by random sample and consensus*. PhD Thesis, Czech Technical University in Prague.

Comaniciu, D., Ramesh, V., & Meer, P. (2003). Kernel-based object tracking. *IEEE Transactions on Pattern Analysis and Machine Intelligence*, *25*(5), 564–575. doi:10.1109/TPAMI.2003.1195991

Computer Aided Desing. (2010). *Wikipedia, The Free Encyclopedia*. Retrieved December 18, 2010, from http://en.wikipedia.org/wiki/CAD

Cootes, T. F., Edwards, G. J., & Taylor, C. J. (1998). Active appearance models. *5th European Conference on Computer Vision* (pp. 484–498).

Dardenne, J., Valette, S., Siauve, N., Burais, N., & Prost, R. (2009). Variational tetrahedral mesh generation from discrete volume data. *The Visual Computer*, *25*(5-7), 401–410. doi:10.1007/s00371-009-0323-7

Davison, A. J., Reid, I. D., Molton, N. D., & Stasse, O. (2007). MonoSLAM: Real-time single camera SLAM. *IEEE Transactions on Pattern Analysis and Machine Intelligence*, *29*(6), 1052–1067. doi:10.1109/TPAMI.2007.1049

Derraz, F., Beladgham, M., & Khelif, M. (2004). Application of active contour models in medical image segmentation. In *International Conference on Information Technology: Coding and Computing, ITCC'04* (p. 679), Los Alamitos, CA: IEEE Computer Society.

Dippel, S., Stahl, M., Wiemker, R., & Blaffert, T. (2002). Multiscale contrast enhancement for radiographies: Laplacian pyramid versus fast wavelet transform. *IEEE Transactions on Medical Imaging*, *21*(4), 343–353. doi:10.1109/TMI.2002.1000258

Droske, M., Meyer, B., Rumpf, M., & Schaller, C. (2001). An adaptive level set method for medical image segmentation. In *17th International Conference on Information Processing in Medical Imaging* (pp. 416–422). London, UK: Springer-Verlag.

Du, G., & Wang, D. (2003). Tetrahedral mesh generation and optimization based on centroidal voronoi tessellations. *International Journal for Numerical Methods in Engineering*, *56*(9), 1355–1373. doi:10.1002/nme.616

Du, Q., Faber, V., & Gunzburger, M. (1999). Centroidal voronoi tessellations: Applications and algorithms. *SIAM Review*, *41*(4), 637–676. doi:10.1137/S0036144599352836

Duda, R. O., Hart, P. E., & Stork, D. G. (Eds.). (2001). *Pattern classification* (2nd ed.). New York, NY: Wiley-Interscience.

Farin, G., Hoshek, J., & Kim, M.-S. (Eds.). (2002). *Handbook of computer aided geometric design*. Amsterdam, The Netherlands: Elsevier Science B.V.

Foley, J. D., Dam, A., Feiner, S. K., & Hughes, J. F. (1995). *Computer graphics: Principles and practice in C* (2nd ed.). Addison-Wesley.

Forsyth, D. A., & Ponce, J. (2003). *Computer vision: A modern approach*. Upper Saddle River, NJ: Pearson Education Inc., Prentice Hall, Inc.

Franke, U., Rabe, C., Badino, H., & Gehrig, S. (2005). *6D-vision: Fusion of stereo and motion for robust environment perception*. DAGM Symposium.

Garland, M. (1999). *Quadric-based polygonal surface simplification*. Ph.D. dissertation, Computer Science Department, Carnegie Mellon University.

Gerig, G., Kubler, O., Kikinis, R., & Jolesz, F. (1992). Nonlinear anisotropic filtering of MRI data. *IEEE Transactions on Medical Imaging*, *11*(2), 221–232. doi:10.1109/42.141646

Gonzalez, R. C., & Woods, R. E. (2006). *Digital image processing* (3rd ed.). Upper Saddle River, NJ: Prentice Hall, Inc.

Hartley, R., & Zisserman, A. (2004). *Multiple view geometry in computer vision*. Cambridge, UK: Cambridge University Press. doi:10.1017/CBO9780511811685

Honec, P., Petyovský, P., Richter, M., Grebeníček, F., & Valach, S. (2001). 3D object surface reconstruction. In *13th International Conference of Process Control*, (pp. 94-95). Bratislava, Slovakia: Slovak University of Technology.

Isard, M., & Blake, A. (1998). Condensation – Conditional density propagation for visual tracking. *International Journal of Computer Vision, 29*, 5–28. doi:10.1023/A:1008078328650

Ito, Y., Shih, A. M., & Soni, B. K. (2004). Reliable isotropic tetrahedral mesh generation based on an advancing front method. In *Proceedings 13th International Meshing Roundtable* (pp. 95–105). Williamsburg, VA: Sandia National Laboratories.

Kalová, I., & Lisztwan, M. (2005). Active triangulation technique. In *5th International Conference of PhD Students,* (pp. 99-104). University of Miskolc.

Kinect. (2010). *Wikipedia, The Free Encyclopedia*. Retrieved December 18, 2010, from http://en.wikipedia.org/wiki/Kinect Kinect–Xbox.com/ (2010). *Xbox, Microsoft*. Retrieved December 18, 2010, from http://www.xbox.com/en-US/kinects

Kobbelt, L. P., Botsch, M., Schwanecke, U., & Seidel, H.-P. (2001). Feature sensitive surface extraction from volume data. In *SIGGRAPH'01: Proceedings of the 28th Annual Conference on Computer Graphics and Interactive Techniques* (pp. 57–66). New York, NY: ACM.

Koch, R. (1995). 3-D surface reconstruction from stereoscopic image sequences. In *IEEE International Conference on Computer Vision, ICCV'95* (p. 109).

Koren, I., Laine, A., Taylor, F., & Lewis, M. (1996). Interactive wavelet processing and techniques applied to digital mammography. *IEEE International Conference on Acoustics, Speech, and Signal Processing, 3*, 1415–1418.

Kraus, K. (2000). *Photogrammetry: Geometry from images and laser scans* (2nd ed.). Berlin, Germany: Walter de Gruyter.

Labelle, F., & Shewchuk, J. R. (2007). Isosurface stuffing: Fast tetrahedral meshes with good dihedral angles. *ACM Transactions on Graphics, 26*(3), 57. doi:10.1145/1276377.1276448

Lachaud, J.-O., & Montanvert, A. (1996). Volumic segmentation using hierarchical representation and triangulated surface. In *ECCV '96: Proceedings of the 4th European Conference on Computer Vision* (pp. 137–146). London, UK: Springer-Verlag.

Leventon, M. E., Faugeras, O., Grimson, W. E. L., & Wells, W. M. (2000). Level set based segmentation with intensity and curvature priors. In *Workshop on Mathematical Methods in Biomedical Image Analysis Proceedings* (pp. 4–11).

Li, X. (2000). *Sliver-free three dimensional delaunay mesh generation*. Doctoral dissertation, UIUC.

Lindstrom, P., & Turk, G. (1998). Fast and memory efficient polygonal simplification. In *IEEE Visualization 98 Conference Proceedings* (pp. 279-286).

Lorensen, W. E., & Cline, H. E. (1987). Marching cubes: A high resolution 3D surface construction algorithm. *SIGGRAPH Computer Graphics, 21*(4), 163–169. doi:10.1145/37402.37422

Low, K.-L., & Tan, T.-S. (1997). Model simplification using vertex-clustering. In *Proceedings of the 1997 Symposium on Interactive 3D graphics* (p. 75). Providence, RI: ACM.

McInerney, T. (1997). *Topologically adaptable deformable models for medical image analysis.* PhD thesis, Dept. of Computer Science, University of Toronto.

McInerney, T., & Terzopoulos, D. (1996). Deformable models in medical imageanalysis: A survey. *Medical Image Analysis, 1*(2), 91–108. doi:10.1016/S1361-8415(96)80007-7

Mikolajczyk, K., & Schmid, C. (2002). An affine invariant interest point detector. In *Proceedings of 8th European Conference on Computer Vision,* (pp. 128-142). Springer Verlag.

Mikolajczyk, K., & Schmid, C. (2004). Scale & affine invariant interest point detectors. *International Journal of Computer Vision, 60*(1), 63–86. doi:10.1023/B:VISI.0000027790.02288.f2

Mikolajczyk, K., Tuytelaars, T., Schmid, C., Zisserman, A., Matas, J., & Schaffalitzky, F. (2005). A comparison of affine region detectors. *International Journal of Computer Vision, 1*(65), 43–72. doi:10.1007/s11263-005-3848-x

Miller, J. V., Breen, D. E., Lorensen, W. E., O'Bara, R. M., & Wozny, M. J. (1991). Geometrically deformed models: A method for extracting closed geometric models form volume data. In *SIGGRAPH'91: Proceedings of the 18th Annual Conference on Computer Graphics and Interactive Techniques* (pp. 217–226). New York, NY: ACM Press.

Mitchell, S. C., Bosch, J. G., Lelieveldt, B. P. F., Van der Geest, R. J., Reiber, J. H. C., & Sonka, M. (2002). 3-D active appearance models: Segmentation of cardiac MR and ultrasound images. *IEEE Transactions on Medical Imaging, 21*(9), 1167–1178. doi:10.1109/TMI.2002.804425

Montemerlo, M., Thrun, S., Koller, D., & Wegbreit, B. (2002). FastSLAM: A factored solution to the simultaneous localization and mapping problem. *Proceedings of the AAAI National Conference on Artificial Intelligence.* Canada: AAAI.

Ng, S.-K., & McLachlan, G. J. (2003). On some variants of the em algorithm for fitting mixture models. *Austrian Journal of Statistics, 32*(1-2), 143–161.

O'Donnell, L. (2001). *Semi-automatic medical image segmentation.* Master's thesis, Massachusetts Institute of Technology.

Paris, S., & Durand, F. (2009). A fast approximation of the bilateral filter using a signal processing approach. *International Journal of Computer Vision, 81*(1), 24–52. doi:10.1007/s11263-007-0110-8

Park, J. Y., McInerney, T., Terzopoulos, D., & Kim, K. H. (2001). A non-selfintersecting deformable surface for complex boundary extraction from volumetric images. *Computers & Graphics, 25*(3), 421–440. doi:10.1016/S0097-8493(01)00066-8

Perona, P., & Malik, J. (1990). Scale-space and edge detection using anisotropic diffusion. *IEEE Transactions on Pattern Analysis and Machine Intelligence, 12,* 629–639. doi:10.1109/34.56205

Pham, D. L., & Prince, J. L. (1999). Adaptive fuzzy segmentation of magnetic resonance images. *IEEE Transactions on Medical Imaging, 18,* 737–752. doi:10.1109/42.802752

Pollefeys, M., Koch, R., Vergauwen, M., & Van Gool, L. (1998). *Metric 3D surface reconstruction from uncalibrated image sequences. 3D Structure from Multiple Images of Large-Scale Environments, LNCS 1506* (pp. 139–154). Berlin, Germany: Springer.

Roy, A., Gale, N., & Hong, L. (2009). Fusion of Doppler radar and video information for automated traffic surveillance. In *Proceedings of the 12th International Conference on Information Fusion* (pp. 1989-1996), Seattle, WA, USA.

Schroeder, W. J., Zarge, J. A., & Lorensen, W. E. (1992). Decimation of triangle meshes. In *Proceedings of the 19th Annual Conference on Computer Graphics and Interactive Techniques, SIGGRAPH'92* (pp. 65-70). New York, NY: ACM.

Shapiro, L., & Stockman, G. (2001). *Computer vision*. NJ: Prentice Hall.

Spanel, M. (2010). *Delaunay-based vector segmentation of volumetric medical images*. Unpublished PhD dissertation, Brno University of Technology, Czech Republic.

Stegmann, M. B. (2000). *Active appearance models: Theory, extensions and cases*. Master's thesis, Informatics and Mathematical Modelling, Technical University of Denmark.

Strecha, C., Hansen, W., Van Gool, L., & Thoennessen, U. (2007). *Multi-view stereo and lidar for outdoor scene modeling*. Photogrammetric Image Analysis.

Tomasi, C., & Kanade, T. (1991). *Detection and tracking of point features*. Carnegie Mellon University Technical Report CMU-CS-91-132.

Tomasi, C., & Manduchi, R. (1998). Bilateral filtering for gray and color images. In *ICCV '98: Proceedings of the Sixth International Conference on Computer Vision* (p. 839). Washington, DC: IEEE Computer Society.

Tournois, J., Srinivasan, R., & Alliez, P. (2009). Perturbing slivers in 3D Delaunay meshes. In *Proceedings of the 18th International Meshing Roundtable* (pp. 157–173). Berlin, Germany: Springer.

Turk, G. (1992). Re-tiling polygonal surfaces. In *Proceedings of the 19th Annual Conference on Computer Graphics and Interactive Techniques, SIGGRAPH'92* (pp. 55-64). New York, NY: ACM.

Vivodtzev, F., Bonneau, G.-P., Linsen, L., Hamann, B., Joy, K. I., & Olshausen, B. A. (2003). Hierarchical isosurface segmentation based on discrete curvature. In *VISSYM'03: Proceedings of the Symposium on Data Visualisation 2003* (pp. 249–258). Aire-la-Ville, Switzerland: Eurographics Association.

Wedel, A., Rabe, C., Vaudrey, T., Brox, T., Franke, U., & Cremers, D. (2008). Efficient dense scene flow from sparse or dense stereo data. *ECCV, 2008*, 739–751.

Williams, D. J., & Shah, M. A. (1992). Fast algorithm for active contours and curve estimation. *CVGIP: Image Understanding, 55*, 14–26. doi:10.1016/1049-9660(92)90003-L

Worth, A. J. (1996). *Brain segmentation in MRI*. Retrieved November, 2010, from http://www.cma.mgh.harvard.edu/seg/

Zhang, J. (1999). *Reconstruction of geometry from cardiac MR images*. Master's thesis. Johns Hopkins University.

Zhang, S. (2005). *High-resolution, real-time 3-D shape measurement*. PhD Dissertation, Stony Brook University.

Zhang, Y., Bajaj, C., & Sohn, B.-S. (2003). Adaptive and quality 3D meshing from imaging data. In *SM'03: Proceedings of the Eighth ACM Symposium on Solid Modeling and Applications* (pp. 286–291). New York, NY: ACM.

Zhang, Z. (2000). A flexible new technique for camera calibration. *IEEE Transactions on Pattern Analysis and Machine Intelligence, 22*, 1330–1334. doi:10.1109/34.888718

## ADDITIONAL READING

Choi, S., Kim, T., & Yu, W. (2009). Performance evaluation of RANSAC family. In *Proceedings of the British Machine Vision Conference (BMVC)*.

Cohen, L., & Cohen, I. (1993). Finite element methods for active contour models and baloons for 2D and 3D images. *IEEE Transactions on Pattern Analysis and Machine Intelligence*, *15*(11), 1131–1147. doi:10.1109/34.244675

Klein, G. (2006). *Visual tracking for augmented reality*. PhD Thesis, University of Cambridge.

Klein, G., & Murray, D. (2007). Parallel tracking and mapping for small AR workspaces. In *Proceedings of the International Symposium on Mixed and Augmented Reality*, ISMAR'07, Nara.

Krysl, P., & Ortiz, M. (1999). Variational delaunay approach to the generation of tetrahedral finite element meshes. *International Journal for Numerical Methods in Engineering*, *50*, 1681–1700. doi:10.1002/nme.91

Li, X.-Y., Teng, S.-H., & Ungor, A., S. (2000). Biting: Advancing front meets sphere packing. *International Journal for Numerical Methods in Engineering*, *49*(1-2), 61–81. doi:10.1002/1097-0207(20000910/20)49:1/2<61::AID-NME923>3.0.CO;2-Y

Lucas, B. D., & Kanade, T. (1981). An iterative image registration technique with an application to stereo vision. *International Joint Conference on Artificial Intelligence* (pp. 674-679).

Peng, T., & Gupta, S. K. (2007). Model and algorithms for point cloud construction using digital projection patterns. *Journal of Computing and Information Science in Engineering*, *7*(4), 372–381. doi:10.1115/1.2798115

Salvi, J., Armangué, X., & Batlle, J. (2002). A comparative review of camera calibrating methods with accuracy evaluation. *Pattern Recognition*, *35*(7), 1617–1635. doi:10.1016/S0031-3203(01)00126-1

Shi, J., & Tomasi, C. (1994). Good features to track. *IEEE Conference on Computer Vision and Pattern Recognition* (pp. 593-600).

Tsai, R. Y. (1987). A versatile camera calibration technique for 3D machine vision. *IEEE Journal on Robotics and Automation*, *3*(4), 323–344. doi:10.1109/JRA.1987.1087109

Watt, A., & Policarpo, F. (Eds.). (1998). *The computer image*. New York, NY: Addison Wesley.

Wu, H., Chellappa, R., Sankaranarayanan, A., & Zhou, S. (2007). *Robust visual tracking using the time-reversibility constraint*. IEEE 11th International Conference on Computer Vision, ICCV.

Yoshizawa, S., Belyaev, A., & Yokota, H. (2010). Fast Gauss bilateral filtering. *Computer Graphics Forum*, *29*(1), 24–52. doi:10.1111/j.1467-8659.2009.01544.x

Zhang, Y., Bajaj, C., & Sohn, B.-S. (2005). 3D finite element meshing from imaging data. *Computer Methods in Applied Mechanics and Engineering*, *194*(48-49), 5083–5106. doi:10.1016/j.cma.2004.11.026

Zhang, Z., & Kanade, T. (1998). Determining the epipolar geometry and its uncertainty: A review. *International Journal of Computer Vision*, *27*, 161–195. doi:10.1023/A:1007941100561

## KEY TERMS AND DEFINITIONS

**AAM:** Active Appearance Model is an algorithm for matching a statistical model of object shape and appearance to a new image. The AAM model is built during a training phase that utilizes a set of annotated images.

**CT:** Computed Tomography is a modern extension of the traditional X-ray examination. The X-ray beam scans a slice of the anatomy from multiple angles. Each slice pixel is then calculated combining the measurements from the multiple angles. The CT produces data in a planar 2D form as a series of slices through the examined part of the patient body. The CT intensity is relative to that of water which is zero.

**Deformable Models:** The deformable models (or active contours) are curves, surfaces, or solids defined within an image or volume domain. They deform under the influence of external and internal forces which are derived from image characteristics. These forces attract the contour to specific image features.

**DT:** Delaunay Triangulation (DT) of a set of vertices in 2D/3D space is a triangulation so that no vertex is inside the circumcircle/circumsphere of any triangle/tetrahedron in the DT. Delaunay triangulations maximize the minimum angle in the triangulation.

**Epipolar Geometry:** Epipolar Geometry is the geometry when two cameras view a 3D scene from two distinct positions. There are many geometric relations between the 3D points and their projections onto the 2D image planes that lead to constraints between the image points. This geometry is motivated by considering the search for corresponding points in stereo matching.

**LIDAR:** Light Detection and Ranging is an optical remote sensing technology that measures distance to an object by emitting pulses of laser light and measuring the delay between emission and detection of the reflected pulses. The measured delay is converted to distance.

**MRI:** Magnetic Resonance Imaging is a technique used to visualize detailed internal structures of human organs and soft tissues. The MRI produces images that represent information of a chemical nature. The different intensities in the image reflect mainly the density of hydrogen atoms. The method has its theoretical basis in advanced nuclear physics and the nuclear magnetic resonance phenomenon.

**NMR:** Nuclear Magnetic Resonance is a phenomenon which occurs when the nuclei of certain atoms are immersed in a static magnetic field and exposed to a second oscillating magnetic field. This causes the nuclei to absorb energy from the second field and radiate this energy back out. The energy radiated back out is at a specific resonance frequency which depends on the strength of the magnetic field and other factors.

**RANSAC:** RANdom SAmple Consensus is an iterative algorithm for robust fitting of models in the presence of many data outliers. The algorithm selects N data items at random, estimates the model parameters and finds out how many data items fit the model within a given tolerance.

**SLAM:** Simultaneous Localization and Mapping is a technique used to build up and update a geometrical map within an unknown environment without a priori knowledge while keeping track of the current location within the map at the same time.

**Stereo Imaging:** Stereo imaging (or stereo vision) stands for a technique of 3D scene reconstruction from a couple of images using a setup of multiple calibrated synchronized cameras with known parameters and a fixed mutual position.

# Chapter 2
# Projective Geometry for
# 3D Modeling of Objects

**Rimon Elias**
*German University in Cairo, Egypt*

## ABSTRACT

*This chapter surveys many fundamental aspects of projective geometry that have been used extensively in computer vision literature. In particular, it discusses the role of this branch of geometry in reconstructing basic entities (e.g., 3D points, 3D lines, and planes) in 3D space from multiple images. The chapter presents the notation of different elements. It investigates the geometrical relationships when one or two cameras are observing the scene creating single-view and two-view geometry. In other words, camera parameters in terms of locations and orientations, with respect to 3D space and with respect to other cameras, create relationships. This chapter discusses these relationships and expresses them mathematically. Finally, different approaches to deal with the existence of noise or inaccuracy in general are presented.*

## INTRODUCTION

Techniques are developed to reconstruct objects/surfaces in 3D space. These techniques use groups of images taken by cameras. Variations of the problem include 3D reconstruction from uncalibrated monocular image sequence (Azevedo, Tavares, & Vaz, 2009, Fitzgibbon, Cross, & Zisserman, 1998,

Pollefeys, Koch, Vergauwen, & Gool, 1998); 3D reconstruction from calibrated monocular image sequence (Nguyen & Hanajik, 1995); and 3D reconstruction from stereo images. This later case includes pairs of images taken at the same time by two cameras or at two different instants by one camera provided that the scene is static. In many cases, the solution is divided into two steps (Zhang, 1995). These steps are:

DOI: 10.4018/978-1-4666-0113-0.ch002

1. Extracting and matching features between corresponding images; and
2. Determining structure from corresponding features.

Projective geometry (O. Faugeras, 1996, R. I. Hartley & Zisserman, 2004, Elias, 2009b) plays a key role in solving different problems in computer vision in general and determining structure from corresponding features in particular. Indeed, using the notation of this branch of geometry simplifies the complicated relationships among different spaces. When a camera takes different shots (i.e., perspective projections) for the same object or scene, geometrical relationships can be established among images. Projective geometry can determine these relationships mathematically in an efficient and easier way.

Consider the situation where two cameras observing a 3D space point of unknown coordinates. In this case, two point projections are formed onto two images. If the locations of these points as well as the locations of the cameras are known, two rays starting at the cameras and passing through the projections may be constructed to intersect in space at the 3D location of the point. This 3D reconstruction process can be handled easily in projective geometry (Beardsley, Zisserman, & Murray, 1997).

Epipolar geometry (O. Faugeras, 1996) is emerged in case of stereo vision with a number of useful relationships and matrices. The fundamental matrix (Luong & Faugeras, 1995) is an example of these matrices that can be used to limit the search for correspondences. When these correspondences are known, different objects can be reconstructed in 3D space.

In this chapter, we will discuss the basics of projective geometry (Elias, 2009a) and the notation of different entities (e.g., points, lines) expressed in 2D as well as 3D spaces. We will also discuss the mathematics of perspective projection when one or two cameras are used to view the same object/scene (i.e., single-view and two-view geometry).

Having those main points explained, we will explain how to use projective geometry in order to reconstruct points, lines and planes in 3D space given their projections onto different images.

New directions of the 3D reconstruction problem include modeling from massive collections of images (e.g., images for famous places obtained from the Web) (Snavely, Seitz, & Szeliski, 2008, 2006a, 2006b) and learning 3D scene structure using clues from a single image (Saxena, Sun, & Ng, 2007). However, such approaches are beyond the scope of this chapter.

## NOTATION

In this section, the notations used to describe points, lines, planes and directions in the rest of the chapter are mentioned. We indicate a 2D point by a bold lowercase letter (e.g., **p**) while a 3D point is indicated by a bold uppercase letter (e.g., **P**). A matrix of any dimensions is represented by a fixed-size letter (e.g., $\mathrm{P}$ ). A scalar variable is represented by an italic letter (e.g., $p$). Finally, corresponding points in different scene views are indicated using the prime notation (e.g., **p**, **p**′).

### 2D Points

A 2D point may be represented in homogeneous or inhomogeneous coordinates. The inhomogeneous point $\dot{\mathbf{p}}$ is identified by a 2D vector $[x,y]^T$ representing the Cartesian coordinates of the point. The same point **p** is represented in homogeneous coordinates as a 3D vector $[x,y,1]^T$. In general, the third term may not be equal to 1 (e.g., $[x,y,s]^T$). In such cases, the Cartesian coordinates of the point can be estimated by dividing all the terms by the third one (e.g., $\left[\dfrac{x}{s},\dfrac{y}{s},1\right]^T$).

### 3D Points

Similar to 2D points, a point in 3D space can be represented in both inhomogeneous and homogeneous coordinates. The inhomogeneous coordinates of a 3D point $\dot{P}$ identify the Cartesian coordinates of the point and are represented as a 3D vector $[x,y,z]^T$. The homogeneous coordinates of the same point are represented by a 4D vector $P=[x,y,z,1]^T$. As mentioned with 2D points, the last term in a homogeneous 3D point may not be 1 in general and the Cartesian coordinates are obtained as we divide all terms by the value of the last term.

### 2D Lines

A line $l$ in 2D space is represented by the equation $ax+by+c=0$. The three coefficients $a$, $b$ and $c$ form a 3D vector representing the same line (i.e., $1=[a,b,c]^T$). Using this notation, a 2D line passing through two points $[x_1,y_1]^T$ and $[x_2,y_2]^T$ is represented as $[y_2-y_1,x_1-x_2,y_1x_2-x_1y_2]^T$; a 2D line whose slope is $m$ and passing through $[x_1,y_1]^T$ is denoted by $[m,-1,y_1-mx_1]^T$; a horizontal line is represented as $[1,0,-x_1]^T$ while a line passing through $[x_1,y_1]^T$ and parallel to another line $[a,b,c]^T$ is represented as $[a,b,-(ax_1+by_1)]^T$.

It is obvious that there is no difference between representing a homogeneous 2D point and a 2D line since both are represented by 3D vectors. This is known as the *duality principle*. Notice that two 2D points determine a line passing through them and two intersecting 2D lines determine a point. Mathematically, this is obtained using the cross product. Thus, the line $l$ passing through the points $\dot{p}_1$ and $\dot{p}_2$ is estimated as $l=p_1 \times p_2$ where $\times$ denotes the cross product. Also, the lines $l_1$ and $l_2$ intersect at $\dot{p}$ such that $p=l_1 \times l_2$.

### Planes

A plane $\Pi$ is represented by the equation $ax+by+cz+d=0$. The first three coefficients $a$, $b$ and $c$ represent the normal vector $N=[a,b,c]^T$ to this plane while the fourth coefficient $d$ indicates the perpendicular distance from the origin to that plane. Similar to the previous notation, the plane $\Pi$ is represented as a 4D vector $[N^T|d]^T=[a,b,c,d]^T$.

### 3D Lines

A 3D line can be considered as the intersection between two planes $\Pi_1$ and $\Pi_2$. Mathematically, a 3D line is represented as a $2\times4$ matrix L indicating the span of the plane vectors $\Pi_1$ and $\Pi_2$ (i.e., $L=[\Pi_1|\Pi_2]^T$).

### Directions

A direction is a point on the *ideal plane* or the plane at infinity. In homogeneous coordinates, the last term of the point vector must be equal to 0 (e.g., $p=[x,y,0]^T$ or $P=[x,y,z,0]^T$).

## SINGLE-VIEW GEOMETRY

Consider Figure 1(a) where a single camera located at the point $\dot{O}$ is observing the space point $\dot{P}$. The projection of this point is formed at the image point $\dot{p}$. Note that the camera location is referred to as the optical center and the line passing through the optical center and perpendicular to the image plane is called the optical axis. The intersection between the optical axis and the image is called the principal point.

## THE PERSPECTIVE PROJECTION MATRIX

Figure 1 depicts two cases for a single camera observing a 3D point. Figure 1(a) shows a general case where the origin of the world coordinate system is placed arbitrarily in space and focal length of the camera is not 1. On the contrary,

*Figure 1. A single camera located at $\dot{\mathbf{O}}$ is observing a point $\dot{\mathbf{P}}$ in 3D space and forming a projection $\dot{\mathbf{p}}$. (a) The general case where the focal length of the camera is different from 1 and the origin of the world coordinate system is located arbitrarily in space. (b) A special case where the focal length of the camera is 1 and the origin of the world coordinate system is located at the optical center of the camera.*

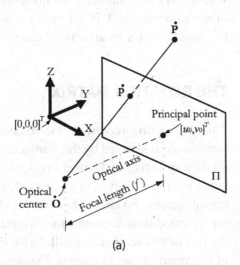

(a)

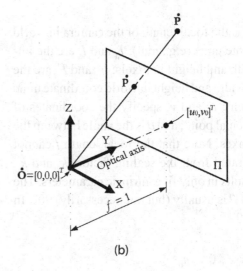

(b)

Figure 1(b) shows the origin of the world coordinate system as located at the position of the camera whose focal length is 1. The question now is how to determine the projection $\dot{\mathbf{p}}$ for the point $\dot{\mathbf{P}}$. The answer is by using what is called the 3×4 perspective projection matrix P (also known as camera matrix (R. I. Hartley & Zisserman, 2004)) where $\dot{\mathbf{p}}$ and $\dot{\mathbf{P}}$ are related as:

$$s\mathbf{p} = P\mathbf{P} \qquad (1)$$

where $\mathbf{p}$ is homogeneous representation of the projection; $\mathbf{P}$ is the homogeneous representation of the 3D point and $s$ is a scaling factor that can take any value. Hence, we can write:

$$\mathbf{p} = P\mathbf{P}. \qquad (2)$$

For the special case mentioned above, the perspective projection matrix P can be regarded as:

$$P = P_c = \begin{bmatrix} 1 & 0 & 0 & 0 \\ 0 & 1 & 0 & 0 \\ 0 & 0 & 1 & 0 \end{bmatrix}. \qquad (3)$$

In the general case where the camera is located arbitrarily in space and the focal length is not 1, the perspective projection matrix is estimated as:

$$P = AP_cD \qquad (4)$$

where A is a 3×3 matrix called the camera calibration matrix and D is a 4×4 matrix responsible for the rotation and translation of the camera.

## THE CALIBRATION MATRIX

This matrix maps the normalized image coordinates to the retinal coordinates. The entries of this matrix are determined by the *intrinsic parameters* of the camera. This matrix is calculated as:

$$A = \begin{bmatrix} fk_u & fk_u \cot\theta & u_0 \\ 0 & \dfrac{fk_v}{\sin\theta} & v_0 \\ 0 & 0 & 1 \end{bmatrix} \text{ such that } k_u = \frac{I_w}{F_w} \ , \ k_v = \frac{I_h}{F_h}$$

$$(5)$$

where $f$ is the focal length of the camera in world coordinate units (e.g., mm); $I_w$ and $I_h$ are the image width and height in pixels; $F_w$ and $F_h$ are the format width and height in world coordinate units (e.g., mm); $u_0$ and $v_0$ specify the coordinates of the principal point; and $\theta$ is the angle between the retinal axes. Note that the focal length $f$ cannot be separated from the scaling factors $k_u$ and $k_v$. This results in only five intrinsic parameters. The value of $\theta$ is usually (but not necessarily) 90°. In case $\theta=90°$:

$$A = \begin{bmatrix} fk_u & 0 & u_0 \\ 0 & fk_v & v_0 \\ 0 & 0 & 1 \end{bmatrix}. \qquad (6)$$

In world coordinate units, the width of a pixel is $\dfrac{F_w}{I_w}$ while its height is $\dfrac{F_h}{I_h}$. Finally, the aspect ratio can be defined as $\dfrac{k_u}{k_v} = \dfrac{I_w F_h}{F_w I_h}$.

## THE ROTATION TRANSLATION MATRIX

The rotation translation matrix D is a 4×4 matrix specifying the location and orientation of the camera in the world coordinate system. This matrix is affected by three parameters representing the rotation of the camera and three others representing its location. These six parameters are known as the *extrinsic parameters* of the camera. The matrix is defined as:

$$D = \begin{bmatrix} R & \mathbf{T} \\ \mathbf{0}_3^T & 1 \end{bmatrix} \qquad (7)$$

where R is a 3×3 matrix representing the rotation of the camera; and $\mathbf{T}$ is 3D vector representing the translation (or location) of the camera.

## THE ROTATION MATRIX

This 3×3 matrix represents the rotation of the camera and is affected by three angles. Different rotation systems may be used to calculate the rotation matrix. However, in all cases, three angles must determine its values. Also, the overall rotation is performed as three consecutive 2D rotations. In the rest of this section, we will derive the terms of this matrix using two rotation systems.

### R **Using** $\omega$, $\phi$ **and** $\kappa$

In this system, the 3D rotation is performed through the following steps:

1. 2D rotation about the $X-$ axis through an angle $\omega$. This is depicted in Figure 2(a) and represented by the rotation matrix $R_\omega$ where:

$$R_\omega = \begin{bmatrix} 1 & 0 & 0 \\ 0 & \cos\omega & \sin\omega \\ 0 & -\sin\omega & \cos\omega \end{bmatrix}. \qquad (8)$$

2. 2D rotation about the $Y_1-$axis through an angle $\phi$. This is depicted in Figure 2(b) and represented by the rotation matrix $R_\phi$ where:

$$R_\phi = \begin{bmatrix} \cos\phi & 0 & -\sin\phi \\ 0 & 1 & 0 \\ \sin\phi & 0 & \cos\phi \end{bmatrix}. \qquad (9)$$

*Figure 2. Rotation is performed as a series of three 2D rotations: (a) Rotation about the X– axis through* $R_{\omega}$. *(b) Rotation about the* $Y_{1}$– *axis through* $R_{\phi}$. *(c) Rotation about the* $Z_{2}$– *axis through* $R_{\kappa}$.

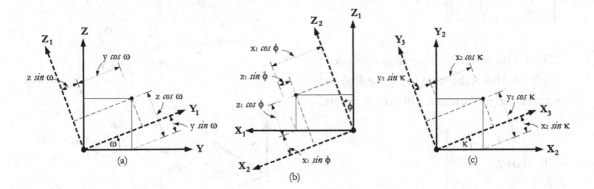

3.  2D rotation about the $Z_{2}$– axis through an angle $\kappa$. This is depicted in Figure 2(c) and represented by the rotation matrix $R_{\kappa}$ where:

$$R_{\kappa} = \begin{bmatrix} \cos\kappa & \sin\kappa & 0 \\ -\sin\kappa & \cos\kappa & 0 \\ 0 & 0 & 1 \end{bmatrix}. \qquad (10)$$

The overall rotation matrix $R$ can be estimated by multiplying the three previous matrices. Thus, we have Equation 11.

# R **Using** $\rho$, $\tau$, **and** $\psi$

In this system, three other angles (Wolf & DeWitt, 2000) are used to estimate the same rotation matrix R. Those are the pan, $\rho$, tilt, $\tau$, and swing, $\psi$, angles shown in Figure 3. In this figure, the principal plane is passing through the optical axis and a vertical line passing the optical center. The angle enclosed between this line and the optical axis is called the tilt, $\tau$. Notice that the principal line is the intersection between the principal plane and the image. Also, the principal plane intersects the $X_{w}Y_{w}$ plane at a line. The angle enclosed between this line and the $Y_{w}$ – axis is called the *pan* or *azimuth*, $\rho$. Finally, the swing, $\psi$, is the angle between the principal line and the direction of $Y_{3}$ – axis. (All the axes are explained below).

Similar to the previous system, the 3D rotation is performed in three steps:

1.  2D rotation about the $Z$ – axis through an angle $\rho$. This is depicted in Figure 4(a) and represented by the rotation matrix $R_{\rho}$ where:

*Equation 11.*

$$R = R_{\kappa}R_{\phi}R_{\omega}$$
$$= \begin{bmatrix} \cos\phi\cos\kappa & \sin\omega\sin\phi\cos\kappa + \cos\omega\sin\kappa & -\cos\omega\sin\phi\cos\kappa + \sin\omega\sin\kappa \\ -\cos\phi\sin\kappa & -\sin\omega\sin\phi\sin\kappa + \cos\omega\cos\kappa & \cos\omega\sin\phi\sin\kappa + \sin\omega\cos\kappa \\ \sin\phi & -\sin\omega\cos\phi & \cos\omega\cos\phi \end{bmatrix} \qquad (11)$$

$$R_\rho = \begin{bmatrix} \cos\rho & \sin\rho & 0 \\ -\sin\rho & \cos\rho & 0 \\ 0 & 0 & 1 \end{bmatrix}. \qquad (12)$$

2. 2D rotation about the $X_1$ − axis through an angle $\tau$. This is depicted in Figure 4(b) and represented by the rotation matrix $R_\tau$ where:

$$R_\tau = \begin{bmatrix} 1 & 0 & 0 \\ 0 & \cos\tau & \sin\tau \\ 0 & -\sin\tau & \cos\tau \end{bmatrix}. \qquad (13)$$

3. 2D rotation about the $Z_2$ − axis through an angle $\psi$. This is depicted in Figure 4(c) and represented by the rotation matrix $R_\psi$ where:

$$R_\psi = \begin{bmatrix} \cos\psi & \sin\psi & 0 \\ -\sin\psi & \cos\psi & 0 \\ 0 & 0 & 1 \end{bmatrix}. \qquad (14)$$

As done with the previous system, the overall rotation matrix R can be estimated by multiplying the three previous matrices. Thus, we have Equation 15.

Note that both systems must result in the same rotation matrix.

## TWO-VIEW GEOMETRY

As depicted in Figure 5, when a space point $\dot{P}$ is observed by two cameras located at $\dot{O}$ and $\dot{O}'$, two projections $\dot{p}$ and $\dot{p}'$ are formed onto the image planes $\Pi$ and $\Pi'$. This setting is referred to *as two-view geometry, stereo vision* or *binocular vision*. The line joining the optical centers $\dot{O}$ and $\dot{O}'$ is called the *baseline*. The baseline intersects both images in two points $\dot{e}$ and $\dot{e}'$ that are called the *epipoles*. The lines joining the point

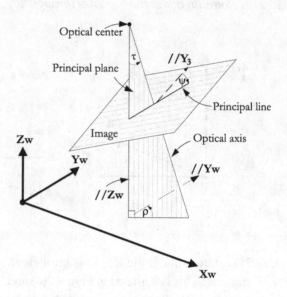

*Figure 3. Pan, $\rho$, tilt, $\tau$, and swing, $\psi$, angles*

projections and the epipoles are called the *epipolar lines*. In the figure shown, the two epipolar lines associated with the point $\dot{P}$ are **l** and **l'**. These lines are called *conjugate epipolar lines*. Note that an image point $\dot{p}$ has its correspondence on the epipolar line **l'** while an image point $\dot{p}'$ has its corresponding point on **l**. Finally, the optical centers along with the space point form a plane that is called the epipolar plane (which intersects the images at the epipolar lines). Different epipolar planes may exist for different points in space; however, all the epipolar planes must intersect at the baseline.

Note that the projection of the optical center $\dot{O}$ is the epipole $\dot{e}'$ and the projection of the optical center $\dot{O}'$ is the epipole $\dot{e}$ so:

$$\mathbf{e} = P\mathbf{O}' \qquad (16)$$

$$\mathbf{e}' = P'\mathbf{O} \qquad (17)$$

where **e** and **e'** are the homogeneous representation of the epipoles; **O** and **O'** are the homogeneous representation of the optical centers; and P and P' are the perspective projection matrices.

*Figure 4. Rotation is performed as a series of three 2D rotations: (a) Rotation about the $Z-axis$ through $R_\rho$. (b) Rotation about the $X_1-axis$ through $R_\tau$. (c) Rotation about the $Z_2-axis$ through $R_\psi$.*

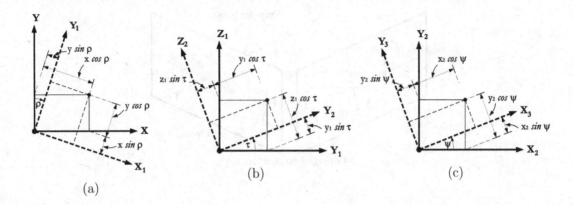

(a)    (b)    (c)

*Equation 15.*

$$R = R_\psi R_\tau R_\rho$$
$$= \begin{bmatrix} \cos\psi\cos\rho + \sin\psi\cos\tau\sin\rho & -\cos\psi\sin\rho + \sin\psi\cos\tau\cos\rho & \sin\psi\sin\tau \\ -\sin\psi\cos\rho + \cos\psi\cos\tau\sin\rho & \sin\psi\sin\rho + \cos\psi\cos\tau\cos\rho & \cos\psi\sin\tau \\ -\sin\tau\sin\rho & -\sin\tau\cos\rho & \cos\tau \end{bmatrix} \quad (15)$$

## The Fundamental Matrix

The fundamental matrix (O. D. Faugeras, 1992, Luong & Faugeras, 1995, Trucco & Verri, 1998, R. I. Hartley & Zisserman, 2004) plays a key role in projective geometry. It relates an image point $\dot{p}$ to its associated epipolar line $l'$ in the other image as:

$$l' = Fp \quad (18)$$

where $F$ is a 3×3 singular matrix called the fundamental matrix; $p$ is a homogeneous point; and $l'$ is an epipolar line in the other image where the corresponding point $\dot{p}'$ resides; i.e., $l'^T p' = p'^T l' = 0$. In other words:

$$p'^T Fp = 0. \quad (19)$$

If $F$ represents the fundamental matrix from one image to another, $F^T$ represents the fundamental matrix in the opposite direction. Thus, we have:

$$p^T F^T p' = 0. \quad (20)$$

There are many methods developed to estimate the fundamental matrix. Some of these methods rely on knowing the camera parameters and others use points correspondences to estimate the matrix.

## Estimating $F$ Using Camera Parameters

The perspective projection matrix $P$ can be partitioned as:

*Figure 5. Stereo vision: Two cameras located at $\dot{\mathbf{O}}$ and $\dot{\mathbf{O}}'$ are observing the space point $\dot{\mathbf{P}}$*

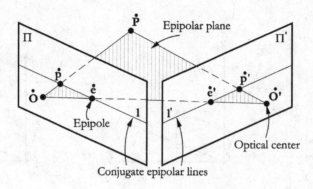

$$P = [AR \mid -AR\dot{O}] \qquad (21)$$

where A is the calibration matrix; R is the rotation matrix; and $\dot{O}$ is the location of the optical center. If AR is a 3×3 invertible matrix, which requires the optical center not to lie on the plane at infinity, then F is estimated as:

$$
\begin{aligned}
F &= [A'R']^{-1T}[\mathbf{O}-\mathbf{O}']_{\times}[AR]^{-1} \\
&= \left[[A'R'][\mathbf{O}-\mathbf{O}']\right]_{\times}[A'R'][AR]^{-1} \qquad (22) \\
&= [A'R']^{-1T}[AR]^{T}\left[[AR][\mathbf{O}-\mathbf{O}']\right]_{\times}
\end{aligned}
$$

where A and A' are the calibration matrices of both cameras; R and R' are the rotation matrices; $\dot{O}$ and $\dot{O}'$ are the optical centers; and $[.]_{\times}$ denotes the cross product matrix. For example, if **T** and **X** are 3D vectors then:

$$[\mathbf{T}]_{\times} = \begin{bmatrix} 0 & -t_3 & t_2 \\ t_3 & 0 & -t_1 \\ -t_2 & t_1 & 0 \end{bmatrix} \text{ such that } [\mathbf{T}]_{\times}\mathbf{X} = \mathbf{T}\times\mathbf{X}$$

$$(23)$$

Also, F can be estimated as:

$$F = [e']_{\times}P'P^{+} \qquad (24)$$

where **e'** is the second epipole; P' is the perspective projection matrix of the second camera; and $P^{+}$ is a 4×3 matrix called the pseudo-inverse of the perspective projection matrix of the first camera P (i.e., $PP^{+}=I$).

Estimating F using *point correspondences*. In case no camera parameters are available, the fundamental matrix F can be estimated if a set of matches between images is obtained. We will discuss two of the algorithms; the 8-point algorithm and RANSAC.

## The Eight-Point Algorithm

This algorithm utilizes the equation:

$$\mathbf{p}'^{T}F\mathbf{p} = 0 \qquad (25)$$

where $\dot{\mathbf{p}} = [x,y]^{T}$ and $\dot{\mathbf{p}}' = [x',y']^{T}$ is a pair of corresponding points. The previous equation can be written as:

$$
\begin{aligned}
x'xf_{11} + x'yf_{12} + x'f_{13} + y'xf_{21} + y'yf_{22} \\
+ y'f_{23} + xf_{31} + yf_{32} + f_{33} = 0
\end{aligned} \qquad (26)
$$

where $f_{ij} \mid i \in \{1,2,3\}$ and $j \in \{1,2,3\}$ are the terms of the fundamental matrix. If n (where $n \geq 8$) corresponding pairs are available and the terms of the fundamental matrix can be written as a 9D vector $\mathbf{F} = [f_{11}, f_{12}, f_{13}, f_{21}, f_{22}, f_{23}, f_{31}, f_{32}, f_{33}]^T$, then (R. I. Hartley & Zisserman, 2004):

$$\mathbb{F}\mathbf{F} = \begin{bmatrix} x_1' x_1 & x_1' y_1 & x_1' & y_1' x_1 & y_1' y_1 & y_1' & x_1 & y_1 & 1 \\ \vdots & \vdots & \vdots & \vdots & \vdots & \vdots & \vdots & \vdots & \vdots \\ x_n' x_n & x_n' y_n & x_n' & y_n' x_n & y_n' y_n & y_n' & x_n & y_n & 1 \end{bmatrix} \mathbf{F} = \mathbf{0} \tag{27}$$

.

A solution for $\mathbf{F}$ can be obtained using singular value decomposition (SVD) for the matrix $\mathbb{F}$. This is the last column of $\mathrm{V}$ in $\mathbb{F} = \mathrm{UDV}^T$.

As mentioned above, the fundamental matrix should be singular (and of rank 2); however, the matrix obtained may not have rank 2. Thus, the matrix $\mathrm{F}$ should be tuned to $\mathrm{F}'$, which minimizes the Frobenius norm $\| \mathrm{F} - \mathrm{F}' \|$ subject to $\det \mathrm{F}' = 0$.

# RANSAC: RANDOM SAMPLE CONSENSUS

The presence of outliers (i.e., mismatches) may affect the accuracy of the fundamental matrix. Thus, the random sample consensus (RANSAC) scheme for estimating the fundamental matrix using a large set of point correspondences is developed to avoid this inaccuracy by preventing outliers from contributing to the fundamental matrix. The steps are:

1. Select seven pairs randomly.
2. Compute the fundamental matrix $\mathrm{F}$ such that:

$$\mathbf{p}'^T \mathrm{F} \mathbf{p} = 0 \tag{28}$$

3. Check other pairs if they agree with the computed $\mathrm{F}$ by testing:

$$d(\mathrm{F}\mathbf{p}, \mathbf{p}') < t_{\mathrm{F}} \tag{29}$$

where $d(.)$ represents the Euclidean distance from $\dot{\mathbf{p}}'$ to the epipolar line $\mathbf{l}' = \mathrm{F}\mathbf{p}$; and $t_{\mathrm{F}}$ is a threshold. All pairs satisfying the previous condition (i.e., those that agree with the computed $\mathrm{F}$) are selected to the support set.

4. Repeat the previous steps and choose the largest support set together with its computed $\mathrm{F}$.

# The Perspective Projection Matrix Revisited

If the fundamental matrix $\mathrm{F}$ is known, the perspective projection matrices $\mathrm{P}$ and $\mathrm{P}'$ may be chosen as:

$$\mathrm{P} = [\mathrm{I} \mid \mathbf{0}] \quad \text{and} \quad \mathrm{P}' = [[\mathbf{e}']_\times \mathrm{F} \mid \mathbf{e}'] \tag{30}$$

where $\mathrm{I}$ is the identity matrix; $\mathbf{0} = [0,0,0]^T$; and $\mathbf{e}'$ is the homogeneous representation of the second epipole.

# The Essential Matrix

The essential matrix $\mathrm{E}$ (Longuet-Higgins, 1981) is a special form of the fundamental matrix $\mathrm{F}$ that exists when the calibration matrices $\mathrm{A}$ and $\mathrm{A}'$ are known. The relationship between $\mathrm{E}$ and $\mathrm{F}$ is given by:

$$\mathrm{E} = \mathrm{A}'^T \mathrm{F} \mathrm{A} \tag{31}$$

Similar to $\mathrm{F}$, we may write:

$$\mathbf{p}'^T \mathrm{E} \mathbf{p} = 0. \tag{32}$$

Note that, using singular value decomposition (SVD), $\mathrm{E}$ can be used to extract the rotation $\mathrm{R}$

and the translation **T** between cameras as (Elias, 2007a):

$$E = [\mathbf{T}]_\times R.$$ (33)

## The Homography Matrix

As shown in Figure 6, a point $\dot{\mathbf{p}}$ in one image can be mapped to its corresponding point $\dot{\mathbf{p}}'$ in the other image using a 3×3 homography matrix $H$:

$$\mathbf{p}' = H\mathbf{p}$$ (34)

The homography matrix $H$ is defined for all points on the plane $\Pi$.

There are many methods that can be used to estimate the homography matrix $H$ according to the type of input available.

### Estimating $H$ Using Four Pairs

Assuming that we have pair of corresponding coplanar points

$$\dot{\mathbf{p}}_i = [x_i, y_i]^T \text{ and } \dot{\mathbf{p}}_i' = [x_i', y_i']^T \mid i \in \{1, 2, 3, 4\},$$

it is required to compute a 3×3 homography matrix, $H$, that maps a source point $\dot{\mathbf{p}}_i$ into another destination one $\dot{\mathbf{p}}_i'$.

Each pair of corresponding points contributes to two linear equations for the elements of $H$. Working with the first pair and removing the scale factor by dividing by the third component, we get:

$$x_1' = \frac{h_{11}x_1 + h_{12}y_1 + h_{13}}{h_{31}x_1 + h_{32}y_1 + h_{33}}$$ (35)

and

$$y_1' = \frac{h_{21}x_1 + h_{22}y_1 + h_{23}}{h_{31}x_1 + h_{32}y_1 + h_{33}}$$ (36)

where $h_{mn}$ is the term at the $m^{th}$ row and $n^{th}$ column of the matrix $H$. Consequently,

$$x_1'(h_{31}x_1 + h_{32}y_1 + h_{33}) = h_{11}x_1 + h_{12}y_1 + h_{13}$$ (37)

and

$$y_1'(h_{31}x_1 + h_{32}y_1 + h_{33}) = h_{21}x_1 + h_{22}y_1 + h_{23}.$$ (38)

The homography matrix, $H$, has eight degrees of freedom; thus, it can be defined using only four corresponding pairs, which results in eight linear

*Figure 6. The positions of the corresponding pair $\dot{\mathbf{p}}$ and $\dot{\mathbf{p}}'$ are related by the homography matrix $H$, which defines the relation for all points on the same plane $\Pi$*

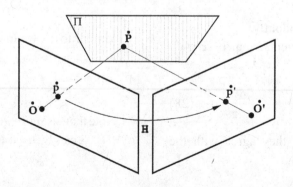

equations. These equations are sufficient to solve for H up to a scale factor. We choose one matrix term to have a certain value; e.g., $h_{33}=1$. Thus, the eight equations can be written as:

$$
\begin{bmatrix}
x_1 & y_1 & 1 & 0 & 0 & 0 & -x_1'x_1 & -x_1'y_1 \\
0 & 0 & 0 & x_1 & y_1 & 1 & -y_1'x_1 & -y_1'y_1 \\
x_2 & y_2 & 1 & 0 & 0 & 0 & -x_2'x_2 & -x_2'y_2 \\
0 & 0 & 0 & x_2 & y_2 & 1 & -y_2'x_2 & -y_2'y_2 \\
x_3 & y_3 & 1 & 0 & 0 & 0 & -x_3'x_3 & -x_3'y_3 \\
0 & 0 & 0 & x_3 & y_3 & 1 & -y_3'x_3 & -y_3'y_3 \\
x_4 & y_4 & 1 & 0 & 0 & 0 & -x_4'x_4 & -x_4'y_4 \\
0 & 0 & 0 & x_4 & y_4 & 1 & -y_4'x_4 & -y_4'y_4
\end{bmatrix}
\begin{bmatrix}
h_{11} \\ h_{12} \\ h_{13} \\ h_{21} \\ h_{22} \\ h_{23} \\ h_{31} \\ h_{32}
\end{bmatrix}
=
\begin{bmatrix}
x_1' \\ y_1' \\ x_2' \\ y_2' \\ x_3' \\ y_3' \\ x_4' \\ y_4'
\end{bmatrix}
\tag{39}
$$

Hence, all the terms of H can be determined.

## Estimating H *Using More Pairs*

In case more corresponding points are available (some of them may be outliers), RANSAC scheme may be used to estimate the homography matrix H. The steps can be summarized as:

1.  Choose four pairs randomly and estimate the homography matrix as done above. Due to the fact that Hp should result in $\mathbf{p}'$ if $\mathbf{p}$ and $\mathbf{p}'$ are a corresponding pair, the homography should be consistent with the relation:

$$
\mathbf{p}' \times H\mathbf{p} = \mathbf{0} \tag{40}
$$

where × indicates the cross product.

2.  Check if other pairs agree with the matrix computed. That is to check:

$$
d(H\mathbf{p}, \mathbf{p}') < t_{H} \tag{41}
$$

where $d(.)$ indicates the Euclidean distance; and $t_{H}$ is a threshold. If the condition above is true, then the pair ( $\dot{\mathbf{p}}$, $\dot{\mathbf{p}}'$ ) agrees with the matrix H.

3.  Repeat the process and pick up the matrix with the maximum number of support pairs.

## Estimating H *Using Plane Equation*

Suppose that the perspective projection matrices are defined by $P = A[I \mid \mathbf{0}]$ and $P' = A'[R \mid \mathbf{T}]$ and the plane equation is $\Pi = [\mathbf{N}^T, d]^T$, then the homography can be estimated as:

$$
H = A'\left[R - \frac{\mathbf{T}\mathbf{N}^T}{d}\right]A^{-1}. \tag{42}
$$

# 3D RECONSTRUCTION

3D reconstruction of objects from images is a fundamental topic in computer vision; e.g., (Morency, Rahimi, & Darrell, 2002, Mckinley, McWaters, & Jain, 2001). Among the varieties of this problem are 3D reconstruction from uncalibrated monocular image sequence (Azevedo et al., 2009, Fitzgibbon et al., 1998, Pollefeys et al., 1998), 3D reconstruction from calibrated monocular image sequence (Nguyen & Hanajik, 1995) and 3D reconstruction from stereo images. Information about camera parameters may range from intrinsic or extrinsic to both. Point correspondences plus the images may be the input to the process that produces the 3D model after reconstruction. According to the available input, the output can be in absolute coordinates, up to an unknown scaling factor or up to unknown projective transformation. For some specific applications, 3D information can be inferred from a single image.

In this section, we will discuss the 3D reconstruction of points, lines and planes.

## 3D Point Reconstruction

We may formulate the problem tackled in this section as follows. Given a stereo pair of images where two projections of some space point are identified, it is required to estimate the 3D position of the point in space whether camera parameters are known or not. Different techniques have been developed to obtain this estimation.

## Projective Reconstruction

In case no camera parameters are available, projective reconstruction can be applied. This type reconstruction may *not* result in a unique output as projective transformation may exist allowing different results to be acceptable.

In this case, if point correspondences are available, the fundamental matrix can be estimated. Hence, the perspective projection matrices may be obtained. Having the $P$ matrix for one image and a point $\dot{p}$, we can write:

$$p = PP$$

$$\begin{bmatrix} \tilde{\mathbf{P}}_1^T \\ \tilde{\mathbf{P}}_2^T \\ \tilde{\mathbf{P}}_3^T \end{bmatrix} \qquad (43)$$

or

$$p \times [PP] = 0 \qquad (44)$$

where $\tilde{\mathbf{P}}_i^T$ is the $i^{th}$ row in $P$; $\mathbf{P}$ is the homogeneous representation of the 3D point required; and $\times$ denotes the cross product. Consequently, for the pair $\dot{p} = [x, y]^T$ and $\dot{p}' = [x', y']^T$, we have:

$$\begin{bmatrix} x\tilde{\mathbf{P}}_3^T - \tilde{\mathbf{P}}_1^T \\ y\tilde{\mathbf{P}}_3^T - \tilde{\mathbf{P}}_2^T \\ x'\tilde{\mathbf{P}}_3'^T - \tilde{\mathbf{P}}_1'^T \\ y'\tilde{\mathbf{P}}_3'^T - \tilde{\mathbf{P}}_2'^T \end{bmatrix} \mathbf{P} = M\mathbf{P} = 0. \qquad (45)$$

Then singular value decomposition (SVD) can be applied to $M$ to get $UDV^T$. $\dot{\mathbf{P}}$ is the last column of $V$.

## Affine Reconstruction

The projective reconstruction can be refined to affine reconstruction where parallel lines remain parallel and ratios along them remain correct. This is done by detecting a plane $\Pi$ (e.g., three intersections of sets of lines that are supposed to be parallel can determine $\Pi$). This plane can be mapped to the plane at infinity $[0,0,0,1]^T$ using a 4×4 transformation matrix $T$. Hence:

$$T^{-1T}\Pi = [0,0,0,1]^T \quad \text{or} \quad T^T[0,0,0,1]^T = \Pi \qquad (46)$$

In other words:

$$\begin{bmatrix} 1 & 0 & 0 \\ 0 & 1 & 0 \\ 0 & 0 & 1 \\ 0 & 0 & 0 \end{bmatrix} \Pi \begin{bmatrix} 0 \\ 0 \\ 0 \\ 1 \end{bmatrix} = \Pi \qquad (47)$$

where $T = \begin{bmatrix} I & | & \mathbf{0} \\ \Pi^T & \end{bmatrix}$ is the transformation to be applied to scene points as well as the perspective projection matrices.

In the methods to follow, we assume the existence of camera parameters.

## Distance Minimization

Assume that the origin of the world coordinate system is placed at the first camera such that $\mathbf{T} = [0,0,0]^T = \mathbf{0}$ and $R = I$ where $I$ is the identity matrix, then a 3D point $\dot{p}$ can be projected onto this image as $PP = A[I \mid \mathbf{0}]P$ where $A$ is the calibration matrix of the first camera. If the motion from the first camera to the second is denoted as a rotation matrix $R'$ and a translation vector $\mathbf{T}'$, then the projection onto the second image is obtained as $P'\mathbf{P} = A'[R' \mid \mathbf{T}']\mathbf{P}$ where $A'$ is the calibration matrix of the second camera. Hence, given the projections $\dot{p}$ and $\dot{p}'$ onto both images, the estimated position of the 3D point can be obtained by minimizing the distance between the image points and the back-projections of initial estimate of the 3D point as (Zhang, 1998):

$$\hat{\mathbf{P}} = \arg\min_{\dot{\mathbf{P}}} \left( \| \mathbf{p} - A[I \mid \mathbf{0}]\mathbf{P} \|^2 + \| \mathbf{p}' - A'[R' \mid \mathbf{T}']\mathbf{P} \|^2 \right) \tag{48}$$

where $\hat{\dot{\mathbf{P}}}$ is the estimated position of the 3D point; and $\mathbf{P}$ is an initial estimate of the point in 3D space. Notice that this method requires an initial estimate for $\dot{\mathbf{P}}$.

## Intersecting Camera Rays

A concept known as triangulation can be used to locate points in 3D space if camera positions as well as point projections are known. Figure 7 shows two rays passing through the optical centers $\dot{O}$ and $\dot{O}'$ and the projections $\dot{p}$ and $\dot{p}'$. Those rays should intersect at the position of the 3D point. (Triangulation, from the perspective, is different from Delaunay triangulation that may be used to generate 3D meshes.)

If the rays $\dot{O}\dot{p}$ and $\dot{O}'\dot{p}'$ intersect the ideal plane at $\dot{\mathbf{P}}_\infty$ and $\dot{\mathbf{P}}'_\infty$ respectively, then, $\mathbf{P}$ can be estimated as (Rothwell, Csurka, & Faugeras, 1995):

$$\mathbf{P} = \alpha_1 \mathbf{O} + \beta_1 \mathbf{P}_\infty = \alpha_2 \mathbf{O}' + \beta_2 \mathbf{P}'_\infty \tag{1.49}$$

where $\mathbf{P}_\infty$ and $\mathbf{P}'_\infty$ are homogeneous directions given by $[\dot{\mathbf{P}}_\infty, 0]^T$ and $[\dot{\mathbf{P}}'_\infty, 0]^T$. Note that $\mathbf{p} = P\mathbf{P}_\infty$

and $\mathbf{p}' = P'\mathbf{P}'_\infty$. Because the last terms in $\mathbf{P}_\infty$ and $\mathbf{P}'_\infty$ are always 0, we can write:

$$\mathbf{p} = \tilde{P}\dot{\mathbf{P}}_\infty \quad \text{and} \quad \mathbf{p}' = \tilde{P}'\dot{\mathbf{P}}'_\infty \tag{50}$$

where $\tilde{P}$ and $\tilde{P}'$ are 3×3 invertible matrices representing the first three columns of $P$ and $P'$. Hence,

$$\dot{\mathbf{P}}_\infty = \tilde{P}^{-1}\mathbf{p} \quad \text{and} \quad \dot{\mathbf{P}}'_\infty = \tilde{P}'^{-1}\mathbf{p}' \tag{51}$$

Thus,

$$\mathbf{P}'_\infty = \frac{\alpha_1}{\beta_2}\mathbf{O} + \frac{\beta_1}{\beta_2}\mathbf{P}_\infty - \frac{\alpha_2}{\beta_2}\mathbf{O}'. \tag{52}$$

These are four equations having three unknowns $\frac{\alpha_1}{\beta_2}$, $\frac{\beta_1}{\beta_2}$ and $\frac{\alpha_2}{\beta_2}$. Then $\dot{\mathbf{P}}$ is obtained by back substitution.

## Nonintersecting Camera Rays

Calculating the point of intersection where optical rays intersect may be the ideal case. In the general case, as shown in Figure 8, the rays are most likely to be skew if the locations of cameras and/or point projections are inaccurate. (This could happen due to sensor problems or noise existence.)

In case rays are skew, the location of the 3D point can be estimated as the midpoint of the perpendicular to both rays as (Beardsley et al., 1997):

$$\dot{\mathbf{P}} = \left[ [I - \dot{\mathbf{P}}_\infty \dot{\mathbf{P}}_\infty^T] + [I - \dot{\mathbf{P}}'_\infty \dot{\mathbf{P}}'^T_\infty] \right]^{-1}$$
$$\left[ \dot{\mathbf{O}} + \dot{\mathbf{O}}' - [\dot{\mathbf{O}}^T\dot{\mathbf{P}}_\infty]\dot{\mathbf{P}}_\infty - [\dot{\mathbf{O}}'^T\dot{\mathbf{P}}'_\infty]\dot{\mathbf{P}}'_\infty \right] \tag{53}$$

where $\dot{\mathbf{P}}$ is the 3D point; $\dot{\mathbf{O}}$ and $\dot{\mathbf{O}}'$ are inhomogeneous representations of camera locations; $\dot{\mathbf{P}}_\infty$

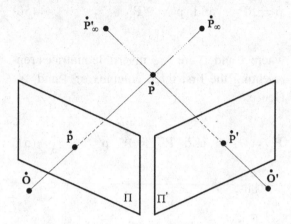

*Figure 7. Triangulation: The location of the reconstructed 3D point $\dot{\mathbf{P}}$ is the intersection between the lines $\langle \dot{\mathbf{O}}\dot{\mathbf{p}} \rangle$ and $\langle \dot{\mathbf{O}}'\dot{\mathbf{p}}' \rangle$*

and $\dot{\mathbf{P}}'_\infty$ are the intersections of the rays with the ideal plane; $\mathbf{I}$ is a 3×3 identity matrix; and $\dot{\mathbf{P}}_\infty$ and $\dot{\mathbf{P}}'_\infty$ are normalized to unit magnitude. This can be generalized to any number of views $n$ (Beardsley et al., 1997) to get:

$$\dot{\mathbf{P}} = \left[ \sum_{i=1}^{n} [\mathbf{I} - \dot{\mathbf{P}}_{i\infty}\dot{\mathbf{P}}_{i\infty}^T] \right]^{-1} \left[ \sum_{i=1}^{n} \dot{\mathbf{O}}_i - \sum_{i=1}^{n} [\dot{\mathbf{O}}_i^T \dot{\mathbf{P}}_{i\infty}\dot{\mathbf{P}}_{i\infty}] \right] \quad (54)$$

where $\dot{\mathbf{P}}$ is the 3D point; $i$ is the view number; $\dot{\mathbf{O}}_i$ represents inhomogeneous representation of camera $i$ location; and $\dot{\mathbf{P}}_{i\infty}$ represents the intersection of different rays with the ideal plane. Again, the directions $\dot{\mathbf{P}}_{i\infty}$ are normalized to unit magnitude.

Note that a better estimate can be obtained when minimizing the residual in the measurement equations (Sutherland, 1974):

$$x_j = \frac{p_{11}^{(j)}X + p_{12}^{(j)}Y + p_{13}^{(j)}Z + p_{14}^{(j)}W}{p_{31}^{(j)}X + p_{32}^{(j)}Y + p_{33}^{(j)}Z + p_{34}^{(j)}W} \quad (55)$$

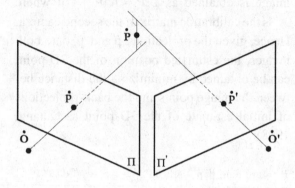

*Figure 8. A 3D point is estimated as the midpoint of the perpendicular to two rays passing through the optical centers and the two projections*

$$y_j = \frac{p_{21}^{(j)}X + p_{22}^{(j)}Y + p_{23}^{(j)}Z + p_{24}^{(j)}W}{p_{31}^{(j)}X + p_{32}^{(j)}Y + p_{33}^{(j)}Z + p_{34}^{(j)}W} \quad (56)$$

where $x_j$ and $y_j$ are feature location, $[X, Y, Z, W]^T$ is the homogeneous point and

$$p_{mn}^{(j)} \mid m \in \{1, 2, 3, 4\}, n \in \{1, 2, 3\}$$

are the perspective projection matrix entries. These equations are multiplied by the denominator and solved as a singular value decomposition or eigenvalue problem.

## 3D LINE RECONSTRUCTION

As done previously with 3D point reconstruction, let us formulate the problem of 3D line reconstruction as follows. Given a stereo pair of images where two projections of the same line are identified, it is required to estimate the 3D line in space if camera parameters are known.

As shown in Figure 9, consider the planes $\Pi$ and $\Pi'$ passing through the optical centers and the projections $\mathbf{l}$ and $\mathbf{l}'$. These planes are given by (Elias, 2004, 2007b):

$$\Pi = \mathbf{P}^T \mathbf{l} \quad \text{and} \quad \Pi' = \mathbf{P}'^T \mathbf{l}' \quad (57)$$

*Figure 9. A 3D line is the intersection between two planes passing through their projections onto images and the optical centers*

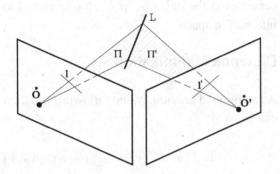

The 3D line $L$ is the intersection between the planes $\Pi$ and $\Pi'$. From the definition of the 3D line, $L$ is represented as:

$$L = \begin{bmatrix} \Pi^T \\ \Pi'^T \end{bmatrix} = \begin{bmatrix} \mathbf{l}^T \mathsf{P} \\ \mathbf{l}'^T \mathsf{P}' \end{bmatrix} \tag{58}$$

## Plane Reconstruction

A plane can be reconstructed using two intersecting lines projected onto both images. The same plane can be determined by three points or a line

and a point. Those last two cases can be turned easily into two intersecting lines.

Let us consider the case where two pairs of intersecting lines $(\mathbf{l}_1, \mathbf{l}_1')$ and $(\mathbf{l}_2, \mathbf{l}_2')$ appear on a pair of stereo images as shown in Figure 10. Each line pair can be used to reconstruct its 3D line in space as done previously to get:

$$L_1 = \begin{bmatrix} \Pi_1^T \\ \Pi_1'^T \end{bmatrix} = \begin{bmatrix} \mathbf{N}_1^T \mid d_1 \\ \mathbf{N}_1'^T \mid d_1' \end{bmatrix} = \begin{bmatrix} \mathbf{l}_1^T \mathsf{P} \\ \mathbf{l}_1'^T \mathsf{P}' \end{bmatrix} \tag{59}$$

and

$$L_2 = \begin{bmatrix} \Pi_2^T \\ \Pi_2'^T \end{bmatrix} = \begin{bmatrix} \mathbf{N}_2^T \mid d_2 \\ \mathbf{N}_2'^T \mid d_2' \end{bmatrix} = \begin{bmatrix} \mathbf{l}_2^T \mathsf{P} \\ \mathbf{l}_2'^T \mathsf{P}' \end{bmatrix}. \tag{60}$$

As $\mathbf{l}_1$ intersects $\mathbf{l}_2$ at $\dot{\mathbf{p}}$ and $\mathbf{l}_1'$ intersects $\mathbf{l}_2'$ at $\dot{\mathbf{p}}'$, the intersection pair $(\dot{\mathbf{p}}, \dot{\mathbf{p}}')$ can be used to reconstruct the intersection point in space $\dot{\mathsf{P}}$ as done above (i.e., $L_1\mathsf{P} = L_2\mathsf{P} = 0$).

The plane equation $\Pi$ can be obtained as:

$$\Pi = \begin{bmatrix} \mathbf{N} \\ d \end{bmatrix} = \begin{bmatrix} [\mathbf{N}_1 \times \mathbf{N}_1'] \times [\mathbf{N}_2 \times \mathbf{N}_2'] \\ [\mathbf{N}_1 \times \mathbf{N}_1'] \times [\mathbf{N}_2 \times \mathbf{N}_2'] \bullet \dot{\mathsf{P}} \end{bmatrix} \tag{61}$$

*Figure 10. A plane is reconstructed using a pair of intersecting 3D lines*

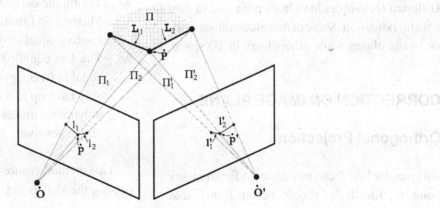

where $\mathbf{N}, \mathbf{N}_1, \mathbf{N}_1', \mathbf{N}_2, \mathbf{N}_2'$ are the normal vectors to $\Pi, \Pi_1, \Pi_1', \Pi_2, \Pi_2'$ respectively; $d$ is the perpendicular distance from the origin to the reconstructed plane; $\dot{\mathbf{P}}$ is the inhomogeneous representation of the intersection point in 3D space; and $\times$ denotes the cross product while $\bullet$ denotes the dot product.

## Plane Given Homography

R. I. Hartley and Zisserman (2004) mentioned that if the perspective projection matrices are given by $\mathtt{P} = [\mathtt{I} \mid \mathbf{0}]$ and $\mathtt{P}' = [\tilde{\mathtt{P}}' \mid \tilde{\mathbf{P}}']$ and the homography induced for the plane $\Pi = [\mathbf{V}, 1]^T$ is $\mathtt{H}$, then $\mathbf{V}$ can be obtained linearly by solving:

$$\lambda \mathtt{H} = \tilde{\mathtt{P}}' - \tilde{\mathbf{P}}' \mathbf{V}^T \tag{62}$$

which are linear in the entries of $\mathbf{V}$ and $\lambda$. The exact solution is obtained if $\mathtt{H}$ satisfies:

$$\mathtt{H}^T \mathtt{F} + \mathtt{F}^T \mathtt{H} = \mathbf{0} \tag{63}$$

or, in other words, if $\mathtt{H}^T \mathtt{F}$ is skew-symmetric.

## INACCURACY CORRECTION

Inaccuracy may exist due to different reasons (e.g., noise or sensor problems). Hence, rays that should intersect in space may turn out to be skew. Different techniques have been proposed to deal with this situation. Some of these techniques work on image planes while others work in 3D space.

## CORRECTION ON IMAGE PLANE

### Orthogonal Projection

An epipolar line $\mathbf{l}'$ can be estimated for an image point $\dot{\mathbf{p}}$. Ideally, $\dot{\mathbf{p}}'$ should lie on $\mathbf{l}'$ such that

$\mathbf{p}'^T \mathbf{l}' = 0$; however, due to inaccuracy, $\dot{\mathbf{p}}'$ may not lie on $\mathbf{l}'$. In this case, the orthogonal projection $\hat{\dot{\mathbf{p}}}'$ from $\dot{\mathbf{p}}'$ onto $\mathbf{l}'$ is computed. Consequently, the rays passing through the optical centers and the pair $(\dot{\mathbf{p}}, \hat{\dot{\mathbf{p}}}')$ are guaranteed to intersect in space.

## Distance Minimization

As mentioned previously, the following equation can be used:

$$\hat{\mathbf{P}} = \arg \min_{\mathbf{P}} \left( \| \mathbf{p} - \mathtt{A}[\mathtt{I} \mid \mathbf{0}]\mathbf{P} \|^2 + \| \mathbf{p}' - \mathtt{A}'[\mathtt{R} \mid \mathbf{T}]\mathbf{P} \|^2 \right) \tag{64}$$

The problem can be reformulated so as to minimize the function (R. I. Hartley & Sturm, 1995, 1994):

$$d(\mathbf{p}, \mathbf{l})^2 + d(\mathbf{p}', \mathbf{l}')^2 \tag{65}$$

where $\mathbf{l}$ and $\mathbf{l}'$ range over all choices of corresponding epipolar lines. This *optimal correction* method has the following steps:

1. Parameterization of the pencil of the epipolar lines in the first image by a parameter $t$;
2. Computing the conjugate epipolar line, $\mathbf{l}'$, of $\mathbf{l}$ using the fundamental matrix $\mathtt{F}$;
3. Expressing the previous equation as a function of $t$;
4. Taking the derivative of the last step;
5. Maxima and minima happen when the derivative equals to 0;
6. The last equality (where the derivative is equal to 0) is a polynomial of degree 6 that may have up to 6 real roots. Solving such a polynomial makes this method computationally expensive.

This method ensures that the two optical rays passing through $\hat{\dot{\mathbf{p}}}$ and $\hat{\dot{\mathbf{p}}}'$ intersect in space.

## Normalization

The normalization method proposed in (R. Hartley, 1997) can be used prior to applying the eight-point algorithm to reduce the pixel noise sensitivity. The experiments in (Boufama & Habed, 2004) have shown the improvement of the accuracy of the recovered 3D structure.

## CORRECTION IN SPACE

As mentioned previously, this is the case where a 3D point is estimated as the midpoint of the perpendicular to skew rays passing through the optical centers and corresponding image points.

## CONCLUSION

In the preceding chapter, we discussed the basic elements of projective geometry that may be needed when reconstructing (or modeling) objects in 3D space from images. We also discussed different methods to deal with inaccuracy that may exist due to different reasons (e.g., noise or sensor problems). The concepts and items discussed can be used together with other steps to solve varieties of the 3D reconstruction problem. For example, if the intrinsic and extrinsic parameters of the camera are known, one can obtain 3D points by intersecting camera rays. In case of inaccuracy and skew camera rays, a 3D point can still be approximated as the nearest point to both rays. A 3D line matrix can also be obtained as the intersection between planes passing through the camera centers and their projections. If 3D lines are estimated, equations for planes containing them can also be estimated. In case that camera parameters are not available, one may use point correspondences to estimate the fundamental matrix, which in turn can be used to get the perspective matrix needed for subsequent steps. If intrinsic camera parameters are available, one can turn the fundamental matrix into its essential counterpart, which in turn can be used to recover extrinsic parameters that may be used for other steps. Note that we emphasized on the reconstruction of the primitives; points, lines, and planes, which can be utilized to build more complex 3D models.

## REFERENCES

Azevedo, T. C. S., Tavares, J. M. R. S., & Vaz, M. A. P. (2009). 3D object reconstruction from uncalibrated images using an off-the-shelf camera. In Tavares, J. M. R. S., & Jorge, R. M. N. (Eds.), *Advances in computational vision and medical image processing* (p. 117).

Beardsley, P. A., Zisserman, A., & Murray, D. W. (1997). Sequential updating of projective and affine structure from motion. *International Journal of Computer Vision, 23*(3), 235–259.

Boufama, B., & Habed, A. (2004). Three-dimensional structure calculation: achieving accuracy without calibration. *Image and Vision Computing, 22*(12), 1039–1049.

Elias, R. (2004). Wide baseline matching through homographic transformation. In *Proceedings of the 17th international conference on pattern recognition* (Vol. 4, p. 130-133). Cambridge, UK: IEEE Computer Society.

Elias, R. (2007a). Enhancing accuracy of camera rotation angles detected by inaccurate sensors and expressing them in different systems for wide baseline stereo. In *Proceedings of 8th International Conference on Quality Control by Artificial Vision* (Vol. 6356, pp. 635617-1:8). Le Creusot, France: SPIE.

Elias, R. (2007b). Sparse view stereo matching. *Pattern Recognition Letters, 28*(13), 1667–1678.

Elias, R. (2009a). Geometric modeling in computer vision: An introduction to projective geometry. In B. Wah (Ed.), *Wiley encyclopedia of computer science and engineering* (Vol. 3, p. 1400-1416). John Wiley & Sons.

Elias, R. (2009b). *Modeling of environments: From sparse views to obstacle reconstruction.* Germany: LAP Lambert Academic Publishing.

Faugeras, O. (1996). *Three-dimentional computer vision, a geometric viewpoint.* Cambridge, MA: MIT Press.

Faugeras, O. D. (1992). What can be seen in three dimensions with an uncalibrated stereo rig. In *Proceedings of the Second European Conference on Computer Vision* (pp. 563–578). London, UK: Springer-Verlag. Retrieved from http://portal.acm.org/citation.cfm?id=645305.648717

Fitzgibbon, A. W., Cross, G., & Zisserman, A. (1998). Automatic 3D model construction for turn-table sequences. In *Lecture Notes in Comuter Science 1506, 3D Structure from Multiple Images of Large-Scale Environments, European Workshop, SMILE'98* (p. 155-170).

Hartley, R. (1997). In defence of the eight-point algorithm. *IEEE Transactions on Pattern Recognition and Machine Intelligence, 19*(6), 580–593.

Hartley, R. I., & Sturm, P. (1994). Triangulation. *American Image Understanding Workshop,* (pp. 957-966).

Hartley, R. I., & Sturm, P. (1995). Triangulation. In *Computer Analysis of Images and Patterns, 6th International Conference* (Vol. 970, p. 190-197). Prague, Czech Republic: Springer.

Hartley, R. I., & Zisserman, A. (2004). *Multiple view geometry in computer vision* (2nd ed.). Cambridge, UK: Cambridge University Press.

Longuet-Higgins, H. C. (1981). A computer algorithm for reconstructing a scene from two projections. *Nature, 293*(10), 133–135.

Luong, Q. T., & Faugeras, O. (1995). The fundamental matrix: Theory, algorithms, and stability analysis. *International Journal of Computer Vision, 17,* 43–75.

Mckinley, T., McWaters, M., & Jain, V. (2001). 3d reconstruction from a stereo pair without the knowledge of intrinsic or extrinsic parameters. *International Workshop on Digital and Computational Video,* (p. 148).

Morency, L. P., Rahimi, A., & Darrell, T. (2002). *3d model acquisition from stereo images. In 3d Data Processing, Visualization and Transmission* (pp. 172–176). Fast.

Nguyen, H. V., & Hanajik, M. (1995). 3-D scene reconstruction from image sequences. In *Lecture Notes in Comuter Science 970, Computer Analysis of Images and Patterns CAIP '95, 6th International Conference* (p. 182-189).

Pollefeys, M., Koch, R., Vergauwen, M., & Gool, L. V. (1998). Metric 3D surface reconstruction from uncalibrated image sequences. In *Lecture Notes in Computer Science 1506, 3D Structure from Multiple Images of Large-Scale Environments, European Workshop, SMILE'98* (p. 139-154).

Rothwell, C., Csurka, G., & Faugeras, O. (1995, April). *A comparison of projective reconstruction methods for pairs of views* (Tech. Rep. No. 2538). Unité de Recherche INRIA-Sophia Antipolis: Institut National de Recherche en Informatique et Automatique, INRIA.

Saxena, A., Sun, M., & Ng, A. Y. (2007). Learning 3-D scene structure from a single still image. In *ICCV Workshop on 3D Representation for Recognition (3DRR07).*

Snavely, N., Seitz, S. M., & Szeliski, R. (2006a). Photo tourism: Exploring photo collections in 3D. In *ACM SIGGRAPH 2006 Papers* (pp. 835–846). New York, NY: ACM. Retrieved from http://doi.acm.org/10.1145/1179352.1141964

Snavely, N., Seitz, S. M., & Szeliski, R. (2006b, July). Photo tourism: Exploring photo collections in 3D. *ACM Transactions on Graphics, 25*, 835–846. Retrieved from http://doi.acm.org/10.1145/1141911.1141964

Snavely, N., Seitz, S. M., & Szeliski, R. (2008, November). Modeling the world from Internet photo collections. *International Journal of Computer Vision, 80*, 189–210. Retrieved from http://portal.acm.org/citation.cfm?id=1412654.1412673

Sutherland, I. E. (1974, September). Three-dimensional data input by tablet. *SIGGRAPH Computer Graphics, 8*, 86–86. Retrieved from http://doi.acm.org/10.1145/988026.988036

Trucco, E., & Verri, A. (1998). *Introductory techniques for 3-D computer vision*. Upper Saddle River, NJ: Prentice Hall PTR.

Wolf, P. R., & DeWitt, B. A. (2000). *Elements of photogrammetry (with applications in GIS)* (3rd ed.). McGraw-Hill Higher Education.

Zhang, Z. (1995). An automatic and robust algorithm for determining motion and structure from two perspective images. In *Lecture Notes in Computer Science 970, Computer Analysis of Images and Patterns CAIP '95, 6th International Conference* (pp. 174-181).

Zhang, Z. (1998). A new multistage approach to motion and structure estimation by gradually enforcing geometric constrains. In R. Chin & T. C. Pong (Eds.), *Third Asian Conference on Computer Vision* (Vol. II, p. 567-574). Hong Kong, China: Springer.

## KEY TERMS AND DEFINITIONS

**Baseline:** The distance between two cameras observing the same scene.

**Calibration Matrix (of a camera):** A 3×3 matrix mapping the normalized image coordinates to the retinal coordinates.

**Conjugate Epipolar Lines:** The epipolar lines in a stereo pair that are associated with the same 3D point.

**Direction:** A point on the ideal plane.

**Epipolar Line:** The line connecting the epipole and the projection of a point onto an image. Also, this line is the intersection between the epipolar plane associated with the 3D point and the image plane.

**Epipolar Plane:** The plane formed by the optical centers and the observed 3D point.

**Epipole:** The intersection between the baseline and each image.

**Essential Matrix:** A 3×3 matrix representing a special form of the fundamental matrix. It exists when the calibration matrices of both cameras are known.

**Extrinsic Parameters (of a camera):** The external parameters of a camera; i.e., orientation and location.

**Fundamental Matrix:** A 3×3 matrix relating a point in one image to its epipolar line in the other image.

**Homography Matrix:** A 3×3 transformation matrix relating the perspective projections of a plane.

**Ideal Plane:** The plane at infinity.

**Ideal Point:** A point on the plane at infinity.

**Intrinsic Parameters (of a camera):** The internal parameters of a camera; e.g., focal length, principal point, etc.

**Line:** In 2D space, a line is represented by a 3D vector denoting the coefficients of the linear equation. In 3D space, a line can be represented as a 2×4 matrix denoting the intersection between two planes.

**Optical Axis:** The line passing through the optical center and perpendicular to the image plane.

**Optical Center:** The camera location.

**Perspective Projection Matrix:** A 3×4 matrix projecting a 3D point onto a 2D image plane. This matrix is sometimes called the camera matrix.

**Point:** In 2D space, a point is represented as a 2D vector in inhomogeneous coordinates and as a 3D vector in homogeneous coordinates. In 3D space, a point is represented as a 3D vector in inhomogeneous coordinates and as a 4D vector in homogeneous coordinates.

**Principal Point:** The intersection between the optical axis and the image plane.

**Rotation Matrix (of a camera):** A 3×3 matrix defining the orientation of a camera.

# Chapter 3
# PDE–Based Image Processing:
## Image Restoration

**Rajeev Srivastava**
*Institute of Technology, Banaras Hindu University (ITBHU), India*

## ABSTRACT

*This chapter describes the basic concepts of partial differential equations (PDEs) based image modelling and their applications to image restoration. The general basic concepts of partial differential equation (PDE)-based image modelling and processing techniques are discussed for image restoration problems. These techniques can also be used in the design and development of efficient tools for various image processing and vision related tasks such as restoration, enhancement, segmentation, registration, inpainting, shape from shading, 3D reconstruction of objects from multiple views, and many more. As a case study, the topic in consideration is oriented towards image restoration using PDEs formalism since image restoration is considered to be an important pre-processing task for 3D surface geometry, reconstruction, and many other applications. An image may be subjected to various types of noises during its acquisition leading to degraded quality of the image, and hence, the noise must be reduced. The noise may be additive or multiplicative in nature. Here, the PDE-based models for removal of both types of noises are discussed. As examples, some PDE-based schemes have been implemented and their comparative study with other existing techniques has also been presented.*

## INTRODUCTION

Image processing is a rapidly growing field which can be defined as the manipulation of an image for the purpose of either extracting information from the image or producing an alternative representation of the image. The scientific structure of any image can be supposed to be based on an intrinsic principles of mathematics i.e. from im-

age analysis to image processing. Image analysis includes modeling and analysis of original image itself, i.e. from image space analysis to different methods to represent image. The various tools of image analysis include spectral analysis, wavelets, statistics, level-sets and partial differential equations (PDEs). On the other hand, image processing is to modify the original image to improve the quality or extracting information from the given

DOI: 10.4018/978-1-4666-0113-0.ch003

image, for example, image restoration, compression, segmentation, shape and texture analysis. There are two dual fields that are directly connected to the image processing in contemporary Computer science. These are Computer vision which is related to the construction of the 3D world from the observed 2D images; and another one is Computer graphics which pursues the opposite direction in designing suitable 2D scene images to simulate our 3D world. Image processing can be considered as the crucial middle way connecting the vision and graphics fields. Image processing can be considered as an input-output system shown in Figure 1.

$I_0$ is the input data which represents an observed or measured single image or image sequences; $\tau$ denotes a typical image processor e.g. restoration, enhancement, segmentation, compression, interpolation, feature extraction, inpainting etc.; and $I$ denotes output which is also an image or an image sequence $(I_1, I_2, I_3, \ldots)$ that contains all the targeted image features. The problem very often encountered in this area is to design an efficient and cost effective and accurate image processor. Typical design tasks include: de-noising, deblurring, edge detection, intensity enhancement, inpainting, interpolation, compression and decompression etc. In addition to these relatively low-level tasks, there are mid- and high-level tasks like disocclusion, shape from shading, motion analysis, image segmentation, and pattern identification and recognition. In image representation (Jain, 2006), one is concerned with characterization of the quantity that each picture element or pixel represents. An image could represent luminance of objects in a scene such as in digital photography, the absorption characteristics of the

body tissue as in X-Ray imaging, the radar cross section of a target in radar imaging, the temperature profile of a region in infrared imaging or the gravitational field in an area in geophysical imaging. In general, any 2D function that contains information can be considered as an image. Image models give a logical or quantitative description of the properties of this function. There are three crucial ingredients of image processing which include modeling, analysis, and efficient implementation of processing tools. The design of a successful image processing technique relies on having a successful model for images. A fundamental issue faced in the design of image analysis techniques is the identification and characterization of the image space. The various approaches to *image modeling and analysis* include statistical representations or random field modeling; spectral and wavelet representations; and scale-space representations or regularity spaces.

The statistical approaches treat images as samples from random fields, which are often modeled by Markov or Gibbs fields or via statistical learning from an image database. The statistical properties of the fields are often established through the filtering technique and learning theory. Statistical models describe an image as a member of an ensemble, often characterized by its mean and covariance functions. This permits development of algorithms that are useful for an entire class or an ensemble of images rather than for a single image. Often the ensemble is assumed to be stationary so that the mean and covariance functions can easily be estimated. Random field modeling is the most appropriate approach for describing natural images with rich texture patterns

*Figure 1. An image processing system*

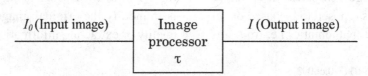

such as trees and mountains. Stationary models are useful in data compression problems such as transform coding, restoration problems such as Wiener filtering (Jain, 2006), and in other applications where global properties of an ensemble are sufficient. A more effective use of these models in image processing is to consider them to be spatially varying or piecewise spatially invariant.

The spectral and wavelet representations are also playing an important role in the design and analysis of an efficient image processor. Wavelet analysis is about analyzing signal with short duration finite energy functions. They transform the signal under investigation into another representation which presents the signal in more useful form. This transformation of the signal is called Wavelet Transform (Gonzalez, 1987) i.e. Wavelet Transforms are based on small waves, called wavelets, of varying frequency and limited duration. Unlike the Fourier transform, we have a variety of wavelets that are used for signal analysis. Choice of a particular wavelet depends on the type of application in hand. Wavelet Transforms provides time-frequency view i.e. provides both frequency as well as temporal (localization) information and exhibits multi-resolution characteristics. Fourier transform is good for periodic or stationary signals and Wavelet is good for transients. Localization property allows wavelets to give efficient representation of transients. In Wavelet transforms a signal can be converted and manipulated while keeping resolution across the entire signal and still based in time i.e. Wavelets have special ability to examine signals simultaneously in both time and frequency. Wavelets are mathematical functions that satisfy certain criteria, like a zero mean, and are used for analyzing and representing signals or other functions. A set of dilations and Translations of a chosen mother wavelet is used for the spatial/frequency analysis of an input signal. The Wavelet Transform uses overlapping functions of variable size for analysis. The overlapping nature of the transform alleviates the blocking artefacts, as each

input sample contributes to several samples of the output. The variable size of the basis functions, in addition, leads to superior energy compaction and good perceptual quality of the decompressed image. Wavelets Transform is based on the concept of sub-band coding (Gonzalez, 1987; Soman, 2004; Topiwala, 1998). The current applications of wavelet include statistical signal processing, Image processing, climate analysis, financial time series analysis, heart monitoring, seismic signal de- noising, de-noising of astronomical images, audio and video compression, compression of medical image stacks, finger print analysis, fast solution of partial differential equations, computer graphics etc.

The scale-space decomposition is a partial differential equation (PDE) based approach to the multi-scale analysis of images. This theory is based on the linear filtering or heat diffusion process, and was highlighted by the famous nonlinear model as proposed by (Perona, & Malik, 1990) for removing small-scale noise images without losing large scale structures like edges. There are other novel theories and trends for image analysis, including regular-space representations by the bounded variation (BV) space, free boundary models, and shape models (Romeny, 1994).

The *first step* of image processing is to *construct suitable models* for the given task. Currently, processing models are being developed using tools like Bayesian decision, variational optimization, inverse problems and the like. These approaches arise from fields such as statistical mechanics, the calculus of variations, nonlinear PDEs, differential geometry and topology, harmonic and functional analysis, and numerical analysis. For example, numerous PDE based methods (Perona, & Malik, 1990; Rudin *et al.*, 1992; Witkin, 1983; Gilboa *et al.*, 2004) have been proposed for image de-noising problem using PDEs. Once an image processing model is selected, the *next step is its analysis*, in order to answer questions of existence and uniqueness, stability, properties of solutions, and so on. Many image processing models are nonlinear or non-convex. Analyzing them requires new mathematical insights. Relatively few image processing models have been analyzed in this way. There is a vast engineering literature of image processors, which were mostly developed based on empirical insights and leaps of good intuition. They require rigorous mathematical analysis that can be crucial for answering questions of great practical significance, such as which among the many techniques proposed for the same task is superior, what effect the various parameters that appear in a method have on its behavior, and under what conditions a given technique can be expected to perform well. Finally, an efficient algorithm for implementing the processing model is devised.

The image restoration is a fundamental pre-processing step of many image processing or computer vision related applications. The goal of image restoration problem is to restore the degraded image for further analysis and use of image data in a specific application. During the capture or formation of an image through an imaging device it may be subjected to various types of noise that may lead to degradation of the observed image. The noise may be additive or multiplicative in nature. The additive noise is easy to remove in comparison to multiplicative one. Image restoration techniques are based on modeling the degradation using a priori knowledge and applying the inverse process in order to restore the original image (Gonzalez, & Wintz, 1987). For some images, the *a priori* information of the degradation phenomenon may not be available that can be further used for modeling the degradation process. In such cases, blind restoration techniques are applied for the restoration of the corrupted image. In blind image restoration technique, the original image is estimated without the explicit knowledge of the underlying degradation process. This process is difficult since information about the original image or the underlying blurring process is not available in many practical applications such as in space exploration and astronomy. Therefore,

to retrieve unknown images one has to incorporate human visual perception mechanism in order to accurately restore the image i.e. restores the image according to the requirement of the desired information. The various possible reasons that can cause the observed image to deviate from the original one may include atmospheric irregularities, instrument aberrations, diffraction limit, detector noise, thermal noise, electronic noise, and intrinsic noise such as Poisson noise. These noises may be additive, multiplicative (speckle noise) or may be distributed according to a specific probability distribution (PDF) function in an image. Several restoration methods such as Weiner Filtering, Inverse Filtering, Constrained Least Squares, and Lucy-Richardson iteration have been proposed in literature (Gonzalez, & Wintz, 1987; Sonka et al, 2007; Lucy, 1974) that remove the noise either using Fourier Transformation in frequency domain or by using optimization techniques. The various methods to estimate the degradation function for use in restoration are observation, experimentation and mathematical modeling. In recent past years, a new idea has been evolved by the research community for image processing in continuous domain using partial differential equation (PDEs) formalism or scale-space decomposition in parallel to the statistical modeling. The scale-space decomposition (Chambolle, 1994; Witkin, 1983) is a PDE approach to the multi-scale analysis of images. These PDE based approaches arise from the fields of mathematical physics such as various transport phenomenon e.g. heat flow, fluid flow, statistical mechanics, the calculus of variations, nonlinear PDEs, and numerical analysis. In PDE based image processing (Caselles *et al.*, 1998), the basic idea is to obtain the processed image as the solution of PDE's, being in general the initial condition a function of the original image. The extensive research on numerical analysis allows us the implementation of these equations, obtaining accurate image processing algorithms. When the image is represented as a continuous signal, PDEs can be seen as the iteration of local filters with an infinitesimal neighborhood. This interpretation of PDEs allows to unify and classify iterated filters as well as to derive new ones (Caselles, 1998). In literature, authors Price *et al.* (1990); Alvarez (1992); Alvarez (1993); Rudin *et al.* (1992); Osher, (1990) have proposed various methods for image restoration and de-noising and edge detection using PDEs formalism including the pioneering work of Perona, & Malik (1990).

The proposed chapter is divided in to five sections. Introduction, gives an introduction of the topic; PDE-based image processing, presents general principles, literature survey, examples and application areas of PDE-based image processing; Performance metrics, gives definitions of various performance metrics that can be used to evaluate the performance of a image processing model; Image restoration, is the main section of the chapter where various PDE-based techniques used to restore an image corrupted with additive and multiplicative noises are discussed. The first subsection, deals with various PDE-based additive noise removal techniques. The second subsection, deals with multiplicative noise reduction from images. The example of multiplicative noise includes speckle noise present in various imaging modalities such as ultrasound imaging, SAR imaging and digital holography. The subsequent next section, examines the statistics of speckle noise patterns for various imaging modalities, discusses the standard speckle reduction techniques available in literature, PDE-based speckle reduction techniques, performance analysis and comparison of PDE-based techniques with other techniques and finally last section, gives the conclusion of the chapter.

# PDE-BASED IMAGE PROCESSING

## General Principles

Partial Differential Equations (PDE's) and Geometry-Driven Diffusion in image process-

ing and analysis is a relatively new area which provides a strong theoretical framework for image processing and analysis. Attention to these methods has increased recently due to the important theoretical and practical results that have been obtained. The use of PDEs and curve or surface evolution theory in image modeling and analysis became a major research topic in recent years. The PDE-based approach permits to unify and extend existent algorithms, as well as to develop novel ones. Extensive research on numerical analysis allows the implementation of these equations, obtaining accurate image processing algorithms. The basic idea is to obtain the processed image as the solution of PDE's, being in general the initial condition a function of the original image.

To explain this (Caselles *et al.*, 1998), suppose $\phi_0: R^2 \rightarrow R$ represent a gray level image, where $\phi_0(x, y)$ is the gray level value. Introducing an artificial time $t$ parameter the image deforms according to

$$\frac{\partial \varphi}{\partial t} = F[\varphi(x, y, t)]; \tag{1}$$

where $\phi(x, y, t) = R^2 \times [0, \tau) \rightarrow R$ is the evolving image, $F: R \rightarrow R$ is an operator characterizing the algorithm and the image $\phi_0(x, y)$ is the initial condition. The solution $\phi(x, y, t)$ of the PDE gives the processed image at scale $t$.

In case of vector valued images, a system of coupled PDEs of the form of (1) is obtained. The same formalism may be applied to planar curves (boundaries of planar shapes), where $\phi(x, y)$ is a function from $R \rightarrow R^2$ or surfaces, functions from $R \rightarrow R^3$. In this case the operator $F$ must be restricted to the curve, and all isotropic motions can be described as a deformation of the curve or surface in its normal direction, with velocity related to its principal curvature(s) and flow of the form

$$\frac{\partial \varphi}{\partial t} = F(k_i) \vec{N}, \tag{2}$$

is obtained, where $k_i$'s are the principal curvatures and $\vec{N}$ is normal to the curve or surface $\phi(x, y)$. A tangential velocity can also be added, which may help the analysis but does not affect the geometry of flow.

The PDEs describing the evolution phenomenon can be obtained from variational problems and for an image processing problem it is formulated as

$$\arg\{Min_\varphi U(\varphi)\}, \tag{3}$$

where $U$ is a given energy.

Let $F(\phi)$ denote the Euler-Lagrange derivative i.e. first variation and under general assumptions, a necessary condition for $\phi$ to be minimizer of $U$ is that $F(\phi)=0$, then the local minima may be computed via the steady state solution of the equation

$$\frac{\partial \varphi}{\partial t} = F(\varphi), \tag{4}$$

where $t$ is an artificial time parameter. One of the most popular example for energy functional $U$, for an image, to be minimized is the Dirichlet integral

$$U(\varphi) = \int \left\| \nabla \varphi \right\|^2 (x)dx, \tag{5}$$

which is associated with the heat equation

$$\frac{\partial \varphi}{\partial t} = \Delta \varphi(x). \tag{6}$$

Extensive research is also being done on the direct derivation of evolution equations which are not necessarily obtained from the energy approaches. This is the case for a number of curvature equations of the form (2).

The ideas on the use of PDEs in image processing (Caselles *et al*, 1998) were introduced very back by Gabor (1965); Jain (1977); and Jain (1978). The notion of scale space i.e. representation of images simultaneously at multiple scales which is now the basis of most of the research in PDEs for image processing was introduced by Koederink (1983) and Witkin (1984) where they shown that the multiscale image representation is obtained by Gaussian filtering which is equivalent to deforming the optimal image via the classical heat equation, which generates an isotropic diffusion flow. Perona and Malik (1990) work on anisotropic diffusion proposed to replace Gaussian smoothing which is equivalent to isotropic diffusion via heat flow, by a directional diffusion that preserves edges. Their work opened a number of theoretical and practical questions that continue to occupy the PDE image processing community. In the same framework, the very good work of Osher and Rudin (1990) on shock filters and Rudin *et al.* (1992) on total variation (TV) decreasing methods explicitly stated the importance and the need for understanding PDEs for image processing applications.

Many other interesting problems in computer vision can be formulated as minimisation problems for energy functional (Shen, 2002). In order to solve these problems, the Euler- Lagrange equations of the functional are computed, resulting in a set of necessary conditions. In effect, these conditions are partial differential equations which are reformulated as a surface evolution problem. Among the first successfully utilised for computer vision problems was Snakes: Active Contours Models (Kass *et al.*, 1988). While originally developed for object segmentation in 2D, this approach can be generalised to 3D. The minimal surfaces may be employed for 3D reconstruction of static objects from multiple views as proposed by Faugeras and Keriven (1998). The basic concepts of curve and surface evolution are as follows (Osher, &Sethian, 1988; Romeny, 1994; Evans, & Spruck,1991):

## Curve Evolution

The curve evolution deals with the task of deforming a curve. Let $C_0: I \rightarrow R^2$ be initial curve and let $p$ denote its parameterisation. To describe an evolution in time, a time parameter $t \geq 0$ is introduced. The curve evolution is defined as

$$\frac{\partial}{\partial t} C(p, t) = \alpha(p, t)\, \vec{t}(p, t) + \beta(p, t)\, \vec{n}(p, t), \tag{7}$$

with the initial curve $C(p, 0) = C_0(p)$.

The movement of each curve point is written in the local coordinate system $(\vec{t}\ ;\ \vec{n})$ of the curve, where $\vec{t}$ denotes the tangential vector and $\vec{n}$ denotes the normal vector. This equation can be simplified to a curve evolution restricted to the normal direction, i.e.

$$\frac{\partial}{\partial t} C(p, t) = \beta(p, t)\, \vec{n}(p, t), \tag{8}$$

if the normal velocity $\beta(p, t)$ only depends on $C(p, t)$ and t. If this is the case, the tangential motion only acts as a re-parameterisation of the curve. The curve evolution in Equation (8) depends on the definition of the velocity (p, t). If, for example (p, t) = 1 for all parameterisations, the evolving curve at a certain time step t is a dilation of the initial curve C0. Erosion can thus be modelled by reverting the sign of (p, t). As another example, (p, t)= k(p, t) yields the prominent Euclidean geometric heat flow or curvature motion. Where k(p, t) denotes the Euclidean curvature.

## Surface Evolution

Analogous to curve evolution, one can define a surface evolution on a surface $S_0 = D \rightarrow R^3$. Let $u$ and $v$ denote the surface parameters and $t \geq 0$ the

necessary time parameter. The surface evolution is then defined by

$$\frac{\partial}{\partial t} S(u, v, t) = \alpha_1(u, v, t)\, \vec{t}_u(u, v, t) \\ + \alpha_2(u, v, t)\, \vec{t}_v(u, v, t) + \beta(u, v, t)\, \vec{n}(u, v, t), \tag{9}$$

with $S(u, v, 0) = S_0(u, v)$.

$\vec{t}_u(u, v, t), \vec{t}_v(u, v, t)$ and $\vec{n}(u, v, t)$ denote the tangential vectors in $u$ and $v$ direction and the surface normal, respectively. Similar as in the case of curves, the tangential components of the surface evolution act only as re-parameterisations and are therefore irrelevant for the geometric shape of the evolving surface. As in the curve evolution case, the constant velocity flows $\frac{\partial}{\partial t} S = \pm \vec{n}$ describe dilations and erosions. As there are two different concepts of curvature on surfaces, one can define different flows, one depending on the mean curvature $H$ and one depending on the Gaussian curvature $k$. Most of the PDEs used in image processing and computer vision are based on moving curves and surfaces with curvature based velocities. In this area, the level set numerical method developed by Osher and Sethian (1988) played a very important role. The basic idea is to represent the deforming curve, surface or image, as the level set of a higher dimensional hyper surface. This technique not only provides more accurate numerical implementations but also solves topological issues that were very difficult to treat before. The representation of objects as level sets (zero-sets) is a fundamental mathematical technique in mathematical morphology (Osher, & Fedkiw, 2001; Evans, & Spruck, 1991). Another key contribution in the PDE formalism has been the general segmentation frame work developed by Mumford and Shah (1989). Their work has unified a large number of image segmentation approaches, and opened as well a large number of theoretical and practical problems. Kimia *et al.* (1990) introduced curve evolution methods in to computer vision for a computational theory of a planar shape. References to works of other authors in related field can be found in (Caselles *et al.*, 1998). The frame work of PDE's and geometry driven diffusion have been applied to many problems in image processing and computer vision, since the seminal works mentioned above. Examples include continuous mathematical morphology, invariant shape analysis, shape from shading, segmentation, object detection, optical flow stereo, image de-noising, image sharpening, contrast enhancement, image interpolation etc.

## Advantages of PDEs Evolution Approaches in Image Analysis (Caselles *et al.*, 1998)

- They bring out a new concept to the area.
- One can think about image processing in continuous domain.
- The problem in hand is then approached as an image deformation task, which help to arrive to novel solutions of classical problems.
- When the image is represented as a continuous signal, PDEs can be seen as the iteration of local filters with an infinitesimal neighborhood. This interpretation of PDEs allows to unify and classify iterated filters as well as to derive new ones.
- PDEs approach allows not only to derive new algorithms, but also to unify previous ones. PDE formulation is natural in order to combine algorithms. If two different image processing schemes are given by $\frac{\partial \Phi}{\partial t} = F_1[\Phi(x,y,t)]$ and $\frac{\partial \Phi}{\partial t} = F_2[\Phi(x,y,t)]$, then they can be combined as $\frac{\partial \Phi}{\partial t} = \alpha F_1 + F_2$, where $\alpha \in R^+$. If F1 and F2 above are the corresponding Euler-Lagrange operators of two energy minimi-

zation problems with energies U1 and U2, then the flow above minimizes the energy $\alpha U_1 + U_2$.

- Another important advantage of the PDE approach is the possibility of achieving high accuracy and stability, with the help of extensive available research on numerical analysis.

## APPLICATION AREAS

Scale-space theory, anisotropic diffusion, vector-valued diffusion, systems of coupled PDE's, PDE based segmentation, image and video enhancement, shape analysis, axiomatic and PDE based theoretical approaches to image analysis, variational and PDE's-from-energy approaches to image processing, curve and surface evolution, PDE's in hybrid systems, comparison of models, image and noise models and adaptation of PDE's, implementations and numerical analysis, Applications (Mathematical morphology, Invariant shape analysis, Shape from shading, Segmentation, Object detection, Optical flow, Image Denoising, Image sharpening, Contrast Enhancement, Image quantization, and Image Compression). Examples of some classical PDE-based algorithms and explanation about how the modeling of curves and surfaces may occur are explained in following sections.

## Image Restoration

A noisy 2D image may be considered for instance as a surface $I: (x, y) \rightarrow (x, y, I(x, y)$. With this kind of model, regularization or smoothing of the image $I$ may be equivalent smooth surface similar enough to the original noisy one. This can be done by minimizing energy functional or directly designing PDE's with specific regularization behaviors that evolve the noisy surface (Perona, & Malik, 1990; Rudin, 1992; Gilboa *et al.*, 2005; You, & Kaveh, 2000).

## Image Segmentation

A classical way of segmenting images with PDEs is to model a closed contour with a 2D curve and then to evolve it from an initial position (random or user defined) until it fits the exact shape of the objects present in the picture. Like image restoration purposes, a PDE is describing the curve evolution and may come from energy minimization or from pertinent local heuristics (Kass *et al.*, 1988; Morel, 1988; Caselles, 1997).

## Image Registration and Optical Flow

The idea is to find a function allowing to transform an image to another one (Zitova, & Flusser, 2003; Brown, 1992). It is used to detect motions in video sequences by registering consecutive frames, or readjust two images in a way that they fit together such as in application medical image analysis. Here, a vector field models the pixel motions between the two images and a PDE is used to describe its evolution until it converges to the expected image transformation.

## Shape from Shading

The problem is reconstructing a 3D representation of an object from a single photograph of it. It is possible if one looks at the intensity variations of the image pixels due to the shadows and the different illumination conditions during the snapshot. PDEs can describe the flow of an originally flat 3D surface converging to the 3D shape of the real object. A survey report on shape and shading is presented in (Zhang, 1999).

## Image and Surface Inpainting

Inpainting refers to technique of modifying an image in an undetectable form. It has numerous applications such as restoration of scratched photographs, removal of undesirable objects, reconstruction of 3D surfaces, etc. Inpainting is done by propagation of information of surrounding structure and intensity. The various methods available in literature includes geometric approach and iterative algorithm. PDE based methods can be used for image and surface inpaintings (Chan, 2005).

*Figure 2. Noisy image (left), and restored image (right)*

*Figure 3. Image segmentation treated as the evolution of a 2D contour curve, original image with initialization curve (left), and segmented image (right)*

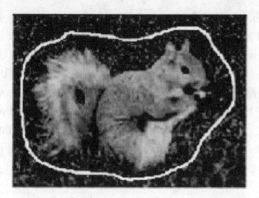 

*Figure 4. Image registration treated as the evolution of a displacement field, Direct superposing of two images (First two images from left), and superposing after image registration (last two images in right)*

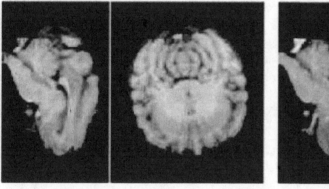 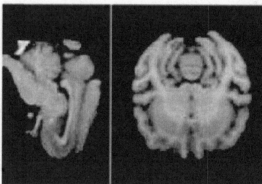

*Figure 5. Image inpainting: original scratched image (left), and inpainted image (right)*

## PERFORMANCE MEASUREMENT METRICS

The various performance measurement metrics for an image of size $m \times n$ used for evaluating the performance and efficacy of the various proposed methods are defined as follows:

### Mean Square Error

$$MSE = \frac{1}{m \times n} \sum_{i=1}^{m} \sum_{j=1}^{n} \left[ I'(i,j) - I(i,j) \right]^2 \tag{10}$$

where $I$ is the observed noisy image and $I'$ is the filtered image.

### Root Mean Square Error

$$RMSE = \sqrt{MSE} \tag{11}$$

### Peak Signal-to-Noise Ratio

$$PSNR = 20 \log_{10} \left[ \frac{255}{RMSE} \right] \tag{12}$$

### Signal-to-Noise Ratio

$$SNR = 10 \log_{10} \left[ \frac{\sum_{i=1}^{m} \sum_{j=1}^{n} I^2(i,j)}{\sum_{i=1}^{m} \sum_{j=1}^{n} (I'(i,j) - I(i,j))^2} \right] \tag{13}$$

### Normalized Mean Square Error

$$NMSE = \frac{\sum_{i=1}^{m} \sum_{j=1}^{n} (I'(i,j) - I(i,j))^2}{\sum_{i=1}^{m} \sum_{j=1}^{n} I^2(i,j)} \tag{14}$$

For optimal performance, measured values of MSE, RMSE and NMSE should be small and PSNR and SNR should be large.

### Speckle Index

Since speckle noise is multiplicative in nature, average contrast of an image may be treated as a measure of speckle removal. Speckle index (SI) is defined as (Dewaele, 1990):

*Figure 6. Image inpainting: original image (left), and inpainted image (right)*

$$SI = \frac{\sqrt{\text{var}(I)}}{E(I)}, \qquad (15)$$

and its discrete version for an image reads

$$SI = \frac{1}{mn} \sum_{i=1}^{m} \sum_{j=1}^{n} \frac{\sigma(i,j)}{\mu(i,j)}, \qquad (16)$$

where $m \times n$ is the size of the image, $\mu$ is the mean and $\sigma$ is the standard deviation.

The speckle index can be regarded as an average reciprocal signal-to noise ratio (SNR) with the signal being the mean value and noise being the standard deviation.

Average SNR=1/$SI$. $\qquad (17)$

## Effective Number of Looks (ENL)

The number of looks (Dewaele, 1990) in an intensity image is a measure of the statistical fluctuations introduced by speckle resulting from the interference between randomly positioned scatterer. Thus ENL gives essentially an idea about the smoothness in the regions on the image that is supposed to have a homogeneous appearance but are corrupted by noise. ENL is generally defined as

$$ENL = \frac{\mu_t^2}{\sigma_t^2} \qquad (18)$$

where $t$ denotes the target area or region of interest, $\mu_t$ and $\sigma_t$ are the pixel mean and standard deviation of a target area of the image. In this paper, target area is the whole image. A large value of ENL reflects better quantitative performance of the filter.

## Correlation Parameter (CP)

CP (Salinas *et al.*, 2007) is a qualitative measure for edge preservation. If one is interested in suppressing speckle noise while at the same time preserving the edges of the original image then this parameter can be used. Therefore, to evaluate the performance of the edge preservation or sharpness, the correlation parameter is defined as follows

$$CP = \frac{\sum_{i=1}^{m}\sum_{j=1}^{n}(\Delta I - \overline{\Delta I}) \times (\Delta \hat{I} - \overline{\Delta \hat{I}})}{\sqrt{\sum_{i=1}^{m}\sum_{j=1}^{n}(\Delta I - \overline{\Delta I})^2 \times \sum_{i=1}^{m}\sum_{j=1}^{n}(\Delta \hat{I} - \overline{\Delta \hat{I}})^2}}$$

$$(19)$$

where $\Delta I$ and $\Delta \hat{I}$ are high pass filtered versions of original image $I$ and filtered image $\hat{I}$ obtained via a 3x3 pixel standard approximation of the Laplacian operator. The $\overline{\Delta I}$ and $\overline{\Delta \hat{I}}$ are the mean values of $I$ and $\hat{I}$, respectively. The correlation parameter should be closer to unity for an optimal effect of edge preservation.

## Structure Similarity Index Map (SSIM)

SSIM (Wang *et al.*, 2004) is used to compare luminance, contrast and structure of two different images. It can be treated as a similarity measure of two different images. The SSIM of two images X and Y can be defined as

$$SSIM(X,Y) = [l(X,Y)]^{\alpha} \cdot [c(X,Y)]^{\beta} \cdot [s(X,Y)]^{\gamma},$$

$$(20)$$

where $\alpha > 0$, $\beta > 0$ and $\gamma > 0$ are parameters and can be used to adjust the relative importance of three components. SSIM of two images X and Y can be calculated as

$$SSIM(X,Y) = \frac{(2\mu_x\mu_y + C_1) \times (2\sigma_{xy} + C_2)}{(\mu_x^2 + \mu_y^2 + C_1) \times (\sigma_x^2 + \sigma_y^2 + C_2)},$$
(21)

where $\mu_i$ (i = X or Y) is the mean intensity, $\sigma_i$ (i=X or Y) is the standard deviation, $\sigma_{xy} = \sigma_x . \sigma_y$ and $C_i$ (i=1 or 2) is the constant to avoid instability when $\mu_x^2 + \mu_y^2$ is very close to zero and is defined as $C_i = (k_i L)^2$ in which $k_i << 1$ and L is the dynamic range of pixel values e.g. L=255 for 8-bit gray scale image. In order to have an overall quality measurement of the entire image, mean SSIM is defined as

$$MSSIM(X,Y) = \frac{1}{mn}\sum_{i=1}^{m}\sum_{j=1}^{n} SSIM(X_{ij}, Y_{ij}).$$
(22)

The MSSIM value should be closer to unity for optimal measure of similarity.

## Histogram Analysis

Though the MSE analysis quantitatively measures the average difference between the original image and the reconstructed image, it is often as important and desirable to know how the errors are distributed in the image. A histogram analysis can be carried out to quantitatively investigate the performance of histogram distribution. Based on the histogram distribution of the zoomed/restored image, one can evaluate the performance of the proposed algorithms.

In a blind image restoration problem a priori information about the degradation process of an image is not known. Only noisy image is available as the input and it has to be restored. Since, we don't have the original image therefore mean-square-error (MSE) and peak signal-to-noise ratio (PSNR) between original (without noise) and restored image can't be calculated and these

criterions can't be used for performance evaluation of the proposed algorithm. Therefore, the performance of the blind restoration algorithms can either be evaluated subjectively by a human observer or by some qualitative procedure that can be used to compare the various restoration algorithms from the information available from noisy image only. In this thesis, the performance measurement metrics used are blurred signal-to-noise ratio (BSNR) and average signal-to-noise ratio (SNR). In addition to BSNR and average SNR, the histogram analysis technique is also used to compare the performances of the various schemes.

## Average Signal-to-Noise Ratio

$$Avg.SNR = \frac{mean(I)}{std.deviation(I)} = \frac{\mu}{\sqrt{\sigma_n^2}}$$
(23)

A higher value of avg. SNR indicates less noise i.e. better restoration. Average SNR is also related to speckle index (SI) which is a measure of speckle noise. It is related as follows:

$$Avg.SNR = \frac{1}{SI}$$
(24)

## Blurred Signal –to-Noise Ratio (BSNR)

$$BSNR = 10\log_{10}\left[\frac{\frac{1}{(M \times N)}\sum\sum[I_{orignoisy} - I_{restored}]^2}{\sigma_n^2}\right]$$
(25)

where $M \times N$ is the size of image, $I_{orignoisy}$ is the original noisy image; $I_{restored}$ is the restored filtered image and $\sigma_n^2$ is the variance of noise in original noisy image (Jain, 2006). A low value of BSNR indicates less blurring or less noise or better restoration.

## IMAGE RESTORATION USING PDES FORMALISM

In this section, 2D image restoration problem is addressed which can be generalized to 3D restoration. The noise present in an image may be additive, multiplicative or may be distributed according to a specific probability distribution function (pdf) depending on the application. For example, additive noise in an image normally follows the Gaussian distribution. Speckle noise which is multiplicative in nature may be present in ultrasound images, synthetic aperture radar (SAR) images, digital holographic images, optical coherence tomography (OCT) images etc. Speckle noise in 2D B-scan ultrasound images follow Rayleigh's probability distribution; speckle noise present in SAR imagery follows k-distribution and noise present in magnetic resonance imaging (MRI) follow Rician distribution. Depending upon the type of noise a specific noise removal filter is required for restoration of a particular image.

Restoration of a digital image from its noisy version is also referred to as regularization or smoothing. In image regularization or smoothing, we simplify the image data in a way that only interesting features are preserved. The regularization term $R$ in PDE formulations like $\frac{\partial I}{\partial t} = R$ introduces additional notion of scale space i.e. the data are iteratively regularized or smoothed and a continuous sequence of smoother images is generated as time $t$ goes by. The regularization PDEs may be seen as nonlinear filters that simplify the image little by little and minimize the image variations. The regularization term constitutes the key elements for solving ill-posed computer vision problems such as restoration, segmentation, registration, surface reconstruction etc. Specifically, the de-noising algorithms are usually based on a regularization term R coupled with a data attachment term *($I_{noisy}$-I)* which is also known as fidelity term and its corresponding PDE is

$$\frac{\partial I}{\partial t} = R + (I_{noisy} - I) \tag{26}$$

Figure 7 shows the examples of various noise patterns present in an image which may have specific noise statistics. Figure 8 shows the histogram plots of various noise patterns in an image. Histogram plot shows the noise variations present in an image.

## ADDITIVE NOISE REMOVAL FROM DIGITAL IMAGES

In PDE based noise removal techniques (Romeny, 1994; Caselles *et al.*, 1998), suppose $I$ is a 2D scalar noisy image that we want to restore and the noise can be considered as high frequency variations σ with low amplitude, added to the pixels of the regular image

$$I_{noisy} = I_{regular} + \sigma . \tag{27}$$

To regularize $I_{noisy}$ a common idea is to minimize its variations estimated by gradient norm of image:

$$\| \nabla I \| = \sqrt{(I_x^{\,2} + I_y^{\,2})} . \tag{28}$$

Then the corresponding variational problem is the minimization of energy functional

$$\min_{I:\Omega \to R} E(I) = \int_{\Omega} \| \nabla I \|^2 d\Omega . \tag{29}$$

The necessary condition for minimizing the energy functional *E(I)* described by Equation (29) can be obtained using Euler-Lagrange minimization that results in following heat equation

$$\frac{\partial I}{\partial t} = c\nabla^2 I = c(I_{xx} + I_{yy}) , \tag{30a}$$

*Figure 7. Various noise patterns present in an image*

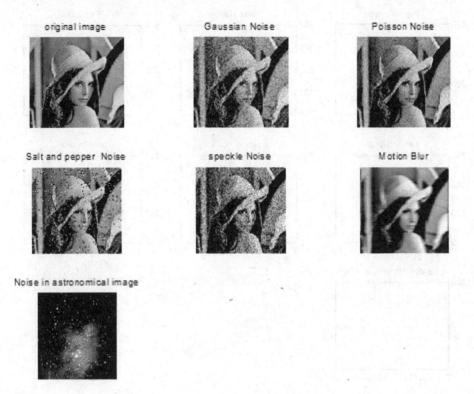

$I_{(t=0)} = I_{noisy}$ with initial condition as the observed noisy image given as:,      (30b)

where $\nabla^2 I$ is Laplacian of image $I$ and $c$ is the diffusion constant and $I(x, y, t) = I(x, y)$. This equation describes the isotropic diffusion process. The basic disadvantage of the $\nabla^2 I$ isotropic diffusion is that in addition to $\nabla^2 I$ noise removal it may also blur the edges and fine structures present in the image after certain iterations.

Koenderink (1984) has shown that the solution of Equation (30) at a particular time $t$ is the convolution of the original image $I_{noisy}$ with a normalized 2D Gaussian kernel $G_\sigma$ with variance $\sigma = \sqrt{2t}$,

$$I_t(x, y) = \iint I_{noisy}(x-u, y-v) * G_\sigma(u, v) du dv,$$
(31)

with $G_\sigma = \dfrac{1}{2\pi\sigma^2} \exp\left(-\dfrac{x^2 + y^2}{2\sigma^2}\right)$ and $\sigma = \sqrt{2t}$

which indicates that regularization is linear based on convolution. Here the image is blurred little by little in an isotropic way during the PDE evolution.

## Some PDE-Based Image Restoration Models for Additive Noise

### Total Variation (TV) Approach

Rudin *et al.* (1992) proposed an algorithm for noise removal based on the minimization of the total first variation (TV) of image *I(x, y, t)* given by following energy functional:

$$E = \underset{\min}{\arg} \int_{image} \sqrt{I_x^2 + I_y^2} dx dy = \underset{\min}{\arg} \int_{image} \|\nabla I\| dx dy.$$
(32)

*Figure 8. Histogram plots of noise patterns present in an image*

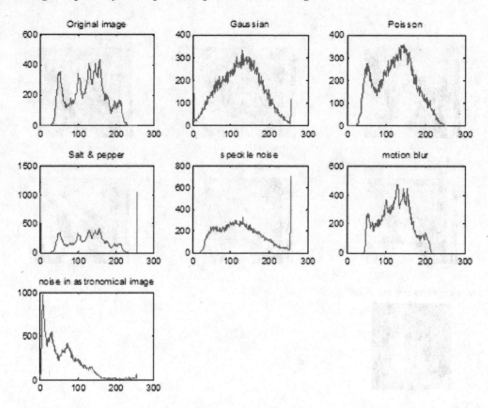

The minimization is performed under certain constraints and boundary conditions (zero flow on the boundary). The constraints they employ are zero mean and given variance of the noise.

The Euler-Lagrange minimization of above energy functional leads to following total variation (TV) based restoration model reads:

$$\frac{\partial I}{\partial t} = \nabla.\left(\frac{\nabla I}{\|\nabla I\|}\right), \qquad (33)$$

with initial condition $I(x, y; 0) = I_{noisy}$.

## Anisotropic Diffusion Based Model

Perona and Malik (1990) proposed a nonlinear diffusion method to avoid blurring and localization problem of linear diffusion filtering which is termed as anisotropic diffusion. Anisotropic dif-

fusion is the opposite of isotropic i.e. to designate a regularization process that does not smooth the image with the same weight in all the spatial directions. This achieves both noise removal and edge enhancement through the use of a non-uniform diffusion which acts as unstable inverse diffusion near edges and as linear heat equation like diffusion in homogeneous regions without edges.

In paper (Perona, &Malik, 1990), authors have used the anisotropic diffusion process which is the extension of isotropic diffusion process to remove additive noise from images. In anisotropic diffusion based filter, the basic idea is that heat Equation (30) for linear diffusion can be written in divergence form:

$$\frac{\partial I}{\partial t} = \nabla^2 I = div(gradI) = \vec{\nabla}.\vec{\nabla} I \qquad (34)$$

The introduction of a conductivity coefficient c in the above diffusion equation makes it possible to make the diffusion adaptive to local image structure:

$$\frac{\partial I}{\partial t} = \vec{\nabla}.c\vec{\nabla}I = c\nabla^2 I + \nabla c.\nabla I \qquad (35)$$

The two possible choices for diffusion coefficient c are:

$$c_1 = \exp\left(-\frac{\parallel \nabla I \parallel}{k^2}\right) \text{ and } c_2 = \frac{1}{1+\frac{\parallel \nabla I \parallel^2}{k^2}} \ ;$$

where k>0    (36)

Both expressions are equal up to first order approximation and $k$ is a fixed gradient threshold that differentiates homogeneous area and regions of contours and edges. The value of conductivity coefficient ranges in between 20-50.

## Fourth Order PDE-Based Model

The second order PDEs such as anisotropic diffusion model (Perona, & Malik, 1990) has side effects of producing the blocky effects during the evolution process (You, & Kaveh, 2000). The fourth order PDEs avoids blocky effect while achieving good trade off between noise removal and edge preservation. The fourth order PDE proposed by (You, & Kaveh, 2000) is derived from a functional which is an increasing function of the Laplacian of the image intensity function i.e. $\nabla^2 I$. The Laplacian of an image at a pixel is zero if the image is planar in its neighbourhood and these PDEs attempt to remove noise and preserve edges by approximating an observed image with a piecewise planar image. The energy functional proposed by You and Kaveh (2000) for additive noise reads

$$\arg_{\min} E(u) = \int_{\Omega} \left\|\nabla^2 I\right\|^2 d\Omega . \qquad (37)$$

The Euler-Lagrange (E-L) minimization of above energy functional leads to following fourth order PDE for edge enhancement and additive noise removal from a digital image.

$$\frac{\partial I}{\partial t} = \nabla^2 \left( C\left(\left\|\nabla^2 I\right\|\right)\nabla^2 I\right), \qquad (38)$$

where the diffusion coefficient is defined as:

$$C\left(\left\|\nabla^2 I\right\|\right) = \frac{1}{1+\left(\frac{\left\|\nabla^2 I\right\|}{k}\right)^2} . \qquad (39)$$

## Complex Diffusion Based Model

In anisotropic diffusion based model (Perona, &Malik, 1990), if real time factor $t$ is replaced by complex time factor $it$ and the diffusion coefficient $c\left(\left\|\nabla I_t^n\right\|\right)$ by $c(\text{Im}(I))$ then it leads to following complex diffusion equation (Gilboa *et al.*, 2004) originally proposed for image enhancement and additive noise removal from digital images.

$$\frac{\partial I}{\partial t} = div\left(c(\text{Im}(I))\nabla I\right) \qquad (40)$$

In *linear* complex diffusion based filter for image enhancement and de-noising, the authors (Gilboa *et al.*,2004) proposed to replace the diffusion coefficient term in equation (40) with a complex diffusion coefficient $c = \exp(i\theta)$, utilizing the approximation $\cos\theta = 1 + O(\theta^2)$ and $\sin\theta = \theta + O(\theta^3)$ and after introducing an operator $\bar{H} = c\Delta$, the equation (40) can be written as: $I_t = \bar{H} I$ with initial condition $I_{t=0} = I_0$. The solution of this PDE is given as $I = \exp(t\bar{H})$. The above assumed approximations generates the following solution

$$I(x, y, t) \approx \exp(t\Delta)(1 + i\theta t\Delta)I_0. \qquad (41)$$

Further separating the real and imaginary parts of the image, $I = I_R + iI_I$, and diffusion coefficient, $c = c_R + ic_I$, the Equation (41) reads

$$I_t = c\nabla^2 I = cI_{xx} + cI_{yy} \qquad (42)$$

can be written in x-component form as follows:

$$I_{Rt} = c_R I_{Rxx} - c_I I_{Ixx}, \ I_{R,t=0} = I_0, \qquad (43a)$$

$$I_{It} = c_I I_{Rxx} + c_R I_{Ixx}, \ I_{I,t=0} = 0, \qquad (43b)$$

where $c_R = \cos\theta$ and $c_I = \sin\theta$. For small $\theta$, relation $I_{Rxx} >> \theta I_{Ixx}$ holds and second term in RHS of Equation (22a) can be omitted. Therefore, under small $\theta$ approximation above equation reduces to

$$I_{Rt} \approx I_{Rxx} \qquad (44a)$$

$$I_{It} \approx \theta I_{Rxx} + I_{Ixx} \qquad (44b)$$

Equation (44) describes the evolution of image using complex diffusion process as proposed by Gilboa *et al*. (2004). The initial condition is the noisy image and after certain number of iterations the de-noised image is evolved according to Equation (44). From Equation (44) it can be observed that evolution of real part of the image is controlled by the linear forward diffusion, whereas evolution of imaginary part of the image is controlled by both the real and imaginary equations. Qualitative

properties of edge detection i.e. second smoothed derivative is described by the imaginary part of the image for small value of $\theta$, whereas real values depicts the properties of ordinary Gaussian scale -space. For large values of $\theta$, the imaginary part feeds back in to the real part creating the wave like ringing effect which is an undesirable property. Here, for experimentation purposes value of $\theta$ is chosen to be $\frac{\pi}{30}$.

For *nonlinear* complex diffusion, the diffusion coefficient is defined as follows (Gilboa *et al*., 2004):

$$c(\text{Im}(I)) = \frac{e^{i\theta}}{1 + \left(\dfrac{\text{Im}(I)}{k\theta}\right)^2}. \qquad (45)$$

Here k is the edge threshold parameter. The value of k ranges from 1 to 1.5 for digital images having additive noise. The value of k is fine tuned according to the application in hand.

## Other PDE-Based Models

Osher and Rudin (1990) proposed an algorithm for image enhancement based on shock filters. In this case the image $\phi(x, y, t)$ evolves according to

$$\frac{\partial\varphi}{\partial t} = -\|\nabla\varphi\| F(L(\varphi)), \qquad (46)$$

where function $F(u)$ satisfies certain technical conditions and $L$ is a 2nd order nonlinear elliptic operator. An image evolving according to above equation develops shocks where L=0. Main goal of this method is to get as close as possible to the inverse heat equation.

Alvarez *et al*. (1992) proposed an algorithm of image selective smoothing and edge detection. In this case the image evolves according to

$$\frac{\partial \varphi}{\partial t} = g(\|G * \nabla \varphi\|) \|\nabla \varphi\| div(\frac{\nabla \varphi}{\|\nabla \varphi\|}), \qquad (47)$$

where G is a smoothing kernel (e.g. Gaussian) and g () is a non increasing function which tends to zero as *t* tends to infinity.

In paper (Beck, &Teboulle, 2009), authors studied gradient-based schemes for image denoising and de-blurring problems based on the discretized total variation (TV) minimization model with constraints. They derived a fast algorithm for the constrained TV-based image de-burring problem. To achieve this task, they combined an acceleration of the well known dual approach to the de-noising problem with a novel monotone version of a fast iterative shrinkage/ thresholding algorithm (FISTA). The resulting gradient-based algorithm shares a remarkable simplicity together with a proven global rate of convergence which is significantly better than currently known gradient projections-based methods. The results are applicable to both the anisotropic and isotropic discretized TV functional. Initial numerical results demonstrate the viability and efficiency of the proposed algorithms on image de-blurring problems with box constraints. Image de-noising methods based on gradient dependent regularizes such as Rudin et al.'s total variation (TV) model often suffer the staircase effect and the loss of fine details. In order to overcome such drawbacks, authors of the paper (Chen *et al.*,2009) presents an adaptive total variation method based on a new edge indicator, named difference curvature, which can effectively distinguish between edges and ramps. In another recent paper (Chang, & Yang, 2009) authors have proposed a Lattice Boltzmann method for image de-noising.

Some other PDE-based model includes: Image Restoration from motion blurred image using PDEs formalism (Srivastava *et al.*, 2009); PDE based Unsharp Masking, Crispening and High Boost Filtering of Digital Images (Srivastava *et al.*, 2009); and Brownian Motion based image modelling and its applications to image regularization (Srivastava *et al.*, 2009).

## Discretization of Models for Digital Implementations

For digital implementations the PDE based models discussed in above section can be discretized using finite differences schemes (Press *et al.*,1992) i.e. Finite Time Centered Scheme (FTCS), where we consider equally spaced points along both the t-axes and x-axes and denote $x_j = x_0 + j\Delta x$, j=0,1,2,....,m and $t_n = t_0 + n\Delta t$, n=0,1,2,....,n where $m \times n$ is the size of image.

The discretized form of anisotropic diffusion based model, given by Equation (35), reads

$$I^{n+1}(x,y) = I^n(x,y) + \Delta t.(\vec{\nabla}.c\vec{\nabla}I) \qquad (48)$$

The second term in R.H.S. of Equation (48) can be further discretized using centred difference scheme as proposed in (Perona, & Malik, 1990).

The discretized form of the fourth order PDE based model, given by Equation (38), reads

$$I^{n+1}(x,y) = I^n(x,y) + \Delta t.$$
$$[div(c(\left\|\nabla^2 I^n(x,y)\right\|)\nabla^2 I^n(x,y))] \qquad (49)$$

The discretized form of the nonlinear complex diffusion based model given by Equations (40) and (45) reads

$$I^{n+1}_{t+1}(i,j) = I^n_t(i,j) + \Delta t.(\nabla.\left(c(\text{Im}(I^n_t(i,j))\nabla I^t_n(i,j)\right) \qquad (50)$$

For the numerical scheme, given by above Equations (49-50) to be stable, the von Neumann analysis (Press *et al.*,1992), shows that we require $\frac{\Delta t}{(\Delta x)^2} < \frac{1}{4}$. If the grid size is set to $\Delta x = 1$, then $\Delta t < \frac{1}{4}$ i.e. $\Delta t < 0.25$. Therefore, the value of $\Delta t$ is set to 0.24 for stability of Equations (48-50).

## RESULTS AND ANALYSIS

### Case I: Anisotropic Diffusion Based Model

The de-noising scheme defined by Equation (35) has been implemented in MATLAB. The both choices of diffusion coefficients ($c_1$ and $c_2$) as defined in Equation (36) have been used. The value of $\Delta t$ was set to 0.24 and value of conductivity coefficient k was set to 50 and k may attain any value in between 20-100 (Perona and Malik, 1990). The performance of the anisotropic diffusion method for image de-noising defined by Equation (35) has been evaluated both qualitatively and quantitatively in terms of various performance measurement metrics such as MSE, RMSE, NMSE, SNR, PSNR and time for different gray images of different resolutions for varying amount of Gaussian noise variance. The mean of noise is considered to be zero. From experimentation it has been tested that the scheme defined by Equation (35) converges to solution at 30-35 iterations for a noise variance of 0.02 for the sample image in consideration. For less variance we obtain the processed de-noised image after 20-25 iterations. Figure 9 shows the visual results. Performance comparisons are shown in Figures 10-11 for both choices of diffusion coefficients. The execution time is less for option 2 of diffusion coefficient (Figure 11). NMSE is less and SNR is high for option 2 of diffusion coefficient (Figure 10). Hence in terms of NMSE, SNR and execution time option 2 of diffusion coefficient is performing better.

### Sample MATLAB Code: Anisotropic Diffusion Based Model

```
%K is the conductivity coefficient
that varies between 20-100; I is the
input image ; and niter is the number
of iterations required for the PDE to
converge to the solution.
```

```
function [Ianiso]=PMAnisoDiff
(I,k,niter)
It=double(I);
dt=0.25;
t=1;
[x y]=size(I);
epsilon=0.0000000001; % epsilon is
added to avoid divide by zero
% k=20-100
for t = 1:niter
    [Ix,Iy]=gradient(It);
     di=sqrt(Ix.^2+Iy.^2+epsilon);%
norm (I)
        c=1./(1.+(di./k).^2);
      F=(c.*gradient(It));%
F=delI/norm(DelI)
        Fdiv=gradient(F);% diver-
gence of F
    It=It+dt.*Fdiv;
  end
  Ianiso=It;
End
```

### Case II: Complex Diffusion Based Model

See Figure 12 and Figure 13 for details about Case II and the complex diffusion based model.

### Case III: Comparative Study of PDE-Based Filters for Additive Noise Removal

In this section, the comparative studies of four PDE based filters in consideration are presented in terms of MSE, PSNR, CP, and MSSIM (see Table 1). The sample image is lena.jpg of size 200x200. Numbers of iterations for TV-based model were chosen to 100 for acceptable quality of results. For anisotropic diffusion based PDE, fourth order PDE, and nonlinear complex diffusion based PDE, the number of iterations were set to 50 for the acceptable quality of images.

*Figure 9. Results of anisotropic diffusion after 35 iterations for noise variance 0.002 for sample image lena.jpg (512x512)*

Original image

Noisy image

Restored image

For more than 50 iterations the performance decreases. The value of diffusion coefficient *k* for anisotropic diffusion based PDE, and fourth order PDE were set to 20 and that of nonlinear complex diffusion was set to 1.5. Figures 14 and 15 give performance comparison of the schemes in consideration.

## MULTIPLICATIVE SPECKLE NOISE REDUCTION FROM DIGITAL IMAGES

### Speckle Noise: Theoretical Background

This section describes the general speckle noise patterns present in various digital images such as ultrasound images and synthetic aperture radar (SAR) images. The speckle noise occurs in coherent imaging of objects whenever surface roughness of the image being imaged is of the

order of the wavelength of the incident radiation (Jain, 2006). The presence of speckle noise in an imaging system reduces its resolution; especially for low contrast images and suppression of speckle noise is an important consideration in the design of coherent imaging systems. For low contrast images speckle noise is multiplicative in nature. Speckle noise may be present in ultrasound medical images, synthetic aperture radar (SAR) imagery and digital holographic images and in other application images. An inherent characteristic of coherent imaging, including ultrasound imaging, is the presence of speckle noise which is a random, deterministic, interference pattern in an image formed with coherent radiation of a medium containing many sub-resolution scatterers. The texture of the observed speckle pattern does not correspond to underlying structure. The local brightness of the speckle pattern, however, does reflect the local echogenicity of the underlying scatterers. Speckle has a negative impact on

*Figure 10. Performance comparison of anisotropic diffusion: SNR vs noise variance; and NMSE vs noise variance for both choices of conductivity coeffs ($c_1$ and $c_2$) for different iterations for the image lena.jpg*

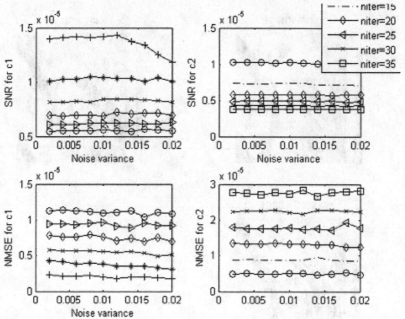

## Speckle Noise in Ultrasound Images

Speckle noise pattern present in ultrasound images are multiplicative in nature and distributed according to Rayleigh's probability distribution function. In ultrasound imaging, speckle leads to reduction in contrast resolution which is responsible for the poorer effective resolution of ultrasound compared to x-ray and MRI. Speckle is present in both RF data and envelope-detected data. Figure 14 conceptually demonstrates the impact of speckle noise on information content (Anderson, 2009). The ultrasound image of a hypoechoic lesion of 5 mm diameter with -9 dB contrast is considered. The echogenicity map corresponding to this object is shown in the top left panel, opposite the corresponding scattering function in the top right panel. The scattering func-

ultrasound imaging and other types of digital imaging e.g. SAR (Synthetic Aperture Radar) imaging and digital holography (Srivastava *et al.*, 2009).

tion represents the population of sub-resolution scatterers being imaged, and that are weighted in amplitude by the echogenicity map. This scattering function convolved with a point spread function to produce the RF echo data is shown in the lower left panel. The RF echo data is zero-mean and thus does not show what is really of interest, i.e. a map of local echogenicity, or local echo magnitude. Envelope detection removes the carrier, producing the desired image of echo magnitude in the lower right panel. The differences between this image and the original echogenicity map arise from speckle noise. The statistics of fully-developed speckle (Anderson, 2009; Goodman, 1984) can be described as follows: For the given stochastic nature of speckle noise, this noise pattern can be described statistically. Each of the diffuse scatterers in the isochronous volume contributes a component to the echo signal in a sum is known as a random walk in the complex plane. If each step in this walk is considered an independent random variable, over many such walks we can

*Figure 11. Performance comparison, Execution time vs noise variance for both choices of conductivity coeffs ($c_1$ and $c_2$) for different iterations for the image lena.jpg*

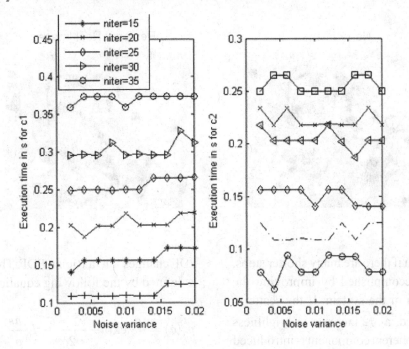

apply the Central Limit Theorem to their sum. Therefore, in fully developed speckle, this complex radio-frequency echo signal from diffuse scatterers alone has a zero mean, two-dimensional Gaussian probability density function (PDF) in the complex plane. The values of the magnitude of *r* for many such scatterer populations follow the Rayleigh PDF. Envelope detection removes the phase component, creating a signal with Rayleigh

amplitude PDF (Anderson, 2009; Goodman, 1984) which reads

$$p_A(a) = \frac{a}{\sigma^2} \exp(-\frac{a^2}{2\sigma^2}), a \geq 0 \qquad (51)$$

where $a$ and $\sigma^2$ are amplitude and variance of the back scatterer signal. Speckle brightness is greater if there are fewer, longer steps in the

*Figure 12. Original image (Left); Real part of the image (Middle); Imaginary part of the image showing edges (Right)*

*Figure 13. Results of linear complex diffusion based filter, original noisy microscopic image (left), restored real image (right)*

Noisy Image

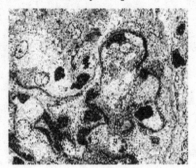

Restored Real Image

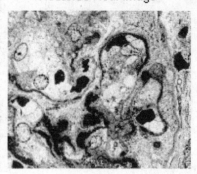

random walk than if there are many shorter steps. This could be accomplished by improving the spatial resolution of the system. If the scatterer density is doubled, a $\sqrt{2}$ increase in brightness results. When a coherent component is introduced to the speckle, it adds a constant strong phasor to the diffuse scatterer's echoes and shifts the mean of the complex echo signal away from the origin in the complex plane. Due to this the Rayleigh

PDF changes into a Rician PDF. The Rician PDF is defined by the following equation:

$$p_A(a) = \frac{a}{\sigma^2} \exp(-\frac{a^2 + s^2}{2\sigma^2}) I_0 \frac{as}{\sigma^2}, a \geq 0$$

(52)

These PDFs are nonzero for $a >= 0$ only. The parameter $s$ is the echo strength of the bright scat-

*Table 1. Performance comparison of additive noise removal techniques (Sample image: lena.jpg, (200x200)*

| Method | Noise Variance | MSE | PSNR [dB] | CP | MSSIM |
|---|---|---|---|---|---|
| Total Variation (TV) | 0.0001 | 290.53 | 23.499 | 0.9132 | 0.5105 |
| | 0.0025 | 290.11 | 23.517 | 0.91604 | 0.50941 |
| | 0.0049 | 289.63 | 23.472 | 0.91668 | 0.510130.5106 |
| | 0.0073 | 294.77 | 23.436 | 0.91552 | 0.51385 |
| | 0.0097 | 291.08 | 23.491 | 0.91862 | |
| Anisotropic Diffusion | 0.0001 | 339.66 | 22.82 | 0.93356 | 0.49915 |
| | 0.0025 | 343 | 22.778 | 0.93562 | 0.49918 |
| | 0.0049 | 339.82 | 22.818 | 0.93311 | 0.502 |
| | 0.0073 | 346.65 | 22.732 | 0.93371 | 0.49723 |
| | 0.0097 | 351.63 | 22.67 | 0.93374 | 0.49347 |
| Fourth Order PDE | 0.0001 | 286.74 | 23.556 | 0.93839 | 0.57417 |
| | 0.0025 | 287.2 | 23.549 | 0.93959 | 0.57937 |
| | 0.0049 | 291.24 | 23.488 | 0.94005 | 0.57761 |
| | 0.0073 | 295.06 | 23.432 | 0.9399 | 0.5762 |
| | 0.0097 | 300.73 | 23.349 | 0.93981 | 0.57484 |
| Nonlinear Complex Diffusion | 0.0001 | 260.21 | 23.978 | 0.935 | 0.58983 |
| | 0.0025 | 259.4 | 23.991 | 0.93492 | 0.58979 |
| | 0.0049 | 254.73 | 24.07 | 0.93719 | 0.59331 |
| | 0.0073 | 260.33 | 23.976 | 0.93478 | 0.58851 |
| | 0.0097 | 263.46 | 23.924 | 0.93466 | 0.58666 |

*Figure 14. Performance comparison of additive noise removal filters; MSE(left), and PSNR (right)*

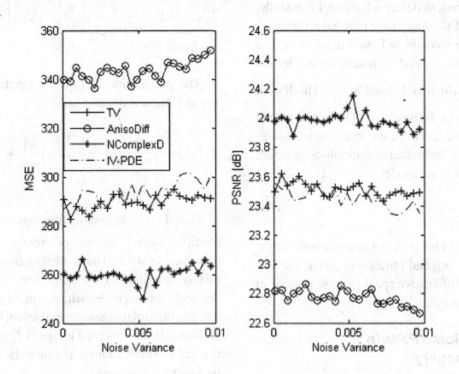

*Figure 15. Performance comparison of additive noise removal filters; CP(left), and MSSIM (right)*

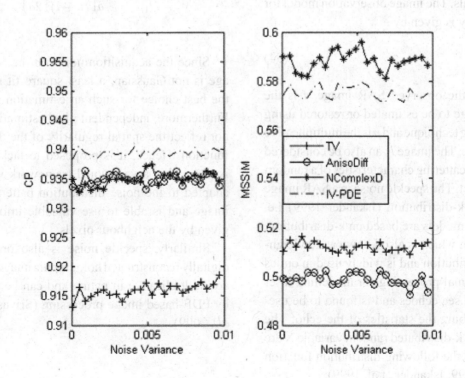

terer, while $\sigma$ is the standard deviation of the complex Gaussian described above, i.e. both the real part and the imaginary part have variances of $\sigma$. $I_0$ is the incomplete Bessel function of zero order. The Rician PDF is parameterized by the variable $k$, which is defined as $\dfrac{s}{\sigma}$. The Rician PDF reduces to the Rayleigh PDF for the special case $s = 0$. The speckle noise in ultrasound imaging is also approximated as multiplicative noise, given by following model:

$$g(x, y) = I(x, y \cdot s(x, y),\tag{53}$$

Here, $g(x, y)$ is the recorded ultrasound image, $I(x, y)$ is the original ultrasound image and $s(x, y)$ is the multiplicative speckle noise present in ultrasound image.

## Speckle Noise Pattern in SAR Imagery

In synthetic aperture radar (SAR) images, the speckle noise is generally caused by the decline of echo signals. The image observation model for SAR imagery is given by

$$I_0 = I \cdot n,\tag{54}$$

where $I_0$ is the observed SAR image, $I$ is the original image to be estimated or restored using some filtering technique and $n$ is the multiplicative speckle noise. The image $I$ can also be considered as the radar scattering characteristics of a random ground object. The speckle noise in a SAR image follows the k-distribution (Iskander 1999) i.e. radar clutter models are based on k-distribution. k-distribution which is also known as Rayleigh-Gamma distribution and is widely used in optics and radar signal processing for modelling laser speckles and sea echoes and is found to be useful in describing the statistics of the echo. The statistics of a k-distributed random variable X are described by the following distribution function (Iskander 1999; Iskander et al. 1999):

$$F_X(x) = 1 - \frac{2}{a\Gamma(v+1)}\left(\frac{x}{2a}\right)^{v+1} K_{v+1}\left(\frac{x}{a}\right), \text{ where}$$
$$x > 0 \text{ and } v > \text{-1}.\tag{55}$$

The probability distribution function of the k-distribution is defined as:

$$f_X(x) = \frac{2}{a\Gamma(v+1)}\left(\frac{x}{2a}\right)^{v+1} K_v\left(\frac{x}{a}\right), \text{ where } x > 0$$
$$\text{and } v > \text{-1}.\tag{56}$$

Here $\Gamma(.)$ is the gamma function, $K_v(.)$ is the modified Bessel function of order $v$ and $a$ is a positive constant. The k-distribution is completely described by the shape parameter $v$ and the scale parameter $a$, which can be estimated using method of moments or maximum likelihood methods. If the observed image is $I_0$ and the estimated or filtered image is $I$ then the pdf given by Equation (56) reads

$$p(I / I_0) = f_{I_0}(I) = \frac{2}{a\Gamma(v+1)}\left(\frac{I}{2a}\right)^{v+1} K_v\left(\frac{I}{a}\right)$$
$$\tag{57}$$

Since the acquisition noise on the SAR image is not Gaussian, a least square fit may not the best choice for such an estimation process. Furthermore, independent pixel estimation does not reflect the spatial regularity of the diffusion function. Hence, it is proposed to tackle these issues within a variational framework which is adapted to the noise distribution pattern in the image and is able to use valuable information given by the neighbour pixels.

Similarly, speckle noise is also present in digitally reconstructed holographic images which are multiplicative in nature and can be reduced by PDE-based image processing (Srivastava *et. al.*, 2009).

## SPECKLE NOISE REDUCTION TECHNIQUES

### General Approaches

In general the speckle noise (Jain, 2006) has complex amplitude given as $a(x,y) = a_R(x,y) + ja_I(x,y)$, where $a_R$ and $a_I$ are zero mean, independent Gaussian random variables for each $(x, y)$ with some variance. The intensity field of speckle noise is given as

$$s(x,y) = |a(x,y)|^2 = a_R^2 + a_I^2 \qquad (58)$$

The general image observation model for speckle noise reads

$$v(x,y) = u(x,y)s(x,y) + \eta(x,y) \qquad (59)$$

where $v(x, y)$ is the observed noisy image, $u(x, y)$ is the original image to be restored, $s(x, y)$ is the intensity of speckle noise and $\eta(x, y)$ is detector noise which is additive in nature. Assuming detector noise to be zero, the general observation model for speckle noise reads

$$v(x,y) = u(x,y)s(x,y). \qquad (60)$$

The speckle noise model given by Equation (60) is a multiplicative noise model. This multiplicative noise model can be converted to additive noise by using homomorphic filtering approach which is easier to implement. Other, effective filters may also be used for the reduction of speckle noise.

The speckle noise can be reduced by multi-look processing, spatial filtering or homomorphic filtering (Jain, 2006). The multi-look processing is usually done during data acquisition stage and speckle reduction by spatial and homomorphic filtering is performed on the image after its acqui-

sition. Irrespective of the methods used to reduce the speckle noise from images, the ideal speckle reduction method must preserve radiometric information and the textural information i.e. the edges between different areas and spatial signal variability. The spatial filters are of two types i.e. adaptive and non-adaptive. Non-adaptive filters take the parameters of the whole image signal into consideration and leave out the local properties of the terrain backscatter or the nature of the sensor. These kinds of filters are not appropriate for non-stationary scene signal. Fast Fourier Transform (FFT) is an example of such filters. The adaptive filters accommodate changes in local properties of the terrain backscatter as well as the nature of the sensor. In adaptive filters, the speckle noise is considered as being stationary but the changes in the mean backscatters due to changes in the type of target are taken into consideration. Adaptive filters reduce speckles while preserving the edges and these filters modify the image based on statistics extracted from the local environment of each pixel. Adaptive filter varies the contrast stretch for each pixel depending upon the Digital Number (DN) values in the surrounding moving kernel. A filter that adapts the stretch to the region of interest produces a better enhancement. Examples of adaptive filters are: Mean, median, Wiener filter (Jain, 2006), Lee filter (Lee, 1983), Frost filter (Frost *et al.*, 1982), Kuan filter (Kuan *et al.*, 1987), Hybrid filter (Rajan *et al.*, 2008) and Speckle Reducing Anisotropic Diffusion (SRAD) based filter (Yu, &Acton, 2002). In a recent paper (Juan *et al.*, 2009), the authors investigate and compile some of the techniques mostly used in the smoothing or suppression of speckle noise in ultrasound images. The basic concepts of these adaptive filters are as follows:

### Mean Filter

The Mean Filter is a simple one and does not remove the speckles but averages it into the data and it is the least satisfactory method of speckle noise reduction as it results in loss of detail and resolution. However, it can be used for applications where resolution is not the first concern.

## Median Filter

The Median filter is also a simple one and removes pulse or spike noises. Pulse functions of less than one-half of the moving kernel width are suppressed or eliminated but step functions or ramp functions are retained.

## Lee-Sigma and Lee Filters

The Lee-Sigma and Lee filters (Lee, 1981; Lee, 1983) utilize the statistical distribution of the DN values within the moving kernel to estimate the value of the pixel of interest. These two filters assume a Gaussian distribution for the noise in the image data. The Lee filter is based on the assumption that the mean and variance of the pixel of interest is equal to the local mean and variance of all pixels within the user-selected moving kernel. The scheme for computing digital number output ($DN_{out}$) is as follows:

$$(DN_{out})=[mean]+k[(DN_{in}-mean]$$ (61)

where mean = average of pixels in a moving window,

$$k = \frac{\mathrm{var}(x)}{(mean)^2 \sigma^2 + \mathrm{var}(x)},$$ (62)

and

$$\mathrm{var}(x) = \left[\frac{\sigma_w + \mu_w^2}{\sigma^2 + 1}\right] - \mu_w^2.$$ (63)

$\mu_w$ and $\sigma_w$ are the mean and variances of pixels within chosen window. The Sigma filter is based on the probability of a Gaussian distribution. It is assumed that 95.5% of random samples are within a two standard deviation range. This noise suppression filter replaces the pixel of interest with the average of all DN values within the moving kernel that fall within the designated range.

## Frost Filter

The Frost filter (Frost *et al.*, 1982) replaces the pixel of interest with a weighted sum of the values within the $n \times n$ moving kernel. The weighting factors decrease with distance from the pixel of interest. The weighting factors increase for the central pixels as variance within the kernel increases. This filter assumes multiplicative noise and stationary noise statistics and follows the following formula:

$$DN = \sum_{n \times n} k\alpha e^{-\alpha|t|},$$ (64)

where $\alpha = (\frac{4}{n\bar{\sigma}^2})(\frac{\sigma^2}{\bar{I}^2})$. (65)

Here $k$ = normalization constant, $I$ = local mean, $\sigma$ = local variance, $\bar{\sigma}$ = image coefficient of variation value, $|t| = |X - X_0| + |Y - Y_0|$, and $n$ = moving kernel size.

## Kuan Filter

Kuan filter (Kuan *et al.*, 1987) first transforms the multiplicative noise model into a signal-dependent additive noise model. Then the minimum mean square error criterion is applied to the model. The resulting filter has the same form as the Lee filter but with a different weighting function. Because Kuan filter made no approximation to the original model, it can be considered to be superior to the Lee filter.

The resulting grey-level value R for the smoothed pixel is:

$$R = I_c * W + I_m * (1 - W),\tag{66}$$

where:

$$W = \left(1 - C_u^2 / C_i^2\right) / \left(1 + C_u^2\right)$$

$$C_u = \sqrt{\frac{1}{NumberofLooks}}$$

$$C_i = \frac{S}{I_m}.$$

$I_c$ = center pixel in filter window, $I_m$ = mean value of intensity within window, and $S$ = standard deviation of intensity within window.

The Kuan filter is used primarily to filter speckled radar data. It is designed to smooth out noise while retaining edges or shape features in the image. Different filter sizes will greatly affect the quality of processed images. If the filter is too small, the noise filtering algorithm is not effective. If the filter is too large, subtle details of the image will be lost in the filtering process. A 7x7 filter usually gives the best results. The *NumberofLooks* parameter is used to estimate noise variance and it effectively controls the amount of smoothing applied to the image by the filter. Theoretically, the correct value for *NumberofLooks* should be the effective number of looks of the radar image. It should be close to the actual number of looks, but may be different if the image has undergone re-sampling. The user may experimentally adjust the *NumberofLooks* value so as to control the effect of the filter. A smaller *NumberofLooks* value leads to more smoothing; a larger *NumberofLooks* value preserves more image features.

## PDE Based Filters

In recent years, several PDE based methods have been developed for removal of additive noise from images (Perona, &Malik, 1990; Gilboa *et al.*,

2004; You, & Kaveh, 2004) which can be used by homomorphic filters to reduce speckle noise. The basic idea behind PDE based noise removal based on energy minimization technique as discussed in section image restoration using PDEs formalism.

## Speckle Reducing Anisotropic Diffusion (SRAD) Filter

In this paper (Yu, &Acton, 2002), the authors provide the derivation of speckle reducing anisotropic diffusion (SRAD), a diffusion method tailored to ultrasonic and radar imaging applications. SRAD is the edge-sensitive diffusion for speckled images, in the same way that conventional anisotropic diffusion is the edge-sensitive diffusion for images corrupted with additive noise. At first authors had shown that the Lee and Frost filters can be cast as partial differential equations, and then SRAD filter is derived by allowing edge-sensitive anisotropic diffusion within this context. SRAD exploits the *instantaneous* coefficient of variation, same as the Lee and Frost filters utilize the coefficient of variation in adaptive filtering. The *instantaneous* coefficient of variation is a function of the local gradient magnitude and Laplacian operators.

## PDE-Based Homomorphic Filtering Approach for Speckle Reduction

Based on the discussions in section Speckle noise: Theoretical background, it can be said that the speckle noise is multiplicative in nature for ultrasound images and SAR images. Assuming detector noise to be zero, the general observation model for speckle noise reads

$$v(x, y)=u(x, y)s(x, y).\tag{67}$$

Since, the direct reduction of multiplicative noise is a difficult task therefore the multiplicative noise is first converted in to additive noise by taking the logarithm of equation (67) i.e. by applying homomorphic transform and reduction of this additive noise by some available filters and finally taking the exponentiation of filter output to produce the speckle reduced image.

The homomorphic filtering approach for speckle reduction can be described as (Srivastava *et al.*, 2009):

Apply the logarithmic transform on equation(67) to convert the multiplicative noise in to additive one which reads

$$\log v(x,y) = \log u(x,y) + \log s(x,y)$$
$$\Rightarrow w(x,y) = I(x,y) + \eta_s(x,y) \qquad (68)$$

where $w(x,y) = \log v(x,y)$ is the observed hologram image in log domain, $I(x,y) = \log u(x,y)$ is the noiseless image in log domain that is to be recovered and $\eta_s(x,y) = \log s(x,y)$ the amount the of the speckle noise which is now an additive noise and is to be minimized.

In this step, an additive noise removal filter (e.g. Wiener filter, median filter, PDE based diffusion filters and other filters) is applied to remove or minimize the additive noise $\eta_s(x,y)$.

Finally, the restored holographic image, $I_{restored}$, can be obtained by taking the exponentiation of output obtained in step ii.

$$I_{restored} = \exp(I(x,y)). \qquad (69)$$

## EXAMPLES

## Non-Linear Complex Diffusion Based Homomorphic Filter for Speckle Reduction from Digital Images

In this section (Srivastava *et al.*, 2009), the nonlinear complex diffusion based homomorphic filter is proposed to be used for speckle reduction from ultrasound and synthetic aperture radar (SAR) images. The performance of the nonlinear complex diffusion based homomorphic filter is evaluated in terms of MSE and PSNR and a comparative study of this scheme with other standard speckle reduction techniques such as Lee filter, Frost filter, Kuan filter and SRAD filter is presented. The obtained results show that the nonlinear complex diffusion based homomorphic filter outperforms all schemes in consideration.

## Methods and Models

As discussed earlier, the nonlinear complex diffusion based PDE reads

$$\frac{\partial I}{\partial t} = \vec{\nabla}.(D(\text{Im}(I))\vec{\nabla} I). \qquad (70)$$

Expressing the above PDE in its tangent and normal forms, the presented model reads

$$\frac{\partial I}{\partial t} = \nabla^2 I(\xi,\xi) + D(\text{Im}(I))\nabla^2 I(\eta,\eta) \qquad (71a)$$

$$I(x,y,0) = I_0 \text{ (Initial Condition)} \qquad (71b)$$

The first term in equation (71a) diffuses the image, I, only in the orthogonal direction of the gradient and the second term diffuses the image, I, in the direction of gradient. The terms $\xi$ and $\eta$ are unit vectors respectively orthogonal and in the direction of the gradient vector $\nabla I$ of the image $I(t,)$. These unit vectors are defined (Perona, 1998) as follows

$$\xi = \frac{\nabla I^{\perp}}{|\nabla I|} = \frac{\langle I_y, -I_x \rangle}{\sqrt{I_x^2 + I_y^2}} \text{ and}$$

$$\eta = \frac{\nabla I}{|\nabla I|} = \frac{\langle I_x, I_y \rangle}{\sqrt{I_x^2 + I_y^2}} \qquad (72)$$

The term $D(\mathrm{Im}(I))$ is the complex diffusion coefficient and $\mathrm{Im}(I)$ is the imaginary part of the image. The diffusion coefficient $D(\mathrm{Im}(I))$ is defined as follows (Gilboa *et al.*, 2004)

$$D(\mathrm{Im}(I)) = \frac{e^{i\theta}}{1 + \left( \dfrac{\mathrm{Im}(I)}{\lambda\theta} \right)} \tag{73}$$

Here $\lambda$ is a threshold parameter and $\theta$ is the small phase angle $(\theta << 1)$. The imaginary value of image $I$ i.e. $\mathrm{Im}(I)$ divided by $\theta$ is used for controlling the diffusion process. For small $t$, this term vanishes and allows stronger diffusion to reduce the noise; with time its influence increases and preserves the ramp features of the image. The function $D(\mathrm{Im}(I))$, known as conductivity coefficient, is a function of local image differential structure that depends on local partial derivatives (Gilboa *et al.*, 2004). The conductivity coefficient controls the diffusion process within the image that can be varied according to image structure i.e lower the diffusion where edges occurs to preserve the edges and enhance the diffusion in smooth region of image. The function D(.) is chosen with values between 0 an 1 according to equation (73). When D(.) = 1, the two diffusion terms in equation (71a) have equal weights and the equation (71a) converts to a 2D isotropic heat equation i.e. Laplacian. When D(.) = 0, only the diffusion in the orthogonal direction of the gradient operates. In homogeneous zones of the image, g (.) will have values near 1.

For simplicity of representation, suppose $I_{\xi\xi} = \nabla^2 I(\xi,\xi)$ represents the diffusion along the normal of the edge and $I_{\eta\eta} = \nabla^2 I(\eta,\eta)$ represents the diffusion along the tangent of the edge. The diffusion along the normal diffuses across the edges and diffusion along the tangent continues along the edges. The blurring of edges of image or area of high frequency content is mainly due to diffusion along the normal. To control the dif-

fusion the diffusion across the edges, $I_{\eta\eta}$, is lowered in comparison to the diffusion along the tangent and this is achieved by varying the values of the diffusion coefficient $D(\mathrm{Im}(I))$ according to equation (73). Further, $I_{\xi\xi}$ and $I_{\eta\eta}$ are defined (Perona, 1998) as follows-

$$I_{\xi\xi} = \frac{I_{xx}I_x^2 - 2*I_{xy}I_xI_y + I_{yy}I_y^2}{I_x^2 + I_y^2} \tag{74}$$

$$I_{\eta\eta} = \frac{I_{xx}I_x^2 + 2*I_{xy}I_xI_y + I_{yy}I_y^2}{I_x^2 + I_y^2}. \tag{75}$$

## Discretization of the Model

For digital implementations, the equation (71) can be discretized using forward time centered scheme (FTCS) and centered difference scheme. Here, we consider equally spaced points along both the t-axes and x-axes and denote $x_j = x_0 + j\Delta x$, j=0,1,2,….,m and $t_n = t_0 + n\Delta t$, n=0,1,2,….,n where $m \times n$ is the size of image. Using the FTCS, the discrete form of equation (70) reads

$$I_{i,j}^{n+1} = I_{i,j}^n + \Delta t.[\nabla^2 I(\xi,\xi) + D(\mathrm{Im}(I))\nabla^2 I(\eta,\eta)]$$

i.e.

$$I_{i,j}^{n+1} = I_{i,j}^n + \Delta t.[I_{\xi\xi} + D(\mathrm{Im}(I))I_{\eta\eta}]. \tag{76a}$$

$$I(x,y,0) = I_0 \quad \text{(Initial Condition)} \tag{76b}$$

For discretizing $I_{\xi\xi}$ and $I_{\eta\eta}$ as defined in equation (74-75), centred difference scheme have been used. For the numerical scheme given by equation (75) to be stable, the von Neumann analysis (Press *et al.*,1992) shows that we require $\frac{\Delta t}{(\Delta x)^2} < \frac{1}{4}$. If the grid size is set to $\Delta x = 1$, then $\Delta t < \frac{1}{4}$ i.e. $\Delta t < 0.25$. Hence, $\Delta t = 0 - 0.25$ for stability of equation (76) during implementation. The basis for selection of the stopping time is that running the diffusion equation on an image I at scale t is equivalent to convolution with Gaussian kernel of standard deviation $\sqrt{2t}$.

The final proposed algorithm reads as follows.

## Algorithm- Complex Diffusion Based Homomorphic Filtering

In first step, logarithm transformation is applied on input given by equation (67) which reads $\log v(x, y) = \log u(x, y) + \log s(x, y)$
$\Rightarrow w(x, y) = I(x, y) + \eta(x, y)$

In second step, input image in log domain is processed using complex diffusion based filter to remove the additive noise. For niter = 1 to n
$w_{i,j}^{n+1} = w_{i,j}^n + \Delta t.[w_{\xi\xi} + D(\text{Im}(w))w_{\eta\eta}]$ , w i t h $w(x, y, 0) = w$
End.

Finally the speckle reduced image, u, is obtained by exponentiation of the output w of step (2) i.e. $u = e^w$.

## RESULTS AND PERFORMANCE COMPARISON

### Test Case I: Speckle Reduction from Ultrasound Images

The first category of images considered for speckle noise reduction is ultrasound images. The proposed algorithm was applied on several ultrasound images and visual results for one sample image Gyn_normal_intrauterine_IUD.jpg (465x589) for varying amount of speckle noise variance e.g. 0.001, 0.002, 0.004, 0.01, 0.02 and 0.04 are shown in Figure15 for speckle noise variance 0.04. The performance of the proposed scheme is also compared with other state of the arts methods available in literature for speckle reduction as shown in Table 2 for test image Gyn_normal_intrauterine_IUD.jpg. Figure16 shows performance comparison of various speckle reduction methods with the proposed scheme for the sample image Gyn_normal_intrauterine_IUD.jpg (465x589) in terms of speckle variance Vs RMSE and speckle variance Vs PSNR and respectively. From Figure16 it can be observed that the proposed homomorphic complex diffusion process for speckle reduction is associated with minimum RMSE and maximum PSNR in comparison to other techniques reported in literature for the sample ultrasound image taken in to consideration and the performance trend remained same for other images too. Therefore, the results show that the proposed complex diffusion based homomorphic filtering scheme performs better than other existing scheme for ultrasound images.

### Test Case II: Speckle Reduction from SAR Images

The second category of images considered for speckle noise reduction is synthetic aperture radar (SAR) images. The proposed algorithm was applied on several SAR images and results for one sample image, SAR.gif (516x416) for varying amount of speckle noise variance e.g. 0.001, 0.002, 0.004, 0.01, 0.02 and 0.04 are presented here. Figure17 shows the visual results for the sample image for speckle noise variance 0.04. Figure18 show performance comparison of various speckle reduction methods with the proposed scheme in terms of speckle variance Vs RMSE and speckle variance Vs PSNR, respectively. From Figure18 it can be observed that the proposed homomorphic complex diffusion process for speckle reduction is associated with minimum RMSE and maximum PSNR in comparison to other techniques in consideration for the sample SAR image. Also, this performance trend remained same for other

*Table 2. Performance comparison of speckle reduction methods (Sample ultrasound image: Gyn_normal_intrauterine_IUD.jpg, (465x589)*

| Method | Speckle Variance | RMSE | PSNR [dB] |
|---|---|---|---|
| Lee Filter | 0.001<br>0.002<br>0.004<br>0.01<br>0.02<br>0.04 | 4.0559<br>4.3344<br>4.8315<br>5.9573<br>7.0466<br>7.9918 | 35.9691<br>35.3922<br>34.4491<br>32.6298<br>31.1712<br>30.0779 |
| Frost Filter | 0.001<br>0.002<br>0.004<br>0.01<br>0.02<br>0.04 | 6.1928<br>6.8972<br>8.1355<br>11.0139<br>14.6570<br>19.8619 | 32.2930<br>31.3573<br>29.9231<br>27.2920<br>24.8099<br>22.1704 |
| Kuan Filter | 0.001<br>0.002<br>0.004<br>0.01<br>0.02<br>0.04 | 4.0580<br>4.3325<br>4.8404<br>5.9526<br>7.0544<br>7.9911 | 35.9646<br>35.3961<br>34.4331<br>32.6367<br>31.1616<br>30.0787 |
| Hybrid Filter<br>(After 02 iterations) | 0.001<br>0.002<br>0.004<br>0.01<br>0.02<br>0.04 | 7.0480<br>7.5056<br>8.3987<br>10.5484<br>17.4995<br>17.5058 | 31.1695<br>30.6231<br>29.6465<br>27.6671<br>23.2703<br>23.2672 |
| SRAD (After 05 iterations)<br>(Anisotropic diffusion based<br>filter) | 0.001<br>0.002<br>0.004<br>0.01<br>0.02<br>0.04 | 9.0476<br>9.0810<br>11.6356<br>10.9302<br>12.9925<br>16.0786 | 29.0001<br>28.9681<br>26.8151<br>27.3583<br>25.8570<br>24.0059 |
| Proposed Method (After 10<br>iterations) | 0.001<br>0.002<br>0.004<br>0.01<br>0.02<br>0.04 | 3.3114<br>3.3804<br>3.5280<br>3.8814<br>4.2837<br>4.9452 | 37.7305<br>37.5516<br>37.1801<br>36.3509<br>35.4945<br>34.2471 |

test images. Therefore, the results show that the proposed complex diffusion based homomorphic filtering scheme performs better than other existing scheme for SAR images too.

Therefore, from above results and discussions it can be concluded that the nonlinear complex diffusion based filter performs better in comparison to other speckle reduction methods for both category of images. This method also performs better for digital holographic images (Srivastava *et al.*, 2009).

## FUTURE RESEARCH DIRECTIONS

The various possible areas where PDE-based image modelling techniques can be applied include: Scale-space theory, image restoration, image sharpening, contrast enhancement, image analysis and feature extraction, segmentation, video processing, shape analysis, axiomatic and theoretical approaches to image analysis, variational and PDE's-from-energy approaches to image processing, curve and surface evolution,

*Figure 16. Impact of speckle noise on information content for ultrasound images*

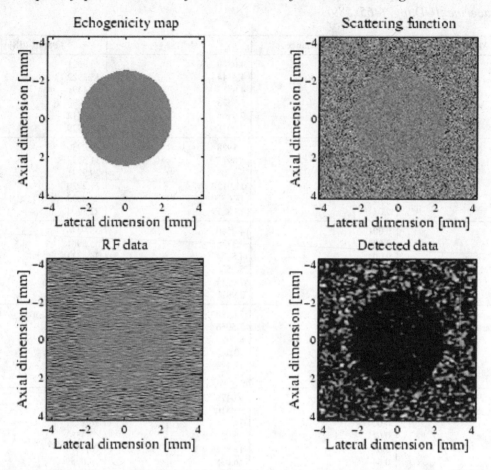

PDE's in hybrid systems, comparison of models, implementations and numerical analysis, mathematical morphology, object detection, optical flow, image compression, shape from shading, 3D reconstruction of views from 2D images, pattern recognition and vision related applications.

PDE-based image modeling techniques can play an important role in analyzing the images obtained from various application areas such as:

## Medical Imaging

The efficient and accurate PDE-based image processing tools can be developed which can aid in to accurate diagnosis of the disease. The some problems of medical imaging that needs further attention include:

- Medical image enhancement and de-noising
- Rician noise removal from MRI images
- Speckle reduction from optical coherence tomography (OCT) images
- Segmentation of an object of interest e.g. Segmentation for Alzheimer's disease detection, segmentation of Iris, segmentation of tissue.
- Medical image registration etc.
- **Synthetic Aperture Radar (SAR) Imaging and Remote Sensing:** Some open problems in this domain include development of efficient PDE-based models for speckle reduction & segmentation, enhancement, restoration etc.

*Figure 17. Original ultrasound image Gyn_normal_intrauterine_IUD.jpg (465x589) (top-left); Speckled image with variance 0.04 (top-right); De-speckled image using proposed scheme (bottom)*

Original image

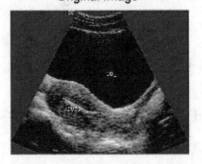

Speckle noised Image-Variance 0.04

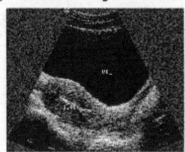

Despeckled Image

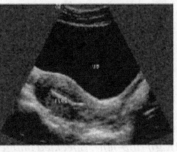

- **Biometrics:** Some open problems in this domain include development of efficient PDE-based models for segmentation, finger prints enhancement & restoration, feature extraction, face detection, identification etc.
- **Optical Information Processing:** Restoration of optical images, speckle reduction and restoration of 3D holograms and image processing of microscopic images.
- **Other application areas:** where the PDE-based image modeling can be applied are:
- Biosignal processing (ECG etc)
- Confocal Microscopy
- Seismic analysis
- Geology and weather monitoring and control
- Robotic vision and many others.

## CONCLUSION

In this chapter, partial differential equation (PDE)-based approaches for image modelling and processing was discussed for image restoration task. The PDE-based approaches can be used in various image processing and computer vision applications such as restoration, segmentation, shape from shading, inpainting, registration, 3D reconstruction of surfaces from multiple views and many more. This chapter is oriented towards the image restoration problem which is an important

*Figure 18. Performance comparison of speckle reduction methods: Speckle Variance Vs RMSE (left), Speckle Variance Vs PSNR(right) for sample ultrasound image: Gyn_normal_intrauterine_IUD.jpg, 465x589*

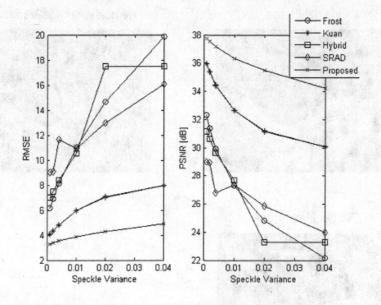

*Figure 19. Original SAR image (Courtesy ESA-ESRIN), SAR.gif (top-left); Speckled image with variance 0.04 (top-right); De-speckled image using proposed complex diffusion based homomorphic filter (bottom)*

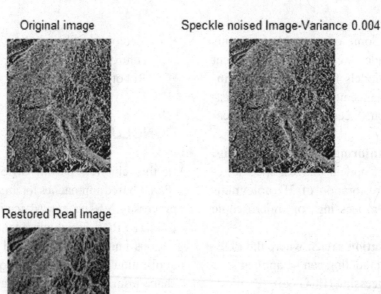

*Figure 20. Performance comparison of speckle reduction methods: Speckle Variance Vs RMSE (left), Speckle Variance Vs PSNR (right) for sample image: SAR.gif, 516x416*

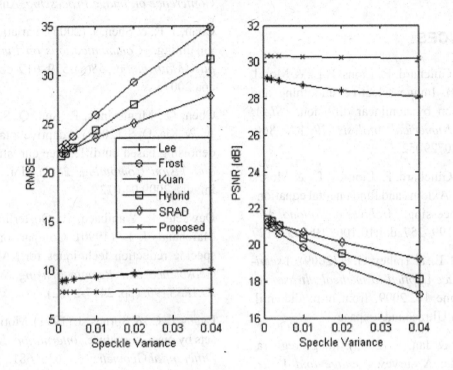

pre-processing task for many applications such as 3-D surface geometry and reconstruction and many more. The introduction part, discussed the basic concepts of image processing and various image modelling techniques. General principles of PDE based image processing and concepts of curve and surface evolution were discussed. Advantages and application areas of PDE-based image processing were presented. The various performance measurement metrics used for comparison purposes were also given. Further, various methods and techniques for removal and reduction of additive and multiplicative noises were discussed. For additive noise removal various popular PDE-based filters such as TV-based approach, anisotropic diffusion based approach, Fourth order PDEs, and complex diffusion based approach were discussed. The performances of

some filters were also evaluated. The complex diffusion based filter is considered to be more efficient filter in comparison to other filters in consideration. For multiplicative or speckle noise, the speckle noise pattern in various imaging modalities such as ultrasound imaging and SAR imaging are discussed. Further, the various methods for speckle reduction were also discussed and finally a comparative analysis of various methods were presented for two cases which concludes that complex diffusion based homomorphic filter performs better in comparison to other methods in consideration. The schemes discussed in this chapter justify the applicability of the PDE-based models in image processing and computer vision which may form the basis for further research in this area for other image processing tasks such as image registration, shape from shading and 3D surface reconstruction.

## REFERENCES

Alvarez, L., Guichard, F., Lions, P. L., & Morel, J. M. (1992). Image selective smoothing and edge detection by nonlinear diffusion. *SIAM Journal on Numerical Analysis*, *29*, 845–866. doi:10.1137/0729052

Alvarez, L., Guichard, F., Lions, P. L., & Morel, J. M. (1993). Axioms and fundamental equations of image processing. *Archives of Rational Mechanics*, *23*, 199–257. doi:10.1007/BF00375127

Anderson, M. E., & Trahey, G. E. (2009). *A seminar on k-space applied to medical ultrasound.* Retrieved June 10, 2009, from http://dukemil.egr.duke.edu/Ultrasound/k-space

Barbara, Z., & Jan, F. (2003). Image registration methods: A survey. *Image and Vision Computing*, *21*, 977–1000. doi:10.1016/S0262-8856(03)00137-9

Beck, A., & Teboulle, M. (2009). Fast gradient-based algorithms for constrained total variation image de-noising and de-blurring problems. *IEEE Transactions on Image Processing*, *18*(11), 2419–2434. doi:10.1109/TIP.2009.2028250

Brown, L. G. (1992). A survey of image registration techniques. *ACM Computing Surveys*, *24*(4), 325–376. doi:10.1145/146370.146374

Caselles, V., Catte, F., Coll, T., & Dibos, F. (1997). A geometric model for active contours. *International Journal of Computer Vision*, *22*, 61–69. doi:10.1023/A:1007979827043

Caselles, V., Morel, J., & Sapiro, G. (1998). Introduction to the special issue on partial differential equations and geometry driven diffusions in image processing. *IEEE Transactions on Image Processing*, *7*(3), 269–273. doi:10.1109/TIP.1998.661176

Chambolle, A. (1994). Partial differential equations and image processing. *IEEE International Conference on Image Processing*, Austin, TX.

Chan, T. F., & Shen, J. (2005). Variational image inpainting. *Communications on Pure and Applied Mathematics*, *58*(5), 579–619. doi:10.1002/cpa.20075

Chen, Q., Montesinos, P., Sun, Q. S., Heng, P. A., & Xia, D. S. (2009). Adaptive total variation denoising based on difference curvature. *Image and Vision Computing*, *28*(3). doi: 10.1016/j.imavis. 2009.04.012

Dewaele, P., Wambacq, P., Oosterlinck, A., & Marchand, J. L. (1990). Comparison of some speckle reduction techniques for SAR images. *Geoscience and Remote Sensing Symposium, IGARSS '90*, (pp. 2417-2422).

Evans, L. C., & Spruck, J. (1991). Motion of level sets by mean curvature. *International Journal of Differential Geometry*, *33*, 635–681.

Frost, V. S., & Stiles, J. A. (1982). A model for radar Images and its application to adaptive digital filtering of multiplicative noise. *IEEE Transactions on Pattern Analysis and Machine Intelligence*, *4*(2), 157–166. doi:10.1109/TPAMI.1982.4767223

Gabor, D. (1965). Information theory in electron microscopy. *Laboratory Investigation*, *14*, 801–807.

Gilboa, G., Sochen, N., & Zeevi, Y. Y. (2004). Image enhancement and denoising by complex diffusion processes. *IEEE Transactions on Pattern Analysis and Machine Intelligence*, *25*(8), 1020–1036. doi:10.1109/TPAMI.2004.47

Gonzalez, R. C., & Wintz, P. (1987). *Digital image processing* (2nd ed.). New York, NY: Academic Press.

Goodman, J. W. (1984). Statistical properties of laser speckle patterns. In Dainty, J. C. (Ed.), *Laser speckle and related phenomena* (pp. 9–75). Berlin, Germany: Springer-Verlag.

Iskander, D. R. (1999). Estimation of the parameters of the k-distribution using higher order and fractional moments. *IEEE Transactions on Aerospace and Electronic Systems, 35*(4), 1453–1457. doi:10.1109/7.805463

Iskander, D. R., Zoubir, A. M., & Boashash, B. (1999). A method for estimating the parameters of k-distribution. *IEEE Transactions on Signal Processing, 47*, 880–884. doi:10.1109/78.752614

Jain, A. K. (1977). Partial differential equations and finite difference methods in image processing, part I: Image representation. *Journal of Optimization Theory and Applications, 23*, 65–91. doi:10.1007/BF00932298

Jain, A. K. (1978). Partial differential equations and finite difference methods in image processing, Part II: Image restoration. *IEEE Transactions on Automatic Control, 23*(5), 817–834. doi:10.1109/TAC.1978.1101881

Jain, A. K. (2006). *Fundamentals of digital image processing*. India: PHI.

Kass, M., Witkin, A., & Terzopoulos, A. (1988). Snakes: active contour models. *International Journal of Computer Vision, 1*, 321–331. doi:10.1007/BF00133570

Kimia, B. B., Tanenbaum, A., & Zucker, S. W. (1990). Lecture Notes in Computer Science: *Vol. 427. Toward a computational theory of shape: An overview*. New York: Springer-Verlag.

Koenderink, J. J. (1984). The structure of images. *Biological Cybernetics, 50*, 363–370. doi:10.1007/BF00336961

Kuan, D. T., & Sawchuk, A. A. (1987). Adaptive restoration of images with speckle. *IEEE Transactions on Acoustics, Speech, and Signal Processing, 35*, 373–383. doi:10.1109/TASSP.1987.1165131

Lee, J. S. (1981). Speckle analysis and smoothing of synthetic aperture radar images. *Computer Graphics and Image Processing, 17*, 24–32. doi:10.1016/S0146-664X(81)80005-6

Lee, J. S. (1983). Digital image smoothing and the sigma filter. *Computer Vision Graphics and Image Processing, 24*, 255–269. doi:10.1016/0734-189X(83)90047-6

Lucy, L. B. (1974). Image restoration of high photometric quality. In R.J Hanisch & R. L. White (Eds.), *Proceedings of the Restoration of HST Images and Spectra STSci*, (pp. 79-85).

Mateo, J. L., & Fernández, C. A. (2009). Finding out general tendencies in speckle noise reduction in ultrasound images. *Expert Systems with Applications, 36*, 7786–7797. doi:10.1016/j.eswa.2008.11.029

Milan, S., Vaclav, H., & Boyle, R. (2007). *Image processing, analysis and machine vision* (2nd ed.). Washington, DC: PWS Publishing.

Morel, J. M., & Solimini, S. (1988). Segmentation of images by variational methods: A constructive approach. *Revista Matematica de Universidad Complutense Madrid, 1*, 169–182.

Mumford, D., & Shah, J. (1989). Optimal approximations by piecewise smooth functions and variational problems. *Communications on Pure and Applied Mathematics, 42*, 577–685. doi:10.1002/cpa.3160420503

Osher, S., & Fedkiw, R. P. (2001). *Level set methods: An overview and some recent results* (pp. 1–65). California, USA: IPAM GBM Tutorials.

Osher, S., & Rudin, L. I. (1990). Feature oriented image enhancement using shock filters. *SIAM Journal on Numerical Analysis*, *27*, 919–940. doi:10.1137/0727053

Osher, S., & Sethian, J. A. (1988). Fronts propagating with curvature dependent speed: Algorithms based on Hamilton-Jacobi formulations. *Journal of Computational Physics*, *79*, 12–49. doi:10.1016/0021-9991(88)90002-2

Perona, P. (1998). Orientation diffusions. *IEEE Transactions on Image Processing*, *7*, 457–467. doi:10.1109/83.661195

Perona, P., & Malik, J. (1990). Scale space and edge detection using anisotropic diffusion. *IEEE Transactions on Pattern Analysis and Machine Intelligence*, *12*, 629–639. doi:10.1109/34.56205

Press, H., Teukolsky, S., Vetterling, T., & Flannery, B. (1992). *Numerical recipes in C: The art of scientific computing* (2nd ed.). Cambridge University Press.

Price, C. B. (1990). Image enhancement and analysis with reaction diffusion paradigm. *Proceedings of the Institution of Electrical Engineers*, *137*, 136–145.

Rajan, J., Kannan, K., & Kaimal, M. R. (2008). An improved hybrid model for molecular image de-noising. *Journal of Mathematical Imaging and Vision*, *31*, 73–79. doi:10.1007/s10851-008-0067-4

Romeny, B. ter H. (1994). *Geometry driven diffusion in computer vision*. Boston, MA: Kluwer.

Rudin, L. I., Osher, S., & Fatemi, E. (1992). Non linear total variation based noise removal algorithms. *Physica D. Nonlinear Phenomena*, *60*, 259–268. doi:10.1016/0167-2789(92)90242-F

Salinas, H., & Fernandez, D. C. (2007). Comparison of PDE-based nonlinear diffusion approaches for image enhancement and de-noising in optical coherence tomography. *IEEE Transactions on Medical Imaging*, *26*(6), 761–771. doi:10.1109/TMI.2006.887375

Shen, T. F., & Vese, L. (2002). *Variational PDE models in image processing*. Joint Math Meeting, San Diego.

Soman, K. P., & Ramachandran, K. I. (2004). *Insight in to wavelets from theory to practice*. India: PHI.

Srivastava, R. (2011). A complex diffusion based nonlinear filter for speckle reduction from optical coherence tomography images. *International Conference on Communication, Computing & Security (ICCCS-2011), Rourkela, India*, (pp. 259-264). ACM Press. ISBN-978-1-4503-0464-1

Srivastava, R., & Gupta, J. R. P. (2010). A PDE-based nonlinear filter adapted to Rayleigh's speckle noise for de-speckling 2D ultrasound images. *International Conference on Contemporary Computing (IC3-2010), Communications in Computer and Information Science* (CCIS), *CCIS-94,* India, (pp. 1-12). Berlin, Germany: Springer-Verlag

Srivastava, R., Gupta, J. R. P., & Parthasarathy, H. (2009). Comparison of PDE based and other techniques for speckle reduction from digitally reconstructed holographic images. *Optics and Lasers in Engineering*, *48*(5), 626–635. doi:10.1016/j.optlaseng.2009.09.012

Srivastava, R., Gupta, J. R. P., Parthasarathy, H., & Srivastava, S. (2011). An adaptive nonlinear PDE based speckle reduction technique for ultrasound images. *International Journal of Biomedical Engineering and Technology*, *6*(3). doi:10.1504/IJBET.2011.041468

Srivastava, R., Gupta, J. R. P., & Parthasarthy, H. (2009). Complex diffusion based speckle reduction from digital images. *IEEE International Conference on Methods and Models in Computer Science (ICM2CS-09)*, Delhi, India, (pp. 43-49).

Topiwala, P. N. (Ed.). (1998). *Wavelet image and video compression*. Kluwer Academic Publishers.

Wang, Z., Bovik, A. C., Sheikh, H. R., & Celli, E. P. S. (2004). Image quality assessment: From error visibility to structural similarity. *IEEE Transactions on Image Processing*, *13*(4), 1–14. doi:10.1109/TIP.2003.819861

Witkin, A. P. (1983). Scale space filtering. *International Joint Conference on Artificial Intelligence*, Germany, (pp. 1019-1023).

You, Y. L., & Kaveh, M. (2000). Fourth order partial differential equations for noise removal. *IEEE Transactions on Image Processing*, *9*, 1723–1730. doi:10.1109/83.869184

Yu, Y., & Acton, S. T. (2002). Speckle reducing anisotropic diffusion. *IEEE Transactions on Image Processing*, *11*(11), 1260–1270. doi:10.1109/TIP.2002.804276

Zhang, R., Tsai, P.-S., Cryer, J. E., & Shah, M. (1999). Shape from shading: A survey. *IEEE Transactions on Pattern Analysis and Machine Intelligence*, *21*(8), 690–706. doi:10.1109/34.784284

## KEY TERMS AND DEFINITIONS

**Additive Noise:** It follows Gaussian distribution.

**Homomorphic Filter:** This filter is used for speckle reduction from digital images using filters defined for additive noise removal in logarithmic domain. In logarithmic domain, the multiplicative noise converts in to additive noise.

**PDE-Based Filters:** Partial differential equation based filters derived using variational calculus by minimizing the energy functional of the image defined in terms of gradient norm of the image.

**Performance Metrics:** The various performance measurement metrics are MSE, PSNR, CP, MSSIM, speckle index and effective number of looks.

**Restoration:** This is one of the digital image processing tasks that removes or reduces the noise from images to improve its visual quality.

**Speckle Noise:** A multiplicative noise that appears in digital holographic images, ultrasound imaging, SAR imaging and many other applications. It degrades the visual quality of the image. This noise is introduced during the formation of image. Speckle noise in ultrasound images follows Rayleigh's distribution.

**Speckle Reduction:** It deals with the methods to reduce speckle noise.

# Section 2
# 3D Reconstruction

*This section contains six chapters that deal with different areas of 3D reconstruction of objects, scenes, and environments. The first chapter of this section describes a surface reconstruction method, which mixes interpolating as well as approximating features and its implementation in graphics hardware. The second chapter explores 3D reconstruction of underwater natural scenes and objects based on stereo vision, whereas the next chapter provides a basic understanding of how 3D statistical visual displays aid in education. The fourth chapter proposes depth estimation for stereo pair of high dynamic range images. The fifth chapter presents fusion of 3D reconstructions generated by two seminal monocular-cue based reconstruction algorithms, and the last chapter proposes a method to extract 3D models from single view perspective images.*

# Chapter 4
# Hybrid GPU Local Delaunay Triangulation through Points Consolidation

**Carlos Buchart**
*CEIT, Spain & TECNUN (University of Navarra), Spain*

**Aiert Amundarain**
*CEIT, Spain*

**Diego Borro**
*CEIT, Spain & TECNUN (University of Navarra), Spain*

## ABSTRACT

*This chapter describes a surface reconstruction method that mixes interpolating and approximating features and its implementation in graphics hardware. Hybrid methods are useful in areas such sculpting, medicine, and cultural heritage, where details must be preserved. Such cases may also contain noise (due to sampling inaccuracies) or duplicated points (in the case of the scan is done from multiple points of view), where hybrid methods provide an interesting solution. The proposed method makes use of a point projection operator to create a regular distributed and noise free set of points, which is reconstructed using local Delaunay triangulations. Both points projection and triangulation methods are studied in its basic serial version, but aiming to design parallel versions (more specifically GPU implementations) that increase their performance. The adaptations required for the parallel reconstruction are discussed, and several implementation details are given.*

## INTRODUCTION

Surface reconstruction is an amazing field of research due to the uncertainty nature of the problem: given a set of points from an unknown surface, how to compute a digital representation as similar as possible to such surface. It faces sev-

eral challenges: incomplete data, inconsistencies, noise, data size, ambiguities, to name a few. It is a vast researching area, and many methods have been already proposed. Unfortunately, surface reconstruction is still an open field since it is too complex and probably impossible to fully recover an unknown surface without previously assuming

DOI: 10.4018/978-1-4666-0113-0.ch004

some kind of information. Almost every single existing method relies on at least one parameter and usually focuses on a subset of problems, so it can better exploit the implicit model's characteristics in order to obtain a proper reconstruction.

It is then important to first consider the goals of the method studied, the information available and the assumptions done:

1. The method must be scalable in terms of the size of the data. One of the most common ways to achieve this kind of goal is the "divide and conquer" approach, so memory and computing power requirements can be reduced.

2. In the last years, graphical hardware accelerated algorithms have become more common and easy to implement in the GPU (Graphics Processing Unit). Then, it is also convenient that the method may be parallelized, much better if it is GPU friendly.

3. The method should be also as noise tolerant as possible, assuming not high amounts of outliers. This is a compromise decision, since some of the most common sources of points are laser scanners and image segmentation, both of them providing few outliers, although noise can be present due to imprecision of the acquiring device or low resolution. Assuming low noise level helps to increase the fidelity of the reconstruction of high detailed areas, since they will not be confused with sampling error.

4. Depending on the source, information such as normals may or not be present. The method should be flexible with the input, performing the necessary steps to compute the missing data. In this sense, only points themselves are a must in this work.

As it will be seen later, combining different processing techniques allows us to design a surface reconstruction method that satisfies with all the goals previously listed.

The user should choose a balance between precision and robustness when facing noise tolerance. In this work, we show how mixing a point consolidation phase and a Delaunay triangulation can produce very good results, both robust against sampling errors and accurate in high frequencies recovery. The Delaunay triangulation only requires a set of points to work, so it also fulfills the last goal.

Regarding the scalability of our method, the triangulation phase is scalable in both terms of memory (a divide and conquer method) and execution time (it is a parallel method that has been implemented in the GPU). The point filter has been adapted to be GPU capable, although its scalability is a bit lower than the triangulation due to its global and iterative nature.

In summary, the main objectives of this chapter include:

- Present local triangulation as a reconstruction alternative,
- Propose a fast filtering scheme for improving local triangulation with global parameter,
- Implement both filtering and triangulation in parallel graphic architecture,
- As such GPU algorithms are still very sensitive to even small optimization, implementation details will be given when they give an important advantage.

## BACKGROUND

As it has been mentioned before, surface reconstruction is an active research field, and many works have been presented. On one hand, if it is assumed that the points have no noise, i.e., they belong to the surface, then it is sufficient to find a relationship among the points (their connectivity) to reconstruct a discrete representation of the surface. These kinds of techniques are called *interpolating*. On the other hand, if noise or incomplete data is present, *approximating* techniques are required. These usually rely on implicit functions to define a similar surface while balancing outliers, noise and high details. Additionally to these two major classes, it is common to filter the point set as a preprocess step, for example, removing outliers. In the rest of this section, we will describe these techniques and enumerate some of the most important related works.

## INTERPOLATING TECHNIQUES

May be the most known and common interpolating technique is the Delaunay triangulation (Delaunay, 1934). The Delaunay triangulation of a set of points $P \in R^D$ is defined as the set of simplices $S$ such that no point in $P$ belongs to the circumscribing hyper-sphere of any simplex of $S$. One important property is that the maximum angle of each triangle is minimized, so Delaunay triangulation produces triangles as regular as possible for the given set of points. Another important definition is the dual of a Delaunay triangulation, the Voronoi diagram of $P$. It is defined as the regions around each point $p \in P$ such that any point inside the region is nearer to $p$ than to any other point of $P$. A general algorithm for computing Delaunay triangulations in $E^d$ has been presented in by Cignoni (1998). It consists on a divide and conquer strategy that reduces the complexity of the problem to an easy case. Then, the methods backtracks the divisions joining the neighboring sections.

One of the most worth citing Delaunay based reconstruction is the Power Crust method proposed by Amenta, Choi and Kolluri (2001). It constructs the Voronoi diagram of the input points, and then extracts a polygonal mesh using the inverse of the medial axis transform obtained from the Voronoi diagram.

The Cocone algorithm (Amenta, Choi, Dey & Leekha, 2000) also relies on Voronoi regions for the reconstruction. It extracts the reconstructed surface by filtering the triangulation as follows: for a sample point $p$ and a Voronoi edge $e$ in the Voronoi cell of $p$, if for the three Voronoi cells adjacent to $e$ have a point $x$ such that the vector $px$ makes a right angle with the normal of $p$, then their dual is included in the reconstruction. Some other improvements to this method have been presented, concretely the Tight Cocone by Dey and Goswami (2003), basically a hole-filling extension; and the Robust Cocone (Dey & Goswami, 2006), that incorporates tolerance against noisy inputs.

In 2000, Gopi, Krishnan and Silva presented a 2D local Delaunay triangulation of the neighborhood of each point of $P$, instead of computing a full 3D triangulation and then extracting the corresponding surface. Assuming a dense sampling of the original object, the neighborhood of $p$ is the same of its projection onto the tangent plane of $p$. Based on this, a lower dimensional triangulation is done in 2D, resulting in a faster reconstruction than in 3D (it is important to note that a 3D Delaunay triangulation is composed of tetrahedras rather than triangles). Following a similar scheme, Buchart, Borro and Amundarain (2008) presented theoretical proof about the validity of that approach, and also proposed a parallel reconstruction algorithm based on concurrent local Delaunay triangulation and its implementation in the GPU by the use of shaders, called GLT (GPU Local Triangulation). Also, Zhang, Liu, Gotsman and Huang (2010) used a similar approach of lower dimensional reconstruction over patches larger than the 1-neighborhood of (Gopi et al., 2000) and (Buchart et al., 2008); those patches are defined as regions where point's tangent plane has small variation.

The main weakness of interpolating methods is the presence of noise. It is interesting to note that isolate outliers are usually discarded by default with proper neighborhood sizes. Sampling inaccuracies, on the other hand, fall into the local support of interpolating methods and are included in the reconstruction. Under certain levels of noise, just a rough surface is obtained. In worse cases, the reconstruction methods may fail to create a consistent surface.

## Approximating Techniques

As mentioned above, if either noise or outliers are present, interpolating techniques fail to generate a correct reconstruction, because all the points are taken into account for the triangulation. Approximating techniques tend to solve this issue at the cost of losing detail (it is also true that many methods can achieve good quality reconstructions, but usually with high memory consumption). Although approximating techniques are out of the scope of this chapter, it is interesting to have a general idea of some of the methods presented so far.

Among the approximating reconstruction we can find many different approaches, but most of them are based on the construction of an implicit function *I(x)* (commonly represented as an scalar field) and on the extraction of a given iso-surface (for example *I(x) = 0*). The iso-surface extraction is usually done using the Marching Cubes algorithm (Lorensen & Cline, 1987) or a polygonizer like (Bloomenthal, 1988).

One of the methods in this area is the work of Hoppe, DeRose, Duchamp, McDonald and Stuetzle (1992). It computes a signed distance field from the points to their tangent planes. Such planes are estimated from the local neighborhood of each point using principal component analysis, and re-oriented using a connectivity graph to consistently propagate a common orientation.

As a more recent example, Wang, Oliveira, Xie and Kaufman (2005) proposed the use of oriented charges to create the signed distance function. The space containing the point set is subdivided using an octree, and in the nodes of the neighborhood of the samples the charges are placed. Such charges are a linear local distance fields. To obtain a global distance field, each charge is weighted by a Gaussian blending function.

Ohtake, Belyaev, Alexa, Turk and Seidel (2005) made use of weighted local shape functions in an adaptive fashion to create a global approximation, and Nagai, Ohtake and Suzuki (2009) followed a similar idea, introducing a Laplacian smoothing term based on the diffusion of the gradient field.

Finally, the Poisson reconstruction (Kazhdan, Bolitho & Hoppe, 2006) is probably one of the best surface reconstruction methods widely available. It performs a global reconstruction by solving a Poisson system.

An adaptive solver is used to adjust the precision of the solution near the surface. It also shares some local fitting characteristics since, in order to create the adaptive conditions, it defines locally supported functions on octree's nodes. One disadvantage of this method is that it relies on the correct orientation of the point's normal.

## Points Preprocessing

There are some interesting works regarding a preprocess step before reconstruction. As mentioned before, one of the major problems concerning all the methods is the quality of the input data. What preprocessing steps try to do is to improve such quality, remove noise and generate a more uniform set of points. It is especially convenient for interpolating methods, due to their dependence on the input data.

Alexa, Behr, Cohen-Or, Fleishman, Levin and Silva (2003) studied the direct visualization of point set surfaces, by defining a projection operator that projects the points near the data set onto the surface, and then constructing a moving least-square surface (Levin, 2003).

In more recent years, Lipman, Cohen-Or, Levin and Tal-Ezer (2007) presented a parameterization-free projection operator called LOP (Locally Optimal Projection) to deal with outliers, and Huang, Li, Zhang, Ascher and Cohen-Or (2009) developed a new WLOP (Weighted LOP), improving the previous operator with a more uniform distribution of points and a clearer convergence. This operator is also used to boost up normal estimation and propagation (Huang et al., 2009). One of the main problems of these operators is that are very expensive in terms of execution time when compared to the time required for the most common reconstruction algorithms. For example, for a simple data set of 35K points, the WLOP operator executes in almost 70 seconds, while the reconstruction using the GLT method is done in less than a second.

Finally, (Zhang et al., 2010) proposed a meshless parameterization and denoising of a set of points by rigid alignment of locally flattered proximity graphs.

## PARALLEL RECONSTRUCTION

As it has seen before, many surface reconstruction algorithms rely on the quality of the used point set. In our case of study, for example, the GPU Local Triangulation (GLT) by (Buchart et al., 2008) excels in execution time but fails to generate good meshes in presence of noisy and non-uniform data sets.

In a move to try to reduce these problems, as well as to provide better input to other methods, it is necessary to have a better distributed and, if possible, noise free set of points. In this sense, the WLOP operator (Huang et al., 2009) provides these two characteristics, but its execution time may contrast too much with the state of the art in surface reconstruction, mainly due to the heavy computational work. On the other hand, although it is an iterative method, if the initial guess is not too far away from the solution, the method converges quickly.

In this chapter, we present a new parallel, accelerated version of the WLOP (called PWLOP, P for Parallel) that speeds it up by one order of magnitude, providing a fast point preprocessing tool for surface reconstruction. We also present an extended version of the GLT method to incorporate the new PWLOP, some improvements in the triangulation as well as a full CUDA implementation of both methods.

## PWLOP: Parallel Weighted Locally Optimal Projection

For a better understanding of the improvements introduced into the projection operator, we will first describe the core of the previously published works on these operators.

Given a set of points $P = \{p_j\}, j \in J = |P|$, an initial guess $X^0 = \{x_i\}, i \in I = |X^0|$, a repulsion parameter $\mu \in [0, 1/2)$ and support radius h, the Locally Optimal Projection (LOP) algorithm presented by (Lipman et al., 2007) computes the projection of X onto P in an iterative way. For each iteration $k \in 1, 2, 3\ldots$, it defines the projection for the i-th point of X:

$$x_i^{(k)} = \frac{\sum_{j \in J} p_j \alpha_{ij}^{(k-1)}}{\sum_{j \in J} \alpha_{ij}^{(k-1)}} + \mu \frac{\sum_{i' \in I \setminus \{i\}} \left( x_i^{(k-1)} - x_{i'}^{(k-1)} \right) \beta_{ii'}^{(k-1)}}{\sum_{i' \in I \setminus \{i\}} \beta_{ii'}^{(k-1)}}, i \in I$$

$$(1)$$

where

$$\alpha_{ij}^{(k)} = \frac{\theta \left( \left\| x_i^{(k)} - p_j \right\| \right)}{\left\| x_i^{(k)} - p_j \right\|} \tag{2}$$

$$\beta_{ii'}^{(k)} = \frac{\theta \left( \left\| x_i^{(k)} - x_{i'}^{(k)} \right\| \right)}{\left\| x_i^{(k)} - x_{i'}^{(k)} \right\|} \left| \frac{\partial \eta}{\partial r} \left( \left\| x_i^{(k)} - x_{i'}^{(k)} \right\| \right) \right|, i' \in I \setminus \{i\}. \tag{3}$$

$\theta(r)$ is a weight function with compact support radius h, that defines the area of influence of the operator; it can be seen as a Gaussian filter applied to the distance function from $x_i^{(k)}$. $\eta(r)$ is a repulsion function that penalizes points going too close to each other. The support radius h is usually set as $h = 4\sqrt{d_{BB} / |P|}$, where $d_{BB}$ is the diagonal length of the bounding box of P (Huang et al., 2009). In the work of (Lipman et al., 2007), such functions are defined as

$$\theta(r) = e^{-r^2/(h/4)^2} \qquad (4)$$

$$\eta(r) = 1/(3r^3) \qquad (5)$$

In their extension of LOP, (Huang et al., 2009) comment that the repulsion force may decrease too fast in many situations, contributing to a non-uniform distribution of points in X. They then propose a new repulsion term "which decreases more gently and penalizes more at larger r, yielding both a better convergence and a more locally regular point distribution" (Huang et al., 2009, p. 3). They also set, empirically, $\mu = 0.45$. The new repulsion function is

$$\eta(r) = -r \qquad (6)$$

which also leads to a simplified $\beta$ term

$$\beta_{ii'}^{(k)} = \frac{\theta\left(\left\|x_i^{(k)} - x_{i'}^{(k)}\right\|\right)}{\left\|x_i^{(k)} - x_{i'}^{(k)}\right\|}, i' \in I \setminus \{i\} \qquad (7)$$

To improve even more the distribution of points, it incorporates locally adaptive density weights $v_j$ for each $p_j \in P$, and $w_i^{(k)}$ for each $x_i^{(k)} \in X^{(k)}$:

$$v_j = 1 + \sum_{j' \in J \setminus \{j\}} \theta\left(\left\|p_j - p_{j'}\right\|\right) \qquad (8)$$

$$w_i^{(k)} = 1 + \sum_{i' \in I \setminus \{i\}} \theta\left(\left\|x_i^{(k)} - x_{i'}^{(k)}\right\|\right). \qquad (9)$$

In this way, the Weighted LOP (WLOP) operator (Huang et al., 2009) is defined as

$$x_i^{(k)} = \frac{\sum_{j \in J} p_j \hat{\alpha}_{ij}^{(k-1)}}{\sum_{j \in J} \hat{\alpha}_{ij}^{(k-1)}} + \mu \frac{\sum_{i' \in I \setminus \{i\}} \left(x_i^{(k-1)} - x_{i'}^{(k-1)}\right) \hat{\beta}_{ii'}^{(k-1)}}{\sum_{i' \in I \setminus \{i\}} \hat{\beta}_{ii'}^{(k-1)}}, i \in I \qquad (10)$$

where

$$\hat{\alpha}_{ij}^{(k)} = \frac{\theta\left(\left\|x_i^{(k)} - p_j\right\|\right)}{\left\|x_i^{(k)} - p_j\right\|} \Big/ v_j \qquad (11)$$

$$\hat{\beta}_{ii'}^{(k)} = \frac{\theta\left(\left\|x_i^{(k)} - x_{i'}^{(k)}\right\|\right)}{\left\|x_i^{(k)} - x_{i'}^{(k)}\right\|} w_i^{(k)}, i' \in I \setminus \{i\} \qquad (12)$$

Once that the bases of the LOP and WLOP operators have been exposed, we will now discuss their performance and the new operator we propose to dramatically reduce the time needed for the projection.

The main issue of both LOP and WLOP is their execution time. Some straightforward optimizations (probably present in the original implementations, but no details are given in the publications) may include computing squared distances instead of the actual distance, and avoid evaluating the weight function θ(r) on the full domain, but only where its weight does not vanish, i.e., evaluate the function in the *h*-vicinity of each point (remember that θ(r) has support radius *h*), although the computation of such vicinity remains an issue.

Even with these optimizations, WLOP is especially slow because it must evaluate the local density weights in each iteration, which means having to recompute the *h*-vicinity of each point several times. We have seen that if a good initial guess $X^0$ is provided (see below for further explanation), the neighborhoods variations are small since the points tend to move just a few (weights do change between iterations). The points that fall into the support of the local density weights of a point have been called the *local support neighborhood* (LSN) of such a point. We propose preloading an *extended LSN* that includes all the points that may fall in the support radius *h* during the iterations of the operator (see Figure 1). Even when some neighbors in the extended LSN may fall outside the support radius (thus computing unnecessarily the weight function), it does worth the time gained by avoiding the costly neighborhood computation. In our tests, an extended radius of $2h$ works well in most of the cases. Also, bounding the maximum number of neighbors is important given the fact that the CUDA matrices are static; in the tests, 64 points of vicinity were enough to correctly project most of the models, while 128 were used in noisy datasets.

The new local weight densities may be expressed in function of their local support neighborhoods as

$$\overline{v}_j^{(k)} = 1 + \sum_{j' \in \overline{J}_j} \theta\left(\left\|p_j - p_{j'}\right\|\right) \tag{13}$$

$$\overline{w}_i^{(k)} = 1 + \sum_{i' \in \overline{I}_i} \theta\left(\left\|x_i^{(k)} - x_{i'}^{(k)}\right\|\right) \tag{14}$$

where $\overline{I}_i$ defines the precomputed neighborhood of $x_i$, and $\overline{J}_j$ is the precomputed neighborhood of $p_j$. To simplify the notation, $\overline{\alpha}_{ij}^{(k)}$ and $\overline{\beta}_{ii'}^{(k)}$ will denote the correspondent new $\hat{\alpha}_{ij}^{(k)}$ and $\hat{\beta}_{ii'}^{(k)}$ terms with precomputed neighborhoods. In the same way, neighborhoods in Equation 10 are replaced by their precomputed counterparts. Experiments reveal that by simply avoiding the expensive neighborhood computation with the previously exposed technique, it is possible to obtain speed up ranges around the 50% in the execution time of the original WLOP operator. This variation of the WLOP operator has been called extended WLOP, or eWLOP for short.

The only problem so far is the initial guess $X^0$. However, a good and easy-to-compute initial set can be obtained by the spatial subdivision of $P$, taking $X^0$ as the centroid of the points inside each cell. This also follows the common sense that a uniform data set may be crudely represented by a grid-based subsampling of the point set.

At this point, it raises the question about parallelization. The less parallelizable part of the

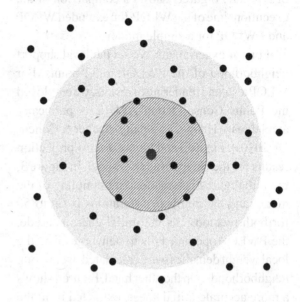

*Figure 1. Local support neighborhood (dark area) vs. the extended LSN (lighter area)*

algorithm is neighborhoods computation, but since we have moved all of them to a preprocessing stage, it must be done just once; in our implementation, we have used the ANN library (Mount & Arya, 2010) to perform the $k$-nearest neighbors ($k$-NN) computation (when talking about neighborhoods, $k$ is the number of neighbors, not the current iteration). The rest of the algorithm is data independent in the same iteration $k$, i.e., a projected point $x_i^{(k)}$ only depends on previously projected points $x_{i'}^{(k-1)}$ and the original points $P$.

Based on the preceding analysis, we have developed a *Parallel WLOP* (PWLOP) that performs an average of 25 times faster than the original WLOP. PWLOP uses graphical hardware acceleration by implementing it on the CUDA architecture. It is worth mentioning that, although the algorithm is dependent between consecutive iterations, there is no need to do CPU processing after an iteration has finished, so the operator can execute completely in the GPU before downloading the projected points into the main memory. Additionally, and for testing purposes, we have also extended the original WLOP introducing the extended LSN, but without the parallelization plus of PWLOP. Figure 2 shows a comparison of the execution time of the WLOP, the extended WLOP and PWLOP for a simple model.

For our experiments, we set the local support neighborhood of the PWLOP to 32 points. For WLOP tests and rendering of results, we employed the Points Consolidation API (it is publically available in (Huang, Li, Zhang, Ascher & Cohen-Or, 2010)). Figure 3 and Figure 4 show projection results for the Happy Buddha model. In Figure 3, the initial guess is a random subsampling of the model and the number of iterations is set to 50 for both methods. As the initial guess is crude, the PWLOP operator fails to converge since the local weight densities were calculated over wrong neighborhoods. On the other hand, Figure 4 shows a more accurate initial guess, extracted from the grid subdivision described above. As the initial guess is near a solution, we reduced the number of iterations to only 10. It can be seen how the results from WLOP and PWLOP are almost identical, while PWLOP executes four times faster than WLOP.

As an additional test, we extended the speed comparison seen in Figure 4, to include the eW-LOP and increase the number of iterations. Results can be seen in Table 1. It shows how PWLOP can execute 50 times more iterations than the original WLOP in the same period of time under equal circumstances (the initial guess set). Also, the average speed up offered by PWLOP against the extended WLOP is of 25 times, ignoring the common neighborhood computation time (6.55s). Finally, we have performed a full speed test over several models and results are shown in Figure 5. There it can be seen how PWLOP is an order of magnitude faster in the worst case. We also found that more than a half of the execution time of PWLOP is spent in the computation of the extended LSN, very reasonable since it is a heavy task and it is done in the CPU instead of the GPU as with the rest of the algorithms.

Concerning the projection of noisy data sets, we defer such analysis to the reconstruction section, since it will be easier to see the changes between original and projected datasets when they are reconstructed.

Finally, as described along this chapter, the validity of the PWLOP operator comes from the use of an eLSN for each point. Figure 3 illustrated what happens if this premise is not valid. In the following experiment, a random set of points is used as the initial set $X^0$ and, instead of computing the eLSN only in the first iteration, it is used for several iterations and it is marked to

*Figure 2. Speed comparison between WLOP, extended WLOP, and PWLOP in the projection of 22K points from the Stanford Bunny (35K points), using different number of iterations*

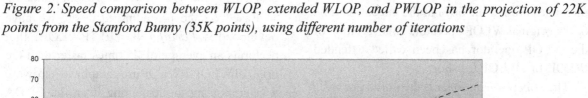
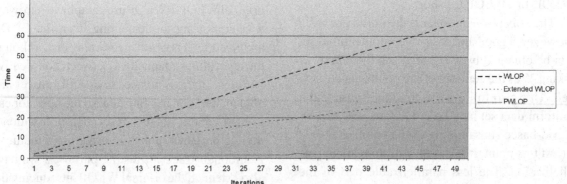

*Figure 3. Projection of the Happy Buddha model (543K) with h = 0.2 and 50 iterations. (a) 10% random subsampling |X⁰|=54K. (b) Using WLOP (91.75s). (c) Using PWLOP (8.9s).*

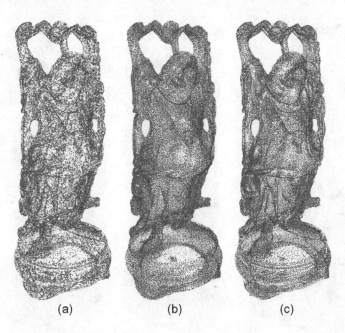

(a)     (b)     (c)

be recomputed each 10 iterations. This leads to a midpoint approach between the original WLOP, that computes the LSN in each iteration, and the PWLOP, that uses only the first eLSN. Results of this experiment are shown in Figure 6. As can be seen, this approach leads to a slightly better projection than WLOP. On the other hand, and as expected, the required time is increased considerably compared with PWLOP, although it remains inferior to the one employed by WLOP.

Implementation details: the PWLOP operator is susceptible to many optimizations that help to speed up the method and to reduce the number of GPU registers used, then incrementing the GPU occupancy and increasing performance. Some of these optimizations include:

- Terms like $\hat{\beta}_{ii}^{(k)}$, where a norm appears several times; this norm may be computed only once.

- Expressions such $\dfrac{\sum\limits_{j \in J} p_j \hat{\alpha}_{ij}^{(k-1)}}{\sum\limits_{j \in J} \hat{\alpha}_{ij}^{(k-1)}}$ can be computed in a single iteration.

- The weight function $\theta(r) = e^{-r^2/(h/4)^2}$ may be expressed as $\theta(r) = e^{-\hat{h}r^2}$, where $\hat{h} = (4/h)^2$ is precomputed. Moreover, the distance $r$ may be used in its squared form, avoiding the costly squared root (in this sense, for example, many $k$-NN algorithms return the squared distance).

- Finally, there are several terms that may produce a division-by-zero when the distance between two points vanishes (more likely between $X$ and $P$). To solve this issue, and to avoid inconvenient branches, given that the divisor is always positive (distances) it is a common practice to add a small value to it.

*Figure 4. Projection of the Happy Buddha model (543K) with h = 0.2 and 10 iterations. (a) grid sub-sampled |X⁰|=55K. (b) Using WLOP (24.63s). (c) Using PWLOP (6.87s)*

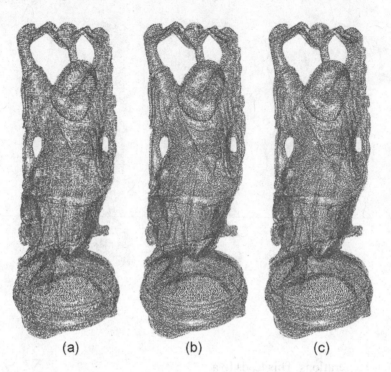

(a)         (b)         (c)

## GLT: GPU Local Triangulation

As it has been mentioned before, GLT is a parallel local surface reconstruction method based on concurrent individual 2D Delaunay triangulations (Buchart et al., 2008). As an overview of the method, it involves, for each point, the computation of the $k$-neighborhood in a radius $\delta$ (value determined by the lowest sampling rate of the data), normal estimation, neighborhood projection onto the tangent plane, radial sorting of projected points around the normal and local Delaunay triangulation. After all points have been processed, the final mesh is assembled from the local triangle fans and normals are uniformly oriented using a propagation based on the connectivity of the points. Although some details are presented bellow regarding the introduced changes, we refer to the original work for a full discussion of the method.

The local nature of this method makes it very favorable to parallelization as it will be seen in the performed tests, but has against it the sensibility to data distribution and noise. The projection operators discussed above help to solve this issue by creating a more uniform set of points, improving the quality of the reconstruction. Also, the PWLOP has an execution time that falls in the same order of magnitude of the reconstruction, which makes it a reasonable choice for a preprocessing stage,

*Table 1. Speed comparison WLOP, improved WLOP and PWLOP when projecting the Happy Buddha model (543K, |X⁰|=55K) with h = 0.2.*

| Iterations | WLOP | Ext. WLOP | PWLOP |
|---|---|---|---|
| 10 | 24.63s | 14.59s | 6.87s |
| 100 | 101.79s | 87.53s | 9.58s |
| 500 | 963.11s | 410.36s | 22.69s |

*Figure 5. Projection of different data sets using WLOP, the Extended WLOP and the proposed PWLOP operators. For all the data sets, 50 iterations were used as well as LSN = 64. The Extended LSN computation times are common for both the Extended WLOP and PWLOP.*

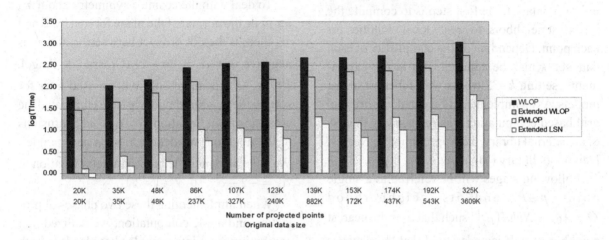

*Figure 6. Projection of the Happy Buddha model (543K) with h = 0.2 and 50 iterations. (a) WLOP (91.75s). (b) PWLOP (8.9s). (c) PWLOP resetting $X^0$ each 10 iterations (41.82s).*

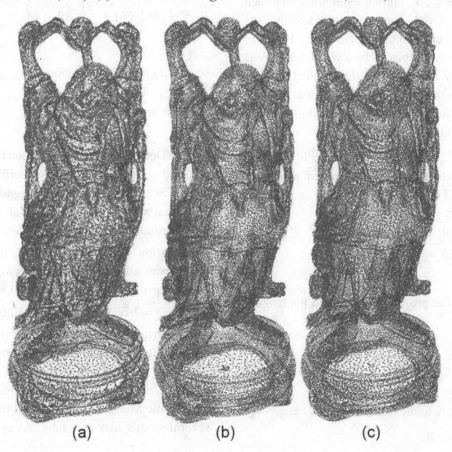

(a)        (b)        (c)

without increasing considerably the total time required to extract the surface.

Once the points are projected to get a more uniform data set, the first step is to compute the *k*-nearest neighbors, to create local vicinities for each point. Depending on the complexity of each data set, *k* may be adjusted. But in our experiments, setting *k=32* works well for most of the models. As an implementation detail, the original grid based computation was replaced by the use of an external library, the Approximating Nearest Neighbors library (Mount & Arya, 2010).

Following stages will be referred to a single point $p \in P$, and its neighborhood $Q = \left\{ q_j \in Nbhd(p) \right\}$, such that $q_0$ is the nearest neighbor of *p*. It is understood that these stages are applied to every single point of *P* to get the final reconstruction.

The second step is to compute the normal $\vec{n}$ of *p*. In this work, normal estimation has been slightly improved. The previous estimator was based on principal component analysis (PCA). In this work, it was replaced by a weighted PCA as proposed by Pauly, Gross & Kobbelt (2002). Similarly to the method by Huang et al. (2009), the weight function is based on the $\theta(r)$ function of the PWLOP operator.

Now, let $Q' = \left\{ q'_j \right\}$ be the minimal rotational projection of *Q* onto the tangent plane of p (see Figure 7):

$$q'_j = p + \frac{\hat{q}_j - p}{\left\| \hat{q}_j - p \right\|} \left\| q_j - p \right\| \qquad (15)$$

where $\hat{q}_j$ is the projection of $q_j$ onto p's tangent plane:

$$\hat{q}_j = q_j + \left\langle p - q_j, \vec{n} \right\rangle \vec{n} - p. \qquad (16)$$

Then, set $\alpha_j$ as the angle between $\vec{v}_j = q'_j - p$ and $\vec{z} = q'_0 - p$

$$\alpha_j = \arccos\left( \left\langle \vec{z}, \vec{v}_j \right\rangle \right) \qquad (17)$$

To deal with the cosine's symmetry about $\pi$, let $\vec{m}$ be the normal of the plane formed by $\vec{z}$ and $\vec{n}$; then, if the dot product between $\vec{v}_j$ and $\vec{m}$ is negative, set $\alpha_j = 2\pi - \alpha_j$ (Crossno & Angel, 1999). As this angle only will be used later for sorting the neighborhood, we have eliminated the arccosine from Equation 17. To avoid confusions in the notation, we denote $\bar{\alpha}_j$ as a new 'angle'. We have also modified the symmetry rotation to $\bar{\alpha}_j = -2 - \bar{\alpha}_j$, so $\bar{\alpha}_j \in (-3,1]$.

When implementing these two phases of projection and angle computation, we realized that combining them into a single phase leads to both mathematical and implementation simplifications. For example, we can express $\vec{v}_j$ as

$$\vec{v}_j = q'_j - p = \frac{\hat{q}_j - p}{\left\| \hat{q}_j - p \right\|} \left\| p - q_j \right\| \qquad (18)$$

so we can simplify Equation 15:

$$q'_j = p + \vec{v}_j. \qquad (19)$$

The Delaunay local triangulation first requires a sorted set of points, more specifically radial sorted. Starting at the nearest neighbor $q_0$ of p, the radial sorting creates a ring of consecutive points around *p*, with sorting key $\bar{\alpha}_j$. As the angle computation was changed above, the order of points was also changed (if keeping the same ascending order), because $\alpha_0 = 0, \alpha_j \in [0, 2\pi)$ while $\bar{\alpha}_0 = 1, \bar{\alpha}_j \in (-3,1]$. As points are sorted around an unoriented normal, either ascending or descending order produces valid results.

In the original version of GLT, the radial sorting is performed using a modified version of the Bitonic Merge Sort, optimized to work with several smalls lists at a time. As our extended

*Figure 7. Minimal rotational projection*

version is implemented in CUDA, the limitation that makes necessary such change (fixed-position scattering) is not longer a barrier. We implemented three different sorting algorithms: the modified Bitonic Merge Sort by (Buchart et al., 2008), Insertion Sort (Knuth, 1998) and the Bubble Sort. Comparing the times of each one, we could see that, even when it has a quadratic complexity, the Bubble Sort produced the best results. It may be due to the fact that the lists are small, and that the other algorithms use more registers, reducing the occupancy of the GPU.

A similar limitation was present in the previous local triangulation implementation, but first let discuss the algorithm. To construct the Delaunay neighborhood of $p$ from $Q$, Gopi et al. (2000) presented a recursive test that indicates whether a neighboring point belongs to the Voronoi region of $p$. Buchart et al. (2008) gave a theoretical proof of the validity of the test and stated that the order of the tests do not affect the final result although temporal results may differ. Both techniques rely on the fact that the nearest neighbor is always a Delaunay neighbor to define a stop condition.

Voronoi test: given three consecutive projected neighbors $q'_{j-1}, q'_j, q'_{j+1}$, define $b_k = q'_k - p$, $o_k = p + b_k/2$ and $\bar{b}_k \perp b_k$, with $k \in \{j-1, j, j+1\}$. Also, let $s$ be the intersection point of the lines that start on $o_{j-1}$ and $o_{j+1}$, with directions $\bar{b}_{j-1}$ and $\bar{b}_{j+1}$, respectively. If the projec-

tion of $s$ onto $b_j$ lies in the region between p than $o_j$, then $q'_j$ is not a Delaunay neighbor of p (see Figure 8). It is important to note that this test only determines if a point is not a Voronoi neighbor of $p$, but if the point passes the test, it is not guaranteed that it is connected to $p$ in the Delaunay triangulation. It comes from the fact that three invalid consecutive points may result in a valid local region. This is solved by repeating the test several times only with the current valid neighborhood.

The GLT performs a concurrent validation scheme using an open ring structure. The open ring is built using the radial sorted neighborhood, repeating the first (nearest) neighbor at the end of the list. In order to satisfy with GPU restrictions, each point has a pointer (index) to the previous and next valid point. The whole ring is sent to the GPU for its validation, where each point is tested independently to others. This process is repeated a few times to mark all the invalid points (there are empirical results that set the number of iterations to 4).

In this work, the previous procedure was replaced by a test loop over the entire neighborhood, one point at a time. This reduces the parallelism of the validation test, but thanks to the improvements in GPU technology, it results in better times due to the higher occupancy of the stream processors. It also reduces the number of

*Figure 8. Voronoi test*

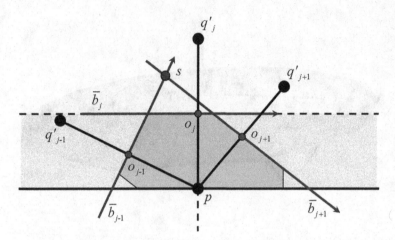

validations performed: each invalidated point is immediately removed from the neighborhood, reducing the false positives. Additionally, now it is easier to establish a stop condition.

At the end of all these phases, the local triangulations are merged and duplicated triangles are removed from the reconstructed mesh. Finally, we have also updated the normal propagation scheme to include the new priority-driven propagation proposed by Huang et al. (2009). It extends the scheme of Hoppe et al. (1992) by introducing the sense of direction of propagation:

$$D_{ij} = 1 - \left| \langle \vec{n}_i, \vec{n}_j \rangle \right| \frac{\max_{r,s \in \{1,2\}} \| m_{rs} - o_{rs} \|}{1 + \| x_i - x_j \|}, r,s \in \{1,2\}$$

(20)

where $m_{rs}$ are the midpoints of the line segments $\overline{x_i^r x_j^s}$, $o_{rs}$ the perpendicular projections of $m_{rs}$ onto the estimated tangent line $\overline{x_i x_j}$, and $x_k^t = x_k + \vec{n}_k (-1)^t$. The normal is then propagated following the minimal spanning tree of the connectivity graph of the mesh, where each edge $E_{ij}$ has cost $D_{ij}$.

To test the integration of the PWLOP operator with GLT, the following methodology was followed: for each model, the initial guess of the projection contains about a third of the number of input points. All the models were then projected using the default support radius $h$, 50 iterations and 64 points for the local support neighborhood (except for the Noisy Foot model, where a 128 points neighborhood and 100 iterations were used). Regarding GLT, the reconstruction radius was fixed to $h/2$. See Figure 9 to Figure 12 for several examples of reconstructed models using our method, and Figure 15 for a full comparison of all our results. Figure 13 compares with more detail the quality of the mesh between the original Hand model and the projected one. And finally, Figure 14 shows the effect of the PWLOP operator in noisy data sets. Note that all the images were rendered with flat shading to emphasize the mesh quality.

## ISSUES, CONTROVERSIES, PROBLEMS

One of the main drawbacks of the proposed operator is the need of a good initial guess. Several tests have been done with random initial sub-samplings from the original point set (see Figure 3c). Although the results show similarities with

*Figure 9. Stanford Dragon*

correct projections, they are not enough evenly distributed and present undesired clustering. As it may be expected, it is due to the fact that in a random distribution points move more, and therefore vicinities change, invalidating the precomputed neighborhood lists.

We have found that the computation of the *k*-nearest neighbors may represent up to 20% of the execution time of both the projection operator and the reconstruction. More on, such computation is linear on the number of points, so we may expect even larger percentages as the size of the data set grows.

As previously remarked by San Vicente, Buchart, Borro and Celigüeta (2009), Delaunay triangulations are not unique under certain input

*Figure 10. Asian Dragon*

*Figure 11. Happy Buddha*

distributions, such as a points aligned on a grid (for example, point sets extracted from medical image segmentations). More on, even if the points are not fully aligned, numerical errors in the validation scheme may produce similar wrong results. When local triangulations are computed on such point sets, it may appear overlapping triangles as well as small holes.

## SOLUTIONS AND RECOMMENDATIONS

Regarding the initial guess assumption, we believe that a hybrid approach would be taken into account if a random or not good enough initial projection is provided. In this sense, neighborhoods may be recomputed in each iteration (as in the original WLOP) and when the projected point distribution is good enough, vicinities may be left static and continue as with the proposed extension. On the counterpart, this approach will not make the most of GPU's power. A direct parallelization of the first stage requires exhaustive tuning to ensure that massive data transfers do not penalize excessively the algorithm.

*Figure 12. Hand model reconstruction comparison. (left) Original model with 327K points. (right) Reconstruction of a 107K projected points.*

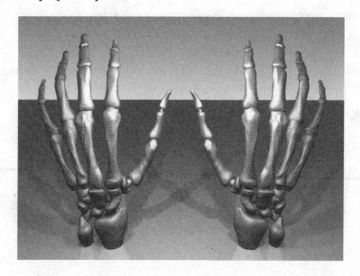

*Figure 13. Hand model detail comparison. (left) Original data set with 327K points. (right) Projected set with 107K points.*

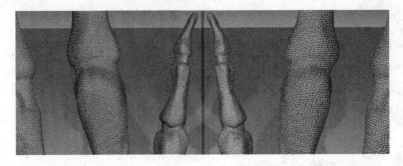

The computation of the *k*-nearest neighbors would be improved using the local support neighborhoods computed in the preprocessing stage. As these local supports are already stored in the GPU memory, a massive transfer of data is avoided. One downside is that such neighborhood is not guaranteed to be sorted, which would lead to a wrong set of Delaunay candidates. It has to be seen if the sorting time in the GPU compensates for the CPU computation of the *k*-NN.

The grid alignment of points is easily solved by applying a small perturbation to the points, as proposed by San Vicente et al. (2009). The points projection operator used solves this problem in most of the cases. It is also possible to combine both schemes: the perturbation should be added before the projection operator (adding it after the operator reduces its effects).

*Figure 14. Noisy Foot with 20K points. From left to right: original data set; self-projected using PW-LOP with LSN=64; self-projected using PWLOP with LSN=128. Bigger neighborhoods are necessary because in noisy data sets the points move more between iterations. It can be seen how the nails are still recognizable. For all the images the number of PWLOP iterations was set to 100.*

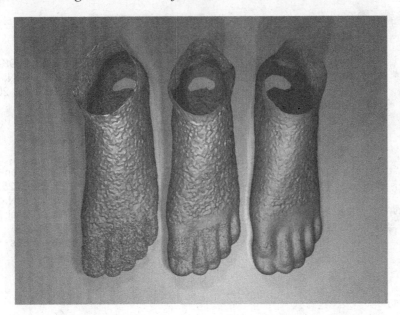

*Figure 15. Results of the proposed PWLOP + GLT reconstruction method*

Noisy Foot 20K
Proj. size: 20K
PWLOP - kNN: 0.81s
PWLOP total: 1.32s
GLT: 0.20s
Total: 1.52s

Hand 327K
Proj. size: 107K
PWLOP - kNN: 6.79s
PWLOP total: 11.10s
GLT: 1.81s
Total: 12.91s

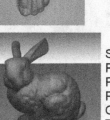

Stanford Bunny 35K
Proj. size: 35K
PWLOP - kNN: 1.50s
PWLOP total: 2.55s
GLT: 0.60s
Total: 3.15s

Stanford Dragon 437K
Proj. size: 174K
PWLOP - kNN: 10.14s
PWLOP total: 19.64s
GLT: 3.04s
Total: 22.68s

Horse 48K
Proj. size: 48K
PWLOP - kNN: 1.92s
PWLOP total: 3.19s
GLT: 0.77s
Total: 3.96s

Armadillo 172K
Proj. size: 153K
PWLOP - kNN: 6.79s
PWLOP total: 14.61s
GLT: 2.57s
Total: 17.18s

Happy Buddha 543K
Proj. size: 192K
PWLOP - kNN: 11.81s
PWLOP total: 22.22s
GLT: 3.41s
Total: 25.63s

Angel 237K
Proj. size: 86K
PWLOP - kNN: 5.71s
PWLOP total: 10.25s
GLT: 1.48s
Total: 11.73s

Blade 882K
Proj. size: 139K
PWLOP - kNN: 13.96s
PWLOP total: 20.38s
GLT: 2.59s
Total: 22.97s

EG'07 Dragon 240K
Proj. size: 123K
PWLOP - kNN: 6.37s
PWLOP total: 12.06s
GLT: 2.09s
Total: 14.15s

Asian Dragon 3609K
Proj. size: 325K
PWLOP - kNN: 47.70s
PWLOP total: 64.52s
GLT: 11.37s
Total: 75.89s

## FUTURE RESEARCH DIRECTIONS

The main goal in future research on local triangulation methods should be to guarantee watertight surfaces without degrading the performance of state-of-the-art algorithms. Some works proposed the use of mesh repairing operators to detect and correct issues such as holes and triangles overlapping. However, we believe that more study on local methods that directly generate watertight surfaces would be very convenient since it has been proved the high parallelization level this kind of methods have.

Another common issue presented in many reconstruction methods is that they rely on both the direction and orientation of normals of the input data to produce correct results. While many of these problems have been studied and solutions have been developed in recent publications (see for example (Huang, 2009)), the robustness of those methods is not 100% guaranteed under some conditions, more specifically in highly noisy point clouds.

## CONCLUSION

We have presented a hybrid reconstruction method by combining interpolating and approximating together in order to be implemented efficiently in parallel architectures (GPUs). By combining a points projection operator and local Delaunay triangulation, convenient approximating and interpolating properties have been added to the reconstruction: an uniformly distributed output independent of the reconstructed data set, at the time that high frequencies are recovered. Our GPU implementation of the PWLOP operator speeds up the original operator by a factor of 25 on average. We have also presented several improvements and a CUDA implementation of the GPU Local Triangulation method.

One of the main drawbacks of point projection operators discussed was their execution time. In this work we have shown how a relatively good initial solution may lead, not only to a faster convergence of the original LOP and WLOP operators (as expected), but also allow the creation of extended local support neighborhood that do not change between iterations and that can be precomputed. The proposed method drastically reduces the execution time of the operator and allows a parallel implementation by the PWLOP operator.

## REFERENCES

Alexa, M., Behr, J., Cohen-Or, D., Fleishman, S., Levin, D., & Silva, T. C. (2003). Computing and rendering point set surfaces. *IEEE Transactions on Visualization and Computer Graphics, 9*, 3–15. doi:10.1109/TVCG.2003.1175093

Amenta, N., Choi, S., Dey, T. K., & Leekha, N. (2000). A simple algorithm for homeomorphic surface reconstruction. In *Proceedings of the Sixteenth Annual Symposium on Computational Geometry*, (pp. 213-222).

Amenta, N., Choi, S., & Kolluri, R. (2001). The power crust. In *Sixth ACM Symposium on Solid Modeling and Applications* (pp. 249-260).

Bloomenthal, J. (1988). Polygonization of implicit surfaces. *Computer Aided Geometric Design, 5*, 341–355. doi:10.1016/0167-8396(88)90013-1

Buchart, C., Borro, D., & Amundarain, A. (2008). GPU local triangulation: An interpolating surface reconstruction algorithm. *Computer Graphics Forum, 27*(3), 807–814. doi:10.1111/j.1467-8659.2008.01211.x

Cignoni, P. (1998). DeWall: A fast divide and conquer Delaunay triangulation algorithm. *Computer Aided Design, 30*, 333–341. doi:10.1016/S0010-4485(97)00082-1

Crossno, P., & Angel, E. (1999). Spiraling edge: fast surface reconstruction from partially organized sample points. In *VIS '99: Proceedings of the Conference on Visualization '99,* (pp. 317-324). IEEE Computer Society Press.

Delaunay, B. (1934). Sur la sphere vide. A la mémoire de Georges Voronoi. *Bulletin of Academy of Sciences of the USSR, 7,* 793–800.

Dey, T. K., & Goswami, S. (2003). Tight cocone: A water-tight surface reconstructor. *Journal of Computing and Information Science in Engineering, 3*(4), 127–134. doi:10.1115/1.1633278

Dey, T. K., & Goswami, S. (2006). Provable surface reconstruction from noisy samples. *Computational Geometry: Theory and Applications, 35,* 124–141.

Gopi, M., Krishnan, S., & Silva, C. T. (2000). Surface reconstruction based on lower dimensional localized Delaunay triangulation. *Computer Graphics Forum, 19*(3), 467–478. doi:10.1111/1467-8659.00439

Hoppe, H., DeRose, T., Duchamp, T., McDonald, J., & Stuetzle, W. (1992). Surface reconstruction from unorganized points. In *Proceedings of ACM SIGGRAPH '92* (pp. 71-78).

Huang, H., Li, D., Zhang, H., Ascher, U., & Cohen-Or, D. (2009). Consolidation of unorganized point clouds for surface reconstruction. *ACM Transactions on Graphics, 28,* 176–182. doi:10.1145/1618452.1618522

Huang, H., Li, D., Zhang, H., Ascher, U., & Cohen-Or, D. (2010). *Points consolidation API.* Retrieved June, 23, 2010, from http://people.cs.ubc.ca/~danli/points_consolidation.htm

Kazhdan, M., Bolitho, M., & Hoppe, H. (2006). Poisson surface reconstruction. In *Proceedings of the Fourth Eurographics Symposium on Geometry Processing (SGP '06),* (pp. 61-70).

Knuth, D. (1998). Section 5.2.1: Sorting by insertion. In *The art of computer programming, Volume 3: Sorting and searching,* 2nd ed., (pp. 80-105). Addison-Wesley.

Levin, D. (2003). Mesh-independent surface interpolation. *Geometric Modeling for Scientific Visualization, 3,* 37–49.

Lipman, Y., Cohen-Or, D., Levin, D., & Tal-Ezer, H. (2007). Parameterization-free projection for geometry reconstruction. *ACM Transactions on Graphics, 26,* 22. doi:10.1145/1276377.1276405

Lorensen, W. E., & Cline, H. E. (1987). Marching cubes: A high resolution 3D surface construction algorithm. In *Proceedings of the ACM SIGGRAPH '87* (pp. 163-169).

Mount, D. M., & Arya, S. (2010). *ANN: A library for approximate nearest neighbor searching.* Retrieved May 20, 2010, from http://www.cs.umd.edu/~mount/ANN/

Nagai, Y., Ohtake, Y., & Suzuki, H. (2009). Smoothing of partition of unity implicit surfaces for noise robust surface reconstruction. *Computer Graphics Forum, 28*(5), 1339–1348. doi:10.1111/j.1467-8659.2009.01511.x

NVIDIA Corporation. (2010). *What is CUDA? Overview.* Retrieved July 15, 2010, from http://www.nvidia.com/object/what_is_cuda_new.html

Ohtake, Y., Belyaev, A., Alexa, M., Turk, G., & Seidel, H. P. (2005). Multi-level partition of unity implicits. *ACM Transactions on Graphics, 22,* 463–470. doi:10.1145/882262.882293

Pauly, M., Gross, M., & Kobbelt, L. P. (2002). Efficient simplification of point-sampled surfaces. In *Proceedings of the Conference on Visualization (VIS'02),* (pp. 163-170).

San Vicente, G., Buchart, C., Borro, D., & Celigüeta, J. T. (2009). Maxillofacial surgery simulation using a mass-spring model derived from continuum and the scaled displacement method. *International Journal of Computer Assisted Radiology and Surgery*, *4*, 89–98. doi:10.1007/s11548-008-0271-0

Wang, J., Oliveira, M. M., Xie, H., & Kaufman, A. E. (2005). Surface reconstruction using oriented charges. *Computer Graphics International*, *2005*, 122–128. doi:10.1109/CGI.2005.1500390

Zhang, L., Liu, L., Gotsman, C., & Huang, H. (2010). Mesh reconstruction by meshless denoising and parameterization. *Computers & Graphics*, *34*, 198–208. doi:10.1016/j.cag.2010.03.006

## ADDITIONAL READING

Alliez, P., Cohen-Steiner, D., Tong, Y., & Desbrun, M. (2007). Voronoi-based variational reconstruction of unoriented point sets. *Proceedings of the Fifth Eurographics Symposium on Geometry Processing (SGP '07), Eurographics Association*, (pp. 39-48).

Amenta, N., & Bern, M. (1999). Surface reconstruction by Voronoi filtering. *Discrete & Computational Geometry*, *22*, 481–504. doi:10.1007/PL00009475

Boubekeur, T., Heidrich, W., Granier, X., & Schlick, C. (2006). Volume-surface trees. *Computer Graphics Forum*, *25*(3), 399–406. doi:10.1111/j.1467-8659.2006.00959.x

Buatois, L., Caumon, G., & Lévy, B. (2006). GPU accelerated isosurface extraction on tetrahedral grids. *International Symposium on Visual Computing*, (pp. 383-392).

Cignoni, P., Montani, C., Perego, R., & Scopigno, R. (1993). Parallel 3D Delaunay triangulation. *Computer Graphics Forum*, *12*(3), 129–142. doi:10.1111/1467-8659.1230129

Dupuy, G., Jobard, B., Guillon, S., Keskes, N., & Komatitsch, D. (2010). Parallel extraction and simplification of large isosurfaces using an extended tandem algorithm. *Computer Aided Design*, *42*, 129–138. doi:10.1016/j.cad.2009.04.016

Fleishman, S., Cohen-Or, D., Alexa, M., & Silva, C. T. (2003). Progressive point set surfaces. *ACM Transactions on Graphics*, *22*, 997–1011. doi:10.1145/944020.944023

Gal, R., Shamir, A., Hassner, T., Pauly, M., & Cohen-Or, D. (2007). Surface reconstruction using local shape priors. *Proceedings of the Fifth Eurographics Symposium on Geometry Processing (SGP '07)*, (pp. 253-262).

Jalba, A. C., & Roerdink, J. B. T. M. (2006). Efficient surface reconstruction from noisy data using regularized membrane potentials. *IEEE Transactions on Image Processing*, *18*, 1119–1134. doi:10.1109/TIP.2009.2016141

Kuo, C., & Yau, H. (2005). A Delaunay-based region-growing approach to surface reconstruction from unorganized points. *Computer Aided Design*, *37*, 825–835. doi:10.1016/j.cad.2004.09.011

Labatut, P., Pons, J.-P., & Keriven, R. (2009). Robust and efficient surface reconstruction from range data. *Computer Graphics Forum*, *28*(8), 2275–2290. doi:10.1111/j.1467-8659.2009.01530.x

McInerney, T., & Terzopoulos, D. (2000). T-snakes: Topology adaptive snakes. *Medical Image Analysis*, *4*, 73–91. doi:10.1016/S1361-8415(00)00008-6

Mederos, B., Amenta, N., Velho, L., & de Figueiredo, L. H. (2005). Surface reconstruction from noisy point clouds. In *Proceedings of the Third Eurographics Symposium on Geometry Processing*.

Musin, O. R. (1997). Properties of the Delaunay triangulation. In *Proceedings of the Thirteenth Annual Symposium on Computational Geometry (SCG'97)*, (pp. 424-426).

Newman, T., & Yi, H. (2006). A survey of the marching cubes algorithm. *Computers & Graphics, 30*, 854–879. doi:10.1016/j.cag.2006.07.021

Ohtake, Y., & Belyaev, A. (2001). Mesh optimization for polygonized isosurfaces. *Computer Graphics Forum, 20*(3), 368–376. doi:10.1111/1467-8659.00529

Petitjean, S. (2001). Regular and non-regular point sets: Properties and reconstruction. *Computational Geometry, 19*, 101–131. doi:10.1016/S0925-7721(01)00016-5

Piegl, L. (2002). Algorithm for finding all k-nearest neighbors. *Computer Aided Design, 34*, 167–172. doi:10.1016/S0010-4485(00)00141-X

Samozino, M., Alexa, M., Alliez, P., & Yvinec, M. (2006). Reconstruction with Voronoi centered radial basis functions. *Proceedings of the Fourth Eurographics Symposium on Geometry Processing (SGP), Eurographics Association* (pp. 51-60).

Sankaranarayanan, J., Samet, H., & Varshney, A. (2006). A fast k-neighborhood algorithm for large point-clouds. *Proceedings of the Third IEEE/Eurographics Symposium on Point-Based Graphics* (pp. 75-84)

Sederberg, T. W., Zheng, J., Bakenov, A., & Nasri, A. (2003). T-splines and T-NURCCs. *ACM Transactions on Graphics, 22*, 477. doi:10.1145/882262.882295

Sethian, J. A. (1999). *Level set methods and fast marching methods. University of California.* Berkeley: Cambridge University Press.

Sharf, A., Alexa, M., & Cohen-Or, D. (2004). Context-based surface completion. *ACM Transactions on Graphics, 23*, 878. doi:10.1145/1015706.1015814

Sharf, A., Lewiner, T., Shamir, A., Kobbelt, L. P., & Cohen-Or, D. (2006). Competing fronts for coarse-to-fine surface reconstruction. *Computer Graphics Forum, 25*(3), 389–398. doi:10.1111/j.1467-8659.2006.00958.x

Vollmer, J., Mencl, R., & Muller, H. (1999). Improved Laplacian smoothing of noisy surface meshes. *Computer Graphics Forum, 18*(3), 131–138. doi:10.1111/1467-8659.00334

Vuçini, E., Möller, T., & Gröller, M. E. (2009). On visualization and reconstruction from non-uniform point sets using B-splines. *Computer Graphics Forum, 28*(3), 1007–1014. doi:10.1111/j.1467-8659.2009.01447.x

Xu, C., & Prince, J. L. (1998). Snakes, shapes, and gradient vector flow. *IEEE Transactions on Image Processing, 7*, 359–369. doi:10.1109/83.661186

Zhou, K., Gong, M., Huang, X., & Guo, B. (2010). Data-parallel octrees for surface reconstruction. *IEEE Transactions on Visualization and Computer Graphics, 17*(5).

## KEY TERMS AND DEFINITIONS

**CUDA (Compute Unified Device Architecture):** "Is NVIDIA's parallel computing architecture that enables dramatic increases in computing performance by harnessing the power of the GPU" (NVIDIA, 2010). It provides the programmer with a programming interface to load and execute highly parallel programs in the GPU.

**Delaunay Triangulation:** The Delaunay triangulation of a set of points $P \in R^D$ is defined as the set of simplices $S$ such that no point in $P$ belongs to the circumscribing hyper-sphere of any simplex of $S$ (Delaunay, 1934).

**GPU (Graphics Processing Unit):** Specialized microprocessor that accelerates computer graphics rendering. Modern GPUs are highly parallel and also allow the modification of the graphics pipeline through the use of special programs (shaders), and may be used as general purpose processing devices by the use of technologies such CUDA.

**$k$-NN:** $k$-nearest neighbors is an object classification method that, given an object, computes the $k$ nearest objects to it, following an specific metric. In surface reconstruction, the objects are usually points and the metric is the Euclidean norm.

**Local Triangulations:** Consist in the triangulation of the 1-neighborhood of a single point at a time. The global triangulation is obtained merging all the individual fans.

**Normal Estimation:** As many point clouds do not provide the normal information, it must be estimated from it. Commonly, this process assumes certain distribution around a point to locally approximate a curve (or surface), from where the normal of the point is estimated.

**Points Projection:** It is the process to derive a new point set from a given point cloud, such that the new set is as similar as possible to the original.

# Chapter 5
# 3D Reconstruction of Underwater Natural Scenes and Objects Using Stereo Vision

**C.J. Prabhakar**
*Kuvempu University, India*

**P.U. Praveen Kumar**
*Kuvempu University, India*

**P.S. Hiremath**
*Gulbarga University, India*

## ABSTRACT

*Over the last two decades, research community of computer vision has developed various techniques suitable for underwater applications using intensity images. This chapter will explore 3D reconstruction of underwater natural scenes and objects based on stereo vision, which will be helpful in mine detection, inspection of shipwrecks, detection of telecommunication cables and pipelines. The general steps involved in 3D reconstruction using stereo vision are provided. The brief summary of papers for 3D reconstruction of underwater environment is presented. 3D reconstruction of underwater natural scenes and objects is challenging problem due to light propagation in underwater. In contrast to light propagation in the air, the light rays are attenuated and scattered, having a great effect on image quality. We have proposed preprocessing technique to enhance degraded underwater images. At the end of the chapter, we have presented the proposed stereo vision based 3D reconstruction technique to reconstruct 3D surface of underwater objects. Ultimately, this chapter intends to give an overview of the 3D reconstruction technique using stereo vision in order to help a reader in understanding stereo vision and its benefits for underwater applications.*

DOI: 10.4018/978-1-4666-0113-0.ch005

## INTRODUCTION

Three dimensional (3D) reconstruction is the process of capturing the shape and appearance of real objects. Recovering 3D surface structure of an object has been a central issue in computer vision. In order to extract 3D information out of 2D images, it is useful to have a set of images showing the target object viewed from different directions. The 3D reconstruction approaches of interest for our application are the so-called optical methods, which perform reconstruction from a set of 2D images. The earliest attempt for 3D reconstruction for general applications is based on volume intersection such as Shape from Silhouette (Laurentini, 1994). The most prominent approaches in 3D reconstruction are the stereo, Voxel Coloring (Slabaugh et al., 2001) and the Space Carving (Kutulakos et al., 1998). The Voxel Coloring and the Space Carving approaches use the color consistency to distinguish surface points from other points in a scene. Cameras with an unoccluded view of a non-surface point see surfaces beyond the point, and hence inconsistent colors, in the direction of the point. Initially, the environment is represented as a discretized set of voxels, and then the algorithm is applied to color the voxels that are part of a surface in the scene. Another promising approach in 3D reconstruction is the Marching Cubes algorithm for rendering iso-surfaces from volumetric scan data (Lorenson et al., 1987). The algorithm produces a triangle mesh surface representation by connecting the patches from all cubes on the iso-surface boundary.

3D scene structures captured by a camera may be detected and acquired observing the apparent motion of brightness patterns from images. In the last fifteen years, theoretical developments in visual motion studies have established a unified framework for the treatment of the Structure from Motion (SFM) and Structure from Stereo (SFS) problems (Faugeras, 1992), also known as 3D

Reconstruction from Multiple Views. 3D reconstruction from multiple views involves extracting target features from one image, matching and tracking these features across two or more images, and using triangulation to determine the position of the 3D target points relative to the camera. Visual motion methods have been well-studied, requiring densely-sampled image sequences. The primary visual motion cue useful for shape acquisition is the perceived movement of brightness patterns, known as optical flow (Horn, 1986), which is an approximation of the 3D world motion field. The 3D reconstruction from differential motion cues requires accurate optical flow computation.

Instead, stereo vision is the more accurate and robust 3D reconstruction method (Scharstein et al., 2002) and the correspondence problem is between the left and right image. A large amount of works has addressed the correspondence problem, attempting to overcome the various difficulties of the large-displacement correspondence problem like occlusions, rotations and disparities, photometric and projective distortions (Lucas et al., 1981; Tomasi et al., 1991).

## STEREO VISION PARADIGM

Stereo vision refers to the ability to infer 3D information of a scene from two images taken from different viewpoints. The simplest demonstration of the essence of stereo vision is to hold an object in front of face and alternatively close the left and right eyes. Observe that the relative position of the object and background seems to change. It is exactly this difference in retinal position that is used by the brain to reconstruct a 3D scene. This is the essence of what we try to duplicate using stereo vision. The generalized stereo vision paradigm, illustrating the steps involved in the stereo vision is shown in Figure 1. These steps are described as follows:

*Figure 1. Generalized stereo vision paradigm*

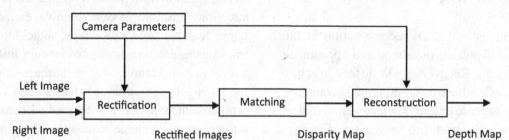

## Camera Calibration

Camera calibration is an important task in computer vision. The purpose of camera calibration is to establish the relation between 3D world coordinates and their corresponding image coordinates. This enables us to infer 3D information from 2D information and vice versa. Thus camera calibration is a prerequisite for any application where 3D information needs to be related to 2D information.

The camera calibration forms the input to the rectification stage and is comprised of two components, the intrinsic parameters and the extrinsic parameters. The intrinsic parameter refers to the internal geometric configuration of the camera. The intrinsic parameters include the focal length, skew, aspect ratio, the position of the principal point and the distortion characteristics of the lens system.

The extrinsic parameters are defined as any set of geometric parameters that identify uniquely the transformation between the unknown camera reference frame and a known reference frame, called the world reference frame. A typical choice of representing the extrinsic parameters are 3×3 orthogonal rotation matrix, $R$, that aligns the corresponding axes of the reference frames and 3D translation vector, $T$ which describes the relative positions of the reference frames.

The classical calibration method makes use of a calibration object with known physical dimensions. A great number of calibration objects have

been used by various researchers. The main difference is whether the calibration routine requires coplanar or noncoplanar data, which requires that the feature points, respectively, must or must not all lie on the same plane in space. This is a direct result of the mathematical approach implemented in the calibration. For the stereo camera calibration the process is very similar, capture from the left and right cameras simultaneously, using a coplanar object. The object is simply moved thought the field of view of both cameras, the only requirement being that it must be visible to both at the same time instant.

There are different techniques of camera calibration available, depending on factors like the accuracy required, the level of human interaction and whether reconstructions need to be metric. Classical calibration algorithms mostly rely on a calibration object with known dimensions which is placed in the camera field of view. This enables us to fully calibrate the camera, resulting in reconstructions which agree with physical measurements.

## Direct Linear Transform (DLT)

This calibration procedure consists of two steps. In the first step the linear transformation from the object coordinates $(x_j, y_j, z_j)$ to image coordinates $(u_{ij}, v_{ij})$ is solved. This matrix is represented by a 3×4 matrix $P_i$ (Projection matrix) for the i-th projection and N fiducial points. The parameters

$p_{11}, ..., p_{34}$ of the DLT matrix can be solved by a homogeneous matrix equation:

$$LP_i = 0, \tag{1}$$

where L is a $N \times 12$ matrix, constituted by corresponding world and image coordinates and $P_i = (p_{11}, ..., p_{34})$. In case of a coplanar control point structure the DLT matrix $P_i$ becomes singular and a $3 \times 3$ submatrix $p_{11}, ..., p_{34}$ has to be used. In this case the decomposition of the submatrix can only deliver a subset of estimates of the camera parameters. After solving the system for these parameters a subset of them can be used as start values for a classical bundle block calibration (Heikkila et al., 1997).

## R. Y. Tsai's Method

The method proposed by R. Y. Tsai (Tsai, 1986) linearizes a huge part of the computation by restricting the lens distortion effect to radial distortion. The model generally does not recognize skewness or lack of orthogonality of the projection. Tsai's two stage calibration technique is fast and no initial guess of the calibration parameters is needed. In the first stage all extrinsic parameters except for $T_z$ are computed by using the parallelism constraint. In the second stage all missing parameters are evaluated by non-linear optimization. The optimization does not use the full camera model in order to speed up performance. Thus the computed residual is quite irrelevant for error measurement, which is done in this case separately by building a full camera model by collecting all resulting parameters of the previous steps. The final error is given here by the difference between back-projected fiducial 3D world points and their corresponding image points. The solution, generally designed for mono-view calibration, was also applied for multiple viewing position calibration. In this case a planar pattern is moved to different levels by a z stage for multiple calibration images.

## Z. Zhang's Method

In contrast to Tsai's technique, we need at least 3 different projections of a planar calibration target. From the image coordinates $\tilde{p} = (u, v, 1)$ and its corresponding known set of world coordinates $\tilde{P} = (X, Y, Z = 0, 1)$, a homography $A = (a_1, a_2, a_3)$ (Zhang, 2000) can be derived:

$$s\tilde{p} = A\tilde{P}, \qquad A = \lambda K(r_1, r_2, t), \tag{2}$$

where $r_1$ and $r_2$ are the first two column vectors of rotation matrix $R$ using the constraint that these two column vectors are orthonormal the following two identities are derived:

$$a_1^T K^{-T} K^{-1} a_2 = 0, \qquad a_1^T K^{-T} K^{-1} a_1 = a_2^T K^{-T} K^{-1} a_2. \tag{3}$$

The image of the absolute conic $B = K^{-T} K^{-1}$ is generally symmetric and can be described as a 6D vector $b = (b_{11}, ..., b_{33})^T$. So far each of the $N$ projections of the target we get a set of 2 equations, to solve for $b$, which implies that we need at least 3 views of the calibration to solve the system for all unknowns.

## Stereo Image Rectification

Given a pair of stereo images, rectification determines a transformation of each image plane such that pairs of conjugate epipolar lines become collinear and parallel to one of the image axes. Image rectification is a transformation process used to project two-or-more images onto a common image plane. It corrects image distortion by transforming the image into a standard coordinate system. The important advantage of rectification is that computing stereo correspondences is reduced to a 1D search problem along the horizontal raster lines of the rectified images. There are two types of rectification techniques, calibrated and uncalibrated stereo image rectification techniques.

## Calibrated Stereo Image Rectification

In the case of calibrated stereo image rectification the camera parameters obtained from camera calibration i.e. intrinsic and extrinsic parameters are used. The perspective projection matrix of left and right camera is calculated. By using the old perspective projection matrix, new perspective projection matrix is found and a suitable transformation matrix is found and applied to the stereo image which gives the rectified stereo images. Fusiello et al., (2000) introduced a rectification algorithm by using the perspective projection matrix obtained by the using the camera calibration parameters (i.e. intrinsic and extrinsic parameters).

## Uncalibrated Stereo Image Rectification

In the case of uncalibrated stereo image rectification the cameras intrinsic and extrinsic parameters are not used. The only information available is image features i.e. points are used to rectify the stereo images. In this technique, the fundamental matrix is found by using image corresponding points. The estimated fundamental matrix is decomposed to give the rotation matrix and translation vector, by using this find the suitable transformation matrix that apply to stereo image such that the resulting images are rectified.

Rectification is a classical problem of stereo vision; however, few methods are available in the computer vision literature. Ayache et al. (1991) introduced a rectification algorithm, in which a matrix satisfying a number of constraints is handcrafted. The distinction between necessary and arbitrary constraints is unclear. Some author report rectification under restrictive assumptions; for instance, Papadimitriou et al. (1996) assume a very restrictive geometry (parallel vertical axes of the camera reference frames). Hartley et al. (1993), Robert et al. (1997) and Hartley (1999) have introduced algorithms which perform rectification given a weakly calibrated stereo rig, i.e. a rig for which only points correspondences between images are given. Loop et al. (1999), Isgro et al. (1999) and Pollefeys et al. (1999) some of this work also concentrates on the issue of minimizing the rectified image distortion.

## Stereo Image Matching

The location of $p_l$ and $p_r$, points formed by projecting the scene point $P$ back into the left and right images, are known and if the orientation of the two cameras are known, then it is possible to find the original coordinates of the point $P$. The issue of identifying corresponding points is a fundamental problem faced by stereo vision problem and is known as the image matching or correspondence problem. The stereo matching algorithm searches for corresponding pixels between the two images and produces a map of the amount each pixel shifts from the left image to the right image. The amount each pixel shifts is its disparity, is inversely proportional to its depth.

Stereo matching is one of the most active research areas in computer vision. Stereo matching is a hard problem due to ambiguity in un-textured and occluded areas. Only dominant features, such as points of interest, can be matched reliably. This motivates the development of progressive approaches (Scharstein et al., 2002). The reduced local disparity in search range makes progressive approaches very efficient in computation and robust. However, the seed initialization remains a computational bottleneck, although, robustness can be improved by enforcing the left-right symmetry constraint.

Stereo matching can be broadly classified into two methods: i) Local methods and ii) Global methods. Local methods also referred to as area-based algorithms; calculate the disparity at each pixel on the basis of the photometric properties of the neighboring pixels. Global methods rely on iterative schemes that carry out disparity assignments on the basis of the minimization of a global cost function. These algorithms yield accurate and dense disparity measurement but exhibit a very high computational cost.

One of the popular local methods is Sum-of-Squared Differences (SSD) method. The SSD method is commonly called as correlation-based matching, the elements to match are image windows of fixed size, and the similarity criterion is a measure of the correlation between windows in the two images (Hannah, 1974). The corresponding element is given by the window that maximizes the similarity criterion within a search region. The general formulation of matching the corresponding point between the two rectified stereo images is given by

$$SSD = \sum_{a=-w}^{w} \sum_{b=-w}^{w} (I_1(i+a, j+b) - I_2(i+a, j+b+disprange))^2,$$
(4)

where, $i, j$ is the size of the image, $I_1$ is the left image, $I_2$ is the right image, $a, b$ size of the search window and *disprange* the range of the disparity that to be searched for the correspondence that is minimum disparity to maximum disparity.

One of the global methods i.e. graph-cut method gives excellent results compared to local methods for stereo matching. Roy et al. (1998) were the first ones to use this algorithm in the context of multi-camera stereovision. In the general case of graph-cut theory, the goal is to find a cut that has a minimum cost among all cuts, by minimizing an energy function.

## Reconstruction

The final stage is the reconstruction where a depth map is computed using the disparity results obtained from the matching process and the parameters of camera calibration for rectified images depth may be computed from:

$$z = \frac{B \times f}{d},$$
(5)

where $z$ is depth, $B$ is baseline length, $f$ is focal length and $d$ is disparity. The stereo baseline is the distance between the centres of the two images and the disparity is the difference in the corresponding image coordinates $I_1$ and $I_2$ of the stereo images. The reconstructed depth map is often referred to as a 2.5D representation rather than a full 3D representation. Since depth information can only be discerned for visible surfaces. No information can be deduced about the extent and shape of objects behind the visible surfaces.

## 3D RECONSTRUCTION OF UNDERWATER NATURAL SCENES AND OBJECTS

Research on 3D reconstruction of objects has been evolved intensively over the last two decades. The researchers have developed many techniques for 3D reconstruction of objects in a controlled environment using optical images. There is less effort to develop technique particularly for 3D reconstruction of underwater objects. However, many researchers have proposed to adopt existing techniques with slight modifications suitable for underwater applications. 3D reconstruction of underwater natural scenes and objects is challenging problem due to underwater imaging conditions, which cause a variety of difficulties that need to be considered. For example, the rigid scene assumption is violated by floating particles, fish, and other moving animals and in case of black smokers sometimes large amounts of smoke. Another challenge arises from the underwater light propagation. In contrast to light propagation in air, the light rays are much more affected by the densely packed water molecules: they are attenuated and scattered, having a great effect on the image colors. In addition, light rays are refracted, when entering the camera housing, causing a different focal length underwater than in air and even 3D distortion effects (Sedlazeck et al., 2009).

In shallow waters, near-the-sea-surface sources of disturbance are of primary concern. First, surface waves often cast complex moving shadow patterns on the targets that are being imaged/inspected. Other difficulties arise from the movement of floating suspended particles and water bubbles that are commonly present in most coastal and harbor waters. On top of these, constant disturbances from wave actions contribute to continuous complex vehicle motions—involving all six degrees-of-freedom (6 DOFs)—that are often difficult to estimate from monocular cues; even without the low quality and contrast of underwater imagery and the complex shadow motions. Where the vehicle has to fight steady currents, reduced thruster power for control action reduces vehicle-maneuvering capability. Because of these factors, the use of existing monocular vision-based technologies—often suitable for deep-sea tasks—can be effectively ruled out because of the unfriendly conditions in most shallow harbor waters. Interestingly, the use of binocular cues offers the unique potential. It allows us to take advantage of visual cues in such a way that the above complexities can be made much less effective in destabilizing the system performance. This motivated various researchers to explore the use of a stereovision system for underwater applications, an operation carried out by Remotely Operated Vehicles (ROV) in the shallow water of ports and harbors (Negahdaripour et al., 2006).

## Applications

Underwater imaging is widely used in scientific research and technology. Computer vision methods are being used in this mode of imaging for various applications, such as mine detection, inspection of underwater power and telecommunications cables, pipelines, nuclear reactors, shipwrecks and columns of offshore platforms. Underwater computer vision is commercially used to help swimming pool life guards. As in conventional computer vision, algorithms are sought for naviga-

tion and control of submerged robots. In addition, underwater imaging is used for research in marine biology, archaeology and mapping.

*In water inspection:* It is an essential task for general maintenance and damage assessment of underwater structures. For example, inspection of ship hulls is necessary as part of periodic maintenance operations. This has become extremely critical with the threat that ships entering ports and harbors for commerce may serve as carriers of nuclear weapons, explosives, deadly chemicals and other hazardous materials, with mass destruction in highly populated cities, national landmarks, and other drastic damages at the nation scale as potentially target activities. To combat this threat, deployment of existing technologies and the development of new ones are sought to implement search and detection systems that can provide no less than 100% success rate. Unlike regular hull maintenance that may be carried out by trained divers, inspection and search for hazardous and (or) deadly materials have to be done with submersible robotics platforms to avoid risk of human lives. In general, it is expected that the deployment of such vehicles, when highly automated, can provide a more effective and efficient solution.

*Inspection of naval mine:* Underwater mine is a self-contained explosive device placed in water to destroy ships or submarines. Unlike depth charges, mines are deposited and left to wait until they are triggered by the approach of or contact with an enemy ship. Naval mines can be used offensively, to hamper enemy ships or lock them into a harbour; or defensively, to protect friendly ships and create "safe" zones.

*Inspect the growth of coral reefs:* Coral reefs are underwater structures made from calcium carbonate secreted by corals. Corals are colonies of tiny living animals found in marine waters containing few nutrients. Most coral reefs are built from stony corals, and are formed by polyps that live together in groups. The polyps secrete a hard carbonate exoskeleton which provides support and protection for the body of each polyp.

Reefs grow best in warm, shallow, clear, sunny and agitated waters.

*In aquatic environment:* The aquatic environment provides a range of recreational activities. In the entertainment industry, the potential applications of 3D reconstruction technology include the reconstruction of underwater scenes for documenting recreational scuba diving expeditions. Many divers videotape their dives using traditional consumer-grade video recording equipment. Automatic 3D reconstruction of the dive could add impact to the experience by increasing the dimensionality of the recording without increasing task-loading on the diver.

## Related Work

The extensive research work has been carried out for reconstruction of 3D surface of underwater objects using different methods for acquisition of shape of a scene or an object. Some of the commonly used optical sensing methods are Shape from Stereopsis (Zhang, 2005), Shape from Photometric stereo (Negahdaripour et al., 2002), Shape from Motion (Khamene et al., 2001) and Active Stereo (Narasimhan et al., 2005). In the non-optical sensing methods acoustic cameras are employed to reconstruct 3D mosaic (Castellani et al., 2004). Josep Forest et al. (2000) have adopted laser range gated imaging system for reconstruction of 3D surface of an underwater object. Dalgleish et al. (2005) have proposed laser line scan method which significantly reduces backscatter in the raw data and enables recovery of the scene's 3D structure by means of triangulation. The similar imaging system was adopted by Carder et al. (2005). Narasimhan et al. (2005) have proposed two methods, which are extensions of the method proposed by (Dalgleish et al., 2005). First, unlike synchronous scanning systems, scanning is performed without any major moving parts and is instead controlled by a spatial light modulator using a digital light processing (DLP) projector. Second, compensation is made for the attenuation of the water when recovering the object radiance. The attenuation depends on the distance of each object point, where distance is recovered using triangulation.

Considering the underwater environment, the methods such as structured lighting or laser range finders need more equipment and provide no flexibility and they are hard to apply. Ultrasonic or sonar is widely used in underwater researches. These methods perform perfectly in long range distances. But in short range, they do not provide detailed results like cameras do. For that reason, studies are performed to combine the data extracted from these two type sensors, optical (e.g. camera) and acoustic sensors (e.g. sonar).

To reconstruct the 3D structure of underwater scene, the sensors like optical cameras, laser light based imaging system and acoustic cameras cannot be used alone to acquire scene information (Trucco et al., 2000; Josep Forest et al., 2000). The researchers have investigated methods for multiple-view 3D reconstruction of underwater scenes and objects that combine Dual frequency IDentification SONar (DIDSON) and stereo imagery (Negahdaripour et al., 2008). The intent is to use the sonar to enhance reconstruction in poor visibility conditions, where visual cues become less informative. DIDSON uses high-frequency sonar (1-2 MHz) to produce range and azimuth 2D measurements that are acquired in a polar coordinate system. Even in turbid water, near optical-quality 2D video can be acquired at operational ranges of 10 to 20 meters. Since the geometry of "acoustic cameras" differs drastically from those of pinhole cameras, the greatest challenge in combining sonar and stereo images is calibrating the system to ensure data model consistency (Negahdaripour, 2005; Kim et al., 2005). Not only do the sensors have different areas of coverage, a pixel in polar coordinates maps to a collection of pixels in the cartesian coordinate system, which further complicates searching and matching of feature points in successive images. Other challenges specific to DIDSON include limited resolution, low Signal Noise Ratio (SNR) and limited range of sight. Kim et al. (2006) developed an algorithm to enhance sonar video sequences by incorporating knowledge of the target object obtained in previously observed frames. This approach involves inter-frame registration, linearization of image intensity, identification of a target object and determining the "maximum posteriori fusion of images" in the video sequence. The Robert Drost et al. (2002) have proposed method to reconstruct the underwater object from a sequence of 2D LIDAR (Light Detection and Ranging) images; the Shape from Silhouette method is used to extract the silhouette information from 2D LIDAR image.

Considering the underwater environment, the methods such as structured lighting or laser range finders need more equipment and provide no flexibility and they are hard to apply. Ultrasonic or sonar is widely used in underwater researches. These methods perform perfectly in long range distances. But in short range, they do not provide detailed results like cameras do. Since underwater provides a limited visibility range, 25 meters in clear water and 3-5 meters in turbid water. It is impossible to cover the research site, for example an archeological site, with this visibility range. For that reason optical camera based imaging systems are developed to capture the images in an appropriate order to get the image of the whole site. Among optical camera based techniques, the stereo vision based methods are efficient techniques to reconstruct 3D model of underwater environment. Barndou et al. (2007) proposed a method for 3D reconstruction of natural underwater scenes using the stereovision system IRIS. For acquiring an image of an underwater scene the authors expose two different ways to generate specific trajectories with the stereovision system which depend on the capabilities offered by the underwater robot equipped with preprogrammed trajectories of the robotic arm. The authors have captured sequence of stereo images of underwater scene and rectified

the stereo images using uncalibrated rectification technique proposed by (Oram, 2001). The dense disparity map is generated by using the stereo matching algorithm proposed by (Roy et al., 1998).

## 3D RECONSTRUCTION OF UNDERWATER OBJECTS USING STEREO VISION

We have proposed 3D reconstruction method to reconstruct 3D surface of underwater objects based on stereo vision (Prabhakar et al., 2010). The proposed method uses the optical imaging system to capture a pair of intensity images of underwater objects. Normally, the captured images are suffered from non uniform illumination, low contrast and blurring. We have proposed image preprocessing technique to enhance the degraded underwater images using suitable filtering techniques (Prabhakar et al., 2010). The enhanced images are rectified by using uncalibrated stereo image rectification technique proposed by (Fusiello et al., 2010) to reduce the 2D correspondence search problem to 1D search problem i.e. along a horizontal direction. The disparity map is computed from rectified images by using stereo correspondence method proposed by (Boykov et al., 2004), which is an energy minimization method. The depth map is obtained from the computed disparity map by using triangulation technique. The 3D surface is reconstructed using Delaunay triangulation. Finally, the texture information is mapped onto 3D surface by using reference image.

## Underwater Image Preprocessing

The underwater images suffer from the limited range, non uniform lighting, low contrast, diminished colors, and important blur. So applying standard computer vision techniques to these images is impossible, so we have to preprocess these images before applying standard computer vision techniques. There has been a great effort from the last ten years to improve the quality of underwater images and many methods have been derived to fulfill the task (Arnold-Bos et al., 2005; Bazeille et al., 2006). Physical properties of the medium cause degradation effects not present in normal images taken in air. Underwater images are essentially characterized by their poor visibility because light is exponentially attenuated as it travels in the water and the scenes result poorly contrasted and hazy. Light attenuation limits the visibility distance at about twenty meters in clear water and five meters or less in turbid water.

We have proposed preprocessing technique to enhance the degraded underwater images. The proposed method is composed of three successive independent processing steps, which correct non uniform illumination, enhance contrast and suppress Gaussian noise by applying filtering technique in each step. To correct non-uniform illumination of light, we apply homomorphic filtering, which simultaneously normalizes the brightness across an image and increases contrast. After correcting non uniform illumination using homomorphic filtering, we use anisotropic filtering to smooth the image in the homogeneous area but preserve image features and enhance them. Finally, we apply wavelet based image denoising technique to denoise the noise present in the underwater image.

## Homomorphic Filtering

The homomorphic filtering is used to correct non uniform illumination and to enhance contrasts in the image. It's a frequency filtering, preferred to other techniques because it corrects non uniform lighting and sharpens the edges at the same time. The homomorphic filtering adopts the illumination and reflectance model. Illumination and reflectance are not separable, but their approximate locations in the frequency domain may be located. Since illumination and reflectance combine multiplicatively, the components are made additive by taking the logarithm of the image intensity, so that these multiplicative components of the image can be separated linearly in the frequency domain. Illumination variations can be thought of as a multiplicative noise, and can be reduced by filtering in the log domain. To make the illumination of an image more even, the high-frequency components are increased and low-frequency components are decreased, because the high-frequency components are assumed to represent mostly the reflectance in the scene (the amount of light reflected off the object in the scene), whereas the low-frequency components are assumed to represent mostly the illumination in the scene. That is, high-pass filtering is used to suppress low frequencies and amplify high frequencies, in the log-intensity domain.

Considering the illumination – reflectance model, we assume that an image is a function of the product of the illumination and the reflectance as described by equation

$$f(x, y) = i(x, y) \cdot r(x, y), \qquad (6)$$

where $f(x, y)$ is the image sensed by the camera, $i(x, y)$ the illumination multiplicative factor, and $r(x, y)$ the reflectance function. If we take into account this model, we can assume that the illumination factor changes slowly through the view field, therefore it represents low frequencies in the Fourier transform of the image. On the contrary reflectance is associated with high frequency components. By multiplying these components by a high-pass filter we can then suppress the low frequencies i.e. the non uniform illumination in the image. The algorithm can be decomposed as follows:

Separation of the illumination and reflectance components by taking the logarithm of the image (Equation 6). The logarithm converts the multiplicative effect into an additive one:

$$g(x,y) = \ln(f(x,y)) = \ln(i(x,y) \cdot r(x,y))$$
$$= \ln(i(x,y)) + \ln(r(x,y)). \tag{7}$$

Computation of the Fourier transform of the log-image

$$G(w_x, w_y) = I(w_x, w_y) + R(w_x, w_y). \tag{8}$$

The High-pass filter is applied to the Fourier transform which decreases the contribution of low frequencies (illumination) and also amplifies the contribution of mid and high frequencies (reflectance), sharpening the edges of the object in the image:

$$S(w_x, w_y) = H(w_x, w_y) \cdot I(w_x, w_y)$$
$$+H(w_x, w_y) \cdot R(w_x, w_y), \tag{9}$$

with,

$$H(w_x, w_y) = (r_H - r_L) \cdot$$
$$\left(1 - \exp\left(-\left(\frac{w_x^2 + w_y^2}{2\delta_w^2}\right)\right)\right) + r_L,$$

where

$$r_H = 2.5$$

and

$$r_L = 0.5$$

are the maximum and minimum coefficients values and $\delta_w$ is a factor which controls the cutoff frequency. These parameters are selected empirically. Computation of the inverse Fourier transform to come back in the spatial domain and then taking the exponent to obtain the filtered image.

## Anisotropic Filtering

Anisotropic filtering allows us to simplify image features to improve image segmentation. This filter smooths the image in homogeneous area but preserves edges and enhances them. It is used to smooth textures and reduce artifacts by deleting small edges amplified by homomorphic filtering. It also removes or attenuates unwanted artifacts. Computation of the nearest-neighbor differences and computation of the diffusion coefficient in the four directions North, South, East, West. Many possibilities exist for this calculation, the easiest way is as follows:

$$\nabla_N I_{i,j} = I_{i-1,j} - I_{i,j}, \quad c_{N_{i,j}} = g(|\nabla_N I_{i,j}|)$$
$$\nabla_S I_{i,j} = I_{i+1,j} - I_{i,j}, \quad c_{S_{i,j}} = g(|\nabla_S I_{i,j}|)$$
$$\nabla_E I_{i,j} = I_{i,j+1} - I_{i,j}, \quad c_{E_{i,j}} = g(|\nabla_E I_{i,j}|)$$
$$\nabla_W I_{i,j} = I_{i,j-1} - I_{i,j}, \quad c_{W_{i,j}} = g(|\nabla_W I_{i,j}|)$$
$$\tag{10}$$

where the function $g$ is defined as: $g(\nabla I) = e^{\left(-\left(\left\|\frac{\nabla I}{K}\right\|\right)^2\right)}$ and with $K$ set to 0.1. This diffusion function favors high contrast edges over low contrast ones. Modification of the pixel value using (Equation 10)

$$I_{i,j} = I_{i,j} + \lambda$$
$$[c_N \nabla_N I + c_S \nabla_S I + c_E \nabla_E I + c_W \nabla_W I]_{i,j}, \tag{11}$$

with $0 \leq \lambda \leq 1/4$.

## WAVELET BASED IMAGE DENOISING

The Gaussian noise (i.e. noise acquisition) is always present in underwater images as like natural images. This noise is further amplified by applying homomorphic filtering. So, a step of denoising is necessary to suppress it. The wavelet denoising method was preferred to many other algorithms because of it performances of speed in comparison of its denoising quality. We proposed to adopt the wavelet based Modified BayesShrink (Prabhakar et al., 2010) to denoise the underwater noisy image. In the proposed method, an image is subjected to the wavelet transform, the wavelet coefficients are found, the components with coefficients below a threshold are replaced with zeros, and the image is then reconstructed.

In particular, the BayesShrink function has been attracting attenuation recently as an algorithm for setting different thresholds for every subband. Here subbands are frequently bands that differ from each other in level and direction. The BayesShrink function is effective for images including Gaussian noise. The observation model is expressed as follows: $Y = X + V$.

Here $Y$ is the wavelet transform of the degraded image, $X$ is the wavelet transform of the original image, and $V$ denotes the wavelet transform of the noise components following the Gaussian distribution $N(0, \sigma^2)$. Here, since $X$ and $V$ are mutually independent, the variances $\sigma_y^2$, $\sigma_x^2$ and $\sigma_v^2$ of $y$, $x$ and $v$ are given by:

$$\sigma_y^2 = \sigma_x^2 + \sigma_v^2. \tag{12}$$

Let us present a method for deriving of the noise: It has been shown that the noise standard deviation $\sigma_v$ can be accurately estimated from the first decomposition level diagonal subband $HH_1$ by the robust and accurate median estimator.

$$\hat{\sigma}_v^2 = \frac{median(|HH_1|)}{0.6745}. \tag{13}$$

The variance of the degraded image can be estimated as

$$\hat{\sigma}_y^2 = \frac{1}{M} \sum_{m=1}^{M} A_m^2, \tag{14}$$

where $A_m$ are the coefficients of wavelet in every scale $M$ is the total number of coefficient of wavelet. The threshold value $T$ can be calculated using

$$T_{MBS} = \frac{\beta \hat{\sigma}_v^2}{\hat{\sigma}_x}, \tag{15}$$

where $\beta = \sqrt{\dfrac{\log M}{2 \times j}}$, $M$ is the total coefficients of wavelet, $j$ is the wavelet decomposition level present in the subband coefficients under scrutiny and $\hat{\sigma}_x = \sqrt{\max(\hat{\sigma}_y^2 - \hat{\sigma}_v^2)}$. Note that in the case where $\hat{\sigma}_v^2 \geq \hat{\sigma}_y^2$, $\hat{\sigma}_x^2$ is taken to be zero, i.e. $T_{MBS} \to \infty$. Alternatively, in practice one may choose $T_{MBS} = \max |A_m|$, and all coefficients are set to zero.

In summary, the Modified BayesShrink thresholding technique performs soft thresholding with adaptive data driven subband and level dependent near optimal threshold given by:

$$T_{MBS} = \begin{cases} \dfrac{\beta \hat{\sigma}_v^2}{\hat{\sigma}_x}, & \text{if } \hat{\sigma}_v^2 < \hat{\sigma}_y^2 \\ \max |A_m|, & Otherwise \end{cases} \tag{16}$$

It is convenient to label the subbands of the transform as shown in Figure 2. The subbands, $HH_k$, $HL_k$, $LH_k$ are called the details, where $k = 1, ..., J$ is the scale, with $J$ being the largest (or coarsest) scale in the decomposition and a subband at scale $k$ has size $N/2^k \times N/2^k$. The subband $LL_J$ is the low resolution residual and is typically chosen large enough such that $N/2^J \leq N$, $N/2^J > 1$.

## Uncalibrated Stereo Image Rectification

Given a pair of stereo images, rectification determines a transformation of each image plane such that pairs of conjugate epipolar lines become collinear and parallel to one of the image axes.

*Figure 2. Subbands of 2D orthogonal wavelet transform*

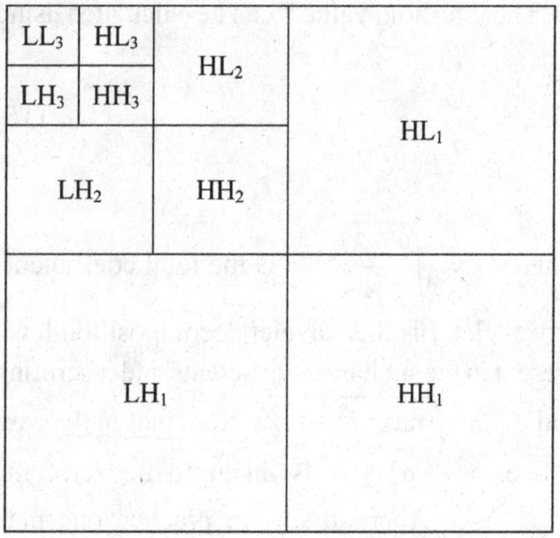

The important advantage of rectification is that computing stereo correspondences is reduced to a 1-D search problem along the horizontal raster lines of the rectified images. In the case of uncalibrated cameras, there are more degrees of freedom in choosing the rectifying transformation and a few competing methods are present in the literature. Each aims at producing a "good" rectification by minimizing a measure of distortion, but none is clearly superior to the others, not to mention the fact that there is no agreement on what the distortion criterion should be. We have proposed to adopt quasi-Euclidean epipolar rectification method for uncalibrated images proposed by Fussiello et al. (2010).

Geometrically, in the Euclidean frame, rectification is achieved by a suitable rotation of both image planes. The corresponding image transformation is the collineation induced by the plane at infinity. As a result, the plane at infinity is the locus of zero-disparity in the rectified stereo pair. This is signified by saying that Euclidean rectification is done with respect to the plane at infinity. In the uncalibrated case the reference plane is generic, as any plane can play the role of the infinity plane in the projective space. Our uncalibrated rectification can be seen as referred to a plane that approximates the plane at infinity.

We assume that intrinsic parameters are unknown and that a number of corresponding points $m_l^j \leftrightarrow m_r^j$ are available. The method seeks the collineations that make the original points satisfy the epipolar geometry of a rectified image pair.

The fundamental matrix of a rectified pair has a very specific form, namely it is the skew-symmetric matrix associated with the cross-product by the vector $u_l = (1,0,0)$:

$$[u_1]_\times = \begin{bmatrix} 0 & 0 & 0 \\ 0 & 0 & -1 \\ 0 & 1 & 0 \end{bmatrix}. \tag{17}$$

Let $H_r$ and $H_l$ be the unknown rectifying collineations. When they are applied to the corresponding tie-points $m_l^j$, $m_r^j$ respectively, the transformed points must satisfy the epipolar geometry of a rectified pair, namely:

$$(H_r m_r^j)^T [u_1]_\times (H_l m_l^j) = 0. \tag{18}$$

The left-hand side of (Equation 18) is an algebraic error, i.e., it has no geometrical meaning, so we used instead the Sampson error, that is a first order approximation of the geometric error. The matrix $F = H_r^T [u_1]_\times H_l$ can be considered as the fundamental matrix between the original images, therefore, in our case, the squared Sampson error for the $j^{th}$ correspondence is defined as:

$$E_j^2 = \frac{(m_r^{jT} F m_l^j)^2}{(F m_l^j)_1^2 + (F m_l^j)_2^2 + (m_r^{jT} F)_1^2 + (m_r^{jT} F)_2^2}, \tag{19}$$

where $(\cdot)_i$ is the $i^{th}$ component of the normalized vector. As this equation must hold for any $j$, one obtains a system of non-linear equations $\{E_j = 0\}$ in the unknown $H_r$ and $H_l$. A least-squares solution can obtained with the Levenberg-Marquardt algorithm, but the way in which $H_r$ and $H_l$ are parameterized is crucial, and characterizes our approach with respect to the previous ones. We force the rectifying collineations to have the same structure as in the calibrated (Euclidean) case, i.e. to be collineations induced by the plane at infinity, namely

$$H_r = K_{nr} R_r K_{or}^{-1} \ ,$$
$$H_l = K_{nl} R_l K_{ol}^{-1}, \tag{20}$$

The old intrinsic parameters $(K_{ol}, K_{or})$ and the rotation matrices $(R_l, R_r)$ are unknown, whereas the new intrinsic parameters $(K_{nl}, K_{nr})$ can be set arbitrarily, provided that vertical focal length and vertical coordinate of the principal point are same. Indeed, it is easy to verify that the matrix $K_{nr}^T [u_1]_\times K_{nl}$ is equal (up to scale) to $[u_1]_\times$, provided that the second and third row of $K_{nr}$ and $K_{nl}$ are the same. Hence it is not necessary to include the matrices $K_{nr}$ and $K_{nl}$ in the parameterization.

Each collineation depends in principle on five (intrinsic) plus three (rotation) unknown parameters. The rotation of one camera along its X-axis, however, can be eliminated. Consider the matrix

$$F = K_{or}^{-T} R_r^T [u_1]_\times R_l K_{ol}^{-1}. \tag{21}$$

Let $R_r'$ and $R_l'$ be the same matrices as $R_r$ and $R_l$ after pre-multiplying with an arbitrary (but the same for both) rotation matrix about the X-axis. It is easy to verify that $R_r^T [u_1]_\times R_l = R_r'^T [u_1]_\times R_l'$. Geometrically, this coincide with rotating a rectified pair around the baseline, which do not alter the rectification, but, in a real camera, it affects the portion of the scene that is imaged. Accordingly, we set to zero the rotation around the X-axis of the left camera.

We further reduce the number of parameters by making as educated guess on the old intrinsic parameters: no skew, principal point in the center of the image, aspect ratio equal to one. The only remaining unknowns are the focal lengths of both cameras. Assuming that they are identical and equal to $\alpha$, we get:

$$K_{or} = K_{ol} = \begin{bmatrix} \alpha & 0 & w/2 \\ 0 & \alpha & h/2 \\ 0 & 0 & 1 \end{bmatrix}, \tag{22}$$

where $w$ and $h$ are width and height (in pixel) of the image. In summary, two collineations are parameterized by six unknowns: five angles and the focal length $\alpha$. Focal length is expected to vary in the interval $[1/3(w+h), 3(w+h)]$, so we consider instead the variable $\alpha' = \log_3(\alpha / (w + h))$ which varies in $[-1,1]$

The minimization of the cost function is carried out using Levenburg-Marquardt, starting with all the unknown variables set to zero. When $\alpha'$ converges outside the boundaries of the interval $[-1,1]$ a random restart is attempted. If the problem persists the minimization is carried out with fixed $\alpha' = 0$.

Finally, the new intrinsic parameters ($K_{nr}$ and $K_{nl}$) are set equal to the old ones: $K_{nr} = K_{nl} = K_{ol}$, modulo a shift of the principal point, that might be necessary to center the rectified images in the customary image coordinate frame. Horizontal translation has no effect on the rectification, whereas vertical translation must be the same for both images.

## Dense Stereo Matching

Stereo matching is one of the classical problems in computer vision and has many potential application areas including robot navigation, 3D modeling, image based rendering and so on. Given two images of the same scene, the goal of stereo matching is to compute the disparity map for the reference image. A disparity describes the difference in the positions of two corresponding pixels. In order to get the disparity map, we have to solve the correspondence problem for each pixel. Generally, in case of stereovision, first rectify the pair of stereo images, so that the epipolar lines become horizontal.

We proposed to employ graph-cut method (Boykov et al., 2004) for computing corresponding points between two rectified images. The graph-cut method gives excellent results; performing better in textureless areas; near discontinuities and out-performing the other optimization methods. The crucial idea of the graph cut algorithm is that for a given configuration $f$ it is possible to find a strong local minimum of the energy function efficiently by using the graph based method. More precisely, we can compute the lowest energy configuration within a single $\alpha$- expansion or $\alpha\beta$- swap move of $f$. The $\alpha$ - expansion algorithm that is the representative graph cuts algorithm repeats such $\alpha$ - expansion local improvement operations for different disparities $\alpha$, until no $\alpha$ - expansion can reduce the energy. It has been proved that such $\alpha$-expansion algorithm can find a label within a known factor of the global minimum.

Let L and R be the sets of pixels in the left and right images, respectively. The goal of stereo matching is to determine a label $f_p$ for each pixel $p$ in the left image, which denotes a disparity value for that pixel. Then, the stereo matching can be formulated as the following energy minimization problem:

$$E(f) = E_{data}(f) + E_{smooth}(f). \qquad (23)$$

The data term, $E_{data}(f)$, measures how consistent the disparity function $f$ is to the input images and can be written as

$$E_{data}(f) = \sum_{p \in L} D_p(f_p), \qquad (24)$$

where $D_p(f_p)$ is a penalty function of the pixel $p$ having the disparity $f_p$. This penalty can be the usual Sum-of-Squared Difference (SSD), Sum-of-Absolute Difference (SAD) or the normalized correlation. The smoothness term, $E_{smooth}(f)$, encodes the smoothness assumption imposed by the algorithm, and can be written as

$$E_{smooth}(f) = \sum_{p,q \in N} V_{p,q} \cdot T(f_p \neq f_q), \qquad (25)$$

where $N$ is a neighborhood system for the pixels of the left image, $V_{p,q}$ is a function that controls the level of smoothness, and $T(.)$ is a binary function that is 1 if its argument is true and 0 otherwise. This is called the potts energy model, and we adopt this smoothness model for its discontinuity preserving nature.

The disparity map gives the dense correspondence map between the stereo images. Thus, the depth map is computed by triangulation with matched point pairs and camera parameters. The disparity map gives us a dense correspondence map between the stereo images. Thus, the depth map is computed by triangulation with matched point is considered independently. Therefore smoothing the surface is important to obtain a spatial coherence.

## Experimental Results

To see the effectiveness of the proposed approach on underwater images, experiment was done in the small water body. The depth at the bottom of the water body is approximately 2m with unknown turbidity characteristics. The stereo setup consists of two identical digital still cameras, which are Canon D10 water proof. The two cameras were installed on the vertical stereo mount and it was kept in the water body. We have selected objects like metal pipes and metal valves for experimentation purpose. These objects were kept at a distance [1m, 2m], near the corner of the water body. We have captured a pair of images of the objects using above mentioned stereo setup. These images present typical noise levels for underwater con-

*Figure 3. The result of 2D wavelet decomposition of underwater image at level 3*

ditions. To preprocess the degraded images, first we have applied homomorphic filtering to correct non-uniform illumination of light. Then, we have applied anisotropic filter, which smooth the image, removes or attenuates unwanted artifacts and remaining noise. Finally, wavelet based shrinkage function was applied to denoise the remaining noise present in the images. Figure 3 shows the result of 2D wavelet decomposition of left image at level 3. We have compared and evaluated different wavelet based shrinkage functions based on PSNR to identify the suitable wavelet based shrinkage function.

The result shows that the Modified Bayes-Shrink performs denoising that is consistent with the human visual system that is less sensitive to the presence of noise in the vicinity of image features. However, the presence of noise in flat regions of the image is perceptually more noticeable by the human visual system. The Modified BayesShrink performs little denoising in high activity subregions to preserve the sharpness of image features but completely denoised the flat sub-parts of the image. The Modified BayesShrink

yields the best results for denoising and also adopts a thresholding strategy that not only performs well. But it is also intuitively appealing as well as the results of simulations performance showed that the Modified BayesShrink preserves image features better than other shrinkage function. In our experimentation, it was demonstrated that spatially adaptive thresholds greatly improves the denoising performance over uniform thresholds.

That is, the threshold value changes for each coefficient. After preprocessing the captured pair of images, we apply sequence of steps to reconstruct the 3D surface of underwater objects as described

*Table 1. Comparison of various wavelet shrinkage functions*

| Wavelet Shrinkage Function | PSNR (dB) |
| --- | --- |
| Modified BayesShrink | 66.5586 |
| BayesShrink | 65.6829 |
| NormalShrink | 60.6853 |
| Adaptive Subband Thresholding | 56.3493 |
| VisuShrink | 40.7303 |
| Wiener | 37.2584 |

in the previous section. Figure 4 shows the result of the complete process of reconstructing the 3D surface of underwater objects. The experimental result shows that the proposed method reconstructs 3D surface of underwater objects accurately.

## FUTURE DIRECTIONS

The 3D reconstruction methods of the underwater scenes have been developed for 20 years in the field of computer vision. Many methods have been developed such as, structured lighting, ultrasonic and laser range finders, etc. Some of the methods mentioned above giving high accuracy but cost more, some of them give inaccurate results beside provides no flexibility. Because of the fast development in computer vision, the 3D reconstruction of the scenes using video sequences has become an effective method compared to image based techniques. It becomes possible to reconstruct a 3D model of the scene from just the video sequence of that scene. The 3D structure of the underwater scenes can be reconstructed using video camera moves through the scene while making an arbitrary motion, from the frames of the video; the 3D model is reconstructed via related computer vision algorithms.

The literature survey reveals that video sequence based techniques are most successful 3D reconstruction techniques. The video sequence based reconstruction techniques reconstruct an underwater scene from uncalibrated video sequences of that scene. The 3D reconstruction based on video sequence consists of the following stages: Image enhancement, feature detection and matching, fundamental matrix estimation, autocalibration, recovery of extrinsic parameters, rectification, stereo matching and dense reconstruction. The feature detection and tracking is an important issue in computer vision, which is required to estimate the fundamental matrix from the uncalibrated video sequences. Feature Tracking algorithms rely on the

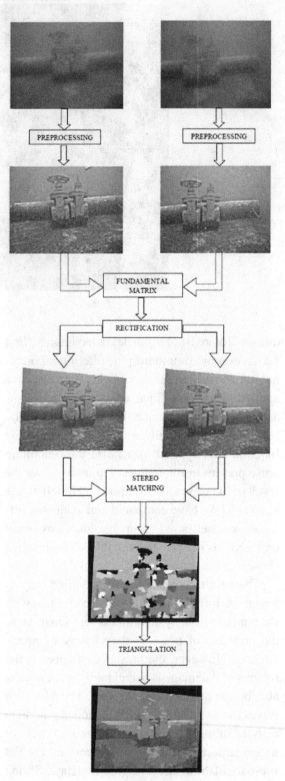

*Figure 4. The result of proposed 3D reconstruction method*

accurate computation of correspondences through a sequence of images. Robust tracking means detecting automatically unreliable matches, or outliers, over an image sequence. Recent examples of such robust algorithms include, which identifies tracking outliers while estimating the fundamental matrix, and which adopts a RANSAC (RANdom SAmple Consensus) approach to estimate outliers for estimating the trifocal tensor. The researchers have proposed the 3D reconstruction techniques based on RANSAC for underwater environment and these methods increase the computational cost of tracking significantly. Tomasi et al. (1991) introduced KLT (Kanade–Lucas–Tomasi) feature tracker based on SSD matching and assuming translational frame-to-frame displacements. The KLT feature tracker can be employed to underwater environment as feature tracker in order to track the features from the video sequences. The KLT based feature tracker system classified a tracked feature as good (reliable) or bad (unreliable) according to the residual of the match between the associated image region in the first and current frames; if the residual exceeded a user-defined threshold, the feature was rejected. Finally, in order to estimate the disparity map from the corresponding pair of sequence of images, Belief Propagation (Jian Sun et al., 2003) method can be adopted instead of Graph Cuts due to running time of Graph cuts takes 4 to 5 times that of Belief Propagation (Joachim Penc et al., 2009).

## CONCLUSION

In this chapter, an overview of the 3D reconstruction of underwater objects and scenes using stereo vision system is presented. 3D reconstruction for underwater applications is a relatively recent research area with a higher complexity than the 3D reconstruction for general applications. This is a very active and growing field of research that brings together challenging problems from the underwater environment and powerful 3D reconstruction techniques from computer vision. Notwithstanding the advance of the field on recent years, its main research challenge remains unsolved due to optical properties of the light in the underwater environment. The huge amount of articles published during the last years involving 3D reconstruction of underwater environment demonstrates the increasing interest in this topic and its wide range of applications. Stereo vision is the more accurate and robust 3D reconstruction method for underwater applications compared to other techniques. In underwater stereo vision, stereo matching is a hard problem due to change of the colour of same point in both left and right images. There is a need for an efficient stereo matching method to match correspondence points in both left and right images. The developed stereo vision based 3D reconstruction technique is expected to be robust enough to reconstruct objects or scenes in a realistic manner. The system is robust in the sense that it should be able to 3D reconstruct the object which is far away and which is captured in turbid water.

## ACKNOWLEDGMENT

The authors are indebted to the referees for their helpful comments and suggestions, which improved the earlier version of this chapter. This work has been supported by the Grants NRB/SC/158/2008-2009, Naval Research Board, DRDO, New Delhi, India.

## REFERENCES

Arnold-Bos, A., Malkasse, J. P., & Kerven, G. (2005). A pre-processing framework for automatic underwater images denoising. In *Proceedings of the European Conference on Propagation and Systems*, France.

Ayache, N., & Lustman, F. (1991). Trinocular stereo vision for robotics. *IEEE Transactions on Pattern Analysis and Machine Intelligence, 13*(1), 73–85. doi:10.1109/34.67633

Bazeille, S., Quidu, I., Jaulin, L., & Malkasse, J. P. (2006). Automatic underwater image pre-processing. *In Proceeding of the Caracterisation du Milieu Marin (CMM '06)*.

Boykov, Y., & Kolmogorov, V. (2004). An experimental comparison of min-cut/max-flow algorithms for energy minimization in vision. *IEEE Transactions on Pattern Analysis and Machine Intelligence, 26*(9), 1124–1137. doi:10.1109/TPAMI.2004.60

Brandou, V., Allais, A. G., Perrier, M., Malis, E., Rives, P., Sarrazin, J., & Sarradin, P. M. (2007). 3D reconstruction of natural underwater scenes using stereovision system IRIS. *IEEE OCEANS'07-EUROPE*, (pp. 1-6).

Carder, K., Reinersman, P., Costello, D., Kalten-bacher, E. M., Kloske, J., & Montes, M. (2005). Optical inspection of ports and harbors: Laser-line sensor model applications in 2 and 3 dimensions. *Proceedings of the Society for Photo-Instrumentation Engineers, 5780*, 49–58.

Castellani, U., Fusiello, A., Murino, V., Papaleo, L., Puppo, E., Repetto, S., & Pittore, M. (2004). Efficient on-line mosaicing from 3D acoustical images. *OCEANS '04. MTTS/IEEE TECHNO-OCEAN'04*, Vol. 2, (pp. 670-677).

Dalgleish, F. R., Tetlow, S., & Allwood, R. L. (2005). Seabed-relative navigation by structured lighting techniques. In Roberts, G. N., & Sutton, R. (Eds.), *Advances in unmanned marine vehicles* (pp. 277–292).

Drost, R., Munson, D. C. Jr, & Singer, A. C. (2002). Shape-from-silhouette approach to imaging ocean mines. In *Proceeding of Ocean Optics* (*Vol. 4488*, pp. 115–122). Remote Sensing and Underwater Imaging.

Faugeras, O. D. (1992). What can be seen in three dimensions with an uncalibrated stereo rig? In *Proceedings of the Second European Conference on Computer Vision*, Vol. 588, (pp. 563-578).

Forest, J., Salvi, J., & Batlle, J. (2000). *Image ranging system for underwater applications*. IFAC Conference on Maneuvering and Control of Marine Craft, Aalborg, Denmark.

Fusiello, A., & Irsara, L. (2010). Quasi-Euclidean epipolar rectification of uncalibrated images. *Machine Vision and Applications, 22*(4), 1–8.

Fusiello, A., Trucco, E., & Verri, A. (2000). A compact algorithm for rectification of stereo pairs. *Machine Vision and Applications, 12*(1), 16–22. doi:10.1007/s001380050120

Hannah, M. J. (1974). *Computer matching of areas in stereo images*. Ph.D. thesis, Comput. Sci. Dept., Stanford Univ., Stanford, CA, July 1974; Tech. Rep. STAN-CS-74-438.

Hartley, R., & Gupta, R. (1993). Computing matched-epipolar projections. In *Proceedings of the IEEE Computer Society Conference on Computer Vision and Pattern Recognition*, (pp. 549-555).

Hartley, R. I. (1999). Theory and practice of projective rectification. *International Journal of Computer Vision, 35*(2), 115–127. doi:10.1023/A:1008115206617

Heikkila, J., & Silven, O. (1997). A four-step camera calibration procedure with implicit image correction. In *Proceedings of the IEEE Computer Society Conference on Computer Vision and Pattern Recognition (CVPR'97), 17-19*, (pp. 1106-1112), San Juan, Pnerto Rico.

Horn, B. (1986). *Robot vision*. MIT Press.

Isgro, F., & Trucco, E. (1999). Projective rectification without epipolar geometry. In *Proceedings of the IEEE Computer Society Conference on Computer Vision and Pattern Recognition (CVPR'99)*, Vol. 1, (pp. 1094-1099).

Jian, S., Zheng, N.-N., & Shum, H.-Y. (2003). Stereo matching using belief propagation. *IEEE Transactions on Pattern Analysis and Machine Intelligence*, *25*(7), 787–800. doi:10.1109/TPAMI.2003.1206509

Khamene, A., Madjidi, H., & Negahdaripour, S. (2001). 3-D mapping of sea floor scenes by stereo imaging. In *Proceedings of the OCEANS '02 MTS/IEEE Conference and Exhibition*, Vol. 4, (pp. 2577-2583).

Kim, K., Neretti, N., & Intrator, N. (2005). Non-iterative construction of super-resolution image from an acoustic camera. *Proceedings of IEEE CIHSPS*, *2005*, 105–111.

Kim, K., Neretti, N., & Intrator, N. (2006). *Video enhancement for underwater exploration using forward looking sonar. Advanced Concepts for Intelligent Vision Systems* (*Vol. 4179*, pp. 554–563). Berlin, Germany: Springer.

Kutulkos, K. N., & Seitz, S. M. (1998). *What do N photographs tell us about 3D shape?* Technical Report TR680, Computer Science department, University of Rochester. USA.

Laurentini, A. (1994). The visual hull concept for silhouette-based image understanding. *IEEE Transactions on Pattern Analysis and Machine Intelligence*, *16*(2), 150–162. doi:10.1109/34.273735

Loop, C., & Zhang, Z. (1999). Computing rectifying homographies for stereo vision. In *Proceedings of the IEEE Computer Society Conference on Computer Vision and Pattern Recognition (CVPR'99)*, Vol. 1.

Lorenson, W. E., & Cline, H. E. (1987). Marching cubes: A high resolution 3D surface construction algorithm. *ACM SIGGRAPH Computer Graphics*, *21*(4), 163–169. doi:10.1145/37402.37422

Lucus, B. D., & Kanade, T. (1981). An iterative image registration technique with an application to stereo vision. In *Proceedings of the Seventh International Joint Conference on Artificial Intelligence*, Vol. 2, (pp. 674-679).

Narasimhan, S. G., Nayar, S. K., Sun, B., & Koppal, S. J. (2005). Structured light in scattering media. In *Proceedings of the Tenth IEEE International Conference on Computer Vision*, Vol. 1, (pp. 420-427).

Negahdaripour, S. (2005). Calibration of DIDSON forward-scan acoustic video camera. *Proceedings of MTS/IEEE OCEANS '05*, Vol. 2, (pp. 1287-1294).

Negahdaripour, S., & Firoozfam, P. (2006). An ROV stereovision system for ship-hull inspection. *IEEE Journal of Oceanic Engineering*, *31*(3), 551–564. doi:10.1109/JOE.2005.851391

Negahdaripour, S., & Taatian, A. (2008). 3-D motion and structure estimation for arbitrary scenes from 2-D optical and sonar video. *Proceedings of IEEE Oceans '08* Quebec City, (pp. 1-8), Canada.

Negahdaripour, S., Zhang, H., & Han, X. (2002). Investigation of photometric stereo method for 3-D shape recovery from underwater imagery. *OCEANS '02 MTS/IEEE*, Vol. 2, (pp. 1010-1017).

Oram, D. (2001). Rectification for any epipolar geometry. In *Proceedings of the 12th British Machine Vision Conference (BMVC 2001)*, (pp. 653-662).

Papadimitriou, D. V., & Dennis, T. J. (1996). Epipolar line estimation and rectification for stereo image pairs. *IEEE Transactions on Image Processing*, *5*(4), 672–676. doi:10.1109/83.491345

Penc, J., Klette, R., Vaudrey, T., & Morales, S. (2009). *Graph-cut and belief-propagation stereo on real-world image sequences*. MI Technical Report.

Pollefeys, M., Koch, R., & Van Gool, L. (1999). A simple and efficient rectification method for general motion. In *Proceedings of the Seventh IEEE International Conference on Computer Vision*, Vol. 1, (pp. 496-501).

Prabhakar, C. J., & Praveen Kumar, P. U. (2010). 3D surface reconstruction of underwater objects. *Abstract Proceedings of Indian Conference on Computer Vision, Graphics and Image Processing – 2010* (ICVGIP – 2010), (pp. 4).

Prabhakar, C. J., & Praveen Kumar, P. U. (2010). Underwater image denoising using adaptive wavelet subband thresholding. In *Proceeding of the International Conference on Signal and Image Processing (ICSIP – 2010),* (pp. 322-327).

Robert, L., Zeller, C., Faugeras, O., & Hebert, M. (1997). Applications of non-metric vision to some visually guided robotics tasks. In Aloimonos, Y. (Ed.), *Visual navigation: From biological systems to unmanned ground vehicles* (pp. 89–134).

Roy, S., & Cox, I. J. (1998). A maximum-flow formulation of the n-camera stereo correspondence problem. In *Proceedings of the Sixth International Conference on Computer Vision*, (pp. 492-499).

Scharstein, D., Szeliski, R., & Zabih, R. (2002). A taxonomy and evaluation of dense two-frame stereo correspondence algorithms. *International Journal of Computer Vision, 47*, 7–42. doi:10.1023/A:1014573219977

Sedlazeck, A., Koser, K., & Koch, R. (2009). 3D reconstruction based on underwater video from ROV Keil 6000 considering underwater imaging conditions. *IEEE OCEANS'09-EUROPE*, (pp. 1-10).

Slabaugh, G., Culberston, B., Malzbender, T., & Schafer, R. (2001). A survey of volumetric scene reconstruction methods from photographs. In *Proceedings of the International Workshop on Graphics*, (pp. 81-100).

Tomasi, C., & Kanade, T. (1991). *Shape and motion from image streams: A factorization method – Part 3 detection and tracking of point features*. Technical Report CMU-CS-91-132, Computer Science Department, Carnegie Mellon University, USA.

Trucco, E., Petillot, Y. R., Tena Ruiz, I., Plakas, K., & Lane, D. M. (2000). Feature tracking in video and sonar subsea sequences with applications. *Computer Vision and Image Understanding, 79*, 92–122. doi:10.1006/cviu.2000.0846

Tsai, R. Y. (1986). An efficient and accurate camera calibration technique for 3D-machine vision. In *Proceedings of the IEEE Conference on Computer Vision and Pattern recognition*. (pp. 364-374), Miami Beach, Florida.

Zhang, H. (2005). Automatic sensor platform positioning and 3-D target modeling from underwater stereo sequences. Ph.D. Thesis, Coral Gables, Florida.

Zhang, Z. (2000). A flexible new technique for camera calibration. *IEEE Transactions on Pattern Analysis and Machine Intelligence, 22*(11), 1330–1334. doi:10.1109/34.888718

## ADDITIONAL READING

Arnold-Bos, A., Malkasse, J. P., & Kervern, G. (2005). Towards a model-free denoising of underwater optical images. In *Proceedings of the IEEE European Oceans Conference*, Vol. 1, (pp.527-532), France.

Boykov, Y., Veksler, O., & Zabih, R. (2001). Fast approximation energy minimization via graph cuts. *IEEE Transactions on Pattern Analysis and Machine Intelligence*, *23*(11), 1222–1239. doi:10.1109/34.969114

Garcia, R., Nicosevici, T., & Cufi, X. (2002). On the way to solve lighting problems in underwater imaging. In *Proceedings of the IEEE OCEANS '02 MTS*, Vol. 2, (pp. 1018-1024).

Hogue, A., German, A., & Jenkin, M. (2007). Underwater environment reconstruction using stereo and inertial data. *IEEE International Conference on Systems, Man and Cybernetics ISIC*, (pp. 2372-2377).

Hou, W., Gray, D. J., Weidemann, A. D., Fournier, G. R., & Forand, J. L. (2007). Automated underwater image restoration and retrieval of related optical properties. In *Proceedings of the IEEE International Geoscience and Remote Sensing Symposium (IGARSS '07)*, (pp. 1889-1892).

Hou, W., Weidemann, A. D., Gray, D. J., & Fournier, G. R. (2007). Imagery-derived modulation transfer function and its applications for underwater imaging. In *Applications of Digital Image Processing, Vol. 6696 of Proceedings of SPIE*, San Diego, California, USA.

Khamene, A., & Negahdaripour, S. (2003). Motion and structure from multiple cues; image motion, shading flow and stereo disparity. *Computer Vision and Image Understanding*, *90*(1), 99–127. doi:10.1016/S1077-3142(03)00028-6

Luong, Q. T., & Faugeras, O. D. (1996). The fundamental matrix: Theory, algorithms and stability analysis. *International Journal of Computer Vision*, *17*(1), 43–75. doi:10.1007/BF00127818

Nicosevici, T., Negahdaripour, S., & Garcia, R. (2005). Monocular-based 3D seafloor reconstruction and ortho-mosaicing by piecewise planar representation. In *Proceedings of the OCEANS MTS/IEEE Conference*, Vol. 2, (pp. 1279-1286).

Perona, P., & Malik, J. (1990). Scale space and edge detection using anisotropic diffusion. *IEEE Transactions on Pattern Analysis and Machine Intelligence*, *12*(7), 629–639. doi:10.1109/34.56205

Schechner, Y. Y., & Karpel, N. (2005). Recovery of underwater visibility and structure by polarization analysis. *IEEE Journal of Oceanic Engineering*, *30*(3), 570–587. doi:10.1109/JOE.2005.850871

Trucco, E., & Olmos, A. (2006). Self-tuning underwater image restoration. *IEEE Journal of Oceanic Engineering*, *31*(2), 511–519. doi:10.1109/JOE.2004.836395

Yu, Y. F. (2000). Measurement of the point spread function of seawater with method of image transmission. *Acta Optica Sinica*, *20*(12), 1649–1651.

## KEY TERMS AND DEFINITIONS

**3D Reconstruction:** 3D reconstruction is the process of capturing the shape and appearance of real objects.

**Absorption:** The physical process in which light rays interacting with particles in suspension in the medium is converted into other forms of energy is called absorption. As a result, the intensity of a point in the image will decay as the distance between the scene and the camera increases.

**Denoising:** Image denoising refers to the recovery of a digital image that has been contaminated by additive white Gaussian noise (AWGN).

**Epipolar Geometry:** Epipolar geometry is the intrinsic projective geometry between two views. It is independent of scene structure, and only depends on the cameras internal parameters and relative pose (position and orientation).

**Rectification:** A transformation process used to project two-or-more images onto a common image plane. It corrects image distortion by transforming the image into a standard coordinate system. It is used in computer stereo vision to simplify the problem of finding matching points between images.

**Scattering:** Scattering is caused by the change in direction of a ray of light after colliding with a particle in suspension. For small angular changes in direction the effect is called forward scattering), whereas for larger angles up to 180 degrees, which

effectively causes the ray to bounce back at the camera, it is called backscattering.

**Stereo Matching:** Given more than two images of the same scene, the goal of stereo matching is to compute the disparity map for the reference image. A disparity describes the difference in the positions of two corresponding pixels.

**Stereo Vision:** A type of techniques for computing depth information based on images captured with two or more cameras. The main idea is to observe a scene from two or more viewpoints and to use the disparity to refer the position, structure and relation of objects in scene.

# Chapter 6
# 3D Reconstruction of Graph Objects, Scenes, and Environments

**Suhana Chikatla**
*Wallace State, USA*

**Ukaiko Bitrus-Ojiambo**
*St. Paul's University, Kenya*

## ABSTRACT

*The purpose of this chapter is to provide a basic understanding of how three-dimensional (3D) statistical visual displays aid in education. The chapter seeks to discuss the importance of surface objects, scenes, and environments reconstructed to enhance the interpretation of charts. Further described are the different types of 3D charts available: bar, line, and pie charts. The chapter also provides enlightenment about two new concepts: the "3D actual" and "3D obvious" charts. Overall, the chapter focuses on the theoretical background, pedagogical practice, usability, and applicability of using 3D surface charts. The chapter, in addition, provides explanations based on research done by Chikatla (2010), Dempsey, Chikatla, and Inpornvijit (2008), Fisher, Dempsey, and Marousky (1997), and Dempsey and Armstrong (1997).*

## INTRODUCTION

The new renaissance, is it here? The big wave of change, attributable to technology innovations, is it here? Growing technology advancements have provided expansions in unattainable areas for humanity. The world of education today is challenged by the growing number of modernized

techniques available to facilitate recreating live settings for educational purposes. We are only a couple of clicks away from creating real world settings to enhance our teaching and learning processes. The latest visual trends in Hollywood and Bollywood have introduced and showcased three dimensional (3D) visual effects to captivate audiences by providing settings closest to

DOI: 10.4018/978-1-4666-0113-0.ch006

reality: the *reel world* is enhanced to recreate *real worlds*. Furthermore, educational videos for children and adults comprise of teachable games and simulations that show clear improvements in providing insights into improved educational purposes. Behind these great technological, virtual advancements are sound mathematical / geometrical principles.

All over the world students are perplexed when dealing with numeric concepts (Trentacosta & Kennedy, 1997). Educators have dedicated a lot of time and resource in trying to find techniques and strategies to revive student interest in numeric concepts. Currently, many educators have been using pictures, videos, games, and simulations to stimulate individual interests in math. Mathematicians and statisticians are facing the dilemma of finding means and tools to stimulate individual interests when interpreting mathematical concepts and statistical graphs (Kosslyn, 1994; Macdonald-Ross, 1977). One strategy that authors are constantly debating is the use of charts. Numerical data can be communicated via chart (Meyers, 1970). For example, language is communicated via words, music via dots, graphic via visuals, and math via symbols. Similarly, when we speak, we use verbal embellishments; simple/complex words, poems, stories, and narration. Likewise, when we use illustrations, we are using *visual embellishments,* that is, through pictorial representation in the form of charts, 3D objects, 3D scenes, and 3D environments (Kosslyn, 1994, Chikatla, 2010).

Charts have been used for ages as a tool to communicate data for problem solving and decision making (Meyers, 1970). Charts are combinations of lines or pictorial forms of columns, bars, or pies that stand for ideas (East, 1952; Pettersson, 1993). Charts have the ability to very effectively show factual data. They help gain audience attention; and are explanatory drawings. They can help make predictions over time showing projections of future possibilities (East, 1942; Meyer, 1970). The visuals, plotted relations, words, and numbers

collectively aid in the comprehension, saves the reader's time, which also enhances communication of concepts provided. Quality charts require fewer explanations and as a result need less time to comprehend (Tufte, 1983). As such, many educators are communicating math concepts and data via charts (White, 1984). Additionally, the flexible nature of charts allows their design process to be easier. According to Spence and Krizel (1994), both children and adults demonstrate success in math learning when exposed to chart data.

In a small group survey conducted by Chikatla (2010), several individuals (Americans and Indians) indicated that pictorial chart images containing 3D objects, scenes, and environments could have made vast differences when comprehending mathematical concepts during their Graduate Record Examination (GRE). In this research, it was also found that participants did not have any problem comprehending when using either 3D pictorial or 2D traditional charts. In another research done by Dempsey, Chikatla, and Inpornvijit (2008) it was found that participants that used charts that included 3D objects and scenes performed better on multiple choice questions compared to their counter parts that used traditional two dimensional (2D) charts. Thus, for this chapter, we are going to focus on the value of reconstructed 3D charts for comprehending math concepts.

## BACKGROUND

This chapter has been developed based on prior research conducted by Chikatla (2010), Dempsey, Chikatla, and Inpornvijit (2008), Dempsey and Armstrong (1997), and Fisher, Dempsey, and Marousky (1997). Research administered by Fisher et al. (1997) indicated that participants used 2D charts more than 3D charts when answering multiple choice questions. A similar series of studies (Dempsey & Armstrong, 1997; Dempsey et al., 2008) indicated that participants neither choose nor used charts that were perceived as being highly 3D. However, in a corresponding research conducted by Dempsey et al. (2008), it was seen that participants that choose the 3D charts performed better compared to the 2D chart environments. Additionally, in a comparative study, on American and Indian participants, conducted by Chikatla (2010) there were a couple of interesting findings. Firstly, it was found that American participants preferred 3D charts more compared to the Indian participants. Secondly, although American participants liked 3D charts it was the Indian participants that ultimately used 3D charts more often during interpretation. In fact Indian participants reported that finding answers in 3D chart environment were not as difficult as they had thought as such they felt comfortable using them. Thirdly, it was found that American participants were more likely to accurately judge 2D or 3D charts compared to the Indian participants due to their familiarity to the jargons, sentence constructions, and pictorial representations.

The need to reconstruct 3D surface charts for the educational purposes arise from arguments discussed from several researchers and theorists. For example, research findings by Chikatla (2010), Dempsey et al. (2008), and Spence and Krizel (1994) indicate that 3D surface charts are suitable to enhance the teaching and learning process. Although, humans have individual differences such as age, intelligence, levels of IQ, socio-cultural beliefs, while interpreting data (Vernon, 1937; Wright 1970). Additionally authors like Clark and Lyons (2004) suggest that individual reasoning can be aided by graphic visuals. Such visuals are eye-catching and gain readers' attention (Kosslyn, 1994). This technique of gaining attention is possible due to the background 3D objects and scenes that are incorporated in the visuals which essentially tell a story (White, 1984). In fact individuals learn better from visuals and words rather than words alone (Clark & Mayer, 2003; Mayer, 2001). Individuals exposed to such environments on the regular basis via games, simulations, television, and internet prove to be more pictorially

literate (Goldsmith, 1987), when exposed to such 3D scenes and environments. Research indicates that charts can be used for all age groups and at any level of competency (Wright, 1970).

Interestingly, all research and theories are subject to refutation. Often, 3D visuals tend to be more decorative than educational. As such, there are several controversial views surrounding the use of 3D surface graphics. For example, in their research, Harp and Mayer (1998) found that extraneous/irrelevant visuals did not aid learning. This finding was consistent with Clark and Mayer's (2003) *Coherence Principle:* extraneous displays hinder learning. In another research, Hegarty, Narayanan, and Freitas (2002), found that visuals that lacked visual learning principles resulted in diminished learning. Additionally, very little difference was seen among the groups that used print-based versus 3D animated version. Michas and Berry (2000) also did not find much difference among three versions of their research: simple graphics and text, simple graphic and arrows, and video demonstration. Clark and Lysons (2004), nonetheless, suggest that decorated visuals neither increase nor decrease learning; their use only hinders our comprehension. Another author asserts that studying pictorial representations require more mental energy and demands higher cognitive drive than purely looking at a picture (Pettersson, 1993). As a result of this debate, this chapter discusses two new terms coined by Spence and Krizel (1999): 3D *apparent* and 3D *effective* dimensions. The authors of this chapter call it "actual charts" and "obvious charts" respectively.

## 3D GEOMETRICAL CHARTS IN TECHNOLOGY AND EDUCATION

The need to motivate individuals to understand numerical concepts has been perplexing for educators, for decades (Spence & Krizel, 1994). Due to the available technology today, many times designers are able to use 3D visual scenes and pictorial environments to stimulate learner interest (Trentacosta & Kennedy, 1997). According to Kosslyn (1994) charts are exceptional visuals that have the ability to overcome the broad learning limitations of the brain. Moreover, technological innovations brilliantly help design numeric concepts to facilitate learning (Mukhopadhyay & Parhar, 2001). The following are brief discussions on 3D geometrical charts and technology, 3D geometrical charts in education, 3D environments and its use and impact on different learners, as defined by one's cultural background.

## 3D Geometrical Charts and Technology

Today's technology can produce exceptional 3D charts, with brilliant colors, shapes, labels, and images with precise accuracy. Previously, designing simple charts was time consuming. Today those same innovations have the ability to reconstruct 3D geometrical charts, making them merely a click away. Tools like MS Excel, MS Expressions Graphic Design, Adobe Illustrator, Graph, Sigma-Plot, SAS, and SPSS are some popular tools that help reconstruct charts. Many times educators, today, forget that technology is only a means to an end. As such, although a lot of money is spent on technology and equipment, educators fail to precisely communicate information to the reader (White, 1984). Fortunately, the current growth in technology helps improve the clarity of chart data and help create teachable and learnable charts.

## 3D Geometrical Charts and Education

Geometrical charts include mathematical expressions. Although mathematical expressions are used by individuals on a daily basis they are fundamentally repugnant to individuals. For example, when we cross the street in front of oncoming traffic, we are actually calculating the distance and the speed of the vehicle that is coming in our direc-

tion. That is, we calculate in our mind if we have enough time to cross the street before the vehicle hits us. The mathematical representation for this example is $d = s * t$ or another representation is $s = d \div t$ (where $d$ is distance, $s$ is speed, $t$ is time, $*$ is the symbol for multiplication, and $\div$ is the symbol for division). Both equations give the same result (Chikatla, 2010). One way to encourage its learning, as discussed earlier, would be allowing individuals to treat math education as learning a new language, the language of symbols and numbers (White, 1984). Mathematical symbols include: 'x or *' for multiplication, '+' for addition, '-' for subtraction, '÷' for division, '=' for equal to, '≤' less than equal to and '≥' for greater than equal to.

Now let us try plotting a basic 2D chart. To do this we first have to plot the linear equation of x + y = p on a chart, given the ordered pair $(x_1, y_1)$ being (3, 2) that satisfy the equation. This equation, when drawn on a chart, forms a straight line. Every equation of the expression x + y = p, with point of intersection p, forms a straight or diagonal line p, and results in the sum of x and y (see *Figure 1*, 2D-Rectangle). While that of circle is $x_1{}^\wedge 2 + y_1{}^\wedge 2 = p^\wedge 2$ (see *Figure 2*, 2D - Circle). Similarly, the mathematical expressions to create 3D objects like sphere is $x_1{}^\wedge 2 + y_1{}^\wedge 2 + z_1{}^\wedge 2 < 1$ (see *Figure 3*, 3D Sphere), cylinder is $x_1{}^\wedge 2 + y_1{}^\wedge 2 < 1$ (see *Figure 4*, 3D Cylinder), and that of cube is $x_1{}^\wedge 2 + y_1{}^\wedge 2 + z_1{}^\wedge 2 < 1$ (see *Figure 5*, 3D Cube).

When showing relationships between three factors or when showing complex unfamiliar objects it often becomes necessary to use 3D charts (Wright 1970). Often pictorial charts show only two factors the *x*- and the *y-axis*. The *z-axis* is often created by adding a background picture which often also acts as an attention gainer. This third dimensional picture representation often provides a sense of reality. Thus, 3D displays have the ability to counteract the *figure-ground* confusion, allowing objects to seem real and solid (Wright, 1970).

*Figure 1. 2D rectangle*

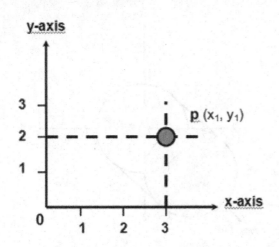

*Figure 2. 2D circle*

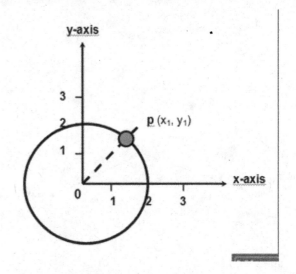

Three-dimensional objects, scenes, and environments are all around us. Today's media have become the core of human learning. Mathematical charts are used regularly via the internet, television, and print media like (news papers) by all age groups. Such forms of media together with audio, video, and television have gradually become the core foundation for educational purposes in respect to the teaching and learning processes. Unfortunately, the problem still remains in that many individuals continue to express fear of understanding mathematical expressions. As such, authors suggest using alternative techniques of using 3D objects, scenes and environments to stimulate learner's interest (Trentacosta & Kennedy, 1997).

## 3D Objects, Scenes, and Environments

Seeing visuals accelerates and boosts learning (East, 1952). To understand this concept, let us consider the old aphorism "a picture is worth a thousand words." For example, any individual would prefer a 2D picture of the Taj Mahal to a thousand word description of the same information. Furthermore, if additional 3D objects, scenes, and environments were added to this image, indi-

viduals would prefer the 3D representation over the 2D representation (Chikatla, 2010).

When we speak, we are free to use simple words as well as complex words. That is, while developing sentences, individuals have the freedom to use metaphors, poetic forms or stories to express themselves. Likewise, to help create meaningful charts (pictorial graphics) freedom should be given to the designer to use 3D objects, scenes, and environments. Charts in general have the ability to instantly provide meaning to data (Kosslyn, 1994; White, 1984). Particularly, when a chart is accurately designed it has been known to attract the learner's attention, motivate, and thus facilitate learning (Burbank & Pett, 1986). With the help of 3D objects, scenes and environments the data might perhaps provide a real world experience; as such, even tell a story. Based on findings, the audiences are known to respond and even get excited about such charts (Chikatla, 2010). So what is the best way of using 3D charts?

For example, the 3D objects, scenes, and environments in the following chart visual (see Figure 6, Chart with Emotional Stimulus) add immediate meaning by stimulating an individual's emotional attention. In Figure 6, food acts as the emotional stimulus. According to Ormrod (2008),

*Figure 3. 3D sphere*

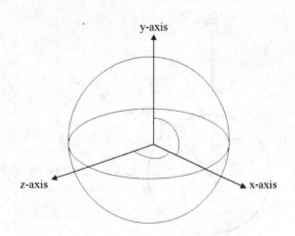

*Figure 4. 3D cylinder*

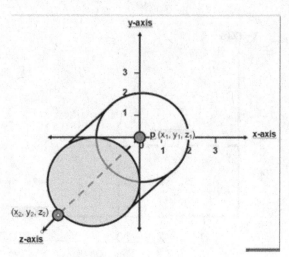

stimuli with strong emotional association attract attention. The initial reaction to the picture would be that the information provided is about eating or chicken. By further studying the picture an individual can even answer questions related to it, for example, "What percentage of respondents DO NOT like fried chicken?" (see Figure 6). Select the Appropriate Answer: a. 70%, b. 59%, c. 38%, and d. 32%.

## 3D Charts and Their Use

This section discusses advantages of 3D charts and raises concerns in using 2D charts. Several researchers encourage the use of 3D charts (Kosslyn, 1994) because 3D charts have the ability to standout and help in gaining attention. White (1994), states that 3D charts are often embedded on a background picture, scene, or environment, which often imitates the real world situations (Kosslyn, 1994) and often tell a story. In this digital age most learners are exposed to games and simulations, as such according to Goldsmith (1987), individuals exposed to graphic environments are more pictorially literate. As a result, individuals are able to assimilate (interpret) the content of a visual in the presence of high apparent or extraneous dimensions (decorated information)

and accommodate (ignore, modify) high apparent or extraneous dimensions while comprehending relevant content of a visual. Furthermore, suggestions are made to use objects, scenes, and environments that act as "picture labels" (Kosslyn, 1994, p. 186). For instance, live objects representing each category can be used to illustrate i.e.; chart showing individuals reasons for an upset stomach, can include take out food depicting spicy food, chicken illustrating fried food (see *Figure 7*, Example for "Picture Labels" of Objects).

Authors have suggested avoiding clashing representations. This is, any form of scenes or environments that have no relevance to the topic should be avoided (Kosslyn, 1994). For example, when depicting the sale of ivory in India, the simplest illustration would be using a picture of an elephant with a trunk rather than using a monkey with a tail because ivory has nothing to do with a monkey neither its tail. An example of visual misrepresentation can be found in the visual showing ketchup bottles as objects, on a vertical bar chart to show burger toppings that include cheese, lettuce, tomato, and cucumber (see Figure 8, Misrepresentation in charts). These types of objects can hinder readers understanding, as readers know lettuce is green and leafy, while tomato is red and round, sliced cucumbers are

*Figure 5. 3D cube*

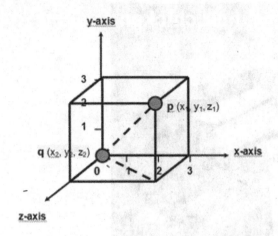

green and round, and cheese is white or yellow and sticky/stringy and none of them look like ketchup bottles (Chikatla, 2010). Such inconsistencies, according to *Visual Communication Theory* (see Figure 8), can be characterized as *noise*.

## 3D Charts in Graduate Record Examination (GRE)

In a small group survey (discussion) conducted on graduate apprentices (Chikatla, 2010), participants who had completed the Graduate Record Examination (GRE) stated that they thought they had done better on the Math, quantitative section, than on the English, verbal section. Even several graduate students from the English department expressed difficulty in the verbal section compared to the quantitative section. The explanations that were discussed by the group were as follows: First, the quantitative section included a narrative format; these story-type questions were more understandable and effective to participants. Second, it was noted that the diagrammatic representation provided next to the question many times helped several individuals answer questions quicker. Finally, when these graduate apprentices were shown the charts, many instantly expressed their

fascination for the 3D chart objects and scenes. Many suggested that these 3D environments could have been a better substitute to the existing displays on the GRE exam. Consider an example of the GRE question: "In 1970, it cost twelve dollars ($12) to purchase 100 pounds of fertilizer. In 1990, it cost thirty four dollars ($34) to purchase 100 pounds of fertilizer. The price of 100 pounds of fertilizer increased, by how many dollars, between 1970 and 1990 (Brownstein, Weiner, & Green, 1999)?" Based on the student's views, such narrative questions, combined with a 3D visual scene would be the best representation for better understanding (see Figure 9). This finding holds true to the *Contiguity Principle* discussed by Mayer. Thus, based on this principle, a visual display with a picture in the background and the data overlaid on the foreground would be an excellent way to communicate to an individual trying to answer the above GRE question.

## 3D Charts and Attention Gaining Techniques

Every educator's top most priority is trying to gain the learners' attention during the teaching and learning process. Decorated colorful displays often attract attention. Often the background displays in a 3D chart provides a real world experience (White, 1984). Thus, allowing the 3D charts to look attractive and show relevance to the content (Kosslyn, 1994).

The objects, scenes, and background environments used to create 3D charts makes the 3D technique more attractive and interesting. Kosslyn (1994) calls these types of displays attention-gaining techniques. Unfortunately, such techniques are not considered an important part of a display and often could make comprehension difficult (Wright, 1970). In any case, the background 3D objects, scenes, and environments aid the brain's sensory registers by catching the eyes of the readers (Kosslyn, 1994). In a research conducted by Chikatla (2010) it was found that American

3D Reconstruction of Graph Objects, Scenes, and Environments

*Figure 6. Chart with emotional stimulus*

participants found 3D charts as more noticeable. Participants argued that the background objects and scenes had instant long term memory storage effect. For instance, the conceptual representations of 3D objects and scenes illustrated the relevant concepts of the chart data. As such, the object

ketchup bottle and images of uniformed football players created a familiarity with concepts thus also making them feel emotionally at ease. Interestingly, American participants reported that they could not believe they were actually participating in a math related activity with so much interest.

*Figure 7. Example for "picture labels" of objects*

People's likes and dislikes are determined by the things that attract them. Often people attend to attractive stimuli (Ormrod, 2008). Changes in visuals in the form of size of font (see Figure 9), unusual stimulus (see Figure 6), or contrasts attract attention (Ormrod, 2008). Such techniques that are used in 3D charts are considered as attention gaining techniques (Kosslyn, 1994). Many times this attraction is the result of our visual sensors (see Figure 6, 7, & 8) and often requires using our visual sensors (Meyers, 1970). Research findings by Chikatla (2010) indicated that American participants liked 3D charts more compared to the Indian participants. American participants were surprised that math activity could seem so much fun. In another research (Dempsey et al., 2008) participants liked as well as used 3D charts while answering multiple choice questions. In a similar research (Dempsey & Armstrong, 1997: Fisher et al., 1997) participants liked 3D charts as well.

## 3D Charts and Comprehension Technique

Charts are known to be used for all age groups and levels of competency (Wright, 1970). An excellent chart would require fewer explanations, as such, require less time to comprehend. The background 3D objects, scenes and environments in a chart give a sense of reality; and instantly tell a story (White, 1984). Furthermore, charts with extra dimensions reduce the time during comprehension. Due to this reason 3D charts take less time to comprehend compared to 1D or 2D charts (Spence, 2004). Moreover, 3D representations come in handy when complex jargons were unfamiliar. For example, in a research conducted by Chikatla (2010) Indian participants reported that the 3D objects and scenes representing unfamiliar jargons labeled on the 3D charts instantly aided their comprehension. For instance, a 3D chart with a background scene of a coffee cup with labels "sweetener" and "cream" created confusion among the Indian participants. Nevertheless, the 3D object of the coffee cup in the background (see *Figure 10*) helped the Indian participants encode the two terms: "sweetener" as sugar substitute and "cream" as "milk cream" rather than 'cream' being "face cream or lotion."

*Figure 8. Misrepresentation in charts (similar chart found in USA Today, 2007 snapshots)*

*Figure 9. Visual representation of GRE question*

## 3D Charts Used by Children and Adults in Education

Charts have been a widely used technique to help interpret mathematical data. As discussed earlier they are available via different media; internet, television, and newspapers. Both children and adults can benefit and learn new information via chart education (Spence & Krizel, 1994). Charts play an important role in the intellectual and educational development of children. Charts are used by children to aid learning. In schools, initially, children use charts to comprehend concepts like fractions, decimals and proportions of *greater than* or *less than*. Later, children use charts to aid in mastering more complex mathematical concepts

such as algebra, geometry, and other higher mathematics (Spence & Krizel, 1994).

Furthermore, pictorial 3D charts are exceptionally helpful when showing simple comparisons of quantities (East, 1952). Such illustrations are good for presenting concrete images for teaching concepts (visual and spatial), while words are good for presenting abstract ideas and concepts that have already been learned (Hartley, 1994). As such their illustrations are considered extremely significance, and their use should not be, in any way, minimized. Its active use can help enhance learning.

Often chart information demonstrates relationships of numeric data between section of parts to a whole (Petterson, 1993). Interestingly both children and adults are able to learn new infor-

*Figure 10. Visually comprehensible chart (similar chart found in USA Today, 2007 snapshots)*

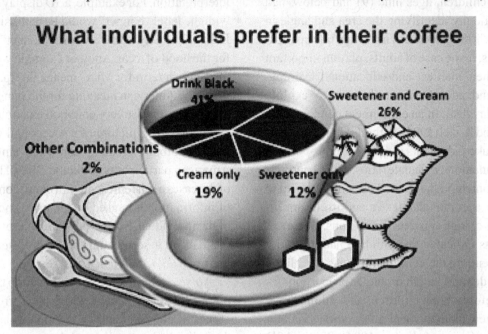

mation through charts and diagrams regularly (Spence & Krizel, 1994). However, a child's perception differs from that of an adult, based on the level of prior experiences and intelligence; as such, children judge chart elements differently than adults. For example, children often fail to make logical connections; their understanding is often more literal and concrete (Piaget, 1952; Spence and Krizel, 1994; Wright, 1970). Based on research it is also true that children below the ages of 10 demonstrate difficulty comprehending the concepts of parts to whole and accurately judging proportions in data (Hart, 1988; Karplus & Karplus, 1972). Even though, these same age groups are exceedingly literate when exposed to pictorial graphics (Goldsmith, 1987). One reason being, children lack skills and experience in dealing with concepts of proportion. Another reason being, many times children in that age group get wrapped up in details found within the scenes and environments of the whole display itself. Young children tend to be misled by irrelevant apparent dimensions when mixed with proportions, scales, weights, and angels (Spence & Krizel, 1994).

This difficulty among children can be associated to Piaget's (1952) *Law of Conservation* during the preoperational stage (ages two, 2, to six, 6, or seven, 7). In this situation, children fail to comprehend the concept of volume.

In contrast, according to Piaget, older children develop abilities to judge, like adults, and have the knowledge to ignore (accommodate) irrelevant information. Older children, in fact, show similar traits as adults, while attending to relevant information (germane load) in the presence of irrelevant information (extraneous load). In a research conducted by Hagen and Hale (1973), it was noted that children age below ten (10) were most of the times able to ignore extraneous information. In this research, it was noted that several children were able to remember more relevant information even with the presence of added distractions in the form of irrelevant information. Thus, researchers conclude that children aged 10 had developed adult abilities of being able to ignore the area and pay more attention to the angle. This age group had little or no difficulty attending to relevant information for pie charts. In contrast, it was noted that younger children, ages nine (9) and below, had more difficulty identifying the area and angle in pie charts in the presence of irrelevant information.

Charts, in the case of adults, play an important role in their intellect and educational learning. Adults and adolescents use charts to explore and display data. In an experiment conducted by Spence and Krizel (1994), both, children and adults had to make judgments in relation to proportion, make estimations, calculate ratios, while interpreting the content in the chart. The adults learned to ignore or accommodate extra and irrelevant dimensions or high apparent dimensions. However, the results indicated that children had difficulty comprehending the concepts of areas or volume (magnitude) and length or angle (proportions).

Therefore, both children and adults have learned new mathematical information via chart education (Spence & Krizel, 1994). Pictorial 3D charts have been outstandingly in presenting designing concrete visuals for teaching visual and spatial concepts (East, 1952); while words are good for presenting abstract ideas and concepts that have already been learned (Hartley, 1994). It is important to remember that children and adults have different needs and prior experiences that limit their comprehension, use, and interpretation of chart data (Piaget, 1952; Spence and Krizel, 1994; Wright, 1970; Hale, 1973). Culture is also a variable that affects chart use and interpretation (Kossly, 1994). Following is a discussion of how culture affects 3D chart reconstruction.

## 3D Chart Reconstruction to Communicate across Cultures

Communicating via 3D charts requires using numbers, words, and symbols. Culturally diverse students decode 3D visuals using familiar learned associations of a particular culture (Kossly, 1994). In different cultural settings words and symbols have cultural connotations. Similarly, individuals' interpretations are impaired by the inconsistencies seen in the 3D object or scene of a display and its interpretation. For example, a 3D display of "hat" with the label "bonnet" would be confusing to an Indian. In many cultures word "bonnet" is used for the hood of a car. Another example would be, the English term for "flat" means the apartment, while the American meaning for the same term is a surface. Another very common example would be, displaying a picture of a soccer ball with the label "football" creating confusion among the American participants (Chikatla, 2010). In either of the cases a misrepresentation or misconception of information is caused by the prior knowledge of the individual. Such type of misinterpretations could result in something known as *noise* according to *Visual Communication Theory.*

*Noise*, as defined by communication theorists (Ormrod, 2008) occurs when the surrounding scenes or environments of the 3D display cause the individual to get distracted or misunderstand, or misinterpret vital information. *Prior Misconceptions,* occur in situations where individuals use unconventional prior knowledge to interpret and elaborate (Ormrod, 2008). In this instance, individuals misrepresent the information communicated with the unconventional prior knowledge causing them to inaccurately interpret information. Consequently, the individual expands or elaborates on a topic being learned by using information they already know or think they know. Through *Elaboration,* (Ormrod, 2008) people perceive information and interpret it in their own way. As a result, individuals have the tendency to learn an extra material than required or even displayed. In communication theory this is once again known as *noise.* Even so, individual often construct *expectations* about things around them, things that are seen or heard (Ormrod, 2008). Often these expectations result from unconventional representation from prior knowledge. This prior knowledge sometimes is a result of *prior misconception.* These *expectations* or *epistemological beliefs* influence individuals while interpreting 3D displays. *Epistemological beliefs* mean understanding individuals' beliefs of their knowledge.

Individual's epistemological beliefs are subject to change over time (Ormrod, 2008). For example, adults believe that knowledge and truth are tentative unlike children who consider knowledge to be absolute truth. Eventually, when these children grow up, they realize that any knowledge is subject to change and any alternative perspective can be equally valid. Individuals subjected to diverse environment have varied epistemological beliefs. As such cultural differences in learners' epistemological beliefs help determine the individual's perceptions/perspective on issues based on their culture beliefs.

## 3D Pie, Bars, and Lines Charts

Several types of charts are available to show representations suitable to a particular situation. The common types of charts are bar, line, and pie. For example, line and bar charts show change over time; pie charts show how segments form a whole of a circle (White, 1984). Any information presented mathematically can also be presented graphically. The main advantage of the graphical form is that it can help in accurate interpretation. Designing graphical representations of charts include using objects, scenes, and environments. According to Garvey (1972), the simple technique in adding 3D to displays is by using actual objects or scenes. Such charts are embedded onto other artistic background that often tends to tell a story. These types of charts are often eye-catching and tend to gain the readers' attention, add meaning and understanding during interpretation. Additionally, such displays are not merely decorations; they are rich in content in terms of detail and relevance (Garvey, 1972; Kosslyn, 1994). While interpreting 3D data, according to Kosslyn (1994), the brain receives sensory signals which allow individuals to interpret data around 3D worlds.

The 3D reconstruction should include object, scenes and environments that can help in the comprehension of chart information. For example, visualize a geometric pie chart with cut out portions

illustrating the number of deaths during the night in the city of New York. Now try embedding this chart on a background of the picture of Statue of Liberty. This type of graphics tends to tell you a story (see Figure 11). Firstly, by looking at the picture of the Statue of Liberty the reader should instantly be able to identify the city as New York. Most people around the world can relate the Statue of Liberty to New York. Secondly, another cue would be the moon behind the statue should tell the reader that the data has something to do with night time. Such charts make communicating statistical learning interesting and challenging. Finally, the last cue would be the moon cut into segments that help interpret the data. In any case, using design principles, in order to enhance learning, a first step to get the learner to pay attention to the data is through visual presentation. In the following section, we will review the characteristics of 3D pie charts, bar charts, and line charts; followed by a discussion on "actual and obvious" 3D charts.

## 3D Pie Charts

*Pie charts* show comparative portions. They include the parts of a whole (Pettersson, 1993). Although, the shape of pie charts varies, the most common shapes are circle or square. Changes in the visual can be made by changing the shades, colors, letterings, and size. The size in a pie does not affect the content because comparisons are made with the angles of each sector, for example, you have the freedom to use varied shapes and forms to depict pies. For instance, a 3D pie (circular) chart can be illustrated by cutting sections of a moon depicting accidents in the night (see Figure 11, 3D Circular Object Depicting Pie Chart) or an octagon shape (see Figure 12, 3D Octagon Object Depicting Pie Chart) or circles such as clock, watch, sun, moon, car or bicycle tire. These charts often emphasize general ideas rather than intricate detail (East, 1952). Interestingly, according to White (1984), 3D pie charts are known to emphasize detail better than the

*Figure 11. 3D circular object and scene depicting pie chart (similar chart found in USA Today, 2007 snapshots)*

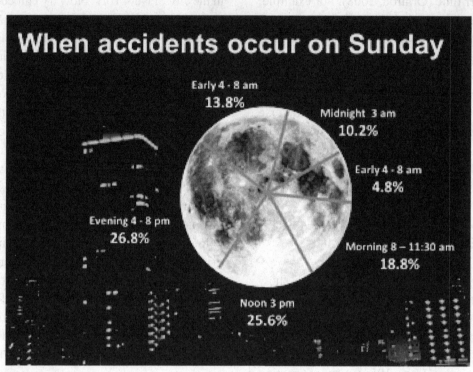

common 2D charts (see Figure 13, 2D Circle Depicting Pie Chart).

## 3D Bar Charts

Commonly, *bar charts* are used for more complex quantitative comparisons. However, when 3D objects or scenes are added they could enhance its clarity (East, 1952). Three-dimensional bar charts are often known as *isotopes*. 3D bar charts contain scenes and environments of columns or rows of 3D objects. There are two forms of bar charts: vertical (see Figures 14 & 15) and horizontal (see Figures 16 & 17). While creating these charts the bars are substituted by objects (see Figures 14 & 16). Unlike the usual rectangles depicting 2D horizontal and vertical bar charts (see Figures 15 & 17), rows of houses, trees, people, pencil, pant, text book, or ketchup bottles are used as decorated backgrounds and objects (see Figures 14 & 16)

depicting 3D horizontal and vertical bar charts (Kosslyn, 1994). For example, using the objects such as a pencil, a text book, and a floppy disk to depict comparisons of items kids need to buys annually is an excellent example of using 3D objects (see Figure 14). According to White (1984) this technique helps in better communicating to the reader. The groupings created by the 3D bars improve visibility and make information clearer. Besides, 3D bar charts if accurately designed can be exceedingly magnificent and can grab individual's attention (Meyers, 1970).

## 3D Line Charts

*Line chart* can precisely show the stages of progressions in situations (East, 1952; White, 1984). The stages in progression can be plotted as a form of a straight line or a smooth curve. Nevertheless, line charts are considered as the most

*Figure 12. 3D octagon object and scene depicting pie chart (similar chart found in USA Today, 2007 snapshots)*

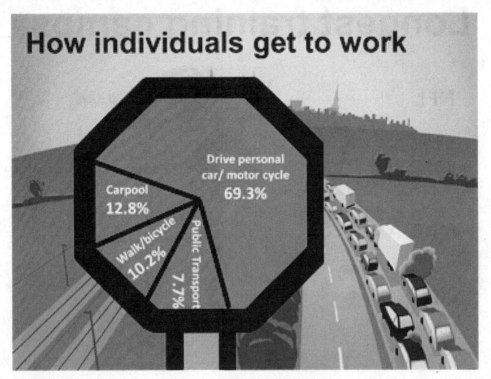

challenging and hardest to interpret. Thus they, should always be clearly drawn and accompany alternative explanations, either oral or written:

i.e., follow the Contiguity Principle. Although, simple 2D line charts are easy to comprehend (see Figure 19), 3D line charts have been known

*Figure 13. 2D circle depicting pie chart*

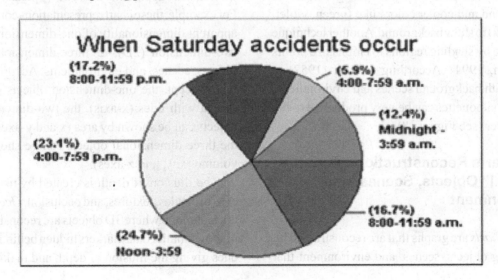

*Figure 14. 3D horizontal objects depicting bar chart*

to be extremely effective, appealing and captivating (see Figure 18). According to White (1984), 3D line charts help improve readers attention. Simple techniques of creating 3D line charts are using dashes, double dashes, solids, dots, colors, objects, and scenes. Kosslyn (1994) suggests using warm colored lines (red, orange) to define foreground and cooler colors like (green, violet, and black) to show background. Another technique would be by shading regions to emphasize points (Kosslyn, 1994). According to East (1952), a graph with background scenes and environments with 3D silhouettes can be very productive to the interpreter (see Figure 18).

## 3D Charts Reconstruction of "Actual" Objects, Scenes, and Environment

*Actual charts* are graphs that are reconstructed by including objects, scenes, and environment that

are actually visible to the naked eye, that is, *height* = x-axis, *width*=y-axis, and *depth*=z-axis. Spence (2004) calls the *actual charts* of objects, scenes, and environments as having *apparent dimensionalities*. In short, apparent charting technique involves showing one-dimensional (1D) representations that are apparently 2D or 3D (Spence, 2004). For example, these chart representations contained apparent dimensionality of one-dimension (1D), two-dimension (2D), or three-dimension (3D) objects, scenes, and environments. According to this concept, the one-dimension objects can be shown with lines (x-axis), the two-dimensional objects can be shown by area (x and y-axes), and the three-dimensional objects can be shown by volume (x, y, and z-axes).

The illusion of depth is created by using 2D cues of shades, textures, and occlusion. *Occlusion* is a technique where 3D objects are reconstructed to show smaller data markers hidden behind larger ones giving the illusion of depth and making the reader feel the object or scene is further away giving a 3D perspective. A 2D chart often shows frequencies, percentages, and proportions in the form of lines, areas of bar, or pie slices. Perceptually these same proportions can be shown using the 3D technique of cylinders, boxes and various objects of volumes. Such perspective reconstructions are apparent 3D charts (Spence, 1990). The most common charts are pie and bar charts. Often these charts do not appear in their traditional form: the pie charts are substituted by a picture of the sun, while bar charts are substituted by soda cans (Spence & Krizel, 1994).

Unfortunately, there is a lack in the use of such displays in today's graphs. Such reconstructions created by added dimensionalities are considered as obstructions to comprehension (Tufte, 1983). Interestingly, this idea was refuted in 1990 by Spence who contradicted based on his concept of *apparent dimensionality* (Spence, 1990), in stating that objects and scenes in charts with extra dimensions aids in reducing the time to better comprehend the chart. Sadly, sometimes, 3D charts fail to illustrate the essential content by including dimensions that do not carry any information, such information is known as *extraneous dimensions or*

*high apparent dimensions* (Spence, 1990). Such *extraneous dimensions* and *elaborations* must be avoided when designing 3D graphs. Fortunately, the time taken to comprehend and process charts with added apparent dimensionality is not effected. The time taken to comprehend 3D graphs with *obvious* objects, scenes and environments is effected.

## 3D Chart Reconstruction of "Obvious" Objects, Scenes, and Environments

*Obvious charts* are graphs that are reconstructed by including objects, scenes and environments that integrates dimensions that shows comparable variance among the categories on the *x*- or the *y-axis* to help make decisions or judgments while interpreting the information provided in the data. Spence (2004) calls the "obvious graphs" as objects, scenes, and environments having *effective dimensionalities*. According to Spence (2004), effective dimensionalities show only one (1) comparable effective dimensionality in the charts and as a result can show singe variance among the categories of the chart. For

*Figure 15. 2D horizontal bar chart*

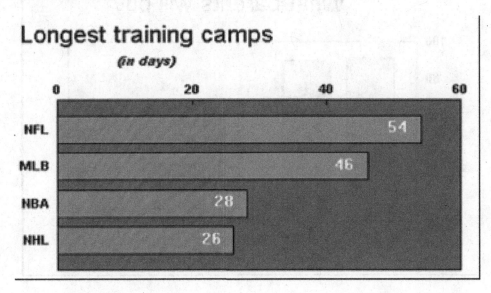

*Figure 16. 3D vertical objects depicting bar chart found in USA Today (2007) snapshots*

example, the single dimension of the *height* is used to depict horizontal or line charts; *length* is used to depict vertical charts; and *angle* is used to depict pie charts.

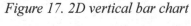

*Figure 17. 2D vertical bar chart*

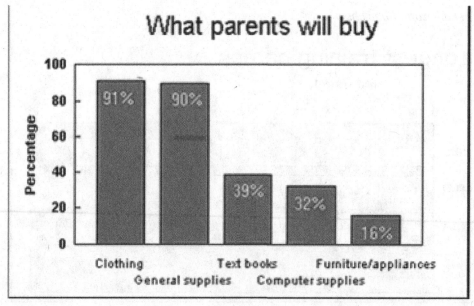

*Figure 19. 2D line chart*

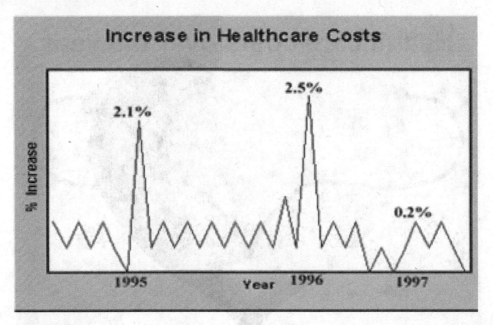

## THEORETICAL AND PRACTICAL VALUES OF 3D OBJECTS, SCENES AND ENVIRONMENTS IN CHARTS

Educational theories provide explanations with practical evidences that result from enhanced teaching and learning processes. Educational processes have undergone changes over the past decade; there has been a mounting challenge to blend the new learned information with learning theories to better meet human needs (Mukhopadhyay & Parhar, 2001). As such, it has become essential to bridge between learning theories and educational practices (Ertmer & Newby, 1993). Growing technological advances have brought about the creation of unimaginable settings in the form of 3D objects, scenes, and environments that were impossible several years ago. For example, flight simulations help train pilots to gain hands-on flight experience. The following is a theoretical perspective applicable to this chapter. This section provides brief theoretical and practical evidences that support the use of 3D objects, scenes, and environments. For example, when designing

3D charts often verbal and visual information is chunked together this is similar to the Principle of *Contiguity* and *Multimedia*.

### Visual Communication Perspective

The *Visual Communication Perspective* (See Figure 20) deals with how visual displays help us make sense of the world around us (Baldwin & Roberts, 2006; Littlejohn, 1999*)*. According to the premise of this theory, there are two approaches to communication. First, is *process theory*: derived from information technology; it views communication as a linear process, where a message is passed from A (sender) to B (receiver). For the purpose of the chapter, the *sender A* of the message is the *3D designer* while the *receiver B* is any *individual (who is using and / or interpreting the visual display)*. Second is *semiotics,* this technique involves the *encoding* of the message that also could often vary from person to person, based on their *prior knowledge*. Visual communication is an on-going process and practiced by individuals on daily basis. Visual communication focuses on

*Figure 18. 3D scene depicting bar chart*

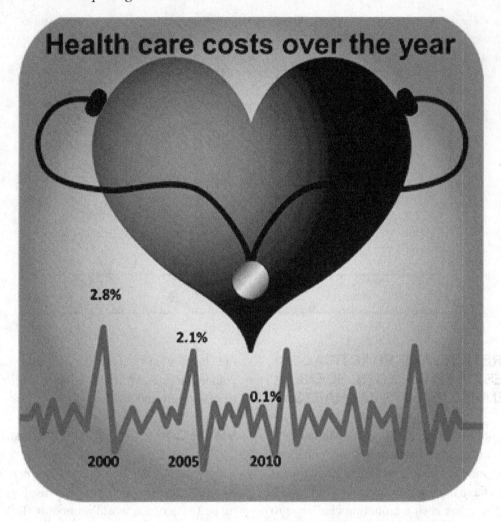

images that help *us* make sense of the world around us. Normally, the process of communication involves sender, receiver, and message (*See* Figure 20). Based on this process we can conclude that the process of visual communication includes the designer (*sender*), audience (*receiver/encoder*), and understanding the design (*message/decoding*).

## Information Process Theory

The receiver is the audience who are required to process the information or message provided to them. *Information Process Theory* (See Figure 20) deals with how individuals process information

that is provided to them in their brain (Atkinson & Shiffrin, 1968). Information is processed in three stages the *Sensory* stage, the *Short-Term Memory* stage, and the *Long-Term Memory* stage. Information being processed from the *Sensory* stage into the *Short-Term Memory* and eventually into the *Long-Term Memory* is subject to the *Multimedia, Contiguity, and Modality Principle*. The *Multimedia Principle* encourages the use of picture instead of only words. The *Contiguity Principle* encourages chunking together the picture and the corresponding text explanations for better process in the short-term memory. While the *Modality Principle* encourages the use of both the senses,

*Figure 20. Amalgamation of theoretical underpinnings for this chapter by Dr. Suhana Chikatla © 2010*

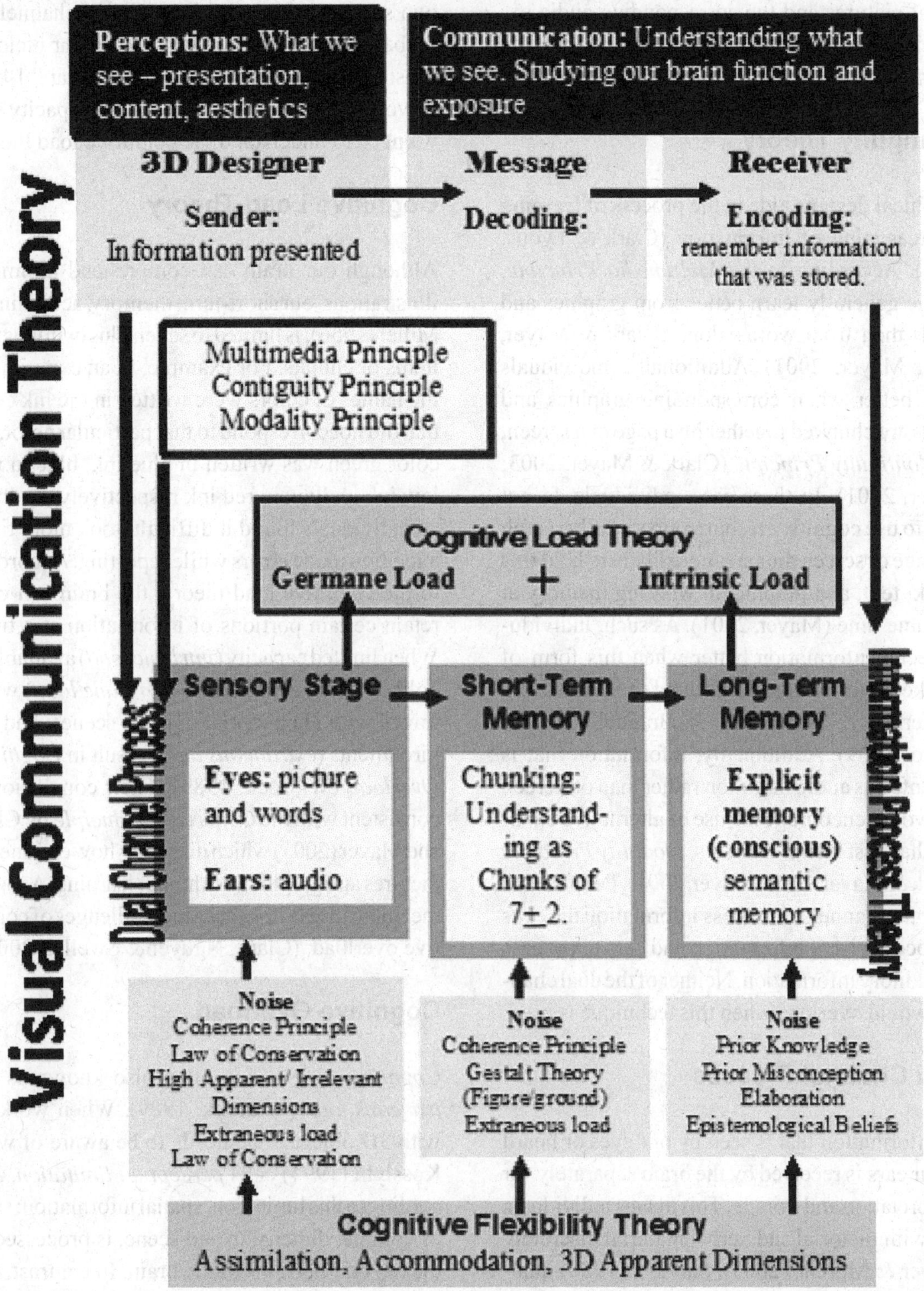

the eyes and the ears; as such, it encourages the use of pictures and the corresponding audio explaining the picture to help process information (Clark & Mayer, 2003; Mayer, 2001).

## Contiguity Theory

Graphical designs aide in the process of learning and reasoning of information (Clark & Lyons, 2004). According to the *Multimedia Principle*, people generally learn better from graphics and words than from words alone (Clark & Mayer, 2003; Mayer, 2001). Additionally, individuals learn better when corresponding graphics and words are chunked together on a page or a screen, the *Contiguity Principle* (Clark & Mayer, 2003; Mayer, 2001). In these case individuals do not have to use cognitive resources to visually search the page or screen thus are more likely to hold this chunk, text, and graphic, in working memory at the same time (Mayer, 2001). As such, individuals recall information better when this form of chunked information is presented simultaneously (Anderson & Bower, 1973; Braddeley, 1986; Paivio, 1969). Additionally, information that is presented as audio narration rather than on screen text would encourage the use of alternative channels than just visual channels, *Modality Principle* (Clark & Mayer, 2003; Mayer, 2001). People have separate channels to process information the eyes to process visual information and ears to process the auditory information. Neither of the dual channels would overload when this technique is used.

## Dual Channel Process

All information that is seen by our eyes or heard by our ears is received by the brain separately for interpretation and storage. This means individuals deal with pictorial and verbal material discretely (Mayer & Moreno, 2003). Paivio's (1986) dual-coding theory has been adapted by many theorists (Graesser, Mills, & Zwaan, 1997; Mayer & Moreno, 2003) to expound the dual-channel process.

According to this theory, our brain consists of two separate channels: the auditory channel for verbal input and the visual channel for pictorial illustration (Graesser, Mills, & Zwaan, 1997). Nevertheless, our brain is limited in capacity thus we need to understand the cognitive load theory.

## Cognitive Load Theory

Although our brain can comprehend unlimited illustrations, our short-term memory, according to Miller (1956), is limited to seven plus or minus two items or chunks. For example, in an experiment, the names of colors were written in the ink color that did not correspond to that particular color, the color green was written in blue ink, blue in yellow ink, yellow in red ink respectively. In doing so individuals found it difficult, took more time, and often made errors while reporting. According to the cognitive load theory, the brain can only retain certain portions of information at a time. When limited capacity (*intrinsic load*) available to hold essential information (*germane load*) when mixed with 3D pictorial objects, scenes, and environments (*extraneous load*) result in *Cognitive Overload* (Wittrock, 1989). Their conclusion is consistent with the *Coherence Principle* by Clark and Mayer (2003) which discusses how extraneous pictures and graphics can hinder learning. As such, meaningful learning faces the challenges of cognitive overload. (Clark, Nguyen & Sweller, 2006).

## Cognitive Overload

*Cognitive overload* is often also known as *extraneous load* (Wittrock, 1989). When working with 3D objects, one needs to be aware of what Kosslyln (1994) calls *perceptual limitation*. According to this limitation, spatial information; such as volume, dimension and scene, is processed in the top rear portions of the brain. In contrast, object properties; such as shape, color and texture, are processed in the temple region of the brain. Nevertheless, the two sequence of information is combined eventually. Although, many times individuals tend to give up trying to simultaneously attention and understand the numerical scale, they ultimately learn to assimilate and accommodate. Until this process takes place individuals experience cognitive overload. Interestingly our brain is flexible enough to make accommodations for such extraneous load.

## Cognitive Flexibility Theory

Our mind is flexible to comprehend any form of information and hold unlimited amount of information. According to Spiro, Coulson, Feltovich, & Anderson (1988) our brain has the ability to reconstruct knowledge by adapting to changing demands in situations. Jean Piaget's research on the development of thinking has greatly impacted the theory of cognitive development (Boeree, 2006). Piaget suggests that, children adapt to situations through the process of *assimilation and accommodation*. As a result, individuals are able to assimilate (*interpret*) the visual content in the presence of high aplparent or extraneous dimensions (decorated information) and accommodate (*ignore, modify*) 3D visuals in the presence of high apparent or extraneous dimensions in the form of 3D objects, scenes, and environments (Spence, 2004).

## SOLUTIONS AND RECOMMENDATIONS FOR THE CHAPTER

In the past, 3D models were primarily used in robotics and computer vision applications (Azevedo, Manuel, & Vaz, 2007). The models of such applications required salient geometric features so that the objects would be recognized. Today, the interest in 3D models for applications focuses more on visualization by humans; using available computer technology, thus making it applicable to a greater variety of fields (Haque, 2002; Pegg,

2010). The demand for constructing 3D models has been steadily growing due to its wide-ranging applications. It is anticipated that academic and technological dialogue will continue beyond this brief chapter presentation. Key to the design of any learning tool (Azevedo et al., 2007; Pegg, 2010; Vella, 2008) is the need for learning needs and resources assessment to find out who the learners are and what end the information is to be used towards. As learners design and develop 3D surfaces and environments, it is important for practice to inform theory (Lecrivain & Slauti, 2008; Pegg, 2010; Vella, 2008); that theory to be directly applicable for users; and that practitioners continue to document and share their findings with others.

## FUTURE RESEARCH DIRECTIONS

The authors of this chapter presented an integrated, multi-disciplinary approach to 3D surface reconstruction; blending the fields of technology, graphic design, education/instructional design, and communication. By way of summary, three recommendations that may entail future research areas are the need to:

1. Incorporate (sound) principles of instructional design (Azevedo et. al, 2007; Vella, 2008) to 3D surface reconstruction (Pegg, 2010; Verbree & Oosterom, 2010); vis-à-vis quality, time, and accuracy (Koch & Frahm, 2001; Pegg, 2010). For example, applying the *Multimedia, Contiguity*, and *Modality principle* while designing a 3D object.
2. Establish further how findings from other fields, such as 3D modeling, reverse engineering (Lecrivain & Slauti, 2008) and cartography (Pegg, 2010), can be adapted to inform the design of 3D reconstructed surfaces and environments (Koch & Frahm, 2001).
3. Analyze the effectiveness of software and available technology in online labs and

learning environments for the self-directed, autonomous learner (Haque, 2002; Lecrivain & Slauti, 2008). Develop tutorials and modules that include animation and visualization techniques. This enhances critical thinking, peer evaluation and interaction, and promotes self-directed, experiential learning for learners who are in an online or hybrid course.

4.  Explore the significance of the design, development, and implementation of 3D animations or 4D objects, scenes, and environments in pedagogical settings.

## CONCLUSION

Technological advancements within the last decade mean that things which were considered impossible have been made possible. Indeed, we are now only a couple of clicks away from creating real world settings to enhance our teaching and learning processes. What does this mean for education? For those struggling to learn numerical concepts (Trentacosta & Kennedy, 1997), it may mean using pictures, videos, games, and simulations to stimulate individual interests. For those who are teaching and researching, it may mean developing 3D models and charts to communicate data for problem solving and decision making (Meyers, 1970). Consistent with research findings (Chikatla, 2010; Dempsey, Chikatla, & Inpornvijit, 2008), visual displays have become widely accepted theoretically. The *Multimedia Principle* states that people learn better from graphics and words than from words alone (Clark & Mayer, 2003; Mayer, 2001). Indeed, the Visual Communication Theory provides a relevant framework from which educators can design and develop a tool to aid learners who need visually representative data via charts, graphs, and pictures to enhance learning.

## REFERENCES

Atkinson, R. C., & Shiffrin, R. M. (1968). Human memory: A proposed system and its control processes. In Spence, K. W., & Spence, J. T. (Eds.), *The psychology of learning and motivation* (*Vol. 2*, pp. 89–195). New York, N Y: Academic Press.

Azevedo, T. C. S., Tavares, J. M. R. S., & Vaz, M. A. P. (2007*). 3D object reconstruction from uncalibrated images using a single off-the-shelf camera*. Retrieved July 28, 2011, from http://repositorioaberto.up.pt/bitstream/10216/4175/2/3D%20 Object%20Reconstruction%20from%20 Uncalibrated%20Images%20using%20a%20Single.pdf

Baldwin, J., & Roberts, L. (2006). *Visual communication: From theory to practice*. Switzerland: AVA Publishing.

Boeree, C. G. (2006). *Personality theories: Jean Piaget*. Retrieved on October 7, 2008, from http://webspace.ship.edu/cgboer/piaget.html

Brownstein, S. C., Weiner, M., & Green, S. W. (1999). *Barron's how to prepare for the GRE*. New Delhi, India: Galgotia Publications.

Chikatla, S. B. P. (2010). *Cross-cultural differences among students from India and the United States on preference, use and other cultural factors involving embodied apparent 2D and embellished apparent 3D USA Today Charts*. Unpublished doctoral dissertation, University of South Alabama.

Clark, R., & Lyons, C. (2004). *Graphics for learning*. San Francisco, CA: Pfeiffer.

Clark, R., & Mayer, R. E. (2003). *e-Learning and the science of instruction*. San Francisco, CA: Pfeiffer.

Dempsey, J. V., Chikatla, S., & Inpornvijit, K. (2008, March). *2D (simple charts) versus 3D (embellished) USA Today charts*. Poster session presented at the USA Research Council's 15th Annual Research Forum, Mobile, AL.

Goldsmith, E. (1987). The analysis of illustration in theory and practice. In Houghton, H. A., & Willows, D. M. (Eds.), *The psychology of illustration* (*Vol. 2*, pp. 53–85). New York, NY: Springer-Verlag. doi:10.1007/978-1-4612-4706-7_2

Haque, M. E. (2002, March). *Contemporary techniques to teach reinforced concrete design.* Session paper presented at the Gulf-Southwest Annual Meeting of American Society for Engineering Education (ASEE), University of Louisiana, Lafayette, USA.

Hegarty, M., Narayanan, N. H., & Freitas, P. (2002). Understanding machines from multimedia and hypermedia presentation. In Otero, J., Leon, J. A., & Graesser, A. C. (Eds.), *The psychology of science text comprehension* (pp. 357–384). Hillsdale, NJ: Erlbaum.

Koch, R., & Frahm, J. (2001). *Visual-geometric 3-D scene reconstruction from uncalibrated image sequences.* Tutorial at DAGM 2001, München Multimedia Information Processing Group: Christian-Albrechts-University of Kiel Germany. Retrieved July 28, 2010, from http://www.mip.informatik.uni-kiel.de

Kosslyn, S. M. (1994). *Elements of graph design.* New York, NY: Freeman and Company.

Lecrivain, G. M., Kennedy, I., & Slaouti, A. (2008). *Hybrid surface reconstruction technique for automotive applications.* IAENG. Retrieved August 1, 2010, from (http://www.engineering-letters.com/issues_v16/issue_1/EL_16_1_16.pdf

Macdonald-Ross, M. (1977). How numbers are shown: A review of research on the presentation of quantitative data in texts. *Audio-Visual Communication Review, 25*, 359–407.

Mayer, R. E. (2001). *Multimedia learning.* New York, NY: Cambridge University.

Mayer, R. E., & Moreno, R. (2003). Nine ways to reduce cognitive load in multimedia learning. *Educational Psychologist, 38*(1), 43–52. doi:10.1207/S15326985EP3801_6

Meyers, C. H. (1970). *Handbook of basic graphs: A modern approach.* Belmont, CA: Dickenson Publishing.

Michas, I. C., & Berry, D. C. (2000). Learning a procedural task: Effectiveness of multimedia presentations. *Applied Cognitive Psychology, 14*, 555–575. doi:10.1002/1099-0720(200011/12)14:6<555::AID-ACP677>3.0.CO;2-4

Mukhopadhyay, M., & Parhar, M. (2001). Instructional design in multi-channel learning system. *British Journal of Educational Technology, 32*(5), 545–559. doi:10.1111/1467-8535.00224

Ormrod, J. E. (2008). *Human learning* (5th ed.). Upper Saddle River, NJ: Prentice Hall.

Pegg, D. (2010*). Design issues with 3D maps and the need for 3D cartographic design principles.* Retrieved August 1, 2010, from http://lazarus.elte.hu/cet/academic/pegg.pdf

Pettersson, R. (1993). *Visual information* (2nd ed.). New Jersey: Educational Technology Publications.

Spence, I. (1990). Visual psychophysics of simple graphical elements. *Journal of Experimental Psychology, 16*(4), 683–692.

Spence, I. (2004). The apparent and effective dimensionality of representations of objects (displays and controls). *Human Factors, 46*(4), 738–748. doi:10.1518/hfes.46.4.738.56809

Spence, I., & Krizel, P. (1994). Children's perception of proportion in graphs. *Child Development, 65*, 1193–1213. doi:10.2307/1131314

Spiro, R. J., Coulson, R. L., Feltovich, P. J., & Anderson, D. (1988). Cognitive flexibility theory: Advanced knowledge acquisition in ill-structured domains. In V. Patel (Ed.), *Proceedings of the 10th Annual Conference of the Cognitive Science Society*. Hillsdale, NJ: Erlbaum.

Trentacosta, J., & Kennedy, M. J. (Eds.). (1997). *Multicultural and gender equity in the mathematics classroom, the gift of diversity*. Reston, VA: National Council of Teachers of Mathematics.

Tufte, E. R. (1983). *The visual display of quantitative information*. Cheshire, CT: Graphics Press.

USA Today. (2007). USA Today snapshot. *USA Today*. Retrieved July 2, 2008, from http://www.usatoday.com/news/snapshot.htm

Vella, J. (2008). *On teaching and learning: Putting the principles and practices of dialogue education into action*. San Francisco, CA: Jossey-Bass.

Verbee, E., & vanOosterom, P. J. (2010). *The Stin method: 3D-surface reconstruction by observation lines and Delaunay Tens*. Delft University of Technology, section GIS-technology. Retrieved August 1, 2010, from http://citeseerx.ist.psu.edu/viewdoc/download?doi=10.1.1.155.2671&rep=rep1&type=pdf

Wagner, K. V. (2008). *Gestalt laws of perceptual organization: Law of Pragnanz*. Retrieved September 28, 2008, from http://psychology.about.com/od/ sensationandperception/ss/gestaltlaws_3.htm

White, J. V. (1984). *Using charts and graphs: 1000 ideas for visual persuasion*. New York, NY: Bowker.

Wittrock, M. C. (1989). Generative processes of comprehension. *Educational Psychology*, *24*, 345–376. doi:10.1207/s15326985ep2404_2

Wright, A. (1970). *Designing visual aid*. New York, NY: Van Nostrand Reinhold.

## ADDITIONAL READING

Bell, A., & Janvier, C. (1981). The interpretation of graphs representing situation. *For the Learning of Mathematics*, *2*(1), 34–42.

Chuang, T., Chen, C., Chang, H., Lee, H., Chou, C., & Doong, J. (2003). Virtual reality serves as a support technology in cardiopulmonary exercise testing. *Teleoperators and Virtual Environments*, *12*(3), 326–331. doi:10.1162/105474603765879567

Cleveland, W. S., & McGill, R. (1987). Graphical perception: The visual decoding of quantitative information on graphical displays of data. *Journal of the Royal Statistical Society A*, *150*(3), 192–229. doi:10.2307/2981473

Cruz, I. F., & Twarog, J. P. (1996). 3D graph drawing with simulated annealing. *Lecture Notes in Computer Science*, *1027*, 162–165. doi:10.1007/BFb0021800

Dwyer, F. M. (1978). *Strategies for improving visual learning. State College*. PA: Learning Services.

Fisher, S. H., Dempsey, J. V., & Marousky, R. T. (1997). Data visualization: Preference and use of two-dimensional and three-dimensional graphs. *Social Science Computer Review*, *15*(3), 256–263. doi:10.1177/089443939701500303

Fontana, F., Moscarini, M., & D'Arcangelo, D. (2006). Virtual environments, objects, and video-communication for e-learning: Virtual world 3D. In E. Pearson & P. Bohman (Eds.), *Proceedings of World Conference on Educational Multimedia, Hypermedia and Telecommunications* (pp. 2699-2705). Chesapeake, VA: AACE.

Kishk, S., & Javidi, B. (2003). Improved resolution 3D object sensing and recognition using time multiplexed computational integral imaging. *Optics Express*, *11*(26), 3528–2541. doi:10.1364/OE.11.003528

Komatitsch, D., & Vilotte, J. (1998). The spectral element method: An efficient tool to simulate the seismic response of 2D and 3D geological structures. *Bulletin of the Seismological Society of America*, *88*(2), 368–392.

Munzner, T. (2002). Exploring large graphs in 3D hyperbolic space. *Computer Graphics and Applications*, *18*(4), 18–23. doi:10.1109/38.689657

Pach, J. (2004). Geometric graph theory. In Goodman, J. E., & O'Rourke, J. (Eds.), *Handbook of discrete and computational geometry* (2nd ed., pp. 219–238). Boca Raton, FL: Chapman & Hall/CRC. doi:10.1201/9781420035315.ch10

Shepard, R. N., & Cooper, L. A. (1982). *Mental images and their transformations*. Cambridge, MA: MIT Press.

Slater, M., & Steed, A. (2003). Computer graphics and virtual environments: From realism to real-time. *Teleoperators and Virtual Environments*, *12*(2), 229–230. doi:10.1162/105474603321640978

Tractinsky, N., & Meyer, J. (1999). Chartjunk or goldgraph? Effects of presentation of objecties and content desirability on information presentation. *Management Information Systems Quarterly*, *23*(3), 397–420. doi:10.2307/249469

Wainer, H. (2005). *Graphic discovery*. Princeton, NJ: Princeton University.

White, J. V. (1984). *Using charts and graphs: 1000 ideas for visual persuasion*. New York, NY: Bowker.

## KEY TERMS AND DEFINITIONS

**3D 'Affective' Dimension/ality:** Also known as *Obvious chart*. (See *Charts*)

**3D 'Apparent' Dimension/ality:** Also known as *Actual chart*. (See *Charts*)

**4D Objects, Scenes, Environments:** A 4D object, scene, and environment shows four factors the a, b, c, and d- axis: where 'a=height,' 'b=width,' and 'c=depth,' and 'd=time.' Thus, d basically shows the changes in a, b, and c factors over time.

**Assimilation and Accommodation:** Based on Jean Piaget's research and theories of cognitive development. Through this process, individuals assimilate (interpret) and accommodate (ignore, modify) 3D visuals in the presence of high apparent or extraneous dimensions in the form of objects, scenes, and environments.

**Bar Charts:** These are used for more complex quantitative comparisons. 3D bar charts, also known as isotopes, contain scenes and environments of columns or rows of 3D objects. Bars are substituted by images.

**Charts:** These are numerical data represented using line, column, bar, or pie formats. *Actual charts* –refers to the number of dimensions that the chart appears to have. Also known as charts with apparent dimensionality (Spence, 2004). *Obvious charts* – refers to the number of dimensions that the chart appears to have. Also, known as charts with effective dimensionality (Spence, 2004).

**Cognitive Flexibility Theory:** The idea that our brain is flexible enough to overcome noise. *Noise* – Interferes with visual, aural and other forms of data transfer. (See *Cognitive Load Theory; Visual Communication Theory, Figure* 9)

**Cognitive Load Theory:** Although our brain can comprehend unlimited illustrations, our short-term memory, is limited to seven plus or minus two items or chunks. (See Figure 9)

**Expectations:** Individuals often construct explanations / perspectives about things around them that are seen or heard; often resulting from unconventional representation from prior knowledge and epistemological beliefs. These can positively or negatively influence the interpretation of 3D displays and objects.

**Coherence Principle:** A concept that adding extraneous audio or visual can hinder learning and comprehension.

**Communication Theory or Principles:** These are concepts derived from communication theory that help to explain factors that enhance or limit one's perceptions and ability to decode visual data. Elaboration: One's ability to take perceived data and interpret it meaningfully. *Noise* - occurs when the surrounding scenes or environments of the 3D display cause the individual to get distracted, misunderstand, or misinterpret vital information. Sometimes results in learning extra material that was not intended to be sent.

**Contiguity Principle:** A concept that encourages placing corresponding words and graphs near each other.

**Contiguity Theory:** View that says individuals learn information better when both visual and verbal information are chunked together.

**Dual Channel Process:** All processed information is received by the brain separately for interpretation and storage, i.e., individuals deal with pictorial and verbal material discretely. Similar to Paivio's (1986) *dual-coding theory*.

**Epistemological Beliefs:** Beliefs relating to knowledge and information about the ways in which we know, and absolute truth. In this chapter, one's culture shapes these beliefs and affects our interpretations of data and information. (See *Expectations*)

**Horizontal/Vertical Charts:** A chart which displays data in the form of bars either vertically or horizontally with the length of the bars relating directly to their value (Market Intelligence Group, 2007).

**Line Chart:** Gives a visual representation of precise stages of progression in situations. The plotting can be done in the form of a straight line or a smooth curve.

**Modality Principle:** A concept which replaces onscreen text with audio narration for better comprehension.

**Multimedia Principle:** A concept that people learn better from graphics and words than from words alone.

**Noise:** See *Communication Theory or Principle*.

**Perceptual Limitation Theory:** Spatial information, such as volume, dimension and scene, are processed in different portions of the brain from Object properties, such as shape, color and texture. Because we cannot simultaneously attend to information, we learn to assimilate and accommodate. (See assimilation and accommodation).

**Pictorial Charts:** These type of graphs help attract attention. It is not an accurate method to help predict data and could also get difficult while making comparisons other than the broadest ones (Wright, 1970).

**Pie Charts:** These are visual/graphic representations that help convey fractions or percentages, which appear on sized slices. They can be shaped in circles or even squares. Pie charts show comparative portions; they include the parts of a whole.

**Prior Misconceptions:** Occur in situations where individuals use unconventional prior knowledge to interpret and elaborate, also referred to as *Expectations (*See *Expectations)*.

**Three-Dimensional (3D) Charts:** A 3D chart shows relationships among three factors the x, y, and z- axis (Wright, 1970). A 3D chart shows apparent dimensionality of three (height, width, and depth) factors with only one effective dimensionality.

**Two-Dimensional (2D) Charts:** 2D charts are referred to as simple charts or traditional charts. A 2D chart show apparent dimensionality of two (height, width) factors with only one effective dimensionality.

**Visual Communication Perspective:** Concept that explains how visual displays help us make sense of the world around us.

**Visual Communication Theory:** Thus the brain only retains certain portions of information at a time. When limited capacity (intrinsic load) available to hold essential information (germane load) when mixed with 3D pictorial objects, scenes, and environments (extraneous load) results in *Cognitive overload* (See *Cognitive overload*).

# Chapter 7
# Depth Estimation for HDR Images

**S. Manikandan**
*Electronics and Radar Development Establishment, Defense Research and Development Organization, India*

## ABSTRACT

*In this chapter, depth estimation for stereo pair of High Dynamic Range (HDR) images is proposed. The proposed algorithm consists of two major techniques namely conversion of HDR images to Low Dynamic Range (LDR) images or Standard Dynamic Range (SDR) images and estimating the depth from the converted LDR / SDR stereo images. Local based tone mapping technique is used for the conversion of the HDR images to SDR images. And the depth estimation is done based on the corner features of the stereo pair images and block matching algorithm. Computationally much less expensive cost functions Mean Square Error (MSE) or Mean Absolute Difference (MAD) can be used for block matching algorithms. The proposed algorithm is explained with illustrations and results.*

## INTRODUCTION

We normally see the world in three dimensions. This is because each eye looks a slightly different view of a scene and the brain converts the information into a 3D image. Stereo pair images contain depth information due to the parallax inherent in the images. Thus it is possible to extract depth information from this stereo image pair. But in image processing, computer graphics and in photography, High Dynamic Range Imaging

(HDRI) is a set of techniques that allows a greater dynamic range of luminance between lightest and darkest areas of an image than standard digital imaging techniques or photographic methods. This wider dynamic range allows HDR images to more accurately represent the wide range of intensity levels found in real scenes, ranging from direct sunlight to faint starlight. The two main sources of HDR imagery are computer renderings and merging of multiple photographs, which in turn are known as Low Dynamic Range (LDR) /

DOI: 10.4018/978-1-4666-0113-0.ch007

Standard Dynamic Range (SDR)) photographs. Tone mapping techniques, which reduce overall contrast to facilitate display of HDR images on devices with lower dynamic range, can be applied to produce images with preserved or exaggerated local contrast for artistic effect.

The natural world presents our visual system with a wide range of colors and intensities. A starlit night has an average luminance level of around $10^{-3}$ candelas/m$^2$, and daylight scenes are close to $10^5$ cd/m$^2$.

Humans can see detail in regions that vary by $1:10^4$ at any given adaptation level, over which the eye gets swamped by stray light (i.e., disability glare) and details are lost. Modern camera lenses, even with their clean-room construction and coated optics, cannot rival human vision when it comes to low flare and absence of multiple paths ("sun dogs") in harsh lighting environments. Even if they could, conventional negative film cannot capture much more range than this, and most digital image formats do not even come close. With the possible exception of cinema, there has been little push for achieving greater dynamic range in the image capture stage, because common displays and viewing environments limit the range of what can be presented to about two orders of magnitude between minimum and maximum luminance. A well-designed CRT monitor may do slightly better than this in a darkened room, but the maximum display luminance is only around 100 cd/m$^2$, which does not begin to approach daylight levels. A high-quality xenon film projector may get a few times brighter than this, but they are still two orders of magnitude away from the optimal light level for human acuity and color perception.

The human eye has two different types of photoreceptors. Cones are responsible for sharp chromatic vision in luminous conditions, or the photopic range. Rods provide less precise vision but are extremely sensitive to light and allow us to see in dark conditions, or the scotopic range. Both rods and cones are active in moderately luminous conditions, known as the mesopic range.

Light adaptation, or simply adaptation, is the (fast) recovery of visual sensitivity after an increase or a small decrease in light intensity. Otherwise, the limited range of neurons results in response compression for (relatively) high luminances. This is why everything appears white during the dazzling observed when leaving a tunnel. To cope with this and to always make the best use of the small dynamic range of neurons (typically 1 to 40, sensitivity is controlled through multiplicative (gaincontrol) and subtractive mechanisms. It is reasonable for the steady state, however since subtractive and multiplicative mechanisms have different time-constants and different effects, they should be differentiated for a more accurate simulation of adaptation. Dark adaptation is the (slow) recovery of sensitivity after a dramatic reduction in light. It can take up to tens of minutes. The classic example of this is the adaptation one experiences on a sunny day upon entering a theater for a matinee. Initially, everything inside appears too dark, and visual acuity is, at best, poor.

Note that all of these mechanisms are local, i.e. they occur independently for single receptors or for small "pools" of receptors. This is motivated by efficiency considerations, but also because considering local adaptation states is extremely challenging. The interaction between local adaptation and eye-gaze movements is very complex and is left as a subject of future research. However, choosing a single adaptation level (or "average" light intensity) is not trivial.

Chromatic adaptation allows us to perceive objects as having a constant color, even if they are observed under illuminants with varying hues. This type of adaptation involves mechanisms in the retina as well as higher level mechanisms. It can be reasonably modeled as a different gain-control for each cone type, which is called Von Kries adaptation. Chromatic adaptation can be complete or partial and takes approximately one minute to completely occur. One of the fascinating aspects of this type of adaptation is that it is not driven by the average color of the stimulus, but by the color of the illuminant: our visual system is somehow able to distinguish the color of the illuminant and discount it, similar to the function of the white balance feature of camcoders.

Tone-mapping algorithms rely on observer models that mathematically transform scene luminances into all the visual sensations experienced by a human observer viewing the scene, estimating the brain's own visual assessments. A Tone Mapping Operator (TMO) tries to match the outputs of one observer model applied to the scene to the outputs of another observer model applied to the desired display image. Tumblin and Rushmeier were the first to bring the issue of tone mapping to the computer graphics community. They offered a general framework for tone reproduction operators by concatenating a scene observer model with an inverse display observer model, and when properly constructed such operators should guarantee the displayed image is veridical: it causes the display to exactly recreate the visual appearance of the original scene, showing no more and no less visual content than would be discernible if actually present to see the original scene.

Unfortunately, visual appearance is still quite mysterious, especially for high contrast scenes, making precise and verifiable tone reproduction operators difficult to construct and evaluate. Appearance, the ensemble of visual sensations evoked by a viewed image or scene, is not a simple one-to-one mapping from scene radiance to perceived radiance, but instead is the result of a complex combination of sensations and judgments, a set of well-formed mental estimates of scene illumination, reflectance, shapes, objects and positions, material properties, and textures. Though all these quantities are directly measurable in the original scene, the mental estimates that make up visual appearance are not.

The most troublesome task of any basic tone reproduction operator is detail-preserving contrast. The Human Visual System (HVS) copes with large dynamic ranges through a process known as visual adaptation. Local adaptation, the ensemble of local sensitivity-adjusting mechanisms in the human visual system, reveals visible details almost everywhere in a viewed scene, even when embedded in scenes of very high contrast. Although most sensations that humans perceive from scene contents, such as reflectance, shape, colour and movement can be directly evoked by the display outputs, large contrasts cannot. As shown in Figure 4, high contrasts must be drastically reduced for display, yet somehow must retain a high contrast appearance and at the same time keep visible in the displayed image all the low contrast details and textures revealed by local adaptation processes.

There are different reasons that make the tone mapping problem not always easy to solve. The most obvious reason is that, as mentioned above the contrast ratio that can be produced by a standard CRT monitor is only about 100:1 which is much smaller than what can exist in the real world. Newspaper photographs achieve a maximum contrast of about 30:1; the best photographic prints can provide contrasts as high as 1000:1. In comparison, scenes that include visible light sources, deep shadows, and highlights can reach contrasts of 100000:1. Another reason that makes tone mapping operators fail in some cases is that the simplest ways to adjust scene intensities for display will usually reduce or destroy important details and textures.

One LDR /SDR image or view of a scene does not contain any information about the depth of various points in the scene. Thus, only with two or more images of a scene, we can extract the depth information. In the stereo image pair the depth information is found in the form of disparity or displacement between projections of same scene point in different images. From this disparity value we can determine the depth. The stereo image pair can be acquired using two cameras displaced from each other by a known distance or using a single moving camera. But the scene must be a static (or still) one.

Stereo vision plays an important role in machine vision applications and robotics. The reasons to go for stereoscopy rather than RADAR and other techniques are as follows:

1.  It is a reliable and effective way to extract range information from the environment (Real time Implementation on low-cost hardware).
2.  It is a passive sensor (no interfaces with other sensoring devices).
3.  It can be easily integrated with other vision routines (object recognition, tracking).

## STEPS INVOLVED IN GAUGING THE DEPTH FROM STEREO IMAGE PAIR

-   Image acquisition and HDR image Processing
-   Image Rectification
-   Stereo matching
-   Disparity map computation
-   Figure 1 shows the block diagram of the proposed Depth estimation algorithm for HDR images.

## Image Acquisition and HDR Image Processing

The image pair can be acquired using two cameras displaced at a known distance or using a single camera which is in motion. Here consider only static or still scenes and only then it is easier to correlate the two images to find the correspondence. If two cameras are used then the relative positions of those cameras must be known. Stereo image pair can be captured using general stereo configuration or canonical configuration.

Computer modelling of the real world appearance involves reproducing high dynamic range (HDR) luminance values in resulting images. Traditionally, such HDR images have been the domain of physics-based global illumination computation, which is very costly. Recent progress towards improving the realism of images that was achieved through the use of captured HDR environment maps and precomputed radiance transfer (PRT) techniques enables to generate HDR image sequences in real time. Furthermore, HDR video of real world scenes can easily be captured using multi-exposure techniques or advanced video sensors and compressed for an efficient storage and later playback. However, contrast in such rendered image sequences and HDR video streams often exceeds capabilities of typical displays and their direct rendering to the screen is not possible. Fortunately, the importance of tone mapping of HDR data is widely understood and many algorithms have already been developed with several implementations achieving real-time performance which is required especially in real-time rendering systems and for HDR video playback. Current real-time approaches to tone mapping are however far from perfect because the perceptual effects typical in everyday observation are generally neglected. The fact that a daylight scene appears very bright and colorful, but during the night everything looks dark and greyish, is obvious for an average observer. Although the lack of sharp vision and color perception in night scenes have already been accounted for in tone mapping, these effects were applied to the whole image with a uniform intensity (globally). This could lead to unrealistic exaggerations if a wide range of luminance was shown in an image. Very appealing results are obtained using the so-called local tone mapping operators, which are very good at preserving fine details in a scene. However, in dimly illuminated scenes such fine details would not be perceivable, because the acuity of human vision is degraded. Therefore, so well reserved details give an unrealistic impression in such cases. On the other hand, certain perceptual effects, like glare, cannot be evoked because the maximum luminance of typical displays is not high enough. However, we are so used to the presence of such a phenomena, that adding glare to an image can increase subjective brightness of the tone mapped image. Clearly, it appears crucial to properly predict and simulate these perceptual effects during the tone mapping process in order to convey a realistic impression of HDR data over a wide range of luminance, when such data are displayed on typical display devices.

The source luminance values Y are first mapped to the relative luminance $Y_r$:

$$Y_r = \alpha \cdot Y / \overline{Y} \quad (1).$$

where $\overline{Y}$ is the logarithmic average of the luminance in the scene, which is an approximation of the adapting luminance, and $\alpha$ is the key value. The relative luminance values are then mapped to the displayable pixel intensities L using the following function:

$$L = Y_r / 1 + Y_r \quad (2).$$

The above formula maps all luminance values to the [0:1] range in such way that the relative luminance $Y_r = 1$ is mapped to the pixel intensity

L=0.5. This property is used to map a desired luminance level of the scene to the middle intensity on the display. Mapping higher luminance level to middle gray results in a subjectively dark image (low key) where as mapping lower luminance to middle gray will give a bright result (high key). Obviously, images which we perceive at night appear relatively dark compared to what we see during a day. After mapping the luminous, the proposed algorithm also looks into enhance the image such as checking for the detail less shadows, enhancing the middle tones of the image and also blown out for the highlights in the image. Initially the upper level threshold, lower level thresholds, middle level thresholds, bound lower and bound upper are set depending on the image luminous values. Based on the thresholds, the luminous values are up sampled and down sampled for image enhancements. And also local edge convolution technique is also used for the tone enhancement of the image.

In Figure 2, two different images of 5 numbers in a set are considered. And these images are acquired at various interval of time and at different

*Figure 1. Block diagram of proposed depth estimation for HDR images*

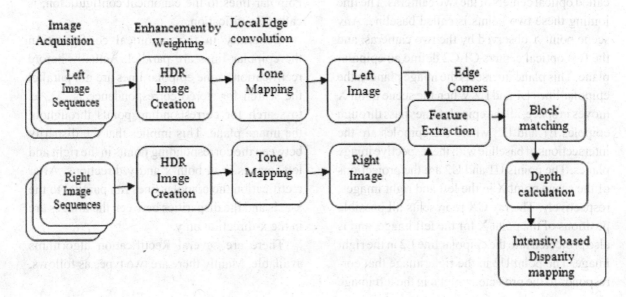

light intensities. And a single image is obtained as output after HDR image processing.

## Stereo Processing and Depth Mapping

Consider the following 2D imaging in which the 3D world is projected in 2D image plane.

In Figure 3(a) C is the optical centre or camera centre. The scene points P and Q on the same viewing line have the same 2D image P' and Q' in the image plane. Thus we cannot make out the depth found between the points P and Q from the 2D image. Thus 2D imaging results in depth information loss. Hence to recover the depth found between the points P and Q, we need another 2D image which is captured at different location as shown below.

In Figure 3(b) $C_1$ and $C_2$ are the camera centers of the two cameras, used to capture the two images. Here we can make out the depth between the points P and Q from the displacement between the locations of the projection points $P_1$' and $Q_1$' in the left image. Thus exact depth can be recovered by correlating these two images.

The geometry of the system with two cameras is shown in Figure 3. In Figure 3(c) C1 and C2 are called optical centers of the two cameras. The line joining these two points is called baseline. Any scene point X observed by the two cameras, and the two optical centers C1,C2 define an epipolar plane. This plane intersects the image plane in the epipolar lines L1 and L2. When the scene point X moves in space, all the epipolar lines pass through epipoles E1 and E2, where the epipoles are the intersections of baseline with the respective image planes. The points U1 and U2 are the projections of the scene point X in the left and right images, respectively. The ray CX represents all possible positions of the point X for the left image, and is also projected into the epipolar line L2 in the right image. The point U2 in the right image that corresponds to the projected point u in the left image

must thus lie on the epipolar line L2 in the right image. This geometry provides a strong epipolar constraint that reduces the dimensionality of the search space for a correspondence between U1 and U2 in the right image from 2D to 1D.

In the general stereo configuration the two cameras are located such that their optical axes are not parallel to each other. In this case the epipolar lines in the two images are also not parallel to each other. Another special arrangement of the stereo rig, called the canonical configuration (Figure 3(d)) may also be used. In this case the baseline is aligned to the horizontal co-ordinate axis, the optical axes of the cameras parallel to each other, the epipoles are at infinity and epipolar lines in the image planes are parallel. In this case Rectification process is not required. A very good example for canonical configuration is our eyes. As the optical axes of the eyes are parallel to each other, we could see only one scene with two eyes. Figure 4 is the block diagram of proposed stereo processing technique.

## Image Rectification

The geometric transformation, which changes a general stereo configuration with non-parallel epipolar lines to the canonical configuration, is called Rectification.

Generally in the canonical configuration the epipolar lines are parallel. Actually before rectification as the epipolar lines are not parallel the search for stereo correspondence is 2D, ie. to search for corresponding points throughout the image plane. This implies that the disparity between the corresponding points in the right and left images is in both x and y directions. After rectification the epipolar lines run parallel to the x-axis and the disparities between the images are in the x-direction only.

There are several Rectification algorithms available. Mainly there are two types as follows,

*Figure 2. Output of the HDR image processing (a) image 1 (b) image 2*

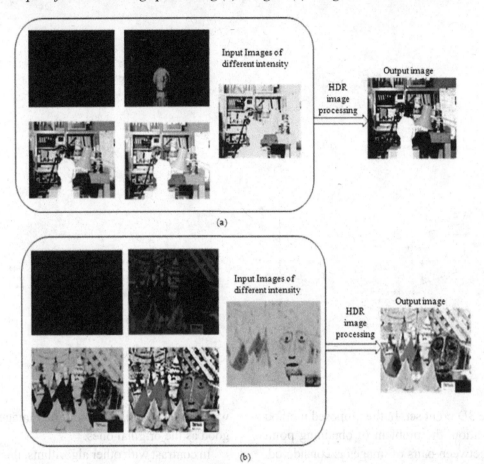

1. Rectification algorithm that requires camera calibration.
2. Rectification algorithm that avoids the necessity for camera calibration.

In the first type of rectification algorithm, camera matrices are used for rectification. In the second type fundamental matrix will be used for rectification.

A new method for image rectification is used, the process of resampling pairs of stereo images taken from widely differing viewpoints in order to produce a pair of "matched epipolar projections (Hartley, R. I. 1999). These are projections in which the epipolar lines run parallel with the x-axis and consequently, disparities between the images are in the x-direction only. The method is based on an examination of the fundamental matrix, which describes the epipolar geometry of the image pair. This is an approach that avoids the necessity for camera calibration. This method involves the determination of a pair of 2D projective transformations ($H_1$ and $H_2$) to be applied to the two images in order to match the epipolar lines.

The advantages include the simplicity of the 2D projective transformation which allows very fast resampling as well as subsequent simplification in the identification of matched points and scene reconstruction. The previous rectification methods start from the assumption that the point matches have already been determined between pairs of images, concentrating on the reconstruc-

*Figure 3. (a) 2D imaging, (b) Stereo vision. (c) General stereo configuration, (d) Canonical configuration*

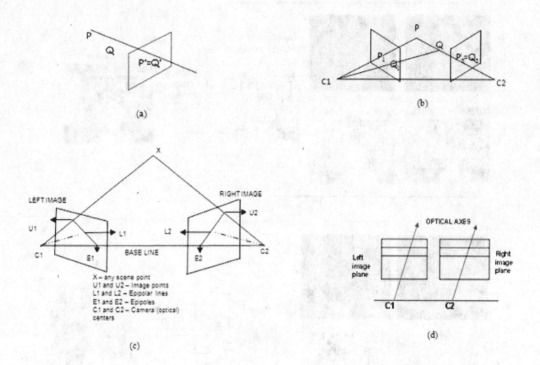

(a)

(b)

(c)

X = any scene point
U1 and U2 – Image points
L1 and L2 – Epipolar lines
E1 and E2 – Epipoles
C1 and C2 – Camera (optical) centers

(d)

tion of the 3D point set. In the proposed method of rectification, the problem of obtaining point matches between pairs of images is considered. In particular in matching images taken from very different locations, perspective distortion and different view point make corresponding regions look very different. The image rectification method described here overcomes this problem by transforming both images to a common reference frame. It may be used as a preliminary step to comprehensive image matching, greatly simplifying the image matching problem. This method of determining the 2D projective transformations to apply to the two images makes use of the fundamental matrix F. The scene may be reconstructed up to a 3D projectivity from the resampled images. In fact, once the two images have been rectified, the original images may be thrown away and the transformations forgotten, since unless parameterized camera models are to be computed (which

we wish to avoid), the resampled images are as good as the original ones.

In contrast with other algorithms, this method does not need the camera matrices, but relies on point correspondences alone. An additional feature of the algorithm described in this method is that it minimizes the horizontal disparity of the points along the epipolar lines so as to minimize the range of search for further matched points. The input is a pair of images containing a common overlap region. The output is a pair of images resampled so that the epipolar lines in the two images are horizontal (parallel with the x- axis), and such that corresponding points in the two images are as close to each other as possible. Any remaining disparity between matching points will be along the horizontal epipolar lines. A top-level outline of the image is as follows.

* Identify a seed set of image-to-image matches $u_{1i} \leftrightarrow u_{2i}$ between the two images.

*Figure 4. Proposed Stereo processing algorithm and block diagram*

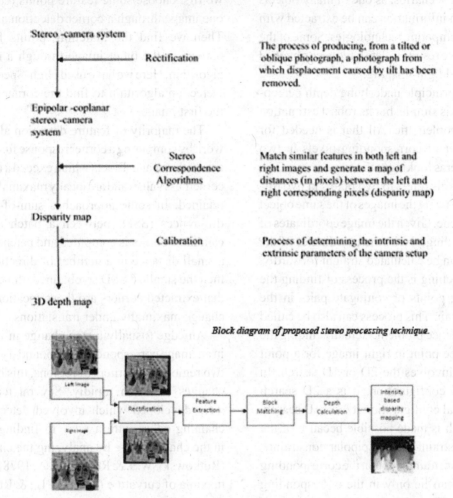

Stereo -camera system

Rectification — The process of producing, from a tilted or oblique photograph, a photograph from which displacement caused by tilt has been removed.

Epipolar -coplanar stereo -camera system

Stereo Correspondence Algorithms — Match similar features in both left and right images and generate a map of distances (in pixels) between the left and right corresponding pixels (disparity map)

Disparity map

Calibration — Process of determining the intrinsic and extrinsic parameters of the camera setup

3D depth map

*Block diagram of proposed stereo processing technique.*

Seven points at least are needed, though more are preferable.

- Compute the fundamental matrix F using the set of matched points and find the epipoles $E_1$ and $E_2$ in the two images using F.
- Select a projective transformation $H_2$ that maps the epipole $p_2$ to the point at infinity, $(1, 0, 0)^T$.
- Find the matching projective transformation $H_1$ that minimizes the Least-squares Distance

$$\sum d(H_1 u_{1i}, H_2 u_{2i})^2 \qquad (3)$$

Resample the first image according to the projective transformation $H_1$ and the second image according to the projective transformation $H_2$.

## Stereo Matching and Disparity Mapping

Depth information is vital for enhancing the level of automation of present day programmable manipulators. Depth perception is the ability to pick up a part from a random orientation and position within work environment of the manipulator. The part may present itself to the manipulator as a single object against a uniform background, or, in more complex scenarios, as one of many objects in a bin. Depth information can be extracted with a number of competing technologies. Some of the most impressive results to date have been obtained with structured light imaging.

The basic principle underlying depth perception via stereo is simple, but its robust estimation has proved problematic. All that is needed for stereo is a pair of corresponding pixels in two different cameras looking at the same scene. Corresponding pixels refers to two pixels in two different cameras being the images of the same object point in the scene. Given the image coordinates of two corresponding pixels, the coordinates of the object point can be calculated straight forwardly.

Stereo matching is the process of finding the corresponding points or conjugate pairs in the stereo image pair. This process can also be called as Correspondence problem. Actually finding the correspondence point in right image for a point in left image involves the 2D or 1D search. In general stereo configuration, it is a 2D search but in canonical configuration it is an 1D search. This 1D search is made possible because of the following constraint called Epipolar constraint.

Epipolar constraint says that the corresponding image points can lie only in the corresponding epipolar lines. This means that the corresponding point for a point in a particular epipolar line (in left image) can be searched in the respective epipolar line in the right image. Thus it is an one dimensional search. So the rectified image reduces the search complexity.

Feature-based Correspondence methods use points or set of points that are striking and easy to find. These features may be like edges, corners etc. Widely, in this method corners of the objects are considered in the images and these corners are matched. An example for Feature-based Correspondence algorithm is PMF algorithm. In this work 'Cooperative algorithm for stereo matching and occlusion detection' which is a type of correlation-based stereo matching algorithm, is used. In order to identify a set of matching points

we first choose some feature points (corners) in one image through a corner detection algorithm. Then we find the matching points for those corners in the other image through a matching algorithm. Here we have used High-Speed Corner Detection algorithm to find the corner points in the first image.

The majority of feature detection algorithms work by computing a corner response function (C) across the image. Pixels which exceed a threshold cornerness value (and are locally maximal) are then retained. In some approaches sum-of-squared-differences (SSD) between a patch around a candidate corner is computed and patches shifted a small distance in a number of directions. C is then the smallest SSD so obtained, thus ensuring that extracted corners are those locations which change maximally under translations.

An edge (usually a step change in intensity) in an image corresponds to the boundary between two regions. At corners of regions, this boundary changes direction rapidly. Several techniques were developed which involved detecting and chaining edges with a view to finding corners in the chained edge by analyzing the chain code (Rutkowski, W.S. & Rosenfeld, A. 1978), finding maxima of curvature (Kitchen, L., & Rosenfeld, A. 1982, Longuet-Higgins, H. C. 1981, Medioni, G., & Yasumoto, Y. 1987), change in direction (Haralick, R.M., & Shapiro, L.G. 1993) or change in appearance(Cooper, J., Venkatesh, S., & Kitchen, L. 1993). Others avoid chaining edges and instead look for maxima of curvature (Zitnick, C. & Kanade,K. 2000) or change in direction (Inanici M, & Galvin.J.2004) at places where the gradient is large. Another class of corner detector works by examining a small patch of an image to see if it "looks" like a corner. Since second derivatives are not computed, a noise reduction step (such as Gaussian smoothing) is not required. Consequently, these corner detectors are computationally efficient since only a small number of pixels are examined for each corner detected. A corollary of this is that they tend to perform poorly on images with only large-scale features such as blurred images.

The method presented in (Guiducci, A. 1988) assumes that a corner resembles a blurred wedge, and finds the characteristics of the wedge (the amplitude, angle and blur) by fitting it to the local image. The idea of the wedge is generalized in (Smith, S.M., & Brady, J.M. 1997), where a method calculating the corner strength is proposed, which computes self similarity by looking at the proportion of pixels inside a disc whose intensity is within some threshold of the centre (nucleus) value. Pixels closer in value to the nucleus receive a higher weighting as shown in Figure 5. This measure is known as the USAN (the Univalue Segment Assimilating Nucleus). A low value for the USAN indicates a corner since the centre pixel is very different from most of its surroundings. A set of rules is used to suppress qualitatively "bad" features, and then local minima of the, SUSANs, (Smallest USAN) are selected from the remaining candidates.

The segment test criterion (Rosten, E., & Drummond, T. 2005, Wang, H., & Brady, M. 1995) operates by considering a circle of sixteen pixels around the corner candidate p. The original detector (Rosten, E., & Drummond, T. 2005) classifies p as a corner if there exists a set of n contiguous pixels in the circle which are all brighter than the intensity of the candidate pixel $I_p$ plus a threshold t, or all darker than $I_p$ - t. That is for each location on the circle x $\in\{1..16\}$, the pixel at that position relative to p (denoted p by x) can have one of three states:

$$S_{p \to x} = \begin{cases} d, & I_{p \to x} \leq I_{p \to t} & (dar\,ker) \\ s, & I_p - t \leq I_{p \to x} < I_p + t & (similar) \\ b, & I_p + t \leq I_{p \to x} & (brighter) \end{cases}$$

(4)

Choosing an x and computing Sp x for all p$\in$P (the set of all pixels in all training images) partitions P into three subsets, $P_d$, $P_s$, $P_b$. n was chosen to be twelve because it admits a high-speed test

which can be used to exclude a very large number of non-corners: the test examines only the four pixels at 1, 5, 9 and 13 (the four compass directions). If p is a corner then at least three of these must all be brighter than $I_{p+t}$ or darker than $I_{p-t}$. If neither of these is the case, then p cannot be a corner. The full segment test criterion can then be applied to the remaining candidates by examining all pixels in the circle.

This detector in itself exhibits high performance, but multiple features are detected adjacent to one another. This can be eliminated by doing Non-maximal Suppression followed by the High-speed corner detection. Since the segment test does not compute a corner response function, non maximal suppression cannot be applied directly to the resulting features. Consequently, a score function, V must be computed for each detected corner, and non-maximal suppression applied to this to remove corners which have an adjacent corner with higher V.

There are several intuitive definitions for V:

- The maximum value of n for which p is still a corner.
- The maximum value of t for which p is still a corner.
- The sum of the absolute difference between the pixels in the contiguous arc and the centre pixel.

Definitions 1 and 2 are very highly quantized measures, and many pixels share the same value of these. For speed of computation, V is given by:

$$V = \max(\sum_{x \in S_{bright}} | I_{p \to x} - I_p | - t, \sum_{x \in S_{dark}} | I_p - I_{p \to x} | - t)$$

(5)

Once the corners are detected in one image, we find the matching points for those corners in the other image using Block matching algorithm. The idea behind block matching is to form a block (window) around each of the corner detected in

*Figure 5. Point segment test corner detection in an image patch. The highlighted squares are the pixels used in the corner detection.*

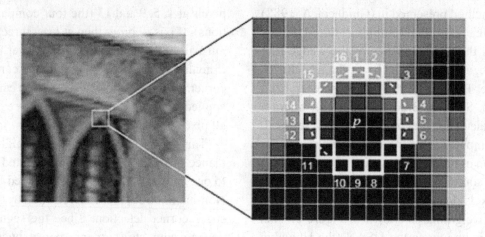

one image and then compared with corresponding block and its adjacent neighbors in the other image to create a vector that shows the displacement between the locations of a macro block in first image and its match block in the other image. The search area for a good macro block match is constrained up to p pixels on all fours sides of the corresponding macro block in the second image. This 'p' is called as the search parameter as shown in Figure 6 a. The matching of one macro block with another is based on the output of a cost function. The macro block that results in the least cost is the one that matches the closest to current block. There are various cost functions, of which the most popular and less computationally expensive is Mean Absolute Difference (MAD) and another cost function is Mean Squared Error (MSE).They are given by,

$$MAD = \frac{1}{N^2} \sum_{i=0}^{N-1} \sum_{j=0}^{N-1} |C_{ij} - R_{ij}| \qquad (6)$$

$$MSE = \frac{1}{N^2} \sum_{i=0}^{N-1} \sum_{j=0}^{N-1} (C_{ij} - R_{ij})^2 \qquad (7)$$

where N is the side of the macro bock, $C_{ij}$ and $R_{ij}$ are the pixels being compared in current macro block and reference macro block, respectively. There are several search methods available for block matching. They are as follows, Exhaustive Search (ES), Three Step Search (TSS), New Three Step Search (NTSS), Simple and Efficient Search (SES), Four Step Search (4SS), Diamond Search (DS), Adaptive Rood Pattern Search (ARPS).

Among these search methods, the Exhaustive search method gives the highest PSNR (Peak Signal to Noise Ratio). So we have employed this method for block matching. This algorithm, also known as Full Search, is the most computationally expensive block matching algorithm of all (Barjatya Aroh 2004). This algorithm calculates the cost function at each possible location in the search window. As a result of which it finds the best possible match and gives the highest PSNR (Peak-Signal-to-Noise-Ratio) amongst any block matching algorithm. Fast block matching algorithms try to achieve the same PSNR doing as little computation as possible.

As shown by Figure 6 (b), 4SS, DS and ARPS come pretty close to the PSNR results of ES. While the ES takes on an average around ~205 searches per macro block, DS and 4SS drop that

*Figure 6. (a) Block matching - a macro block of side mbsize pixels and a search parameter of size p pixels, (b) PSNR performance of fast block matching algorithms.*

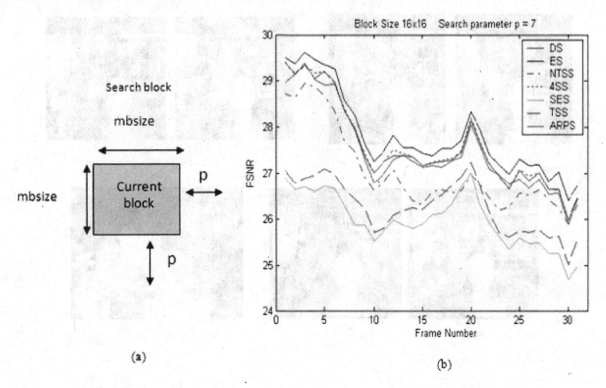

(a)                                                                    (b)

number by more than an order of magnitude. ARPS further drops by a factor of 2 compared to DS. NTSS and TSS although do not come close in PSNR performance to the results of ES, but even they drop down the number of computations required per macro block by almost an order of magnitude. SES takes up less number of search point computations amongst all but ARPS. It however also has the worst PSNR performance.

Once the corresponding points are found, we can find the Disparity between the matched points. Disparity is the displacement between the locations of the conjugate pair or corresponding points in the right and left images. That is the distance between the points of a conjugate pair when the two images are superimposed. As said earlier the disparity and depth are proportional to each other. In fact, they are inversely proportional to each other. Thus if we map the disparity of each point in an image, we get the disparity map showing the depth variations in the scene. So it can also said to be Depth map. The depth variations can be shown as the intensity variations in the image.

Here the objects in bright colour (with high intensity values) are at the front and the objects in dark colour (with low intensity values) are at the back. So as the depth increases the brightness (or intensity value) decreases.

## EXPERIMENTAL RESULTS

Figure 7 and 8 gives the result of the proposed stereo algorithm and its intensity based disparity mapping. Figure 7(a & b) and 8(a & b) are the input stereo pairs (left and right images). Figure 7(c) and 8(c) are the corner detected points of left images with minimum threshold of 7 points. Figure 7(d) and 8(d) are the matched corners of the right image. With reference of the corner points,

*Figure 7. (a)Left image (b) Right image (c) Corner detected in left image (d) Matched corner points in right image (e) Rectified left image (f) Rectified right image (g) Disparity map image*

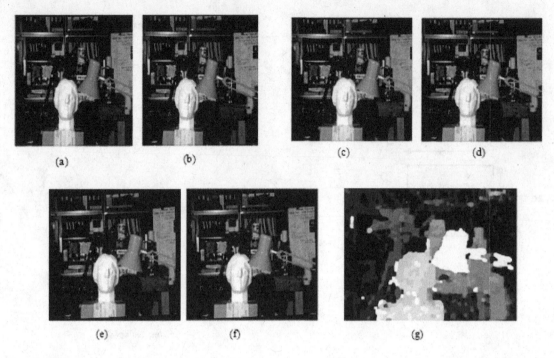

*Figure 8 (a)Left image (b) Right image (c) Corner detected in left image (d) Matched corner points in right image (e) Rectified left image (f) Rectified right image (g) Disparity map image*

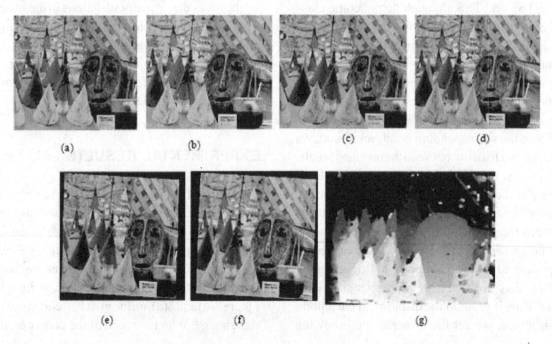

the left image and the right image are tilted to the reference plane in Figure 7(e & f) and 8(e & f). The disparity mapped image is given in Figure 7(d) and 8(d). Experiments are carried out on a Pentium IV 2.1 GHz PC with 512 MB RAM. The algorithm has been implemented using Matlab7 for the images from the Computer Vision and Image Media Laboratory, University of Tsukuba, Japan.

## FUTURE RESEARCH DIRECTIONS

This chapter provides a solution for the depth estimation for HDR images. The results of the proposed technique can be improved by providing the best algorithms at each stage. The HDR image conversion can be done with better tone mapping techniques. And also the feature detection can be done with latest computer vision algorithms such as SIFT, SURF and etc. The matching algorithm can be performed with other cost functions. As in this work, the computation of Disparity map using offline images has been done, it can be extended in future by taking real time images and the actual depth can be computed using Triangulation. This algorithm can be used for the different applications.

## CONCLUSION

A very simple stereo matching algorithm has been developed that analyses grayscale or color images to estimate the disparity map for 3D scene reconstruction. Moreover, the proposed algorithm can work even for the image pair taken with uncalibrated cameras. To cope the uncalibration problem, the simple and well efficient corner detection and Block matching algorithms are used. The feature detection algorithms can be improved for better accuracy. The Stereo matching algorithm yields dense and continuous disparity map. Stereoscopy finds numerous applications in the real world. Some of the applications are Robot Navigation, Space research photography,

3D movies, Autonomous vehicle control, Military applications to trace missiles etc, Medical Imaging (like 3D x-ray imaging) and in many other machine vision applications.

## REFERENCES

Barjatya, A. (2004). *Block matching algorithms for motion estimation*. DIP 6620 Spring Final Project Paper.

Cooper, J., Venkatesh, S., & Kitchen, L. (1993). Early jump-out corner detectors. *IEEE Transactions on Pattern Analysis and Machine Intelligence, 15*, 823–828. doi:10.1109/34.236246

Faugeras, O., & Maybank, S. (1990). Motion from point matches: Multiplicity of solutions. *International Journal of Computer Vision, 4*, 225–246. doi:10.1007/BF00054997

Gonzalez Rafael, C., Woods, R. E., & Eddins, S. L. (2004). *Digital image processing using MATLAB*. Pearson Education.

Guiducci, A. (1988). Corner characterization by differential geometry techniques. *Pattern Recognition Letters, 8*, 311–318. doi:10.1016/0167-8655(88)90080-3

Haralick, R. M., & Shapiro, L. G. (1993). *Computer and robot vision (Vol. 1)*. Addison-Wesley.

Hartley, R. (1992). Estimation of relative camera positions for uncalibrated cameras. In G. Sandini (Ed.), *Proceedings of ECCV-92, LNCS Vol. 588*, (pp. 579–587). Springer-Verlag.

Hartley, R. I. (1999). Theory and practice of projective rectification. *International Journal of Computer Vision, 35*(2), 1–16. doi:10.1023/A:1008115206617

Inanici, M., & Galvin, J. (2004). *Evaluation of high dynamic range photography as a luminance mapping technique*. Paper LBNL-57545.

Kitchen, L., & Rosenfeld, A. (1982). Gray-level corner detection. *Pattern Recognition Letters, 1*, 95–102. doi:10.1016/0167-8655(82)90020-4

Langridge, D. J. (1987). Curve encoding and detection of discontinuities. *Computer Vision Graphics and Image Processing, 20*, 58–71.

Longuet-Higgins, H. C. (1981). A computer algorithm for reconstructing a scene from two projections. *Nature, 293*.

Medioni, G., & Yasumoto, Y. (1987). Corner detection and curve representation using cubic b-splines. *Computer Vision Graphics and Image Processing, 39*, 279–290. doi:10.1016/S0734-189X(87)80181-0

Mokhtarian, F., & Suomela, R. (1998). Robust image corner detection through curvature scale space. *IEEE Transactions on Pattern Analysis and Machine Intelligence, 20*, 1376–1381. doi:10.1109/34.735812

Reinhard, E., Ashikhmin, M., Gooch, B., & Shirley, P. (2001). Color transfer between images. *IEEE Computer Graphics and Applications, 21*, 34–41. doi:10.1109/38.946629

Rosten, E., & Drummond, T. (2005). Fusing points and lines for high performance tracking. *10th IEEE International Conference on Computer Vision*, Vol. 2, (pp. 1508-1515). Beijing, China: Springer

Rosten, E., & Drummond, T. (2006). *Machine learning for high speed corner detection*. 9th European Conference on Computer Vision. Springer.

Rutkowski, W. S., & Rosenfeld, A. (1978). *A comparison of corner detection techniques for chain coded curves*. Technical Report 623, Maryland University.

Smith, S. M., & Brady, J. M. (1997). SUSAN - A new approach to low level image processing. *International Journal of Computer Vision, 23*, 45–78. doi:10.1023/A:1007963824710

Wang, H., & Brady, M. (1995). Real-time corner detection algorithm for motion estimation. *Image and Vision Computing, 13*, 695–703. doi:10.1016/0262-8856(95)98864-P

Zitnick, C., & Kanade, K. (2000). A cooperative algorithm for stereo matching and occlusion detection. *IEEE Transactions on Pattern Analysis and Machine Intelligence, 22*(7), 675–684. doi:10.1109/34.865184

## KEY TERMS AND DEFINITIONS

**Corner Detection:** Corners points features for stereo matching.

**Depth Mapping:** Ability to pick up a part from a random orientation and position within work environment of the manipulator.

**Exhaustive Search:** Block matching technique which is fast in computation.

**High Dynamic Range Imaging (HDRI):** A techniques that allows a greater dynamic range of luminance between lightest and darkest areas of an image.

**Mean Square Error (MSE):** Cost function used for block matching

**Stereo Matching:** The corresponding points or conjugate pairs in the stereo image pair.

**Tone Mapping:** Mathematically transform scene luminance.

# Chapter 8
# Monocular–Cues Based
# 3–D Reconstruction:
## A Comparative Review

**Sudheer Tumu**
*State University of New York-Albany, USA*

**Viswanath Avasarala**
*GE Global Research, USA*

**Sai Tejaswi Jonnalagadda**
*Hetero Med Solutions, India*

**Prasad Wadekar**
*Mahindra Satyam, USA*

## ABSTRACT

*3-D reconstruction from images has traditionally focused on using multiple images. However, in recent years, some interesting breakthroughs have been made in constructing depth maps of images using monocular cues. This chapter summarizes the recent work in this evolving research domain. The chapter also presents results from an initial exploratory study based on fusing the 3-D reconstructions generated by two seminal monocular-cue based reconstruction algorithms. With new testing data, the fusion approach improved the 3-D estimation accuracy significantly as compared to the original approaches. The authors use the improved estimation accuracy produced by the fusion algorithm as a motivating evidence for future work: the use of non-parametric Bayesian regression for 3-D reconstruction.*

## INTRODUCTION

Traditionally, computational vision algorithms for constructing 3D structure from images have focused on using multiple images of a scene. Based on triangulation, these techniques including

'Structure from Motion (SFM)' or 'Stereovision' calculate the depth maps of images. These approaches are not applicable to situations where only single images of a particular scene are available. On the other hand, humans are adept at analyzing the 3D structure of even a single

DOI: 10.4018/978-1-4666-0113-0.ch008

image. For this purpose, human brain relies on a number of monocular cues including properties related to image texture, known object sizes/shapes, occlusion, vanishing points etc. Many of these monocular cues depend not only on the local properties of image but also it's global properties and are therefore difficult to model. Because of the difficulty in understanding/modeling these monocular cues, automating the identification of the 3D structure from a single image is a difficult problem. However, in recent years, researchers have made significant progress in developing solutions for this problem. Particularly, the work done by Saxena et al. (Saxena, A., Sun, M., Ng, A. Y., 2009; Saxena, A.,Chung, S.H., Ng, A. Y., 2007, & Saxena, A.,Chkeung, S.H., Ng, A. Y., 2005) and Hoiem et al. (Hoiem, D., Efros, A., & Herbert, M., 2005 & Hoiem, D., Efros, A., & Herbert, M., 2006) has significantly improved the state of the art in calculating 3D structure from monocular cues. Both these approaches rely on sophisticated machine learning algorithms to learn the feature patterns useful for estimating 3D structure of images. In this chapter, we summarize the two above seminal approaches to 3D construction from monocular cues and discuss their comparative performance. We also present results of our fusion algorithm that combines the two results to produce better depth estimates. Section II provides a brief literature review of both monocular and multi-view based 3-D reconstruction approaches. Section III describes the Saxena et al. (2009)'s *Make3D* algorithm and Hoiem et al. (2006)'s geometric image labeling work (referred to as *HEH* in the rest of this chapter) in greater detail. We describe the design of our fusion algorithm and results from an experimental study in the results section. We are currently investigating non-parametric Bayesian approaches for monocular depth estimation. This approach is introduced in the future work session.

## BACKGROUND

The 3-D reconstruction problem can be formulated in multiple ways (Zhang, R., Tsai, P.-S., Cryer, J., & Shah, M., 1999). A common formulation requires the calculation of depth value at each coordinate. The depths can be expressed as the distance of the surface point to the camera or from any other standard surface like the x-y plane. Other ways to express 3-D structure is by using surface normals, surface gradients or surface slant and tilt angles. In addition to these quantitative approaches, 3-D reconstruction algorithms can simply generate geometric/qualitative labels that allow the organization of the image into a 3-D hierarchy.

In this section, we provide a high level review of previous work on 3-D reconstruction both using binocular or multiple views and monocular views.

## 3-D Reconstruction from Multiple Images

Many techniques for constructing 3-D geometry based on two or more images of a scene have been successfully developed. Stereovision algorithms are the most common 3-D reconstruction algorithms.

As a first step, cameras are calibrated and image rectification is performed so that image planes become coplanar. Correspondence algorithms are used to match stereo pairs between images (Faugeras, O., & Luong, Q.T., 2001; Hartley, R. I., & Zisserman, A., 2000). The correspondence algorithms are usually pixel-based (refer to Scharstein, D., & Szeliski, R., 2002 for a good survey). Frequency domain-based correspondence algorithms, particularly using Gabor Filters or FFTs (Udo Ahlvers, U.Z, 2005) exhibit sub-pixel accuracy and are also used. Depth values or the inversely related disparity values of pixels can be calculated using epipolar constraints (other approaches are described in Scharstein, D., et al., 2002). The disparity calculation uses a minimization procedure that minimizes the aggregate of matching costs between the multiple images and smoothing constraints within a single image (based on the assumption that physical world consists of piecewise smooth surfaces). Different approaches like Simulated Annealing (Barnard, 1989), Graph Cuts (Vladimir Kolmogorov, R.Z., 2004; Hong, L., Chen G., 2004) or Probabilistic Diffusion (Scharstein, D. & Szeliski, R., 1998) can be used to solve the minimization problem.

Another interesting approach for 3-D reconstruction from multiple images is the Structure from Motion approaches (Faugeras, O., 1993), which uses temporal relationships within a sequence of image (as compared to spatial relationship in Stereovision). The perceived motion of objects across the field of view is called motion parallax (Loomis, J. & Eby, D., 1989). Motion parallax provides cues that can be used to calculate depth values. The earliest algorithms for SFM were for two-frame correspondences only (Longuet-Higgins, H. C., 1981). Algorithms based on SVD-based factorization (Tomasi, C., & Kanade, T., 1992) and global optimization algorithms (Spetsakis, M. E., & Aloimonos, J. Y., 1991; Szeliski, R., & Kang, S. B., 1994; Oliensis, J., 1999; Triggs, B., et al., 1999) have later been developed to extend SFM framework to multi-view frames. Photogrammetry inspired techniques like Bundle Alignment (Snavely, N., Seitz, S. M., Szeliski, R., 2006) can be used to refine the SFM solution by minimizing a global cost function based on original estimates of the camera position and structure parameters. For the photo-tourism application, Snavely, N., Seitz, S.M., & Szeliski, R. (2007); Breiman, L., (2001) have developed powerful SFM approaches that are applicable to a large number of views obtained under widely varying imaging conditions.

## 3-D Reconstruction from a Single Image

Both stereovision and structure from motion require multiple images of a scene for 3-D reconstruction. In general, constructing a 3-D structure from a 2-D image is an ill-posed problem. For example, the image of another image of a 3-D scene does not provide information that the underlying structure has only two dimensions. However, most images of the physical world have many important monocular cues. Using these cues, humans can easily reconstruct a 3-D scene, given its 2-D image. For this purpose, humans rely on properties related to image texture, known object sizes/shapes, occlusion, vanishing points etc. Researchers have developed special purpose algorithms for depth estimation from monocular cues. Many of these algorithms can be characterized as '*shape from x*' where $x$ can be stereo, motion, shape, texture or specular reflections.

Shape from shading approaches recover 3-D structure of one or more images using the variation in the shading of the image (Zhang, R., Tsai, P.-S.,Cryer, J., & Shah, M., 1999; Kozera, R., 1998). In this comprehensive review, Zhang et al. (1999) have categorized this research into four broad categories.

a. Minimization approaches: These approaches minimize an energy function over the entire image where the energy functions encode contextual constraints like the brightness constraint (at each surface point, the original image and the reconstructed image should not differ significantly in the brightness value), the smoothness constraint (the reconstructed surface should have smooth changes in depth) etc.

b. Propagation approaches: Using a single/ collection of initial points whose shape is known or can be calculated because of singularities, these approaches propagate shape information to the rest of the image.

c. Local Shape Approaches: Based on assumptions about the local surface type (for example, by assuming that local surfaces are spherical), these approaches derive image structure.

d. Linear approaches: These approaches solve a linearization of the reflectance map, obtained by ignoring higher order components.

More sophisticated algorithms for SFS have been developed since then for application to non-Lambertian surfaces, eliminating the concave/convex ambiguity (Ahmed, A., & Farag. A., 2006), for perspective projections (Kindermann, R., Snell, J.L., 1980) and for images taken using a pinhole camera with light source at the optical center (Tankus, A., Sochen, N., & Yeshurun. Y., 2005).

A related approach is shape from texture, which measures the texture distortion of a monocular image and constructs the 3-D coordinates based on this distortion (Gibson. J., 1950; Garding. J.,1992; Hwang, W., Lu, C.-S., & Chung, P.-C., 1998; Kanatani, K. & Chou, T., 1989; Malik, J., & Rosenholtz, R., 1997;Permuter, H., & Franoos, J., 2000;Clerc M., Mallot S.,2002). Similarly, researchers have also investigated the use of specular reflections to recover 3-D structure (Fleming, R. W., Torralba, A., & Adelson, E. H., 2004).

However, the above algorithms are special-purpose algorithms that are not easy to apply to real images, for example, the image of an outdoor scene downloaded from the Internet. This precludes the development of applications like photo-tourism (see Snavely, N., Seitz, S.M., & Szeliski, R. 2007 for a SFS-based photo-tourism work) based on monocular cues. In the next section, we will review two monocular-cue based 3-D reconstruction approaches that do not have restrictive applicability constraints.

## 3-D Reconstruction From Monocular Cues

### HEH: Generating Geometric Labels from Monocular Cues

The algorithm developed by Hoiem et al. (Hoiem, D., et al., 2005 & 2006) does not identify the 3D depth but only categorizes the image into set of geometric classes that are related to 3D structure. The labels generated by this approach are shown in Figure 1. The authors have selected seven different surface geometry related labels:

- Support surface (ground)
- Sky
- Vertical
  - Planar: facing LEFT (←), CENTER (↑) and RIGHT (→)

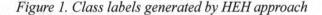

*Figure 1. Class labels generated by HEH approach*

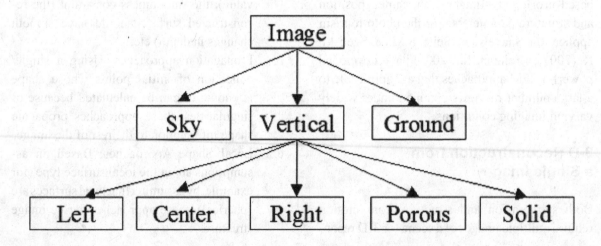

○ Non-planar: SOLID (X) and POROUS or wiry (O)

The HEH algorithm first uses a segmentation algorithm to over-segment the image into small, nearly-uniform image regions known as superpixels. (Felzenszwalb, P. & Huttenlocher, D., 2004). Starting from a single-pixel region, the super pixel generation algorithm creates larger regions by merging two regions if the maximum intensity disparity within a region is lesser than the minimum intensity difference across the boundary. This over-segmentation algorithm usually groups large, homogenous regions into a single super-pixel, while dividing heterogeneous regions to smaller super pixels. The superpixels though likely to belong to a similar geometric label are too small to allow calculation of complex geometric features that can inculcate context from large regions. Using a standard segmentation algorithm to generate larger homogenous image regions will not suffice, since these algorithms also use local image properties. To overcome this drawback, the authors used a very interesting multi-hypothesis segmentation approach. The authors first over-segmented the image into superpixels. Using fifty training images which are manually assigned class labels shown in *Figure 1*, the authors trained a logistic form of Adaboost algorithm to estimate the probability that two superpixels have the same class label. For each new image, multiple segmentation hypotheses are generated using the following approach.

1. Select $n$ superpixels randomly and initialize $n$ "regions" with the selected superpixels
2. Assign the remaining super-pixels to the region with which it has the maximum average pair wise log likelihood of belonging to the same label (calculated using logistic regression)

Using different values of $n$ and repeating the above process generates multiple segmentation hypotheses.

For each region, homogeneity likelihood (the probability that a region has a single label) and label likelihood (the probability that the region has a particular label) are learned using logistic regression models. Finally, for each super pixel, the likelihood of each label is calculated as the average of the label likelihoods of all regions it belongs to, weighted by the likelihood of the homogeneity of that region

The authors have used color, texture, location and shape-based features and attributes related to vanishing points (properties of lines and their intersections in the image plane) as input data for their pattern recognition algorithm. The color features used by HEH are mean RGB values, mean HSV values, 5-bin histogram and entropy of the hue and 3-bin histogram and entropy of the saturation. HEH uses 15 texture features. These include the mean absolute response of the 12 DOOG filters, the mean value of these responses, the argument of their maximum and the difference between their maximum and median. The location features used by HEH are the normalized mean of horizontal (x) and vertical coordinates (y), $10^{th}$ and $90^{th}$ percentile of the norm of x and y coordinates, $10^{th}$ and $90^{th}$ percentile of the norm of y with respect to the horizontal. The shape features used by HEH are number of superpixels in the region, number of sides of convex hull, the number of pixels per area of the convex hull and a binary value indicating the contiguous nature of the region. The 3D orientation of an image plane can be calculated using its vanishing line. HEH used statistics of straight lines and their intersections as a proxy for the vanishing line. Using the algorithm proposed by Kosecka and Zhang, 2002, the authors first identify long straight lines in the image. The authors then calculated the total number of long lines in the region, % of nearly parallel pairs of lines (defined as lines with less than $\prod/8$ difference in orientation), historgram over 12 orientations and entropy of line intersections, % of line intersections to the right of center, % of line intersections above the center, % of line intersections far from center (distance of at least 1.5 times the image size) at 8 orientations, % of line intersections very far from center (distance of at least 5 times the image size) at 8 orientations. In addition, the authors use the x and y texture gradient of the region center.

With this approach, the authors have achieved 86% accuracy in predicting the main class and 52% accuracy in predicting the sub class on their test images.

## MAKE3D: 3-D Reconstruction from Monocular Cues

In their latest and most sophisticated work, Saxena et al. (2009) used monocular cues to reconstruct both 3-D location and orientation of image regions. Similar to HEH, Make3D first uses a segmentation algorithm to over-segment the image into superpixels (Felzenszwalb, P. & Huttenlocher, D., 2004).

Make3D algorithm uses 524 features per super-pixel for depth recognition. The kurtosis and energies of seventeen filters (9 Law masks, 2 YCbCr space color channels and 6 oriented edges) are used to generate a feature vector of length 34 per superpixel. The authors also included the filter outputs of the four largest neighbors of a super pixel, so as to provide contextual information to the 3D reconstruction algorithm. In addition, the authors utilized the super-pixel's eccentricity and also the shape and location features used by HEH algorithm. Each of these features is calculated at three spatial scales resulting in a final feature vector of 524 length. Using these features, the authors use a multi-tier learning algorithm for 3-D reconstruction. As the first step, the authors trained a logistic regression model to learn the probability that an occlusion boundary exists

between two neighboring superpixels. In a parallel step, another logistic regression model is learnt to calculate the confidence of the depth estimation based on local super-pixel features. In the final regression model, the authors used the superpixel features to estimate depth. The values generated by the logistic regression models are used as parameters in the final prediction algorithm to adjust the reliance of the prediction on the corresponding superpixel properties. However, relying only on local features is not sufficient since global properties also provide depth cues. To capture global cues, the authors used a two-pronged approach. As explained earlier, the authors use the features of not only a particular super-pixel but also its neighboring super-pixels at three scales to train the learning algorithm. In addition, the authors modeled the depth-related neighborhood relationships between super-pixels using Markov Random Fields (MRFs) (Kindermann, R., Snell, J. L., 1980; Li, S., 1995). Markov Random Fields is a graphical reasoning algorithm that uses an undirected graph model to represent relationships between a set of random variables. Many computer vision problems, including segmentation, stereovision etc can be posed as labeling problems, i.e. association of either discrete or continuous labels to each image pixel. MRF theory provides a convenient framework for representing the prior and posterior distribution properties of such labeling problems. Using MRFs, the contextual constraints of the problem can be coded as part of the prior label distribution. The data, as represented by the image features, is then used to calculate the posterior distribution using Bayesian calculus. The predicted labels are generated using a *maximum a posteriori* (*MAP*) estimate of the posterior distribution. The authors use the MRF technique to capture the following neighborhood properties.

a.  Neighboring superpixels are highly likely to be connected to each other, unless occlusion occurs.

b.    Neighboring superpixels with similar features and without separating edges are more likely to be co-planar.

c.    The probability that long, straight lines in the image are caused by straight lines in the 3D model, is high.

To learn the parameters of the MRF model, the authors use an approximate learning technique Multi-Conditional Learning (MCL), which use a product of several marginal conditional likelihoods to represent the model (Paul, M.K.C, Wang, X., & McCallum, A., 2006; McCallum, A., Pal, C., Druck, G.,& Wang, X., 2006). The authors reported a relative error percent of 37% on their test data that consisted of several images collected in diverse outdoor settings.

## Fusion Approach

We are investigating non-parametric Bayesian regression models for 3-D reconstruction from monocular cues. Du, L., Ren, L., Dunson, D., & Carin, L. (2009) have used a Hierarchical Dirchlet Process (HDP) based clustering for object segmentation across multiple images. In comparison to standard Bayesian non-parametric clustering models, their approach allows the representation of spatial relationships; for example, the belief that contiguous image segments are more likely to have similar depth properties, can be statistically modeled. We believe that this capability is a key advantage for 3-D reconstruction also. We are currently extending this HDP process to cluster-wise Dirchlet Regression. (Kang, C., & Ghosal, S., 2009). In addition to having flexible number of component mixtures, the above regression approach works well for high-dimensional regressor variables. Both these capabilities are crucial for depth regression. Our approach is based on the hypothesis that clustering the image into spatially homogeneous regions (regions that are closely related in depth) as a preprocessing step will improve the accuracy of the regression for depth.

An uncomplicated way to test this hypothesis is to if providing the label information generated by *HEH* approach can improve the regression output generated by *Make3D*. Since *HEH* provides information similar to depth-based image clustering, an improvement in *Make3D*'s output when fused with *HEH* labels will provide positive evidence regarding our approach. To test our hypothesis, we developed a Random Forest based fusion method.

The fusion algorithm is based on Random Forest, which is a tree-based machine-learning algorithm. The Random Forest is an ensemble of tree predictors, which outputs the average of the individual tree predictors as the final output (Breiman, L., 2001). Using the bagging technique developed by Breiman L., (1996), each tree is generated using a subset of the training data. At each node, only a subset of the total number of predictor variables are considered and the variable that generates the best split in terms of decrease in entropy (or any similar metric) is used to branch further. Each of the predictor trees is grown without pruning (as compared to normal tree-based predictors like CART). In general, Random Forests have low generalization error and can be used seamlessly for both categorical and continuous variables. Since *HEH* generates categorical labels and *Make3D* generates continuous values, we used Random Forest to fuse the results of the two algorithms. For the feature vector, we used the

1.    Depth maps of the corresponding pixel and its four corresponding neighbors

2.    Labels of the corresponding pixel and its four neighbors

Hoiem et al (2005 & 2006)'s approach requires that image requires that the training data contain sky, ground and vertical structures in similar proportions. We down-selected images that meet Hoiem's constraints from the image collection provided by Saxena et al (2005), Saxena et al (2007)

& Saxena et al (2009) at (http://www.cs.cornell. edu/~asaxena/learningdepth/data.html). Out of these images, we randomly selected 60 images. We used 45 images out of this collection as training data and 15 as test images. The parameters used for the random forest algorithm are in Table 1.

Akin to Saxena's approach, we trained three different regression models for the upper, middle and lower portions of the image. This allows the regression models to associate different depth priors based on image region (For example, a blue region in the upper part of the image is likely to be part of the sky whereas the blue region in the bottom part of the image is more likely to be a water body). Since the top most rows of the image consisted mainly of sky in the selected images, we used 50% of the image to train the upper regression model. The rest of the image was split equally between the other two regression models.

For training the regression model, we used a 10 dimensional feature vector for each pixel, consisting of the following elements:

a. *Make3D*'s depth prediction for the pixel
b. The depth prediction corresponding to the pixel's *m* closest neighbors.
c. *HEH*'s geometric label for the pixel
d. The geometric label corresponding to its *m* closed neighbors.

We used a value of four for *m*. Increasing the value of *m* did not appreciably affect our experimental results. For a comparison of the fusion algorithm performance, we use the average mean square error of the regression models. The fusion algorithm generated around 72% lower mean square error in training data and around 70% lower mean square error on the testing images, when compared to *Make3D*. Laser-generated ground truth data had a constant depth value of 80 for sky region whereas *Make3D* predictions had significant variability. To verify that this improvement is not only an artifact of an improved Sky prediction, we also calculated the per-label

*Table 1. Random forest parameters*

| Parameter | Value | |
|---|---|---|
| Ntrees | 250 | Number of ensemble trees |
| Nvars | 5 | Number of variables considered at each node |
| maxVar | 5 | Maximum cardinality of the leaf node |

mean square error improvement produced by the fusion of *Make3D* and *HEH* algorithms. Table 2 shows the decrease in percent mean square for data corresponding to a particular *HEH* label. As expected, the biggest improvements are noticed in delineating the sky (90% improvement), since *HEH* is highly accurate in detecting the sky region. The depth predictions corresponding to ground and vertical structure labels have also improved marginally (with 40% and 37% improvements respectively). Thus, fusion algorithm generated improvements in prediction across the spectrum of *HEH* labels.

Figure 2 shows an illustrative sample from our test images. These images include examples of outdoor scenes with and without buildings. The second column in the image shows *HEH* labels. The color code for *HEH* labels is green (ground), blue (sky) and red (vertical structures). Superimposed labels that indicate vertical sub-structures are '*o*' (porous), '*x*' (solid) and arrows (planar orientation). The third column shows *Make3D* output. The fourth column shows the fusion algorithm's output. Since *HEH* generated labels for vertical sub-structures change extensively even in a small image region, the fusion output also exhibited a similar trend. For smoother visualization, the fusion algorithm was modified using the morphological dilation operator with a disk size of two (The regression errors were calculated without the dilation operation). The final column shows the ground truth generated using a laser

*Table 2. Fusion results per individual HEH labels. The table shows that the fusion improved results across all HEH labels in the testing data.*

| HEH Label | Percent Decrease in Mean Square Error |
|---|---|
| Sky | 90.3212 |
| Ground | 44.6447 |
| Vertical Structures | 38.1775 |

(Saxena et al, 2009). Clearly, the fusion algorithm has better depth prediction for the sky region. The improvement for the other regions though subtler is also noticeable. The artifacts of the laser-generated ground data (inability to distinguish sky and far-away objects) are also overcome to a certain extent by the fusion algorithm because of the *HEH* labels (see the first and second examples).

## APPLICATIONS

3-D reconstruction from monocular cues has been used to provide context to image classification tasks. For example, an object detection algorithm can learn contextual information like "Pedestrians are likely to be on the Ground and are vertical non porous surfaces" if 3-D structural cues are provided to it. By simply augmenting the object detection classifier with contextual features related to 3-D surface layouts generated by HEH, Hoiem, D., Efros, A., and Herbert, M., (2007) showed that object detection performance can be drastically improved. Heitz, G., and Koller, D., (2008) suggest the use of 3-D construction for providing scale context to their TAS algorithm (though their current version uses only 2-D information). For the pedestrian identification problem in urban settings, Perko, R., and Leonardis, A., (2007) have used HEH to provide spatial context to their detection problem.

Hoiem, D., Stein, A. N., Efros, A. A., and Herbert, M. (2007) have used the geometric class

confidence values for each region generated by HEH algorithm as part of the feature vector to learn occlusion boundaries. These features are useful since variation in 3-D surface characteristics between two tow adjoining regions indicates a high-likelihood of an occlusion boundary. One of the challenges of the object detection tasks is that there can be a lot of scale variations amongst the objects. A 3-D reconstruction approach can be used to provide the scale context to improve the results of the object detection class. Heitz, G., and Koller, D., (2008) suggest the use of 3-D construction for providing scale context to their TAS algorithm (though their current version uses only 2-D information).

Scene understanding algorithms attempt to recover multiple image properties like surface orientation and depth, occlusion boundaries, object recognition, illumination and scene categorization etc. These image properties are interrelated. For example, occlusion boundary and object detection can benefit by surface reconstruction as shown in Hoiem et al. (2007a) and Hoiem et al. (2007b). Similarly, 3-D surface reconstruction can also benefit from occlusion boundary detection and object detection steps. For example, the existence of a car object implies the highly likelihood of a supporting ground surface. Therefore, inferring these multiple image properties simultaneously can produce more comprehensive results. In Hoiem, D., Efros, A., and Herbert, M., (2008), authors used a simple iterative inference algorithm where during each iteration, surface estimation using HEH, Occlusion estimation using algorithm proposed in (Hoiem, D., Efros, A., & Herbert, M. 2007b) and object/viewpoint estimation using the algorithm in (Hoiem, D., Efros, A., & Herbert, M. 2008b) are recalculated in that order. For each of these individual algorithms, the feature vectors are augmented with estimates from the other steps. The authors have reported impressive improvements in occlusion boundary detection whereas surface estimation and object detection results have improved marginally. Li, C., Kowdle, A.,

*Figure 2. A comparative visualization of the depth estimated generated by Make3D and the fusion approach. From left, the first column shows the original image; the second column shows the labels generated by HEH; the third column shows the depth map produced by Make3D; the fourth column shows the depth map generated by fusion of Make3D and HEH; the final column shows the ground truth.*

Saxena, A., & Chen, T. (2010) has used a similar approach for holistic scene understanding. Their Cascaded Classification Model (CCM) estimates scene categorization, object detection, multiclass image segmentation and 3D structure of an image. The CCM uses n-tier structure where each tier has multiple classifiers for each subtask of interest. The classifiers in the first tier operate in a standalone mode operating only on the image features, whereas lower tier classifiers receive both image features and model outputs from the previous tiers. Since the sub-tasks are inter-related, this augmented information provides context to the subtask classifiers, allowing them to improve their performance.

Another interesting application of 3-D reconstruction is robot manipulation and path planning. Nabbe, B., Hoiem D., Efros, A.A., & Hebert M. (2006) have used HEH generated 3-D structural labels to optimize the mobile robots path planning algorithm. Since standard mobility sensors such as LADAR or stereo have a very short depth resolution, current path planning algorithms are very myopic in nature and use only local obstacle avoidance based approaches. However, HEH generated labels can be used to improve these algorithms beyond the standard sensor horizons. Michels, J., Saxena, A., & Ng, A.Y. (2005) estimate depths from monocular cues and then use reinforcement learning to learn control policy for selecting steering directions. The authors train the monocular depth reconstruction algorithm on a combination of real and synthetic images, estimate the depth of obstacles in a scene using the trained algorithm and drive the car at multiple locations.

A novel application of the ability to learn complex image attributes from 2-D features is the robotic grasping system built by Saxena, A., Driemeyer, J., Kearns, J., & Ng, A.Y., (2006). Inspired by the success of Make3D in generating descriptive 3-D properties based on a 2-D image, the authors have developed an algorithm that learns the technique to grasp a novel object without constructing a dense 3-D model.

An obvious application of 3-D reconstruction is to generate 3-D models of scenes that can be used to improve browsing experience. Hoiem, D., Efros, A., & Herbert, M. (2005b) have developed the automatic pop up algorithm that first lays the image on the grouped plane and then "pops" up regions classified as being vertical by HEH. Saxena (Saxena et al., 2009) has used Make3D algorithm to improve the results generated by the "pop up algorithm". More complex applications to convert 2-D video to 3-D video have also been developed, mainly for converting traditional 2-D movies to their pseudo 3-D versions (Comanducci, D., Maki, A., Colombo, C., & Cipolla, R. 2010). Comanducci et al. (2010) present an algorithm for generating a stereo image pairs that have disparities matching the depth of the scene depicted by an input image. The algorithm takes as input two images of a same scene that are not in stereoscopic system configuration. Using the image pair, epipolar geometry and camera self calibration are first calculated. HEH algorithm is then used to identify the ground region in both images. Homography induced by the ground plane is then used to generate ground plane equation. The stereoscopic images of the ground plane are calculated using the ground plane and calibration data. After that, the background and foreground images are rendered using the rendered ground plane images. Stereoscopic image pairs are then displayed by merging the rendered images.

Many other interesting applications are being developed based on monocular cue based 3D structural properties including tools for photo navigation (Hsieh, C.C., Cheng, W.H., Chang, C.H., Chuang, Y.Y., & Wu, J.L. 2008) and internet photo montaging (Chen, T., Ming, C. M., Tan, P., Shamir, A., & Hu, S.M. 2009).

## FUTURE RESEARCH DIRECTIONS

As shown in the previous section, our fusion approach improved *Make3D*'s output marginally. However, we found that a considerable disparity in the ability of *HEH* labels in impacting the accuracy of the *Make3D*'s depth estimation. Considering the fact that *HEH* and *Make3D* work are unrelated and *HEH* labels were not designed to provide the most useful label information to *Make3D*, the improvements we obtained by fusion provide positive evidence that clustering the image into spatially homogeneous regions as a simultaneous/preprocessing step to 3-D depth estimation has the potential to improve estimation accuracy.

We are in the initial stages of generalizing HDP based clustering to regressing for depth estimates. Few of the advantages of our approach are

1.  Dirchlet process based clustered has the ability to dynamically adjust the number of clusters based on evidence (image data in our case). Compared to conventional techniques like *k-means* which require the number of clusters as an input parameter, the dynamic cardinality of Dirchlet clusters provides a significant advantage for our problem. This allows us to model the possibility of an arbitrarily complex image with any number of spatially homogenous 3-D clusters.

2.  Spatial relations can be expressed in statistical terms using HDPs (Du, L., 2009). As proven by Saxena et al's work (2008), enforcing neighborhood relationships between superpixels using the MRF framework was a key contributor to their overall performance. HDPs provide a statistically rigorous model for enforcing neighborhood relationships.

3.  Our approach is based on the premise that spatial clusters and depth estimation regression models should be learnt as part of a single parameter estimation process, with the objective of maximizing depth estimation accuracy. The fusion approach presented in this chapter suffered from the handicap of having to deal with evidence generated by two independent estimation models, whose performance was simultaneously optimized. For example, *HEH* generated vertical subclasses are not significantly useful to the fusion model, since they did not complement *Make3D*'s depth estimates. However, since *HEH* approach was trained for images that have all three main classes (ground, sky and vertical structures) in significant proportions, the fusion approach had the same applicability constraint. We hope that a unified approach will produce significant improvements in the final estimation since both clustering and estimation processes can be fine-tuned together.

## CONCLUSION

In this chapter, we provided a brief review of research literature on 3-D reconstruction, with a particular emphasis on monocular-cues based reconstruction. Two recent 3-D reconstruction techniques that used machine-learning algorithms trained by monocular cues were explained in detail. These techniques were chosen, since they do not have restrictive applicability constraints. The success of these algorithms is their ability to not only use local features of image regions but also their global context in relation to the entire image. The HEH algorithm relies on multiple segmentation hypothesis to overcome the pitfall of using a single local feature based segmentation based hypothesis. Make3D uses a MRF algorithm to enforce structural constraints on the 3D properties of an image region. Recognizing the importance of incorporating global context into 3D reconstruction, we are exploring non parametric techniques for further advance the state of the art in this domain. In this book chapter, We presented results from an initial fusion-based approach that uses the output generated by the two seminal approaches to generate a even more accurate depth prediction..

## REFERENCES

Ahmed, A., & Farag, A. (2006). A new formulation for shape from shading for non-Lambertian surfaces. *Conference on Computer Vision and Pattern Recognition*, (pp. 1817–1824).

Barnard, S. T. (1989). Stochastic stereo matching over scale. *International Journal of Computer Vision, 3*(1), 17–32. doi:10.1007/BF00054836

Breiman, L. (1996). Bagging predictors. *Machine Learning, 24*(2), 123–140. doi:10.1007/BF00058655

Breiman, L. (2001). Random forests. *Machine Learning*, *45*(1), 5–32. doi:10.1023/A:1010933404324

Chen, T., Ming, C. M., Tan, P., Shamir, A., & Hu, S. M. (2009). Sketch2photo: Internet image montage. *ACM Transactions on Graphics*, *28*(5). doi:10.1145/1618452.1618470

Clerc, M., & Mallot, S. (2002). The texture gradient equation for recovering shape from texture. *IEEE Transactions on Pattern Analysis and Machine Intelligence*, *24*, 536–549. doi:10.1109/34.993560

Comanducci, D., Maki, A., Colombo, C., & Cipolla, R. (2010). 2D-to-3D photo rendering for 3D displays. *Proceedings of International Symposium on 3D Data Processing, Visualization and Transmission* (3DPVT).

Du, L., Ren, L., Dunson, D., & Carin, L. (2009). A Bayesian model for simultaneous image clustering, annotation and object segmentation. In Bengio, Y., Schuurmans, D., Lafferty, L., Williams, C. K. I., & Culotta, A. (Eds.), *Advances in Neural Information Processing Systems, 22* (pp. 486–494).

Faugeras, O. (1993). *Three-dimensional computer vision*. Cambridge, MA: MIT Press.

Faugeras, O., & Luong, Q.-T. (2001). *The geometry of multiple images*. Cambridge, MA: MIT Press.

Felzenszwalb, P., & Huttenlocher, D. (2004). Efficient graph-based image segmentation. *International Journal of Computer Vision*, *59*.

Fleming, R. W., Torralba, A., & Adelson, E. H. (2004). Specular reflections and the perception of shape. *Journal of Vision (Charlottesville, Va.)*, *4*(9), 798–820. doi:10.1167/4.9.10

Fraser, C. (1999). *Automated vision metrology: A mature technology for industrial inspection and engineering surveys*. In 6th South East Asian Surveyors Congress Fremantle. Department of Geomatics, University of Melbourne, Western Australia.

Garding, J. (1992). Shape from texture for smooth curved surfaces in perspective projection. *Journal of Mathematical Imaging and Vision*, *2*, 327–350. doi:10.1007/BF00121877

Gibson, J. (1950). *The perception of the visual world*. Boston, MA: Houghton Mifflin.

Hartley, R. I., & Zisserman, A. (2000). *Multiple view geometry*. Cambridge, UK: Cambridge University Press.

Heitz, G., & Koller, D. (2008). Learning spatial context: Using stuff to find things. In *Proceedings of the European Conference on Computer Vision*.

Hoiem, D., Efros, A., & Herbert, M. (2005a). *Geometric context from a single imag*. International Conference on Computer Vision (ICCV).

Hoiem, D., Efros, A., & Herbert, M. (2005b). *Automatic photo pop-up*. In ACM SIGGRAPH.

Hoiem, D., Efros, A., & Herbert, M. (2006). *Putting objects in perspective. Computer Vision and Pattern Recognition*. CVPR.

Hoiem, D., Efros, A., & Herbert, M. (2007a). Recovering surface layout from an image. *International Journal of Computer Vision*, *75*(1). doi:10.1007/s11263-006-0031-y

Hoiem, D., Efros, A., & Herbert, M. (2008a). *Closing the loop on scene interpretation*. CVPR.

Hoiem, D., Efros, A. A., & Herbert, M. (2008b, December). Putting objects in perspective. *International Journal of Computer Vision*, *80*(1). doi:10.1007/s11263-008-0137-5

Hoiem, D., Stein, A. N., Efros, A. A., & Herbert, M. (2007b). *Recovering occlusion boundaries from an image.* International Conference on Computer Vision (ICCV).

Hong, L., & Chen, G. (2004). Segment-based stereo matching using graph cuts. *IEEE Computer Society Conference on Computer Vision and Pattern Recognition*, Vol. 1, (pp. 74-81).

Hsieh, C. C., Cheng, W. H., Chang, C. H., Chuang, Y. Y., & Wu, J. L. (2008). Photo navigator. In *Proceeding of the 16th ACM International Conference on Multimedia*, (pp. 419–428). New York, NY: ACM.

Hwang, W., Lu, C.-S., & Chung, P.-C. (1998). Shape from texture: Estimation of planar surface orientation through the ridge surfaces of continuous wavelet transform. *IEEE Transactions on Image Processing*, 7, 773–780. doi:10.1109/83.668032

Kanatani, K., & Chou, T. (1989). Shape from texture: General principle. *Artificial Intelligence*, 38, 1–48. doi:10.1016/0004-3702(89)90066-0

Kang, C., & Ghosal, S. (2008, November). Clusterwise regression using Dirichlet mixtures. In A. Sengupta (Ed.), Advances in multivariate statistical methods (pp. 305–325). Singapore: World Scientific Publishing Company.

Kolmogorov, V., & Zabih, R. (2002). *Multi-camera scene reconstruction via graph cuts.* European Conference on Computer Vision.

Kosecka, J., & Zhang, W. (2002). Video compass. In *Proceedings of the European Conference on Computer Vision.* Springer-Verlag.

Kozera, R. (1998). An overview of the shape from shading problem. *Machine Graphics and Vision*, 7(1), 291–312.

Li, C., Kowdle, A., Saxena, A., & Chen, T. (2010). *Towards holistic scene understanding: Feedback enabled cascaded classification models. Neural Information Processing Systems.* NIPS.

Li, S. (1995). *Markov random field modeling in computer vision.* Springer-Verlag.

Longuet-Higgins, H. C. (1981). A computer algorithm for reconstructing a scene from two projections. *Nature, 293*, 133–135. doi:10.1038/293133a0

Loomis, J., & Eby, D. (1989, March). Relative motion parallax and the perception of structure from motion. In *Proceedings of IEEE Workshop on Visual Motion,* Irvine, CA, (pp. 204–211).

Malik, J., & Rosenholtz, R. (1997). Computing local surfaces orientation and shape from texture for curved surfaces. *International Journal of Computer Vision, 23*(2), 149–168. doi:10.1023/A:1007958829620

McCallum, A., Pal, C., Druck, G., & Wang, X. (2006). *Multi-conditional learning: Generative/discriminative training for clustering and classification.* AAAI.

Michels, J., Saxena, A., & Ng, A. Y. (2005*). High speed obstacle avoidance using monocular vision and reinforcement learning.* International Conference on Machine Learning (ICML).

Nabbe, B., Hoiem, D., Efros, A. A., & Hebert, M. (2006). *Opportunistic use of vision to push back the path-planning horizon. Intelligent Robots and Systems.* IROS.

Oliensis, J. (1999). A multi-frame structure-from-motion algorithm under perspective projection. *International Journal of Computer Vision, 34*(2–3), 163–192. doi:10.1023/A:1008139920864

Paul, M. K. C., Wang, X., & McCallum, A. (2006). *Multi-conditional learning for joint probability models with latent variables.* NIPS Workshop Advances Structured Learning Text and Speech Processing.

Perko, R., & Leonardis, A. (2007, December). On text driven focus of attention for object detection. In L. Paletta & E. Rome (Eds.), *Attention in Cognitive Systems. Theories and Systems from an Interdisciplinary Viewpoint (WAPCV 2007), LNAI 4840*, (pp. 216–233). Springer.

Permuter, H., & Franoos, J. (2000). Estimating the orientation of planar surfaces: Algorithms and bounds. *IEEE Transactions on Information Theory, 46*(5). doi:10.1109/18.857800

Prados, E., & Faugeras, O. (2005). Shape from shading: A well-posed problem? In *Proceedings of the IEEE Conference on Computer Vision and Pattern Recognition (CVPR)*, San Diego, California, Vol. 2, (pp. 870–877).

Ross, K., & Laurie, S. J. (1980). *Markov random fields and their applications*. American Mathematical Society.

Saxena, A., Chung, S. H., & Ng, A. Y. (2005). *Learning depth from single monocular images. Neural Information Processing Systems*. NIPS.

Saxena, A., Chung, S. H., & Ng, A. Y. (2007). 3-D depth reconstruction from a single still image. *International Journal of Computer Vision, 76*(1), 53–69. doi:10.1007/s11263-007-0071-y

Saxena, A., Driemeyer, J., Kearns, J., & Ng, A. Y. (2006). *Robotic grasping of novel objects using vision. Neural Information Processing Systems*. NIPS.

Saxena, A., Sun, M., & Ng, A. Y. (2009). Make3D: Learning 3D scene structure from a single still image. *IEEE Transactions on Pattern Analysis and Machine Intelligence, 30*(5), 824–840. doi:10.1109/TPAMI.2008.132

Scharstein, D., & Szeliski, R. (1998). Stereo matching with nonlinear diffusion. *International Journal of Computer Vision, 28*(2), 155–174. doi:10.1023/A:1008015117424

Scharstein, D., & Szeliski, R. (2002). A taxonomy and evaluation of dense two-frame stereo correspondence algorithms. *International Journal of Computer Vision, 47*(1), 7–42. doi:10.1023/A:1014573219977

Snavely, N., Seitz, S. M., & Szeliski, R. (2006). Photo tourism: Exploring photo collections in 3D. *ACM Transactions on Graphics, 25*(3), 835–846. doi:10.1145/1141911.1141964

Snavely, N., Seitz, S. M., & Szeliski, R. (2007). Modeling the world from Internet photo collections. *International Journal of Computer Vision, 80*(2), 189–210. doi:10.1007/s11263-007-0107-3

Spetsakis, M. E., & Aloimonos, J. Y. (1991). A multiframe approach to visual motion perception. *International Journal of Computer Vision, 6*(3), 245–255. doi:10.1007/BF00115698

Szeliski, R., & Kang, S. B. (1994). Recovering 3D shape and motion from image streams using nonlinear least squares. *Journal of Visual Communication and Image Representation, 5*(1), 10–28. doi:10.1006/jvci.1994.1002

Tankus, A., Sochen, N., & Yeshurun, Y. (2005, June). Shape-from shading under perspective projection. *International Journal of Computer Vision, 63*(1), 21–43. doi:10.1007/s11263-005-4945-6

Tomasi, C., & Kanade, T. (1992). Shape and motion from image streams under orthography: a factorization method. *International Journal of Computer Vision, 9*(2), 137–154. doi:10.1007/BF00129684

Triggs, B., McLauchlan, P. F., Hartley, R. I., & Fitzgibbon, A. W. (1999, September). Bundle adjustment—A modern synthesis. *International Workshop on Vision Algorithms* (pp. 298–372).

Udo Ahlvers, U. Z. (2005). *Inclusion of magnitude information for improved phase-based disparity estimation in stereoscopic image pairs*. Hamburg, Germany: Department of Signal Processing and Communications Helmut-Schmidt University.

Zhang, R., Tsai, P.-S., Cryer, J., & Shah, M. (1999, August). Shape from shading: A survey. *IEEE Transactions on Pattern Analysis and Machine Intelligence*, *21*(8), 690–706. doi:10.1109/34.784284

## ADDITIONAL READING

Forsyth, D. A., & Ponce, J. (2003). *Computer vision: A modern approach*. Prentice Hall.

## KEY TERMS AND DEFINITIONS

**AdaBoost:** It is a machine learning algorithm used to construct a strong classifier using linear combination of weak classifiers.

**Image Segmentation:** Dividing image into different regions or into set of pixels. At the end of this process, each pixel of the image will be assigned a label such that all the pixels belong to same label share same visual characteristics.

**Markov Random Field (MRF):** Markov Random Fields is a graphical reasoning algorithm that uses an undirected graph model to represent relationships between a set of random variables.

**Monocular Vision:** A kind of vision which involves two eyes getting used separately. The field of view is increased in this vision but the depth perception is limited.

**Random Forest:** A tree-based machine-learning algorithm which is an ensemble of tree predictors and outputs the average of the individual tree predictors as the final output.

**Stereo Vision:** The task exploiting the difference between two slightly different projections of the world onto the retinas of the two eyes. It involves two steps: Combining the features observed by two eyes and reconstructing their three-dimensional figure.

**Structure from Motion (SFM):** A technique to obtain 3-d locations of the points. In this, two or more photographs will be taken to find correspondences between the images. Finally triangulation will be used to obtain 3-d locations of the points.

# Chapter 9
# Image Based 3D Modeling and Rendering from Single View Perspective Images

**S. Mohan**
*Dr.N.G.P Institute of Technology, India*

**S. Murali**
*Maharaja Institute of Technology, India*

## ABSTRACT

*In computer vision, 3D modeling refers to the process of developing 3D representation of the real world objects with systematic procedure. The 3D models can be built based on geometric information about the object or scene to be modeled using CAD/CAM software. However, this approach needs prior knowledge of the objects in the scene like dimension, size of objects, distance from the object to camera, et cetera. To make the 3D models more photo realistic and convenient, images of the objects can be used to build the 3D models. In this chapter, the authors propose a method to extract 3D model from single view perspective image. The approach is based on edge length and exploiting symmetric objects in the scene. Later, an application of touring into picture is discussed with the proposed method.*

## INTRODUCTION

There are mainly two reasons for the diversion from stereovision – 3D modelling with multiple images, to monocular vision – 3D modelling with a single image. Firstly, it allowed researchers to clearly understand the importance of monocular cues and how useful it would be when combined with binocular cues. 3D reconstruction will be more visually pleasing when monocular cues are combined with binocular cues. Secondly, it allowed researches to elucidate what sorts of monocular cues are useful for depth perception. Monocular cues are interesting and important. Further, monocular cameras are cheaper, and their installation is less complex then stereo cameras. Using single view images, reconstruction of 3D works well even at larger distances. But in stereo

DOI: 10.4018/978-1-4666-0113-0.ch009

vision, the accuracy is limited by the baseline distance between the two cameras. When the distance between the cameras becomes large, surfaces in the images exhibit, different degrees of occlusion, large disparities, etc, all of which makes it more difficult for a computer to accurately determine the depth of the scene. Due to all these reasons, recent work on 3D reconstruction is done mainly using single view images. It is called as Single View Modeling (SVM).

SVM refers to building three dimensional models from single image. It is inferred from the literature (Seitz, 2001, Criminisi, 1999, & Debevec, 1996) that 3D reconstruction from a single image must necessarily be through an interactive process in which the user provides information about the scene structure. Such information may be in terms of vanishing points or vanishing lines, co-planarity, spatial inter-relationship of features, surface normal, and camera parameters. Some of the traditional approaches based on shape, shading and texture have complicated user interaction in terms of specifying the inputs.

Recent works deal with various kinds of 3D modeling methods – a little user interactivity is effective in reconstructing a 3D model (Seitz, 2001) were high quality results were obtained on images with limited perspective distortion but only visible surfaces in an image could be modelled in the 3D thus leading to holes near the occluded boundaries. Another algorithm was introduced later by Feng Han which reconstructed 3D shapes and scenes of an object with prior experience or knowledge using Bayesian reconstruction (Han, 2003). Derek Hoiem later proposed a fully automatic method for creating virtual walkthroughs from a single photograph. Though the algorithm proposed did not work on every single image, surprising results were obtained on a wide range of images (Hoiem, Derek, 2005). The approach proposed by Tal Hassner was interesting as 3D reconstruction was done with the help of a database of 2D images. Hassner's approach also provided accurate results but did not do well on unstructured objects

(hands). A large set of probable images (Hassner, & Basri, 2006) were stored in the database with their depth maps. The input image is compared with the images in the database and the most probable match is selected and the probable depth is estimated. Another reconstruction technique was proposed recently by A. Saxena were the Markov Random Field (MRF) algorithm was used given only the 2D image as input. No particular assumptions were made in this approach which was beneficiary (Saxena, & Ng, 2007). This approach created 3D models which were visually pleasing to the user's eye.

Perspective image in simple terms is an approximate representation of an image as seen by the human eye. A point in the perspective image to which the parallel lines not parallel to the image plane appear to converge is called the vanishing point. Hence, in the single view perspective images, parallel lines converge at vanishing point. The line which is passing through more than one vanishing points and parallel to the ground plane is known as the horizon line (Criminisi, 1999), (Hartley, 2003). The lines perpendicular to the horizon line may contribute a vanishing point which may be very far from the image boundary (Figure 1). In Figure 1, the edges 1, 2 and 3 are of equal length in the world space. But they appear to be in different lengths due to perspective distortion.

It can also be observed that the length of these vertical edges (edges 1, 2 and 3) decrease towards the vanishing point. With this observation, it is found that there is a scope for estimating the 3D coordinates from single view perspective images by measuring the vertical edges and its lengths.

Generally, images considered for modeling contains building images and hence the vertical edges would be present. The core of the investigation could be on extracting the vertical edges, measuring its lengths and assigning a relative intensity to depict the depth. The length of the vertical edges may not be used as the scale of depth because the length may vary depending on the resolution of the image. But the intensity can

*Figure 1. Visual clues in terms of edges in perspective image*

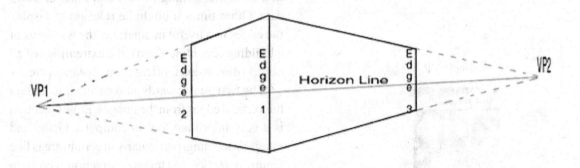

be assigned as a relative scale because the range of values is fixed and can be assigned based on the length of the line segments.

The chapter is organized as follows: Initially a method of constructing 3D wireframes using length of the edges is discussed. The edge length here is used to assign an intensity which helps in extracting approximate 3D coordinates. Later part of the chapter unveils the method of constructing 3D walk through from single view images based on very minimal user interaction using cuboids meshes. Though these two portions are independent, both can be used in constructing the 3D structure from single view images.

## APPROACH FOR BUILDING THE 3D WIREFRAME USING EDGE LENGTH

With the observation from a perspective image, it is understood that the vertical edges and its length constitute major features to estimate the depth information. When the perspective images are observed, there may be more than one vanishing point present in the scene based on the orientation of parallel lines. The possible cases of vanishing points are shown in Figure 2.

Multiple vanishing points are common in particular situations. Formations of single and double vanishing points are most common in the scenario where objects of planar surfaces are considered. Three vanishing points cases might occur when the horizontal edges form two vanishing points and the vertical edges form one vanishing point on convergence as in figure 2 c.

In most of the single perspective images with planar surfaces, it is observed that there will be at the most two vanishing points which are formed by the horizontal edges as in Figure 2 b. In such cases, the vertical edges may not lead to third vanishing point. Even if it appears to converge, the vanishing point will be very far from the boundary of the image. The vanishing points contribute in estimating the length of the vertical edges as the lengths of vertical edges vary depending on the position of vanishing points. Also it can be observed that the length of the vertical edges decrease towards the vanishing point.

An edge is described as "the external limit of an object, area or surface; a place or part farthest away from the center of something" (Oxford American Dictionary). In digital images, an edge can be seen as local changes in color intensity, also called "brightness discontinues". In an image without edges, the colors would either be continuous in intensity (called a gradient) or a flat image of one color. If an image does contain edges, these would be shown as local gradients (if the edges are, more or less, blurred) or a sudden change in brightness or color intensity. Edge detection is used in many applications for computer vision, using image processing. The intention is to recognize

*Figure 2. Various cases of vanishing point formation*

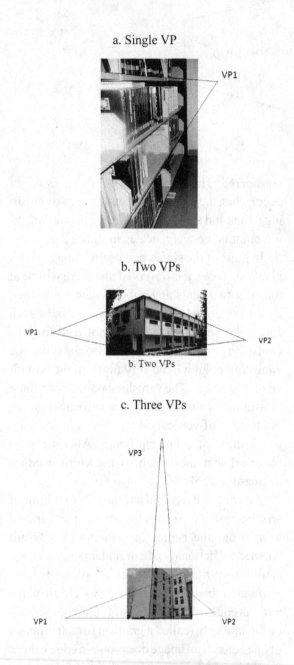

a. Single VP

b. Two VPs

b. Two VPs

c. Three VPs

and take apart objects from one another, and also recognition of these shapes. One could imagine having an application, where a camera captures a DVD cover, and identifies it by calculating its position, then the position of the barcode and finally, by reading its barcode and comparing it to a database, getting its title and other relevant data. Other times it might be relevant to display the edges in a useful manner, i.e. the windows of a building (counting them), the extremities of an object (dimensions, orientation, distance, etc.).

The first goal towards automating is to extract the vertical edges from the images. Edge detection is a very important tool in computer vision and image processing, particularly in certain areas like feature detection and feature extraction. The main aim is to identify points in the image where the image brightness changes sharply and has other discontinuities. The purpose of edge detection is to capture important events and changes in the properties of the world. To extract the vertical edge segments, a pre-processing is required by applying edge detection methods like canny, sobel or prewitt. The sobel operator is usually used in image processing for detecting edges. It is a discrete differentiation operator which computes the approximation of the gradient of the image intensity. This operator is based on convolving the image entered with a very small, separable integer valued filter, both in the horizontal and vertical direction and is hence in terms of computation very inexpensive. Thus, the gradient of the image intensity at each point is calculated by the operator which gives the rate of change in that direction. Hence, the result specifies how abruptly and smoothly the image changes at that point at the probability of an edge at that point. The orientation of the edge can also be calculated using the Sobel operator. The prewitt edge detector is very similar to sobel edge detector, both sobel and prewitt return a number of false edges, they have very little practical differences with each other. In most of the cases Canny method performs better by extracting edges. The canny edge detector used a multi-stage algorithm to detect a wide range of edges in images. Canny edge detector used a filter based on the first derivative of Gaussian to reduce noise. The Canny algorithm is adaptable to various environments, thus canny is widely used in most algorithms. Edge detection results in extracting all edges including trivial and non vertical edges as in Figure 3. The vertical edges from the image can be extracted by applying a suitable filter. There are standard filters like line detection mask to extract only vertical edges. As this filter may extract small segments, it may not be useful for extracting vertical edges in this case. Hence alternative approaches should be used to solve this problem.

## Vertical Edge Extraction

From the extracted set of edges, the basic intention is to filter only the vertical edge segments. The standard method of detecting vertical lines is using the mask as given in Figure 4.

The drawback of the filter is that it cannot be generalized. Based on the size of the mask, the length of the vertical lines may vary. It might filter trivial edges which may not contribute the actual vertical edges. Hence a more convenient filter has to be designed to extract the vertical edges.

The basic property of vertical edges is the angle of inclination with respect to X-axis and the number of pixels which forms the line segments. By keeping these two parameters as the key component, a filter to extract vertical edge segments can be designed. The parameters consist of two components: length ($l$) and the angle ($\theta$). As the vertical lines are to be considered, the angle of inclination with respect to X axis could be typically 90˚. Since many discontinuities might occur along the vertical edge segments, the length parameter can be fixed at a value which could either extract a portion or whole line.

It is observed that if the length parameter chosen for filtering is more, then many small edge segments may be missed out. Similarly if the length parameter for filtering is small, then some of the trivial edges may be selected.

As the outcome of the filtering parameters, a line in the image may appear as disconnected line in the resultant image. Also the discontinuity occurs due to the orientation of the vertical edges in the images. It can be observed from the Figure 5 that some of the vertical edges are not perpendicular (90˚) to the X axis. It can be verified by manually drawing a line perpendicular to horizon line as in Figure 5. Applying the filtering to these vertical lines will result in disconnected line segments.

To resolve the problem of discontinuity there are some approaches proposed in the literature (Lee, 1990), (Vernon, 1991), and (Yuan-Hui, 2006) in which most of the approaches are based on either gradient filtering or Hough transform. Following them, the Hough transform based rotation could be used as one of the solutions to first fit the straight lines and then rotate the image for an angle equal to the angle of inclination between any of the straight lines with X-axis (or horizon line).

The consequence of this approach is that the whole image is rotated based on any one of the vertical edge's orientation. Other vertical edges may not be rectified to 90˚. For example applying Hough transform based rotation to the image in 5 will result in an image as in Figure 6. Again it can be observed by drawing vertical lines perpendicular to horizon line manually over the edges. In Figure 6 edges on the right side are 90˚ to the X-axis where as the edges on the left side are not vertical after rotation. The reason behind this is that the vertical edges are not parallel in the image space. They appear to converge at a vanishing point farther from image boundary.

Other method could be a heuristic approach based on the orientation of each line segment. In this case a threshold along the X axis called *Xdiff* can be considered for connecting the line segments. As we know, each line segment can be represented with a pair of coordinates as (*Xstart, Ystart*) and (*Xend, Yend*). Since the disconnected line may contain more than one line segments, there may be more than one pair of coordinates on the line segment. If the *Xstart* and *Xend* of any line segment fall within certain threshold *Xdiff*, then it

*Figure 3. Image with edges using canny operator*

a. Original Image

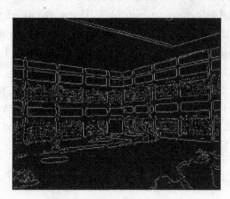

b. Edge image

can be considered to be a part of length line segment.

As long as the line segments are within the threshold, their Y coordinates can be traced to find the end. With all the line segments within the threshold, the *Ystart* of the first line segment and the *Yend* of the last line segments can be considered as the Y coordinate of two end points of a single line segment.

In figure 7, there are seven line segments within the threshold value *Xdiff*. The actual length of the line segment after applying this method becomes equal to the sum of all the small line segments and finally these are considered to be a single line.

The procedure based on the above approach can be given as

Procedure *ConnectLine*

1. Assign *Threshold* with the maximum Xdiff and count with 1 for counting unique line segments
2. For each line segment
   a. while (Xend-XStart) is less than *Threshold* do
      i. Store the Y coordinate in YVal
      ii. Increment X coordinate
   b. X min = Xstart
   c. Y min = minimum(YVal)
   d. X max= X coordinate
   e. Y max = Maximum(YVal)
   f. Increment count
3. length of each unique line is calculated as
   a. |Ymax-Ymin|
4. Total number of unique lines = count

*Figure 4. Vertical line detection mask*

| -1 | 2 | -1 |
|----|---|----|
| -1 | 2 | -1 |
| -1 | 2 | -1 |

*Figure 5. Vertical edge segments not perpendicular to X-axis*

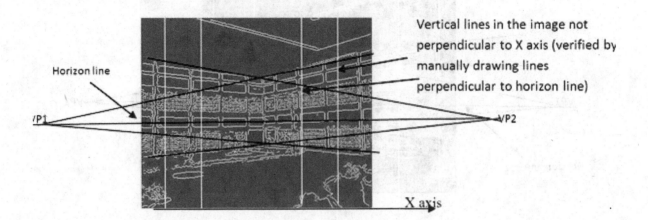

## Intensity Assignment to Vertical Edges

The length of each vertical line extracted during filtering can be found by counting the number of pixels on each line segment. Since only vertical edges are required for line length, the pixels along the Y axis can be counted by tracing neighborhood pixels with value 1 (which represent the edges in a binary image). When all the line lengths are identified, the intensity depth cueing method can be applied to assign the intensity which is the representative of approximate depth information. As discussed in chapter 4, representing the intensity with 256 levels has lot of advantages and hence the same can be followed while assigning the intensity.

The intensity can be assigned by first identifying the longest line segment in the image. The longest line segment should be assigned with the highest intensity. All the other line segments can be assigned with intensities relative to its length. The intensity to each line segment is computed as

$$Ix = Imax / Lmax * Lx \qquad (1)$$

where $Ix$ is *Intensity of current line,*

*Imax* is the *Maximum Intensity* (usually 255),

Lmax is the Length of longest line and Lx is length of current line

Here the *maximum intensity* is the upper limit of the intensity value (usually 255), *length of the longest line* segment and *current line segment* are extracted after filtering. The intensity depth cueing is assigned to each of the line segments as above. Hence all the pixels along each line segments get the same values as intensities. Similar to the simple depth cueing method, here also the lines retain the perspective distortion as the X and Y coordinates of each line segments are directly taken from image space. The procedure based on the above investigation is given as follows

Procedure *AutoEstimate*

1.  Consider the image f(x,y). Apply high pass filter to sharpen the edge. Call the sharpened image fs(x,y).

2.  Apply edge detector (canny, Sobel or Prewitt) to extract the edges from the image. Call the resultant image as fse(x,y)

3.  Apply the vertical edge detection method as below on fse(x,y)

*Figure 6. After rotation. Vertical lines on left are not parallel and vertical lines on right are parallel with manually drawn lines.*

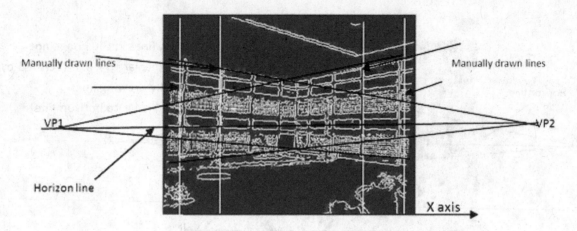

a. Consider a structure element S with length 10 and angle 90' for filtering
b. Apply filtering using S on fse(x,y)
c. For all pixels (x,y)
   i. While fse(x,y) = 1 (indicating presence of edge) do
1. increment value of y by 1
   ii. store the start and end of y value
   iii. length(current line) = end of y value – start of y value
4. If disconnected line segments are there, call procedure *connectline,* else continue step 5.
5. Assign the intensity to each line segment as below
   a. Find the longest line segment lmax
   b. Assign highest intensity Imax to lmax.
   c. For all the remaining line segments do
      i. Intensity (current line)=(Imax/length(Lmax)) * length(current line)
6. The coordinates of each line segment are assigned as below
   a. X = (Xstart, Xend) of current line
   b. Y = (Ystart, Yend) of current line
   c. Z = intensity of current line

## Using Symmetric Clues: Method for Rectifying the Aspect Ratio of Perspective Images

A homography is an invertible transformation from the real projective plane to the projective plane that maps straight lines to straight lines. According to the studies in the field of computer vision, any two images of the same planar surface in space are related by a homography. There are many practical applications, few of which are image rectification, image registration, or computation of camera motion—rotation and translation—between two images. Once camera rotation and translation have been extracted from an estimated homography matrix, this information may be used for navigation, or to insert models of 3D objects into an image or video, so that they are rendered with the correct perspective and appear to have been part of the original scene The results of plane homography (Xiang, 2005) applied on the perspective images are the images retained where the parallel lines are rectified. Finding the final boundary on which the image to be mapped involves homography estimation. If the reference plane and its coordinates of an image are known as described by (Criminisi, 1999), the mapping

*Figure 7. Discontinuity of oriented line due to filtering parameters*

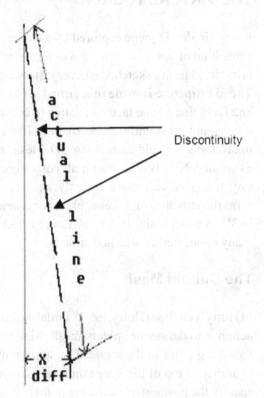

could result in recovering the aspect ratio of the surface. In our case, there is no known reference from the site of the scene and hence a geometrical manipulation can be applied to rectify the surface to its actual aspect ratio. The presence of symmetric patterns in the images like circle, square, hexagon, etc can be exploited as clues while recovering the aspect ratio of the surface. Using the clues there is a possibility of finding the aspect ratio. Consider the Figure 8.a) where the circular object remains as ellipse after applying the perspective trans-formation. The ellipse can be rectified to a circle by scaling either along the minor or major axis of the ellipse. In both the cases, the factor could be to equalize both the axes so that the length of the axes becomes the radius of the circle. If the ellipse is enclosed by an optimally fit rectangle, the major and minor axes can be identified as in Figure 8 b. If the ratio between the major and minor axis is known, then the scaling factor can be accordingly determined.

The correction can be carried out either by increasing the minor axis (Figure 8.b) such that it is equal to the major axis or by decreasing the major axis such that it is equal to the minor axis. In both the ways the ellipse will become a circle. The strategy adopted for correcting the circle is applicable to the entire image. The amount of increase or decrease in the shape gives a valuable input for the image which contains the circular object to resize to its relatively true size (Figure 8.c).

The ratio between major and minor axis is used to either increase or decrease the shape of the whole image.

It is calculated as below.

When Major axis is greater than minor axis

$$R=H/W \qquad (2)$$

When Minor axis is greater than major axis

$$R=W/H \qquad (3)$$

where R- Ratio between height and width, H-Height of rectangle encloses circle, W- Width of rectangle encloses circle.

The new Height (H') and width (W') of the boundary enclosed by rectangle can be computed in two ways as

## Case 1: To Increase the Minor Axis (Width)

$$W'=W * R \qquad (4)$$

$$H'=H$$

where W'-New width, H'-New Height, W-Width of rectangle encloses circle, R- Ratio calculated from either Eq 6.10 or 6.11

## Case 2: To Decrease the Major Axis (Height)

$$H'=H * R \qquad (5)$$

$$W'=W$$

where H'-New height, W'-New width, H-Height of rectangle encloses circle, R- Ratio calculated from either Equation 2 or 3.

Now the height (H') and width (W') of the object become same and hence the ellipse became a circle. The amount of increase in height and width is passed on to the next step to find the true size of the image. Here the image which was rectified by perspective warping is resized to the new height (H') and width (W').

## Virtual Touring into Picture: Introduction

A virtual tour is a simulation of a 3D scene. Creating 3D animations with photo realistic results from single image is a complex and tedious for the animators. They need to create the 3D models on iterative basis that closely resemble the actual scene. To create walk through into the 3D model, the virtual camera position should be known. Extracting camera parameters from single image becomes one of the preconditions for 3D modeling. Without camera parameters, the scene can be modeled with the vague information like scene structure, approximate dimension of surfaces. But the resultant model will lose the photorealistic results in such cases. So a more straightforward approach without camera parameters and tedious user interaction is needed in order to generate virtual walkthrough from single image.

## PROPOSED METHOD TO SIMPLIFY THE VIRTUAL TOURING

Every single 3D scene captured by a camera has some kind of structure in it – a wireframe, which is modeled from a sketch, design or just a scheme. The 3D structure is made of a virtual set of lines and faces that can be faceted enough to construct curves and apparently crude shapes. There are many tools that aid in making 3D Mesh, such as splines, NURBS, etc, but it all comes back to tiny triangles, and more recently squares, that form the structure of a scene, object or character in 3D. A mesh is similar to web or net which has many connected or attached strands.

### The Cuboid Mesh

In Horry's method (Horry,1997), initial user interaction is to define the spidery mesh using single vanishing point in the scene. The spidery mesh is drawn on top of the image and the user has to specify the position of vanishing point if it is not found properly (Figure 9 a). An inner rectangle is drawn with four points which also need to be adjusted using interaction (Figure 9 b). Based on the position of vanishing point, the mesh is approximately drawn to cover the surfaces. If the alignment of mesh is not proper, then the user has to adjust it to fit the surfaces. The spidery mesh is made of large number of vertical and horizontal lines as in Figure 9 c. The lines converge towards the vanishing point and based on the vanishing point the camera parameters are extracted.

It is understood from the study on the types of images considered for modeling that there are one back ground surface and four surfaces covering all the four sides as in a box (Figure 9). Once the background and other surfaces are indentified, then the rest of the process of extracting depth information can be simplified. Each surface in the scene is perspective distorted. Since all the surfaces can be mapped on to a box, they need to have the same depth from the view point. If any-

*Figure 8. a. Circle appears as ellipse b. Ellipse enclosed in a rectangle c. Circular object rectified*

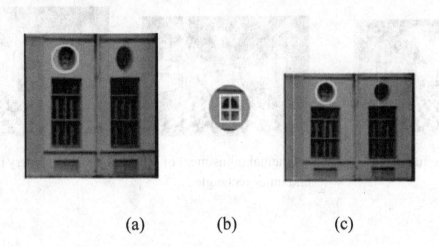

(a)        (b)        (c)

one surface is rectified to the scale using perspective rectification using symmetric objects, then remaining surfaces can be recovered. Hence there is a significant scope in improving the way the mesh is drawn and the surfaces can be rectified to the scale in contrast to the Horry method where the surfaces are mapped approximately. Instead of spidery mesh, a simple cuboid connecting all the surfaces can be drawn. The significance of cuboid mesh and various regions are explained in the following section

## THE REGIONS AND NAMING CONVENTIONS OF CUBOID MESH

In an image to be modeled, the innermost plane is considered to be the back ground and the border of the image is considered to be the foreground. Both background and foreground surfaces can be defined by drawing two rectangles. This can be drawn as part of the user interaction. Remaining four surfaces are the regions connecting foreground and background surfaces. There are five regions formed in the image as in figure 10. The foreground appears hallow from where the viewer perceives the scene.

The surfaces are named as *Region 1 to 4*, from left to right counter clock wise direction as in Figure 10. Each region is represented by the co-ordinates of inner and outer rectangles drawn during user interaction. The coordinates of inner and outer rectangles are represented by specifying *top left* and *bottom right* of the boundaries. There are only four inputs required to draw two rectangles during user interaction. The coordinates of each region and boundaries are given in table 1. All the regions and their vertices are shown in Figure 10.

## EXTRACTION AND RECTIFICATION OF REGIONS FROM CUBOID MESH

The notations in Table 1 and Figure 10 can be generalized for any perspective image which forms single vanishing point at the centre and five regions which cover the vanishing point. Each region in the cuboids mesh has to be extracted for rectification process. The surface in each region is perspective distorted. Applying the perspective rectification method (Xiang, 2005), each surface can be rectified to the scale. The assumption is that any one of the surfaces in the image contains

*Figure 9. User interaction and the spidery mesh in TIP method*

a. Initial setup of VP        b. Manual adjustment of VP      c. Complex spidery mesh
                               and inner rectangle

symmetric patterns which will be used to rectify the surfaces to the scale. It can be understood from Figure 11 that the width of region 1 and 3 and height of region 2 and 4 are same in the world space

The distance between inner and outer rectangle gives the depth of surfaces looked from outer rectangle. The distance between two rectangles is equal to the height of region 2 and 4 or width of region 1 and 3. Since all the surfaces are distorted – perspective distortion, the actual dimension of each surface will be known only after the perspective correction. Since all the surfaces are at the same dimension, rectifying any one

*Figure 10. Regions and the naming in a cuboid mesh*

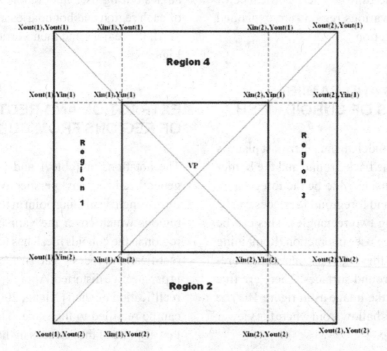

*Table 1. Coordinates of each region in the cuboid mesh*

| Region | Vertex 1 | | Vertex 2 | | Vertex 3 | | Vertex 4 | |
|---|---|---|---|---|---|---|---|---|
| | X | Y | X | Y | X | Y | X | Y |
| Inner Rectangle | Xin(1) | Yin(1) | Xin(1) | Yin(2) | Xin(2) | Yin(2) | Xin(2) | Yin(1) |
| Outer Rectangle | Xout(1) | Yout(1) | Xout(1) | Yout(2) | Xout(2) | Yout(2) | Xout(2) | Yout(1) |
| Region 1 | Xout(1) | Yout(1) | Xout(1) | Yout(2) | Xin(1) | Yin(2) | Xin(1) | Yin(1) |
| Region 2 | Xin(1) | Yin(2) | Xout(1) | Yout(2) | Xout(2) | Yout(2) | Xin(2) | Yin(2) |
| Region 3 | Xin(2) | Yin(1) | Xin(2) | Yin(2) | Xout(2) | Yout(2) | Xout(2) | Yout(1) |
| Region 4 | Xout(1) | Yout(1) | Xin(1) | Yin(1) | Xin(2) | Yin(1) | Xout(2) | Yout(1) |

surface to the scale will be sufficient to estimate the distance between two rectangles. With the distance between two rectangles and dimension of surfaces, the cube in the 3D space can be drawn. In the cube box, all the rectified surfaces can be texture mapped and rendered to create novel views.

In the rectification process, each region is enclosed by a rectangular boundary as in Table 2.

Since the boundaries enclosing each region is known, the process of perspective transformation (Xiang, 2005) can be carried out without user interaction. Each region is transformed into their respective enclosed rectangle. Transformation of coordinates in each region is shown in Figure 12.

After the projective transformation, the parallel lines in each surface are rectified. But they are not rectified to the scale. Using symmetric object in any of the surfaces, rectification to the scale is achieved in all the remaining surfaces also. This is based on the fact that all the surfaces have the same dimension between foreground and background. The scaling factor which is used to scale the symmetric object is used as input to scale all the surfaces. Finally the inner rectangle can be scaled according to the width of region 2 (or 4) and height of region 1 (or 3).

## WIREFRAME OF CUBOID

As the 3D model is enclosed in a cube box, the wireframe of a general cube can be drawn on 3D space as in Figure 13. The vertices of the cube are fixed based on the height and width of surfaces after rectification.

The rectified surfaces can now be texture mapped onto the respective surfaces of the wireframe and the necessary user interaction can be set for the virtual 3D walk through. Texture mapping is a method for adding detail, surface texture, or color to a computer-generated graphic or 3D model. Texture mapping is one of the most successful new techniques in high quality image synthesis. Its use can enhance the visual richness of raster scan images immensely. The technique has been applied to a number of surface attributes: surface color, surface normal, transparency, etc. Texture mapping can be split into two topics: the geometric mapping that warps a texture onto a surface, and the filtering that is necessary in order to avoid aliasing. Texture mapping means the mapping of a function onto a surface in 3D or interpolation. The domain of the function can be one, two, or three-dimensional, and it can be represented by either an array or by a mathematical function. For example, a 1D texture can simulate rock strata; a 2D texture can represent waves, vegetation, or surface bumps; a 3D texture can represent clouds, wood, or marble. Currently

*Figure 11. Width and height of each region used to extract the depth*

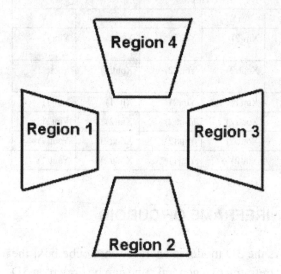

textures will usually be 2D arrays. The source image (texture) is mapped onto a surface in 3D object space, which is then mapped to the destination image (screen) by the viewing projection.

Since the interaction is given based on the keyboard navigation, a random coordinate which covers the model in the scene has been fixed as the initial camera origin. During navigation, depending on the user input, the camera centre is recalculated. In summary, the scene is completely modelled with respect the 3D coordinates, keeping one of the vertices as reference and the camera centre is fixed in such a way that it faces the scene for a possible walk through or fly-through. Some of the screenshots of the walk through are given in Figure 14.

## FUTURE RESEARCH DIRECTIONS

The 3D modelling has wide potential as it has been applied in various fields like architecture, archaeology and entertainment like movies, advertisements and gaming. The conventional modelling methods strongly depends on sophisticated software like maya, studio max etc. However the methods which apply the image based approaches are light in terms of resource consumption and time required to build the models. In addition, the users need not be an expert in using the system. Hence there is a strong scope in developing more approaches for 3D modelling as an integrated system. For example, a tourist can feed the pictures he collected from a heritage or ancient place and the system can build a complete 3D walk through of the scene using the pictures.

The approaches suggested here and the methods existing in literature have somewhat uses user interaction for building the 3D models. Coming out with a system which could build the 3D models from photographs without any user interaction could be a challenging task and the same could be addressed in the future research. Also the methods that discussed were assuming certain types of images like building images, irregular shapes, etc. A method which develops 3D models from any type of images could be really challenging. Such an invariant to objects method could be one of possible development in the future.

Considering the potential of web users and the optimal web objects, loading 3D worlds (second life for example) in lesser time and available bandwidth could be taken well as a research problem. Modeling the 3D world, integrating real pictures in the virtual world, dynamic scene building using natural scenes are some of major upcoming research areas.

*Table 2. Vertices of enclosed rectangle of each region*

| Region | Top left | | Bottom right | |
|---|---|---|---|---|
| | X | Y | X | Y |
| Region 1 | Xout(1) | Yout(1) | Xin(1) | Yout(2) |
| Region 2 | Xout(1) | Yin(2) | Xout(2) | Yout(2) |
| Region 3 | Xin(2) | Yout(1) | Xout(2) | Yout(2) |
| Region 4 | Xout(1) | Yout(1) | Xout(2) | Yin(1) |

*Figure 12. Projection of coordinates on to the enclosed rectangle in each region*

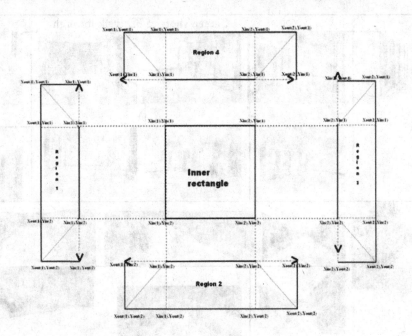

*Figure 13. Cube with all regions*

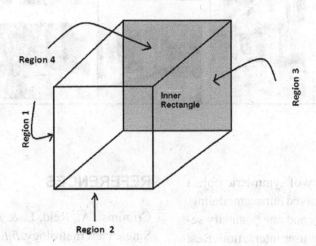

## CONCLUSION

In this chapter, a method to construct 3D wire-frames from single view perspective image based on edge length is proposed. Also a method for rectifying the perspective distortion has been discussed. The rectification is possible only in the presence of symmetric objects. As we have taken, images of building and planar objects, we have found the symmetric objects in most of the cases. Using these two methods, a complete walk through of a single picture can be generated.

In the virtual touring, the user interaction involved is very simple. Drawing two rectangles

*Figure 14. 3D walkthrough of various scenes*

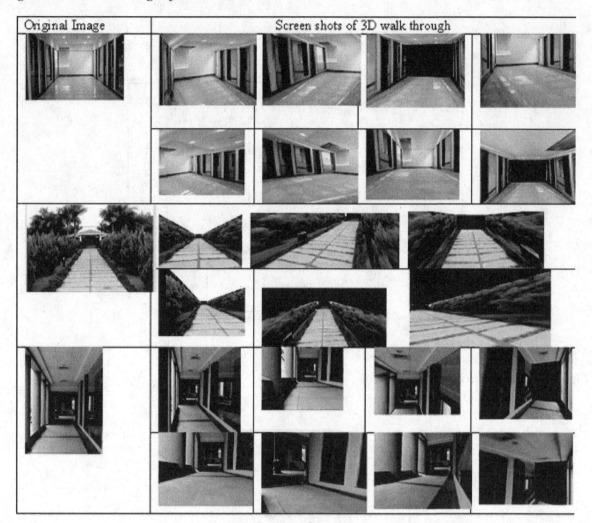

and selecting the boundary of symmetric object is the only interaction involved during modeling. Typically it has four clicks and one boundary selection as the input during user interaction. Rest of the processes is automated. Since the method is based on images having single vanishing point, other kinds of images which contribute more than one vanishing point cannot be modeled. Also there can be at the most five regions that could be texture mapped. Sometimes, the regions may overlap if the inner and outer rectangles are not properly selected.

## REFERENCES

Criminisi, A., Reid, I., & Zisserman, A. (1999). Single view metrology. *International Conference on Computer Vision*, (pp. 434-442).

Debevec, P., Taylor, C., & Malik, J. (1996). Modeling and rendering architecture from photographs: A hybrid geometry- and image-based approach. *In Proceedings of SIGGRAPH*, (pp. 11-20).

Delage, E., Lee, H., & Ng, Y. A. (2006). A dynamic Bayesian network model for autonomous 3D reconstruction from a single indoor image. *Computer Vision and Pattern Recognition*, (pp. 2418-2428).

Forsyth, D. A., & Ponce, J. (2003). *Computer vision: A modern approach*. Prentice Hall.

Gonzalez, R. C., & Woods, R. E. (2002). *Digital image processing* (2nd ed.). Prentice Hall.

Han, F., & Zhu, S. C. (2003). Bayesian reconstruction of 3d shapes and scenes from a single image. In *ICCV Workshop Higher-Level Knowledge in 3D Modeling Motion Analysis*, (pp. 12-21).

Hartley, R. I. (2003). *Multiple view geometry*. Cambridge University Press.

Hassner, T., & Basri, R. (2006). Example based 3D reconstruction from single 2D images. *Computer Vision and Pattern Recognition Workshop (CVPRW)*, (pp. 15-22).

Hoiem, D., Efros, A., & Hebert, M. (2005). Automatic photo pop-up. In *Association for Computing Machinery's Special Interest Group on Computer Graphics and Interactive Techniques*, (pp. 577 – 584).

Horry, Y., Anjyo, K., & Arai, K. (1997). Tour into the picture: Using a spidery mesh interface to make animation from a single image. *Proceedings of the 24th Annual Conference on Computer Graphics and Interactive Techniques*, (pp. 225–232).

Lee, D. (1990). Coping with discontinuities in computer vision: Their detection, classification, and measurement. *IEEE Transactions on Pattern Analysis and Machine Intelligence, 12*(4), 321–344. doi:10.1109/34.50620

Saxena, A., Sun, M., & Ng, A. Y. (2007). Learning 3D scene structure from a single still image. In *ICCV Workshop on 3D Representation for Recognition (3dRR-07)*, (pp. 1-8).

Saxena, J. A., & Ng, A. Y. (2005). High speed obstacle avoidance using monocular vision and reinforcement learning. In *International Conference on Machine Learning (ICML)*, (pp. 713-717).

Vernon, D. (1991). *Machine vision*. Prentice-Hall.

Wang, X., Klette, R., & Rosenhahn, B. (2005). Geometric and photometric correction of projected rectangular pictures. In B. McCane (Ed.), *International Conference on Image and Vision Computing 2005 (IVCNZ)*, (pp. 223-228).

Yu, Y., & Chang, C. (2006). A new edge detection approach based on image context analysis. *Image and Vision Computing, 24*(10), 1090–1102. doi:10.1016/j.imavis.2006.03.006

Zhang, L., Dugas-Phocion, G., Samson, J., & Seitz, S. M. (2001). Single view modeling of free-form scenes. *Computer Vision and Pattern Recognition, 1*, 990–997.

Zhang, L., Dugas-Phocion, G., Samson, J., & Seitz, S. M. (2002). Single view modeling of free-form scenes. *Journal of Visualization and Computer Animation, 13*(4), 225–235. doi:10.1002/vis.291

## KEY TERMS AND DEFINITIONS

**3D Modeling:** In three dimensional computer graphics, 3D modeling is the procedure of developing a mathematical representation of a three dimensional surface of any object – it can be man-made or natural using any specialized software. It is a process of creating a wireframe model that represents the three dimensional object which is man-made, alive or natural. A three dimensional model is created using a set of points in 3D space, which are connected by various geometric data such as lines, and curved surfaces. It can be displayed as a two-dimensional image through a process called 3D rendering or used in a computer simulation of physical phenomena.

**Monocular Vision:** Monocular vision in general language mean 'vision with one eye'. By using each eye individually as opposed to binocular vision (using two eyes), the field of view is greater than before and the depth insight is inadequate. There are a few monocular cues that provide depth information when viewing the scene with one eye: Motion parallax, Depth from motion, Perspective, Relative Size, Occlusion, texture gradient, etc.

**Perspective Image:** Perspective images are a fairly accurate representation of in the least any kind of objects on a flat surface (such as a paper), as it is seen by the naked eye. There are two main characteristic qualities in a perspective image: (1) the objects are drawn smaller as the distance from the viewer increases, (2) the size of an object's dimensions along the line of sight are comparatively shorter than dimensions across the line of sight.

**Pixel:** A pixel is the smallest distinct constituent of an image or picture on a CRT screen (it is more often than not a colored spot). As the number of pixels per inch of an image increases the resolution also increases.

**Stereovision:** Stereovision or stereopsis is the method of visual insight leading to the sense of distance downwards from the two slightly different projections of the world onto the retinas of the two eyes. That is two separate images from two eyes are effectively combined onto one image in the brain. Stereovision is regular healthy vision. Both the eyes when aimed at a particular object because the two eyes are located in different positions, each eye take a unique view from its own perspective. The two images are then sent to the brain for processing where it is combined to form a single unique picture. The ensuing image is three dimensional because it has added depth information.

**Wireframe:** Wireframe is a visual model of an electronic arrangement of a three-dimensional object. It can also be called a visual guide used to propose the layout of basic elements in a particular object structure.

**Vanishing Point:** Vanishing point is the point in linear perspective at which all imaginary lines of perspective converge. In simple terms the vanishing point is the point at which a thing disappears or ceases to exist. A man-made environment has two distinguishing properties: Many lines in the landscape are parallel and a variety of edges in the prospect are orthogonal. In an indoor environment this is true for shelves, doors, windows, passage borders, etc. Outdoor environments like streets, buildings and pavements also satisfy this statement. This means that vanishing points provide strong cues for inferring information about the 3D structure of a scene. If e.g. the camera geometry is known, each vanishing point corresponds to a course of direction in the scene and vice versa.

# Section 3
# Real-World Applications

*This section consists of five chapters, describing the application of 3D reconstruction in various domains. The first chapter presents the use of discrete basis functions in surface modelling and its application to real-time automatic surface inspection. The second chapter introduces two kinds of applications of red, green, and blue as a carrier and their testing by measuring the shape of objects' surface. The next chapter discusses the representation of obstacles in an environment with planar ground through wide baseline set of images in the context of teleoperation, whereas the fourth chapter presents an algorithm for identifying complementary site of objects broken into two parts and subsequently, reassembly of 3D fragments. The last chapter explains the use of an inexpensive passive method involving 3D surface reconstruction from video images taken at multiple views and the utility of the developed methodology for prosthetic designers.*

# Chapter 10
# Surface Modelling Using Discrete Basis Functions for Real–Time Automatic Inspection

**Paul O'Leary**
*Institute for Automation, University of Leoben, Austria*

**Matthew Harker**
*Institute for Automation, University of Leoben, Austria*

## ABSTRACT

*This chapter presents an introduction to discrete basis functions and their application to real-time automatic surface inspection. In particular, discrete polynomial basis functions are analyzed in detail. Emphasis is placed on a formal and stringent mathematical background, which enables an analytical a-priori estimation of the performance of the methods for specific applications. A generalized synthesis algorithm for discrete polynomial basis functions is presented. Additionally a completely new approach to synthesizing constrained basis functions is presented. The resulting constrained basis functions form a unitary matrix, i.e. are optimal with respect to numerical error propagation and have many applications, e.g. as admissible functions in Galerkin methods for to solution of boundary value and initial value problems. Furthermore, a number of case studies are presented, which show the applicability of the methods in real applications.*

## 1.1 SURFACE MEASUREMENT

The methods presented in this chapter are generally applicable to any data which lies on a regular grid, more precisely called an invariant lattice (see Figure 1). The term regular or invariant refers to the fact that there is a constant number of data points in each of the the two dimensions

of the grid; it is not necessary that the points be equally spaced. In the case of image processing we will most commonly be dealing with grids with constant spacing in the $x$ and $y$ directions, simply because of the structure of the pixels in a camera chip. However, polynomially distorted grids, see Figure 1c, are encountered in non-rigid registration. Also conformal mappings such as

DOI: 10.4018/978-1-4666-0113-0.ch010

polar coordinates can be dealt with using the methods presented here.

In this chapter we work primarily with data acquired using a laser scanning device. The device uses a plane of light, also called light sectioning, to acquire cross sectional profiles. This, combined with motion, enables the acquisition of complete surfaces. The data acquired in this manner have in general different resolutions in the *x* and *y* directions. The resolution along the laser line is determined by the camera, whereby the resolution in the other direction is determined by the rate at which the sections can be measured and the speed of the material being observed.

### 1.1.1 Laser Profiling

The basic principle is shown in Figure 2, a variety of manes are used for this type of device, e.g. laser plane of light, light sectioning etc. The principle is very simple: a laser with a line optics projects a plan of light. This light is scattered when it impinges upon a surface and a camera mounted with an appropriate position and orientation observes the light scattered from the surface.

A typical image, as acquired by the camera, is shown in Figure 3. In this image some of the background, including the machinery, can be seen; this is due to ambient light. The signal to noise ratio of the image is dramatically improved by inserting an optical interference filter into the optical path. This is most simply achieved by mounting the filter on the lens of the camera. In general the energy of the ambient light is spread over a large wavelength bandwidth, whereas the laser is almost mono-chromatic. Consequently, an interference filter whose passband is matched to the wavelength of the laser will remove almost all the ambient light, see Figure 4.

The position of the laser line in the image, i.e. the pixel coordinates, is usually determined on a column by column basis. Computing the first moment of the intensity in each column for all pixels with an intensity above a threshold gives a good estimate for the position of the laser-line in the image. The method used to determine the threshold depends on the application, the aim is

*Figure 1. Some examples of invariant grids: a) an invariant grid with equal spacing in the x and y directions; b) exponential spacing in the x and y directions; c) a polynomially distorted grid; d) polar grid, here the terms x and y directions are not appropriate*

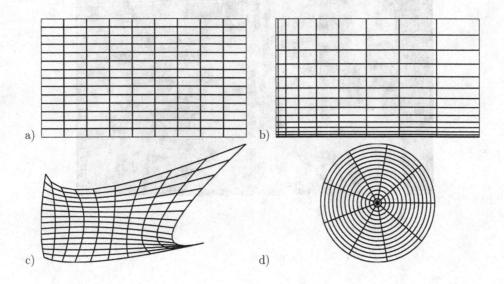

a)

b)

c)

d)

*Figure 2. Basic principle of a laser plan of light measurement unit*

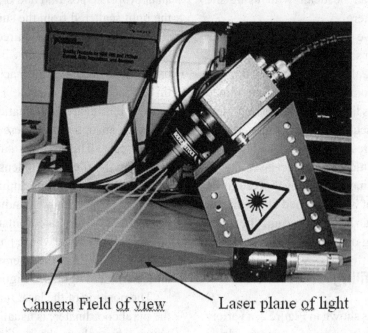

*Figure 3. Image acquired by a camera observing the laser light scattered from the surface. This image was acquired without the use of an interference filter*

*Figure 4. The same scene as in Figure 3, but with an interference filter matched to the wavelength of the laser*

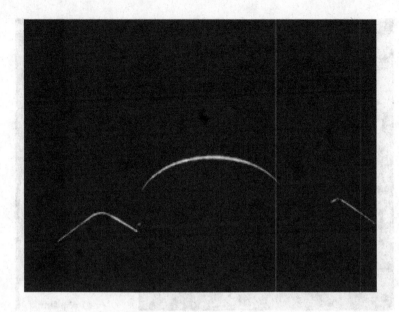

to reduces the effect of background illumination. In some applications it may be a global threshold and in others it may be relative to the maximum intensity in the relevant column. This procedure yields a vector for the $x_c$ and $y_c$ coordinates of the laser line as seen by the camera with sub-pixel accuracy. Whereby, the accuracy is limited to approximately 1/10 of a pixel; the camera coordinates have the dimension pixels.

In general the data is then segmented so as to extract the desired portion of the data. This will require the integration of some a-priory knowledge into the image processing. An example of the result of such measurements can be seen in Figure 5.

The camera coordinates must now be mapped to real world coordinates. The detection device in the camera is planar and all points observed are on the plane defined by the laser. Consequently, the mapping between the pixel coordinates $x_c$ and $y_c$ and the real world coordinates $x_r$ and $y_r$ is a projection between two planes. Now representing all points as column vectors in homogeneous coordinates,

$$\boldsymbol{p}(i) = \begin{bmatrix} x_c(i) \\ y_c(i) \\ 1 \end{bmatrix} \quad \text{and} \quad \boldsymbol{p}(i)_{hr} = \begin{bmatrix} x_{hr}(i) \\ y_{hr}(i) \\ w_{hr}(i) \end{bmatrix}$$

$$(1.1)$$

enables the representation of the projection, which is called a homography, as a $3 \times 3$ matrix denoted **H**, such that,

$$\begin{bmatrix} x_{hr}(i) \\ y_{hr}(i) \\ w_{hr}(i) \end{bmatrix} = \begin{bmatrix} h_{11} & h_{12} & h_{13} \\ h_{21} & h_{22} & h_{23} \\ h_{31} & h_{32} & h_{33} \end{bmatrix} \begin{bmatrix} x_c(i) \\ y_c(i) \\ 1 \end{bmatrix},$$

$$(1.2)$$

$$\boldsymbol{p}_c = \mathbf{H}\,\boldsymbol{p}_{hr} \qquad (1.3)$$

The affine real world coordinates, i.e. the measurement result, is obtained by computing,

$$x_r(i) = \frac{x_{hr}(i)}{w_{hr}(i)} \quad \text{and} \quad y_r(i) = \frac{y_{hr}(i)}{w_{hr}(i)}$$

$$(1.4)$$

*Figure 5. Typical image where the region of interest has been determined and the first moment of intensity has been computed*

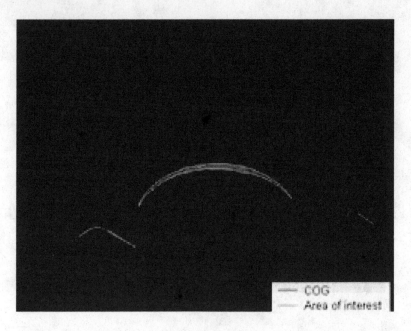

The result of such a measurement and computation can be seen in Figure 6.

Two examples of plan of light measurement devices, constructed according to this principle, are show in Figure 7. Both of these units were designed for the measurement of fine structures. The system on the right has two measurement heads, each of which is equipped with two lasers.

*Figure 6. Result of the plane of light measurement: (red) measurement points; (black) result of the circle fit*

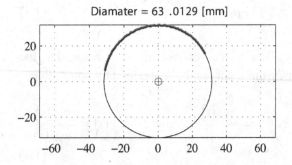

This enables the determination of the orientation of the sample being measured.

Additionally motion is required to enable the acquisition of a complete surface. The implicit motion of the material in the production environment is commonly used, such an industrial scanner system is shown in Figure 8. This is an application in a steel rolling mill. The geometry of the edge of the billet is measured with aim of detecting cracks. This device has been designed to fulfill the IP-65 standard. It is also equipped with a heat shield, to ensure that the radiant heat from the billets do not disturb the measurement.

This scanner in Figure 8 is capable of measuring 3500 cross sections per second. In this manner the surface of the billet can be acquired in real time while it is moving through the production plant. The individual cross sectional data are sequentially assembled to form the complete surface model, see Figure 9. This two dimensional data set is used during the surface analysis process.

*Figure 7. Examples of small plane of light measurement devices. Left: for small geometries. Right: two plane of light units each equipped with two lasers. The use of two lasers enables additionally the determination of the orientation of the material being measured*

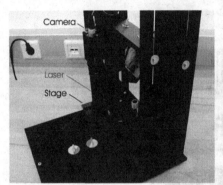
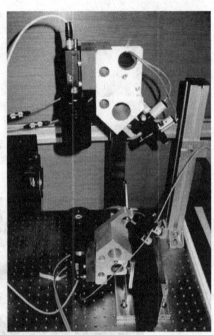

## 1.1.2 Calibration

The values contained in the matrix H must be determined by a calibration process. This requires a calibration target and a calibration procedure. The aim is to eliminate the necessity for adjustment of the position and orientation of the camera or laser. The necessary data should be determined by the calibration process and computationally corrected by the values in the homography. There are three coordinate frames which need to be considered:

1.  The real world coordinate system. This is usually some reference frame in the production plant, e.g. it should be aligned with the motion of the material or orthogonal to the axes of the material;
2.  The laser plane coordinate frame. Due to production and assembly tolerances the laser my not have exactly the orientation which is desired. This error should be determined by the calibration procedure and computationally corrected;
3.  The camera coordinate frame, i.e. the pixel coordinates of the observed laser line in pixels.

A projection between two planes is uniquely defined if four corresponding points in each of the two planes are known. The numerical accuracy of the result can be improved by using a redundant set of points. Consider the calibration target shown in Figure 10left: The target consists of three horizontal planes, each with eight LEDs, the top layer has an additional LED which defines a unique orientation. The target is placed in the production line with the desired calibration orientation, see Figure 10 right. The eight LEDs permit the fitting of a homography for the projection onto each layer. Furthermore,

*Figure 8. Example of an industrial surface scanner: a) view of the laser scanner; b) laser scanner in protective housing; c) laser scanner in the production plant. In this application the inherent movement of the billet during the production process provides the linear motion.*

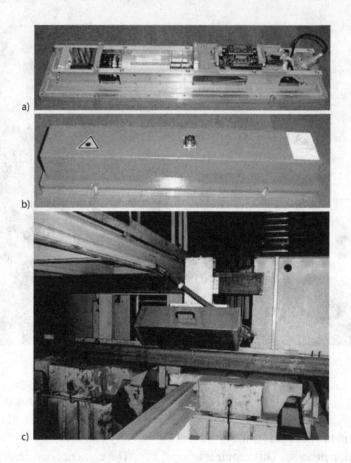

*Figure 9. Surface data acquisition; showing the assembly of the 3D surface from the sequence of individual 2D-sections*

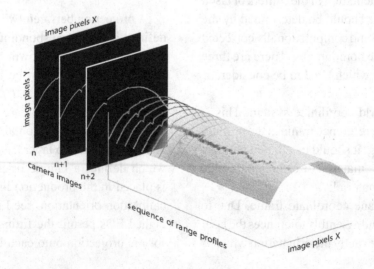

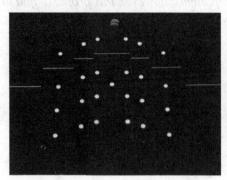

*Figure 10. Left: A calibration target consisting of three horizontal planes each with eight LEDs. The red laser line can be seen towards the top of the target. Right: The target placed in the production plant to enable in-line calibration of the system*

the laser line on the target can be detected. The three homographies are then used to determine the position and orientation of the laser relative to the target. Then the homography representing the projection from the camera coordinates to the real world coordinates is determined.

### 1.1.3 Surface Model

The basis of the mathematical modelling is to regard the acquired surface data as consisting of the addition of three components: **G** a global surface geometry; **A** local anomalies and **S** a stochastic component (see Figure 11).

The mathematical framework, presented in the following sections, enables the separation of the three components in the original measurement data. Furthermore, this task is performed in real time during the production process.

### 1.2 FUNDAMENTALS OF DISCRETE BASIS FUNCTIONS

Most Engineers and Scientists are familiar with approximating a set of data by linear or polynomial regression, i.e., fitting a straight line or polynomial to a set of measurement data.

$$y \approx a_0 + a_1 x + a_2 x^2 \dots a_n x^n. \tag{1.5}$$

The aim is to have a curve which represents the data, so that it is not necessary to work with the discrete data directly. Usually while fitting it is desirable to reduce the effects of perturbations (noise). The advantage of having an equation to describe the data is that analytical techniques can be applied to determine properties of the measurement data and in turn to deduce behavior of the process being observed. This task is very closely related to approximating a function by a Taylor or Maclaurin series,

$$y = f(x) \approx f(a) + \dot{f}(a)(x-a) + \frac{\ddot{f}(a)}{2!}(x-a)^2 + \frac{f^{(3)}(a)}{3!}(x-a)^3 \dots + \frac{f^{(d)}(a)}{d!}(x-a)^d, \tag{1.6}$$

if $a = 0$, then the Tayloy series become a Maclauren series,

$$y = f(x) \approx f(0) + \dot{f}(0)x + \frac{\ddot{f}(0)}{2!}x^2 + \frac{f^{(3)}(0)}{3!}x^3 \dots + \frac{f^{(d)}(0)}{d!}x^d. \tag{1.7}$$

Later it will be seen that local polynomial approximation can be used to estimate regularized derivatives from noise data. In many cases we wish to determine which function lies behind

*Figure 11. Illustration of the principle of the surface model: (a) acquired surface data consisting of the addition of all three components* **D = G + A + S** *(Patch size: 32×24 data points); (b) least squares approximation to the global surface geometry* **G***; (c) local anomalies* **A** *and stochastic component* **S***. This figure needs to be regenerated showing all three components, however, this proposal had to be generate at such short notice that this was not presently possible.*

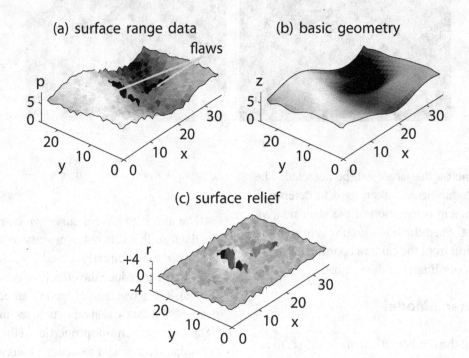

a set of measurement data, or we know a-priory how a system behaves, e.g., we have its transfer function, and we wish to evaluate the data incorporating this knowledge.

The task is complicated by the fact that the measurement data $\hat{y}$ is perturbed by noise, i.e.,

$$\hat{y} = y + \delta_y, \tag{1.8}$$

where $y$ is the ideal value and $\delta_y$ is Gaussian noise. Most commonly, independent and identically distributed (i.i.d.) Gaussian noise is assumed. There are a number of reasons why a Gaussian distribution is assumed:

1. The central limit theorem is used as a justification for this assumption. The central limit theorem states, somewhat simplified, that the mean of a sufficiently large number of independent random variables is normally distributed, independent of the nature of the distributions of the individual variables. That is, the perturbations of a complex measurement with multiple influences will have a Gaussian distribution. Some care must be taken since this condition is not always fulfilled;

2. At least squares approximation delivers a maximum likelihood predictors if the perturbations ar Gaussian. This is very convenient, however, this is also one of the main sources of error. A least squares approximation will

have a systematic bias if the above condition is not fulfilled;

3. There are a number of simple linear algebraic methods available to perform least square approximations under the assumption that the error is Gaussian;

4. But probably the most important reason for using the Gaussian distribution is that it is the only distribution for which commonly Engineers and scientists have some knowledge and understanding.

## 1.2.1 Notation and Nomenclature

Before proceeding with derivations, we wish to introduce the notation used in this chapter:

1. A scalar value is represented by a simple letter, e.g., $x$ or $y$;

2. A set of $n$ values of a variable, e.g., $x$ will always be considered as a column vector and represented by $x$;

3. The $i^{th}$ entry in a vector will be represented as $x_i$ or $x(i)$;

4. A vector with a tilde, e.g. $\tilde{y}$ is an approximation for $y$;

5. A vector with an over-hat, e.g., $\hat{y}$ is a perturbed vector $y$;

6. Matrices are represented by upright letters in a font without serifs, e.g., $\mathbf{B}$;

7. The notation $\mathbf{B}(:,i) = b_i$ refers to the $i^{th}$ column of $\mathbf{B}$, i.e., a column vector $b_i$;

8. Similarly $\mathbf{B}(k,:)$ refers to the $k^{th}$ row of $\mathbf{B}$, i.e., a row vector.

## 1.2.2 Polynomial Regression

An algebraic analysis of polynomial regression is an appropriate starting point, to understanding approximation via basis functions. Consider a set of $n$ data points $p$, where each data points $p_i = [x_i, y_i]^T$ is perturbed by independent identically distributed (i.i.d.) Gaussian noise. The aim of polynomial

regression of degree $d$, is to model the data by a sum of monomials, i.e.,

$$\tilde{y} = a_0 + a_1\,x + a_2\,x^2 \ldots a_d\,x^d = \sum_{i=0}^{d} a_i\,x^i. \tag{1.9}$$

this is called the design equation. Linear regression is a special case of polynomial regression for $d = 1$. Since the data points $y_i$ are perturbed they in general do not lie exactly on the polynomial. Consequently, there is a residual $r_i$ associated with each point,

$$r_i = y_i - \tilde{y}_i = y_i - \sum_{i=0}^{d} a_i\,x^i. \tag{1.10}$$

Note: This equation assumes that only the $y$ coordinate is perturbed, i.e., the $x$ values is known without error. Now writing the systems of equations associated with the $n$ points yields,

$$\begin{bmatrix} r_1 \\ \vdots \\ r_n \end{bmatrix} = \begin{bmatrix} y_1 \\ \vdots \\ y_n \end{bmatrix} - \begin{bmatrix} 1 & x_1 & x_1^2 & \ldots & x_1^d \\ \vdots & \vdots & \vdots & \vdots & \vdots \\ 1 & x_n & x_n^2 & \ldots & x_n^d \end{bmatrix} \begin{bmatrix} a_0 \\ a_1 \\ \vdots \\ a_n \end{bmatrix}. \tag{1.11}$$

It is now convenient to introduce an algebraic approach, i.e., describing the data and set of equations by vectors and matrices: let $x$ be a column vector of known $x$ values, these are the *nodes* at which the system of equations will be solved; similarly $y$ is a column vector containing the $y$ data. in general measurement data; the design matrix $\mathbf{B}$ and the coefficient vector $s$ are defined as,

$$\mathbf{B} = \begin{bmatrix} 1 & x_1 & x_1^2 & \ldots & x_1^d \\ \vdots & \vdots & \vdots & \vdots & \vdots \\ 1 & x_n & x_n^2 & \ldots & x_n^d \end{bmatrix} \quad \text{and} \quad s = \begin{bmatrix} a_0 \\ a_1 \\ \vdots \\ a_n \end{bmatrix}. \tag{1.12}$$

consequently,

$$\tilde{y} = \mathbf{B}s. \tag{1.13}$$

It is now helpful to find the connections between the notations generally used in fitting literature and in spectral analysis bases on basis functions. The design matrix $\mathbf{B} = [\boldsymbol{b}_0, \boldsymbol{b}_1, \ldots \boldsymbol{b}_d]$ is the Vandermonde matrix, and each column of which is a polynomial basis function $\boldsymbol{b}_i$. In the case of simple polynomial regression the basis functions are not orthogonal in a discrete sense, i.e., $\boldsymbol{b}_i^T \boldsymbol{b}_j \neq 0$ for $i \neq j$. This is equivalent to saying that the matrix $\mathbf{S} = \mathbf{B}^T\mathbf{B}$ is not a diagonal matrix. The coefficient vector $s$, known as the spectrum is connection with basis functions, are the coefficients required with each basis function so as to approximate the data.

Now using this notation in Equation 1.11 yields,

$$r = y - \tilde{y} = y - \mathbf{B}s \tag{1.14}$$

The task now is to determine values for the coefficient vector $z$, i.e., for $a_0, \ldots a_n$, such that the cost function $E$ is minimized,

$$E = \sum_{i=1}^{n} r_i^2 = \boldsymbol{r}^T \boldsymbol{r}. \tag{1.15}$$

Substituting for $r$ yields,

$$E = \left( \boldsymbol{y} - \mathbf{B}s \right)^T \left( \boldsymbol{y} - \mathbf{B}s \right) \tag{1.16}$$

Expanding

$$E = \boldsymbol{y}^T \boldsymbol{y} - 2 s^T \mathbf{B}^T \boldsymbol{y} + s^T \mathbf{B}^T\mathbf{B}s \tag{1.17}$$

Evaluating the partial derivative with respect to $z$ and equating to zero, yielding the normal equations for this problem,

$$\mathbf{B}^T \mathbf{B} s = \mathbf{B}^T \boldsymbol{y}. \tag{1.18}$$

The matrix $\mathbf{B}^T \mathbf{B}$ is positive semi definite, consequently a solution to the set of equations can be found,

$$s = \left( \mathbf{B}^T \mathbf{B} \right)^{-1} \mathbf{B}^T \boldsymbol{y} = \mathbf{B}^+ \boldsymbol{y}. \tag{1.19}$$

The term $(\mathbf{B}^T \mathbf{B})^{-1} \mathbf{B}^T$ is called the Moore and Penrose pyseudo-inverse and is denoted by $\mathbf{B}^+$. It is a least squares approximation to the inverse of a rectangular matrix.

Now given the coefficient vector $z$ the estimated values for $\tilde{y}$ can be computed as,

$$\tilde{y} = \mathbf{B}s \tag{1.20}$$

$$= \mathbf{B}\,\mathbf{B}^+ \boldsymbol{y}. \tag{1.21}$$

This simple algebraic derivation for polynomial regression reveals some of the fundamental algebraic structures associated with approximation by basis functions. The two fundamental equations in the above sections are:

$$\tilde{y} = \mathbf{B}s \quad \text{and} \quad z = \mathbf{B}^+ y. \tag{1.22}$$

The column vectors forming the matric $\mathbf{B}$ are the basis functions. The use of geometric polynomials as basis functions is intuitively easy to grasp and leads to the Vandermonde matrix as $\mathbf{B}$. However, there are a number of problems associated with the Vandermonde matrix which limit its practical usability: the basis functions, i.e., the polynomials, are not orthogonal. This requires the computation of $\mathbf{D}^+$ which is computationally expensive and quickly becomes numerically degenerate as the degree of the polynomial increases, making it impossible to compute a usable inverse, e.g., the condition number of the Vandermonde matrix is $\kappa_2(V) > 10^9$, for degree $d = 10$ and $n =$

100 points equally spaced such that $[-1 \leq x \leq 1]$. Consequently, the Vandermonde (Geometric) polynomials are not suitable basis functions when solving large scale problems.

This brief analysis also opens the question as to which properties should a set of basis functions have, and if different basis functions have the same properties what are the criteria for selecting a set of basis functions in a specific application. Much has been written on different polynomial bases for image processing and pattern recognition. It is important to note that in this chapter the processing and analysis of measurement data is bing considered. Consequently, much emphasis is being placed on analytical properties of the methods and bases being proposed.

The quality of polynomial bases have been tested in *all* of the following papers (Mukundan et al., 2001, Yap and Raveendren, 2003, Mukundan, 2004, Yap and Raveendren, 2005, Ong and Raveendren, 2005, Yang et al., 2006, Hosny, 2007, Bayraktar et al., 2007, Zhu et al., 2007a) using specifically selected images. However, the result of such tests is a combination of the properties and information content of the selected image and the quality of the polynomial basis. Neither an objective evaluation of the quality of the bases functions, nor an estimate of performance is possible in this manner. The Fourier basis functions are virtually the only set of basis functions for which a solid and objective evaluation has been performed. This chapter presents the first systematic algebraic framework to enable an objective measure of the quality of any set of discrete basis functions.

## 1.2.3 Literature Survey

The concept of moment invariants for pattern recognition was introduced in 1962 by Hu (Hu, 1962). In his computations Hu used a geometric polynomial basis set $f(x) = \sum_{i=1}^{n} c_n x^n$ to determine the polynomial moments. The name Vandermonde basis is used here, since a matrix

$\mathbf{B}_v$ containing the geometric basis functions as columns is a Vandermonde matrix. The use of this name is advantageous since it ties the polynomials to the theory and difficulties in inverting the matrix $\mathbf{B}_v$. It should be noted that the Fourier basis is also a Vandermonde matrix; however, computed on a set of nodes lying on the unit circle in the complex plane. Hu's method is fundamentally a polynomial regression; however, he defined the moments in terms of continuous integrals but computed using discrete samples functions; basically he ignored or avoided dealing with all the potential difficulties od mapping continuous to discrete domains.

In the years ensuing Hu's publication there was some development in the understanding of Polynomial moments and their relationship to least square approximation (Eden et al., 1986). With time new polynomials were introduced for moment computations (Mukundan et al., 2001, Yap and Raveendren, 2003, Yap and Raveendren, 2005, Yang et al., 2006, Zhu et al., 2007a, Hosny, 2007), this enabled the computation of moments of higher degree on larger images; for example Zhu (Zhu et al., 2007b) was able to compute global moments for images with a size of 256×256. In particular the Legendre (Yap and Raveendren, 2005, Hosny, 2007, Yang et al., 2006) and Tchebichef(Mukundan et al., 2001, Mukundan, 2004, Lang et al., 2009, Huang et al., 2010, Nakagaki and Mukundan, 2007) polynomials have become popular in literature, actually the term Discrete Tchebichef Transform is becoming very popular although the name is clearly incorrect.

The Legendre polynomials arise as solutions to the Legendre differential equation,

$$\left(1-x^2\right) \frac{\mathrm{d}^2 y}{\mathrm{d}\,x^2} - 2x \, \frac{\mathrm{d}\,y}{\mathrm{d}\,x} + n\left(n+1\right) y = 0.$$

$$(1.23)$$

This is a second-order ordinary differential equation; consequently, there are two linearly independent solutions, i.e. the Legendre functions of the first $P_n(x)$ and second kind $Q_n(x)$. If $n$ is an integer the Legendre functions of the first kind reduce to the Legendre polynomials, they are defined on the interval $x \in [-1, 1]$. They can be synthesized using Bonnet's recurrence relationship,

$$(n+1)P_{n+1}(x) = (2n+1)\, x\, P_n(x) - nP_{n-1}(x). \tag{1.24}$$

The synthesis starts using $P_0 = 1$ and $P_1 = x$. The first six Legendre polynomials are shown in Figure 12

The Legendre fulfil the orthogonality condition,

$$\int_{-1}^{1} P_m(x) P_n(x)\, \mathrm{d}x = \frac{2}{2n+1}\,\delta(n, m) \tag{1.25}$$

where $\delta(n,m)$ is the Kronecker delta. Many image processing papers (Yap and Raveendren, 2005, Hosny, 2007, Yang et al., 2006) use the above recurrence relationship to generate discrete basis functions starting from a discrete set of nodes. However, the synthesized functions are not or-

thogonal in a discrete sense. This can be verified by computing by setting up a vector $x$ of uniformly spaced nodes in the interval $[-1, 1]$, then use $x$ in the above recurrence relationship to synthesize the first the first $m$ Legendre polynomials. Each polynomial is used as a column vector to form the matrix $\mathbf{B} = [p_0, \ldots p_m]$. The matrix of residual errors resulting from the basis functions not being orthogonal can be computed as,

$$\mathbf{R} = \mathbf{B}^{\mathrm{T}}\,\mathbf{B} - \mathrm{diag}\{\mathbf{B}^{\mathrm{T}}\,\mathbf{B}\} \tag{1.26}$$

The result is shown for the Legendre polynomials of up to degree $d = 10$ computed on $n = 100$ equidistant points in the interval $[-1,1]$ in Figure 13. The polynomials generated in this manner are clearly not orthogonal.

Mukundan introduced the use of the Chebyshev polynomials to compute moments. However, the polynomials he suggests are actually the Gram (Gram, 1883) and not the Chebyshev polynomials. There is considerable confusion in literature as to the use of the names Gram- and Chebyshev-polynomials. Indeed, modified discrete orthogonal Chebyshev polynomials (Boyd, 2001, Jerri, 1998) do exist, but these do not have a uniform norm. Unfortunalty, the name Chebyshev poly-

*Figure 12. The first six Legendre polynomials*

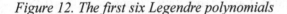

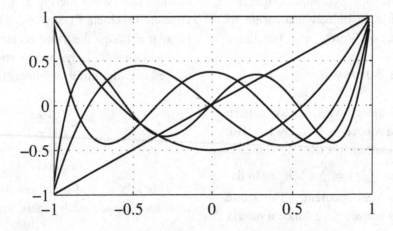

nomials is becoming popular (Nakagaki and Mukundan, 2007, Huang et al., 2010, Lang et al., 2009) although incorrect. We consider the use of the name Gram polynomials as appropriate since they are generated using a modified Gram-Schmidt orthogonalization. Furthermore, Gram's original paper (Gram, 1883) from 1883 would appear to be the earliest publication of such polynomials. The Chebyshev polynomials arise, in a similar manner as do the Legender polynomials, as solutions to the Chebyshev differential equation,

$$\left(1 - x^2\right) \frac{d^2 y}{d x^2} - x \frac{d y}{d x} + \alpha y = 0. \quad (1.27)$$

The solutions for $y$ is the linear combination of two independent solutions,

$$y = c_1 \cos\left\{ \alpha \cos^{-1}(x) \right\} + c_2 \sin\left\{ \alpha \sin^{-1}(x) \right\} \quad (1.28)$$

the Chebyshev polynomials of the first $T_\alpha(x)$ and second kind $U_\alpha(x)$ are defined such that,

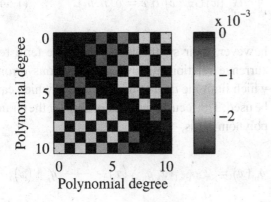

$$y = c_1 \, T_\alpha(x) + c_2 \sqrt{1 - x^2} \; U_\alpha(x). \quad (1.29)$$

It is the Chebyshev polynomials of the first kind which are used in image processing, i.e.,

$$T_\alpha(x) = \cos\left\{ \alpha \cos^{-1}(x) \right\}. \quad (1.30)$$

The Chebyshev polynomials of the first kind can be synthesized from the recurrence relationship,

$$P_{n+1}(x) = 2 \, x \, P_n(x) - P_{n-1}(x). \quad (1.31)$$

The synthesis starts using $P_0 = 1$ and $P_1 = x$. The first six Chebyshev polynomials are shown in Figure 14.

The Chebyshev polynomials belong to the classe of weighted polynomials, i.e., they are orthogonal with respect to a weighting function,

$$\int_{-1}^{1} P_n(x) \, P_m(x) \, W(x) \, d x = w(n) \, \delta(n,m). \quad (1.32)$$

In the case of the Chebyshev polynomials the weighting function is,

$$W(x) = 1 \Big/ \sqrt{\left(1 - x^2\right)},$$

consequently,

$$\int_{-1}^{1} \frac{T_n(x) \, T_m(x)}{\sqrt{1 - x^2}} \, d x = \begin{cases} 0 & n \neq m \\ \pi & n = m = 0 \\ \frac{\pi}{2} & n = m \neq 0 \end{cases}. \quad (1.33)$$

The Chebsschev polynomials are not orthogonal in a discrete sense if computed on a set of equidistant nodes in the interval $x \in [-1, 1]$. The roots of the $n^{th}$ degree polynomial are called the Chebyschev points, synthesizing the polynomials

*Figure 14. The first six Chebyshev polynomials*

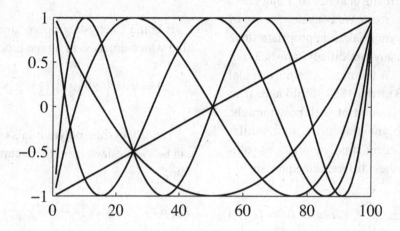

on these points, but applying them to uniformly spaced samples, generates the cosine basis, which are orthogonal in a discrete sense.

The above methods are all related to global approximation of data or functions. In 1964 Savitzky and Golay (Savitzky and Golay, 1964) introduced local polynomial approximation to smooth and evaluate the derivatives noisy spectrometer data. The smoothing was based on fitting a geometric polynomial (Vandermonde basis set) of low degree $d$ to a data set of limited length. The original paper used a maximum degree of $d_{max} = 6$ and the data length of $l_s = 25$ also known as the support length, or in filtering literature, as the bandwidth. Modden (Madden, 1978) pointed out some errors in the original paper and extended the method to larger support lengths. The method was extended to image processing by a number of groups, e.g. by Rajagopalan (Rajagopalan and Robb, 2003). All these applications are limited by the properties of the Vandermonde basis and limits their applicability to low degree approximations.

In 1990 two groups (Meer and Weiss, 1990, Gorry, 1990), apparently independently, proposed the use of Gram polynomials (Barnard et al., 1998) in place of the Vandermonde basis for Savitzky-Golay smoothing. Meer and Weiss (Meer and Weiss, 1990) state that the Chebyschev and Gram polynomials are synonymous for the same set of basis functions; this is only partially correct. The modified discrete Chebyschev polynomials (Boyd, 2001, Jerri, 1998) do not have a uniform scaling, where as the Gram polynomials do. Nevertheless, the use of Gram polynomials is an important step in the improvement of the performance of orthogonal polynomials and their corresponding spectra.

The Gram polynomials are a synthetic set of polynomials, generated by the Gram-Schmidt orthogonalization process. They have not been derived from the solution to a differential equation. Theoretically the Gram polynomials should form an ideal basis, fulfilling an ideal orthogonality condition,

$$\int_{-1}^{1} G_n\left(x\right) G_m\left(x\right) \, \mathrm{d}x = \delta\left(n, m\right). \qquad (1.34)$$

however, their synthesis via the three term recurrence relationship introduces serious errors which limit the degree of polynomial which can be used: The recurrence relationship for the Gram polynomials is,

$$g_n\left(x\right) = 2 \, \alpha_{n-1} \, x \, g_{n-1}\left(x\right) - \frac{\alpha_{n-1}}{\alpha_{n-2}} \, g_{n-2}\left(x\right), \qquad (1.35)$$

whereby,

$$\alpha_{n-1} = \frac{m}{n} \left( \frac{n^2 - 1/2}{m^2 - n^2} \right)^{1/2} \quad (1.36)$$

and

$$g_0(x) = 1, \quad g_{-1}(x) = 0 \quad \text{and} \quad \alpha_{-1} = 1, \quad (1.37)$$

$x$ is computed on equidistant points,

$$x = -1 + \frac{(2k-1)}{m}, \quad 1 \leq k \leq m. \quad (1.38)$$

Note that, these points do not span the full range [−1, 1]. The bases functions are scaled by $\sqrt{m}$ yielding a unitary bases set. Now consider the matrix $\mathbf{G}_n = [g_0(x), \dots g_n(x)]$, whereby the $i^{th}$ column corresponds to the $i^{th}$ basis function $g_i(x)$. It $\mathbf{G}$ contains an ideal unitary bases set then, $\mathbf{G}^T \mathbf{G} = \mathbf{I}$, and consequently, the $\mathbf{G}^T \mathbf{G} - \mathbf{I} = 0$ should yield a matrix which is uniformly zero. To demonstrate the limits associated with the generation of the Gram recurrence relationship a basis was computed for $m = 100$ and $n = 40$ the associated error is shown in Figure 15. The errors are in the range $\varepsilon = 10^{-13}$; these are small but already three orders of magnitude larger than the computational accuracy available[1], indicating that the errors associated with the recurrence relationship are now dominant. The highest feasible degree for a Gram polynomial generated in this manner was $n = 20$ when computed for $m = 100$ points; at higher degrees the error exceeded the numerical accuracy available. With this, the Savitzky-Golay method remains a local polynomial approximation with limited degree, unable to reach the dimensions associated with global approximations.

Mukundan (Mukundan, 2004) published a synthesis algorithm which produces a high qual-ity basis with almost arbitrary degree. However, the errors are concentrated at lower degrees and the algorithm is limited to regular nodes. In 2008 O'Leary and Harker (O'Leary and Harker, 2008b) published an algorithm which enabled the synthesis of a virtually perfect unitary discrete orthogonal basis function on arbitrary nodes lying in the complex plane: a more formal proof for this algorithm is presented here and the algorithm is extended to the generation of the basis function derivatives.

Locally weighted polynomial regression—an extension of the Savitzky Golay smoothing—has become popular for the design of lowpass filters (Proitte and Luati, 2009, Eilers, 2003). All the work on such filters also use the Vandermonde basis, with all its associated limitations. The method has also been applied in physical chemistry for the smoothing of spectroscopic data (Seah et al., 1988). Here a new analysis is presented and the relationship to weighted polynomials is derived.

The literature survey has made it clear that there is presently no systematic approach to the

*Figure 15. The error $\mathbf{G}^T \mathbf{G} - \mathbf{I}$ associated with the Gram basis set for $m = 100$ and $n = 40$. The errors are in the range $\varepsilon = 10^{-13}$; these are small but already three times larger than the computational accuracy available, indicating that the errors associated with the recurrence relationship are now dominant.*

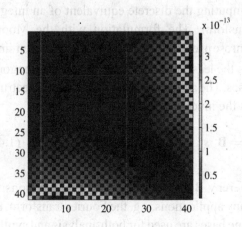

application of discrete basis functions in image processing and surface modelling.

## 1.2.4 Algebraic Framework

Past analysis of polynomial moments has focused on their application in pattern recognition and not on filtering (Hu, 1962, Mukundan et al., 2001, Yap and Raveendren, 2003, Yap and Raveendren, 2005, Ong and Raveendren, 2005, Ping et al., 2005, Zhu et al., 2007a, Bayraktar et al., 2007). Polynomial moments have been proposed for filtering (Thurston and Brawn, 1992); however, no formal analysis has been performed for such applications. In contrast, Savitzky-Golay smoothing focused on filtering but payed no attention to the global characteristics of the polynomial approximations. The aim in this section is to develop a theoretical framework which unifies both aspects. At this point no assumptions are made with respect to the basis function set being used. Some examples of suitable basis functions are: the Fourier basis; discrete orthogonal polynomials; the Bessel functions and the Haar functions. The most appropriate basis functions depend on the nature of the application at hand. The most general formulation of a discrete equivalent of an integral-transform is,

$$s = \mathbf{B}_a^+ \, y. \tag{1.39}$$

The spectrum $s$ of the data $y$ is determined by computing the discrete equivalent of an integral transform. The formulation with the Moore-Penrose pseudo inverse $\mathbf{B}_a^+$ has been chosen since it is the least squares solution for non-orthogonal bases. The synthesis of a signal from its spectrum, i.e. the inverse transform is computed as,

$$\hat{y} = \mathbf{B}_s \, s \tag{1.40}$$

whereby $\mathbf{B}_s$ contains the synthesis functions. In many applications, e.g. the Fourier transform, the same bases are used for both analysis and synthe-

sis $\mathbf{B} = \mathbf{B}_a = \mathbf{B}_s$. Hereby, unitary bases, i.e. $\mathbf{B}^T \mathbf{B} = \mathbf{I}$ play a special role due to their error propagation properties. Gabor filters are a notable case where different analysis and synthesis functions are used to implement orientational selective filters.

### Completeness and Invertibility

Equations 1.39 and 1.40 can be combined to yield,

$$\hat{y} = \mathbf{B}_s \, s = \mathbf{B}_s \, \mathbf{B}_a^+ \, y. \tag{1.41}$$

The reconstruction error $r = y - \hat{y}$ is,

$$\begin{aligned} r &= y - \mathbf{B}_s \, \mathbf{B}_a^+ \, y \\ &= \left( \mathbf{I} - \mathbf{B}_s \, \mathbf{B}_a^+ \right) \, y \end{aligned} \tag{1.42}$$

Consequently, perfect reconstruction is given if the projection onto the orthogonal complement $\mathbf{I} - \mathbf{B}_s \, \mathbf{B}_a^+ = 0$. This can be achieved using a unitary[2] and complete[3] basis for analysis and reconstruction; i.e. $\mathbf{B} = \mathbf{B}_a = \mathbf{B}_s$ such that,

$$r = \left( \mathbf{I} - \mathbf{B} \, \mathbf{B}^T \right) \, y = 0. \tag{1.43}$$

In general, the complex conjugate transpose[4] of any complete unitary basis is its inverse. Ideally the residuals should be exactly zero; however, the computation of the projection onto the orthogonal complement is subject to numerical errors. The matrix of errors,

$$\mathbf{\Delta}_p = \mathbf{I} - \mathbf{B} \, \mathbf{B}^T, \tag{1.44}$$

reveals information on the quality of the synthesized basis.

### Unitary Bases and Condition Number

The fundamental aim of this section is to provide algebraic techniques which enable the objective evaluation of the quality of a set of basis functions. All papers on moments use specific images to test the quality of the basis being used. This is not an acceptable approach since the results are a mixture of the information content of the image and the quality of the basis functions.

If the basis is unitary then the matrix **B** has the condition number of 1. This insures a minimization of the propagation of numerical errors (O'Leary and Harker, 2008d) in matrix computations. Computing the matrix of errors $\Delta$,

$$\Delta = \mathbf{B}^T \mathbf{B} - \mathbf{I}, \tag{1.45}$$

will reveal numerical errors which occured during the synthesis of the set of basis functions, see Figure 15 for an example of the errors associated with the generation of the Gram basis from the standard three term recurrence relationship.

## Plancherel's Theorem

Consider two vectors of data $x$ and $y$ respectively,

$$x^T y = (\mathbf{B}\, s_x)^T \mathbf{B}\, s_y \tag{1.46}$$

$$= s_x^T \mathbf{B}^T \mathbf{B}\, s_y \tag{1.47}$$

if the basis is unitary,

$$x^T y = s_x^T s_y \tag{1.48}$$

Parsival's theorem is a special case where $x = y$

## Covariance Propagation in Linear Transformations

The computation of spectra, be it a Fourier Gram or other spectrum, is performed via a linear transformation; also spectral filtering and function approximations using basis functions are implemented via such transformations. Consequently, it is important to investigate the covariance propagation through a linear transformations. Consider the signal $y$ perturbed by independent and identically distributed (i.i.d.) Gaussian noise, then the covariance of $y$ is,

$$\Lambda_y = \text{diag}\left\{ \sigma_y^2, ...., \sigma_y^2 \right\}$$

$$= \sigma_y^2\, \mathbf{I}_m \tag{1.49}$$

where $\mathbf{I}_m$ is an $m \times m$ identity matrix. Now applying the linear transformation $\mathbf{L}$ to $y$, i.e.,

$$z = \mathbf{L}\, y, \tag{1.50}$$

yields the vector $z$. The noise present in $z$ is also Gaussian, since it is generated from a linear combination of $y$ which is perturbed by i.i.d. noise. The covariance propagates to $z$ as,

$$\Lambda_z = \frac{\partial z}{\partial y} \Lambda_y \left( \frac{\partial z}{\partial y} \right)^T \tag{1.51}$$

where $\frac{\partial z}{\partial y}$ is the Jacobian of $z$ with respect to $y$. Consequently, the required Jacobian is,

$$\frac{\partial z}{\partial y} = \mathbf{L}. \tag{1.52}$$

Substituting this result into Equation 1.51 yields,

$$\Lambda_z = \mathbf{L}\, \Lambda_y\, \mathbf{L}^T, \tag{1.53}$$

$$= \sigma_y^2\, \mathbf{L}\, \mathbf{L}^T. \tag{1.54}$$

In general a linear transformation will yield a signal $z$ which is heteroscedastic when the input is i.i.d., with the exception if the matrix $\mathbf{L}$ is unitary; an example for the covariance propagation in polynomial approximations is shown in

Figure 16. Recall that the spectrum $s$ of the signal $y$ is computed as, $s = \mathbf{B}^+ y$, and consequently the covariance of the spectrum is,

$$\Lambda_s = \sigma^2\, \mathbf{B}^+\, \mathbf{B}. \tag{1.55}$$

If the set of basis functions contained in the $m \times n$ matrix $\mathbf{B}$ are orthonormal, then the covariance is,

$$\Lambda_s = \sigma^2\, \mathbf{I}_n. \tag{1.56}$$

This proof states that gaussian noise has a flat power spectral density for all unitary basis function sets, independent of their nature, i.e., Parseval's theorem is true for all unitary bases. This fact is well known for the Fourier and Cosine Bases. However, the new algebraic approach to analyzing discrete basis functions enables the extension of this theory to all unitary bases, e.g., Gram or the normalized Haar basis functions.

*Figure 16. Example of the covariance matrix associated with a degree, d = 4, Gram polynomial approximation of a data set with n = 20 points. Note the nonuniform covariance propagation as the border of the support is approached.*

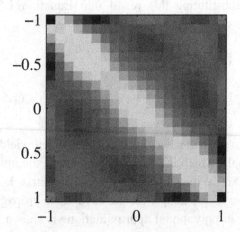

## Frequency Response of Linear Transformations

Thurston (Thurston and Brawn, 1992) made a rudimentary attempt to relate two dimensional polynomial spectra to their Frequency response, but failed to present a systematic approach. Local polynomial approximation has also been applied to the design of low-pass filters (Eilers, 2003, Proitte and Luati, 2009): in filter design a continuous stream of data is assumed and the problem associated at the start and end of the support are ignored. However, for finite measurement data it is important to deal with these regions correctly. Here a systematic approach to computing the frequency response of generalized linear operator is presented. It deals with all points in the data correctly. It also reveals the tendency of polynomial approximations to oscillate at the borders of the support.

Consider the linear transformation $z = \mathbf{L}\, y$, each output point is a linear combination of all input values,

$$z(i) \;=\; \sum_{k=1}^{n} \mathbf{L}(i,k)\, y(k) \tag{1.57}$$

$$= \mathbf{L}(i,:)\, y. \tag{1.58}$$

Consequently, the $i^{th}$ row of the matrix L corresponds to the coefficients of an FIR filter relating $z[i]$ to all the input values $y$. Given the coefficients of a FIR filter the frequency response can be simply computed. In general each output position may have a different frequency response depending on the structure of $\mathbf{L}$, (see Figure 17 for an example). A uniform frequency response is only given when $\mathbf{L}$ is circulant.

### 1.2.5 Condition Number and Error Propagation

The representation of discrete basis functions as a matrix enables the use of algebraic techniques to determine bounds on error propagation. In this section the condition number of a matrix (possibly a set of basis functions) is used to predict a bound on the propagation of errors from the input to output of a general algebraic operator.

It is possible to determine an upper-bound(Golub and Van Loan, 1996) for the reconstruction error as a function of the condition number $\kappa_2(\mathbf{P})$ of the matrix $\mathbf{P}$. It is demonstrative to examine the 1D case: the residual vector is,

$$r = y - \mathbf{P}\,\mathbf{P}^+ y \qquad (1.59)$$

Say the basis matrix $\mathbf{P}$ is perturbed by,

$$\mathbf{P}(\varepsilon) = \mathbf{P} + \varepsilon\mathbf{F} \qquad (1.60)$$

where $\mathbf{F}$ is a matrix of perturbations and $\varepsilon$ is small. Expanding $r(\varepsilon)$ in a Taylor series,

$$r(\varepsilon) = r + \varepsilon r'(0) + O(\varepsilon^2) \qquad (1.61)$$

So, truncating for the purpose of a first order analysis and rearranging

$$r(\varepsilon) - r \cong \varepsilon r'(0). \qquad (1.62)$$

Differentiating Equation 1.59 yields

$$r'(\varepsilon) = -\frac{\partial}{\partial \varepsilon}\Big(\mathbf{P}(\varepsilon)\,\mathbf{P}(\varepsilon)^+\Big)\,y \qquad (1.63)$$

$$= -\Big[\mathbf{A}_p^{\perp}(\varepsilon)\,\mathbf{P}'(\varepsilon)\,\mathbf{P}^+(\varepsilon) + \big(\mathbf{A}_p^{\perp}(\varepsilon)\,\mathbf{P}'(\varepsilon)\,\mathbf{P}^+(\varepsilon)\big)^{T}\Big]\,y \qquad (1.64)$$

where $\mathbf{A}_p^{\perp}(\varepsilon) \triangleq \mathbf{I} - \mathbf{P}(\varepsilon)\,\mathbf{P}(\varepsilon)^+$, i.e. the projection onto the orthogonal complement of $\mathbf{P}(\varepsilon)$. So,

$$r'(0) = -\Big[\mathbf{A}_p^{\perp}\,\mathbf{F}\,\mathbf{P}^+ + (\mathbf{A}_p^{\perp}\,\mathbf{F}\,\mathbf{P}^+)^{T}\Big]\,y \qquad (1.65)$$

From Equation 1.62 the relative error in the residuals is,

$$\frac{\|r(\varepsilon) - r\|}{\|r\|} \cong \frac{|\varepsilon|\,\|r'(0)\|}{\|r\|} \qquad (1.66)$$

*Figure 17. Magnitude frequency response of a degree, d = 4, Gram polynomial approximation for a data set with n = 20 points. The oscillatory behavior of the polynomial approximation at the ends of the support is clearly visible*

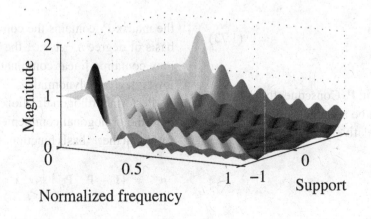

$$= \frac{\left|\, \varepsilon \,\right| \, \left\| \, \left[ \mathbf{A}_p^{\perp} \, \mathbf{F} \, \mathbf{P}^{+} + \left( \mathbf{A}_p^{\perp} \, \mathbf{P} \mathbf{F} \mathbf{P}^{+} \right)^T \right] \, \boldsymbol{y} \, \right\|}{\left\| \, \mathbf{A}_p^{\perp} \, \boldsymbol{y} \, \right\|} \tag{1.67}$$

$$\leq \left|\, \varepsilon \,\right| \frac{\left( \left\| \mathbf{A}_p^{\perp} \right\| \, \left\| \mathbf{F} \right\| \left\| \mathbf{P}^{+} \right\| \, \left\| \boldsymbol{y} \right\| + \left\| \mathbf{P}^{+T} \right\| \, \left\| \mathbf{F}^T \right\| \, \left\| \mathbf{A}^{\perp, T} \right\| \, \left\| \boldsymbol{y} \right\| \right)}{\left\| \mathbf{A}_p^{\perp} \, \boldsymbol{y} \right\|} \tag{1.68}$$

$$\leq 2 \left|\, \varepsilon \,\right| \left\| \mathbf{F} \right\| \, \left\| \mathbf{P}^{+} \right\| \left( \frac{\left\| \mathbf{A}_p^{\perp} \right\| \, \left\| \boldsymbol{y} \right\|}{\left\| \mathbf{A}_p^{\perp} \, \boldsymbol{y} \right\|} \right) \tag{1.69}$$

$$\leq 2 \left|\, \varepsilon \,\right| \frac{\left\| \mathbf{F} \right\|}{\left\| \mathbf{P} \right\|} \, \left\| \mathbf{P} \right\| \, \left\| \mathbf{P}^{+} \right\| \tag{1.70}$$

The two-norm condition number of the matrix $\mathbf{P}$ is defined as

$$\kappa_2(\mathbf{P}) \triangleq \left\| \mathbf{P} \right\| \, \left\| \mathbf{P}^{+} \right\| = \frac{\tilde{\mathbf{A}}_{max}}{\tilde{\mathbf{A}}_{min}} \tag{1.71}$$

where $\sigma_{max}$ and $\sigma_{min}$ are the maximum and minimum singular values respectively. With this definition, the relative error reads,

$$\frac{\left\| \, \boldsymbol{r}(\varepsilon) - \boldsymbol{r} \, \right\|}{\left\| \, \boldsymbol{r} \, \right\|} \leq 2 \, \rho_p \, \kappa_2(\mathbf{P}) \tag{1.72}$$

where the quantity,

$$\rho_p = \frac{\left|\, \varepsilon \,\right| \left\| \, \mathbf{F} \, \right\|}{\left\| \, \mathbf{P} \, \right\|} \tag{1.73}$$

is the relative error in $\mathbf{P}$. Consequently, the error in the residuals can be as large as the condition number times the relative error in[5] $\mathbf{P}$.

## 1.2.6 Polynomial Basis, One and Only One

Before proceeding to a procedure for synthesizing polynomial basis functions it is valuable to show that there is one and only one polynomial basis which is orthonormal (unitary). Much literature has been published on different polynomial basis for moment computation e.g., Hahn (Ong and Raveendren, 2005, Zhu et al., 2007c), Gram (Gram, 1883, Barnard et al., 1998), Tchebychev (Mukundan et al., 2001, Nakagaki and Mukundan, 2007, Huang et al., 2010, Lang et al., 2009), Krawtchouk (Yap and Raveendren, 2003), Racan (Zhu et al., 2007b), Legendre (Yap and Raveendren, 2005), etc. much of which we feel is superfluous. Here we prove explicitly that there is one and only one unitary polynomial basis which is a sum of monomials.

All the polynomials proposed for image analysis and representation can be synthesized from a functional analysis point of view using the three term recurrence relationship (Gautschi, 2004),

$$\boldsymbol{p}_n = \alpha_n \, \boldsymbol{x} \circ \boldsymbol{p}_{n-1} + \beta_n \, \boldsymbol{p}_{n-2}, \tag{1.74}$$

whereby $\circ$ indicates the Hadamard product. Different values for $\alpha$ and $\beta$ deliver different polynomials. The recurrence relationship can be formulated in a more general form,

$$\boldsymbol{p}_n = \alpha_n \, \boldsymbol{x} \circ \boldsymbol{p}_{n-1} + \mathbf{P}_c \, \beta_n, \tag{1.75}$$

the matrix $\mathbf{P}_c$ contains the complete polynomial basis of degree $n - 1$, i.e., the basis of degree $n$ may contain a linear combination of any of the lower degree polynomials.

Perform orthogonalization by projecting $\boldsymbol{p}_n$ onto the orthogonal complement of $\mathbf{P}_c$[6], this ensures that the $n^{th}$ basis function is orthogonal to $\mathbf{P}_c$,

$$\boldsymbol{p}_n^{\perp} = \left( \mathbf{I} - \mathbf{P}_c \, \mathbf{P}_c^{+} \right) \left\{ \alpha_n \, \boldsymbol{x} \circ \boldsymbol{p}_{n-1} + \mathbf{P}_c \, \beta_n \right\}. \tag{1.76}$$

The projection of $\mathbf{P}_c$ onto its own orthogonal complement must be zero, i.e.

$$\left(\mathbf{I} - \mathbf{P}_c \ \mathbf{P}_c^+\right) \mathbf{P}_c = 0. \qquad (1.77)$$

Consequently,

$$\boldsymbol{p}_n^\perp = \alpha_n \left(\mathbf{I} - \mathbf{P}_c \ \mathbf{P}_c^+\right) \boldsymbol{x} \circ \boldsymbol{p}_{n-1} \qquad (1.78)$$

This proves that the generation of a unitary basis is independent of the value used for $\beta$. The new polynomial is normalized to ensure a unitary basis that is correspondingly perfectly conditioned,

$$\hat{\boldsymbol{p}}_n^\perp = \frac{\boldsymbol{p}_n^\perp}{\left\| \boldsymbol{p}_n^\perp \right\|_2}$$

$$= \frac{\alpha_n \left(\mathbf{I} - \mathbf{P}_c \ \mathbf{P}_c^+\right) \boldsymbol{x} \circ \boldsymbol{p}_{n-1}}{\sqrt{\alpha_n^2 \left(\boldsymbol{x} \circ \boldsymbol{p}_{n-1}\right)^T \left(\mathbf{I} - \mathbf{P}_c \ \mathbf{P}_c^+\right) \left(\boldsymbol{x} \circ \boldsymbol{p}_{n-1}\right)}} \qquad (1.79)$$

Since $\alpha_n / \sqrt{\alpha_n^2} = \text{sign}\left(\alpha_n\right)$ we have that,

$$\hat{\boldsymbol{p}}_n^\perp = \frac{\left(\mathbf{I} - \mathbf{P}_c \ \mathbf{P}_c^+\right) \boldsymbol{x} \circ \boldsymbol{p}_{n-1}}{\sqrt{\left(\boldsymbol{x} \circ \boldsymbol{p}_{n-1}\right)^T \left(\mathbf{I} - \mathbf{P}_c \ \mathbf{P}_c^+\right) \left(\boldsymbol{x} \circ \boldsymbol{p}_{n-1}\right)}}. \qquad (1.80)$$

This proves that the generation of a unitary orthogonal basis is independent of both $\alpha_n$ and $\beta$, i.e. there is one and only one polynomial basis that is perfectly conditioned.

### 1.2.7 Universal Synthesis Algorithm

Here we document the first algorithm which can generate a unitary set of basis functions for an arbitrary set of nodes in the complex plane. Examples of the resulting basis functions are: the Gram basis, the discrete cosine basis (polynomials on the Tchebychev points) and the Fourier basis. The possible set of basis functions is not limited to this list.

Many different orthogonal basis functions can be computed via recurrence relationships from nodes in the complex plane: e.g., the Fourier basis is equivalent to the Vandermonde basis where the nodes, $x$, are evenly spaced on the unit circle in the complex plane (Golub and Van Loan, 1996); using the Tchebychev points as nodes yields the cosine basis (Boyd, 2001); the Gram polynomials (Barnard et al., 1998) can be synthesized from a set of nodes lying on the real line in the interval $[-1,1]$.

The limiting factor for three term recurrence relationships is that numerical round-off errors accumulate, making it impossible to synthesize bases of higher degree. Orthogonalization using the (modified) Gram-Schmidt (Golub and Van Loan, 1996) algorithm was proposed to eliminate this problem; however, this requires the complete basis to be available prior to orthogonalization.

Here a new generalized recurrence relationship is derived which can be used to synthesize a basis for arbitrary nodes and of virtually unlimited degree. The concept of the three term recurrence relationship is extended so that the basis function $b_n$ is a linear combination[7] of $b_{n-1} \circ x$ and of all previously generated basis functions, $\mathbf{B}_{n-1}$. $\mathbf{B}_{n-1}$ is a matrix whose columns contain the basis functions $[b_0 \dots b_{n-1}]$. The new recurrence relationship is:

$$\boldsymbol{b}_n = \alpha \left(\boldsymbol{b}_{n-1} \circ \boldsymbol{x}\right) + \mathbf{B}_{n-1}\beta, \qquad (1.81)$$

whereby $\alpha$ is a scalar and $\beta$ a vector. There are two constraints placed on the basis functions:

$$C_1 : \qquad \mathbf{B}_{n-1}^T \boldsymbol{b}_n = \mathbf{0} \qquad (1.82)$$

the orthogonality condition, and

$$C_2 : \qquad \boldsymbol{b}_n^T \boldsymbol{b}_n \doteq 1, \qquad (1.83)$$

the unit norm condition. Substituting Equation 1.81 into the constraint $C_1$ yields

$$\mathbf{B}_{n-1}^T \left\{ \alpha \left( \boldsymbol{b}_{n-1} \circ \boldsymbol{x} \right) + \mathbf{B}_{n-1} \, \beta \right\} = 0 \, . \quad (1.84)$$

Expanding the above equation yields

$$\alpha \, \mathbf{B}_{n-1}^T \left( \boldsymbol{b}_{n-1} \circ \boldsymbol{x} \right) + \mathbf{B}_{n-1}^T \, \mathbf{B}_{n-1} \, \beta = 0 \, . \quad (1.85)$$

Since the functions already generated are orthonormal, Substituting $\mathbf{B}_{n-1}^T \, \mathbf{B}_{n-1} = \mathbf{I}$, and solving for $\beta$ yields

$$\beta = - \, \alpha \, \mathbf{B}_{n-1}^T \left( \boldsymbol{b}_{n-1} \circ \boldsymbol{x} \right) . \quad (1.86)$$

Now substituting Equation 1.81 into the constraint $C_2$ yields

$$\left\{ \alpha \left( \boldsymbol{b}_{n-1} \circ \boldsymbol{x} \right) + \mathbf{B}_{n-1} \, \beta \right\}^T \left\{ \alpha \left( \boldsymbol{b}_{n-1} \circ \boldsymbol{x} \right) + \mathbf{B}_{n-1} \, \beta \right\} = 1 . \quad (1.87)$$

Expanding and using the condition $\mathbf{B}_{n-1}^T \, \mathbf{B}_{n-1}$ yields,

$$\alpha^2 \left( \boldsymbol{b}_{n-1} \circ \boldsymbol{x} \right)^T \left( \boldsymbol{b}_{n-1} \circ \boldsymbol{x} \right)$$

$$+ \, 2 \, \alpha \left( \boldsymbol{b}_{n-1} \circ \boldsymbol{x} \right)^T \mathbf{B}_{n-1} \, \beta + \beta^T \, \beta = 1 \quad (1.88)$$

Substituting Equation 1.86 into above yields,

$$\alpha^2 \left\{ \left( \boldsymbol{b}_{n-1} \circ \boldsymbol{x} \right)^T \left( \boldsymbol{b}_{n-1} \circ \boldsymbol{x} \right) - \left( \boldsymbol{b}_{n-1} \circ \boldsymbol{x} \right)^T \mathbf{B}_{n-1} \, \mathbf{B}_{n-1}^T \left( \boldsymbol{b}_{n-1} \circ \boldsymbol{x} \right) \right\} = 1 \quad (1.89)$$

thus,

$$\alpha^2 \left( \boldsymbol{b}_{n-1} \circ \boldsymbol{x} \right)^T \left\{ \mathbf{I} - \mathbf{B}_{n-1} \, \mathbf{B}_{n-1}^T \right\} \left( \boldsymbol{b}_{n-1} \circ \boldsymbol{x} \right) = 1 \, . \quad (1.90)$$

A projection is by definition symmetric and idempotent, i.e.

$$\left\{ \mathbf{I} - \mathbf{B}_{n-1} \, \mathbf{B}_{n-1}^T \right\} \left\{ \mathbf{I} - \mathbf{B}_{n-1} \, \mathbf{B}_{n-1}^T \right\}^T = \left\{ \mathbf{I} - \mathbf{B}_{n-1} \, \mathbf{B}_{n-1}^T \right\} . \quad (1.91)$$

Consequently, Equation 1.90 can be solved for $\alpha$ yielding,

$$\alpha = \frac{1}{\left\| \left\{ \mathbf{I} - \mathbf{B}_{n-1} \, \mathbf{B}_{n-1}^T \right\} \left( \boldsymbol{b}_{n-1} \circ \boldsymbol{x} \right) \right\|_2} \, . \quad (1.92)$$

Substituting Equation 1.86 into Equation 1.81 yields the final recurrence relation,

$$\boldsymbol{b}_n = \alpha \left\{ \mathbf{I} - \mathbf{B}_{n-1} \, \mathbf{B}_{n-1}^T \right\} \left( \boldsymbol{b}_{n-1} \circ \boldsymbol{x} \right) , \quad (1.93)$$

The term $\mathbf{I} - \mathbf{B}_{n-1} \, \mathbf{B}_{n-1}^T$ is the projection onto the orthogonal complement of $\mathbf{B}_{n-1}$, i.e. all correlations in $\boldsymbol{b}_{n-1} \circ \boldsymbol{x}$ with $\mathbf{B}_{n-1}$ are removed. This is important since the rounding (quantization) errors occurring during computation are generally correlated with $\mathbf{B}_{n-1}$.

This is an incremental orthogonalization process, i.e., during the synthesis of each basis function all correlations with previous basis functions are eliminated. Equation 1.93 is a general recurrence relationship whereby the selection of the nodes $x$ determines the functions being synthesized. The nodes may lie in the complex plane.

The ability of the new synthesis procedure to generate sets of virtually perfect basis functions from arbitrary nodes in the complex plane is demonstrated with a number of examples:

1.  The Gram polynomials are generated from uniformly spaced nodes on the real axis, $x(i) = -1 + (2k-1)/m$, $1 \le i \le m$ for $m$ points (see Figure 18). This result shows that polynomial

*Figure 18. a) The nodes for the computation of the Gram basis are defined in Equation 1.38 (only 20 nodes are shown here); b) the real and imaginary components of the 6 basis functions first; c) the error matrix* $\Delta = \mathbf{B}^{\mathrm{T}}\,\mathbf{B} - \mathbf{I}$ *for 1000 Gram basis functions*

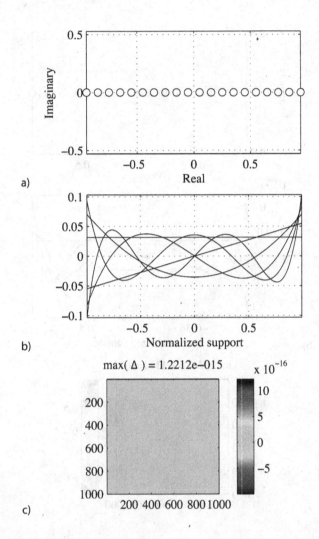

basis of degree 1000 can be synthesized with virtually no errors;

2. A set of unitary basis functions generated from arbitrary nodes, $x_a(i) = x(i)\sqrt{|(x(i))|}$, is shown in Figure 19. The discrete cosine basis can be synthesized in a similar manner using the Tchebychev points as nodes. The ability to generate unitary bases from arbitrary nodes enables, e.g., the computation of Fourier spectra for irregularly samples

data. Furthermore, interpolation can be performed;

3. The Fourier basis functions can be synthesized from a set of nodes uniformly distributed on the unit circle in the complex plane, see Figure 20. There are indeed more efficient methods of synthesizing the Fourier basis, the point at issue here is the universality of the method;

4. Also bases of fractional degree can be synthesized, see Figure 21 for an example. Here

*Figure 19. a) The nodes for the computation this set of basis functions are $x_a(i)=x(i)\sqrt{|(x(i))|}$; b) the real and imaginary components of the 6 basis functions first; c) the error matrix $\Delta = B^T B - I$ for 1000 basis functions*

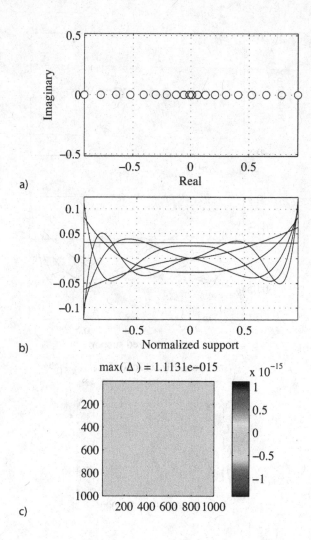

a)

b)

c)

the the bases are synthesized from $\sqrt{(x(i))}$, whereby $x(i)$ is uniformly distributed such that $0 \leq x(i) \leq 1$. The power of 1/2 is arbitrary and was chosen for demonstration purposes only. As far as we could determine, this is the first procedure which can synthesize orthonormal basis functions for polynomials of non-integer degrees.

## 1.2.8 Spectral Compactness

Filters can be implemented using either Fourier or polynomial basis function sets, among others. The question is: which basis is better suited for a specific given application? To answer this question we must know the behavior of the bases with respect to noise and with respect to the nature of the signal which is to be processed.

The approximation of a signal with a set of discrete orthogonal basis functions is an incremental

*Figure 20. a) Nodes in the complex plane for the Fourier basis (here only 20 nodes are shown; b) the real and imaginary components of the 6 basis functions first; c) the error matrix* $\mathbf{\Delta}=\mathbf{B}^{\mathrm{T}}\,\mathbf{B}-\mathbf{I}$ *for 1000 Fourier basis functions*

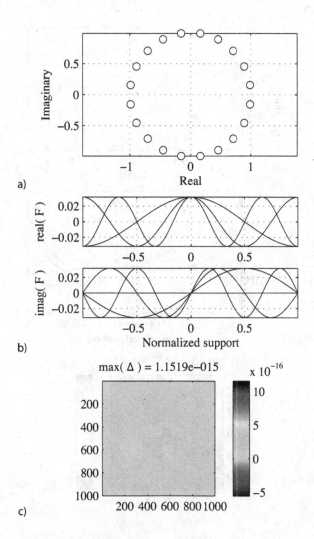

least squares approximation (O'Leary and Harker, 2008e). The Gibbs phenomena occurs where the basis functions are unable to model portions of the signal; this occurs with the Fourier and Polynomial basis functions at discontinuities. It is the ability of a set of basis functions to describe a signal which determines its suitability; there can be no general statements as to one set of basis functions being fundamentally better than another. To support understanding this fact, consider the Fourier series for a saw wave of length $2L$,

$$f\left(x\right) = \frac{x}{2L} = \frac{1}{2} - \frac{2}{2\pi}\sum_{n=1}^{\infty}\frac{1}{n}\,\sin\left(\frac{n\pi x}{L}\right).$$

(1.94)

This is a simple ramp function $f\left(x\right) = \frac{x}{2L}$, it could be modelled by a single linear polynomial component. However, it requires an infinite set of Fourier basis functions to describe it. On the other hand, consider the Taylor expansion for $f(x) = e^{-jx}$,

*Figure 21. a) The nodes for the computation this set of basis functions are √(x(i)) for 0≤x(i)≤1; b) the real and imaginary components of the 6 basis functions first; c) the error matrix $\Delta = \mathbf{B}^T \mathbf{B} - \mathbf{I}$ for 1000 fractional degree basis functions*

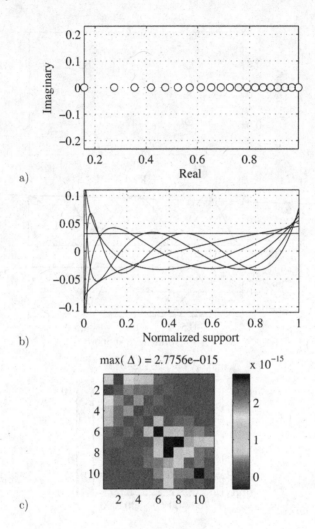

$$f\left(x\right) = e^{-\mathrm{j}x} = 1 + \sum_{n=1}^{\infty} \frac{\left(-\mathrm{j}x\right)^n}{n\,!} \;. \qquad (1.95)$$

$$C_s = \frac{n_\sigma}{n}. \qquad (1.96)$$

A single Fourier basis function can model this signal; however, a infinite polynomial series would be required.

*"Spectral compactness"* is defined here as the ratio of the number of discrete spectral components $n_\sigma$ required to model a given percentile $\sigma$ of the signal, to the number of points, $n$, available,

To better understand this issue it may be helpful to consider the example signal shown in Figure 22.

A geometric function has been chosen to demonstrate the differences between the Fourier and polynomial spectra. Both the classical Fourier spectrum and the polynomial spectrum have been computed for this signal. Furthermore, the number of components required to model 95% of the

*Figure 22. Top: An example signal generated by $y=-1.6x^2+2x+0.1$ computed for 200 points on the support $-1 \leq x \leq 1$. Mid-left: the Fourier spectrum of the signal. Mid-right: the Polynomial spectrum of the signal. Lower-left: Proportional sum of signal power in the Fourier spectral components. Lower-right: Proportional sum of signal power in the polynomial spectral components. The boundary for 95% signal power is shown for both cases. The polynomial basis has been generated using the method proposed in (O'Leary and Harker, 2008a).*

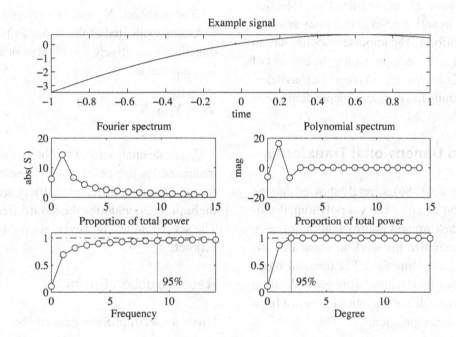

signal power has been determined. It can be seen in Figure 22 that the Fourier spectrum requires $n_\sigma = 10$ components to describe the signal, and polynomial spectrum requires $n_\sigma = 3$. The signal bandwidth required is larger for the Fourier basis than for the polynomial basis. Consequently, the noise bandwidth is smaller for the polynomial basis functions making them a better candidate to model this signal. Since the noise power is evenly distributed over all spectral components, the noise power gain is equal to the spectral compactness. This is a new result for polynomial moments. It enables an objective comparison of different bases with respect to their signal to noise ratio.

Consequently, the selection of the appropriate basis functions enables the embedding of a-priori knowledge into the solution. This improves the signal to noise ratio of the solution.

In the application presented in this paper it is known a-priory that the deformation of the global surface can be modelled using a geometric model, i.e. the surface deformation is not periodic. Consequently, it is prudent to choose a polynomial basis to model the surface.

## 1.2.9 Gibbs Error for Polynomial Basis Functions

The Gibbs error is well known for the Fourier basis. Here the Gibbs error is analyzed for polynomial basis functions. It is shown that the Gibbs error is only invariant to position for bases which are circulant.

The $i^{th}$-column $c_i$ of the projection matrix $\mathbf{P}$, is the impulse response of the filter to an impulse at the $i^{th}$ position in $y$. The matrix corresponding to the linear operator for the cyclic Savitzky-Golay are cyclically uniform, and hence, the Gibbs error will also be cyclically uniform; this effect is shown in Figure 23. In contrast, the projection matrix for conventional Savitzky-Golay smoothing is non-uniform. The impulse response has an increasing amplitude approaching the borders of the support. Consequently, conventional Savitzky-Golay smoothing has positional dependent Gibbs errors; see Figure 24.

### 1.2.10 Two Dimensional Transforms

Eden(Eden et al., 1986) correctly showed that the reconstruction of an image via polynomial moments is a least squares approximation process. Here, we generalize his work to show that his proof is generally true for all orthogonal bases independent of their nature. This generalization also leads to the idea of anisotropic spectra (moments) and to interpolation.

If the data $\mathbf{Z}$ (image) all lie on a separable lattice, the spectra can be computed using separable basis functions,

$$\mathbf{S} = \mathbf{Y}_a^+ \, \mathbf{Z} \, \mathbf{X}_a^{+T} \tag{1.97}$$

The matrices $\mathbf{X}_a$ and $\mathbf{Y}_a$ contain the basis functions evaluated at the nodes for the $x$ and $y$ directions respectively. Two dimensional synthesis is computed as,

$$\hat{\mathbf{Z}} = \mathbf{Y}_s \, \mathbf{S} \, \mathbf{X}_s^T . \tag{1.98}$$

Separate analysis and synthesis functions are maintained at this point; it will be seen later that for interpolation, different matrices are used, i.e. the basis functions are evaluated at different nodes. The sets of nodes, however, are not completely disjoint.

### Reconstruction Errors

Given a spectrum $\mathbf{S}$ the data can be synthesized as $\hat{\mathbf{Z}}$ (reconstructed) according to Equation 1.98; the matrix of reconstruction errors is,

*Figure 23. Response of the cyclic Savitzky-Golay filter to a step function, $l_s = 33$ of degree $d=4$, this demonstrates the uniform and cyclic Gibbs error associated with the cyclic smoothing*

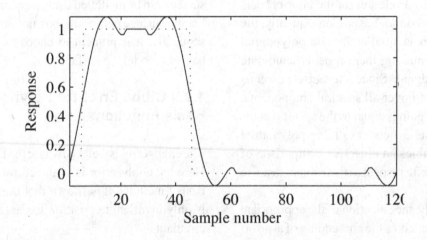

$$\mathbf{R} = \mathbf{Z} - \mathbf{Y}_s \, \mathbf{S} \, \mathbf{X}_s^T . \tag{1.99}$$

The aim is to determine the properties required for the basis functions so that the reconstruction process is a least squares approximation. We define the cost function,

$$E = \sum_{i=1}^{n_y} \sum_{j=1}^{n_y} \mathbf{R}(i,j)^2 = \left\| \mathbf{Z} - \mathbf{Y}_s \, \mathbf{S} \, \mathbf{X}_s^T \right\|_F^2 \tag{1.100}$$

where $\| \, . \, \|_F^2$ is the squared Frobenius norm of the matrix, i.e. the sum of the squares of all elements of the matrix. Evaluating the Frobenius norm yields,

$$
\begin{aligned}
E ={}& trace \left\{ \left( \mathbf{Z} - \mathbf{Y}_s \, \mathbf{S} \, \mathbf{X}_s^T \right) \left( \mathbf{Z} - \mathbf{Y}_s \, \mathbf{S} \, \mathbf{X}_s^T \right)^T \right\} \\
={}& trace \left\{ \mathbf{Z} \, \mathbf{Z}^T \right\} - trace \left\{ \mathbf{Y}_s \, \mathbf{S} \, \mathbf{X}_s^T \, \mathbf{Z}^T \right\} \\
& - trace \left\{ \mathbf{Z} \, \mathbf{X}_s \, \mathbf{S}^T \, \mathbf{Y}_s^T \right\}
\end{aligned}
\tag{1.101}
$$

$$+ \; trace \left\{ \mathbf{Y}_s \, \mathbf{S} \, \mathbf{X}^T \mathbf{X}_s \, \mathbf{S}^T \, \mathbf{Y}_s^T \right\} . \tag{1.102}$$

Differentiating the cost-function with respect to the matrix $\mathbf{S}$ and setting it equal to zero yields the matrix equation,

$$\frac{d\mathbf{E}}{d\mathbf{S}} = 2 \left( \mathbf{Y}_s^T \, \mathbf{Y}_s \, \mathbf{S} \, \mathbf{X}_s^T \mathbf{X}_s - \mathbf{Y}_s^T \mathbf{Z} \, \mathbf{X}_s \right) = 0. \tag{1.103}$$

Consequently,

$$\mathbf{S} = \left( \mathbf{Y}_s^T \, \mathbf{Y}_s \right)^{-1} \mathbf{Y}_s^T \, \mathbf{Z} \, \mathbf{X}_s \left( \mathbf{X}_s^T \mathbf{X} \right)_s^{-1} \tag{1.104}$$

$$= \mathbf{Y}_s^+ \, \mathbf{Z} \left( \mathbf{X}_s^+ \right)^T . \tag{1.105}$$

It should be noted that this proof is completely general and makes no assumptions about the basis functions and their evaluations at the nodes, except that they are not degenerate.

*Figure 24. Response of the Savitzky-Golay filter to a step function, $l_s = 33$, of degree $d = 4$, this demonstrates the positional dependence of the Gibbs error for Savitzky-Golay filtering*

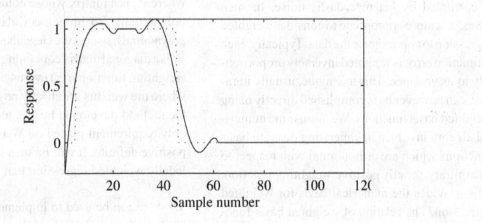

Filtering in the Fourier domain can be explained with this equation; the image is transformed using a complete set of basis functions; a selected number of the spectral components are set to zero; and the image is then reconstructed. This is equivalent to reconstruction with an incomplete set of harmonic functions. The result is a least squares approximation of the image by the selected basis functions. Similarly, discrete polynomial moments can be used to perform polynomial filtering. There is no requirement that the basis functions in the $x$ and $y$ directions be of the same nature. This opens the possibility of anisotropic moments, should a data set be better modelled by different types of basis functions along different axes.

### 1.2.11 Anisotropic Moments

The methods presented above make no assumptions on the nature of the basis functions used. Consequently different basis functions may be used in each direction of the lattice. This enables the implementation of anisotropic moments. There are specific applications, such as seismic exploration (O'Leary and Harker, 2008c) where the data has different characteristics in different directions.

### 1.3 MODIFIED BASES

It occurs often in measurement tasks that the data is corrupted by heteroscedastic noise. In such cases, it is more appropriate to consider weighted regression to approximate the data. Typically, each estimation error is weighted inversely proportionally to its variance. This technique, usually iterative, can however be accomplished directly using weighted basis functions. We discuss the numerical algebra involved in generating discrete basis functions which are orthonormal with respect to an arbitrary, strictly positive weighting function. This provides the numerical basis for weighted regression. The relation of weighted basis functions to spectral windowing is also discussed.

Often in Engineering problems, it is known that the solution must satisfy certain constraints or boundary conditions. An effective approach to such problems is to use constrained basis functions. It is shown how these can also be generated using techniques from numerical linear algebra such that they are orthonormal, and thereby have ideal properties with respect to error propagation.

### 1.3.1 Synthesizing Weighted Polynomials

The orthogonality condition for weighted polynomials is defined in a continuous sense as,

$$\int_{x_1}^{x_2} w(x)\, p_j(x)\, p_i(x)\, \mathrm{d}x = \begin{cases} C_i : j = i, \\ 0 : j \neq i, \end{cases}$$

$$(1.106)$$

where, $w(x)$ is a weighting function, and $p_j(x)$ and $p_i(x)$ are polynomials of degree $j$ and $i$ respectively. Weighted polynomials are most commonly encountered as being solutions to specific differential equations; e.g. Hermite with $w(x) = e^{-x2}$ and Gegenbauer polynomials with $w(x)=(1-x^2)^{(\lambda-1/2)}$. In this paper discrete weighted polynomials are defined to be orthonormal in the following manner,

$$\mathbf{P}_w^T\ \mathbf{W}\mathbf{P}_w = \mathbf{I}, \qquad (1.107)$$

where $\mathbf{P}_w$ is a matrix whose columns contain the polynomials. To implement classical weighted polynomials, such as the Gegenbauer polynomials, $\mathbf{W}$ is a diagonal matrix containing the values of the weighting function $w(x)$ evaluated at the nodes $x$, where the weights are strictly positive. However, the method developed here is more general, the only requirement placed on $\mathbf{W}$ is that it must be positive definite. It will be seen in the section on locally weighted regression that

$\mathbf{W}=\Lambda^{-1/2}$ can be used to implement optimal bases for heteroscedastic data.

The task now is, given $\mathbf{W}$, to synthesize a set of basis functions $\mathbf{P}$ that are strictly polynomial and fulfill Equation 1.107. If $\mathbf{P}_w$ is sorted according to increasing degree then the relationship to the Gram polynomials is,

$$\mathbf{P}_w = \mathbf{G}\,\mathbf{C}, \tag{1.108}$$

where $\mathbf{C}$ is upper triangular. Substituting Equation 1.108 into Equation 1.107 yields,

$$\mathbf{C}^T\mathbf{G}^T\mathbf{W}\,\mathbf{G}\,\mathbf{C} = \mathbf{I}. \tag{1.109}$$

Consequently,

$$\mathbf{G}^T\mathbf{W}\,\mathbf{G} = \mathbf{C}^{-T}\mathbf{C}^{-1} \tag{1.110}$$

A unique Cholesky factorization of $\mathbf{A} = \mathbf{R}^T\mathbf{R}$ exists if the matrix $\mathbf{A}$ is symmetric positive definite. The matrix $\mathbf{G}^T\mathbf{W}\,\mathbf{G}$ is positive definite, since $\mathbf{G}$ is orthonormal and $\mathbf{W}$ is positive definite. Thus if $\mathbf{R}\,\mathbf{R}^T$ is the Cholesky factorization of $\mathbf{G}^T\mathbf{W}\,\mathbf{G}$ where $\mathbf{R}$ is lower triangular, then $\mathbf{C} = \mathbf{R}^{-T}$ is the upper triangular matrix sought. The weighted polynomials are generated as $\mathbf{P}_w = \mathbf{G}\,\mathbf{C}$, and are orthogonal according to Equation 1.107.

This is a completely new approach to synthesizing weighted polynomials and delivers basis functions which are correct up to the computational resolution available. The condition number of the weighted basis functions depends on the ratio of the maximum to minimum values of the weighting matrix, i.e. it is not unity.

## 1.3.2 Synthesizing Constrained Orthonormal Basis Functions

In many engineering applications there are constraints placed on the object being measured. This results in constraints on the measurement data, e.g., when measuring the deformation of a cantilever. The aim here is to develop a method of synthesizing a set of basis functions which fulfil an arbitrary set of constraints. These basis functions may then be used to perform a least squares evaluation of the data, while taking the a-priori known constraints into account.

To generate a set of constrained orthonormal basis functions $\mathbf{B}_c$, it is necessary to determine $\mathbf{B}_c$ such that,

$$\mathbf{C}^T\,\mathbf{B}_c = 0 \quad and\, \mathbf{B}_c^T\,\mathbf{B}_c = \mathbf{I}, \tag{1.111}$$

where for $n$ data points and $p$ constraints, the matrix $\mathbf{C}$ is the $n \times p$ matrix containing discrete coefficients which implement the desired constraints and is of rank[8] $p$. Since adding constraints to a set of basis functions will reduce the number of degrees of freedom, the constrained basis is related to a full $m \times m$ basis by the relation,

$$\mathbf{B}_c = \mathbf{B}\,\mathbf{X}, \tag{1.112}$$

where the matrix $\mathbf{X}$ is $m \times n$, with $n = m - p$. Substituting this relation into the constraint equation yields,

$$\mathbf{C}^T\mathbf{B}\,\mathbf{X} = 0. \tag{1.113}$$

To fulfil the above equation, the matrix $\mathbf{X}$ must lie in the null space of $\mathbf{C}^T\,\mathbf{B}$. Performing $\mathbf{QR}$ decomposition on $\mathbf{B}^T\,\mathbf{C}$, yields,

$$\mathbf{Q}\,\mathbf{R} = \mathbf{B}^T\mathbf{C}, \tag{1.114}$$

and with this,

$$\mathbf{R}^T\mathbf{Q}^T\mathbf{X} = 0. \tag{1.115}$$

Since $\mathbf{C}$ has rank $p$, the matrix $\mathbf{R}$ may be partitioned such that,

$$\mathbf{R} = \begin{bmatrix} \mathbf{R}_1 \\ \mathbf{0} \end{bmatrix}, \tag{1.116}$$

where $\mathbf{R}_1$ is $p \times p$ a full rank upper triangular matrix. It now convenient to define $\mathbf{Y}$ such that,

*Figure 25. The Gegenbauer polynomials as example of weighted polynomials: b) the first 6 Gegenbauer polynomials; c) the error matrix* $\Delta = \mathbf{B}^{\mathrm{T}}\mathbf{B} - \mathbf{I}$ *for 1000 Gegenbauer basis functions*

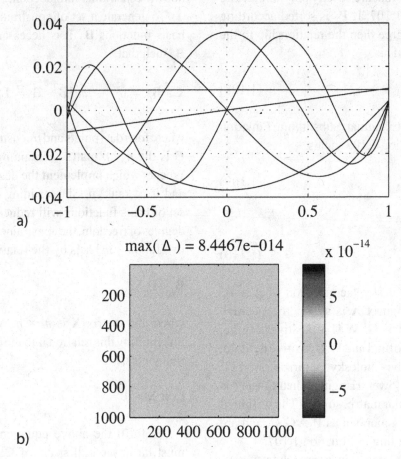

$\mathbf{Y} = \mathbf{Q}^{\mathrm{T}}\mathbf{X}$ and thus $\mathbf{X} = \mathbf{Q}\mathbf{Y}$     (1.117)

and to partition these matrices so that they are compatible with the partitioning of $\mathbf{R}$

$$\begin{bmatrix} \mathbf{X}_1 \\ \mathbf{X}_2 \end{bmatrix} = \begin{bmatrix} \mathbf{Q}_{11} & \mathbf{Q}_{12} \\ \mathbf{Q}_{21} & \mathbf{Q}_{22} \end{bmatrix} \begin{bmatrix} \mathbf{Y}_1 \\ \mathbf{Y}_2 \end{bmatrix} \tag{1.118}$$

Substituting $\mathbf{Y}$ into Equation 1.115, yields,

$$\begin{bmatrix} \mathbf{R}_1^{\mathrm{T}} & 0 \end{bmatrix} \begin{bmatrix} \mathbf{Y}_1 \\ \mathbf{Y}_2 \end{bmatrix} = \mathbf{0} \tag{1.119}$$

Since $\mathbf{R}_1$ is full rank this requires $\mathbf{Y}_1 = \mathbf{0}$ and as a consequence,

$$\begin{bmatrix} \mathbf{X}_1 \\ \mathbf{X}_2 \end{bmatrix} = \begin{bmatrix} \mathbf{Q}_{12} \mathbf{Y}_2 \\ \mathbf{Q}_{22} \mathbf{Y}_2 \end{bmatrix} \tag{1.120}$$

If we add the condition, that the number of roots of the constrained basis functions is strictly increasing[9], then we have the additional requirement that $\mathbf{X}_2$ is upper triangular. Thus, let the **RQ** decomposition[10] of $\mathbf{Q}_{22}$ be,

$$\mathbf{Q}_{22} = \tilde{\mathbf{R}}\,\tilde{\mathbf{Q}}, \tag{1.121}$$

where $\tilde{\mathbf{Q}}$ is orthonormal, and $\tilde{\mathbf{R}}$ is upper triangular. Letting $\mathbf{Y}_2 = \tilde{\mathbf{Q}}^T$ yields,

$$\mathbf{X} = \begin{bmatrix} \mathbf{X}_1 \\ \mathbf{X}_2 \end{bmatrix} = \begin{bmatrix} \mathbf{Q}_{12}\,\tilde{\mathbf{Q}}^T \\ \tilde{\mathbf{R}} \end{bmatrix}, \qquad (1.122)$$

and with this the required matrix $\mathbf{X}$ is fully determined. Finally, we verify the requirement that the basis is orthonormal,

$$\mathbf{B}_c \mathbf{B}_c = \mathbf{X}^T \mathbf{B}^T \mathbf{B}\, \mathbf{X} = \mathbf{X}^T \mathbf{X} = \mathbf{Y}^T \mathbf{Q}^T \mathbf{Q}\, \mathbf{Y} = \mathbf{Y}^T \mathbf{Y} = \tilde{\mathbf{Q}}\,\tilde{\mathbf{Q}}^T = \mathbf{I}, \qquad (1.123)$$

i.e., the basis is unitary. To summarize, teh algorithm requires a **QR** decomposition of $\mathbf{B}^T\mathbf{C}$ and an **RQ** decomposition of $\mathbf{Q}_{22}$.

The constraints associated with the bending of a cantilever, i.e., $y(-1) = 0$, $\dot{y}(-1) = 0$, $\ddot{y}(1) = 0$ and $y(1) = 0$, were applied to Gram polynomials to demonstrate the potential of this procedure (the results can be seen in Figure 26). There are $n - 4$ orthonormal basis functions, as would be expected since $p = 4$ and the basis is virtually free from errors. Such basis functions can be used as admissible functions to solve boundary value problems and initial value problems. It should be noted that this procedure can be applied to any orthonormal set of basis functions, and not only to polynomials.

### 1.3.3 Windowing

Windowing is commonly used in Fourier analysis to suppress or reduce the Gibbs effect (Jerri, 1998). The aim here is to derive a generalized convolution theorem valid for all bases which can be synthesized via the recurrence relationship. A signal can be synthesized from a set of basis functions $\mathbf{B}$ and its spectrum[11] $s$ as $y = \mathbf{B}\,s$. Consequently, given the signal the spectrum is computed as,

$$s = \mathbf{B}^+ y. \qquad (1.124)$$

The window function $w$ can be expressed as a diagonal matrix $\mathbf{W}$. The spectrum of the windowed data is,

$$s_w = \mathbf{B}^+ \mathbf{W}\, y. \qquad (1.125)$$

Consequently the relationship between the windowed and original spectrum is,

$$s_w = \mathbf{B}^+\,\mathbf{W}\,\mathbf{B}s. \qquad (1.126)$$

This is the completely general case true for all bases.

### 1.3.4 Weighted Regression

The concept of weighted regression arises when we have a set of measurements, $y$, which are corrupted by anisotropic noise with covariance $\Lambda$. Then the measured values, $\hat{y}$, are the ideal values plus the additive noise, i.e.,

$$\hat{y} = y + v. \qquad (1.127)$$

The aim is to model the measured values, $\hat{y}$, by a linear system $\mathbf{A}\,\alpha$. Thus, we define the residual, $r$, as the difference between the two, i.e.,

$$r = \hat{y} - \mathbf{A}\alpha. \qquad (1.128)$$

According to the noise model, we thus have,

$$r = y + v - \mathbf{A}\,\alpha. \qquad (1.129)$$

Assuming there is no systematic error in modelling the ideal measurements with a linear system, $y - \mathbf{A}\alpha = \mathbf{0}$, and thus,

$$r = v. \qquad (1.130)$$

That is, the residual vector, as defined, is a Gaussian random variable with covariance $\Lambda$. Naïvely applying a Least Squares minimization to the residual is not appropriate, since Gauss's

*Figure 26. Example of a set of constrained polynomials; the constraints placed on these polynomials are y(−1) = 0, ẏ(−1) = 0, ÿ(1) = 0 and, ⃛y(−1) = 0. There are the constraints corresponding to the solution of the differential equation for a cantilever. a) the first 6 constrained (polynomials) basis functions; b) the error matrix $\Delta = B^T B - I$ for 1000 constrained basis functions*

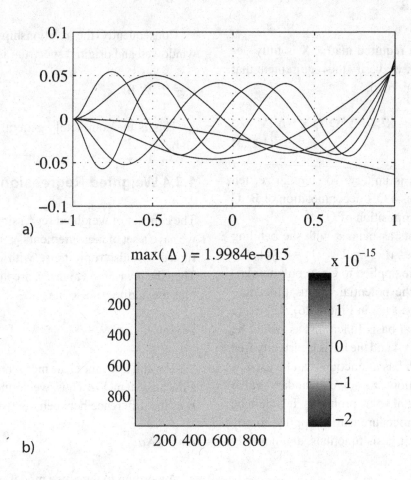

a)

b)

minimum variance theorem only applies to i.i.d. noise. We thus define the modified residual,

$$r' = \Lambda^{-\frac{1}{2}} r,$$  (1.131)

and hence

$$r' = \Lambda^{-\frac{1}{2}} \Lambda^{\frac{1}{2}} u,$$  (1.132)

$$= u,$$  (1.133)

which is the i.i.d. residual which was sought. From Equations (1.128) and (1.131), the residual function which is appropriate for Least Squares minimization is,

$$r' = \Lambda^{-\frac{1}{2}} \left( \hat{y} - A\alpha \right).$$  (1.134)

The Weighted Least Squares cost function is thus defined as,

$$\varepsilon = \left\| \Lambda^{-\frac{1}{2}} \left( \hat{y} - \mathbf{A}\alpha \right) \right\|_2^2 . \tag{1.135}$$

In the special case where the noise is independent, but not identically distributed, we have

$$\Lambda^{-\frac{1}{2}} = \mathrm{diag}\{w_1, \ldots, w_n\} \tag{1.136}$$

and the cost function reads,

$$\varepsilon = \sum_{i=1}^{n} w_i (\hat{y}_i - \tilde{y}_i)^2 , \tag{1.137}$$

where $\tilde{y}_i$ is the mathematical model for the measurment data. This is the Weighted Regression cost function which is common to the literature.

## 1.3.5 Weighted Regression via Basis Functions

The cost function for locally weighted polynomial regression is,

$$\varepsilon = \left( \hat{y} - \mathbf{A}\pm \right)^{\mathrm{T}} \mathbf{W} \left( \hat{y} - \mathbf{A}\pm \right). \tag{1.138}$$

where $\mathbf{W} = \Lambda^{-1}$, $\Lambda$ is the covariance of the heteroscedastic data $\hat{y}$. Expanding and simplifying the cost function yields,

$$\varepsilon = \hat{y}^{\mathrm{T}} \mathbf{W} \hat{y} - 2\alpha^{\mathrm{T}} \mathbf{A}^{\mathrm{T}} \mathbf{W} \hat{y} + \alpha^{\mathrm{T}} \mathbf{A}^{\mathrm{T}} \mathbf{W} \mathbf{A}\alpha \tag{1.139}$$

To find the minimum, differentiate with respect to $\alpha$, yielding,

$$\frac{\partial \varepsilon}{\partial \alpha} = -2\mathbf{A}^{\mathrm{T}} \mathbf{W} \hat{y} + 2\mathbf{A}^{\mathrm{T}} \mathbf{W} \mathbf{A}\alpha . \tag{1.140}$$

Equating the partial derivatives to zero, yields the so-called normal equations for regression,

$$\mathbf{A}^{\mathrm{T}} \mathbf{W} \mathbf{A}\alpha = \mathbf{A}^{\mathrm{T}} \mathbf{W} \hat{y} . \tag{1.141}$$

Clearly, if the matrices $\mathbf{A}$ and $\mathbf{W}$ are full rank, the system of equations can be solved for $\alpha$ by matrix inversion. However, in regression problems, the solution is known to have a particular form (e.g., linear, quadratic, sinusoidal etc.). In this case, the matrix $\mathbf{A}$ may be a set of discrete basis functions (e.g., polynomial), which are orthogonal with respect to the weighting function, $\mathbf{W}$. In the regression problem we let $\mathbf{A} = \mathbf{B}_w$ such that

$$\mathbf{B}_w^{\mathrm{T}} \mathbf{W} \mathbf{B}_w = \mathbf{I} . \tag{1.142}$$

The normal equations then read,

$$\mathbf{B}_w^{\mathrm{T}} \mathbf{W} \mathbf{B}_w \alpha = \mathbf{B}_w^{\mathrm{T}} \mathbf{W} \hat{y} . \tag{1.143}$$

Clearly, by definition of the weighted basis functions, no matrix inversion is necessary to solve the system, and therefore,

$$\alpha = \mathbf{B}_w^{\mathrm{T}} \mathbf{W} \hat{y} . \tag{1.144}$$

Substituting this expression for the maximum likelihood values of $\alpha$ into the original model for the data yields,

$$y = \mathbf{B}_w \mathbf{B}_w^{\mathrm{T}} \mathbf{W} \hat{y} . \tag{1.145}$$

There are two cases which are of note. If the set of basis functions are complete, i.e., if the matrix $\mathbf{B}_w$ is $n \times n$ and full rank, then from the orthogonality relation we have,

$$\mathbf{W} = \mathbf{B}_w^{-T}\, \mathbf{B}_w^{-1} \qquad (1.146)$$

or

$$\mathbf{W}^{-1} = \mathbf{B}_w\, \mathbf{B}_w^{T}\,. \qquad (1.147)$$

Clearly in this case the coefficient matrix of the regression data is the identity. Thus, when a full set of basis functions is used, the weighting has no influence on the result, as is to be expected. In the alternative case where the basis functions are not complete, the important fact to note is that the approximation given in Equation (1.145) is always the least squares minimizer (maximum likelihood estimator) for that set of basis functions (e.g., polynomials up to degree two). This follows as a direct consequence of the derivation.

## 1.4 APPLICATION RELEVANT ISSUES

There are a number of issues relevant when considering applications, these are presented in this section.

### 1.4.1 Incomplete Grids and Interpolation

In this paper the theory of computing spectra on regular grids but with missing data points is generalized for all complete basis functions. Furthermore, it is shown that interpolation can be performed by performing analysis with basis functions evaluated on the incomplete set of nodes, and performing synthesis with the basis functions evaluated on the complete set of nodes.

Consider a complete set of $n$ nodes on which $m$ values of $y$ are given as $y_m$ for $n > m$, i.e. there are $n - m$ missing points. The index of the $k^{th.}$ known value of $y$ is $\rho(k)$. We wish to compute the spectrum of $y_n$ from $y_m$ and to perform interpolation i.e. generate $y_n$ for the complete set of $n$ nodes.

The known points should remain unchanged by interpolation, i.e.

$$y_m = \mathbf{P}y_n \qquad (1.148)$$

where $\mathbf{P}$ is an $m \times n$ permutation matrix,

$$\mathbf{P}(i,j) = \begin{cases} 1 & : \text{if } i = k \text{ and } j = \rho(k) \\ 0 & : \text{otherwise.} \end{cases} \qquad (1.149)$$

The matrix $\mathbf{P}$ is eliminating the $y$ values from $y_n$ which are generated by interpolation. The spectra of the known and interpolated data must be identical with the exception of some zero entries, since interpolation does not create any new information, hence

$$s_n = \mathbf{Q}s_m \qquad (1.150)$$

where $\mathbf{Q}$ is an $n \times m$ permutation matrix,

$$\mathbf{Q}(i,j) = \begin{cases} 1 & : \text{if } i = \alpha(k) \text{ and } j = k \\ 0 & : \text{otherwise,} \end{cases} \qquad (1.151)$$

whereby $\alpha(k)$ is the index of the $k^{th}$ basis function representing the known data $y_m$. This is the most general case of zero padding(Oppenheim and Schafer, 1989), whereby Q inserts zeros at the appropriate place in the spectrum $s_n$. To implement Lagrangian interpolation, i.e, for discrete polynomial bases, the zeros are simply concatenated to the end of the spectrum.

The values of $y_n$ at all $n$ points can be synthesized from its spectrum $s_n$ using a unitary and complete basis B, i.e., $y_n = \mathbf{B}\, s_n$, Substituting this relationship into Equation 1.148 yields,

$$y_m = \mathbf{P}\,\mathbf{B}\, s_n \qquad (1.152)$$

now substituting Equation 1.150 for $s_n$ yields,

$$y_m = \mathbf{P}y_n = \mathbf{P}\,\mathbf{B}\,\mathbf{Q}s_m, \qquad (1.153)$$

consequently,

$$s_m = \{\,\mathbf{P}\,\mathbf{B}\,\mathbf{Q}\,\}^+ y_m. \qquad (1.154)$$

Hence,

$$s_n = \mathbf{Q}\,\{\,\mathbf{P}\,\mathbf{B}\,\mathbf{Q}\,\}^+ y_m. \qquad (1.155)$$

This derivation is completely general, there are no assumptions made about the basis functions used. It can be applied with any unitary and complete set of basis functions. It delivers a direct solution for computing the Fourier spectrum of a signal with missing data points. Furthermore, the complete interpolation process can be formulated as,

$$y_n = \{\,\mathbf{B}\,\mathbf{Q}\,\}\,\{\,\mathbf{P}\,\mathbf{B}\,\mathbf{Q}\,\}^+ y_m. \qquad (1.156)$$

This derivation is valid for any unitary and complete set of basis functions. Lagrange and harmonic interpolation are special cases, where polynomial or Fourier basis functions are used respectively.

## 1.4.2 Interpolation on 2D Latices

The computation of spectra on 2D latices, assumes that the data is so structured that separable $x$ and $y$ basis functions can be used. This is also true for interpolation, i.e. the regions to be interpolated must consist of full columns or full rows. The spectra of an image with missing rows can be computed as,

$$\mathbf{S} = \mathbf{Y}_{PQ}^{+}\,\mathbf{Z}\,\mathbf{X} \qquad (1.157)$$

whereby $\mathbf{Y}_{PQ} = \mathbf{P}\,\mathbf{Y}\,\mathbf{Q}$, and similarly for missing columns,

$$\mathbf{S} = \mathbf{Y}^T\,\mathbf{Z}\mathbf{X}_{PQ}^{+T}. \qquad (1.158)$$

The interpolation process is the same in both cases,

$$\hat{\mathbf{Z}} = \mathbf{Y}\,\mathbf{S}\mathbf{X}^T. \qquad (1.159)$$

This algorithm provides a means of performing interpolation independent of the nature of the basis being used.

## 1.4.3 Local Approximation

Local approximation is when the support length is shorter than the number of points available in the data set. Consequently, an extended linear operator is required in such applications. The implementation proposed can be used with any of the projection matrices proposed in this paper, is not limited to local polynomial approximation (Savitzky-Golay smoothing).

Given a set of $n$ data points and the projection $\mathbf{P}$ associated with a linear operator of support length $l_s$: The extended linear operator $\mathbf{S}$ is an $n \times n$ matrix,

$$\hat{y} = \mathbf{S}\,y. \qquad (1.160)$$

The data can be segmented into three portions, each of which has a corresponding partition in the projection matrix:

1. The first and last $(l_s - 1)/2$ points. Savitzky and Golay did not present a solution for these points. Most implementations reduce the support length in this region and reduce the degree of the approximation, e.g., the tri-diagional matrix used to approximate a discrete differential operator is degree two in the core and only degree one at the end of the support; this leads to significant errors.

The correct solution is to maintain the support length and degree of approximation while moving the point of the Taylor expansion towards the border of the support. The upper partition of the projection matrix **P** delivers the correct solution for the start of the support and the lower portion for the end of the support;

2. The central row of the projection is used for the complete core of the extended linear operator. An example is shown in Figure 27 for $l_s = 7$, $d = 2$ and for $n = 20$.

We are not proposing to implement an application in this manner, since this matrix contains many zeros and would be very inefficient for long data vectors. However, all the presented algebraic techniques can be applied to the matrix,

making it an excellent means of analyzing local regression and predicting performance.

A highly efficient implementation for long data vectors is obtained from observing that the central portion of the linear operator **P** is circulant and only the top and bottom $(l_s - 1)/2$ rows are not. Consequently, the circulant portion can be computed as a cyclic convolution using a FFT, then the first and last $(l_s - 1)/2$ points are corrected.

### 1.4.4 Cyclic Local Approximation

Each of the four above methods can be used to perform cyclic local smoothing. The first step is to compute the corresponding linear operator matrices. Consider smoothing a set of $n$ data points, using a support length of $l_s$ and a polynomial of degree $d$. To support understanding, the example with $n = 10$, $l_s = 5$ and $d = 3$ is presented

*Figure 27. Left: Structure of the projection matrix* **P=B B**$^T$ *associated with the Gram basis with $l_s = 7$ and $d = 2$. The matrix has been partitioned into three segments. Right: structure of the linear operator S for local polynomial regression with $l_s = 7$, $d = 2$ and for $n = 20$ data points. This example corresponds to Savitzky-Golay smoothing.*

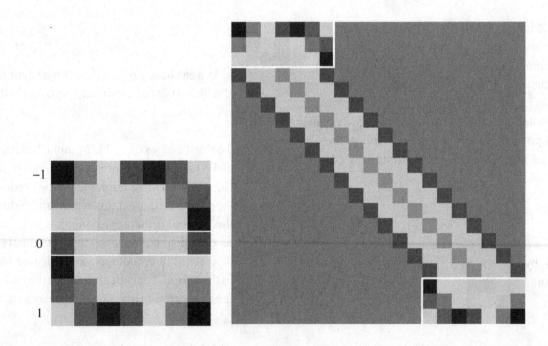

graphically in Figure 28. The projection matrix $\mathbf{P}_{SG} = \mathbf{G}\,\mathbf{G}^T$, is an $l_s \times l_s$ matrix. The center row of $\mathbf{P}$ corresponds to computing the projection at the center of the support $\mathbf{P}_{x=0}$: here called the *core coefficients*. These coefficients are used to weight the data as long as the point for which the smoothing is being performed is further than ($l_s$ $-1)/2$ from the start or end of the data-set. Since the start and end points are adjacent for cyclic data sets, the coefficients are wrapped around to use the needed points from the start and end of the data respectively. In this manner the linear operator matrices are circulant, see Figure 28.

Circulant matrices form a special class of matrices that are cyclic convolutions. All rows are phase shifted copies of the previous row. The computation $y_f = \mathbf{P}y$ can be computed via the Fast Fourier Transform (Golub and Van Loan, 1996) (FFT), although the bases are polynomial,

$$y_f = FFT^{-1}\{\,FFT\{\,\boldsymbol{P}_{x=0}\,\} \circ FFT\{y\}\},$$

$$(1.161)$$

whereby the FFT of the coefficients can be computed in advance. In this manner local cyclic polynomial smoothing can be performed with the same numerical efficiency as filtering via the elliptical fourier descriptors. There are, however, a number of advantages associated with the local polynomial approximation:

1. The Gibbs error associated with a discontinuity is limited to the length $2l_s - 1$, whereas with elliptical descriptors the Gibbs error can be distributed over the whole data set;
2. The local polynomial filtering is polynomial preserving;
3. Local derivatives with implicit regularization can be computed from the local polynomial approximation (Savitzky and Golay, 1964).

To summarize four different filtering procedures have been analyzed: their respective linear operators are:

$$Savitzky\text{--}Golay\,\mathbf{L}_{SG} = \mathbf{G}\,\mathbf{G}^T; \qquad (1.162)$$

*Figure 28. Left: structure of the linear operator for Cyclic Savitzky-Golay Smoothing. Right: example linear operator for support length $l_s = 7$, of degree $d = 2$, and $n = 20$ points*

*Spatial windowing* $\mathbf{L}_{SW} = \mathbf{G}\ \mathbf{G}^T\ \mathbf{W}$;

$$(1.163)$$

*Weighted regression* $\mathbf{L}_{WR} = \mathbf{B}_w\ \mathbf{B}_w^T\ \mathbf{W}$;

$$(1.164)$$

*Constrained bases* $\mathbf{L}_c = \mathbf{B}_c\ \mathbf{B}_c^T$ $\qquad(1.165)$

Each of these procedures will deliver filter coefficients, which can be used for cyclic Savitzky-Golay smoothing. To demonstrate the possibilities offered, a weighting function $w(x) = e^{-x2/\sigma2}$ with $\sigma = 0.8$, has been chosen. Gaussian functions are the most commonly used weighting in literature. The filter coefficients for the four linear operators with $l_s = 101$ and $d = 4$ are shown in Figure

29. The corresponding frequency responses are shown in Figure 30.

## 1.5 CASE STUDIES

In this section case studies are presented where the possibilities offered by discrete orthogonal basis functions are utilized. The aim is to show the reader how the theory may be applied in real applications.

### 1.5.1 Inhomogeneous Lighting in Metallographic Images

This simple example shows the application of discrete basis functions to the correction of inho-

*Figure 29. The correlation coefficients for the four linear operators:* $\mathbf{P}_{SG}$ *(black);* $\mathbf{P}_{SW}$ *(green) and* $\mathbf{P}_{WR}$ *(red), for* $l_s = 101$ *and* $d = 4$

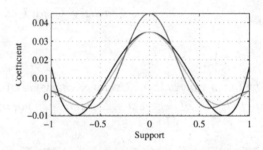

*Figure 30. Frequency response of the linear operators from Figure 29:* $\mathbf{P}_{SG}$ *(black);* $P_{SW}$ *(green) and* $P_{WR}$ *(red), for* $l_s = 101$ *and* $d = 4$

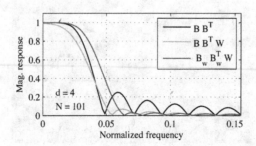

mogeneous lighting in metallographic images. The primary task in this application is to determine the orientation of primary dendrites from a sample taken from a metal casting process, see Figure 31

The sample is photographed under a microscope and the images are used to determine the local orientation of the dendrites. There are considerable intensity variations within the original image P. These variations are detrimental when performing binary morphology.

A Gram tensor polynomial is used to perform intensity correction. The Gram bases for the $x$ and $y$ directions respectivly are $\mathbf{G}_x$ and $\mathbf{G}_y$. The corrected image $\mathbf{P}_c$ is computed as,

$$\mathbf{P}_c = \mathbf{P} - \mathbf{G}_y \, \mathbf{G}_x^T \, \mathbf{P} \, \mathbf{G}_x \mathbf{G}_x^T . \tag{1.166}$$

The resulting image is better suited for global binary morphology.

## 1.5.2 Seismic Processing and Anisotropic Moments

This case study presents the application of discrete basis functions to the processing of seismic data for geological prospection. A typical seismic measurement has approximately 200 geophones on a linear baseline, each geophone acquires the acoustic response of the ground to the shot. The signals from all the geophones are stacked beside each other to form a data set on an invariant lattice.

This data set is inherently anisotropic: the vertical dimension is a time dimension and the signals are periodic due to their acoustic nature; the horizontal correlations in the data set are associated with the subsurface structures and are geometric in nature. Furthermore, it is typical that there are missing channels or corrupted channels in the data set which need to be eliminated.

In this application a Fourier basis is used in the vertical direction and a Gram polynomial basis in the horizontal direction. This yields anisotropic moments having lower Gibbs error than using a conventional Fourier spectrum approach. Additionally interpolation is performed together with simultaneous filtering so as to generate data for the missing channels, in this manner the result of the processing still lies on an invariant lattice.

## 1.5.3 Real-Time Inspection of Copper Plates

Copper refinement is generally performed in large scale electrolysis "farms". Each bath contains a large number of cathodes made from stainless steel. There are two major sources of defects and errors in the refinement process: the electrodes may be deformed, i.e., non-planar, this leads to a non-uniform spacing between the electrodes over the area of the cathode, which in turn leads to a varying rate of copper deposition; secondly;

*Figure 31. This figure shows the place from where the metal sample is taken*

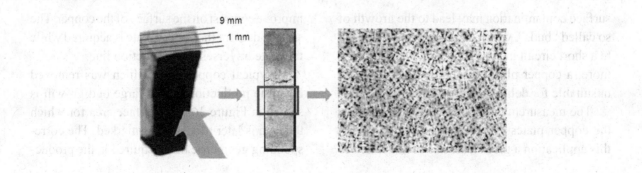

*Figure 32. Left: The original photomicrograph prior to processing. Right: Image after intensity correction using a Gram tensor polynomial of degree 15*

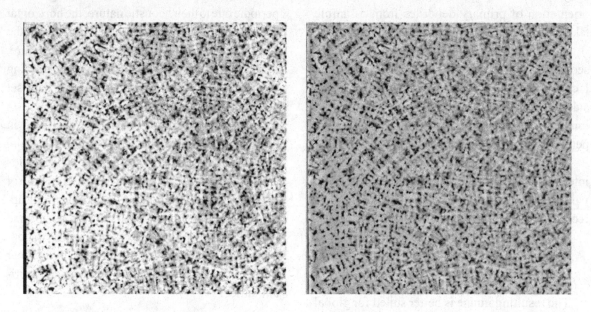

*Figure 33. Seismic data-set prior to processing, the lattice is of size $n_x=44$ $n_y=851$. Note, there are five missing channels (11, 12, 18, 19 and 20).*

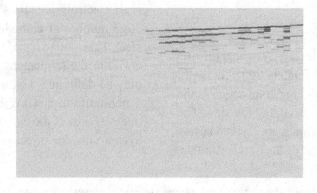

surface contamination may lead to the growth of so called "buds", which above a certain size lead to a short circuit in the electrolysis bath. Furthermore, a copper plate with buds is also deemed unsuitable for delivery to a customer.

The measurement setup for the inspection of the copper plates can be seen in Figure 35. In this application a green laser has been applied to

improve contrast on the surface of the copper. The surface data for the copper plate is acquired while the plate traverses the production line.

A typical copper plate which was removed from the production due to large bud-growth is shown in Figure 36. The surface area for which the data is later processed is marked. The corresponding geometric data acquired in the produc-

*Figure 34. Seismic data-set after interpolation for the missing channels and simultaneously filtering. A polynomial basis of degree $d_x$=18 is used in the x direction and a DFT basis with 830 components is used in the y direction.*

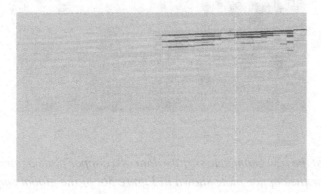

*Figure 35. Copper plate inspection system in the production line. Here a green laser has been used to improve the visibility on the surface.*

tion line is shown in Figure 37(a). The aim is to seperate the global surface geometry from the local anomalies. In this application the global geometry of the surface is modelled by a 2D ten-

sor gram polynomial of degree $d_x$=16 in the x direction and $d_y$=4 in the y direction. This 2D surface model, see Figure 37(b) is used to determine if the electrode carrying the copper is de-

*Figure 36. A typical copper plate which is removed from the production due to large bud-growth*

*Figure 37. a) Example of the raw geometric surface data of a copper plate acquired inline in the production line. This data is for the copper plate shown in Figure 36. b) the global surface model determined using least squares approximation of the data by a 2D tensor Gram polynomial, $d_x$=16 and $d_y$=4. c) the local anomalies which are used to determine the positions and sizes of the buds.*

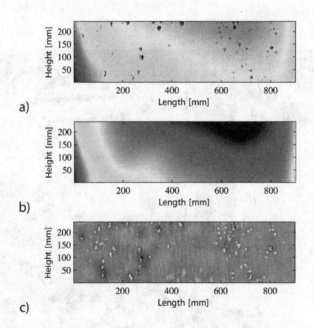

formed. The local anomalies on the surface are then used to determine the positions and sizes of the buds, see Figure 37(c).

## 1.5.4 Extraction of 3D Embossed Digits

Embossed digits are used in the steel industry to identify slabs and blocks, a similar system is used for the identification of beer kegs. The embossed digits have a three dimensional geometry making them less sensitive to harsh environments and handling.

This case study presents an application in a seamless pipe production plant. A three component surface model consisting of a global geometry, local anomalies and measurement perturbations is used. The unitary property of discrete

*Figure 38. a) The original data. b) The global surface model. c) The local anomalies, i.e. the difference between the original data and the global surface model. The number of points in the x and y directions are $n_x$ and $n_y$. The surface model is generated with a tensor polynomial of degree $d_x=180$ and $d_y=2$.*

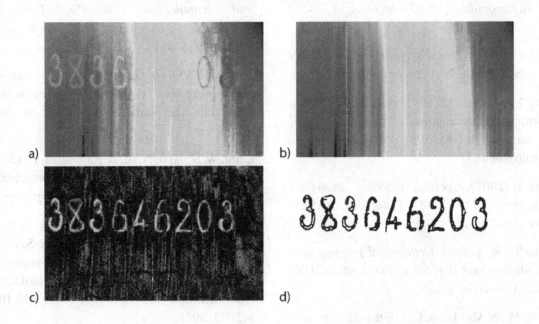

basis functions is utilized to separate the local anomalies (the digits) from the global geometry and to simultaneously reduce the effects of the perturbations. This implementation enables the extraction of the data associated with the digits from a cluttered background.

## 1.6 DISCUSSION

This chapter has presented an in depth discussion of discrete polynomial basis functions and some of their possible applications. The advantage of the methods presented here, is that they are computationally efficient, while enabling an a-priori analytical estimation of performance. The new algebraic framework is a very useful tool which simplifies the analysis of basis functions and their applications.

The focus of the applications in this chapter is on surface modelling and automatic inspection. The reader should however be aware that discrete

basis functions have many other applications, e.g. as admissible function in Galarkin methods for the solution of initial value, and boundary value problems.

Presently research is being performed on the use of discrete polynomial basis functions for the solution of ill-conditioned problems involving partial differential equations. In particular, new solutions for the evaluation of seismic data in geophysical prospection are emerging.

## REFERENCES

Barnard, R., Dahlquist, G., Pearce, K., Reichel, L., & Richards, K. (1998). Gram polynomials and the Kummer function. *Journal of Approximation Theory*, *94*(1), 128–143. doi:10.1006/jath.1998.3181

Bayraktar, B., Bernas, T., Robinson, P., & Rajwa, B. (2007). A numerical recipe for accurate image reconstruction from discrete orthogonal moments. *Pattern Recognition, 40*, 659–669. doi:10.1016/j.patcog.2006.03.009

Boyd, J. (2001). *Chebyschev and Fourier spectral methods*. Mineola, NY: Dover Publications Inc.

Eden, M., Unser, M., & Leonardi, R. (1986). Polynomial representation of pictures. *Signal Processing, 10*, 385–393. doi:10.1016/0165-1684(86)90046-0

Eilers, P. (2003). A perfect smoother. *Analytical Chemistry, 75*(14), 1383–1386. doi:10.1021/ac034173t

Gautschi, W. (2004). *Orthogonal polynomials, computation and approximation*. Oxford, UK: Oxford University Press.

Golub, G., & Van Loan, C. (1996). *Matrix computations* (3rd ed.). Baltimore, MD: John Hopkins University Press.

Gorry, P. (1990). General least-squares smoothing and differentiation by the convolution (Savitzky-Golay) method. *Analytical Chemistry, 62*, 570–573. doi:10.1021/ac00205a007

Gram, J. (1883). Ueber die entwicklung realler funktionen in reihen mittelst der methode der kleinsten quadrate. *Journal fuer dei reine und angewandte Mathematik*, 150- 157.

Hosny, K. (2007). Exact Legendre moment computation for gray level images. *Pattern Recognition, 40*(12). doi:10.1016/j.patcog.2007.04.014

Hu, M.-K. (1962). Visual pattern recognition by moment invariants. *I.R.E. Transactions on Information Theory, 8*, 179–187. doi:10.1109/TIT.1962.1057692

Huang, W., Chen, S., & Zheng, G. (2010). A fast 2D discrete tchebichef transform algorithm. *International Conference on Innovative Computing and Communication and Asia-Pacific Conference on Information Technology and Ocean Engineering*, (pp. 358–361).

Jerri, A. (1998). *The Gibbs phenomenon in Fourier analysis, splines and wavelet approximations*. Dordrecht, The Netherlands: Kluver Academic Publishers.

Lang, W. S., Abu, N. A., & Rahmalan, H. (2009). Fast 4x4 tchebichef moment image compression. *International Conference of Soft Computing and Pattern Recognition*, (pp. 295–300).

Madden, H. (1978). Comments on the Savitzky-Golay convolution method for least-squares-fit smoothing and differentiation of digital data. *Analytical Chemistry, 50*(9), 1383–1386. doi:10.1021/ac50031a048

Meer, P., & Weiss, I. (1990). Smoothed differentiation filters for images. In *IEEE I10th International Conference on Pattern Recognition*, Vol. 2, June 1990, (pp. 121-126). Atlantic City, NJ, USA.

Mukundan, R. (2004). Some computational aspects of discrete orthogonal moments. *IEEE Transactions on Image Processing, 13*(8), 1055–1059. doi:10.1109/TIP.2004.828430

Mukundan, R., Ong, S., & Lee, P. (2001). Image analysis by Tchebichef moments. *IEEE Transactions on Image Processing, 10*(9), 1357–1363. doi:10.1109/83.941859

Nakagaki, K., & Mukundan, R. (2007). A fast 4 × 4 forward discrete tchebichef transform algorithm. *IEEE Signal Processing Letters, 14*(10), 684–687. doi:10.1109/LSP.2007.898331

O'Leary, P., & Harker, M. (2008a). *An algebraic framework for discrete basis functions in computer vision*. In IEEE Indian Conference on Computer Vision, Graphics and Image Processing, Bhubaneswar, Dec.

O'Leary, P., & Harker, M. (2008b). An algebraic framework for discrete basis functions in computer vision. *Indian Conference on Computer Vision, Graphics and Image Processing*, (pp. 150-157).

O'Leary, P., & Harker, M. (2008c). An algebraic framework for discrete basis functions in computer vision. *Indian Conference on Computer Vision, Graphics and Image Processing*, (pp. 150–157).

O'Leary, P., & Harker, M. (2008d). Discrete polynomial moments for real-time geometric surface inspection. *Journal of Electronic Imaging*, 18.

O'Leary, P., & Harker, M. (2008e). Discrete polynomial moments for real-time geometric surface inspection. *Journal of Electronic Imaging*, 18.

Ong, S., & Raveendren, P. (2005). Image feature analysis by Hahn orthogonal moments. *Lecture Notes in Computer Science, 3656*, 524–531. doi:10.1007/11559573_65

Oppenheim, A., & Schafer, R. (1989). *Discrete-time Signal Processing*. Upper Saddle River, NJ, USA: Prentice Hall.

Ping, Z., Ren, H., Zou, J., Sheng, Y., & Bo, W. (2005). Generic orthogonal moments: Jackobi-Fourier moments for invariant image description. *Pattern Recognition, 40*, 1245–1254. doi:10.1016/j.patcog.2006.07.016

Proitte, T., & Luati, A. (2009). Low-pass filter design using locally weigthed polynomial regression and discrete spheroidal sequences. *MPRA Paper No. 15510*, (pp. 1 – 23).

Rajagopalan, S., & Robb, R. (2003). Image smoothing with Savitzky-Golay filters. In *Medical Imaging 2003: Visualization, Image-Guided Procedures, and Display*, Vol. 5029, May 2003, (pp. 773-781).

Savitzky, A., 7 Golay, M. (1964). Smoothing and differentiation of data by simplified least squares procedures. *Analytical Chemistry, 36*(8), 1627–1639. doi:10.1021/ac60214a047

Seah, M. P., Dench, W. A., Gale, B., & Groves, T. E. (1988). Towards a single recommended optimal convolutional smoothing algorithm for electron and other spectroscopies. *Journal of Physics. E, Scientific Instruments, 21*(4), 351–363. doi:10.1088/0022-3735/21/4/003

Thurston, J., & Brawn, J. (1992). The filtering characteristics of least-squares polynomial approximation for regional/residual separation. *Canadian Journal of Exploration Physics, 28*(2), 71–80.

Yang, G., Shu, H. C., Han, G., & Luo, L. (2006). Efficient Legendre moment computation for grey level images. *Pattern Recognition, 39*, 74–80. doi:10.1016/j.patcog.2005.08.008

Yap, P.-T., & Raveendren, P. (2003). Image analysis by Krawtchouk moments. *IEEE Transactions on Image Processing, 12*(11), 1367–1377. doi:10.1109/TIP.2003.818019

Yap, P.-T., & Raveendren, P. (2005). An efficient method for the computation of Legendre moments. *IEEE Transactions on Pattern Analysis and Machine Intelligence, 27*(12), 1996–2002. doi:10.1109/TPAMI.2005.232

Zhu, H., Shu, H., Liang, J., Luo, L., & Coatrieus, J.-L. (2007a). Image analysis by discrete orthogonal Racah moments. *Signal Processing, 87*, 687–708. doi:10.1016/j.sigpro.2006.07.007

Zhu, H., Shu, H., Zhou, J., Luo, L., & Coatrieus, J.-L. (2007b). Image analysis by discrete orthogonal Racah moments. *Pattern Recognition Letters, 2007*, 1688–1704. doi:10.1016/j.patrec.2007.04.013

Zhu, H., Shu, H., Zhou, J., Luo, L., & Costrieux, J. (2007c). Image analysis by discrete orthogonal dual Hahn moments. *Pattern Recognition Letters Archive, 28*, 1688–1704. doi:10.1016/j.patrec.2007.04.013

## ENDNOTES

[1] These computations were performed using MATLAB with a relative error in floating point numbers of *eps* = $10^{-16}$

[2] Unitary implies $\mathbf{B}^T \mathbf{B} = \mathbf{I}$, i.e. an orthogonal matrix.

[3] A unitary and complete matrix fulfills the condition $\mathbf{B}^T \mathbf{B} = \mathbf{B} \mathbf{B}^T = \mathbf{I}$.

[4] The transpose $(.)^T$ always refers to the complex conjugate transpose in this paper.

[5] A similar proof for a slightly different set of equations has been presented by Golub (Golub and Van Loan, 1996).

[6] note for a perfectly conditioned basis $\mathbf{P}_c$ that $\mathbf{P}_c^+ = \mathbf{P}_c^T$.

[7] The symbol ∘ represents the Hadamard product.

[8] Without loss of generality, it may be assumed that all constraints are independent, it is the rank of $\mathbf{C}$ which is relevant. The synthesis procedure does not require the constraints to be independent; it will automatically identify the independent portions.

[9] In the case of polynomials this would mean that the constrained polynomials are sorted to be according to increasing degree

[10] It should be noted that this is $\mathbf{RQ}$ and not $\mathbf{QR}$ decomposition, the two methods are related via row and column permutations.

[11] The word spectrum here is used to denote a spectrum with respect to a specific set of basis functions and not only the Fourier spectrum.

# Chapter 11
# Application of Red, Green, and Blue Color Channels in 3D Shape Measurement

**Zonghua Zhang**
*Hebei University of Technology, China*

## ABSTRACT

*Optical full-field measurement techniques have been widely studied in academia and applied to many actual fields of automated inspection, reverse engineering, cosmetic surgery, and so on. With the advent of color CCD cameras and DMD (Digital Micromirror Device) based color DLP (Digital Light Processing) projectors, their major red, green, and blue channels have been used as a carrier to code fringe patterns. Since three fringe patterns can be simultaneously projected and captured at one shot, the acquisition time reduces to 1/3 of the value by the gray fringe pattern projection. This chapter will introduce two kinds of applications of red, green, and blue as a carrier: 1) modulation and demodulation method of coding sinusoidal fringe patterns into RGB channels of a composite color image; and 2) modulation and demodulation method of coding sinusoidal and binary fringe patterns into RGB channels of multiple composite color images. Experiments on testing the two kinds of applications were carried out by measuring the shape of objects' surface. The results confirm that red, green, and blue channels can be used as a carrier to reduce the acquisition time.*

## INTRODUCTION

Optical full-field measurement techniques, especially phase-based fringe projection, have been widely studied and applied to fields of automated inspection, reverse engineering, cosmetic surgery and so on owing to the advantages of non-contact operation, fast acquisition, high precision and automatic processing (Chen, Brown & Song, 2000; Petrov, Talapov, Robertson, Lebedev, Zhilyaev & Polonskiy, 1998; Blais, 2004). With the increasing demands of the accuracy, speed and surface properties, such as color texture and shiny surface, new measuring techniques and methods

DOI: 10.4018/978-1-4666-0113-0.ch011

have emerged to satisfy with these requirements. In fringe projection techniques, unambiguous absolute phase calculation of objects having surface discontinuities and/or spatially isolated surfaces is one of the most challenging problems (Gorthi & Rastogi, 2010). Several strategies, including temporal phase unwrapping (Saldner & Huntley, 1997), optimum multi-frequency selection method (Towers, Towers & Jones, 2005), and spatiotemporal phase unwrapping (Zhang, Lalor & Burton, 1999), have been developed to solve such problems of the absolute phase discontinuities. The temporal phase unwrapping technique (Saldner & Huntley, 1997) used a sequence of binary fringe patterns with the fringe numbers of geometric series to determine the fringe order of each sinusoidal fringe pattern, so it need to capture more images to calculate the absolute phase map. The optimum multi-frequency selection method (Towers, Towers & Jones, 2005) greatly reduced the required images by using a geometric series of synthetic wavelengths. However, these methods need to capture more multiple fringe pattern images, so that the acquisition time is much longer than spatial phase unwrapping methods. For fast capturing 3D shape data or measuring dynamic objects, multiple fringe pattern images projection and acquisition techniques are not an ideal choice.

With the advent of color CCD cameras and DMD (Digital Micromirror Device) based DLP (Digital Light Processing) projectors, the major color channels (mostly red, green and blue) have been used to facilitate identification as spatial identifier (Wong, Niu & He, 2005; Koninckx & Gool, 2006) or to code fringe patterns as a carrier (Hausler & Ritter, 1993; Huang, Hu, Jin & Chiang, 1999; Skydan, Lalor & Burton, 2002; Zhang, Towers & Towers, 2006; Karpinsky & Zhang, 2010). All these methods use color information to generate different structured color patterns and then projected them onto a measured object surface. For the techniques of using color channels as identifier (Wong, Niu & He, 2005; Koninckx & Gool, 2006), the color patterns should have a

minimum size to be easily identified, so that the measured data has small resolution. In order to increase resolution, the structured color patterns should contain enough entries. However, the depth resolution reported to date does not compare with that from phase measurement of projected sinusoidal fringe patterns. Processing errors can also be introduced due to hue variations of the object surface.

For the techniques of taking color channels as a carrier (Hausler & Ritter, 1993; Huang, Hu, Jin & Chiang, 1999; Skydan, Lalor & Burton, 2002; Zhang, Towers & Towers, 2006; Karpinsky & Zhang, 2010), fringe patterns are coded into the red, green and blue channels of a color image to generate composite RGB images. A DLP projector projected the composite RGB fringe pattern images onto the measured object's surface. From another viewpoint, the fringe patterns are deformed with respect to the measured shape. A color CCD camera captures the deformed composite fringe patterns into its red, green and blue color channels for post processing. Since one color image can code three fringe patterns, the required images are less than the gray fringe projection. Hausler et al presented a color-coded triangulation method, which is simple, fast, and without moving mechanical parts. Whilst this approach uses a single frame, the dynamic range is limited to <200 (Hausler & Ritter, 1993). Huang et al proposed a color-encoded fringe projection technique using three patterns, one in each color channel, with a phase shift of $2\pi / 3$ between neighboring channels. The wrapped phase map and unwrapped phase map are calculated by the three-step phase-shifting algorithm and spatial phase unwrapping method, respectively. Therefore, the 3D surface contour information can be retrieved from a single image snapshot of the object surface (Huang, Hu, Jin & Chiang, 1999). Skydan et al presented a method with up to three fringe patterns projected on the three primary color channels from three different video projectors at different viewpoints to overcome shadowing effects on the object. The used system is expensive since three projectors are used (Skydan, Lalor & Burton, 2002). However, the approaches described by Huang et al and Skydan et al only produce wrapped phase maps, so spatial phase unwrapping methods are required to generate the 3D shape of an object and hence these methods cannot be applied to objects with large slope or discontinuity. Karpinsky et al demonstrated that an arbitrary 3-D shape can be represented as a single composite color image, with the red and green channel being represented as sine and cosine fringe images, and the blue channel encoded as a phase unwrapping stair function (Karpinsky & Zhang, 2010).

Su and Chen et al described a composite fringe pattern projection method that combined encoded color strips and sinusoidal intensity fringes into the same fringe pattern for single snapshot 3D shape acquisition (Chen, Zhang, Lv & Fang, 2007; Su, 2007), as simulated illustrations in Figure 1(a) and (b), respectively. The color strips offered absolute depth, whilst sinusoidal fringes give sub-wavelength phase information. Since the strips and sinusoidal fringes are overlapped at each pixel, the captured color strips and fringe modulation depth have low intensity. Therefore, it is difficult to identify the edge of the color strips and to obtain accurate phase information. In order to measure dynamic and spatially isolated objects, Su presented another encoding composite fringe pattern method by overlapping sinusoidal fringes, binary stripes and color grids at each pixel position into one image (Su, 2008). However, the use of binary stripes and color grids offered even lower intensity levels, and hence edges became more difficult to identify.

Towers et al introduced the principle of optimum multi-frequency selection method to determine the absolute fringe order by using much less fringe pattern images (Towers, Towers & Jones, 2003). Later, the authors applied the principle to fringe projection technique by a DLP projector (Towers, Towers & Jones, 2005). The numbers of projected fringe to be:

$$N_{fi} = N_{f0} - \left(N_{f0}\right)^{(i-1)/(n-1)}, \text{ for } i=1,\dots,n\text{-}1,$$

(1)

where $N_{f0}$ and $N_{fi}$ are the maximum number of fringes and the number of fringes in the ith fringe set, respectively, and $n$ is the number of fringe sets used. When three fringe sets are used, it is usually referred to as the optimum three-frequency method and the optimum fringe numbers are $N_{f0} = N$, $N_{f1} = N - 1$, $N_{f2} = N - \sqrt{N}$. For example, if $N_{f0} = 49$ and $n=3$, the other two fringe sets have fringe numbers of $N_{f1} = 48$ and $N_{f2} = 42$. This method resolves fringe order ambiguity as the beat obtained between $N_{f0}$ and $N_{f1}$ is a single fringe over the full field of view and the reliability of the obtained fringe order is maximized as fringe order calculation is performed through a geometric series of beat fringes with 1, 7 and 49 fringes. The fringe order calculation is reliable to 6σ providing the phase noise to one standard deviation is better than 1/59th of a fringe (Towers, Towers & Jones, 2003).

Combining the optimum 3-frequency selection method (Towers, Towers & Jones, 2003; Towers, Towers & Jones, 2005) and the three primary color channels, a time-efficient color fringe projection system was developed to acquire shape and color information of an object (Zhang, Towers & Towers, 2006). This system uses an off-the-shelf CCD camera and a DLP projector, therefore it is easy to assemble them together. The phase information having the three optimum fringe numbers can be modulated into the red, green and blue channels, respectively, so it is possible to use one image for Fourier transform and four images for a four-frame phase shifting algorithm to implement the acquisition. On the one hand, the acquisition time is less than the white light and single color methods, and objects with discontinuities can be

*Figure 1. Simulated composite fringe pattern images. (a) color-encoded fringe patterns by Su and (b) composite pattern by color encoded stripes and cosinoidal intensity fringes by Chen*

measured to get the absolute phase; on the other hand, the obtained phase has a high dynamic range and the color information of the surface can be extracted. However, further investigation is required to determine the range of colors that are measurable and explore the effect that the varying modulation depth in the different color channels has on the noise floor and reliability of the shape data obtained.

In this chapter, two kinds of applications of red, green and blue as a carrier will be presented. The first application is coding three sinusoidal fringe patterns having the optimum three fringe numbers into red, green and blue channels of a composite RGB image. The composite color image is projected onto a measured object surface and the deformed fringe patterns are simultaneously captured as a color image from another viewpoint. Three deformed fringe patterns are extracting from the red, green and blue color channels of the captured color image. Three wrapped phase maps are calculated by using the Fourier transform algorithm and then the absolute phase map by the optimum three fringe number method. Since the

absolute phase is calculated pixel by pixel, the proposed method can measure objects having discontinuous and/or isolated surfaces by one snapshot acquisition.

The second application codes sinusoidal and binary fringe patterns into RGB channels of several composite color images. Multiple-step phase-shifting algorithm will be used to calculate the wrapped phase data at each pixel position from the sinusoidal fringe patterns. The fringe numbers in binary fringe patterns are geometric series, so that the absolute fringe order of sinusoidal fringe pattern can be determined pixel by pixel. Combining the obtained wrapped phase map and the absolute fringe order, this kind of modulation and demodulation method can measure objects having discontinuous and/or isolated surfaces. Although multiple composite RGB fringe pattern images need to be projected and captured, this method can give high precise phase even at the edges and large slopes of an object surface.

This chapter will first introduce the principle of the two kinds of applications of red, green and blue channels as a carrier. The modulation and demodulation methods of coding three sinusoidal fringe patterns having the optimum fringe numbers into a single composite RGB image, and coding sinusoidal and binary fringe patterns into four composite RGB images will be presented in detail separately. Then experiments on testing the two kinds of applications were carried out by measuring the shape of objects' surface. The results confirm that red, green and blue channels can be used as a carrier to reduce the acquisition time for general object measurement. Finally, the future research trends of using three color channels in measuring 3D shape of objects is given and the effects of chromatic aberration and crosstalk between color channels are discussed in the last section.

## APPLICATION OF RGB COLOR CHANNELS

Both applications are based on triangulation relationship between the imaging axis and the projecting axis. That is, the projected straight fringe patterns onto an object surface are deformed from another viewpoint with respect to the shape of the object surface. Demodulating the deformed fringe patterns by Fourier transform or multiple-step phase-shifting techniques can obtain a wrapped phase map, which needs to be unwrapped for 3D shape calculation. Phase unwrapping procedure is a challenging problem of measuring objects having discontinuous and/or isolated surfaces. The chapter presents two solutions: the optimum three fringe number selection method and utilization of binary fringe pattern having the geometric series fringe numbers.

### Sinusoidal Fringe into a RGB Image

Three sinusoidal fringe patterns having the optimum three fringe numbers are coded into the red, green and blue channels of a color image to generate a composite RGB fringe image, as illustrated in Figure 2. The optimum fringe numbers in red, green and blue channels are 42, 48 and 49, respectively. Projecting via a DLP projector this composite RGB image onto an object surface, a color CCD camera can simultaneously capture and save the deformed composite RGB fringe pattern image for post processing. Three deformed fringe patterns are extracted from the red, green and blue color channels of the captured color image. Three wrapped phase maps are calculated by using the Fourier transform algorithm and then the absolute phase map by the optimum three fringe number method. After calibration, the absolute phase map can be converted to 3D shape data.

Since red, green and blue channels are used as a carrier to code three independent fringe patterns, ideally there would be no crosstalk between color channels in order to get the correct phase information. However, most off-the-shelf DLP projectors and CCD cameras have overlapping spectra between color channels to cover all wavelengths, which means crosstalk is unavoidable. The regions between the color bands are often at different wavelengths in CCD cameras and those in DLP projectors. Hence, the information captured in each of the three color channels is not independent. Therefore, the directly extracted fringe

*Figure 2. Generated composite RGB fringe pattern image. The optimum fringe numbers in red, green and blue channels are 42, 48 and 49, respectively.*

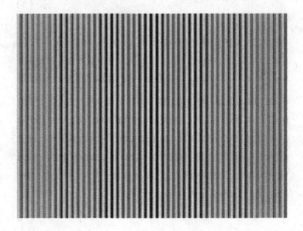

patterns from each color channel cannot be applied for phase calculation. Here a software-based crosstalk compensation method is applied to the three color channels of the captured composite RGB image to get the correct sinusoidal shape of fringe pattern.

The image intensity captured in each channel can be represented as:

$$I_i(m,n) = a_i(m,n) + b_i(m,n)\cos\{2\pi m / p_i + \Delta\phi_i(m,n)\} + \sum k_{i,j}[a_j(m,n) + b_j(m,n)\cos\{2\pi m / p_j + \Delta\phi_j(m,n)\}] \quad (2)$$

where $i,j = R, G, B$ with $j \neq i$, $k_{i,j}$ is the coupling effect from light in the jth color illumination channel into the ith channel, $a_i$ and $b_i$ are the average intensity and intensity modulation, respectively; $\Delta\phi_i$ is the phase corresponding to the object height; $p_i$ is the fringe period; (m, n) are the pixel index; and $a_j$, $b_j$, $\Delta\phi_j$, $p_j$ have the same meanings as the corresponding terms in the chosen channel i. The coupling effect $k_{i,j}$ can be calibrated beforehand by sequentially projecting red, green and blue fringe patterns onto a flat white surface (Zhang, Towers & Towers, 2006). Hence, a first order compensation for the crosstalk can be implemented by calculating a modified intensity for each color channel, $I_i'$ as:

$$I_i'(m,n) = I_i(m,n) - \sum k_{i,j}I_j(m,n)$$
$$\cong a_i(m,n) + b_i(m,n)\cos(2\pi m / p_i + \Delta\phi_i(m,n)) \quad (3)$$

Providing the crosstalk coefficients are $<<1$ the residual crosstalk is negligible (the maximum value of $k_{i,j} \times k_{j,k}$ is 0.019). Therefore, three compensated fringe patterns are obtained from one composite RGB fringe pattern image. Each compensated fringe image can be regarded as a sinusoidal fringe pattern from a single projected fringe pitch and in the following for brevity the channel index i is omitted:

$$I(m,n) = a(m,n) + b(m,n)\cos[2\pi m / p + \Delta\phi(m,n)] \quad (4)$$

In order to easily understand Fourier transform technique, Equation (4) is changed into the following complex form

$$I(m,n) = A(m,n) + C(m,n)\exp[i2\pi m / p] + C^*(m,n)\cdot\exp[-i2\pi m / p] \quad (5)$$

where $A(m,n) = a(m,n)$, and

$$C(m,n) = \frac{1}{2}b(m,n)\cdot\exp[i\Delta\phi(m,n)] \quad (6)$$

where $C^*(m,n)$ is the complex conjugate of $C(m,n)$.

Because of the limited width of the fringe pattern, leakage will occur at the edges of the image when using Fourier phase analysis. Windowing the original fringe pattern before taking the Fourier transform can reduce the leakage errors (Berryman, Pynsent & Cubillo, 2004). A Blackman window is applied two dimensionally to the image generating a new windowed fringe pattern, $I_w(m,n)$. The 2D Fourier transform of $I_w(m,n)$ gives the spatial frequency spectrum of the fringe pattern:

$$\tilde{I}_w(f_m, f_n) = \tilde{A}_w(f_m, f_n) + \tilde{C}_w(f_m - f_0, f_n) + \tilde{C}_w^*(f_m + f_0, f_n) \quad (7)$$

The functions $\tilde{I}_w$, $\tilde{A}_w$, and $\tilde{C}_w$ represent the Fourier spectra of $I_w$, $A_w$, and $C_w$, $f_m$ and $f_n$ are the spatial frequencies in the row and column directions, and $f_0 = 1 / p$ is a carrier-frequency. From Equation (7), the spectrum is composed of three parts. The $\tilde{C}_w(f_m - f_0, f_n)$ and $\tilde{C}_w^*(f_m + f_0, f_n)$ are the side lobes, which involve the phase information $\Delta\phi(m,n)$. Since $C_w^*(m,n)$ is the complex conjugate of $C_w(m,n)$, only one side lobe is needed to calculate the phase information. As the spatial frequency of $a(m,n)$ is much lower than $f_0$, a band-pass filtering process can be applied to isolate the function $\tilde{C}_w(f_m - f_0, f_n)$. Applying the Band Pass Filter ($BPF[\cdot]$) at the spectral position $f_0$ obtains

$$BPF[\tilde{I}_w(f_m, f_n)] = \tilde{C}_w(f_m - f_0, f_n). \qquad (8)$$

Taking the inverse Fourier transform of Equation (8) gives:

$$B_w(m,n) = C_w(m,n)\exp[i2\pi m / p]. \qquad (9)$$

Therefore, the phase at each pixel position is obtained by the following equation:

$$\theta(m,n) = 2\pi m / p + \Delta\phi(m,n)$$
$$= \tan^{-1}\left(\mathrm{Im}\left(B_w(m,n)\right) / \mathrm{Re}\left(B_w(m,n)\right)\right),$$
(10)

where Im($\cdot$) and Re($\cdot$) represent the imaginary and real parts of a complex number. It is not straightforward to precisely define the size of the window when applying the Band Pass Filter, rather, there is a compromise in setting the window shape and size. For example, if the dimensions of the window are too small, the side lobe cannot be completely captured giving errors in the obtained phase; on the other hand, if the dimension of the window is too large, crosstalk arises from the background information and higher frequency noise is introduced to the phase.

Due to the internal properties of the discrete Fourier transform on a finite image size, leakage effects are inevitable, especially near edges or discontinuities (Su & Chen, 2001; Vanlanduit, Vanherzeele, Guillaume, Cauberghe & Verboven, 2004), which causes errors in the calculated phase. As the fringe order is determined from the wrapped

phases at each frequency via the optimum three-frequency method, the presence of phase errors in the neighborhood of edges or discontinuities can lead to fringe order mis-calculation. These pixels can be removed by setting an appropriate low modulation threshold to identify valid data. Modulation depth has been used previously to identify pixels having an incorrect phase value (Towers, Towers & Jones, 2003) and it has also been shown to facilitate identification of pixels at the edges or discontinuities of an object (Takeda, Gu, Kinoshita, Takai & Takahashi, 1997). The energy of such pixels is spread out in the frequency domain. When the Band Pass Filter window size is small and applied to the first order side lobe, some energy from these pixels is filtered out, so the corresponding modulation depth obtained has a smaller value than for other pixels. In order to get the modulation depth at each pixel position, Equations (8)-(10) are applied to the crosstalk compensated fringe pattern $I(m,n)$ (the windowed image is not used as the modulation depth in the windowed fringe pattern $I_w(m,n)$ becomes smaller at the boundaries) to get $B(m,n)$ and then the modulation is obtained by:

$$b(m,n) = 2 * |B(m,n)|, \qquad (11)$$

where $|\cdot|$ is the magnitude of a complex number. A window with a smaller size is used in this case to isolate the first order side lobe and increase the contrast between pixels near edges and discontinuities from the rest of the image.

The optimum three-frequency method is applied to calculate the absolute phase pixel by pixel (Towers, Towers & Jones, 2003; Towers, Towers & Jones, 2005). Since three fringe patterns having the optimum fringe numbers of $N - \sqrt{N}$, N-1, N are coded into the three color channels, three wrapped phase maps $\theta_r(m,n), \theta_g(m,n), \theta_b(m,n)$ can be calculated from one composite fringe pattern image and the absolute phase data obtained using the optimum three-frequency method. The points near the discontinuity have been masked by setting an appropriate threshold on the image derived from Equation (11).

## Combination of Sinusoidal and Binary Fringe into RGB Images

In order to independently determine the absolute fringe order of sinusoidal fringe patterns, binary fringe patterns having geometric series fringe numbers can be used. The binary fringe patterns utilize two gray levels: one has a high value, the other a low value. Although binary patterns are insensitive to the noise and can directly measure discontinuities and/or isolated surfaces, the low spatial resolution and low dynamic range limit the applications to the high accurate 3D shape measurement. While the multiple-step phase shift

algorithm gives high accurate phase information of each pixel position. The obtained modulo $2\pi$ phase information needs to be unwrapped, which is a challenging task for large slopes and discontinuities. Therefore, combining the two kinds of fringe projection techniques can utilize their advantages. On the one hand, the phase information calculated from the sinusoidal fringe patterns gives accurate value and high dynamic range; on the other hand, the binary fringe patterns determine each sinusoidal fringe order, so that objects having discontinuities and/or isolated surfaces can be measured.

In principle, the sinusoidal and binary fringe patterns can be coded into any color channel of a RGB image. However, when the sinusoidal and binary fringe patterns are coded into the same RGB image, the crosstalk between color channels has great effects on the modulation and DC intensity of the sinusoidal fringe pattern. The calculated phase information from the extracted sinusoidal

*Figure 3. Four generated composite RGB fringe pattern images. The top two images contain six sinusoidal fringe patterns with fringe numbers of 64. The bottom two images contain six binary fringe patterns with fringe numbers of 1, 2, 4, 8, 16 and 32.*

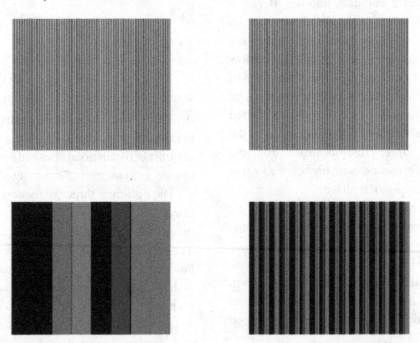

fringe patterns is not accurate. Therefore, the sinusoidal fringe patterns are coded into the red, green and blue channels of the same color images. Even so, the crosstalk and the chromatic aberration destroy the sinusoidal shape after they have been compensated by software-based methods. The four-step phase shift algorithm has been widely used to calculate the wrapped phase, but it is sensitive to phase shift miscalibration and nonlinear response of the CCD camera and DLP projector. In order to decrease the effects of non-sinusoidal shape on phase calculation, a six-step phase shift algorithm will be used.

If the sinusoidal fringe patterns have 64 projected fringe numbers, six binary fringe patterns with fringe numbers of 1, 2, 4, 8, 16 and 32 can determine the absolute fringe order. Therefore, there are six sinusoidal fringe patterns and six binary fringe patterns coded into twelve channels, which generate four composite RGB fringe pattern images. On the one hand, all the color channels are used in the four composite RGB fringe pattern images; on the other hand, a six-step phase shift algorithm (which called 6A-frame method in the literature (Schmit & Creath, 1995)) can calculate the wrapped phase with the advantage of high tolerance for phase shift miscalibration and no sensitivity to first-order and second-order detector nonlinearity. The sinusoidal fringe patterns with $\pi/2$ phase shift in between are coded into two composite RGB fringe pattern images, while the binary fringe patterns are coded into the other two images, as illustrated in Figure 3. The four composite RGB fringe pattern images are projected onto a measured object surface. From a different viewpoint, a color CCD camera captures and saves the four deformed fringe pattern images.

Demodulating the captured composite RGB fringe pattern images can get sinusoidal fringe patterns and binary fringe patterns. The binary fringe patterns are directly extracted from the composite RGB images because they are insensi-

tive to the crosstalk; while the crosstalk between sinusoidal fringe patterns needs to be compensated for in order to get correct sinusoidal shape. Six sinusoidal and six binary fringe patterns are extracted from the four acquired composite RGB images. Crosstalk between color channels has effects on the sinusoidal shape of the sinusoidal fringe patterns, so a software-based compensation method (Zhang, Towers & Towers, 2010) is used to reduce the effects on phase calculation. Wrapped phase information is calculated from the obtained sinusoidal fringe patterns by using the six-step phase shift algorithm. Each binary fringe pattern has two gray values and can be directly extracted from the composite images. The six extracted binary fringe patterns independently determine the absolute fringe order even the measured objects have discontinuities and/or spatially isolated surfaces. Combining the wrapped phase and the absolute fringe order obtains the absolute phase map of the measured object's surface even it has complex surface shape. Figure 4 shows the flowchart of the fringe demodulation procedure.

## EXPERIMENTS AND RESULTS

### Hardware System

The hardware setup comprises a portable DLP (Digital Light Processing) video projector, a 3-CCD color camera with IEEE 1394 port and a personal computer (PC), as illustrated in Figure 5. The projector is from BenQ (Model CP270) with one-chip digital micro-mirror device (DMD) and a resolution of up to 1024 x 768 pixels (XGA). The colors of red, green, and blue are produced by rapidly spinning a color filter wheel in the projector and synchronously modifying the state of the DMD. The 3-CCD camera from Hitachi (Model HV-F22F) has a resolution of 1360 x 1024 pixels. A color image whose RGB components are three

*Figure 4. Flowchart of calculating the absolute phase map from four captured composite RGB fringe pattern images*

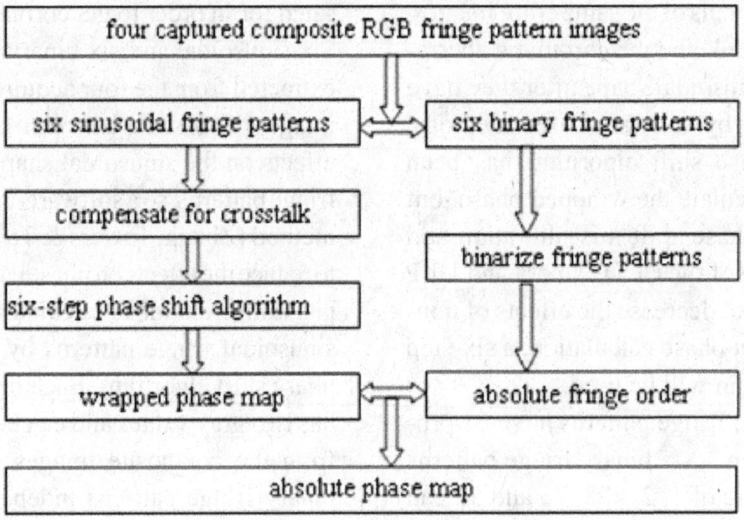

fringe patterns with different spatial frequency is generated in the PC and projected onto an object surface, for example a manufactured step, by the DLP projector.

## Experimental Results

Due to the optical properties of the DLP projector and CCD camera lens, chromatic aberration between color channels is unavoidable and potentially has a severe effect on the absolute phase calculation. In fact, chromatic aberration will zoom in the red fringe pattern and zoom out the blue fringes with respect to the green channel. A software-based compensation method is applied to eliminate the chromatic aberration by changing the numbers of fringes by -0.18% and -0.31% in the green and red channels respectively (Zhang, Towers & Towers, 2010). The uneven fringe projection method is employed in the system for calibration between the absolute phase and surface depth (Zhang, Towers & Towers, 2007). Therefore, on the one hand, the calibration to build up the relationship between phase and depth is simple

and accurate; and on the other hand, the Fourier transform will give more accurate phase data because of the constant period of the projected fringes in the measurement field.

Two flat white boards having different depths were located in the field of view as shown in Figs. 6, 7 and 8. A composite RGB fringe pattern with fringe numbers of 42, 48, and 49 in the red, green and blue channels is projected onto the two discrete surfaces and the deformed fringe patterns are captured by a 3-chip CCD camera from another viewpoint, as illustrated in Figure 6(a). Three sinusoidal fringe patterns coded in the red, green and blue channels are extracted by using Equation (2) to reduce the crosstalk, as shown in Figure 6(b)-(d) respectively. Applying Fourier transform phase analysis as described in section 2.1 to the three fringe patterns and the optimum three-frequency method with the corrected numbers of projected fringes as 49, 47.914, and 41.870, the absolute unwrapped phase map is obtained as illustrated in Figure 7. The modulation depth at each pixel is calculated by applying a smaller Hamming window to the fundamental frequency

*Figure 5. The hardware setup of the 3-D imaging system including a DLP projector, a color 3CCD camera and a personal computer.*

(Equation (10)). The pixels on the discontinuities and edges having smaller modulation depth are marked as black. The absolute phase map can be easily converted into actual 3D shape data by using the calibration method as detailed in (Zhang, Towers & Towers, 2007; Zhang, Ma, Zhang, Guo, Towers & Towers, 2011). Figure 8 displays a 3D representation of the object by gradient shading of the surface profile from two different viewpoints.

Since shape data are obtained from a single composite RGB fringe pattern, the proposed method can measure moving objects. A sequence of composite RGB fringe pattern images of a moving hand of the first author were captured at a rate of 7.5 frames per second. Each frame was processed by the proposed method to obtain the phase (shape) information. Figure 9 shows a single composite fringe pattern from the image sequence of the hand and Figure 10 illustrates the calculated 3D shape with gradient shading.

It clearly shows that the proposed snapshot composite fringe projection method reliably measures the shape information of objects with discontinuities and/or isolated surfaces.

In order to test the other application of combining sinusoidal and binary fringe patterns into composite RGB images, a mask and a toy were positioned in the same field of view of a color 3D imaging system. The four generated composite RGB fringe pattern images were projected onto their surfaces to show the ability of measuring isolated surfaces. The four deformed fringe patterns were captured by a color 3-CCD camera from a different viewpoint, as illustrated in Figure 11. The top two composite fringe pattern images contain six sinusoidal fringe patterns. While the below two images are the six binary fringe patterns with projected fringe numbers of 1, 2, 4, 8, 16 and 32 (The captured fringe numbers are less because of the small field of view). Six sinusoidal fringe patterns are extracted from the red, green and blue channels of the top two composite images after compensating for the crosstalk between color channels. The six-step phase shift algorithm calculates the wrapped phase map, as illustrated

*Figure 6. The captured composite fringe pattern on two flat boards and the corresponding color channels. (a) composite fringe pattern, (b) red channel, (c) green channel, and (d) blue channel.*

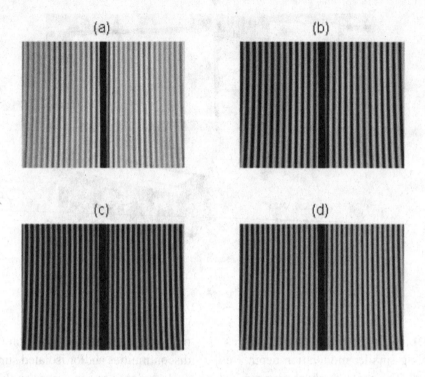

in Figure 12. Because each color channel has two values in binary fringe patterns, the crosstalk has no effect on calculating fringe order. The six binary fringe patterns are extracted from the red, green and blue channels of the bottom two composite images in Figure 11. After binarization, six binary images are obtained as shown in Figure 13. The obtained binary fringe patterns independently determine each sinusoidal fringe order, so an absolute phase map as illustrated in Figure 14 is obtained from the four composite RGB fringe pattern images. Even the two objects are isolated, the binary fringe patterns correctly determine the sinusoidal fringe order and then the absolute phase map is correctly unwrapped.

Because the red, green and blue channels of color images are used, the acquisition time reduces to 1/3 of the value by the gray fringe pattern projection technique. In order to alleviate the effects of crosstalk on the phase information, the six-step phase shift algorithm is applied to calculate the wrapped phase. However, the three-step phase shift algorithm can calculate the phase information at each pixel, so that the absolute phase is obtained from three composite RGB fringe pattern images.

## FUTURE RESEARCH DIRECTIONS

Although red, green and blue channels have been widely studied as a carrier to code fringe pattern, chromatic aberration and crosstalk between color channels have great effects on the extracted fringe patterns (Zhang, Towers & Towers, 2006; Zhang, Towers & Towers, 2010). The main future research directions are how to compensate for chromatic aberration and reduce the crosstalk between color channels. One can consider software- and hardware-based methods to solve the two problems. The three color channels can also be used as a carrier to measure objects having colorful

*Figure 7. The unwrapped phase information of the two measured boards*

*Figure 8. 3D shading representation of the two measured boards from two viewpoints*

(a)

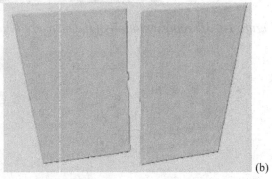

(b)

surface (Zhang, Towers & Towers, 2008; Chen, Nguyen, Zhang & Lin, 2010).

In any refractive optical system with multiple color channels based on chromatic separation, the presence of dispersion leads to chromatic aberration. Chromatic aberration can be categorized into lateral chromatic aberration and longitudinal chromatic aberration. Longitudinal chromatic aberration affects the sharpness of the fringes (different color fringes are focused at different distances) and in practice is found to give an acceptable reduction in the modulation depth of the fringes. However, lateral chromatic aberration has a large effect on fringe order calculation since it changes the overall magnification of the fringe patterns, giving a zoomed in or out variation between the color channels. Therefore, the numbers of projected fringes used in the three color channels to determine the fringe order number should be different from the number of fringes used to form the image projected by the projector. For the color fringe projection system, chromatic aberration comes from the lenses of the Digital Light Processing (DLP) video projector and the 3-chip color CCD camera. Using high quality lenses for the camera and projector can

reduce but not eliminate the measured phase errors from lateral chromatic aberration. The chromatic aberration between color channels will change the relevant fringe numbers in the field of view and can be compensated by changing the projected fringe numbers (Zhang, Towers & Towers, 2010).

Another effect on phase calculation is from the crosstalk between color channels. Ideally there would be no crosstalk between color channels in order to get the correct phase information. However, most off-the-shelf DLP projectors and CCD cameras are designed to have overlapping spectra between color channels in order to cover all wavelengths, which means crosstalk is unavoidable. The regions between the color bands are often at different wavelengths in CCD

*Figure 9. Composite RGB fringe pattern on a human hand*

*Figure 10. 3D representation of the measured hand with gradient shading*

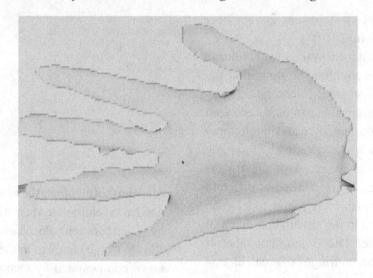

cameras and those in DLP projectors. Hence, the information captured in each of the three color channels is not independent. Software-based and hardware-based compensation methods can be used to decrease the coupling effects (Pan, Huang & Chiang, 2006). Hardware-based methods require the internal filters on the spinning wheel of a DLP projector to be replaced in order to have no overlapped spectra between color channels and match the spectra of the color CCD camera. This is a problematic modification as the inertia of the new filter wheel must be comparable to the original as well as the chromatic properties of the filters optimized. The software-based compensation schemes reported to date have only provided partial recovery of the potential phase resolution in each color channel, to approximately 1/75th of a fringe when a single color measurement gives ~1/150th of a fringe (Zhang, Towers & Towers, 2006). Therefore, although crosstalk between color channels is compensated by a software-based method in this chapter, it can be greatly reduced

*Figure 11. The four captured composite RGB fringe pattern images on a mask and a toy. The top two images contain six sinusoidal fringe patterns with π/2 phase shift in between; the below two images contain six binary fringe patterns with projected fringe numbers of 1, 2, 4, 8, 16 and 32.*

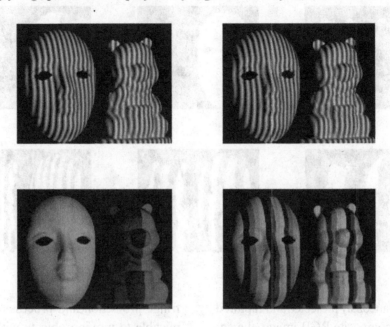

*Figure 12. The calculated wrapped phase map on the mask and the toy*

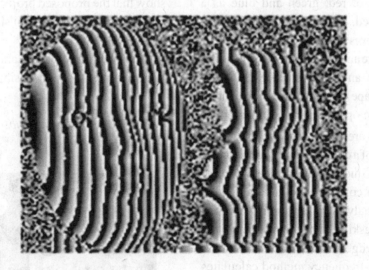

by using a hardware-based method. Also, the hybrid of hardware- and software-based methods can be used to eliminate the crosstalk between color channels.

## CONCLUSION AND DISCUSSION

This chapter presents the application of red, green and blue channels as a carrier in measuring 3D shape of objects surface. Since three fringe pat-

*Figure 13. The processed binary fringe patterns on the mask and the toy with projected fringe numbers of 1, 2, 4, 8, 16 and 32.*

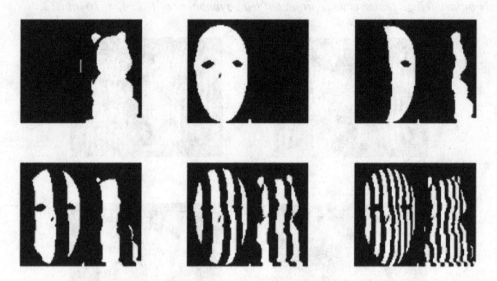

terns can be simultaneously projected and captured through a single composite RGB image, the acquisition time reduces to 1/3 of the value by the gray fringe pattern projection. Two kinds of application methods of red, green and blue as a carrier are discussed. One is coding three sinusoidal fringe patterns into red, green and blue channels to generate and project a composite RGB fringe image onto an object surface to obtain absolute phase (shape) information. Three fringe patterns having the optimum fringe numbers of $N - \sqrt{N}$, N-1, N are coded into the red, green and blue channels of a color image and simultaneously projected onto the object's surface. Wrapped phase data in each color channel are calculated by Fourier phase analysis and an algorithm introduced to enable masking of bad data areas in the neighborhood of edges and discontinuities. As the optimum three-frequency method calculates the unwrapped phase map on a pixel by pixel basis, objects having discontinuities and/or isolated surfaces can be measured using this technique. Since a single composite RGB image is required to obtain shape information, the proposed

fringe projection and processing method is applicable to moving objects with discontinuities and/or isolated surfaces. Experimental results on a static scene with two boards at different depths show that the proposed projection and processing method can reliably obtain shape information of these objects.

The other modulation and demodulation application method codes sinusoidal and binary

*Figure 14. The measured absolute unwrapped on the mask and the toy*

fringe patterns into red, green and blue channels to generate composite RGB fringe pattern images. Six sinusoidal fringe patterns having the constant $\pi/2$ phase shift in between are coded into the red, green and blue channels of two composite RGB fringe pattern images. While six binary fringe patterns with the fringe numbers of 1, 2, 4, 8, 16, and 32 are coded into the three color channels of the other two composite images. The four generated composite RGB images are projected onto the measured object's surface by a DLP projector. A 3-chip color CCD camera captures the four deformed composite RGB fringe pattern images from a different viewpoint. Six sinusoidal fringe patterns and six binary fringe patterns are extracted from the four captured composite images. A six-step phase shift algorithm calculates the wrapped phase information and the six binary fringe patterns determine each sinusoidal fringe order. Therefore, the absolute phase information can be obtained even the measured objects have surface discontinuities and/or spatially isolated surfaces. Experimental results on two isolated objects show that the proposed fringe projection and processing method has the ability to measure discontinuities and/or spatially isolated surfaces, and quicker acquisition time than the gray fringe pattern projection technique.

## ACKNOWLEDGMENT

The author would like to thank "the Scientific Research Foundation for the Returned Overseas Chinese Scholars, State Education Ministry", "the Key Project of Chinese Ministry of Education", "Scientific Research Foundation for the Returned Overseas Scholars, Hebei Province", "Research Project supported by Hebei Education Department (NO: ZD2010121)" and "State Key Laboratory of Precision Measuring Technology and Instruments".

## REFERENCES

Berryman, F., Pynsent, P., & Cubillo, J. (2004). The effect of windowing in Fourier transform profilometry applied to noisy images. *Optics and Lasers in Engineering, 41*, 815–825. doi:10.1016/S0143-8166(03)00061-7

Blais, F. (2004). Review of 20 years of range sensor development. *Journal of Electronic Imaging, 13*, 231–240. doi:10.1117/1.1631921

Chen, F., Brown, G. M., & Song, M. (2000). Overview of three-dimensional shape measurement using optical methods. *Optical Engineering (Redondo Beach, Calif.), 39*, 10–22. doi:10.1117/1.602438

Chen, H. J., Zhang, J., Lv, D. J., & Fang, J. (2007). 3-D shape measurement by composite pattern projection and hybrid processing. *Optics Express, 15*, 12318–12330. doi:10.1364/OE.15.012318

Chen, L. C., Nguyen, X. L., Zhang, F. H., & Lin, T. Y. (2010). High-speed Fourier transform profilometry for reconstructing objects having arbitrary surface colours. *Journal of Optics, 12*, 095502. doi:10.1088/2040-8978/12/9/095502

Gorthi, S. S., & Rastogi, P. (2010). Fringe projection techniques: Whither we are? *Optics and Lasers in Engineering, 48*(2), 133–140. doi:10.1016/j.optlaseng.2009.09.001

Hausler, G., & Ritter, D. (1993). Parallel three-dimensional sensing by use of color-coded triangulation. *Applied Optics, 32*, 7164–7169. doi:10.1364/AO.32.007164

Huang, P. S., Hu, Q. Y., Jin, F., & Chiang, F. P. (1999). Color-encoded digital fringe projection technique for high-speed three-dimensional surface contouring. *Optical Engineering (Redondo Beach, Calif.), 38*, 1065–1071. doi:10.1117/1.602151

Karpinsky, N., & Zhang, S. (2010). Composite phase-shifting algorithm for three-dimensional shape compression. *Optical Engineering (Redondo Beach, Calif.)*, *49*(6), 063604-1–6. doi:10.1117/1.3456632

Koninckx, T. P., & Gool, L. V. (2006). Real-time range acquisition by adaptive structured light. *IEEE Transactions on Pattern Analysis and Machine Intelligence*, *28*, 432–445. doi:10.1109/TPAMI.2006.62

Pan, J. H., Huang, P. S., & Chiang, F. P. (2006). Color phase-shifting technique for three-dimensional shape measurement. *Optical Engineering (Redondo Beach, Calif.)*, *45*, 013602. doi:10.1117/1.2151160

Petrov, M., Talapov, A., Robertson, T., Lebedev, A., Zhilyaev, A., & Polonskiy, L. (1998). Optical 3D digitizers: Bringing life to the virtual world. *IEEE Computer Graphics and Applications*, *18*, 28–37. doi:10.1109/38.674969

Saldner, H. O., & Huntley, J. M. (1997). Temporal phase unwrapping: application to surface profiling of discontinuous objects. *Applied Optics*, *36*, 2770–2775. doi:10.1364/AO.36.002770

Schmit, J., & Creath, K. (1995). Extended averaging technique for derivation of error-compensating algorithms in phase-shifting interferometry. *Applied Optics*, *34*, 3610–3619. doi:10.1364/AO.34.003610

Skydan, O. A., Lalor, M. J., & Burton, D. R. (2002). Technique for phase measurement and surface reconstruction by use colored structured light. *Applied Optics*, *41*, 6104–6117. doi:10.1364/AO.41.006104

Su, W. H. (2007). Color-encoded fringe projection for 3D shape measurements. *Optics Express*, *15*, 13167–13181. doi:10.1364/OE.15.013167

Su, W. H. (2008). Projected fringe profilometry using the area-encoded algorithm for spatially isolated and dynamic objects. *Optics Express*, *16*, 2590–2596. doi:10.1364/OE.16.002590

Su, X., & Chen, W. (2001). Fourier transform profilometry: A review. *Optics and Lasers in Engineering*, *35*, 263–284. doi:10.1016/S0143-8166(01)00023-9

Takeda, M., Gu, Q., Kinoshita, M., Takai, H., & Takahashi, Y. (1997). Frequency-multiplex Fourier-transform profilometry: A single-shot three-dimensional shape measurement of objects with large height discontinuities and/or surface isolations. *Applied Optics*, *36*, 5347–5354. doi:10.1364/AO.36.005347

Towers, C. E., Towers, D. P., & Jones, J. D. C. (2003). Optimum frequency selection in multifrequency interferometry. *Optics Letters*, *28*, 887–889. doi:10.1364/OL.28.000887

Towers, C. E., Towers, D. P., & Jones, J. D. C. (2005). Absolute fringe order calculation using optimised multi-frequency selection in full-field profilometry. *Optics and Lasers in Engineering*, *43*, 788–800. doi:10.1016/j.optlaseng.2004.08.005

Vanlanduit, S., Vanherzeele, J., Guillaume, P., Cauberghe, B., & Verboven, P. (2004). Fourier fringe processing by use of an interpolated Fourier-transform technique. *Applied Optics*, *43*, 5206–5213. doi:10.1364/AO.43.005206

Wong, A. K. C., Niu, P. Y., & He, X. (2005). Fast acquisition of dense depth data by a new structured light scheme. *Computer Vision and Image Understanding*, *98*, 398–422. doi:10.1016/j.cviu.2004.09.003

Zhang, H., Lalor, M. J., & Burton, D. R. (1999). Spatiotemporal phase unwrapping for the measurement of discontinuous objects in dynamic fringe-projection phase-shifting profilometry. *Applied Optics*, *38*, 3534–3541. doi:10.1364/AO.38.003534

Zhang, Z. H., Ma, H. Y., Zhang, S. X., Guo, T., Towers, C. E., & Towers, D. P. (2011). Simple calibration of a phase-based 3D imaging system based on uneven fringe projection. *Optics Letters, 36*(5), 627–629. doi:10.1364/OL.36.000627

Zhang, Z. H., Towers, C. E., & Towers, D. P. (2006). Time efficient color fringe projection system for 3D shape and color using optimum 3-frequency selection. *Optics Express, 14,* 6444–6455. doi:10.1364/OE.14.006444

Zhang, Z. H., Towers, C. E., & Towers, D. P. (2007). Uneven fringe projection for efficient calibration in high-resolution 3D shape metrology. *Applied Optics, 46,* 6113–6119. doi:10.1364/AO.46.006113

Zhang, Z. H., Towers, C. E., & Towers, D. P. (2008). Shape and colour measurement of colourful objects by fringe projection. In J. Schmit, K. Creath & C. E. Towers (Ed.), *The Conference of Interferometry XIV: Techniques and Analysis, Vol. 7063.* Doi:10.1117/12.794561

Zhang, Z. H., Towers, C. E., & Towers, D. P. (2010). Compensating lateral chromatic aberration of a color fringe projection system for shape metrology. *Optics and Lasers in Engineering, 48*(2), 159–165. doi:10.1016/j.optlaseng.2009.04.010

## KEY TERMS AND DEFINITIONS

**3D Imaging:** A technique to get not only x,y coordinates, but also depth or range of an object surface, from one or more captured images by using active or passive imaging methods. Therefore, 3D data description of an object can be obtained by 3D imaging techniques.

**Composite RGB Fringe Image:** Three generated fringe patterns coded into the red, green and blue channels of a color image is called a composite RGB fringe image. Here, the three color channels are regarded as a carrier, so the acquisition time can reduce to $1/3^{rd}$ of the technique by gray fringe pattern projection.

**Fourier Transform:** A mathematical operation that decomposes a signal into its constituent frequencies. In the technique of fringe projection, Fourier transform converts the sinusoidal fringe pattern from spatial domain into frequency domain.

**Fringe Projection:** A technique to project some kind of fringe patterns onto an object surface by using a DLP (Digital Light Processing) or LCOS (Liquid Crystal On Silicon) projector. The fringe patterns can be sinusoidal, binary, trapezoidal and triangular.

**Phase Calculation:** The method to calculate the phase data of a sinusoidal fringe pattern. Mostly used methods include multiple phase-step, Fourier transform, windowed Fourier transform, regularized phase-tracking and wavelet transform. The obtained phase is modulo $2\pi$ and needs to be unwrapped.

**Phase Shifting:** Any change that occurs in the phase of one quantity, or in the phase difference between two or more quantities. For fringe projection technique, phase shifting refers to the phase change among the multiple projected fringe pattern images.

**Shape Measurement:** A technique to obtain the 3D shape of an object surface by contact or non-contact measurement methods. In this chapter, 3D shape is obtained by projecting optical fringe patterns onto the measured object surface.

# Chapter 12
# Widely–Separated Stereo Views Turn into 3D Objects:
## An Application

**Rimon Elias**
*German University in Cairo, Egypt*

## ABSTRACT

*This chapter discusses the representation of obstacles in an environment with planar ground through wide baseline set of images in the context of teleoperation. The camera parameters are assumed to be known approximately within some range according to the error margins of the sensors used such as inertial devices. The technique proposed in this chapter is based on detecting junctions in all images using the so-called the JUDOCA operator, and through homographic transformation, correlation is applied to achieve point correspondences. The match set is then triangulated to obtain a set of 3D points. Point clustering is then performed to achieve a bounding box for each obstacle, which may be used for localization purposes by itself. Finally, voxel occupancy scheme is applied to get volumetric representation of the obstacles.*

## INTRODUCTION

Teleoperation refers to a machine operation that can be controlled remotely. This could be the answer for machinery operating in harsh environments; e.g., mining, waste disposal, forestry, and/or oil platform maintenance environments. In such environments, equipments may operate over a relatively flat work surface. Rocks of different sizes and shapes may exist to constitute obstacles that have to be avoided when moving the equipment. Therefore, it is not an easy task for a robotic vehicle to navigate in these conditions.

DOI: 10.4018/978-1-4666-0113-0.ch012

The complex machine-environment interactions produce continual operator-equipment dialogs that require the operator's constant attention. Moreover, collisions or control errors may result from the direct nature of the transactions. Also, a great deal of data is transmitted to and from the operator (e.g., commands and images); a task that slows down the operation. Such transmission delay to and from the operator's site affects the efficiency, relevance and safety of the specifications. This suggests that more global representation of the environment should be inferred using less data (e.g., a limited number of images).

Following this idea, only a small number of natural images of widely separated views of the work site may be taken using cameras mounted on the navigating robotic vehicles. This is combined with approximate camera parameters information; i.e., position and orientation, at every viewpoint. However, the accuracy of these measurements is limited by the error tolerance of the measuring devices. Any information inferred from these measurements therefore has to take these uncertainties into account.

Our goal is to build a 3D representation of the work area in which obstacles are localized and their volumes of occupancy are specified. This is to provide the operator with a virtual synthesized sequence of images of the extended portion of the terrain. In other words, we aim to move a virtual camera along a path determined by the operator to generate the synthesized sequence of images. We will assume that the ground surface, where the obstacles reside, is flat. Furthermore, we will assume that the available views are widely separated (i.e., the differences among successive camera poses are large) so that the amount of data transmitted to the human operator is reduced. For each view, the camera parameters are known approximately. This includes three parameters that determine its position and three others representing its orientation about all three axes. Based on the sensor specifications, the values of these parameters are within a certain range.

Our system is different from photo-tourism (Snavely *et al.*, 2006, 2008) in certain aspects. While photo-tourism uses hundreds and sometimes thousands of images, one of our main constraints is to use as few images as possible. Such a constraint forces us to work with wide baseline images; a setting that imposes additional difficulties. Another difference between those systems is that we use approximate camera parameters while photo-tourism uses a procedure to recover the camera parameters.

The rest of this chapter is organized as follows. Section Background is a literature review of different approaches to detect obstacles and to reconstruct them in 3D space using multiple images. Section Scene Modeling Approach discusses the scene modeling approach we propose, which has several steps that are discussed in its subsections. Experimental results will be provided following the explanation of each step. Section Discussion provides discussion about important points mentioned while Section Conclusion provides a final conclusion.

## BACKGROUND

Since our proposed system is dealing with detection and reconstructing objects in 3D space, we will go over the important concepts found in the literature concerning these two problems.

Many researchers have tackled the problem of detecting objects residing on a ground plane (or detecting the ground plane alternatively). Different approaches have been developed to solve such a problem for different settings. Color information can be used for ground detection as in (Hoffmann *et al.*, 2005). Stereo pairs can be used for detection as in (Sabe *et al.*, 2004; Mandelbaum *et al.*, 1998; Bertozzi *et al.*, 1996). Monocular vision approaches also have been developed. Optical flow can be used in this case as in (Kim & Kim, 2004) where the surface normals for different image areas are computed and grouped to identify the ground plane. Homography can also be used with monocular sequence of images to identify the ground plane as in (Zhou & Li, 2006). However, this previous approach is restricted to a camera fixed on a mobile robot with a flexibility to rotate horizontally only.

Techniques developed to reconstruct objects in 3D space can be divided into two main classes (Niem & Wingbermuhle, 1997); *active methods* that use laser scanners; and *passive methods* that use groups of images taken by cameras. We will restrict ourselves to the second class, which we address in this chapter. Furthermore, reconstruction from images can be categorized into four categories (Cross & Zisserman, 2000): reconstruction from contours; texture correlation; feature based matching; and space carving.

As an example of the first category, Niem *et al.* (1997) performed 3D object modeling based on shape reconstruction and texture mapping. In order to achieve shape reconstruction, they suggested to use *shape from silhouettes* or *method of occluding contours* (Chien & Aggarwel, 1986; Szeliski, 1993). They proceeded by first forming a convex hull representing the bounding pyramid. This one was determined by the lines of sight from the focal point of the camera and the contours of the silhouette. The pyramids were intersected resulting in an approximate bounding volume. Then, a mesh growing algorithm was used to transform that bounding volume into a surface model consisting of a mesh of triangles. Finally, texture mapping was used to render each mesh triangle patch. In the previous system, a rotationally symmetrical pattern should be arranged around the object under consideration for calibration purposes. Also, some criteria must be met; e.g., the pattern and the object must be separable with no occlusion of object by the pattern and object and pattern must be in depth of focus. In such a system, it is predictable that a small number of input wide baseline images would make difficulties with intersecting pyramids.

Another algorithm based on the *shape from silhouette* approach is presented in (Matsumoto, 1997). This algorithm uses a turntable that is used along with an object of known shape to acquire camera parameters. This is done through a *multi-level extraction* scheme. In the ordinary silhouette extraction scheme, a pixel-level subtraction between the object image and the background image is to be performed. However, they proposed to add a new stage to this one. They called it *region-level extraction* where region segmentation is performed and the average of the absolute subtraction at each pixel is calculated. According to a threshold, the whole region may be decided if it is a part of the silhouette. This may avoid misjudging pixels similar to its background image while its neighborhood differs.

An example of a texture correlation category is presented in (Koch, 1995) where Koch uses a stereoscopic image sequence. This method is based on image correspondence that uses cross correlation of a small image patch as a similarity measure; disparity estimation that results in a disparity map and hence a depth map; surface segmentation according to surface orientation; depth interpolation; surface approximation by a triangular mesh; and finally texture mapping. Such a system is limited to the use of stereo pairs to extract the depth information.

Ayache and Faugeras (1987) use three cameras mounted on a robot to recognize the environment. The triplet of images is analyzed by a program presented in (Ayache & Faverjon, 1987; Ayache & Lustman, 1987). This program outputs 3D line segments expressed in a coordinate system attached to the three cameras. Thus, for *n* robot positions, we have *n* line segments. (The authors called combining coherently various sources of information at different times and from different places *Visual Fusion problem*.) They apply transformations to relate various 3D line segments for the same real line at different robot locations in order to express all segments in one coordinate system attached to a given robot position. Through some representation of uncertainty of both 3D line segment positions and rigid motions among various positions, they can combine various representations to decide if they are for the same segment and hence enhance the accuracy and abandon the redundant information.

Another development is *space carving* (Cross & Zisserman, 2000) or *volumetric scene reconstruction* (Dyer, 2001). While *shape from silhouette* approach is usually used with binary silhouette images, *shape from photo consistency* combined with visibility testing is for color images. In this category, the scene is often discretized into voxels and a voxel occupancy scheme is to be developed to determine the volumetric model from silhouette or from color information. Photometric information resides in color or gray-scale images can be used to enhance the model achieved.

Cross and Zisserman (2000) presented an approach to reconstruct a surface of an object from a number of views. This system combines information from apparent contours and surface texture and used a voxelization technique. Through this, deficiencies of using one source can be overcome by the strength of the other. However, such an approach has its own limitations; e.g., in case of under segmentation (if parts of contours are missing) or over segmentation; in which case, parts of the actual object will be removed.

Granger-Piche *et al.* (2004) presented an interactive reconstruction system based on space carving. In this system, silhouette carving is performed and then representative images are stored in a hemispherical structure for balanced color carving. This system requires that the object to reconstruct be placed in a room corner marked with feature points for calibration. Also, wide baseline setup is not an issue in this case.

The approach that we propose in this chapter combines different aspects of these previous four categories aiming to merge their strengths and obtain a volumetric representation of the detected obstacles.

## SCENE MODELING APPROACH

Our task is to model the scene under consideration. In order to obtain a good model, requirements like detecting, localizing and representing obstacles on the ground plane should be fulfilled as sub-goals or transition stages. There are two main phases to achieve a solution to represent an obstacle. These phases include: extracting and matching features among images; and determining structure from corresponding features. Hence, we propose to use the system described in Figure 1. This system starts with detecting junctions in all images (Junction Detection) and calculating ground plane homography (Ground Plane Representation). Then, it proceeds with selecting junctions that belong to obstacles; i.e., excluding junctions that are part of the ground plane through homography estimation (Junction Selection). Those selected junctions are then matched among views (Junction Matching). Every pair of points corresponds to a 3D point in space that can be determined through triangulation (Three-Dimensional Point Reconstruction). This results in a set of 3D points that should belong to the surfaces of the obstacles. This set of points is then clustered according to some proximity criterion. Thus, a bounding box containing every obstacle can be obtained (3D Point Clustering). Finally and according to a voxel occupancy scheme, a volumetric representation of an obstacle can be achieved (Volumetric Representation of Obstacles). Notice that, in Sec. Junction Detection, we work on individual images. In Sec. Junction Selection and Sec. Junction Matching, pairs of images are considered while in Sec. 3D Point Clustering, more pairs are used and in Sec. Volumetric Representation of Obstacles, all available images are put to contribution in order to achieve good voxelization results.

Because it is a multi-step process that includes a great deal of details, we will discuss every step and provide the experimental result related to it at the end of its explanation. In our experiments,

*Figure 1. Steps of the proposed technique*

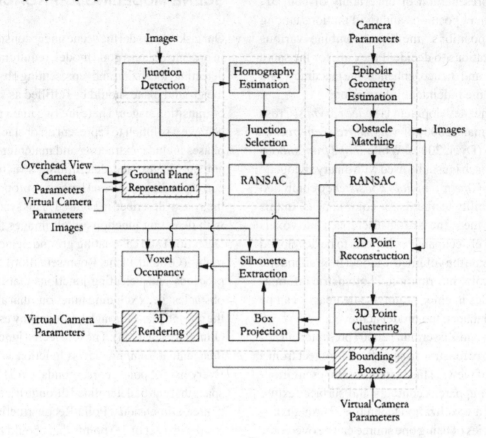

we selected two scenes; each containing one obstacle as shown in Figure 2 and Figure 3.

## Junction Detection

In order to detect junctions, we used the so-called JUDOCA operator (Laganiere & Elias, 2004). This operator uses the gradient images to detect intersecting ridges that form the junctions. To do so, two binary images are used; **B**, obtained by imposing a threshold on the gradient magnitude and **B⁺**, obtained by retaining the directional local maxima of **B**. As shown in Figure 4, a circular mask is centered at every point in **B**. The list of points in **B⁺** located on the circumference of this mask is obtained. The radial segment that joins each of these points to the central point is scanned. If all points along this segment belong to the set **B**, then a junction edge is found. A junction is identified when at least two such junction edges are found. This operator outperforms other corner detectors as it provides junctions of good accuracy in terms of their locations, number of edges forming each junction and their orientations as well.

## Experimental Results

In order to test our algorithm, consider the "box" pair shown in Figure 2(b) and 2(f) and the "cubes" pair shown in Figure 3(e) and 3(f). The images were processed to detect junctions using the JU-DOCA operator. Figure 5 shows those pairs where junctions are superimposed on images.

*Figure 2. Images of a scene. Through inaccurate sensors, the error margins are assumed to be ±10 mm, ±10 mm, ±10 mm, ±0.8°, ±0.8° and ±0.8° for ΔX, ΔY, ΔZ, Δω, Δφ and Δκ, respectively, where X, Y, and Z represent the location; and ω, φ and κ represent the orientation*

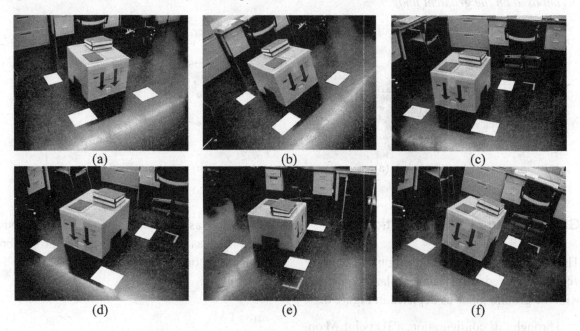

(a)        (b)        (c)

(d)        (e)        (f)

*Figure 3. Images of another scene. Through inaccurate sensors, the error margins are assumed to be ±10 mm, ±10 mm, ±10 mm, ±0.8°, ±0.8° and ±0.8° for ΔX, ΔY, ΔZ, Δω, Δφ and Δκ, respectively*

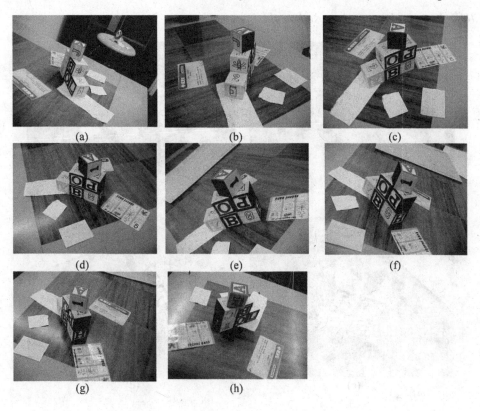

(a)        (b)        (c)

(d)        (e)        (f)

(g)        (h)

*Figure 4. An example of a 3-edge Y-junction. (a) One corner of a box that produces a Y-junction. (b) A circular mask is centered at the position of the junction* $\dot{\mathbf{p}}$ *with three points on the circumference (superimposed on the gradient image).*

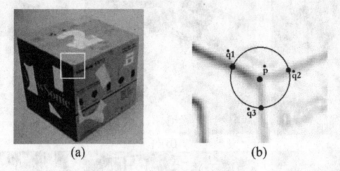

(a)  (b)

## Ground Plane Representation

The world coordinate system origin can be conveniently placed so that the *xy*-plane coincides with the ground plane as depicted in Figure 6.

Through this configuration, a 3D point $\dot{\mathbf{M}}$ on the ground can be expressed in inhomogeneous coordinates as $[X, Y, 0]^T$ and in homogeneous coordinates as $\mathbf{M} = [X, Y, 0, 1]^T$. The projection of this point on the image, $\mathbf{m} = [x, y, 1]^T$, is obtained using:

$$s\mathbf{m} = \mathbf{P}\mathbf{M} \tag{1}$$

*Figure 5. JUDOCA results superimposed on the images*

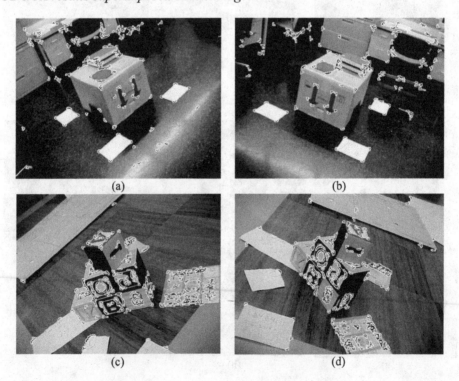

(a)  (b)

(c)  (d)

*Figure 6. (a) The plane under consideration: The origin of world coordinate system origin is placed at the lower left corner of the overhead view.* **M** *is an arbitrary point on the plane; (b) 3D representation of (a). Note that Z-coordinate is always 0. The image plane showed is formed using rotation angles of 90°, 0° and 0° for ω, φ and κ (or 90°, 0° and 0° for the tilt, τ, pan, ρ, and swing ψ respectively).*

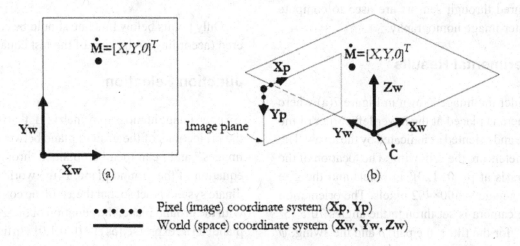

where $s$ is a scaling factor; and **P** is the perspective projection matrix. No matter what the values in the third column of matrix **P** are, their products by the third term of the vector **M** will always be 0. As a result, the matrix **P** can be reduced to a 3×3 matrix, **H**$_z$, that we call the *planar perspective matrix* (Elias & Laganiere, 2003). Following the same idea, **M** is reduced to a 3D vector **m'** = [$X$, $Y$, 1]$^T$. Rewriting Eq. (1), we get:

$$sm = H_z m'$$  (2)

Eq. (2) relates a point in an overhead view to its perspective projection onto an image. In other words, the matrix **H**$_z$ can be used to display the ground plane in the final synthesized image. This matrix can be estimated by calculating the 3×4 perspective projection matrix and eliminating the third column in this matrix to obtain **H**$_z$.

Different rotation systems may be used in order to calculate the perspective projection matrix (Elias, 2007). More information on this matrix can be found in (Elias & Laganiere, 2003). In addition to displaying the perspective image of the ground

plane, the same matrix can be used to determine feature points that belong to the ground and those that belong to the obstacles as explained later.

In order to display the perspective image of the ground plane, the intersection between that plane and the plane at infinity; i.e., the line at infinity, must be detected. The line at infinity is the vanishing line of the ground plane. Only the points below this line must be considered when generating a perspective view of the plane. Hence, the last row of **H**$_z^{-1}$ represents the equation of the line at infinity, **l**$_\infty$. That is:

$$l_\infty = \left[ h_{31}, h_{32}, h_{33} \right]^T$$  (3)

where $h_{3i} \mid i \in \{1,2,3\}$ are the terms of the last row of **H**$_z^{-1}$.

## Parameters and Thresholds

In order to estimate the planar perspective matrix, intrinsic and extrinsic camera parameters should be known. Note that this matrix is used to display the perspective projection of the ground plane as well as to compute the original inter-image homography of the ground plane. In case of displaying the ground plane, virtual camera parameters are used while camera parameters measured through sensors are used to compute the inter-image homography.

## Experimental Results

Consider the image shown in Figure 7(a) where a camera is placed at the lower left corner of the image and oriented as indicated by the arrow. The parameters are the following. The location of the camera is at $[0, 0, 120]^T$ in pixels and the size of the image is 400×402 pixels. The orientation of the camera is set through the angles 70°, 45° and 0° for the tilt, $\tau$, the pan, $\rho$ and the swing, $\psi$ respectively. The focal length along both $x$ and $y$ directions is 160 pixels. The perspective view of that image as seen by a camera given the above parameters can be generated as seen in Figure 7(b) using the planar perspective matrix.

Applying the planar perspective matrix, we get:

$$H_z^{-1} = \begin{bmatrix} -90.3 & 30.88 & -7634.98 \\ 90.3 & 30.88 & -25694.71 \\ 0.0 & -1.0 & 41.76 \end{bmatrix} \qquad (4)$$

Note that, according to Eq. (3), the equation of the line at infinity is:

$$y = 41.76 \qquad (5)$$

Only points below this line should be considered (according to the sign of the last equation).

## Junction Selection

An inter-image homography matrix $\mathbf{H}_{ij}$ that relates the projections of the ground plane between two images $i$ and $j$ can then be obtained through the equation of the ground plane. If the world coordinate system is set so that the $xy$-plane coincides with the ground plane, the equation of the ground plane can be expressed as $\Pi = [0,0,1,0]^T$. In the first camera coordinate system, this can be expressed as (Elias, 2004):

$$\Pi_{new}^T = \begin{bmatrix} \mathbf{N}_{new}^T & | d_{new} \end{bmatrix} = \begin{bmatrix} 0 & 0 & 1 & 0 \end{bmatrix} \begin{bmatrix} \mathbf{R}'^{-1} & -\mathbf{R}'^{-1}\mathbf{T}' \\ 0_3^T & 1 \end{bmatrix} \qquad (6)$$

where $\mathbf{N}_{new}$ is the normal to the ground plane; $d_{new}$ is the distance to the ground plane from the origin; both expressed in the first camera coordinate system; $\mathbf{R}'$ is the rotation of the second camera; and $\mathbf{T}'$ is the translation of the second camera; both

*Figure 7. (a) The top view. The position of the camera is the lower left corner. (b) The perspective view generated using the planar perspective matrix.*

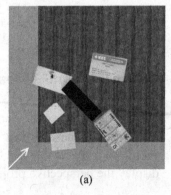
(a)

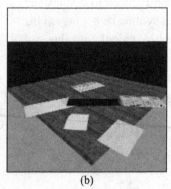
(b)

expressed in the world coordinate system. The rotation matrix and the translation vector of the second camera can be expressed with respect to the first camera using the same 4×4 transformation matrix as:

$$\left[\mathbf{R}'_{new} \quad | \ \mathbf{T}'_{new}\right] = \mathbf{A}'^{-1} \ \mathbf{P}' \begin{bmatrix} \mathbf{R}'^{-1} & -\mathbf{R}'^{-1}\mathbf{T}' \\ \mathbf{0}_3^{\mathbf{T}} & 1 \end{bmatrix} \tag{7}$$

where $\mathbf{R}'_{new}$ is the new rotation matrix; $\mathbf{T}'_{new}$ is the new translation vector both expressed in the first camera coordinate system; $\mathbf{A}'$ is the calibration matrix; and $\mathbf{P}'$ is the projection matrix of the second camera. The homography of the ground plane that relates an overhead view $i$ to an arbitrary view $j$ can then be expressed as (Hartley & Zisserman, 2006):

$$\mathbf{H}_{ij} = \mathbf{A}' \left[ \mathbf{R}'_{new} - \frac{\mathbf{T}'_{new}\mathbf{N}_{new}^T}{d_{new}} \right] \mathbf{A}^{-1} \tag{8}$$

The above equation assumes that $\mathbf{R}'_{new}$, $\mathbf{T}'_{new}$, $\mathbf{N}_{new}$ and $d_{new}$ are all expressed in the first camera coordinate system (i.e., where $\mathbf{P} = \mathbf{A}[\mathbf{I} \mid \mathbf{0}]$).

Alternatively, $\mathbf{H}_{ij}$ may be obtained through the planar perspective matrices $\mathbf{H}_{z\,i}$ and $\mathbf{H}_{z\,j}$ using:

$$\mathbf{H}_{ij} = \mathbf{H}_{zj}\mathbf{H}_{zi}^{-1} \tag{9}$$

Using this homography matrix, $\mathbf{H}_{ij}$, and taking into account the camera parameter error margins, a set of candidate junctions in one image; e.g., image $j$, can be obtained for each junction in the other image, $i$. Variance normalized correlation (VNC) is then applied to select the correct candidates. This step allows identifying matches that belong to the ground plane. According to some threshold, junctions with low correlation values are rejected. This is to check:

$$\frac{\sum_{m,n=-\frac{N}{2}}^{\frac{N}{2}} \left[ I_l(x+m, y+n) - \overline{I_l(x,y)} \right] \left[ I_r(\dot{\mathbf{k}}^T + \mathbf{t}_{lr}^T) - \overline{I_r(\mathbf{m}'^T + \mathbf{t}_{lr}^T)} \right]}{\sqrt{\sum_{m,n=-\frac{N}{2}}^{\frac{N}{2}} \left[ I_l(x+m, y+n) - \overline{I_l(x,y)} \right]^2} \sqrt{\sum_{m,n=-\frac{N}{2}}^{\frac{N}{2}} \left[ I_r(\mathbf{k}^T + \mathbf{t}_{lr}^T) - \overline{I_r(\mathbf{m}'^T + \mathbf{t}_{lr}^T)} \right]^2}} \geq t_g \tag{10}$$

where $(N+1)^2$ is the area correlated in the left image; the inhomogeneous point $\dot{\mathbf{m}} = [x, \ y]^T$ is the left point; the homogeneous point $\mathbf{m}'$ in the right image is equal to $\mathbf{H}_{ij} \mathbf{m} = \mathbf{H}_{ij} [x, y, 1]^T$; $\mathbf{t}_{lr}$ is the translation vector from the inhomogeneous $\dot{\mathbf{m}}'$ to the correlated right point; $\dot{\mathbf{m}}' + \mathbf{t}_{lr}$ is the correlated right point; $\overline{I_l(x,y)}$ is the mean of the neighborhood surrounding $[x,y]^T$; $\mathbf{k}$ is $\mathbf{H}_{ij} [x+m, y+n, 1]^T$; $\overline{I_r\left(\mathbf{m}'^T + \mathbf{t}_{lr}\right)}$ is the mean of the neighborhood surrounding $\mathbf{m}' + \mathbf{t}_{lr}$; and $t_g$ is a threshold. The above correlation is applied for both direction; i.e., left-right and right-left. The matches accepted are those approved in both phases.

At this point, match pairs on the ground plane should have been identified; however, other ground features that did not contribute to match pairs might have leaked off the process. In order to identify these features, the homography matrix needs to be estimated accurately. The so-called RANSAC scheme is then applied to the obtained match set as follows (Vincent & Laganiere, 2001; Hartley & Zisserman, 2006):

1.  Randomly choose four pairs of corresponding points.
2.  Compute the homography matrix.
3.  Compute the number of inliers consistent with the above-estimated homography matrix using a threshold $t_H$.
4.  Repeat these steps for the rest of samples.

According to the above RANSAC method, the homography matrix that supports the largest number of inliers will be chosen to represent a refined version of the previously-estimated homography matrix. VNC correlation represented in (10) is re-applied again with the updated version of the homography matrix to the other junctions that do not represent ground matching pairs.

Consequently, more ground features may be detected. Knowing this information, feature points on the obstacles can be identified as the complement set of those on the ground.

## Parameters and Thresholds

In addition to camera parameters, the error margins play an important role at this step. Moreover, $t_g$ is a threshold used to detect feature points on the ground plane and $t_H$ is a threshold used with RANSAC to obtain an enhanced homography matrix while $N$ determines the size of the correlation window.

## Experimental Results

The aim of this step is to identify junctions on the ground plane versus those on obstacles. In order to achieve this goal, junctions were processed to find matches on the ground plane. The results are shown in Figure 8 where disparity vectors are shown.

We tested the effect of the correlation window size and the correlation threshold, $t_g$, on the overall results of detecting ground features. As depicted in Figure 9, the experiments have shown that the larger the size of the correlation window, the better the results. Also, larger correlation thresholds tend to provide better results.

Updated homography matrices were obtained through RANSAC as mentioned above. Consequently, more features on the ground plane were detected through correlation.

For the "cubes" pair, 429 and 409 junctions were detected for both images. Having to work with the inaccurate homography matrix resulted in 32 ground feature matches. This represents 7.5% and 7.8% of the total number of junctions. Some of these matches are repeated due to the fact that 3-edge junctions are split into three 2-edge junctions. After applying RANSAC, only 24 different pairs were recorded. Hence, the resulting

*Figure 8. Match results for ground features*

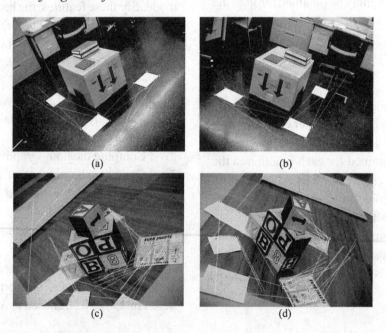

(a)                          (b)

(c)                          (d)

*Figure 9. The "cubes" pair: The behavior of the percentages of correct matches through different correlation window sizes and correlation thresholds*

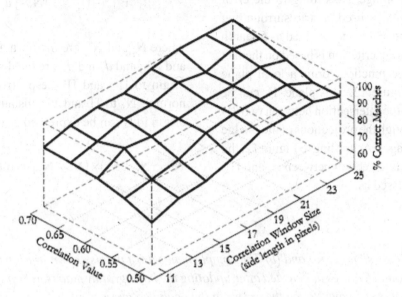

homography matrix is used to detect more ground features that reached 146 and 161 for the left and right images respectively. These last figures represent 34.0% and 39.4% of the total number of junctions. The bar chart of Figure 10 depicts these relationships. Figure 11 shows the effect of

this step in excluding many junctions as a relief operation for arbitrary plane matching.

## Junction Matching

Based on the epipolar geometry derived from the available approximate parameters, a junction has

*Figure 10. The cubes" pair: Bar chart shows the number of junctions in total and after segmenting into ground and obstacle sets.*

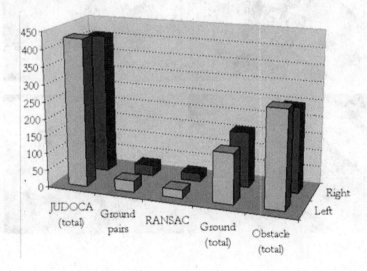

its corresponding one on or around its epipolar line in the other image. According to the error margins of the sensor used, a strip surrounding each epipolar line can be determined as a search range. The matching criterion is based on the fact that every 2-edge junction forms a local plane as depicted in Figure 12. This plane, $\Pi$, can be reconstructed as the intersection between two 3D lines formed through the projections of the 2-edge junction onto images. According to Figure 12, the 3D line $\mathbf{L}_1$ is the intersection between $\Pi_1$ and $\Pi'_1$ and can be expressed as:

$$L_1 = \begin{bmatrix} \mathbf{l}_1^T\, P \\ \mathbf{l}_1'^T\, P' \end{bmatrix} \doteq \begin{bmatrix} \Pi_1^T \\ \Pi_1'^T \end{bmatrix} = \begin{bmatrix} \mathbf{N}_1^T \mid d_1 \\ \mathbf{N}_1'^T \mid d_1' \end{bmatrix} \tag{11}$$

where $\mathbf{N}_1$ and $\mathbf{N'}_1$ are the normal vectors to $\Pi_1$ and $\Pi'_1$; and $d_1$ and $d'_1$ are the distances from the origin to $\Pi_1$ and $\Pi'_1$ respectively. Hence, the normal, $\mathbf{N}$, to $\Pi$ and the distance, $d$, from origin to $\Pi$ can be expressed as (Elias, 2004):

$$\mathbf{N} = \left(\mathbf{N_1} \times \mathbf{N_1'}\right) \times \left(\mathbf{N_2} \times \mathbf{N_2'}\right) \quad \text{and} \quad d = -\mathbf{N} \bullet \dot{\mathbf{M}} \tag{12}$$

*Figure 11. The "cubes" pair: (a) and (b) The complement sets of points shown in Figure 8(c) and 8(d). (c) and (d) All ground features as detected after updating the homography matrix. (e) and (f) The complement sets of the previous row. Notice the errors in the occluded areas.*

*Figure 12. Every 3D line, $L_p$ is the intersection of two planes, $\Pi_l$ and $\Pi'_p$ formed by the optical centers and the projections of the line, $l_l$ and $l'_p$ onto both images. Two 3D lines form the plane of the junction.*

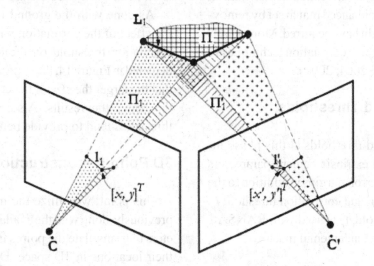

where × denotes the cross product; · denotes the dot product; $N$ should be normalized to unit magnitude and $\dot{M}$ is an *estimation* for the 3D point in space (refer to Eq. (15)). Similar to Eq. (8), the homography matrix of that plane, $H$, is calculated as (Hartley & Zisserman, 2006):

$$H = A' \left[ R' - \frac{T'N^T}{d} \right] A^{-1} \qquad (13)$$

where $A$ and $A'$ are the calibration matrices; $R'$ is the rotation matrix of the second camera; $T'$ is the translation vector of the second camera; $N$ is the normal to the plane; and $d$ is the distance to the origin. This equation assumes that the origin of the world coordinate system is placed at the first optical center where $P = A [I \mid 0]$. Thus, a 4×4 transformation matrix should be applied to get the transformed $R'$, $T'$, $N$ and $d$ as done in Sec. **Junction Selection**. Consequently, homographic correlation is applied to determine the best match for a given junction as done in (10).

Alternatively, SAD correlation can be performed as:

$$\sum_{m,n=-\frac{N}{2}}^{\frac{N}{2}} \left| I_l \left( x+m, y+n \right) - I_r \left( \dot{k}^T \right) \right| \le t_{SAD} \qquad (14)$$

where $N+1$ is the side length of the correlation window in pixels; $k = H [x+m, y+n, 1]^T$; and $t_{SAD}$ is a threshold.

An additional RANSAC phase may be applied at this point to enforce the epipolar constraint and get an updated version of the fundamental matrix. The steps are as follows (Roth & Whitehead, 2000; Vincent & Laganiere, 2001):

1.  Seven points are randomly selected.
2.  The fundamental matrix is computed from this set.
3.  Pairs that satisfy the computed $F$ are selected to the support set. The pair is satisfying the matrix $F$ if the point in one image lies within some threshold $t_F$ (e.g., 1 pixel) from the computed epipolar line.
4.  The preceding steps are repeated and the largest support set along with its fundamental matrix, $F$ are returned.

The above-mentioned RANSAC steps should result in a more accurate fundamental matrix, which results in an enhanced match set by removing outliers that might have occurred. More details about this homographic correlation technique are discussed in (Elias, 2004, 2007).

## Parameters and Thresholds

The parameters and thresholds at this phase include intrinsic and extrinsic camera parameters and the associated error margins in addition to the window size $(N+1)^2$ and correlation threshold $t_g$. Moreover, a threshold, $t_F$ is used with RANSAC to obtain enhanced fundamental matrix.

## Experimental Results

The complement sets of the ground features detected in the previous step are used here as candidates to the matching process (refer to Figure 11(e) and 11(f)). Matches that belong to arbitrary planes are shown in Figure 13 for the "box" and "cubes"

pairs. In both cases, the correlation threshold used is 0.75. Disparity vectors are indicated.

As done with the ground features, we tested the effect of the correlation window size and the correlation threshold on the overall results. As depicted in Figure 14, the experiments have shown that the larger the size of the correlation window, the better the results. Also, larger correlation thresholds tend to provide better results.

## 3D Point Reconstruction

At this point, we utilize the match set obtained previously along with the available camera parameters to triangulate the points in order to estimate their locations in 3D space. Due to the possible inaccuracy in camera parameters, the two rays produced by these points may not intersect. In this case, the 3D point can be calculated as the middle point of the perpendicular to both rays. Thus, the 3D point can be estimated as (Beardsley *et al.*, 1997):

*Figure 13. Matches that belong to arbitrary planes*

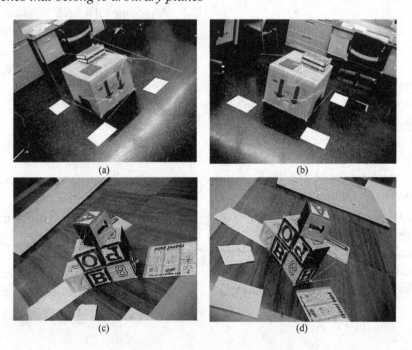

(a)  (b)

(c)  (d)

$$\dot{\mathbf{M}} = \left( \left[ \mathbf{I} - \dot{\mathbf{M}}_\infty \dot{\mathbf{M}}_\infty^T \right] + \left[ \mathbf{I} - \dot{\mathbf{M}}_\infty' \dot{\mathbf{M}}_\infty'^T \right] \right)^{-1} \left( \dot{\mathbf{C}} + \dot{\mathbf{C}}' - \left[ \dot{\mathbf{C}}^T \dot{\mathbf{M}}_\infty \right] \dot{\mathbf{M}}_\infty - \left[ \dot{\mathbf{C}}'^T \dot{\mathbf{M}}_\infty' \right] \dot{\mathbf{M}}_\infty' \right)$$

(15)

where $\dot{\mathbf{M}}$, $\dot{\mathbf{C}}$, $\dot{\mathbf{C}}'$, $\dot{\mathbf{M}}_\infty$ and $\dot{\mathbf{M}}_\infty'$ are the inhomogeneous representation of the point in 3D space, the optical centers and the intersection of the rays with the plane at infinity respectively; $\mathbf{I}$ is a 3×3 identity matrix; and $\dot{\mathbf{M}}_\infty$ and $\dot{\mathbf{M}}_\infty'$ are normalized to unit magnitude. Hence, for every match pair, we obtain a 3D point. The 3D point set obtained from all image pairs is then clustered. This is discussed in the following subsection.

## 3D Point Clustering

The obtained 3D points are grouped according to some proximity criterion to form clusters through a hierarchical structure (Elias, 2003). An example of this structure is shown in Figure 15. The idea of building such a structure is based on the concept of irregular pyramids.

Each level of the structure is represented as a graph. At the base, the graph consists of a number of cluster nodes where each node shares a graph edge with every other node and where every node contains only one space point. The process of building subsequent levels -- and how the inter-level links are established -- is controlled through some rules. These rules are:

1.  Two neighbors on the same level may both survive at the next level (i.e., the parent level) if and only if some certain binary variable is set to zero during the decimation process. Note that this is different from the case of the adaptive and disparity pyramids (Jolion & Montavert, 1991; Elias & Laganiere, 1999).

2.  For each nonsurviving node, there exists at least one surviving node in its neighborhood (to be promoted to the parent level). This is true in the case of the adaptive and disparity pyramids.

Suppose that the set of clusters at a given level, $L_i$, is $L_{(i)} = \{ C_{(i,1)}, C_{(i,2)}, ..., C_{(i,n)} \}$ where $i$ is the level number; $n$ is the number of clusters at a level $L_i$; and $C_{(i,j)}$, where $j \in \{ 1, ..., n \}$, is a cluster consisting of a number of space points. Further-

*Figure 14. The behavior of correct matches as affected by the size of correlation window and the correlation threshold*

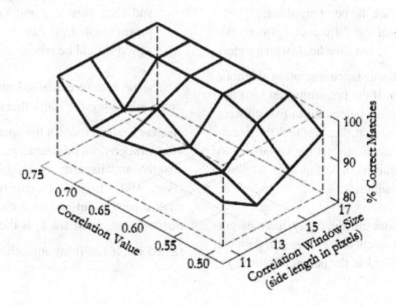

*Figure 15. The hierarchical structure*

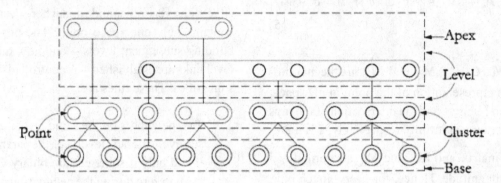

more, a cluster $C_{(i,j)}$ is defined as $C_{(i,j)} = \left\{ \dot{\mathbf{M}}_{(i,j,1)}, \dot{\mathbf{M}}_{(i,j,2)}, \cdots, \dot{\mathbf{M}}_{(i,j,m)} \right\}$ where $i$ is the level number; $j$ is the cluster number, $j \in \{1, ..., n\}$; $m$ is the number of points in cluster; and $\dot{\mathbf{M}}$ is a 3D vector representing the point in 3D space. Then, for every two clusters, $C_{(i,j)}$ and $C_{(i,k)}$, at level $L_i$, we reset a binary variable $q$ to 0 and perform the following check among the points contained in these clusters. This is by checking:

$$\left\| \dot{\mathbf{M}}_{(i,j,a)} - \dot{\mathbf{M}}_{(i,k,b)} \right\| < t_{\dot{\mathbf{M}}} \qquad (16)$$

where $i$ is the level number; $j$ and $k$ are the cluster numbers; $a$ and $b$ are the point numbers; $\|.\|$ represents the norm of the difference between the two vectors; and $t_{\dot{\mathbf{M}}}$ is a threshold, which determines the maximum distance separating neighbor points in a cluster. If the proximity test (16) between any two points belonging to two clusters results in a true condition, then we break the search for the current clusters and set the variable $q$ to 1; otherwise, $q$ remains 0. At this step, we have the following possibilities:

- If $q = 1$ and one cluster; e.g., $j$, has a parent while the other cluster, $k$, does not, then we link the cluster $k$ to the parent of cluster $j$.

- If $q = 1$ and neither cluster $j$ nor cluster $k$ has a parent, then a new node at the next level is to be created and linked to both clusters.

- If $q = 1$ and each cluster ($j$ and $k$) has a different parent created previously, then we link both to one parent and delete the other.

- If $q = 0$ and one cluster; e.g., $j$, has a parent while the other cluster, $k$, does not, then a new node is to be created at the next level and linked to cluster $k$.

- If $q = 0$ and neither cluster $j$ nor cluster $k$ has a parent, then a new node at the next level is to be created for each one and linked to the corresponding cluster.

- The last possibility happens when $q = 0$ and each cluster ($j$ and $k$) has a different parent created previously. In this case, no action should be taken.

The procedure explained above is repeated iteratively using the same threshold $t_{\dot{\mathbf{M}}}$ until all clusters become roots at the apex. This is a common property to this structure as well as the adaptive and disparity pyramids (Jolion & Montavert, 1991; Elias & Laganiere, 1999). In our case, a root is defined as a cluster that is at a distance $\geq t_{\dot{\mathbf{M}}}$ -- where $t_{\dot{\mathbf{M}}}$ is the threshold mentioned in (16) -- from any other cluster. In this case; i.e., at the apex, one cluster should exist for each object in space.

Through 3D point clustering, outliers -- caused by mismatches -- may be detected and removed as they will likely result in isolated points in space. Moreover, if isolated true matches that belong to the ground leaked off the step mentioned in Sec. **Junction Selection**, clustering may discard these cases as well. As a result of point clustering, a 3D bounding box for every obstacle can be obtained (see Figure 16). Clusters containing a number of points less than some threshold are rejected. This bounding box may serve as localization information for the obstacle. For some applications, such a bounding box may be sufficient for robot navigation. For others, a more accurate occupancy model may be required. This is what we discuss in Sec. \ref{obstacle reconstruction}.

## Parameters and Thresholds

The hierarchical structure proposed to cluster points in space controls the operation through the threshold $t_M$. The legitimate range for this threshold varies considerably according to the scene under consideration and also according to the measuring units of the camera parameters. For example, if the translation of each camera is measured in millimeters, the locations of 3D points will be produced in millimeters and the threshold $t_M$ should reflect that. The threshold value would differ for the same scene if inches were used instead. Also, the density and the number of 3D points influence the value of this threshold.

In addition to the above threshold, another threshold may be imposed on the number of points in the resulting clusters in order to exclude isolated point that might result from outliers.

## Experimental Results

The match sets previously detected were triangulated and then clustered to obtain bounding boxes.

In order to examine the process, the results were superimposed on the images. Also, we added to the top, side and perspective views for one of the scenes as shown in Figure 16. In this case, the clustering threshold used is 600mm. This figure shows that wrong clusters were obtained. Those clusters have one common feature; that is the small number of points contained. Thus such clusters could be easily abandoned by imposing a threshold as mentioned above. At the end only one bounding box representing one real cluster is obtained.

Notice that in Figure 17(a), only partial bounding box was obtained using the points of the pair shown in Figure 11 and a threshold of 60mm. The pair shown in Figure 3(a) and 3(b) was used to add points to the 3D point set. Using a threshold

*Figure 16. 3D points are clustered through a hierarchical structure. Results through a threshold of 600mm: (a) Top projection. (b) Perspective view. (c) and (d) Side views. All clusters are shown. (e) The cluster with the maximum number of points superimposed on the original image as a bounding box.*

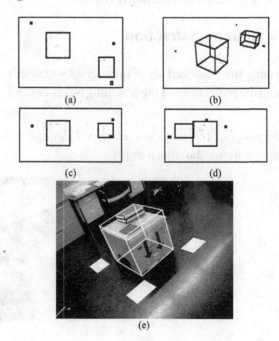

of 80mm, this resulted in a bounding box that covered the whole volume of the obstacle.

## Volumetric Representation of Obstacles

The hierarchical structure suggested provides a bounding box for every obstacle in the scene according to the features extracted. However, this bounding box is built according to the overall maximum and minimum coordinates -- of the feature points detected on that obstacle -- along the three axes. In other words, an obstacle can be contained in the bounding box but may not occupy its whole volume. Hence, the need may arise to determine the sub-volume that could better represent the obstacle. In order to reach this goal, we propose an algorithm that is based on a voxelization scheme. In this approach, the projection matrices may be updated according to the accurate matrices obtained using the RANSAC scheme. Then, we proceed with extracting silhouettes for the obstacles. This is followed by determining the occupied voxels through shape from silhouettes and color consistency scheme and finally, determining hidden and occluded voxels.

## Silhouette Extraction

Using the enhanced set of homography matrices and the projections of the bounding boxes onto all images in the set, we can extract silhouette-like images for the obstacles corresponding to every image in the set.

For each obstacle, the corners are projected onto images using the projection matrices. Then the convex hull is determined for each of them. This could be done through any well-known algorithm; e.g., Graham Scan (Sedgewick, 1988). However, we have a small number of points. Moreover, in fact, the lines that represent the edges of the convex hull are a subset of the projections of the edges of the bounding box. This makes it simpler to obtain the convex hull. In order to check if an edge is a part of the convex hull, its linear equation may be used. This equation can be easily obtained through its two end points. Thus, applying the coordinates of the other projected points (only 6 points) to this linear equation can determine whether this edge is a part of the convex hull or not. This to check the sign of:

$$\mathbf{m}_{ijb}^{T}\mathbf{l}_{pq} = \mathbf{m}_{ijb}^{T}\left[\mathbf{m}_{pjb} \times \mathbf{m}_{qjb}\right] = \begin{bmatrix} x_{ijb} & y_{ijb} & 1 \end{bmatrix} \begin{bmatrix} y_{qjb} - y_{pjb} \\ x_{pjb} - x_{qjb} \\ y_{pjb}x_{qjb} - y_{qjb}x_{pjb} \end{bmatrix}$$

(17)

where $\mathbf{l}_{pq}$ is the equation of the line connecting points $\mathbf{\dot{m}}_{pjb}$ and $\mathbf{\dot{m}}_{qjb}$; and $\mathbf{\dot{m}}_{ijb}$, $\mathbf{\dot{m}}_{pjb}$ and $\mathbf{\dot{m}}_{qjb}$ are the projections on image $j$ of three different corners of the bounding box, $b$; i.e., $i$, $p$, $q \in \{1, 2,$

*Figure 17. 3D points are clustered through a hierarchical structure. Results through a threshold of 60mm in (a) and 80mm in (b).*

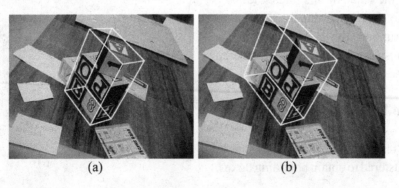

(a)                              (b)

..., 8} and $i \neq p \neq q$. If the sign of the result of Eq. (17) is the same for all $i \in \{1, 2, ..., 8\}$ such that $i \neq p \neq q$, then the line $\mathbf{l}_{pq}$ is an edge of the convex hull; otherwise, it lies inside its boundaries. The last point to mention at this step is that we keep track of the sign of the internal direction of each edge of the convex hull as this will be used in the next step.

Knowing the edges of the convex hull, a pixel can be identified to lie inside the boundaries of the convex hull. As in Eq. (17), applying the pixel coordinates to the linear equations of all edges of the convex hull determines if this pixel lies inside the convex hull if all signs are consistent with the corresponding signs of the last step. To reduce consuming time, the smallest rectangle enclosing the convex hull may serve as a range for candidate pixels.

The homography of the ground plane between two images $j$ and $k$ can be obtained through the concatenation of the available set of homography matrices. Thus, given a set of homography matrices $\{\mathbf{H}_1, \mathbf{H}_2, ..., \mathbf{H}_i, ..., \mathbf{H}_j, ..., \mathbf{H}_g\}$ where $\mathbf{H}_i$ represents the ground plane homography between images $i$ and $i+1$, and in order to calculate the homography from image $i$ to image $j$, $\mathbf{H}_{ij}$, we use the relation:

$$\mathbf{H}_{ij} = \prod_{h=j-1}^{i} \mathbf{H}_h \qquad (18)$$

Note that Eq. (8) and Eq. (9) may be used also at this step to get the inter-image homography $\mathbf{H}_{ij}$. Knowing the positions of the pixels inside the convex hull and the inter-image homography, cross correlation that is based on the sum of absolute differences (SAD) can be applied as follows:

$$\sum_{m,n=-\frac{N}{2}}^{\frac{N}{2}} \left| I_i\left(x_{ib}+m, y_{ib}+n\right) - I_j\left(\mathbf{j}^T\right) \right| > t_S \qquad (19)$$

where $N+1$ is the side length of the correlation window in pixels; $\mathbf{j} = \mathbf{H}_{ij} [x_{ib}+m, y_{ib}+n, 1]^T$; and $t_s$ is a threshold.

There are a few possibilities at this point. If the colors of two corresponding pixel are close to each other; i.e., false condition in (19), the examined pixel may be a part of the ground plane. If the colors are far from each other according to $t_s$; i.e., true condition in (19), then there is a good chance that the examined pixel is a part of the silhouette. Another possibility may happen where the location of the corresponding pixel lie outside the image.

This correlation step is to be repeated between that given pixel and its corresponding location in every other possible image. Different counters are to be initialized to record every comparison resulting in the above three possibilities; i.e., being part of the ground plane, $\Sigma_{grd}$; being part of the obstacle, $\Sigma_{obs}$; being outside range, $\Sigma_{out}$, in addition to the total number of comparisons, $\Sigma_{all}$. The outcome can be summarized in Table 1. Hence, an approximation of the silhouette for each obstacle can be obtained on each image plane.

## Voxel Occupancy Determination

At this point, each bounding box is split into voxels, which are then projected onto image planes. If the voxel projection is not part of the silhouette in a number of images $\geq t_{nS}$ (where $t_{nS}$ is a threshold) then this voxel is not occupied. Otherwise, there is a good chance that this voxel is a part of the obstacle and hence we perform a color consistency test through interpolation. This is done by checking if the color of the pixel is consistent in $t_{nI}$ or more images where $t_{nI}$ is a threshold. (Checking color consistency is controlled by a threshold $t_I$.) If a voxel is occupied, a binary flag must be set to indicate occupancy. The color of the voxel is the average intensity of all its projections. Notice that the thresholds $t_{nI}$ and $t_{nS}$ are different. This is due to the fact that the projection of a voxel could be part of the silhouette while it is vacant. This

*Table 1. Possible cases to decide if a pixel is a part of the ground plane or obstacle. $\Sigma_{grd}$ is being part of the ground plane. $\Sigma_{obs}$ is being part of the obstacle. $\Sigma_{out}$ is being outside range. $\Sigma_{all}$ is the total counter. In our application, we added cases "1" and "4" to the ground plane.*

| # | Case | Interpretation |
|---|------|----------------|
| 1 | $\Sigma_{out} = \Sigma_{all}$ | No info |
| 2 | $\Sigma_{obs} = \Sigma_{all}$ | Obstacle |
| 3 | $\Sigma_{obs} > \Sigma_{grd}$ | Obstacle |
| 4 | $\Sigma_{obs} = \Sigma_{grd}$ | Obstacle or Ground |
| 5 | $\Sigma_{obs} < \Sigma_{grd}$ | Ground |
| 6 | $\Sigma_{grd} = \Sigma_{all}$ | Ground |

happens when the projection of another occupied voxel coincides with that of the vacant one. In this case, the color consistency test mentioned above and the threshold $t_{nI}$ will have the impact rather than the threshold $t_{nS}$.

## Hidden Voxel Determination

There are two points pertinent to hidden or occluded voxel determination issue. The first point is that some voxels may be occluded all the time. This happens when the six sides of the voxel are occupied by other voxels. If so, and in order to avoid further calculation with this voxel, another binary flag is set to exclude this voxel from further consideration.

The second point is that sometimes, some voxels may be hidden behind others. In other words, voxel $\dot{\mathbf{V}}_m$ may be occluded by another voxel $\dot{\mathbf{V}}_n$ for some virtual camera viewpoint, $\dot{\mathbf{C}}$. In this case, we check if:

$$\left\| \dot{\mathbf{V}}_m - \dot{\mathbf{C}} \right\| < \left\| \dot{\mathbf{V}}_n - \dot{\mathbf{C}} \right\| \tag{20}$$

where $\dot{\mathbf{V}}_m$ and $\dot{\mathbf{V}}_n$ are the centers of the voxels in space; and $\dot{\mathbf{C}}$ is the virtual optical center. If (20) results in a true condition, then the intensity of the pixel is supplied from the voxel $\dot{\mathbf{V}}_m$; otherwise, the voxel $\dot{\mathbf{V}}_n$ is used instead.

## Parameters and Thresholds

In order to extract silhouettes, the threshold $t_S$ is used, which measures SAD correlation utilized to extract silhouettes. Assume that the correlation window side is $N+1$ pixels, then the legitimate range for the threshold $t_S$ resides in the interval $[0, 255(N+1)^2]$ with 0 represents the perfect case and $255(N+1)^2$ represents the worst case.

At the voxelization step, more parameters and thresholds are used. These are $\varepsilon$, $t_{nS}$, $t_I$ and $t_{nI}$. The parameter $\varepsilon$ determines the size of a voxel. In other words, it determines the resolution at which a bounding box may split and the number of the resulting voxels. Selecting too low value for $\varepsilon$ will certainly increase the accuracy of the voxelization; however, this comes with the cost of more space to be utilized and more execution time to be consumed. The value of $\varepsilon$ may get affected by some factors. For example, if the resolution of the resulting synthesized image is too high, one may have to lower the value of this parameter to increase accuracy. Other values; e.g., the focal length of the virtual camera, may have a similar role affecting the choice of the parameter $\varepsilon$.

Another threshold used with the color consistency test at the voxelization step is $t_I$. This test checks how close two voxels are in terms of intensity or color. Thus, the range of this threshold can be represented by the interval $[0, 255]$ with 0 represents identical intensities and 255 represents the maximum difference possible. In our experiments, we found that setting this threshold around 50 to 60 would result in a good outcome.

Two more thresholds used at the voxelization step are $t_{nS}$ and $t_{nI}$. The threshold $t_{nS}$ restricts the maximum number of images allowed for the projection of a voxel to deviate from the silhouette if the voxel is considered occupied. The threshold $t_{nl}$ determines the minimum number of images where the color or intensity is consistent for a given voxel. It is obvious that the maximum number of images available represents the upper limit for the last two thresholds. However, the ideal value for each of these thresholds differs according to the poses of the cameras. In addition to the above-mentioned parameters, window size $(N+1)^2$ and virtual camera parameters should be determined.

## Experimental Results

Extracting silhouettes is shown in Figure 18 for one image. The corners of the bounding box were projected onto the image and the convex hull was determined as shown in Figure 18(b). A binary image showing all points that lie inside the convex hull of the bounding box projected onto the image is shown in Figure 18(c) while Figure 18(d) shows a gray-scale version of the silhouette where the brighter the pixel the closer it gets to be an obstacle point. The silhouette of the obstacle as a binary version is shown in Figure 18(e). In order to show the accuracy of this step, we used the obtained silhouette to extract the object as shown in Figure 18(f). Finally, volumetric representation results; as bounding boxes and as voxels are shown in Figure 19 and Figure 20.

## DISCUSSION

As our system consists of a series of steps, we will analyze the complexity of each of these steps.

1. **Representing the ground plane:** Obviously, it takes constant time; i.e., $O(1)$, to turn the virtual camera parameters into the planar perspective matrix to display the ground surface in the resulting synthesized image.

2. **Junction detection:** If the number of pixels in the input image is $N_p$ and every pixel is processed to determine if a junction is present at that location, then the time consumed by this junction detection step is linear. In other words, the cost of this step is $O(N_p)$.

3. **Ground feature matching:** Junctions detected in two images form two disjoint sets that contribute to a bipartite graph. At the ground feature matching step, a link is sought between two candidates; each from a different set. If the number of junctions in the left image is $N_l$ and the number of junctions in the right image is $N_r$, then the time spent by this step is $O(N_l N_r)$ taking into consideration that a number of operations is required to be performed for each pair of candidates.

4. **Matching on arbitrary planes:** Matching on arbitrary planes has the same time complexity as the previous step; i.e., $O(N_l N_r)$ taking into consideration the number of operations to be performed for SAD and VNC

5. **Point reconstruction:** At this step, constant time; i.e., $O(1)$, is required to reconstruct a point in space through its projections onto images. If the number of match pairs is $N_m$, then the time consumed by this step is $O(N_m)$.

6. **Point clustering:** The cost of merging two clusters into a larger one is quadratic since all points in one cluster are checked against all points in the other cluster. Suppose that the number of points in clusters $C_1$ and $C_2$ are $N_{C1}$ and $N_{C2}$, then the time cost will be $O(N_{C1} N_{C2})$ taking into account that several clusters may be present at each level of the hierarchical structure.

7. **Volumetric representation:** For the silhouette extraction phase, if the number of images is $N_i$ and the number of pixels to be processed is $N_p$, then the time required to extract a silhouette is $O(N_p N_i)$ taking into account the number of operations to be per-

*Figure 18. Silhouette extraction. (a) An image shown in Figure 3(e). (b) The convex hull of the bounding box. (c) Points inside the convex hull. (d) A gray-scale version of the silhouette where the brighter the pixel the closer it gets to be an obstacle point. (e) The silhouette of the obstacle as a binary version of (d). (f) The obstacle detected using (e).*

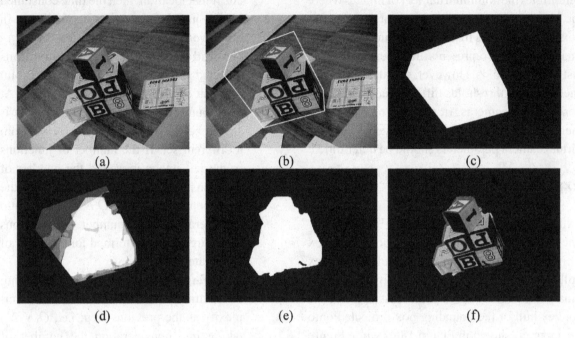

formed for correlation. For the voxelization phase, if the number of images is $N_i$ and the number of voxels is $N_v$, then the time required to process all voxels is $O(N_i N_v)$.

It is evident from the complexity analysis that the steps with quadratic time complexity are the dominating factors; i.e., those that require the largest amount of processing. However, one should notice that inputs to different steps are quite diverse. While the inputs to the junction detection step are pixels of input images and the inputs to the matching step are sets of junctions and pairs of images, the inputs to the point reconstruction step are locations of junctions and for the point clustering step is a set of 3D points. Finally, the inputs to the voxelization step are a group of images in addition to bounding boxes; i.e., a variable number of voxels. Thus, the amount of time consumed by every step depends not only on the complexity but on the type of inputs as well. For

example, although the complexity to merge two clusters is quadratic, all clusters together can be processed in real time in most cases since usually the number of points is not large at this step. Also, while the time complexity of Step 2 is linear, this operation can be performed in real time as we work on two binary images, which reduce the time spent considerably. Moreover, although the complexities of Step 3 and Step 4 are the same, the time consumed by Step 3 is expected to be more than that of Step 4 since at Step 3, all junctions are to be processed while only a selected set of the junctions is processed in Step 4.

The rest of this section is dedicated to discuss more points in more details.

## Binary, Gray-Scale, and Color Images

Binary versions of the edge maps are used at the junction detection stage to accelerate the process.

*Figure 19. (a) A part of the top view of the scene shown in Figure 2. (b) The obstacle represented as a bounding box. (c) through (f) The reconstructed object represented as voxels from different viewpoints and orientations.*

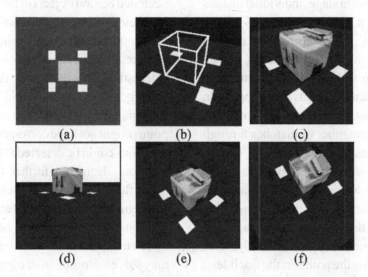

*Figure 20. (a) A part of the top view generated for the scene shown in Figure 3. (b) The obstacle represented as a bounding box. (c) through (f) The reconstructed object represented as voxels from different viewpoints.*

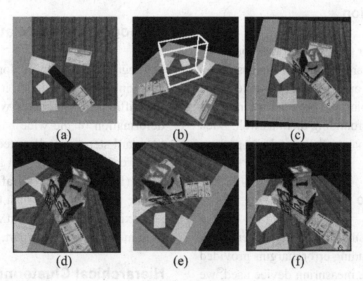

In order to perform matching, gray-scale as well as color images are used to collect information from the intensity and color channel values. Color channels may be used in the wide baseline matching phase that often produce better match set comparing to using the gray-scale versions of the images. However, the following stage; i.e., clustering, may not be affected if gray-scale or color images are used as the information inferred from the images are irrelevant in this case. Color images play a major and key role at the voxel occupancy determination stage.

## Number of Images

At the junction detection stage, individual images are to be operated on separately. Pairs of images are used at the homographic correlation stage to detect both ground and obstacle matches. Notice that, because of the wide baseline constraint, a small number of feature points may appear in more than two views. One of our concerns was to obtain the largest number of matches through the minimum processing time we could. Thus, a minimum number of images are used to match features in order to obtain the largest match set to be used for reconstruction. Considering this fact, pairs -- rather than triplets -- of images are considered at the matching phase. Finally, after this stage and locating the points in the Euclidean 3D space, all available images are exploited in order to achieve a good volumetric representation for a given obstacle.

## Feature Detection

Any corner detector provides information about the locations of interest points in images; however, the JUDOCA operator not only detects the locations of such points but provides information about the edges surrounding them as well. Such rich information makes the matching process much easier.

## Ground Feature Detection

Through the approximate camera parameters along with their corresponding error margins provided by the sensor or the measuring device used, we can remove most of the possible matches that belong to the ground plane. Although at this stage, it is not our primary goal to detect match points on the ground plane, the existence of such a step relieves some pressure off the next step; i.e., the matching step. Few of the ground features may leak to the next step. There are some reasons why

this step may not detect all ground features. One reason is that some of the real matches might be occluded behind objects in the other image or having their correspondences outside the boundaries of the other image. Also, the inaccuracy in camera parameters reflects on the homography matrix calculation. This may cause the correlation value to trigger the given threshold and hence abandon right matches. Another reason is that some feature points might not have correspondences because no junctions could be detected at their corresponding locations. Hence, a further RANSAC phase is used afterwards to update the homography matrix and remove other ground feature points that do not constitute match pairs. Moreover, using the updated versions of the homography matrices may solve the problem of triggering the threshold due to the inaccuracy in camera parameters. In our experiments, we found that enlarging the correlation window at this stage as well as applying conservative thresholds may enhance the results.

## Homographic Correlation

Homographic transformation is utilized before performing the correlation in order to overcome the difficulty that comes with the perspective deformation of the wide baseline stereo setup. Standard stereo matching techniques would fail in our case. Scale-invariant feature transform or SIFT (Lowe, 1999) with affine transformation can be used; however, such transformation may approximate the process but won't be as accurate as homographic counterpart.

## Hierarchical Clustering

The concept of irregular pyramids, used usually on images, is used in a different way on a set of space points. Clustering of space points is done hierarchically according to a proximity criterion. This results in more global information pertinent to each obstacle separately. Hence, this stage may be used to localize obstacles by itself and may be used as a final result for a robot to navigate safely in its environment.

## Voxelization

Note that the error margins of camera parameters may be used with the initial rough estimates of the ground homography matrix to extract the silhouettes by searching for the right match within a specific range. However, extracting silhouettes this way might be expensive in terms of run time. Instead, finding matches that belong to the ground plane and hence applying RANSAC to get an accurate version of a homography matrix before using it to extract silhouettes may save time. Moreover, at this stage, the whole bounding box volume may digitized into voxels and checked for color consistency. However, we find that the silhouette extraction step plays a key role in determining the occupancy of a voxel by assuring whether a voxel is vacant. Finally, experiments show that checking the connectivity of a voxel may considerably save space and hence memory when processing and displaying the final synthesized image.

Notice that one may argue that the images of the vacant voxels within the bounding box of a particular obstacle may correspond to other objects in the environment and not necessarily the ground. However, such a vacant voxel may appear as a part of other obstacles in one or two images but not all of them. This is why we used the thresholds of the voxelization step. For example, the threshold $t_{nl}$ determines the minimum number of images where the color or intensity is consistent for the voxel. If the voxel is vacant, the color will not be consistent to be accepted by the threshold. At the same time, we must note that although such thresholds are used successfully, errors still occur around occupied voxels with regions of flat colors as shown in Figure 20.

## Updating Calculations

RANSAC scheme is used twice in our algorithm; once to update the homography matrices of the ground plane and another time to update the fundamental matrices following the matching process. The enhanced homography matrices are used twice; once to detect the ground features before matching features on obstacles and another time to extract silhouettes. Updated fundamental matrices may also be used twice; once to exclude mismatches that might occur at the matching stage and another time to update the projection matrices for subsequent voxelization and silhouette extraction steps. In our experiments, skipping RANSAC step applied to the match set to get enhanced fundamental matrices may not affect the clustering process as clustering space points may exclude possible mismatches as those mismatches will likely result in isolated 3D points.

## Performance Issues

Execution time varies from one phase to another in our system. Using a Pentium 4 machine running at 1.8 GHz, we measured 1.01 and 0.93 seconds to detect 322 and 301 junctions for the pair shown in Figure 3(e) and 3(f) where both images are of size 640×480 pixels. 32.50 seconds were consumed to detect ground feature matches between the same pair of images. Processing with the updated homography matrix consumes 15.66 seconds. Furthermore, homographic VNC correlation takes 4.25 seconds to execute both directions as opposed to 1.61 seconds for the homographic SAD to execute both directions. Execution time for clustering the output of 2 pairs; that is 23 points, is 0.38 seconds.

Of course, at the voxelization stage, the resolution plays a key role resulting in different number of voxels and hence affects the execution time. In the same example, using size of 1 mm for a voxel side length results in 947376 voxels, which takes 59.62 seconds to detect all surface voxels.

The most expensive step in voxelization is the silhouette extraction stage. Again, depending on the area of the projected bounding box onto the image, the execution time for silhouette extraction may vary significantly. For example, the execution time for the image shown in Figure 3(e) is 838.39 seconds. Unlike the previous steps, the correlation here is applied to all pixels, which results in extended execution time.

## Training

Our algorithm does not require any training data as compared to other approaches; e.g., Saxena *et al.* (2007) use Markov Random Fields (MRF), trained via supervised learning, to infer a set of plane parameters.

## Limitations

The algorithm is a multi-stage technique where steps depend on their predecessors. For example, a junction may not be detected at the start due to different reasons (e.g., occlusion, noise, etc.). Consequently, the matching step will be affected as well as the outcome of the point reconstruction step and so on.

## CONCLUSION

This chapter presented the different steps proposed to perform scene modeling through wide baseline set of images. The assumptions are that the ground is planar and the camera parameters are known approximately. Due to the existence of perspective deformation among corresponding points in the case of wide baseline pairs of images, measures of invariance are needed to overcome this difficulty. We proposed to use homographic transformation to achieve good outcome. This is used to determine points that belong to the obstacles rather than to the ground plane and hence to perform homographic correlation among them to obtain a

match set. The match set is used to obtain a set of 3D points, which is clustered to obtain bounding boxes containing obstacles. Finally, a voxelization scheme is applied to determine a volumetric representation for each obstacle.

## REFERENCES

Ayache, N., & Faugeras, O. D. (1987). Building a consistent 3D representation of a mobile robot environment by combining multiple stereo views. In *International Joint Conference on Artificial Intelligence* (pp. 808-810).

Ayache, N., & Faverjon, B. (1987). Efficient registration of stereo images by matching graph descriptions of edge segments. *International Journal of Computer Vision*, *1*(2), 107–131. doi:10.1007/BF00123161

Ayache, N., & Lustman, F. (1987). Trinocular stereovision: Recent results. In *International Joint Conference on Artificial Intelligence* (pp. 826-828).

Beardsley, P. A., Zisserman, A., & Murray, D. W. (1997). Sequential updating of projective and affine structure from motion. *International Journal of Computer Vision*, *23*(3), 235–259. doi:10.1023/A:1007923216416

Bertozzi, M., Broggi, A., & Fascioli, A. (1996). A stereo vision system for real-time automotive obstacle detection. In *IEEE International Conference on Image Processing: Vol. II.* (pp. 681-684).

Chien, C. H., & Aggarwel, J. K. (1986). Identification of 3D Objects from multiple silhouettes using quadtrees/octrees. *Computer Vision Graphics and Image Processing*, *36*(2), 256–273. doi:10.1016/0734-189X(86)90078-2

Cross, G., & Zisserman, A. (2000). Surface reconstruction from multiple views using apparent contours and surface texture. In A. Leonardis, F. Solina, & R. Bajcsy (Eds.), *NATO Advanced Research Workshop on Confluence of Computer Vision and Computer Graphics* (pp. 25-47). Ljubljana, Slovenia.

Dyer, C. R. (2001). Volumetric scene reconstruction from multiple views. In Davis, L. S. (Ed.), *Foundations of image understanding* (pp. 469–489). Boston, MA: Kluwer. doi:10.1007/978-1-4615-1529-6_16

Elias, R. (2003). Clustering points in *n*D space through hierarchical structures. In *IEEE Canadian Conference on Electrical and Computer Engineering: Vol. 3* (pp. 2079-2081).

Elias, R. (2004). Wide baseline matching through homographic transformation. In *International Conference on Pattern Recognition: Vol. IV* (pp. 130-133).

Elias, R. (2007). Enhancing accuracy of camera rotation angles detected by inaccurate sensors and expressing them in different systems for wide baseline stereo. In *International Conference on Quality Control by Artificial Vision: Vol. 6356* (pp. 17:1-8). Le Creusot, France.

Elias, R. (2007). Sparse view stereo matching. *Pattern Recognition Letters, 28*(13), 1667–1678. doi:10.1016/j.patrec.2007.04.009

Elias, R., & Laganiere, R. (1999). The disparity pyramid: An irregular pyramid approach for stereoscopic image analysis. In *Vision Interface Conference* (pp. 352-359).

Elias, R., & Laganiere, R. (2003). *The planar perspective matrix: Derivation through different rotation systems*. Technical Report TR-2003-02, VIVA Lab, School of Information Technology and Engineering, University of Ottawa. Ottawa, Ontario, Canada.

Granger-Piche, M., Epstein, E., & Poulin, P. (2004). Interactive hierarchical space carving with projector-based calibrations. In *Vision, Modeling, and Visualization Conference* (pp. 159-166).

Hartley, R. I., & Zisserman, A. (2006). *Multiple view geometry in computer vision*. Cambridge University Press.

Hoffmann, J., Jungel, M., & Lotzsch, M. (2005). Vision based system for goal-directed obstacle avoidance. In *LNCS, RoboCup 2004: Robot Soccer World Cup VIII: Vol. 3276* (pp. 418-425). Springer.

Jolion, J. M., & Montavert, A. (1991). The adaptive pyramid: A framework for 2D image analysis. *CVGIP: Image Understanding, 55*(3), 339–348. doi:10.1016/1049-9660(92)90031-W

Kim, Y., & Kim, H. (2004). Layered ground floor detection for vision-based mobile robot navigation. In *International Conference on Robotics and Automation: Vol. 1* (pp. 13-18).

Koch, R. (1995). 3D surface reconstruction from stereoscopic image sequences. In *International Conference Computer Vision* (pp. 109-114).

Laganiere, R., & Elias, R. (2004). The detection of junction features in images. In *International Conference on Acoustics, Speech, and Signal Processing: Vol. III* (pp. 573-576).

Lowe, D. G. (1999). Object recognition from local scale-invariant features. In *International Conference on Computer Vision: Vol. 2* (pp. 1150–1157).

Mandelbaum, R., McDowell, L., Bogoni, L., Beich, B., & Hansen, M. (1998). Real-time stereo processing, obstacle detection, and terrain estimation from vehicle-mounted stereo cameras. In *Workshop on Applications of Computer Vision* (pp. 288-289).

Matsumoto, Y., Terasaki, H., Sugimoto, K., & Arakawa, T. (1997). A portable three-dimensional digitizer. In *International Conference on Recent Advances in 3-D Digital Imaging and Modeling* (pp. 197-204).

Niem, W., & Wingbermuhle, J. (1997). Automatic reconstruction of 3D objects using mobile monoscopic camera. In *International Conference on Recent Advances in 3-D Digital Imaging and Modeling* (pp. 173-180).

Roth, G., & Whitehead, A. (2000). Using projective vision to find camera positions in an image sequence. In *Vision Interface Conference* (pp. 255-232).

Sabe, K., Fukuchi, M., Gutmann, J.-S., Ohashi, T., Kawamoto, K., & Yoshigahara, T. (2004). Obstacle avoidance and path planning for humanoid robots using stereo vision. In *International Conference on Robotics and Automation: Vol. 1* (pp. 592-597).

Saxena, A., Sun, M., & Ng, A. Y. (2007) Learning 3-D scene structure from a single still image. In *ICCV Workshop on 3D Representation for Recognition.* (pp. 1-8).

Sedgewick, R. (1988). *Algorithms*. Addison-Wesley.

Snavely, N., Seitz, S. M., & Szeliski, R. (2006). Photo tourism: Exploring photo collections in 3D. In *SIGGRAPH Conference* (pp. 835-846).

Snavely, N., Seitz, S. M., & Szeliski, R. (2008). Modeling the world from (Internet) photo collections. *International Journal of Computer Vision*, *80*(2), 189–210. doi:10.1007/s11263-007-0107-3

Szeliski, R. (1993). Rapid octree construction from image sequences. *CVGIP: Image Understanding*, *58*(1), 23–32. doi:10.1006/ciun.1993.1029

Vincent, E., & Laganiere, R. (2001). Detecting planar homographies in an image pair. In *International Symposium on Image and Signal Processing and Analysis* (pp. 182-187).

Zhou, J., & Li, B. (2006). Robust ground plane detection with normalized homography in monocular sequences from a robot platform. In *International Conference on Image Processing* (pp. 3017-3020).

## ADDITIONAL READING

Baker, H. H., & Binford, T. O. (1981). Depth from edge and intensity based stereo. In *International Joint Conference on Artificial Intelligence* (pp. 631-636).

Chiang, K. K., & Chan, K. L. (2006). Volumetric model reconstruction from unrestricted camera views based on the photo-consistency of 3D voxel mask. *Machine Vision and Applications*, *17*(4), 229–250. doi:10.1007/s00138-006-0034-2

Faugeras, O., & Keriven, R. (1998). Complete dense stereovision using level set methods. In *European Conference on Computer Vision: Vol. 1* (pp. 379-393).

Giblin, P., & Weiss, R. (1987). Reconstruction of surfaces from profiles. In *International Conference Computer Vision* (pp. 136-144).

Hornung, A., & Kobbelt, L. (2006). Robust and efficient photo-consistency estimation for volumetric 3D reconstruction. In *LNCS, European Conference on Computer Vision: Vol. 3952* (pp. 179-190).

Kutulakos, K., & Seitz, S. (1999). A theory of shape by space carving. In *International Conference on Computer Vision: Vol. 1* (pp. 307-314).

Liu, X., Yao, H., & Gao, W. (2007). Shape from silhouette outlines using an adaptive dandelion model. *Computer Vision and Image Understanding*, *105*(2), 121–130. doi:10.1016/j.cviu.2006.09.003

Martin, W. N., & Affarwal, J. K. (1983). Volumetric description of objects from multiple views. *IEEE Transactions on Pattern Analysis and Machine Intelligence, 5*(2), 150–158. doi:10.1109/TPAMI.1983.4767367

Michels, J., Saxena, A., & Ng, A. Y. (2005). High speed obstacle avoidance using monocular vision and reinforcement learning. In *International Conference on Machine Learning* (pp. 593- 600).

Saxena, A., Chung, S. H., & Ng, A. Y. (2005). Learning depth from single monocular images. In *Neural Information Processing Systems, 18*.

Saxena, A., Chung, S. H., & Ng, A. Y. (2008). 3-D depth reconstruction from a single still image. *International Journal of Computer Vision, 76*(1), 53–69. doi:10.1007/s11263-007-0071-y

Saxena, A., Schulte, J., & Ng, A. Y. (2007). Depth estimation using monocular and stereo cues. In *International Joint Conferences on Artificial Intelligence* (pp. 2197-2203).

Saxena, A., Sun, M., & Ng, A. Y. (2007). Learning 3-D scene structure from a single still image. In *ICCV workshop on 3D Representation for Recognition* (pp. 1-8).

Seitz, S. M., & Dyer, C. R. (1997). Photorealistic scene reconstruction by voxel coloring. In *International Conference on Computer Vision and Pattern Recognition* (pp. 1067-1073).

Zheng, J. Y., & Kishino, F. (1992). 3D models from contours: Further identification of unexposed areas. In *International Conference Pattern Recognition* (pp. 349-353).

Ziegler, R., Matusik, W., Pfister, H., & McMillan, L. (2003). 3D reconstruction using labeled image regions. In *Eurographics Symposium on Geometry Processing* (pp. 1–12)

## KEY TERMS AND DEFINITIONS

**3D Modeling (3D Reconstruction):** Building 3D models.

**Baseline:** The distance between two cameras observing the same scene.

**Correlation:** Techniques used to find corresponding points.

**Homographic Transformation:** The process by which a homography matrix is used for transformation.

**Homography Matrix:** A $3 \times 3$ transformation matrix relating the perspective projections of a plane.

**Point Clustering:** The process by which points are classified into groups.

**Point Matching (or Point Correspondences):** Finding image points that correspond to the same 3D point in space.

**Stereo Views:** Pairs of images taken for the same scene.

**Voxel:** Volume element.

**Voxelization:** The process that splits the space into voxels.

**Wide Baseline (Sparse View) Matching:** Point matching problem when cameras are widely separated.

**Wide Baseline:** The distance between cameras is wide with respect to the observed scene.

**Widely-Separated Stereo Views:** Wide baseline stereo images.

# Chapter 13
# Complementary Part Detection and Reassembly of 3D Fragments

**Vandana Dixit Kaushik**
*Harcourt Butler Technological Institute, India*

**Phalguni Gupta**
*Indian Institute of Technology Kanpur, India*

## ABSTRACT

*This chapter presents an algorithm for identifying complementary site of objects broken into two parts. For a given 3D scanned image of broken objects, the algorithm identifies the rough sites of the broken object, transforms the object to a suitable alignment, registers it with its complementary part which belongs to the same object, and finds the local correspondence among the fragmented parts. The presented algorithm uses multiple granularity descriptors and edge extraction to detect the exact location of multiple cleavage sites in the object. It greatly reduces the amount of information to be matched and also helps in identification of the parts; as a result it reduces the computational time in the processing. It is also applicable to all triangulated surface data even in the presence of noise.*

## INTRODUCTION

Recent advances in the field of computer vision, image processing and pattern recognition have led to substantial research in object identification and feature extraction from 2D images for different applications. In order to design efficient methods for solving problems in the field of 2D image processing, it is essential to have the good quality of image which is dependent on the image acquisition system and the environment. Generally, 2D methods are found to be efficient under controlled environment where the input images are acquired in almost fixed orientation, distance, camera calibration, illumination, fixed atmospheric condition etc. However, in reality it

DOI: 10.4018/978-1-4666-0113-0.ch013

is expected that the acquired images which are to be processed do not possess good quality and fixed environment. Further, information available in 2D images may not be sufficient to generate needful result for a given application. This has motivated people to explore the possibility of analyzing 3D images. The most obvious difference between a 3D image and a 2D image of a particular object is its depth information. The 2D image provides only monocular depth information while a 3D image consists of both monocular and binocular depth information. This binocular depth information should also be considered for the study on images. Moreover, a 2D image is very sensitive to changes due to illumination or lighting conditions and change in orientation of image being captured. Since any 3D image considers the overall geometry of the image being captured, therefore, it is insensitive to the above mentioned changes. However, there are many challenges associated with 3D images; out of which handling large volume of data, high computational cost to process these data, inconvenient 3D acquisition systems and the digital archiving of 3D image data (Terry, 1995) are most important. There exists a large number of 3D scanners (Boehler, & Marbs, 2002) that can be used to scan any type of objects - from a small-sized object to a life-sized artifact (Levoy, 2000). Features are extracted from this scanned data for further processing.

This chapter deals with the problem of detecting the complementary part and to reassemble the broken 3D fragments. It has many applications in the fields like archeology where multiple broken fragments are obtained from the sites and parts belonging to the same object are to be identified. Along with this, automatic reassembly is required in art restoration, forensics, computer-aided design, chemistry, medicine etc. (Barequet, & Sharir, 1997). Generally, the reconstruction of arbitrary objects from their fragments may have many constraints. Some of these are mentioned below.

- Arbitrary shapes of parts (fragments)
- Unknown shape and number of the final objects
- Arbitrary number of fractured faces per fragment
- Missing fragments
- Probably flawed or weathered surfaces
- Non-existence of strict assemblage rules

Solutions to any assembly problem should be able to handle above mentioned challenges. The problem considered in this chapter can be formally defined as follows: Consider a 3D image consisting of multiple objects scanned using a 3D laser scanner and each object is broken into two pieces. The problem is to detect the complement of a broken part of a given object. Detection of complementary parts in the multiple broken objects is an important phase during the reassembly. Here, the rough site/ cleavage site in any fragment is identified and then an attempt is made to detect its complementary rough site in the other fragment. The detected complementary parts are aligned for reassembly. For example Figure 1 shows the multiple broken fragments. Fragment A and A' belong to one object. This chapter presents an algorithm for the detection of A and A' which are the complementary parts of same object. The result of detection is shown in Figure 2 (a) and (b) respectively.

## BACKGROUND

There have been lot of studies in the area of reassembly and reconstruction of broken 3D objects due to advances in the field of 3D scanners and 3D imaging devices. In the last decade there have been significant technological advances in the design of tools for digitizing and modeling 3D shape of objects. Modeling of 3D shapes also includes regeneration and reassembly of broken objects. Given multiple pieces of some 3D scanned

*Figure 1. Multiple broken fragments*

A

A'

*Figure 2. (a) Fragment A (b) Fragment A' [Complementary of A]*

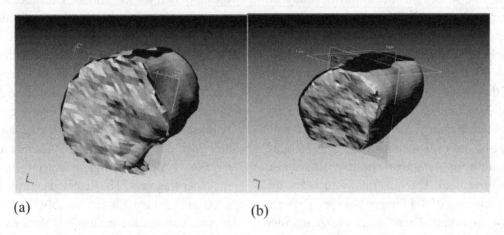

(a)                                        (b)

objects, the problem considered in this chapter is to detect all complementary parts of each broken object and to reassemble these detected parts. In order to identify and reassemble the complementary parts, it considers the property of broken fragments which leave the cleavage site rougher as compared to remaining surface and based on this property, the rough site of each broken fragment is determined.

The work described here is mainly based on an efficient surface inspection algorithm for cleavage/rough site detection in broken 3D objects. The algorithm captures differences in the geometric structure in different parts of the 3D object represented by polygon meshes. Most of the work in the field of roughness analysis of 3D meshes has been done in context of visualization, finding

surface defects to assess the visual quality of watermarked 3D objects. Rogowitz & Rushmeier have proposed the perceptual metric which is based on the estimation of roughness of the surface of the watermarked 3D objects (Rogowitz, & Rushmeier, 2001). Perceptual considerations have been used in Computer Graphics for various operations such as mesh simplification (Bolin, & Meyer, 1998, Lindstrom, & Turk, 2000, Nicolas, et. al. 2002, Scopigno, et. al., 1998, Williams, et. al., 2003) and perceptually guided rendering. Mesh simplification aims at reducing the number of vertices of a polygonal mesh model while preserving as much as possible its visual appearance. In general, the simplification process is driven by a similarity metric that measures the impact of changes of the model after each simplification step. Hausdorff distance is often used as a metric to evaluate the distortions due to mesh simplification. Nicolas et. al. have proposed two tools for geometric mesh comparison (Nicolas, et. al. 2002). This chapter takes triangular meshes representing the surfaces in terms of triangles [known as facets] as inputs and determines all rough facets [obtained through some threshold value] which form the cleavage site of the fragment. This cleavage site is used to detect the complementary part of a given broken object. The meshes representing surfaces at different levels are shown in Figure 3(a-d)

Wu, et. al. have obtained the roughness of a single facet using a dihedral angle based approach (Wu, et. al., 2001). In this work, some conclusion can be drawn on cleavage sites on the surfaces by assigning a roughness level to each facet. This metric does not take into account the scale of roughness. In other words, The proposed metric measures 'bumpiness' of a surface with granularity close to the size of single facet and this is one major drawback of this metric. Corsini et. al. have proposed a new metric which takes into account multi-scale roughness along with the roughness at single facet level (Corsini, Gelasca, Ebrahimi,

*Figure 3. Meshes at different levels*

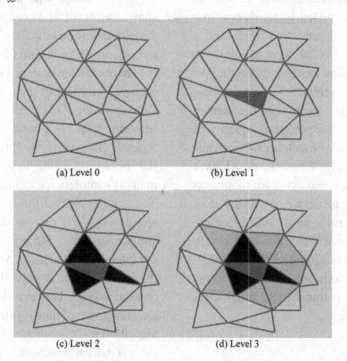

(a) Level 0      (b) Level 1

(c) Level 2      (d) Level 3

*Figure 4. Roughness at various levels of granularity*

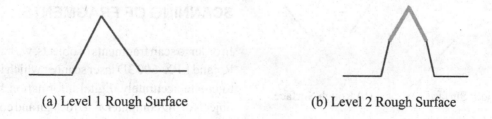

(a) Level 1 Rough Surface      (b) Level 2 Rough Surface

2005). Multi-scale roughness refers to bump size in a rough surface. For example, bumps or grains in a brick are larger than those in a ceramic material. Figure 4 illustrates the rough surfaces at various levels of granularity.

Generally, roughness of a facet can be obtained as a function of the dihedral angles made with neighboring facets, variation of these dihedral angles and the area of facets under consideration. In order to obtain the roughness of a facet, the above said metric only considers the area of facet whose roughness is being calculated and not the area of neighboring facets. It does not take into account the direction of neighbouring facets which is very important as this may lead to wrong detection of smooth surface as rough surface. In order to explain it more clearly, let us consider Figure 5 representing a smooth surface and a rough surface. Corsini et. al. have ignored the direction of neighbouring facets to determine the roughness value and it provides same roughness value for both the cases. Since both the metrics discussed above focus on perceptual quality of 3D meshes, they may not be suitable for cleavage site detection. However, Kaushik, et. al have proposed a metric which makes uses of roughness detection at single facet level along with different granularity levels (Kaushik, et. al., 2007). Further, it also takes into account the direction of neighbouring facets thereby assigning a different roughness values to a smooth surface and a rough surface. Therefore, it is found to be suitable for cleavage site detection.

*Figure 5. Different surfaces*

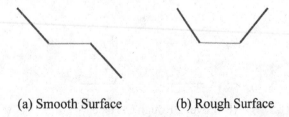

(a) Smooth Surface     (b) Rough Surface

The detected cleavage sites in 3D fragments help to reassemble 3D broken objects. This chapter first determines cleavage site or sites in broken 3D scanned fragments, and then identifies complementary parts in two broken objects at the cleaved sites which reduce the area to be matched considerably and finally proposes a new process to register these complementary parts for reassembly. It can be noted here that registration plays an important role in 3D model acquisition, object recognition, and geometry processing. For the two sets of points representing two scanned fragments, the registration process tries to find suitable transformation composed of a rotation matrix and a translation vector that aligns a scanned fragment to get best match with another one. Figure 6(a) shows two sets P and Q of points. After applying the registration process the set P of points is aligned to Q as shown in Figure 6(b).

There exist several well known algorithms for registration. Most of them are based on Iterative Closest Points [ICP] (Besl, & McKay, 1992). Masuda, & Yokoya have used Least Median of Squares (Rogowitz, & Rushmeier 2001) in the ICP based algorithm to overcome the original method's intolerance to outlier data (Masuda, & Yokoya, 1995). Even though the above algorithms along with ICP can work for registration of similar surfaces, but they may not work for complementary surfaces. Another drawback with the ICP is that it is very slow to determine the correspondence between two sets of points and may not give real time results. Also, the ICP based algorithm involves processing of all the points in the set which makes the processing time extremely high.

## SCANNING OF FRAGMENTS

In order to scan fragments of objects, we have used Roland LPX-600 3D laser scanner which is found to create accurately digital information from an object for 3D computer aided design and computer

*Figure 6. Registration process*

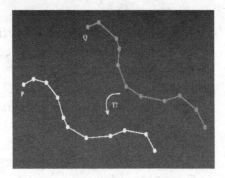 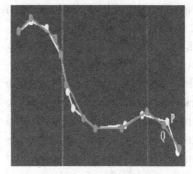

(a)  Sets P and Q of Points          (b)  Set P Aligned to Set Q

graphics applications. Since the scanner can scan the objects having maximum height of 16 inch and diameter of 10 inch, we have selected fragments accordingly. It has a door to insert objects to be scanned to place on a rotating plate. It scans the object and creates a 3D point cloud data. Figure 7 shows the image of the scanner.

## ROUGHNESS DETECTION DESCRIPTOR

An efficient algorithm for detecting the rough site of a broken fragment has been presented. It also considers the direction of the facets properly and therefore the desired rough site is obtained

*Figure 7. Roland LPX-600 3D laser scanner*

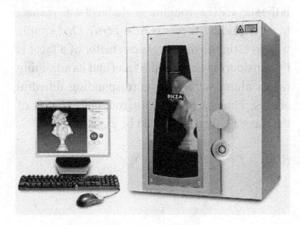

efficiently. The proposed algorithm consists of the following major steps. Firstly, the roughness factor for each facet both at single granularity and multiple granularity level is calculated. Secondly, the facet's final roughness factor is computed which can be defined as the maximum value of roughness factors of the facets at different levels. Then, using a roughness histogram a dynamic roughness threshold is obtained to mark portions of surface as rough. In this process due to the presence of noise, a smooth portion may be incorrectly marked as rough. Therefore, in order to avoid such wrongly detected rough portions from the broken fragment, a roughness consolidation algorithm along with a noise removal algorithm is used. The detailed description to calculate roughness factor at each step is given below.

### Measuring Roughness

Roughness can be defined in terms of dihedral angles (Wu, et. al., 2001), stochastic models (Jafari, 2003, Waechter, et. al., 2004) and fractals (Arrault, Arnéodo, Davis, & Marshak, 1997) which are all based on perceptual quality of a mesh or facet. However, since primary aim of cleavage detection algorithm is to decrease computations, perfect roughness modeling is not required. Keeping this issue in mind, the dihedral angle based approach to determine roughness factor has been modified which is found to be very efficient. Figure 8 shows a cleavage site in a broken object obtained from an archaeological site.

A rough surface is the surface with high concentration of 'bumps' of different sizes (Corsini, Gelasca, Ebrahimi, 2005). It is difficult to define a suitable metric that can help to differentiate between roughness due to natural texture and roughness due to cleavage. Since most fragments obtained from an archeological site are weathered and eroded, it becomes difficult to ascertain whether roughness is due to the natural texture or not. However, there exist fundamental differences in roughness generated through natural texture and roughness due to cleavage. Following are the observations about rough surfaces obtained through experiments.

1.  Composition of materials in the fragment and the effect of external agents in the weathered fragments are the major reasons for natural roughness of a surface. It can be noted that weathering agents have a smoothing effect on surface texture.
2.  Bumps of different sizes follow Gaussian distribution.
3.  In natural unbroken surfaces, over a long measurement range; most of the smaller bumps average out each other while the larger bumps are retained. This is shown in Figure 9.
4.  Natural rough surfaces obey fractal property which is computationally complex and is difficult to use.
5.  In case of a cleaved surface, high roughness both at lower and at higher granularity levels is visible.

## Computation of Roughness of Single Facet

Consider a regular triangular mesh $M$. Let $F$ be the facet or the triangle under consideration. An adjacent/ adjoining facet of $F$ is the facet which shares one edge with the facet $F$ and is shown in Figure 10.

Let $\theta$ be the dihedral angle between two facets $F_i$ and $F_j$. Finding the value of the angle $\theta$ involves inverse trigonometric function which is computationally expensive. However, the value of $\theta$ can be found through the angle function which is given by $(1 - \cos\theta)$. Let $N_{F_i}$ and $N_{F_j}$ be the normals of the facets $F_i$ and $F_j$ respectively. Then $\omega_{ij}$ is given by

$$w_{ij} = 1 - \left( \frac{N_{F_i}.N_{F_j}}{\mid N_{F_i}\mid . \mid N_{F_j}\mid} \right) \qquad (1)$$

The value of the dihedral angle $\omega_{ij}$ is lying between 0 and 1. Smaller the value of $\omega_{ij}$, smoother is the surface (i.e. roughness of a facet with respect to its adjoining facets is near zero). One simple way to estimate the roughness factor of a facet is by considering areas of the facet and its adjoining facets along with their corresponding dihedral angles. Thus, if $R(F_i)$ is the roughness factor of the facet $F_i$, then $R(F_i)$ can be expressed as

$$R(F_i) = f_n\{ \omega_{ij} * ( A_{F_i} ; A_{F_j} )\}$$

*Figure 8. Cleavage site in a broken object (Kaushik, et. al., 2007)*

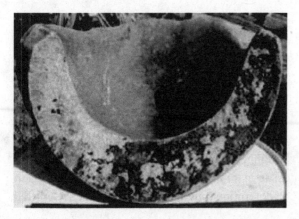

*Figure 9. Example of single and multilevel roughness (Kaushik, et. al., 2007)*

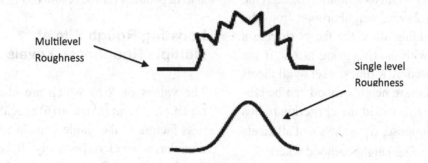

where $A_{F_i}$ is the area of facet $F_i$ under consideration and $A_{F_j}$ is the area of facet $F_j$, $\forall j = 1, 2, 3$.

It may be observed that the value of $\omega_{ij}$ can be very small. Hence, even though there exists a roughness of a facet with respect to its neighbouring facets, but the difference between the roughness factors of a smooth facet and a rough facet may be very small. Thus, to highlight the cleavage site consisting of such type of rough facets, we need to use proper multiplicative factor to upgrade the roughness factor $R(F_i)$.

In this work, we have considered the roughness of facet $F_i$, $R(F_i)$, as the product of $M(F_i)$ and $V(F_i)$ as

$$R(F_i) = M(F_i) * V(F_i) \qquad (2)$$

where $M(F_i)$ and $V(F_i)$, can be computed by

$$M(F_i) = \frac{1}{3} \sum_{F_j \in A(F_i)} (\omega_{ij}) * (A_{F_i} + A_{F_j}) \qquad (3)$$

$$V(F_i) = \sum_{F_j \in A(F_i)} \frac{1}{3} (\omega_{ij}.(A_{F_i} + A_{F_j}) - M(F_i))^2 \qquad (4)$$

It can be observed that value of $R(F_i)$ is not fixed. Thus, to apply a threshold for roughness, there is a need to normalize the value of $R(F_i)$ to the interval [0,1]. This can be done by

$$R'(F_i) = \frac{R(F_i) - \min(R(F_i))}{\max(R(F_i)) - \min(R(F_i))} \qquad (5)$$

## Multi-Granularity Roughness Estimation

Corsini et. al. have defined the rough surface as the surface having high concentration of steep crests and troughs (Corsini, Gelasca, Ebrahimi, 2005). If one considers multi-scale roughness i.e. bump size which is exceeding the dimension of single facet, then the effects of local crest and an adjacent local trough cancel each other by making minimum effect on overall bumpiness of the considered collective facets. Thus, the idea of roughness estimation can be extended from roughness of single facet to $N$ levels of roughness estimation which is known as estimation of multi-granularity roughness.

*Figure 10. Adjoining Facets (Kaushik, et. al., 2007)*

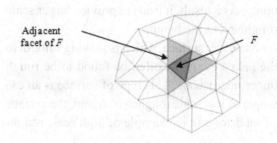

Let a $(N,1)$-ring neighborhood of a facet $F$ comprise of facet $F$ and its adjoining facets. One can create a $(N,2)$-ring neighborhood from the $(N,1)$-ring by adding all of the facets sharing a common edge with the $(N,1)$-ring facets. If the process is repeated by $K$ times, a set of all facets within the $(N,K)$-ring neighborhood can be created. The value $K$ is called the clustering radius of $(N,K)$-ring. Suppose, $S_F^N$ is the set of all facets within the $(N,N)$-ring neighbourhood where $N$ is the radius of $(N,N)$-ring for the facet $F$. Roughness of $(N,N)$-ring or estimation of multi-granularity roughness at level $N$ is given by

$$R^N(F_i) = \frac{1}{|S_F^N|} \sum_{F_i \in S_F^N} (-1)^{1+Z_{ij}} R(F_j) \qquad (6)$$

where $|S_F^N|$ is the number of facets in $(N,N)$-ring and the Boolean variable $Z_{ij}$ indicates whether the facet is downward sloping or upward sloping, i.e.,

$$Z_{ij} = \begin{cases} 1 & \text{if the facet } F_j \text{ is upward sloping with respect to } F_i \\ 0 & \text{if the facet } F_j \text{ is downward sloping with respect to } F_i \end{cases}$$

$Z_{ij}$ can be computed by

$$Z_{ij} = \left\lfloor 1 + \frac{N_{F_i}.(C_{F_j} - C_{F_i})}{|N_{F_i}|.|(C_{F_j} - C_{F_i})|} \right\rfloor \qquad (7)$$

where $\lfloor . \rfloor$ is the floor function, $C_{F_i}$ and $C_{F_j}$ are the centroid of facet $F_i$ and $F_j$ respectively. It can be noted that the complementary (upward and downward sloping) surfaces local bumps, as shown in Figure 11, may cancel each other's effect and this leads to contribute higher scale roughness to the bump. As a result, it leads to provide larger scale roughness to the bump.

Also, any surface, which is looking smooth to the naked eye, may often be found to be rough under microscope. This type of surface is an example of low scale roughness. Again, the surface of sandstone is an example of high scale rough-

ness. However, it can be noted that this scale is also dependent on the resolution of the scanner.

## Locating Rough Site at Multiple Roughness Levels

The values of $R(F)$ which are obtained using Equation (5) and Equation (6) provide the roughness factors of the single granularity and multi-granularity level respectively. It can be noted that the value of $R(F)$ is directly related with the roughness, i.e. more the value of $R(F)$, more is the roughness. Thus the cluster of faces which is having the values of roughness more than roughness threshold can be found in the surface and that can be labeled as rough area. Hence the cleavage site can be determined which is shown in Figure 12.

## Roughness Histogram

These roughness values of all facets can be used to compute its histogram. For a particular roughness granularity, the roughness distribution in that fragment can be seen from the computed histogram. It can be noted that roughness value is always found to be the least at and near the centre position. The roughness threshold $H$ is selected from the roughness level corresponding to this minimum value. A facet is marked as rough if its roughness value is greater than the threshold $H$.

Figure 14 shows the roughness histogram of the object considered in Figure 13. Note that the thick line in the center represents threshold value $H$ which is used to determine the cleavage site. It is shown in the highlighted area of Figure 12.

## Consolidation of Roughness Patches

Due to the presence of noise, some small spurious patches on smooth area can be formed. It is important to remove such type of noise from the cleavage site. Suppose, there are $\Psi$ rough facets in an $(N,K)$-ring having $T$ facets. If the value of $\Psi$ is

*Figure 11. Bumps with different scales (Kaushik, et. al., 2007)*

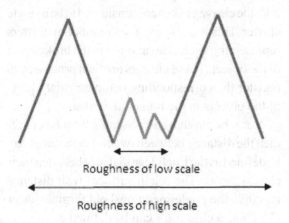

*Figure 12. Roughness values of facets and highlighting cleavage site using threshold as 0.5914 (Kaushik, et. al., 2007)*

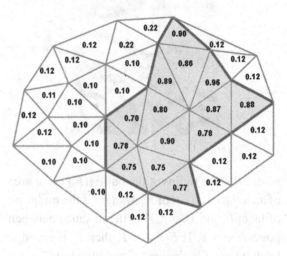

very small then one can assume that all *T* facets in that ring are smooth. In other words, all *T* facets of an *(N,K)*-ring in a fragment are considered to be smooth if for a predefined threshold value *u*, $0<u<1$, it satisfies the following:

$\Psi < T*u.$

Again, it can be observed that for any given threshold value *H* obtained from roughness histogram, the roughness detection algorithm may not produce continuous roughness areas in an *(N,K)*-ring; i.e. some scattered roughness patches, say *Ψ*, can be found in *(N,K)*-ring through this algorithm as shown in Figure 10. A continuous rough area which forms a cleavage site can be obtained by merging these scattered patches. All *T* facets of an *(N,K)*-ring can be marked as rough if for some predefined threshold *v* lying between 0 and 1, it satisfies the following

$\Psi > T*u.$

Based on the above discussion the algorithm for roughness detection of a single facet *F* of a broken surface has been given in Algorithm 1. It can be noted that the time complexity of the

algorithm is *O(n)* where *n* is the number of facets in the cleavage site.

## CLEAVAGE SITE DETECTION

During the detection of the rough surface, the edge facets are also detected as rough because of their higher dihedral angle and angle function. A cleavage site from a rough surface of a given 3D broken object is determined by removing these edge facets. This approach can be used to find all cleavage sites of a 3D broken object.

### Edge Descriptor

A hypothetical ball of *(N,N)*-ring diameter is moved over the entire surface of the object and the number of facets lying within it is used to extract edges. The ball is centered at the midpoint of every facet and the area lying within the ball is used for edge detection. The edge descriptor, $E(F_i)$ for the facet $F_i$ can be defined mathematically as follows

$$E(F_i) = \sum A(F_j) \; \forall j \; \ni \; Dist(Mid(F_j), Mid(F_i)) \; < \; R$$

(8)

*Figure 13. Source surface used to generate Figure 12 (Kaushik, et. al., 2007)*

where $R$ is the radius of the ball, $A(F_j)$ is the area of an adjacent facet of $F_i$, $Mid(F_i)$ is the midpoint of facet $F_i$ and $Dist(X,Y)$ is the distance between point $X$ and $Y$. If $E(F_i) > T$, then $F_i$ is an edge facet where $T$ is the predefined threshold.

The cleavage site is detected by removing all detected edge facets from its corresponding rough surface. Figure 15(a) shows the broken 3D object while Figure 15(b) shows the detected rough surface of applying roughness detection algorithm and Figure 15(c) gives the rough surface after removing its edge facets.

## Clustering

Clustering is used to obtain the multiple cleavage sites (if any) in the broken 3D object. The process of grouping a set of physical or abstract objects into classes of similar objects is called clustering. More clearly, a cluster is a collection of data objects that are similar to each other within the same cluster and are dissimilar to the objects in other clusters. That is, a cluster of data objects can be treated collectively as one group.

Advantages of clustering are that it is adaptable to changes and helps to identify useful features that distinguish different groups. In this case groups are multiple cleavage sites and the feature that distinguishes them is the minimum distance between them. The Euclidean distance among all closest pairs of rough facets is used to determine

the distance between two cleavage sites. If the distance is lying within some predefined threshold, both the cleavage sites are considered to be a single cluster. This process creates a number of clusters representing each cleavage site in the broken part of the object. These clusters are then processed to register the corresponding complementary parts of the objects in the registration phase.

Let $S_i$ be a rough surface and $F_j$ be a facet in $S_i$ then the distance between two rough surfaces can be defined as the Euclidean distance between their closest facets. The rough surfaces with distance less than the predefined threshold form a cluster $C_m$. Thus, a cluster $C_m$ can be defined as

$$C_m = U_{k=0}^n S_k :: \forall S_i \ni S_j \ni Dist(S_i, S_j) < \text{threshold where } 0 \le i,j \le n \qquad (9)$$

These clusters $C_m$ represent different cleavage sites in the broken 3D object. Figure 16(a) shows the broken object with two cleavage site while Figure 16(b) shows the result of clustering on a broken object.

*Figure 14. Roughness histogram (Kaushik, et. al., 2007)*

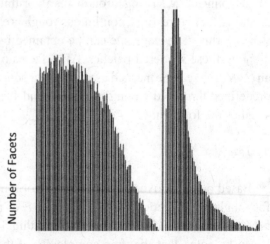

*Algorithm 1. Roughness-Detection (F)*

---

**Step 1:** *Compute the roughness factor at single level R(F) using the formula*

$$R'(F_i) = \frac{R(F_i) - \min(R(F_i))}{\max(R(F_i)) - \min(R(F_i))}$$

*where R(F) is defined in Equation (2)*

**Step 2:** *Compute the roughness factor at multiple levels using the following formula*

$$R^N(F_i) = \frac{1}{|S_F^N|} \sum_{F_i \in S_F^N} (-1)^{1+Z_{ij}} R - (F_j)$$

**Step 3:** *Generate the roughness histogram.*
**Step 4:** *Select threshold roughness value H.*
**Step 5:** *Mark facets having roughness more than computed threshold.*
**Step 6:** *Consolidate all rough patches and remove noise to detect rough surface.*

---

*Figure 15. Detection of cleavage site from broken 3D object*

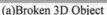

(a)Broken 3D Object      (b)Rough Surface      (c) Detected Cleavage Site

## COMPLEMENTARY PART DETECTION

The complementary part detection problem is to identify parts of $P$ and $Q$ of a given 3D object that represents the same physical part of the scanned object. The correspondence descriptor is used to obtain the complementary parts from multiple broken objects.

Assume that the objects are broken into two parts, $P$ and $Q$, and parts are point-sampled. Let parts $P$ and $Q$ consist of $n$ points $\{p_1, p_2, ....., p_n\}$ and $\{q_1, q_2, ....., q_n\}$ respectively. A pair of points from $P$ and $Q$ is in correspondence by assigning to $p_i$ a corresponding point $q_i$. This descriptor, termed as correspondence descriptor, is the mean of the Euclidean distances of facets from the center of the cleavage site which is given by

*Figure 16. Detected cleavage sites after clustering*

(a) Broken Object      (b) Cleavage Sites Detection

*Figure 17. Initial orientation of fragments*

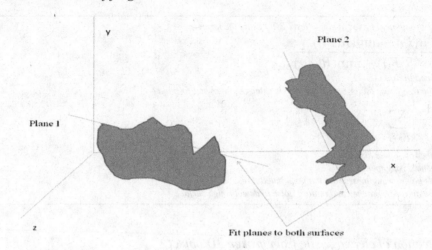

*Figure 18. Two cleavage sites in common orientation with respect to ZX-plane*

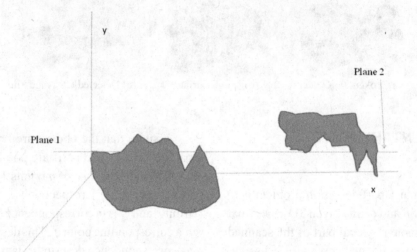

$$C_d = \frac{\sum E_F}{n}$$

where $n$ is the total number of facets in the cleavage site and $E_F$ is the Euclidean distance of all facets from the center of a given cleavage site.

## REGISTRATION

After detection of complementary cleavage sites, these complementary parts need to be aligned so that they can be registered to regenerate the original object. This phase registers the cleavage sites of the detected complementary parts by realignment and translation of the broken parts. The steps for registration are discussed here.

## Changing to Common Orientation

The initial orientation of the complementary cleavage sites is random; hence they need to be transformed to a common orientation. The registration phase first aligns the cleavage sites of the broken fragments parallel to the ZX-plane. This is done by fitting a plane on the cleavage site as

*Figure 19. Cleavage sites with maximum and minimum Y-coordinate*

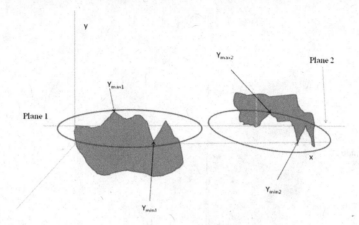

*Figure 20. Aligned cleavage sites*

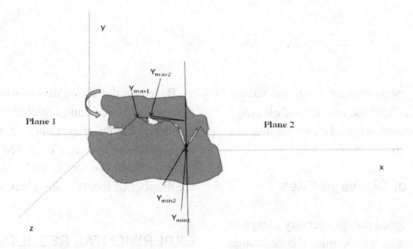

shown in Figure 17. The plane is fitted by taking weighted average of the normals of the rough facets with their corresponding area. Let there be $n$ facets in the cleavage site. Then average of normals is given by

$$\bar{N} = \frac{\sum_{k=1}^{n} N_k A_k}{\sum_{k=1}^{n} A_k} \qquad (11)$$

where $N_k$ and $A_k$ are the normal and the area of the $k^{th}$ facet in the cleavage site. Once the plane is fitted, it needs to be aligned parallel to a refer-

ence plane which in this case is the $ZX$-plane, as shown in Figure 18.

## Aligning Cleavage Sites

Cleavage sites which are in a common orientation, i.e. parallel to $ZX$-plane, further needs to be aligned such that one cleavage site is above the $ZX$-plane while other one is below it. This is done by considering two points having maximum and minimum values of the $Y$-coordinate on each cleavage site. Figure 19 shows these coordinates. The cleavage sites are aligned first by translating the minimum $Y$-coordinate values of both the cleavage sites with respect to the origin and then

*Figure 21. Registered cleavage sites*

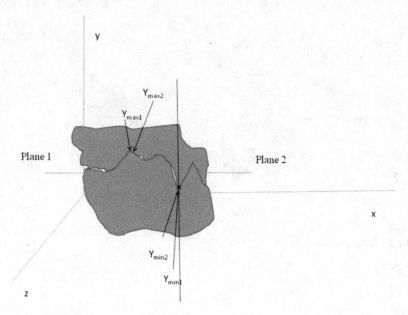

by matching the corresponding maximum values of $Y$-coordinate so that these two aligned cleavage sites can be registered. Aligned cleavage sites are shown in Figure 20.

## Registration of Cleavage Sites

To register the aligned complementary cleavage sites, the corresponding maximum $Y$-coordinates are matched. This is achieved by rotating one of the objects about $Y$-axis with its axis perpendicular to the plane fitted on the cleavage site passing through the minimum $Y$-coordinates.

Consider a vector for each cleavage site which is formed by joining the maximum and minimum $Y$-coordinates. Then the angle between the projections of the two vectors of the corresponding cleavage sites on the $ZX$-plane (by the dot product method) is found. Further, one cleavage site is rotated by that angle about the $Y$-axis so that the corresponding maximum $Y$-coordinates are matched with each other. This process makes the registration of two complementary cleavage sites as shown in Figure 21.

Based on the above discussion the algorithm for registration of complementary cleavage sites of broken 3D fragments surface has been given in Algorithm 2. It can be noted that the time complexity of the algorithm is $O(n)$ where $n$ is the number of facets in the cleavage site.

## EXPERIMENTAL RESULTS

The proposed roughness detection algorithm has been tested on more than 50 scanned fragments.

*Figure 22. Two original fragments*

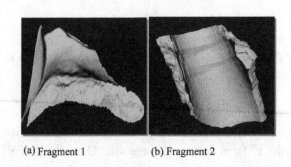

(a) Fragment 1       (b) Fragment 2

*Figure 23. Roughness detected fragments*

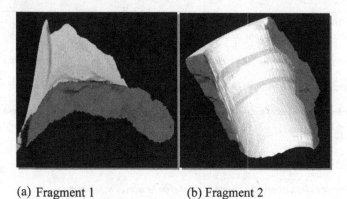

(a) Fragment 1          (b) Fragment 2

*Figure 24. Fragment with two cleavage sites*

 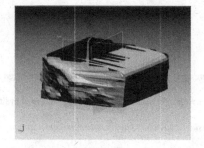

(a)    Cleavage Site 1        (b) Cleavage Site 2

All the fragments are scanned using 3D laser LPX 600 Roland scanner. The results have shown that the proposed algorithms are well suited for detecting cleavage sites in broken objects in a much accurate and efficient manner. To illustrate the performance of the algorithm, the original fragment's surface as marked in Figure 13 has been considered. The calculated roughness values of a single facet as well as multiple facets are shown in Figure 12. Using these roughness values of all the facets, a roughness histogram is constructed as shown in Figure 14. The minimum value near the center is chosen as the threshold value with H = 0.5914. Now all the facets having roughness values more than H are highlighted which form a rough site as shown in Figure 12.

In order to illustrate the consolidation of roughness patches, another example is considered.

First the value of clustering radius $K$ is chosen according to the size of model and the values of $u$ and $v$ have been experimentally estimated for consolidation and noise removal as shown in Table 1. The values of $u$ and $v$ depend on the type of material. Table 1 depicts these values for half baked clay fragments of different sizes. Since values for a particular material are applicable for all materials having similar texture, so these values need not be found each time.

*Table 1. Values of u and v for varying clustering radii (K)*

| $K$ | $V$ | $U$ |
|---|---|---|
| 3 | 0.44 | 0.22 |
| 4 | 0.50 | 0.16 |
| 5 | 0.60 | 0.10 |

*Algorithm 2. Registration*

---

***Step 1:*** *Detect the cleavage sites of broken 3D fragments following the steps given below*

    ***Step 1.1:*** *Use Roughness Detection algorithm as discussed above*

    ***Step 1.2:*** *Determine cleavage site from a rough surface by removing these edge facets as discussed above*

    ***Step 1.3:*** *Use clustering to obtain all multiple cleavage sites in the broken 3D object using the method discussed*

***Step 2:*** *Determine the complementary parts of the detected cleavage sites using the correspondence descriptor given by*

$$C_d = \frac{\sum E_F}{n}$$

***Step 3:*** *Bring both complementary cleavage sites to common orientation by using the following steps*

    ***Step 3.1:*** *Fit a plane on each cleavage site by taking weighted average of the normals of the rough facets with their corresponding area which is given by*

$$\bar{N} = \frac{\sum_{k=1}^{n} N_k A_k}{\sum_{k=1}^{n} A_k}$$

    ***Step 3.2:*** *Using these planes fitted on the cleavage sites, align them parallel to the ZX-plane*

***Step 4:*** *Align the cleavage sites such that one cleavage site is above the ZX-plane while other one is below it using*

    ***Step 4.1:*** *Consider two points having maximum and minimum values of the Y-coordinate on each cleavage site*

    ***Step 4.2:*** *Translate the minimum Y-coordinate values of both the cleavage sites with respect to the origin*

***Step 5:*** *Register the aligned complementary cleavage sites by following the steps given below*

    ***Step 5.1:*** *Form a vector for each cleavage site by joining the maximum and minimum Y-coordinates*

    ***Step 5.2:*** *Compute the angle between the projections of the two vectors of the corresponding cleavage sites on the ZX-plane*

    ***Step 5.3:*** *Rotate one cleavage site by the angle computed in the above step about the Y-axis in order to match the corresponding maximum Y-coordinates*

---

*Figure 25. Corresponding cleavage sites of fragments shown in Figure 24*

(a) Detected Cleavage Site 1       (b) Detected Cleavage Site 2

*Figure 26. Multiple broken fragments*

*Figure 27. First fragment with its cleavage site*

*Figure 28. Second fragment with its cleavage site*

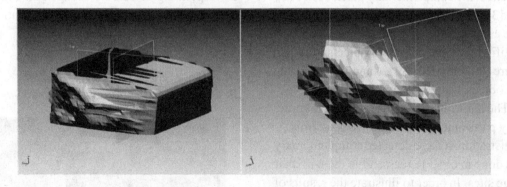

Figure 22 shows two original earthen-ware fragments. The roughness values at single facet level and multiple facet level are computed. Corresponding fragments after roughness consolidation and facet de-noising are shown in Figure 23.

The roughness is calculated at $(N, N)$-ring radius of 2.

From each of the above two earthen-ware fragments, only one cleavage site is detected. There may be more than one cleavage site in a broken fragment. As shown in Figure 24 there are

*Table 2. Broken objects and their complementary parts*

| 3D Broken Object | Complementary Part |
|---|---|
| | |
| | |
| | |

two cleavage sites in the scanned fragment. The detected cleavage sites are shown in Figure 25.

To detect the complementary parts, each of 50 scanned 3D objects has been broken into two parts and the cleavage site of each of these fragments is identified. Sample of broken objects is shown in Figure 26. Table 2 shows some results of the broken objects after applying the proposed algorithm. The algorithm could detect all the complementary parts among the objects successfully.

Registration of these detected complementary parts is done in order to reassemble them at their cleavage sites. In order to illustrate the results of registration, four experiments are given.

## Experiment 1

The first object considered for our experiment is an earthenware rectangular object having height 2.0", width 0.5" and length 1" approximately.

The object is broken into two fragments. Figure 27 and Figure 28 show the fragments with their corresponding detected cleavage site. Figure 29 depicts both the fragments after registration.

*Figure 29. Registration of both fragments*

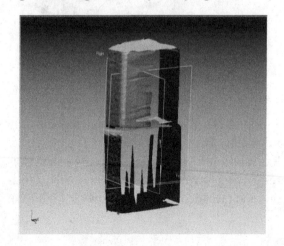

*Figure 30. First fragment with its cleavage site*

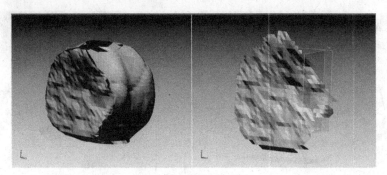

*Figure 31. Second fragment with its cleavage site*

## Experiment 2

Next object considered in our experiment is a clay pottery which has the size of approximately 1.5 inches in height and 0.5 inches in diameter. This object is broken into two fragments. Figure 30 shows the first fragment with its detected cleavage site while the other fragment with its cleavage site is given in Figure 31. Both the fragments with their respective detected cleavage sites are registered and its result is shown in Figure 32.

## Experiment 3

In this experiment, we have also considered a clay pottery. It is approximately 2.5" in height and 1" diameter. This object is also broken into two fragments. Both the fragments along with their respective cleavage sites are shown in Figure 33 and Figure 34. Registered fragments are shown in Figure 35.

## Experiment 4

The object considered in this experiment is a piece of chalk. The chalk is broken into two fragments. It can be noted that this chalk piece is a good example of multi-granularity roughness. Frag-

*Figure 32. Result after registration*

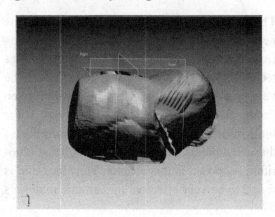

*Figure 33. First fragment with its cleavage site*

*Figure 34. Second fragment with its cleavage site*

ments with their respective detected cleavage sites are shown in Figure 36 and Figure 37 while the object obtained from fragments after registration is depicted in Figure 38.

## FUTURE WORK

The work discussed in this chapter opens up some new directions of research which are ranging from theoretical issues to the latest cutting edge technologies. The problem studied is found to be very useful for archeologists who obtain broken fragments especially in case of potteries at the time of excavations. Automatic reassembly of these fragments can be done through the algorithm proposed in this chapter. The algorithm is found to be very effective for ceramic materials

and earthen-ware. However, it is not well suited for metallic objects and crystalline solids because the roughness in case of metallic broken objects is difficult to obtain.

*Figure 35. Registration of fragments*

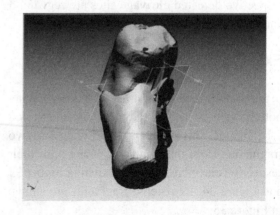

*Figure 36. First fragment with its cleavage site*

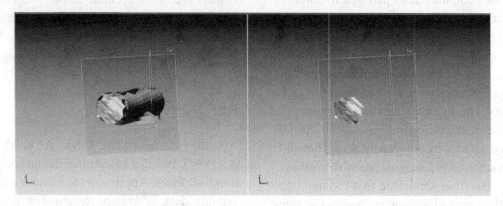

*Figure 37. Second fragment with its cleavage site*

Cleavage site detection algorithm is found to reduce the area to be matched drastically by identifying the portions where we should attempt to fit complementary fragments. This algorithm can further be enhanced by taking into account the sharp edges found on cleavage site boundaries. But it requires careful evaluation because all fragments may not have sharp cleavage boundaries. Further, the algorithm for registration can be improved by taking into consideration the boundaries of the obtained cleavage sites and applying the 3D image correlation on it. This may further improve the accuracy of the registration of the broken complementary pieces.

## CONCLUSION

The chapter has explored a problem for deter-

*Figure 38. Object after registration*

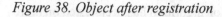

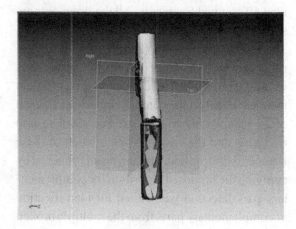

mining the complementary part of a fragment of an object and of reassembling them to form the object. It has proposed an efficient surface inspection algorithm which detects the corresponding cleavage sites of fragments and registers them so that the object can be formed from the given fragments. The algorithm captures differences in the geometric structure in different parts of the 3D object represented by polygon meshes. These differences are used to find most probable cleavage/fracture sites. It is applicable to all triangulated surface data even in presence of noise. The algorithm is found to be very effective on objects of ceramic material and archeological artifacts. The work already done in the field of reconstruction of ceramic material or archeological artifacts is through reassembly is either on 2D reassembly or reassembly of 3D thin walled objects. However, the problem described in this chapter can efficiently handle thick walled objects as well. In this work, not only few existing algorithms for roughness detection were enhanced, but the generated data was consolidated and cleaned to make it suitable for entirely new application of cleavage site detection. As such 3D fragment reassembly is a complex problem, involving matching and registration of complementary surfaces. Cleavage site detection algorithm reduces the area to be matched drastically by identifying the portions where we should attempt to fit complementary fragments. To validate and optimize, the proposed roughness detection algorithm has been tested on more than 50 scanned fragments. All the fragments are scanned using 3D laser LPX 600 Roland scanner. The results have shown that the proposed algorithms are well suited for detecting cleavage sites in broken objects in a much accurate and efficient manner. To detect the complementary parts, each of 50 scanned 3D objects has been broken into two parts and the cleavage site of each of these fragments is identified. Further, results obtained by applying the proposed algorithm for complementary part detection well suited for identification of complementary parts from the multiple broken

objects in a much accurate and efficient manner. After the detection of complementary parts, final registration of these complementary parts is done in order to reassemble them at their cleavage sites.

## REFERENCES

Arrault, J., Arnéodo, A., Davis, A., & Marshak, A. (1997). Wavelet based multifractal analysis of rough surfaces: Application to cloud models and satellite data. *Physical Review Letters*, *79*(1), 75–78. doi:10.1103/PhysRevLett.79.75

Barequet, G., & Sharir, M. (1997). Partial surface and volume matching in three dimensions. *IEEE Transactions on Pattern Analysis and Machine Intelligence*, *19*(9), 929–948. doi:10.1109/34.615444

Besl, P. J., & McKay, N. D. (1992). A method for registration of 3D shapes. *IEEE Transactions on Pattern Analysis and Machine Intelligence*, *14*(2), 239–256. doi:10.1109/34.121791

Boehler, W., & Marbs, A. (2002). 3D scanning instruments. In *CIPA WG6 International Workshop on Scanning for Cultural Heritage Recording (CIPA2002)* (pp. 9-12).

Bolin, M. R., & Meyer, G. W. (1998). A perceptually based adaptive sampling algorithm. In *ACM SIGGRAPH* (pp. 299–309). ACM Press.

Corsini, M., Gelasca, E. D., & Ebrahimi, T. (2005). A multi-scale roughness metric for 3D watermarking quality assessment. In *Workshop on Image Analysis for Multimedia Interactive Services*, (pp. 13-15).

Jafari, G. R. (2003). Stochastic analysis and regeneration of rough surfaces. *Physical Review Letters*, *91*(22), 1–4. doi:10.1103/PhysRevLett.91.226101

Kaushik, V. D., Singh, A. K., Varshney, J., Pandey, P., Rao, K. P., & Pathak, V. K. (2007). Cleavage site detection in broken 3D objects. In *International Conference on Advanced Computing and Communications (ADCOM 2007)* (pp. 339–344).

Levoy, M., Pulli, K., Curless, B., Rusinkiewicz, S., Koller, D., & Pereira, L. ... Fulk, D. (2000). The digital Michelangelo project: 3D scanning of large statues. In *ACM SIGGRAPH* (pp.131-144). ACM Press.

Lindstrom, P., & Turk, G. (2000). Image-driven simplification. *ACM Transactions on Graphics, 19*(3), 204–241. doi:10.1145/353981.353995

Masuda, T., & Yokoya, N. (1995). A robust method for registration and segmentation of multiple range images. *Computer Vision and Image Understanding, 61*(3), 295–307. doi:10.1006/cviu.1995.1024

Nicolas, A., Santa-Cruz, D., & Ebrahimi, T. (2002). Mesh: Measuring error between surfaces using the Hausdorff distance. In *IEEE International Conference on Multimedia and Expo (ICME): Vol. I* (pp. 705–708). IEEE Press.

Rogowitz, B., & Rushmeier, H. (2001). Are image quality metrics adequate to evaluate the quality of geometric objects? In Rogowitz, B. E., & Pappas, T. N. (Eds.), *SPIE on Human Vision and Electronic Imaging VI* (*Vol. 4299*, pp. 340–348). SPIE. doi:10.1117/12.429504

Scopigno, R., Cignoni, P., & Rocchini, C. (1998). Metro: Measuring error on simplified surfaces. *Computer Graphics Forum, 17*(2), 167–174. doi:10.1111/1467-8659.00236

Terry, W. (1995). The challenge of 3D digitizing. *Computer Graphics World, 18*(11), 21–25.

Waechter, M., Riess, F., Schimmel, T., Wendt, U., & Peinke, J. (2004). Stochastic analysis of different rough surfaces. *The European Physical Journal B- Condensed Matter and Complex Systems, 41*(2), 259-277.

Williams, N., Luebke, D., Cohen, J. D., Kelley, M., & Schubert, B. (2003). Perceptually guided simplification of lit, textured meshes. In *Symposium on Interactive 3D Graphics* (pp. 113-121). ACM Press.

Wu, J., Hu, S., Tai, C., & Sun, J. (2001). An effective feature-preserving mesh simplification scheme based on face constriction. In *9th Pacific Conference on Computer Graphics and Applications* (pp. 12 - 21). IEEE Press.

## KEY TERMS AND DEFINITIONS

**Cleavage Site:** It consists of all rough facets in a fragment.

**Complementary Part Detection:** The method of obtaining the corresponding fragments belonging to the same 3D object.

**Facet:** If a surface is represented by triangular meshes, then each triangle is it is termed as facet.

**Fragment:** Each broken piece of a 3D object is known as fragment.

**Multi-Level Granularity:** It is the roughness having more than one level in a fragment.

**Registration:** Alignment of complimentary parts of fragments.

**Roughness Factor:** A metric to measure the roughness of a surface of a 3D object.

# Chapter 14
# 3D Surface Reconstruction from Multiviews for Prosthetic Design

**Nasrul Humaimi Bin Mahmood**
*Universiti Teknologi Malaysia, Malaysia*

## ABSTRACT

*Existing methods that use a fringe projection technique for prosthetic designs produce good results for the trunk and lower limbs; however, the devices used for this purpose are expensive. This chapter investigates the use of an inexpensive passive method involving 3D surface reconstruction from video images taken at multiple views. The design and evaluation methodology, consisting of a number of techniques suitable for prosthetic design, is developed. The method that focuses on fitting the reference model (3D model) of an object to the target data (3D data) is presented. The 3D model is obtained by a computer program while the 3D data uses the shape-from-silhouette technique in an approximately circular motion. The modification of existing model-based reconstruction – mainly on the deformation process of vertices – is discussed, and the results of different objects show a good possibility for using a passive method in prosthetic devices. The methodology developed is shown to be useful for prosthetic designers as an alternative to manual impression during the design.*

## INTRODUCTION

Three-dimensional (3D) digitalisation systems applied to the orthopaedic domain allow for the freeing from the necessity of making manual impressions of the socket during prosthetic design. The work carried out in these fields aims to find the best fitting of the socket into the portion of the arm or leg remaining after an amputation (residual limb or stump), during the prosthetic design by using a multiview method. A prosthetic device is an artificial substitute for a missing body part such as an arm, leg, hand or foot, and is used for functional or cosmetic reasons, or both. Most of the previous works on prosthetic design are based on manual design and use Computer-Aided Design (CAD)

DOI: 10.4018/978-1-4666-0113-0.ch014

systems (Lusardi and Nielson, 2007; Seymour (2002)). With a manual design, the most common way of defining the shape of a residual limb is to make a mould of the residual limb itself. A trained practitioner can then manipulate the mould in order to correctly spread out the pressure that the mould exerts on the patient. One of the advantages in CAD is the reduced need for cast modifications and is, thus, a time saver. However, computer-aided systems increase the initial cost and training that is needed to operate the system. This initial cost and training is decreased if there is a system that can capture the residual limb shapes and give the actual dimension of the limb for the design. This can be realized using a reconstructed image of the limb for orthotic and prosthetic design. The cost of training will be reduced as the image is analysed automatically. Using the reconstructed 3D image would also be more comfortable for the patient when compared to using a traditional fabrication, as the latter might cause more injury during the design. In this chapter, the shapes of objects which are similar to a limb are used as a starting point of this research. A cylinder, cone or a combination of these are suitably similar shapes to the limb. This chapter provides 3D reconstruction system that capable to produce the measurement of the limb as well as creating a model of the limb. The finding will help the practitioner or prosthetist in designing the prosthetic device.

## ORTHOTIC AND PROSTHETIC

Orthotic and prosthetic devices have existed for many years. Originally, orthotic and prosthetic devices were simply replacements for missing limbs or used as supports for the human body, but now they enable people to have active lives. Prosthetics involves the design, fabrication and fitting of custom-made artificial limbs or other assistive devices for patients who have lost limbs as a result of traumatic injuries, vascular diseases, diabetes, cancer or congenital disorders. These

devices will restore — as completely as possible — the function and appearance of a full or partially missing limb. Because of the vast differences in human anatomy, the fabrication of prostheses is an intricate, custom procedure requiring a high degree of skill combined with sophisticated technology. Orthotics involves the design, fabrication, fitting and supervised use of devices that provide external support or assist weak or abnormal joints and/or muscle groups. Musculoskeletal disorders, joint weakness, back problems, or the inability of any joint or muscle group to function correctly can detrimentally affect an individual's quality of life and mobility. These problems can be caused by congenital factors, traumatic injury, chronic conditions, sports injuries, or degenerative disease.

Many improvements have been made possible because of new surgical techniques, the advancement of components for making prosthetics, and creative engineering ideas (Lusardi and Nielson, 2007). Improved materials and technologies are enabling many individuals with disabilities to return to activities they previously enjoyed. Custom fabricated and custom fitted prostheses and orthoses require high strength and low weight. Advancements in technology continue to improve patient care. Technological breakthroughs such as electronic knees and computer imaging are changing the way orthoses and prostheses enable patients to fulfil their potential.

Materials used in each device depend on the weight of the user, their desired activities and their personal preferences. Flexible polymers provide increased comfort for patients. Carbon fibre, Kevlar® and titanium are all used for reducing the weight and increasing the strength and durability of the device.

CAD/CAM technology is increasingly being used to help design and fabricate models from which orthoses and prosthetic sockets are produced. Measurements can be scanned by laser or by using a special hand-held wand. This information describing the size and shape of the limb allows the prosthetist and orthotist to design the device for the patient by using a computer. The design can then be downloaded to an automated carver to make the orthosis or prosthesis. Many arm prostheses have electrically powered hands and elbows (Mahmood, 2009). Simple switches may be used to control these, but it is also possible to use sensors on the skin to detect signals generated by muscles (myoelectric signals) to control the prosthesis. In some instances, microprocessors are used in analyzing and processing the myoelectric signals. Users of this kind of 'bionic arm' can have both the delicate touch to pick up an egg and the strength to grasp a heavy object.

Electronic knee joints for prostheses can now be programmed for the individual patient. A computer chip allows the knee joint to sense changes in position, speed and force, enabling patients with amputations to walk down stairs and hills with confidence. There are also prosthetic feet made especially for running, golfing, or swimming.

Orthosis can be made with patterns and colours to make wearing them more fun for children. The ranges of options available today require the prosthetist/orthotist be well trained and educated to analyse the individual needs of each patient and to develop appropriate recommendations. Considerable skill is needed in working with the device and the patient to ensure that optimal fit and function are achieved.

## 3D RECONSTRUCTION FROM MULTIVIEWS

3D object reconstruction from multiviews is the process of estimating the shape of a 3D object from different views. Its applications include virtual reality, digital preservation of cultural heritage and medical imaging. The use of such an approach for 3D digitisation can be categorised into two groups: active and passive (Hartley and Zisserman, 1998). Active methods make use of calibrated light sources such as lasers or coded light; the most typical example of which is the shape from the structured light method. Passive methods, on the other hand, rely solely on two-dimensional (2D) images of the scene taken at different camera views to extract surface information. The common passive methods include shape from silhouette (SfS), shape from stereo and shape from shading. In this chapter, the SfS method (Laurentini, 1994 and 1997; Wong and Cipolla, 2001) is adopted because it offers the use of low cost hardware (i.e., a video camera and a turntable) and adequate accuracy in the object reconstruction.

## The Camera Model

In this work, the perspective camera model is adopted in the SfS method. The model corresponds to an ideal pinhole camera (Hartley and Zisserman, 1998). The object reconstruction process is completely determined by choosing a perspective projection/camera centre $C$ and an image plane $R$. The projection of a scene point $M$ is then obtained as the intersection of a line connecting this point and the centre of the projection $C$ with the image plane, as shown in Figure 1. The optical axis is the line going through $C$ perpendicular to the image plane $R$. It pierces the plane at the principal point $p$. An orthonormal system of coordinates in the image plane centred at $p$ is used to define a 3D orthonormal system of coordinates (called the camera coordinate system) which is centred at the projection centre $C$ with two axes of coordinates (i.e., X and Y) parallel to the image plane and the third (i.e., Z) parallel to the optical axis. The focal length $f$ is the distance between point $C$ and the image plane $R$.

The relationship between the coordinates of a scene point $M$, i.e., $(X, Y, Z)^T$, and those of its projection $m$, i.e., $(x, y)^T$, is given by the Tales theorem (Faugeras, 1993):

*Figure 1. The pinhole camera model*

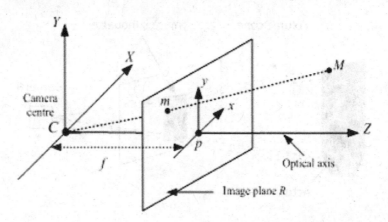

$$x = f \bullet \frac{X}{Z} \qquad (1)$$

A point *m* in an image represents an incoming light ray; called the optical ray of *m*. Since the optical ray passes the optical centre, to define its position in the camera coordinate system only requires another point along the ray to be specified, e.g., $(X, Y, Z)^T$. However, any point of coordinates $(\lambda X, \lambda Y, \lambda Z)^T$ lie along the ray and are projected to the same 2D point *m*. The coordinates of *m* are $(x, y, 1)^T$ which represent a point in 3D on the optical ray of *m*. Using the homogeneous representation of a point, the following linear projection equation is obtained:

$$m = \begin{bmatrix} x \\ y \\ 1 \end{bmatrix} = \begin{bmatrix} 1 & 0 & 0 & 0 \\ 0 & 1 & 0 & 0 \\ 0 & 0 & 1 & 0 \end{bmatrix} \begin{bmatrix} X \\ Y \\ Z \\ 1 \end{bmatrix} \qquad (2)$$

where $(X, Y, Z)$ is a world point and $(x, y)$ is the corresponding image point.

## Shape from Silhouette

A 2D silhouette is a closed contour that outlines the projection of a 3D object onto the image plane.

The object lies within the cone (bounding volume) formed by its silhouette and the camera centre as illustrated in Figure 2. SfS starts with an image acquisition step where images of the object are taken from different camera locations around it. For each of these images, the object silhouette is extracted using a simple differencing or an image segmentation technique. The computed silhouettes of every image together with the corresponding camera centre are then used to define a bounding volume. The intersection of these bounding volumes yields a reasonable approximation of the real object. This intersection volume is referred to as the visual hull (Laurentini, 1994) and describes the maximal object that gives the same silhouette of the object from any possible camera viewpoints.

## Approximate Circular Motion

In this chapter, the silhouettes of an object in motion are employed in order to improve accuracy of the reconstructed shape. In some related works, images of the object placed on a turntable are captured by rotating the turntable (Fremont and Chellali, 2004; Shin and Tjahjadi, 2005). The changing relative positions between the camera and the object are described by the rotation parameter of a turntable. Throughout the circular motion of the turntable, the camera's internal

*Figure 2. The bounding volume constraints the shape of an object*

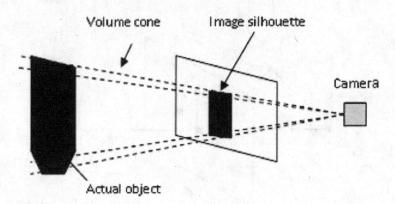

parameters remain identical. This facilitates the camera calibration process by enabling the camera's parameters to be estimated using the same internal parameters and 3D camera position with respect to the reference camera position.

Turntable calibration requires the acquisition of a second image sequence of the object placed on the turntable axis with the same camera adjustments. The extrinsic calibration parameters related to this rotation sequence are then determined. The intrinsic parameters are not computed again since the camera adjustments remain unchanged. This provides a rigid transformation which relates the calibration pattern coordinate system to the fixed camera coordinate system for each view of the pattern in the rotation sequence. The rotation axis is then computed from the set of rigid transformations through the numerical procedure detailed by (Shin and Tjahjadi, 2005).

In turntable motion, the physical imperfection of the turntable as well as measurement error affects the accuracy of the object reconstruction. Hence, a modified projection matrix introduced in (Shin and Tjahjadi, 2005) is used. If circular motion of the turntable is assumed, then a projection matrix at a rotated position α, $P(\alpha)$, is

$$P(\alpha) = KR\left[R(\alpha) \quad -\vec{o}_\alpha\right] \qquad (3)$$

where $K$ is a 2D affine homography which includes the internal parameters of the camera and $R$ is the 3D rotation matrix relating the world frame and camera frame. The 2D similarity homography $R(\alpha)$ represents a pure 2D rotation term of the circular motion. The 3D camera origin with respect to the world frame is represented as $\vec{o}_\alpha$.

In Figure 3, $I(0)$ is the reference image plane, $I(\alpha)$ and $I(\alpha')$ respectively represent the estimated and true image planes that have been rotated by α degrees from $o_{ref}$. Although the true camera origin $o_{\alpha'}$ cannot be determined from images, the 2D homography between $I(\alpha)$ and $I(\alpha')$ can be estimated when there are at least four pairs of correspondences, i.e., $x^{\alpha'} \leftrightarrow x^w$, where

$$x^{\alpha'} = H_p KR[R(\alpha) \quad -\vec{o}_\alpha]x^w \qquad (4)$$

and $H_p$ is a projective homography with 8 degrees of freedom because the lines at infinity $\vec{l}_h$ in $I(\alpha)$ and $I(\alpha')$ are not identical. Using the Direct Linear Transform algorithm (require a reference) when more than 4 points are detectable to derive a linear solution of $H_p$, the modified projection matrix for an approximate circular motion is formulated as

*Figure 3. Geometrical illustration of circular motion*

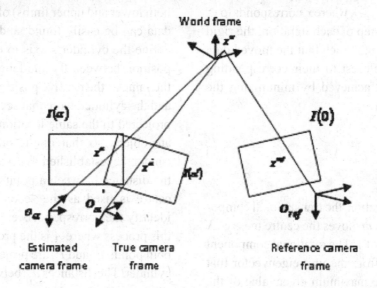

$$P'(\alpha) = H'_p \left[ R(\alpha) \quad -\vec{o}_\alpha \right] \tag{5}$$

where $H'_p = H_p KR.$.

The following decision function of two projection matrices

$$d\left(P(\alpha), P'(\alpha)\right) = \sum_i \left\| \left(P(\alpha) - P'(\alpha)\right) x_i^w \right\| \tag{6}$$

is introduced in order to achieve an accurate object reconstruction. If $d\left(P(\alpha), P'(\alpha)\right)$ is greater than zero, then $P'(\alpha)$ replaces $P(\alpha)$, otherwise the estimated projection matrix remains unchanged.

## SURFACE DEFORMATION

The variations in the shape of a residual limb make it difficult to extract the features and segment of the limb, thus a reference model is used to provide prior knowledge to refine the 3D reconstruction of the limb. The surface model is obtained by deforming the reference model with constraints

imposed by the SfS-based reconstruction. Two methods are used to obtain the reference model of the limb and other objects similar to a limb. The first uses the octree data generated by the SfS reconstruction technique in (Shin and Tjahjadi, 2005). For simple object such as a cone or cylinder, the reference model is generated by a simple computer program (Mahmood and Tjahjadi, 2010, 2009 and 2006).

Two data sets are involved in the reconstruction: the reference model (referred to as the model) and the target objects (referred to as the data). These need to be registered in order to merge them before a deformation process is applied to refine the reconstruction. This is achieved using the iterative corresponding point (ICP) algorithm (Rusinkiewicz and Levoy, 2001), an improved version of the iterative closest point (ICP) algorithm (Besl and McKay, 1992).

The ICP algorithm rigidly moves (i.e., registers and positions) the points of the data to be in best alignment with the corresponding points of the model. This is done iteratively. In the first step of each iteration, the closest point on the surface of the model $Y=(y_1, y_2, ...)$ is computed for every data point $X=(x_1, x_2, ...)$, where $x_i$ corresponds to $y_i$.

In the second step of each iteration, the rigid motion $m$ is computed such that the moved data points $m(x_i)$ are closest to their corresponding points, $y_i$. This is achieved by minimizing the objective function

$$F = \sum_{i=1}^{N} \left\| m\left( x_i \right) - y_i \right\|^2. \qquad (7)$$

In this minimization, the translational component of the motion $m$ moves the centre mass of $X$ to the centre mass of $Y$. The rotational component of $m$ is obtained from the unit eigenvector that corresponds to the maximum eigenvalue of the symmetric 4×4 matrix.

The solution eigenvector is the unit quaternion of the rotational component of $m$. Following the second step, the positions of the data points are updated via $X_{new} = m(X_{old})$. Step 1 and step 2 are then repeated, using the updated data points, until the change in the mean-square error falls below a preset threshold. Since the value of the objective function decreases both in steps 1 and 2, the ICP algorithm always converges monotonically to a local minimum.

## Pre-Processing

Following registration, a pre-processing is applied to achieve a better correspondence between the registered data sets to find the feature points on the model that correspond to the points on the data. Although the registration between two datasets produces good results, a further correspondence analysis is needed because ICP only performs a rigid registration and there is no non-rigid movement or re-sampling of the vertices. A model point corresponds to a data point if both points project to the same location on the intermediate object, where a cylinder with the unit radius is used as the intermediate object.

The most prominent points on the limbs (for both lower and upper limbs) of the model and the data can be easily found, and these are used to define the cylinder's axis to ensure the relative position between the model and the cylinder is the same as the relative position between the data and the cylinder. Note that several points may be projected to the same location on the intermediate object, so that one-to-one correspondence cannot be established. To solve this problem, the distance between a point and the projection centre is used as the secondary parameter to identify the correspondence. Figure 4 illustrates this process where $A$ is the projection centre and both points $P_1$ and $P_2$ are projected onto C on the cylinder. The distances $d_1$ (between $P_1$ and $A$) and $d_2$ (between $P_2$ and $A$) are also used to identify their corresponding points. For some cases, the cone is a suitable intermediate object if the apex can be easily determined between both data sets.

After the correspondence between the model and data is established, the model needs to be deformed to match the data to generate a modified model that matches all the points on the data contours. The simple constrained deformation

*Figure 4. Using a cylinder as the intermediate object for correspondence analysis*

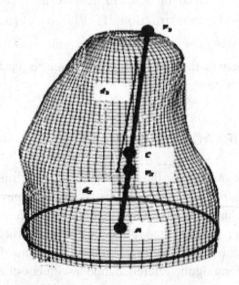

methods operate on a 3D volume without considering the object's geometry and topology inside the volume (Borrel and Rappaport, 1994). As a result, the influence a feature point imposes on the points within its influence region is a function of the Euclidean distance between the two points. However, the Euclidean distance alone does not reflect the actual relationship between two points, especially when the constraint point is on the surface of an object. There are cases when two points are close in Euclidean distance but remote to one another in surface distance. In these cases, the deformation will be incorrect. Another problem with these techniques is that each point is only influenced by a small number of given constraint points without considering the constraints imposed by its neighbouring points. As a result, the inherent connectivity between neighbouring points may be violated.

To address these problems, a modified technique based on simple constrained deformation is introduced. In the proposed algorithm, instead of defining the influence region within a 3D volume the influence region is defined by the object surface. This addresses the problem where two points are close in Euclidean distance but remote in surface distance. The influence region of a constraint point consists of all points on the model whose surface distance to the constraint point is smaller than a given radius. The surface distance between two points is calculated by adding all the distances along triangle along the shortest surface path between them. The deformation is calculated by accumulating the influences propagated through neighbouring points.

For each data point paired with a model feature point, the displacement of a feature point is\

$$d(C)=\|K-C\| \tag{8}$$

where $d(C)$ is the displacement vector of feature point $C$, and $K$ is the corresponding data point of $C$. A point has direct influence only on its neighbouring points. Let $C$ be a feature point and $P$ be one of its neighbouring points. Thus the displacement of P from C is

$$d(P) = d(C) * f\left(\frac{\|P - C\|}{r}\right) \tag{9}$$

where $f(x)$ is a decreasing function with $f(0)=1$ and $f(x)=0$ for $x \geq 1$; $r$ is the radius of an influence region. $f(x)$ is zero for $\|P-C\| \geq r$ (i.e., points whose distance from $C$ is greater than or equal to the radius $r$) and $f(x)$ is 1 when $\|P-C\|=0$ (i.e., when $P$ is the feature point itself). Point $P$ will in turn influence its own neighbouring points, i.e., using (9) but with $P$ as the feature point. This process

*Figure 5 (a) Modified 3D model of the dummy limb after deformation process. (b) Measuring the approximate position of an actual dummy limb.*

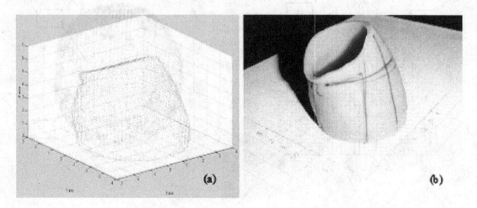

continues until the displacement of $P$, $d(P)$, is less than a threshold $t$ or the surface distance between point $P$ and feature point $C$ exceeds $C$'s influence radius, $R_c$.

Let $P_n$ be any point that is influenced by feature point $C$, and $P_1, P_2, ..., P_{n-1}$ the points on the surface path between $P_n$ and $C$. The displacement of $P_n$ is thus given by

$$d(P_n) = d(C) * f\left(\frac{\|P_1 - C\|}{r}\right) * f\left(\frac{\|P_2 - P_1\|}{r}\right) * ... f\left(\frac{P_n - P_{n-1}}{r}\right)$$

(10)

where * denotes convolution.

## MULTIVIEWS RECONSTRUCTION OF LOWER AND UPPER LIMB

### Lower Limb

In prosthetic design, it is necessary to perform quantitative analysis and measurements. The length, angle, area of region, 3D surface area and volume of the limb need to be measured. The analysis and measurements are employed to ensure that the 3D model created will fit the actual limb. In order to evaluate the experimental results, the modified 3D model created after the deformation process and the actual limb data are compared. The evaluation is done by comparing some selected points on the actual limb with the

*Figure 6 The measurement of 15 cross sections of modified model (a) x-y plane (b) z-x plane (c) z-y plane and (d) top view. Each labelled line represents the measurement of the length in Table 1.*

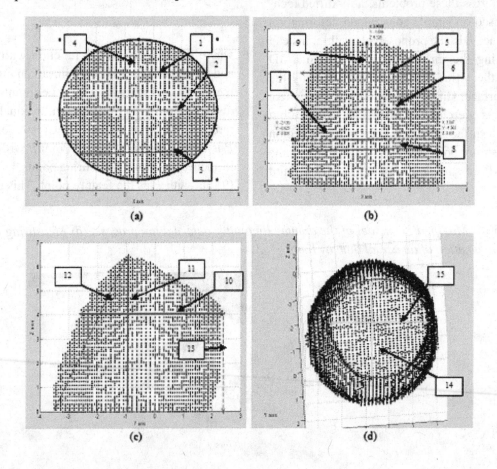

*Figure 7. (a) Modified model of upper limb after deformation process. (b) Measuring the approximate position of an actual dummy limb.*

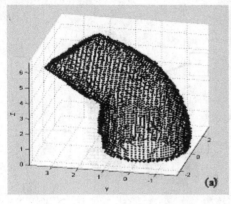
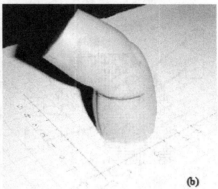

corresponding points on the modified model. To facilitate the comparison, a grid is superimposed onto the modified model as shown in Figure 5(a). The actual limb is positioned to correspond to the modified model as illustrated in Figure 5(b).

Fifteen measurements of cross sections of the model in the x-y plane (as shown in Figure 6(a)),

*Table 1. Differences between the modified model and the lower limb data*

| Length | Modified 3D model (cm) | Actual limb (cm) ± errors | Difference (cm) |
|---|---|---|---|
| 1 | 4.8 | 4.8 ± 0.2 | 0.0 ± 0.2 |
| 2 | 5.5 | 5.4 ± 0.1 | 0.1 ± 0.1 |
| 3 | 4.1 | 4.1 ± 0.1 | 0.0 ± 0.1 |
| 4 | 5.8 | 5.9 ± 0.1 | 0.1 ± 0.1 |
| 5 | 4.4 | 4.4 ± 0.1 | 0.0 ± 0.1 |
| 6 | 4.8 | 4.7 ± 0.2 | 0.1 ± 0.2 |
| 7 | 5.3 | 5.3 ± 0.1 | 0.0 ± 0.1 |
| 8 | 4.0 | 4.0 ± 0.1 | 0.0 ± 0.1 |
| 9 | 6.3 | 6.2 ± 0.0 | 0.1 ± 0.0 |
| 10 | 5.1 | 5.0 ± 0.1 | 0.1 ± 0.1 |
| 11 | 6.5 | 6.4 ± 0.1 | 0.1 ± 0.1 |
| 12 | 7.2 | 7.3 ± 0.2 | 0.1 ± 0.2 |
| 13 | 4.0 | 4.0 ± 0.1 | 0.0 ± 0.1 |
| 14 | 4.1 | 4.0 ± 0.2 | 0.1 ± 0.2 |
| 15 | 4.0 | 4.0 ± 0.2 | 0.0 ± 0.2 |

in the z-x plane (as shown in Figure 6(b)), in the z-y plane (as shown in Figure 6(c)) and from the top view (as shown in Figure 6(d)) were made. The corresponding cross sections on the actual dummy limb were also made. Both sets of measurements were scaled to centimetre (cm) unit and are shown in Table 1.

Table 1 shows that the differences between the two sets of measurements are small. The small error between the model and actual limb is dependent on several factors such as resolution and processing of the actual 3D image data, thickness and distance between vertices, the method of reconstruction (i.e., control parameters of the decimation algorithm or triangulation), and factors associated with marking the measurement points by a human.

## Upper Limb

The modified model of the upper limb is shown in Figure 7(a) and the actual limb is shown in Figure 7(b).

Figure 8 (a) shows the z-y plane of the modified model. The 3D point (0.7813, 1.563, 2.734) is the most obvious point that can be determined in both the 3D model and actual limb. Measurements for others cross sections were made as shown in Figure 8 (b) and 8 (c).

*Figure 8. The measurement of 15 cross sections of modified model (a) z-y plane (b) z-x plane and (c) x-y plane. Each labelled line represents the measurement of the length in Table 2.*

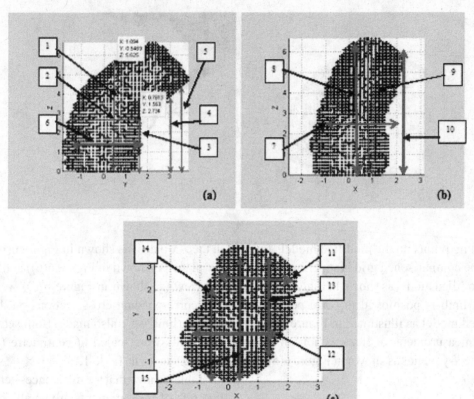

The fifteen measurements of both the modified data and the corresponding measurements on the actual limb are shown in Table 2.

Table 2 shows that the differences in the two sets of measurements are small demonstrating that good fitting of the model to the data during the deformation process has been adequately achieved. The correlation coefficient between 15 measurements of the modified model and the actual limb is 0.99928.

Instead of demonstrated on lower and upper limb, the new proposed method for the deformation process was applied to four different objects, which are a candle, a spherical candle, a box and a fruit. Table 3 summarised the percentage of non-matching vertices for these six objects after the deformation process. The table shows that for a large number of object vertices (i.e., a candle) and the object which have lot of sharp corner (i.e., a fruit), it is difficult to fit their model to the data. Both of these objects almost have a half percentage of non-matching vertices after the deformation process which are 50% for a candle and 47% for a fruit. The rest of the objects have below 30% of non-matching vertices and are considered low. However, there are plenty of opportunities to improve this percentage.

The experimental results show that the movement of model vertices to fit the data vertices depends on some of the cases below:

1.  If a few vertices' locations are different, the method performs very well, where almost all the vertices can fit or move towards the data.

*Table 2. Differences between the modified model and the upper limb data*

| Length | 3D new model (cm) | Actual limb (cm) ± errors | Difference (cm) ± errors |
|---|---|---|---|
| 1 | 5.6 | 5.5 ± 0.2 | 0.1 ± 0.2 |
| 2 | 3.0 | 2.8 ± 0.1 | 0.2 ± 0.1 |
| 3 | 2.9 | 2.9 ± 0.2 | 0.0 ± 0.2 |
| 4 | 3.8 | 3.8 ± 0.1 | 0.0 ± 0.1 |
| 5 | 4.6 | 4.5 ± 0.3 | 0.1 ± 0.3 |
| 6 | 3.9 | 3.9 ± 0.2 | 0.0 ± 0.2 |
| 7 | 3.2 | 3.2 ± 0.1 | 0.0 ± 0.1 |
| 8 | 6.1 | 6.0 ± 0.1 | 0.1 ± 0.1 |
| 9 | 6.8 | 6.8 ± 0.1 | 0.0 ± 0.1 |
| 10 | 3.1 | 3.0 ± 0.2 | 0.1 ± 0.2 |
| 11 | 2.8 | 2.9 ± 0.1 | 0.1 ± 0.1 |
| 12 | 3.6 | 3.6 ± 0.1 | 0.0 ± 0.1 |
| 13 | 3.8 | 3.8 ± 0.2 | 0.0 ± 0.2 |
| 14 | 2.5 | 2.4 ± 0.0 | 0.1 ± 0.0 |
| 15 | 3.9 | 3.7 ± 0.2 | 0.2 ± 0.2 |

*Table 3. The percentage of non-matching vertices of six objects*

| Objects | Non-matching vertices (approx.) | Total registered vertices (approx.) | Percentage of non-matching vertices (%) |
|---|---|---|---|
| Candle | 47650 | 82156 | 58 |
| Spherical candle | 1363 | 4808 | 28 |
| Box | 900 | 4200 | 21 |
| Fruit | 3094 | 6584 | 47 |
| Lower Limb | 1720 | 6373 | 26 |
| Upper Limb | 1023 | 4265 | 24 |

2.  As the differences between the model and the data vertices increase, it becomes difficult for the model to fit to the data.
3.  For a dummy limb, the fitting of the model with the data shows a satisfactory result. The results of 15 measurements show that both the upper and lower limbs have a correlation coefficient close to 1, i.e. both the model and the actual limb data are highly correlated.

The major contribution of this chapter is the introduction of a new methodology of prosthetic design using multiviews technique. The technique is passive and reduces the cost of using a laser scanner or any other active device. The technique avoids direct contact with the residual limb — as in casting with plaster — gives a better result and can quickly choose the desired prosthetic socket if the method of fitting the model and data is applied successfully. On registration, by applying the deformation process, the rigid registration of

the ICP algorithm is extended into a non-rigid registration. The influence region introduced during the deformation process solves the problem for the two points that are close in Euclidean distance but are far apart in surface distance.

## CONCLUSION AND FUTURE WORK

This chapter presents an alternative approach to designing prosthetic devices using multiviews reconstruction method and offering a significant advance for orthotic and prosthetic design by using an image processing technique. The passive method of reconstruction is used to avoid the expensive devices found in the active method. In order to demonstrate the application of the proposed algorithm, models of the dummy limbs are used. First, the 3D data of these limbs (upper and lower limbs) are obtained by using a turntable-based system and the data is then reconstructed using the shape-from-silhouette technique. The object to be reconstructed is placed on the turntable and the images of the object are taken at fixed intervals while the turntable rotates around a vertical axis. The marching cubes technique is used to obtain the surface of the 3D mesh data. The model of the limb (which is cylindrical) has been created to fit with the 3D limb data. After pre-processing the 3D data, the 3D model and 3D data are registered for a further reconstruction process. The 3D data and model are registered using an ICP algorithm. Once the 3D data is registered with the 3D model, the 3D model is then deformed to match the 3D data. In this step, a new method that transforms the 3D model's feature points to match their 3D data counterparts is proposed.

As a conclusion, a method of generating a 3D model of a limb which involves fitting and modifying a reference model generated by either a SfS based reconstruction technique or a simple program, and a deformation process is successfully presented. The experimental results show that the use of the deformation process to reshape the 3D model of a limb produces good fit with the actual limb data, especially for a limb that has a small number of vertices. For real applications on limb data, if the model of the residual limb of a patient is available, a prosthetist can use the proposed method to fit model to the current patient's limb data. If the available model is similar to the limb data, then the deformation process will achieve a better performance. The reconstruction from multiviews in this paper uses a turntable system, which in practice is difficult for obtaining 3D data of real human limbs. In future, rotating the camera instead of the object is a possible approach to overcome this problem. Another consideration is introducing the Graphical User Interface (GUI) for the program.

## REFERENCES

Besl, P., & McKay, N. (1992). A method for registration of 3D shapes. *IEEE Transactions on Pattern Analysis and Machine Intelligence, 14*(2), 239–255. doi:10.1109/34.121791

Borrel, P., & Rappoport, A. (1994). Simple constrained deformations for geometric modeling and interactive design. *ACM Transactions on Graphics, 13*(2), 137–155. doi:10.1145/176579.176581

Faugeras, O. (1993). Three-dimensional computer vision: A geometric viewpoint. MIT Press. Fremont, V., & Chellali, R. (2004). Turntable-based 3D object reconstruction. *IEEE Conference on Cybernetics and Intelligent Systems* (pp. 1277-1282).

Hartley, R., & Zisserman, A. (1998). *Multiple view geometry in computer vision*. Cambridge University Press.

Laurentini, A. (1994). The visual hull concept for silhouettes - based image understanding. *IEEE Transactions on Pattern Analysis and Machine Intelligence, 16*(2), 150–162. doi:10.1109/34.273735

Laurentini, A. (1997). How many 2D silhouettes does it take to reconstruct a 3D object? *Computer Vision and Image Understanding, 67*(1), 81–87. doi:10.1006/cviu.1996.0508

Lusardi, M., & Nielson, C. (2007). *Orthotics and prosthetics in rehabilitation* (2nd ed.). Elsevier.

Mahmood, N. H. (2009). *3D surface reconstruction from multiviews for orthotic and prosthetic design*. University of Warwick. Ph.D Thesis.

Mahmood, N. H., & Tjahjadi, T. (2006). 3D reconstruction from multiple views for orthotic and prosthetic design: An overview. *4th Student Conference on Research and Development* (pp. 70–75).

Mahmood, N. H., & Tjahjadi, T. (2009). Prosthetic design of lower limb using 3D surface reconstruction. *ICSESC, 2009*, 263–267.

Mahmood, N. H., & Tjahjadi, T. (2010). 3D reconstruction for prosthetic design. *Second International Conference on Computer Engineering and Applications* (pp. 431–435).

Rusinkiewicz, S., & Levoy, M. (2001). Efficient variants of the ICP algorithm. In *Proceedings of the 3rd International Conference on 3D Digital Imaging and Modeling* (pp. 145- 152).

Seymour, R. (2002). *Prosthetics and orthotics - Lower limb and spinal*. Lippincott Williams & Wilkins.

Shin, D., & Tjahjadi, T. (2005). 3D object reconstruction from multiple views in approximate circular motion. *Proceedings of IEE SMK UK-RI Chapter Conference on Applied Cybernetics* (pp. 70-75)

Wong, K., & Cipolla, R. (2001). Structure and motion from silhouettes. *Computer Vision, ICCV*, 217–222.

## KEY TERMS AND DEFINITIONS

**3D Surface Reconstruction:** A method to generate a piecewise linear surface from a 3d point set.

**Circular Motion:** Circular motion is rotation along a circle, a circular path or a circular orbit. It can be uniform, that is, with constant angular rate of rotation, or non-uniform, that is, with a changing rate of rotation. The rotation around a fixed axis of a three-dimensional body involves circular motion of its parts. The equations describing circular motion of an object do not take size or geometry into account, rather, the motion of a point mass in a plane is assumed. In practice, the center of mass of a body can be considered to undergo circular motion.

**Iterative Closest Point:** Iterative Closest Point (ICP) is an algorithm employed to minimize the difference between two clouds of points.

**Model-Based Reconstruction:** A reconstruction process based on a model that is similar with the object.

**Prosthetic Devices:** Prosthetic devices are artificial components designed to replace a part of the human body that is missing, either due to accident or a birth defect.

**Residual Limb:** The portion of the arm or leg remaining after an amputation, sometimes referred to as a stump or residuum.

**Shape from Silhouettes:** Shape-From-Silhouette (SFS), also known as Visual Hull (VH) construction, is a popular 3D reconstruction method which estimates the shape of an object from multiple silhouette images. The original SFS formulation assumes that the entire silhouette images are captured either at the same time or while the object is static. This assumption is violated when the object moves or changes shape.

# Compilation of References

Ahmed, A., & Farag, A. (2006). A new formulation for shape from shading for non-Lambertian surfaces. *Conference on Computer Vision and Pattern Recognition*, (pp. 1817–1824).

Alexa, M., Behr, J., Cohen-Or, D., Fleishman, S., Levin, D., & Silva, T. C. (2003). Computing and rendering point set surfaces. *IEEE Transactions on Visualization and Computer Graphics*, 9, 3–15. doi:10.1109/TVCG.2003.1175093

Alliez, P., Cohen-Steiner, D., Yvinec, M., & Desbrun, M. (2005). Variational tetrahedral meshing. *ACM Transactions on Graphics*, 24(3), 617–625. doi:10.1145/1073204.1073238

Alvarez, L., Guichard, F., Lions, P. L., & Morel, J. M. (1992). Image selective smoothing and edge detection by nonlinear diffusion. *SIAM Journal on Numerical Analysis*, 29, 845–866. doi:10.1137/0729052

Alvarez, L., Guichard, F., Lions, P. L., & Morel, J. M. (1993). Axioms and fundamental equations of image processing. *Archives of Rational Mechanics*, 23, 199–257. doi:10.1007/BF00375127

Amenta, N., Choi, S., & Kolluri, R. (2001). The power crust. In *Sixth ACM Symposium on Solid Modeling and Applications* (pp. 249-260).

Amenta, N., Choi, S., Dey, T. K., & Leekha, N. (2000). A simple algorithm for homeomorphic surface reconstruction. In *Proceedings of the Sixteenth Annual Symposium on Computational Geometry*, (pp. 213-222).

Anderson, M. E., & Trahey, G. E. (2009). *A seminar on k-space applied to medical ultrasound*. Retrieved June 10, 2009, from http://dukemil.egr.duke.edu/Ultrasound/k-space

Armangué, X., & Salvi, J. (2003). Overall view regarding fundamental matrix estimation. *Image and Vision Computing*, 21(2), 205–220. doi:10.1016/S0262-8856(02)00154-3

Arnold-Bos, A., Malkasse, J. P., & Kerven, G. (2005). A pre-processing framework for automatic underwater images denoising. In *Proceedings of the European Conference on Propagation and Systems*, France.

Arrault, J., Arnéodo, A., Davis, A., & Marshak, A. (1997). Wavelet based multifractal analysis of rough surfaces: Application to cloud models and satellite data. *Physical Review Letters*, 79(1), 75–78. doi:10.1103/PhysRevLett.79.75

Atkinson, R. C., & Shiffrin, R. M. (1968). Human memory: A proposed system and its control processes. In Spence, K. W., & Spence, J. T. (Eds.), *The psychology of learning and motivation* (*Vol. 2*, pp. 89–195). New York, N Y: Academic Press.

Ayache, N., & Faugeras, O. D. (1987). Building a consistent 3D representation of a mobile robot environment by combining multiple stereo views. In *International Joint Conference on Artificial Intelligence* (pp. 808-810).

Ayache, N., & Lustman, F. (1987). Trinocular stereovision: Recent results. In *International Joint Conference on Artificial Intelligence* (pp. 826-828).

Ayache, N., & Faverjon, B. (1987). Efficient registration of stereo images by matching graph descriptions of edge segments. *International Journal of Computer Vision*, 1(2), 107–131. doi:10.1007/BF00123161

Ayache, N., & Lustman, F. (1991). Trinocular stereo vision for robotics. *IEEE Transactions on Pattern Analysis and Machine Intelligence*, 13(1), 73–85. doi:10.1109/34.67633

Azevedo, T. C. S., Tavares, J. M. R. S., & Vaz, M. A. P. (2007). *3D object reconstruction from uncalibrated images using a single off-the-shelf camera*. Retrieved July 28, 2011, from http://repositorioaberto.up.pt/bitstream/10216/4175/2/3D%20Object%20Reconstruction%20from%20 Uncalibrated%20Images%20 using%20a%20Single.pdf

Baldwin, J., & Roberts, L. (2006). *Visual communication: From theory to practice*. Switzerland: AVA Publishing.

Bankman, I. N. (Ed.). (2000). *Handbook of medical imaging: Processing and analysis*. Orlando, FL: Academic Press, Inc.

Barbara, Z., & Jan, F. (2003). Image registration methods: A survey. *Image and Vision Computing, 21*, 977–1000. doi:10.1016/S0262-8856(03)00137-9

Barequet, G., & Sharir, M. (1997). Partial surface and volume matching in three dimensions. *IEEE Transactions on Pattern Analysis and Machine Intelligence, 19*(9), 929–948. doi:10.1109/34.615444

Barjatya, A. (2004). *Block matching algorithms for motion estimation*. DIP 6620 Spring Final Project Paper.

Barnard, R., Dahlquist, G., Pearce, K., Reichel, L., & Richards, K. (1998). Gram polynomials and the Kummer function. *Journal of Approximation Theory, 94*(1), 128–143. doi:10.1006/jath.1998.3181

Barnard, S. T. (1989). Stochastic stereo matching over scale. *International Journal of Computer Vision, 3*(1), 17–32. doi:10.1007/BF00054836

Bayraktar, B., Bernas, T., Robinson, P., & Rajwa, B. (2007). A numerical recipe for accurate image reconstruction from discrete orthogonal moments. *Pattern Recognition, 40*, 659–669. doi:10.1016/j.patcog.2006.03.009

Bazeille, S., Quidu, I., Jaulin, L., & Malkasse, J. P. (2006). Automatic underwater image pre-processing. *In Proceeding of the Caracterisation du Milieu Marin (CMM '06)*.

Beardsley, P. A., Zisserman, A., & Murray, D. W. (1997). Sequential updating of projective and affine structure from motion. *International Journal of Computer Vision, 23*(3), 235–259. doi:10.1023/A:1007923216416

Beck, A., & Teboulle, M. (2009). Fast gradient-based algorithms for constrained total variation image denoising and de-blurring problems. *IEEE Transactions on Image Processing, 18*(11), 2419–2434. doi:10.1109/TIP.2009.2028250

Berryman, F., Pynsent, P., & Cubillo, J. (2004). The effect of windowing in Fourier transform profilometry applied to noisy images. *Optics and Lasers in Engineering, 41*, 815–825. doi:10.1016/S0143-8166(03)00061-7

Bertozzi, M., Broggi, A., & Fascioli, A. (1996). A stereo vision system for real-time automotive obstacle detection. In *IEEE International Conference on Image Processing: Vol. II.* (pp. 681-684).

Besl, P., & McKay, N. (1992). A method for registration of 3D shapes. *IEEE Transactions on Pattern Analysis and Machine Intelligence, 14*(2), 239–255. doi:10.1109/34.121791

Bileschi, S. (2009). Fully automatic calibration of LIDAR and video streams from a vehicle. *IEEE 12th International Conference on Computer Vision Workshops (ICCV Workshops)* (pp. 1457-1464). Institute of Electrical and Electronics Engineers.

Blais, F. (2004). Review of 20 years of range sensor development. *Journal of Electronic Imaging, 13*, 231–240. doi:10.1117/1.1631921

Bloomenthal, J. (1988). Polygonization of implicit surfaces. *Computer Aided Geometric Design, 5*, 341–355. doi:10.1016/0167-8396(88)90013-1

Boehler, W., & Marbs, A. (2002). 3D scanning instruments. In *CIPA WG6 International Workshop on Scanning for Cultural Heritage Recording (CIPA2002)* (pp. 9-12).

Boeree, C. G. (2006). *Personality theories: Jean Piaget*. Retrieved on October 7, 2008, from http://webspace.ship.edu/cgboer/piaget.html

Bolin, M. R., & Meyer, G. W. (1998). A perceptually based adaptive sampling algorithm. In *ACM SIGGRAPH* (pp. 299–309). ACM Press.

Borrel, P., & Rappoport, A. (1994). Simple constrained deformations for geometric modeling and interactive design. *ACM Transactions on Graphics, 13*(2), 137–155. doi:10.1145/176579.176581

Boufama, B., & Habed, A. (2004). Three-dimensional structure calculation: achieving accuracy without calibration. *Image and Vision Computing, 22*(12), 1039–1049.

Boyd, J. (2001). *Chebyschev and Fourier spectral methods*. Mineola, NY: Dover Publications Inc.

Boykov, Y., & Kolmogorov, V. (2004). An experimental comparison of min-cut/max-flow algorithms for energy minimization in vision. *IEEE Transactions on Pattern Analysis and Machine Intelligence, 26*(9), 1124–1137. doi:10.1109/TPAMI.2004.60

Brandou, V., Allais, A. G., Perrier, M., Malis, E., Rives, P., Sarrazin, J., & Sarradin, P. M. (2007). 3D reconstruction of natural underwater scenes using stereovision system IRIS. *IEEE OCEANS'07-EUROPE*, (pp. 1-6).

Bredno, J., Lehmann, T. M., & Spitzer, K. A. (2003). General discrete contour model in two, three, and four dimensions for topology-adaptive multichannel segmentation. *IEEE Transactions on Pattern Analysis and Machine Intelligence, 25*(5), 550–563. doi:10.1109/TPAMI.2003.1195990

Breiman, L. (1996). Bagging predictors. *Machine Learning, 24*(2), 123–140. doi:10.1007/BF00058655

Breiman, L. (2001). Random forests. *Machine Learning, 45*(1), 5–32. doi:10.1023/A:1010933404324

Brown, L. G. (1992). A survey of image registration techniques. [CSUR]. *ACM Computing Surveys, 24*(4), 325–376. doi:10.1145/146370.146374

Brownstein, S. C., Weiner, M., & Green, S. W. (1999). *Barron's how to prepare for the GRE*. New Delhi, India: Galgotia Publications.

Buchart, C., Borro, D., & Amundarain, A. (2008). GPU local triangulation: An interpolating surface reconstruction algorithm. *Computer Graphics Forum, 27*(3), 807–814. doi:10.1111/j.1467-8659.2008.01211.x

Carder, K., Reinersman, P., Costello, D., Kaltenbacher, E. M., Kloske, J., & Montes, M. (2005). Optical inspection of ports and harbors: Laser-line sensor model applications in 2 and 3 dimensions. *Proceedings of the Society for Photo-Instrumentation Engineers, 5780*, 49–58.

Caselles, V., Catte, F., Coll, T., & Dibos, F. (1997). A geometric model for active contours. *International Journal of Computer Vision, 22*, 61–69. doi:10.1023/A:1007979827043

Caselles, V., Morel, J., & Sapiro, G. (1998). Introduction to the special issue on partial differential equations and geometry driven diffusions in image processing. *IEEE Transactions on Image Processing, 7*(3), 269–273. doi:10.1109/TIP.1998.661176

Castellani, U., Fusiello, A., Murino, V., Papaleo, L., Puppo, E., Repetto, S., & Pittore, M. (2004). Efficient on-line mosaicing from 3D acoustical images. *OCEANS '04. MTTS/IEEE TECHNO-OCEAN '04*, Vol. 2, (pp. 670-677).

Cavalcanti, P. R., & Mello, U. T. (1999). Three-dimensional constrained delaunay triangulation: A minimalist approach. In *Proceedings of the 8th International Meshing Roundtable* (pp. 119–129), Lake Tahoe, CA: Sandia National Laboratories.

Chambolle, A. (1994). Partial differential equations and image processing. *IEEE International Conference on Image Processing*, Austin, TX.

Chan, T. F., & Shen, J. (2005). Variational image inpainting. *Communications on Pure and Applied Mathematics, 58*(5), 579–619. doi:10.1002/cpa.20075

Chen, Q., Montesinos, P., Sun, Q. S., Heng, P. A., & Xia, D. S. (2009). Adaptive total variation denoising based on difference curvature. *Image and Vision Computing, 28*(3). doi: 10.1016/j.imavis. 2009.04.012

Chen, F., Brown, G. M., & Song, M. (2000). Overview of three-dimensional shape measurement using optical methods. *Optical Engineering (Redondo Beach, Calif.), 39*, 10–22. doi:10.1117/1.602438

Chen, H. J., Zhang, J., Lv, D. J., & Fang, J. (2007). 3-D shape measurement by composite pattern projection and hybrid processing. *Optics Express*, *15*, 12318–12330. doi:10.1364/OE.15.012318

Chen, L. C., Nguyen, X. L., Zhang, F. H., & Lin, T. Y. (2010). High-speed Fourier transform profilometry for reconstructing objects having arbitrary surface colours. *Journal of Optics*, *12*, 095502. doi:10.1088/2040-8978/12/9/095502

Chen, T., Ming, C. M., Tan, P., Shamir, A., & Hu, S. M. (2009). Sketch2photo: Internet image montage. *ACM Transactions on Graphics*, *28*(5). doi:10.1145/1618452.1618470

Chien, C. H., & Aggarwel, J. K. (1986). Identification of 3D Objects from multiple silhouettes using quadtrees/octrees. *Computer Vision Graphics and Image Processing*, *36*(2), 256–273. doi:10.1016/0734-189X(86)90078-2

Chikatla, S. B. P. (2010). *Cross-cultural differences among students from India and the United States on preference, use and other cultural factors involving embodied apparent 2D and embellished apparent 3D USA Today Charts.* Unpublished doctoral dissertation, University of South Alabama.

Choi, S., Kim, T., & Yu, W. (2009). Performance evaluation of RANSAC family. In *Proceedings of the British Machine Vision Conference (BMVC).*

Chum, O. (2005). *Two-view geometry estimation by random sample and consensus.* PhD Thesis, Czech Technical University in Prague.

Cignoni, P. (1998). DeWall: A fast divide and conquer Delaunay triangulation algorithm. *Computer Aided Design*, *30*, 333–341. doi:10.1016/S0010-4485(97)00082-1

Clark, R., & Mayer, R. E. (2003). *e-Learning and the science of instruction.* San Francisco, CA: Pfeiffer.

Clark, R., & Lyons, C. (2004). *Graphics for learning.* San Francisco, CA: Pfeiffer.

Clerc, M., & Mallot, S. (2002). The texture gradient equation for recovering shape from texture. *IEEE Transactions on Pattern Analysis and Machine Intelligence*, *24*, 536–549. doi:10.1109/34.993560

Comanducci, D., Maki, A., Colombo, C., & Cipolla, R. (2010). 2D-to-3D photo rendering for 3D displays. *Proceedings of International Symposium on 3D Data Processing, Visualization and Transmission* (3DPVT).

Comaniciu, D., Ramesh, V., & Meer, P. (2003). Kernel-based object tracking. *IEEE Transactions on Pattern Analysis and Machine Intelligence*, *25*(5), 564–575. doi:10.1109/TPAMI.2003.1195991

Computer Aided Desing. (2010). *Wikipedia, The Free Encyclopedia.* Retrieved December 18, 2010, from http://en.wikipedia.org/wiki/CAD

Cooper, J., Venkatesh, S., & Kitchen, L. (1993). Early jump-out corner detectors. *IEEE Transactions on Pattern Analysis and Machine Intelligence*, *15*, 823–828. doi:10.1109/34.236246

Cootes, T. F., Edwards, G. J., & Taylor, C. J. (1998). Active appearance models. *5th European Conference on Computer Vision* (pp. 484–498).

Corsini, M., Gelasca, E. D., & Ebrahimi, T. (2005). A multi-scale roughness metric for 3D watermarking quality assessment. In *Workshop on Image Analysis for Multimedia Interactive Services*, (pp. 13-15).

Criminisi, A., Reid, I., & Zisserman, A. (1999). Single view metrology. *International Conference on Computer Vision*, (pp. 434-442).

Cross, G., & Zisserman, A. (2000). Surface reconstruction from multiple views using apparent contours and surface texture. In A. Leonardis, F. Solina, & R. Bajcsy (Eds.), *NATO Advanced Research Workshop on Confluence of Computer Vision and Computer Graphics* (pp. 25-47). Ljubljana, Slovenia.

Crossno, P., & Angel, E. (1999). Spiraling edge: fast surface reconstruction from partially organized sample points. In *VIS '99: Proceedings of the Conference on Visualization '99*, (pp. 317-324). IEEE Computer Society Press.

Dalgleish, F. R., Tetlow, S., & Allwood, R. L. (2005). Seabed-relative navigation by structured lighting techniques. In Roberts, G. N., & Sutton, R. (Eds.), *Advances in unmanned marine vehicles* (pp. 277–292).

Dardenne, J., Valette, S., Siauve, N., Burais, N., & Prost, R. (2009). Variational tetrahedral mesh generation from discrete volume data. *The Visual Computer, 25*(5-7), 401–410. doi:10.1007/s00371-009-0323-7

Davison, A. J., Reid, I. D., Molton, N. D., & Stasse, O. (2007). MonoSLAM: Real-time single camera SLAM. *IEEE Transactions on Pattern Analysis and Machine Intelligence, 29*(6), 1052–1067. doi:10.1109/TPAMI.2007.1049

Debevec, P., Taylor, C., & Malik, J. (1996). Modeling and rendering architecture from photographs: A hybrid geometry- and image-based approach. *In Proceedings of SIGGRAPH,* (pp. 11-20).

Delage, E., Lee, H., & Ng, Y. A. (2006). A dynamic Bayesian network model for autonomous 3D reconstruction from a single indoor image. *Computer Vision and Pattern Recognition,* (pp. 2418-2428).

Delaunay, B. (1934). Sur la sphere vide. A la mémoire de Georges Voronoi. *Bulletin of Academy of Sciences of the USSR, 7,* 793–800.

Dempsey, J. V., Chikatla, S., & Inpornvijit, K. (2008, March). *2D (simple charts) versus 3D (embellished) USA Today charts.* Poster session presented at the USA Research Council's 15th Annual Research Forum, Mobile, AL.

Derraz, F., Beladgham, M., & Khelif, M. (2004). Application of active contour models in medical image segmentation. In *International Conference on Information Technology: Coding and Computing, ITCC'04* (p. 679), Los Alamitos, CA: IEEE Computer Society.

Dewaele, P., Wambacq, P., Oosterlinck, A., & Marchand, J. L. (1990). Comparison of some speckle reduction techniques for SAR images. *Geoscience and Remote Sensing Symposium, IGARSS '90,* (pp. 2417-2422).

Dey, T. K., & Goswami, S. (2003). Tight cocone: A water-tight surface reconstructor. *Journal of Computing and Information Science in Engineering, 3*(4), 127–134. doi:10.1115/1.1633278

Dey, T. K., & Goswami, S. (2006). Provable surface reconstruction from noisy samples. *Computational Geometry: Theory and Applications, 35,* 124–141.

Dippel, S., Stahl, M., Wiemker, R., & Blaffert, T. (2002). Multiscale contrast enhancement for radiographies: Laplacian pyramid versus fast wavelet transform. *IEEE Transactions on Medical Imaging, 21*(4), 343–353. doi:10.1109/TMI.2002.1000258

Droske, M., Meyer, B., Rumpf, M., & Schaller, C. (2001). An adaptive level set method for medical image segmentation. In *17th International Conference on Information Processing in Medical Imaging* (pp. 416–422). London, UK: Springer-Verlag.

Drost, R., Munson, D. C. Jr, & Singer, A. C. (2002). Shape-from-silhouette approach to imaging ocean mines. In *Proceeding of Ocean Optics* (*Vol. 4488,* pp. 115–122). Remote Sensing and Underwater Imaging.

Duda, R. O., Hart, P. E., & Stork, D. G. (Eds.). (2001). *Pattern classification* (2nd ed.). New York, NY: Wiley-Interscience.

Du, G., & Wang, D. (2003). Tetrahedral mesh generation and optimization based on centroidal voronoi tessellations. *International Journal for Numerical Methods in Engineering, 56*(9), 1355–1373. doi:10.1002/nme.616

Du, L., Ren, L., Dunson, D., & Carin, L. (2009). A Bayesian model for simultaneous image clustering, annotation and object segmentation. In Bengio, Y., Schuurmans, D., Lafferty, L., Williams, C. K. I., & Culotta, A. (Eds.), *Advances in Neural Information Processing Systems, 22* (pp. 486–494).

Du, Q., Faber, V., & Gunzburger, M. (1999). Centroidal voronoi tessellations: Applications and algorithms. *SIAM Review, 41*(4), 637–676. doi:10.1137/S0036144599352836

Dyer, C. R. (2001). Volumetric scene reconstruction from multiple views. In Davis, L. S. (Ed.), *Foundations of image understanding* (pp. 469–489). Boston, MA: Kluwer. doi:10.1007/978-1-4615-1529-6_16

Eden, M., Unser, M., & Leonardi, R. (1986). Polynomial representation of pictures. *Signal Processing, 10,* 385–393. doi:10.1016/0165-1684(86)90046-0

Eilers, P. (2003). A perfect smoother. *Analytical Chemistry, 75*(14), 1383–1386. doi:10.1021/ac034173t

Elias, R. (2003). Clustering points in *n*D space through hierarchical structures. In *IEEE Canadian Conference on Electrical and Computer Engineering: Vol. 3* (pp. 2079-2081).

Elias, R. (2004). Wide baseline matching through homographic transformation. In *Proceedings of the 17th international conference on pattern recognition* (Vol. 4, p. 130-133). Cambridge, UK: IEEE Computer Society.

Elias, R. (2007). Enhancing accuracy of camera rotation angles detected by inaccurate sensors and expressing them in different systems for wide baseline stereo. In *International Conference on Quality Control by Artificial Vision: Vol. 6356* (pp. 17:1-8). Le Creusot, France.

Elias, R. (2009a). Geometric modeling in computer vision: An introduction to projective geometry. In B. Wah (Ed.), *Wiley encyclopedia of computer science and engineering* (Vol. 3, p. 1400-1416). John Wiley & Sons.

Elias, R., & Laganiere, R. (1999). The disparity pyramid: An irregular pyramid approach for stereoscopic image analysis. In *Vision Interface Conference* (pp. 352-359).

Elias, R., & Laganiere, R. (2003). *The planar perspective matrix: Derivation through different rotation systems.* Technical Report TR-2003-02, VIVA Lab, School of Information Technology and Engineering, University of Ottawa. Ottawa, Ontario, Canada.

Elias, R. (2007). Sparse view stereo matching. *Pattern Recognition Letters, 28*(13), 1667–1678. doi:10.1016/j.patrec.2007.04.009

Elias, R. (2009b). *Modeling of environments: From sparse views to obstacle reconstruction.* Germany: LAP Lambert Academic Publishing.

Evans, L. C., & Spruck, J. (1991). Motion of level sets by mean curvature. *International Journal of Differential Geometry, 33*, 635–681.

Farin, G., Hoshek, J., & Kim, M.-S. (Eds.). (2002). *Handbook of computer aided geometric design.* Amsterdam, The Netherlands: Elsevier Science B.V.

Faugeras, O. (1993). Three-dimensional computer vision: A geometric viewpoint. MIT Press. Fremont, V., & Chellali, R. (2004). Turntable-based 3D object reconstruction. *IEEE Conference on Cybernetics and Intelligent Systems* (pp. 1277-1282).

Faugeras, O. D. (1992). What can be seen in three dimensions with an uncalibrated stereo rig? In *Proceedings of the Second European Conference on Computer Vision,* Vol. 588, (pp. 563-578).

Faugeras, O. (1996). *Three-dimentional computer vision, a geometric viewpoint.* Cambridge, MA: MIT Press.

Faugeras, O., & Luong, Q.-T. (2001). *The geometry of multiple images.* Cambridge, MA: MIT Press.

Faugeras, O., & Maybank, S. (1990). Motion from point matches: Multiplicity of solutions. *International Journal of Computer Vision, 4*, 225–246. doi:10.1007/BF00054997

Felzenszwalb, P., & Huttenlocher, D. (2004). Efficient graph-based image segmentation. *International Journal of Computer Vision, 59*.

Fitzgibbon, A. W., Cross, G., & Zisserman, A. (1998). Automatic 3D model construction for turn-table sequences. In *Lecture Notes in Comuter Science 1506, 3D Structure from Multiple Images of Large-Scale Environments, European Workshop, SMILE'98* (p. 155-170).

Fleming, R. W., Torralba, A., & Adelson, E. H. (2004). Specular reflections and the perception of shape. *Journal of Vision (Charlottesville, Va.), 4*(9), 798–820. doi:10.1167/4.9.10

Foley, J. D., Dam, A., Feiner, S. K., & Hughes, J. F. (1995). *Computer graphics: Principles and practice in C* (2nd ed.). Addison-Wesley.

Forest, J., Salvi, J., & Batlle, J. (2000). *Image ranging system for underwater applications.* IFAC Conference on Maneuvering and Control of Marine Craft, Aalborg, Denmark.

Forsyth, D. A., & Ponce, J. (2003). *Computer vision: A modern approach.* Upper Saddle River, NJ: Pearson Education Inc., Prentice Hall, Inc.

Franke, U., Rabe, C., Badino, H., & Gehrig, S. (2005). *6D-vision: Fusion of stereo and motion for robust environment perception.* DAGM Symposium.

Fraser, C. (1999). *Automated vision metrology: A mature technology for industrial inspection and engineering surveys.* In 6th South East Asian Surveyors Congress Fremantle. Department of Geomatics, University of Melbourne, Western Australia.

Frost, V. S., & Stiles, J. A. (1982). A model for radar Images and its application to adaptive digital filtering of multiplicative noise. *IEEE Transactions on Pattern Analysis and Machine Intelligence*, *4*(2), 157–166. doi:10.1109/TPAMI.1982.4767223

Fusiello, A., & Irsara, L. (2010). Quasi-Euclidean epipolar rectification of uncalibrated images. *Machine Vision and Applications*, *22*(4), 1–8.

Fusiello, A., Trucco, E., & Verri, A. (2000). A compact algorithm for rectification of stereo pairs. *Machine Vision and Applications*, *12*(1), 16–22. doi:10.1007/s001380050120

Gabor, D. (1965). Information theory in electron microscopy. *Laboratory Investigation*, *14*, 801–807.

Garding, J. (1992). Shape from texture for smooth curved surfaces in perspective projection. *Journal of Mathematical Imaging and Vision*, *2*, 327–350. doi:10.1007/BF00121877

Garland, M. (1999). *Quadric-based polygonal surface simplification*. Ph.D. dissertation, Computer Science Department, Carnegie Mellon University.

Gautschi, W. (2004). *Orthogonal polynomials, computation and approximation*. Oxford, UK: Oxford University Press.

Gerig, G., Kubler, O., Kikinis, R., & Jolesz, F. (1992). Nonlinear anisotropic filtering of MRI data. *IEEE Transactions on Medical Imaging*, *11*(2), 221–232. doi:10.1109/42.141646

Gibson, J. (1950). *The perception of the visual world*. Boston, MA: Houghton Mifflin.

Gilboa, G., Sochen, N., & Zeevi, Y. Y. (2004). Image enhancement and denoising by complex diffusion processes. *IEEE Transactions on Pattern Analysis and Machine Intelligence*, *25*(8), 1020–1036. doi:10.1109/TPAMI.2004.47

Goldsmith, E. (1987). The analysis of illustration in theory and practice. In Houghton, H. A., & Willows, D. M. (Eds.), *The psychology of illustration* (*Vol. 2*, pp. 53–85). New York, NY: Springer-Verlag. doi:10.1007/978-1-4612-4706-7_2

Golub, G., & Van Loan, C. (1996). *Matrix computations* (3rd ed.). Baltimore, MD: John Hopkins University Press.

Gonzalez Rafael, C., Woods, R. E., & Eddins, S. L. (2004). *Digital image processing using MATLAB*. Pearson Education.

Gonzalez, R. C., & Wintz, P. (1987). *Digital image processing* (2nd ed.). New York, NY: Academic Press.

Gonzalez, R. C., & Woods, R. E. (2006). *Digital image processing* (3rd ed.). Upper Saddle River, NJ: Prentice Hall, Inc.

Goodman, J. W. (1984). Statistical properties of laser speckle patterns. In Dainty, J. C. (Ed.), *Laser speckle and related phenomena* (pp. 9–75). Berlin, Germany: Springer-Verlag.

Gopi, M., Krishnan, S., & Silva, C. T. (2000). Surface reconstruction based on lower dimensional localized Delaunay triangulation. *Computer Graphics Forum*, *19*(3), 467–478. doi:10.1111/1467-8659.00439

Gorry, P. (1990). General least-squares smoothing and differentiation by the convolution (Savitzky-Golay) method. *Analytical Chemistry*, *62*, 570–573. doi:10.1021/ac00205a007

Gorthi, S. S., & Rastogi, P. (2010). Fringe projection techniques: Whither we are? *Optics and Lasers in Engineering*, *48*(2), 133–140. doi:10.1016/j.optlaseng.2009.09.001

Gram, J. (1883). Ueber die entwicklung realler funktionen in reihen mittelst der methode der kleinsten quadrate. *Journal fuer dei reine und angewandte Mathematik*, 150-157.

Granger-Piche, M., Epstein, E., & Poulin, P. (2004). Interactive hierarchical space carving with projector-based calibrations. In *Vision, Modeling, and Visualization Conference* (pp. 159-166).

Guiducci, A. (1988). Corner characterization by differential geometry techniques. *Pattern Recognition Letters*, *8*, 311–318. doi:10.1016/0167-8655(88)90080-3

Han, F., & Zhu, S. C. (2003). Bayesian reconstruction of 3d shapes and scenes from a single image. In *ICCV Workshop Higher-Level Knowledge in 3D Modeling Motion Analysis*, (pp. 12-21).

Hannah, M. J. (1974). *Computer matching of areas in stereo images*. Ph.D. thesis, Comput. Sci. Dept., Stanford Univ., Stanford, CA, July 1974; Tech. Rep. STAN-CS-74-438.

Haque, M. E. (2002, March). *Contemporary techniques to teach reinforced concrete design*. Session paper presented at the Gulf-Southwest Annual Meeting of American Society for Engineering Education (ASEE), University of Louisiana, Lafayette, USA.

Haralick, R. M., & Shapiro, L. G. (1993). *Computer and robot vision* (*Vol. 1*). Addison-Wesley.

Hartley, R. (1992). Estimation of relative camera positions for uncalibrated cameras. In G. Sandini (Ed.), *Proceedings of ECCV-92, LNCS Vol. 588*, (pp. 579–587). Springer- Verlag.

Hartley, R. I., & Sturm, P. (1994). Triangulation. *American Image Understanding Workshop*, (pp. 957-966).

Hartley, R. I., & Sturm, P. (1995). Triangulation. In *Computer Analysis of Images and Patterns, 6ᵗʰ International Conference* (Vol. 970, p. 190-197). Prague, Czech Republic: Springer.

Hartley, R., & Gupta, R. (1993). Computing matched-epipolar projections. In *Proceedings of the IEEE Computer Society Conference on Computer Vision and Pattern Recognition*, (pp. 549-555).

Hartley, R. (1997). In defence of the eight-point algorithm. *IEEE Transactions on Pattern Recognition and Machine Intelligence, 19*(6), 580–593.

Hartley, R. I. (1999). Theory and practice of projective rectification. *International Journal of Computer Vision, 35*(2), 115–127. doi:10.1023/A:1008115206617

Hartley, R. I. (2003). *Multiple view geometry*. Cambridge University Press.

Hartley, R. I., & Zisserman, A. (2006). *Multiple view geometry in computer vision*. Cambridge University Press.

Hassner, T., & Basri, R. (2006). Example based 3D reconstruction from single 2D images. *Computer Vision and Pattern Recognition Workshop (CVPRW)*, (pp. 15-22).

Hausler, G., & Ritter, D. (1993). Parallel three-dimensional sensing by color-coded triangulation. *Applied Optics, 32*, 7164–7169. doi:10.1364/AO.32.007164

Hegarty, M., Narayanan, N. H., & Freitas, P. (2002). Understanding machines from multimedia and hypermedia presentation. In Otero, J., Leon, J. A., & Graesser, A. C. (Eds.), *The psychology of science text comprehension* (pp. 357–384). Hillsdale, NJ: Erlbaum.

Heikkila, J., & Silven, O. (1997). A four-step camera calibration procedure with implicit image correction. In *Proceedings of the IEEE Computer Society Conference on Computer Vision and Pattern Recognition (CVPR '97), 17-19,* (pp. 1106-1112), San Juan, Pnerto Rico.

Heitz, G., & Koller, D. (2008). Learning spatial context: Using stuff to find things. In *Proceedings of the European Conference on Computer Vision*.

Hoffmann, J., Jungel, M., & Lotzsch, M. (2005). Vision based system for goal-directed obstacle avoidance. In *LNCS, RoboCup 2004: Robot Soccer World Cup VIII: Vol. 3276* (pp. 418-425). Springer.

Hoiem, D., Efros, A., & Hebert, M. (2005). Automatic photo pop-up. In *Association for Computing Machinery's Special Interest Group on Computer Graphics and Interactive Techniques*, (pp. 577 – 584).

Hoiem, D., Efros, A., & Herbert, M. (2005a). *Geometric context from a single imag*. International Conference on Computer Vision (ICCV).

Hoiem, D., Stein, A. N., Efros, A. A., & Herbert, M. (2007b). *Recovering occlusion boundaries from an image*. International Conference on Computer Vision (ICCV).

Hoiem, D., Efros, A. A., & Herbert, M. (2008b, December). Putting objects in perspective. *International Journal of Computer Vision, 80*(1). doi:10.1007/s11263-008-0137-5

Hoiem, D., Efros, A., & Herbert, M. (2006). *Putting objects in perspective. Computer Vision and Pattern Recognition*. CVPR.

Hoiem, D., Efros, A., & Herbert, M. (2007a). Recovering surface layout from an image. *International Journal of Computer Vision, 75*(1). doi:10.1007/s11263-006-0031-y

Hoiem, D., Efros, A., & Herbert, M. (2008a). *Closing the loop on scene interpretation*. CVPR.

Honec, P., Petyovský, P., Richter, M., Grebeníček, F., & Valach, S. (2001). 3D object surface reconstruction. In *13th International Conference of Process Control*, (pp. 94-95). Bratislava, Slovakia: Slovak University of Technology.

Hong, L., & Chen, G. (2004). Segment-based stereo matching using graph cuts. *IEEE Computer Society Conference on Computer Vision and Pattern Recognition*, Vol. 1, (pp. 74-81).

Hoppe, H., DeRose, T., Duchamp, T., McDonald, J., & Stuetzle, W. (1992). Surface reconstruction from unorganized points. In *Proceedings of ACM SIGGRAPH '92* (pp. 71-78).

Horn, B. (1986). *Robot vision.* MIT Press.

Horry, Y., Anjyo, K., & Arai, K. (1997). Tour into the picture: Using a spidery mesh interface to make animation from a single image. *Proceedings of the 24th Annual Conference on Computer Graphics and Interactive Techniques*, (pp. 225–232).

Hosny, K. (2007). Exact Legendre moment computation for gray level images. *Pattern Recognition, 40*(12). doi:10.1016/j.patcog.2007.04.014

Hsieh, C. C., Cheng, W. H., Chang, C. H., Chuang, Y. Y., & Wu, J. L. (2008). Photo navigator. In *Proceeding of the 16th ACM International Conference on Multimedia*, (pp. 419–428). New York, NY: ACM.

Huang, H., Li, D., Zhang, H., Ascher, U., & Cohen-Or, D. (2010). *Points consolidation API.* Retrieved June, 23, 2010, from http://people.cs.ubc.ca/~danli/points_consolidation.htm

Huang, W., Chen, S., & Zheng, G. (2010). A fast 2D discrete tchebichef transform algorithm. *International Conference on Innovative Computing and Communication and Asia-Pacific Conference on Information Technology and Ocean Engineering*, (pp. 358–361).

Huang, H., Li, D., Zhang, H., Ascher, U., & Cohen-Or, D. (2009). Consolidation of unorganized point clouds for surface reconstruction. *ACM Transactions on Graphics, 28*, 176–182. doi:10.1145/1618452.1618522

Huang, P. S., Hu, Q. Y., Jin, F., & Chiang, F. P. (1999). Color-encoded digital fringe projection technique for high-speed three-dimensional surface contouring. *Optical Engineering (Redondo Beach, Calif.), 38*, 1065–1071. doi:10.1117/1.602151

Hu, M.-K. (1962). Visual pattern recognition by moment invariants. *I.R.E. Transactions on Information Theory, 8*, 179–187. doi:10.1109/TIT.1962.1057692

Hwang, W., Lu, C.-S., & Chung, P.-C. (1998). Shape from texture: Estimation of planar surface orientation through the ridge surfaces of continuous wavelet transform. *IEEE Transactions on Image Processing, 7*, 773–780. doi:10.1109/83.668032

Inanici, M., & Galvin, J. (2004). *Evaluation of high dynamic range photography as a luminance mapping technique.* Paper LBNL-57545.

Isard, M., & Blake, A. (1998). Condensation – Conditional density propagation for visual tracking. *International Journal of Computer Vision, 29*, 5–28. doi:10.1023/A:1008078328650

Isgro, F., & Trucco, E. (1999). Projective rectification without epipolar geometry. In *Proceedings of the IEEE Computer Society Conference on Computer Vision and Pattern Recognition (CVPR'99)*, Vol. 1, (pp. 1094-1099).

Iskander, D. R. (1999). Estimation of the parameters of the k-distribution using higher order and fractional moments. *IEEE Transactions on Aerospace and Electronic Systems, 35*(4), 1453–1457. doi:10.1109/7.805463

Iskander, D. R., Zoubir, A. M., & Boashash, B. (1999). A method for estimating the parameters of k-distribution. *IEEE Transactions on Signal Processing, 47*, 880–884. doi:10.1109/78.752614

Ito, Y., Shih, A. M., & Soni, B. K. (2004). Reliable isotropic tetrahedral mesh generation based on an advancing front method. In *Proceedings 13th International Meshing Roundtable* (pp. 95–105). Williamsburg, VA: Sandia National Laboratories.

Jafari, G. R. (2003). Stochastic analysis and regeneration of rough surfaces. *Physical Review Letters, 91*(22), 1–4. doi:10.1103/PhysRevLett.91.226101

Jain, A. K. (1977). Partial differential equations and finite difference methods in image processing, part I: Image representation. *Journal of Optimization Theory and Applications, 23*, 65–91. doi:10.1007/BF00932298

Jain, A. K. (1978). Partial differential equations and finite difference methods in image processing, Part II: Image restoration. *IEEE Transactions on Automatic Control, 23*(5), 817–834. doi:10.1109/TAC.1978.1101881

Jain, A. K. (2006). *Fundamentals of digital image processing*. India: PHI.

Jerri, A. (1998). *The Gibbs phenomenon in Fourier analysis, splines and wavelet approximations*. Dordrecht, The Netherlands: Kluver Academic Publishers.

Jian, S., Zheng, N.-N., & Shum, H.-Y. (2003). Stereo matching using belief propagation. *IEEE Transactions on Pattern Analysis and Machine Intelligence, 25*(7), 787–800. doi:10.1109/TPAMI.2003.1206509

Jolion, J. M., & Montavert, A. (1991). The adaptive pyramid: A framework for 2D image analysis. *CVGIP: Image Understanding, 55*(3), 339–348. doi:10.1016/1049-9660(92)90031-W

Kalová, I., & Lisztwan, M. (2005). Active triangulation technique. In *5th International Conference of PhD Students,* (pp. 99-104). University of Miskolc.

Kanatani, K., & Chou, T. (1989). Shape from texture: General principle. *Artificial Intelligence, 38*, 1–48. doi:10.1016/0004-3702(89)90066-0

Kang, C., & Ghosal, S. (2008, November). Clusterwise regression using Dirichlet mixtures. In A. Sengupta (Ed.), Advances in multivariate statistical methods (pp. 305–325). Singapore: World Scientific Publishing Company.

Karpinsky, N., & Zhang, S. (2010). Composite phase-shifting algorithm for three-dimensional shape compression. *Optical Engineering (Redondo Beach, Calif.), 49*(6), 063604-1–6. doi:10.1117/1.3456632

Kass, M., Witkin, A., & Terzopoulos, A. (1988). Snakes: active contour models. *International Journal of Computer Vision, 1*, 321–331. doi:10.1007/BF00133570

Kaushik, V. D., Singh, A. K., Varshney, J., Pandey, P., Rao, K. P., & Pathak, V. K. (2007). Cleavage site detection in broken 3D objects. In *International Conference on Advanced Computing and Communications (ADCOM 2007)* (pp. 339–344).

Kazhdan, M., Bolitho, M., & Hoppe, H. (2006). Poisson surface reconstruction. In *Proceedings of the Fourth Eurographics Symposium on Geometry Processing (SGP '06),* (pp. 61-70).

Khamene, A., Madjidi, H., & Negahdaripour, S. (2001). 3-D mapping of sea floor scenes by stereo imaging. In *Proceedings of the OCEANS '02 MTS/IEEE Conference and Exhibition*, Vol. 4, (pp. 2577-2583).

Kim, Y., & Kim, H. (2004). Layered ground floor detection for vision-based mobile robot navigation. In *International Conference on Robotics and Automation: Vol. 1* (pp. 13-18).

Kimia, B. B., Tanenbaum, A., & Zucker, S. W. (1990). Lecture Notes in Computer Science: *Vol. 427. Toward a computational theory of shape: An overview*. New York: Springer-Verlag.

Kim, K., Neretti, N., & Intrator, N. (2005). Non-iterative construction of super-resolution image from an acoustic camera. *Proceedings of IEEE CIHSPS, 2005*, 105–111.

Kim, K., Neretti, N., & Intrator, N. (2006). *Video enhancement for underwater exploration using forward looking sonar. Advanced Concepts for Intelligent Vision Systems* (*Vol. 4179*, pp. 554–563). Berlin, Germany: Springer.

Kinect. (2010). *Wikipedia, The Free Encyclopedia*. Retrieved December 18, 2010, from http://en.wikipedia.org/wiki/Kinect Kinect – Xbox.com/ (2010). *Xbox, Microsoft*. Retrieved December 18, 2010, from http://www.xbox.com/en-US/kinects

Kitchen, L., & Rosenfeld, A. (1982). Gray-level corner detection. *Pattern Recognition Letters, 1*, 95–102. doi:10.1016/0167-8655(82)90020-4

Knuth, D. (1998). Section 5.2.1: Sorting by insertion. In *The art of computer programming, Volume 3: Sorting and searching,* 2nd ed., (pp. 80-105). Addison-Wesley.

Kobbelt, L. P., Botsch, M., Schwanecke, U., & Seidel, H.-P. (2001). Feature sensitive surface extraction from volume data. In *SIGGRAPH '01: Proceedings of the 28th Annual Conference on Computer Graphics and Interactive Techniques* (pp. 57–66). New York, NY: ACM.

Koch, R. (1995). 3-D surface reconstruction from stereoscopic image sequences. In *IEEE International Conference on Computer Vision, ICCV '95* (p. 109).

Koch, R., & Frahm, J. (2001). *Visual-geometric 3-D scene reconstruction from uncalibrated image sequences*. Tutorial at DAGM 2001, München Multimedia Information Processing Group: Christian-Albrechts-University of Kiel Germany. Retrieved July 28, 2010, from http://www.mip.informatik.uni-kiel.de

Koenderink, J. J. (1984). The structure of images. *Biological Cybernetics*, *50*, 363–370. doi:10.1007/BF00336961

Kolmogorov, V., & Zabih, R. (2002). *Multi-camera scene reconstruction via graph cuts*. European Conference on Computer Vision.

Koninckx, T. P., & Gool, L. V. (2006). Real-time range acquisition by adaptive structured light. *IEEE Transactions on Pattern Analysis and Machine Intelligence*, *28*, 432–445. doi:10.1109/TPAMI.2006.62

Koren, I., Laine, A., Taylor, F., & Lewis, M. (1996). Interactive wavelet processing and techniques applied to digital mammography. *IEEE International Conference on Acoustics, Speech, and Signal Processing*, *3*, 1415–1418.

Kosecka, J., & Zhang, W. (2002). Video compass. In *Proceedings of the European Conference on Computer Vision*. Springer-Verlag.

Kosslyn, S. M. (1994). *Elements of graph design*. New York, NY: Freeman and Company.

Kozera, R. (1998). An overview of the shape from shading problem. *Machine Graphics and Vision*, *7*(1), 291–312.

Kraus, K. (2000). *Photogrammetry: Geometry from images and laser scans* (2nd ed.). Berlin, Germany: Walter de Gruyter.

Kuan, D. T., & Sawchuk, A. A. (1987). Adaptive restoration of images with speckle. *IEEE Transactions on Acoustics, Speech, and Signal Processing*, *35*, 373–383. doi:10.1109/TASSP.1987.1165131

Kutulkos, K. N., & Seitz, S. M. (1998). *What do N photographs tell us about 3D shape?* Technical Report TR680, Computer Science department, University of Rochester. USA.

Labelle, F., & Shewchuk, J. R. (2007). Isosurface stuffing: Fast tetrahedral meshes with good dihedral angles. *ACM Transactions on Graphics*, *26*(3), 57. doi:10.1145/1276377.1276448

Lachaud, J.-O., & Montanvert, A. (1996). Volumic segmentation using hierarchical representation and triangulated surface. In *ECCV '96: Proceedings of the 4th European Conference on Computer Vision* (pp. 137–146). London, UK: Springer-Verlag.

Laganiere, R., & Elias, R. (2004). The detection of junction features in images. In *International Conference on Acoustics, Speech, and Signal Processing: Vol. III* (pp. 573–576).

Lang, W. S., Abu, N. A., & Rahmalan, H. (2009). Fast 4x4 tchebichef moment image compression. *International Conference of Soft Computing and Pattern Recognition*, (pp. 295–300).

Langridge, D. J. (1987). Curve encoding and detection of discontinuities. *Computer Vision Graphics and Image Processing*, *20*, 58–71.

Laurentini, A. (1994). The visual hull concept for silhouette-based image understanding. *IEEE Transactions on Pattern Analysis and Machine Intelligence*, *16*(2), 150–162. doi:10.1109/34.273735

Laurentini, A. (1997). How many 2D silhouettes does it take to reconstruct a 3D object? *Computer Vision and Image Understanding*, *67*(1), 81–87. doi:10.1006/cviu.1996.0508

Lecrivain, G. M., Kennedy, I., & Slaouti, A. (2008). *Hybrid surface reconstruction technique for automotive applications*. IAENG. Retrieved August 1, 2010, from (http://www.engineeringletters.com/issues_v16/issue_1/EL_16_1_16.pdf

Lee, D. (1990). Coping with discontinuities in computer vision: Their detection, classification, and measurement. *IEEE Transactions on Pattern Analysis and Machine Intelligence*, *12*(4), 321–344. doi:10.1109/34.50620

Lee, J. S. (1981). Speckle analysis and smoothing of synthetic aperture radar images. *Computer Graphics and Image Processing, 17*, 24–32. doi:10.1016/S0146-664X(81)80005-6

Lee, J. S. (1983). Digital image smoothing and the sigma filter. *Computer Vision Graphics and Image Processing, 24*, 255–269. doi:10.1016/0734-189X(83)90047-6

Leventon, M. E., Faugeras, O., Grimson, W. E. L., & Wells, W. M. (2000). Level set based segmentation with intensity and curvature priors. In *Workshop on Mathematical Methods in Biomedical Image Analysis Proceedings* (pp. 4–11).

Levin, D. (2003). Mesh-independent surface interpolation. *Geometric Modeling for Scientific Visualization, 3*, 37–49.

Levoy, M., Pulli, K., Curless, B., Rusinkiewicz, S., Koller, D., & Pereira, L. … Fulk, D. (2000). The digital Michelangelo project: 3D scanning of large statues. In *ACM SIGGRAPH* (pp.131-144). ACM Press.

Li, X. (2000). *Sliver-free three dimensional delaunay mesh generation*. Doctoral dissertation, UIUC.

Li, C., Kowdle, A., Saxena, A., & Chen, T. (2010). *Towards holistic scene understanding: Feedback enabled cascaded classification models. Neural Information Processing Systems*. NIPS.

Lindstrom, P., & Turk, G. (1998). Fast and memory efficient polygonal simplification. In *IEEE Visualization 98 Conference Proceedings* (pp. 279-286).

Lindstrom, P., & Turk, G. (2000). Image-driven simplification. *ACM Transactions on Graphics, 19*(3), 204–241. doi:10.1145/353981.353995

Lipman, Y., Cohen-Or, D., Levin, D., & Tal-Ezer, H. (2007). Parameterization-free projection for geometry reconstruction. *ACM Transactions on Graphics, 26*, 22. doi:10.1145/1276377.1276405

Li, S. (1995). *Markov random field modeling in computer vision*. Springer-Verlag.

Longuet-Higgins, H. C. (1981). A computer algorithm for reconstructing a scene from two projections. *Nature, 293*.

Loomis, J., & Eby, D. (1989, March). Relative motion parallax and the perception of structure from motion. In *Proceedings of IEEE Workshop on Visual Motion,* Irvine, CA, (pp. 204–211).

Loop, C., & Zhang, Z. (1999). Computing rectifying homographies for stereo vision. In *Proceedings of the IEEE Computer Society Conference on Computer Vision and Pattern Recognition (CVPR'99),* Vol. 1.

Lorensen, W. E., & Cline, H. E. (1987). Marching cubes: A high resolution 3D surface construction algorithm. In *Proceedings of the ACM SIGGRAPH '87* (pp. 163-169).

Low, K.-L., & Tan, T.-S. (1997). Model simplification using vertex-clustering. In *Proceedings of the 1997 Symposium on Interactive 3D graphics* (p. 75). Providence, RI: ACM.

Lowe, D. G. (1999). Object recognition from local scale-invariant features. In *International Conference on Computer Vision: Vol. 2* (pp. 1150–1157).

Lucus, B. D., & Kanade, T. (1981). An iterative image registration technique with an application to stereo vision. In *Proceedings of the Seventh International Joint Conference on Artificial Intelligence*, Vol. 2, (pp. 674-679).

Lucy, L. B. (1974). Image restoration of high photometric quality. In R.J Hanisch & R. L. White (Eds.), *Proceedings of the Restoration of HST Images and Spectra STSci,* (pp. 79-85).

Luong, Q. T., & Faugeras, O. (1995). The fundamental matrix: Theory, algorithms, and stability analysis. *International Journal of Computer Vision, 17*, 43–75.

Lusardi, M., & Nielson, C. (2007). *Orthotics and prosthetics in rehabilitation* (2nd ed.). Elsevier.

Macdonald-Ross, M. (1977). How numbers are shown: A review of research on the presentation of quantitative data in texts. *Audio-Visual Communication Review, 25*, 359–407.

Madden, H. (1978). Comments on the Savitzky-Golay convolution method for least-squares-fit smoothing and differentiation of digital data. *Analytical Chemistry, 50*(9), 1383–1386. doi:10.1021/ac50031a048

Mahmood, N. H. (2009). *3D surface reconstruction from multiviews for orthotic and prosthetic design*. University of Warwick. Ph.D Thesis.

Mahmood, N. H., & Tjahjadi, T. (2006). 3D reconstruction from multiple views for orthotic and prosthetic design: An overview. *4th Student Conference on Research and Development* (pp. 70–75).

Mahmood, N. H., & Tjahjadi, T. (2010). 3D reconstruction for prosthetic design. *Second International Conference on Computer Engineering and Applications* (pp. 431–435).

Mahmood, N. H., & Tjahjadi, T. (2009). Prosthetic design of lower limb using 3D surface reconstruction. *ICSESC, 2009*, 263–267.

Malik, J., & Rosenholtz, R. (1997). Computing local surfaces orientation and shape from texture for curved surfaces. *International Journal of Computer Vision, 23*(2), 149–168. doi:10.1023/A:1007958829620

Mandelbaum, R., McDowell, L., Bogoni, L., Beich, B., & Hansen, M. (1998). Real-time stereo processing, obstacle detection, and terrain estimation from vehicle-mounted stereo cameras. In *Workshop on Applications of Computer Vision* (pp. 288-289).

Masuda, T., & Yokoya, N. (1995). A robust method for registration and segmentation of multiple range images. *Computer Vision and Image Understanding, 61*(3), 295–307. doi:10.1006/cviu.1995.1024

Mateo, J. L., & Fernández, C. A. (2009). Finding out general tendencies in speckle noise reduction in ultrasound images. *Expert Systems with Applications, 36*, 7786–7797. doi:10.1016/j.eswa.2008.11.029

Matsumoto, Y., Terasaki, H., Sugimoto, K., & Arakawa, T. (1997). A portable three-dimensional digitizer. In *International Conference on Recent Advances in 3-D Digital Imaging and Modeling* (pp. 197-204).

Mayer, R. E. (2001). *Multimedia learning*. New York, NY: Cambridge University.

Mayer, R. E., & Moreno, R. (2003). Nine ways to reduce cognitive load in multimedia learning. *Educational Psychologist, 38*(1), 43–52. doi:10.1207/S15326985EP3801_6

McCallum, A., Pal, C., Druck, G., & Wang, X. (2006). *Multi-conditional learning: Generative/discriminative training for clustering and classification*. AAAI.

McInerney, T. (1997). *Topologically adaptable deformable models for medical image analysis*. PhD thesis, Dept. of Computer Science, University of Toronto.

McInerney, T., & Terzopoulos, D. (1996). Deformable models in medical imageanalysis: A survey. *Medical Image Analysis, 1*(2), 91–108. doi:10.1016/S1361-8415(96)80007-7

Mckinley, T., McWaters, M., & Jain, V. (2001). 3d reconstruction from a stereo pair without the knowledge of intrinsic or extrinsic parameters. *International Workshop on Digital and Computational Video,* (p. 148).

Medioni, G., & Yasumoto, Y. (1987). Corner detection and curve representation using cubic b-splines. *Computer Vision Graphics and Image Processing, 39*, 279–290. doi:10.1016/S0734-189X(87)80181-0

Meer, P., & Weiss, I. (1990). Smoothed differentiation filters for images. In *IEEE 110th International Conference on Pattern Recognition*, Vol. 2, June 1990, (pp. 121-126). Atlantic City, NJ, USA.

Meyers, C. H. (1970). *Handbook of basic graphs: A modern approach*. Belmont, CA: Dickenson Publishing.

Michas, I. C., & Berry, D. C. (2000). Learning a procedural task: Effectiveness of multimedia presentations. *Applied Cognitive Psychology, 14*, 555–575. doi:10.1002/1099-0720(200011/12)14:6<555::AID-ACP677>3.0.CO;2-4

Michels, J., Saxena, A., & Ng, A. Y. (2005). *High speed obstacle avoidance using monocular vision and reinforcement learning*. International Conference on Machine Learning (ICML).

Mikolajczyk, K., & Schmid, C. (2002). An affine invariant interest point detector. In *Proceedings of 8th European Conference on Computer Vision*, (pp. 128-142). Springer Verlag.

Mikolajczyk, K., & Schmid, C. (2004). Scale & affine invariant interest point detectors. *International Journal of Computer Vision, 60*(1), 63–86. doi:10.1023/B:VISI.0000027790.02288.f2

Mikolajczyk, K., Tuytelaars, T., Schmid, C., Zisserman, A., Matas, J., & Schaffalitzky, F. (2005). A comparison of affine region detectors. *International Journal of Computer Vision*, *1*(65), 43–72. doi:10.1007/s11263-005-3848-x

Milan, S., Vaclav, H., & Boyle, R. (2007). *Image processing, analysis and machine vision* (2nd ed.). Washington, DC: PWS Publishing.

Miller, J. V., Breen, D. E., Lorensen, W. E., O'Bara, R. M., & Wozny, M. J. (1991). Geometrically deformed models: A method for extracting closed geometric models form volume data. In *SIGGRAPH'91: Proceedings of the 18th Annual Conference on Computer Graphics and Interactive Techniques* (pp. 217–226). New York, NY: ACM Press.

Mitchell, S. C., Bosch, J. G., Lelieveldt, B. P. F., Van der Geest, R. J., Reiber, J. H. C., & Sonka, M. (2002). 3-D active appearance models: Segmentation of cardiac MR and ultrasound images. *IEEE Transactions on Medical Imaging*, *21*(9), 1167–1178. doi:10.1109/TMI.2002.804425

Mokhtarian, F., & Suomela, R. (1998). Robust image corner detection through curvature scale space. *IEEE Transactions on Pattern Analysis and Machine Intelligence*, *20*, 1376–1381. doi:10.1109/34.735812

Montemerlo, M., Thrun, S., Koller, D., & Wegbreit, B. (2002). FastSLAM: A factored solution to the simultaneous localization and mapping problem. *Proceedings of the AAAI National Conference on Artificial Intelligence*. Canada: AAAI.

Morel, J. M., & Solimini, S. (1988). Segmentation of images by variational methods: A constructive approach. *Revista Matematica de Universidad Complutense Madrid*, *1*, 169–182.

Morency, L. P., Rahimi, A., & Darrell, T. (2002). *3d model acquisition from stereo images. In 3d Data Processing, Visualization and Transmission* (pp. 172–176). Fast.

Mount, D. M., & Arya, S. (2010). *ANN: A library for approximate nearest neighbor searching*. Retrieved May 20, 2010, from http://www.cs.umd.edu/~mount/ANN/

Mukhopadhyay, M., & Parhar, M. (2001). Instructional design in multi-channel learning system. *British Journal of Educational Technology*, *32*(5), 545–559. doi:10.1111/1467-8535.00224

Mukundan, R. (2004). Some computational aspects of discrete orthogonal moments. *IEEE Transactions on Image Processing*, *13*(8), 1055–1059. doi:10.1109/TIP.2004.828430

Mukundan, R., Ong, S., & Lee, P. (2001). Image analysis by Tchebichef moments. *IEEE Transactions on Image Processing*, *10*(9), 1357–1363. doi:10.1109/83.941859

Mumford, D., & Shah, J. (1989). Optimal approximations by piecewise smooth functions and variational problems. *Communications on Pure and Applied Mathematics*, *42*, 577–685. doi:10.1002/cpa.3160420503

Nabbe, B., Hoiem, D., Efros, A. A., & Hebert, M. (2006). *Opportunistic use of vision to push back the path-planning horizon. Intelligent Robots and Systems*. IROS.

Nagai, Y., Ohtake, Y., & Suzuki, H. (2009). Smoothing of partition of unity implicit surfaces for noise robust surface reconstruction. *Computer Graphics Forum*, *28*(5), 1339–1348. doi:10.1111/j.1467-8659.2009.01511.x

Nakagaki, K., & Mukundan, R. (2007). A fast 4 × 4 forward discrete tchebichef transform algorithm. *IEEE Signal Processing Letters*, *14*(10), 684–687. doi:10.1109/LSP.2007.898331

Narasimhan, S. G., Nayar, S. K., Sun, B., & Koppal, S. J. (2005). Structured light in scattering media. In *Proceedings of the Tenth IEEE International Conference on Computer Vision*, Vol. 1, (pp. 420-427).

Negahdaripour, S. (2005). Calibration of DIDSON forward-scan acoustic video camera. *Proceedings of MTS/IEEE OCEANS '05*, Vol. 2, (pp. 1287-1294).

Negahdaripour, S., & Taatian, A. (2008). 3-D motion and structure estimation for arbitrary scenes from 2-D optical and sonar video. *Proceedings of IEEE Oceans '08* Quebec City, (pp. 1-8), Canada.

Negahdaripour, S., Zhang, H., & Han, X. (2002). Investigation of photometric stereo method for 3-D shape recovery from underwater imagery. *OCEANS '02 MTS/IEEE*, Vol. 2, (pp. 1010-1017).

Negahdaripour, S., & Firoozfam, P. (2006). An ROV stereovision system for ship-hull inspection. *IEEE Journal of Oceanic Engineering*, *31*(3), 551–564. doi:10.1109/JOE.2005.851391

Ng, S.-K., & McLachlan, G. J. (2003). On some variants of the em algorithm for fitting mixture models. [UK: Blackwell Publishing Ltd.]. *Austrian Journal of Statistics*, *32*(1-2), 143–161.

Nguyen, H. V., & Hanajik, M. (1995). 3-D scene reconstruction from image sequences. In *Lecture Notes in Comuter Science 970, Computer Analysis of Images and Patterns CAIP'95, 6th International Conference* (p. 182-189).

Nicolas, A., Santa-Cruz, D., & Ebrahimi, T. (2002). Mesh: Measuring error between surfaces using the Hausdorff distance. In *IEEE International Conference on Multimedia and Expo (ICME): Vol. 1* (pp. 705–708). IEEE Press.

Niem, W., & Wingbermuhle, J. (1997). Automatic reconstruction of 3D objects using mobile monoscopic camera. In *International Conference on Recent Advances in 3-D Digital Imaging and Modeling* (pp. 173-180).

NVIDIA Corporation. (2010). *What is CUDA? Overview*. Retrieved July 15, 2010, from http://www.nvidia.com/object/what_is_cuda_new.html

O'Donnell, L. (2001). *Semi-automatic medical image segmentation*. Master's thesis, Massachusetts Institute of Technology.

O'Leary, P., & Harker, M. (2008c). An algebraic framework for discrete basis functions in computer vision. *Indian Conference on Computer Vision, Graphics and Image Processing*, (pp. 150–157).

O'Leary, P., & Harker, M. (2008e). Discrete polynomial moments for real-time geometric surface inspection. *Journal of Electronic Imaging*, 18.

Ohtake, Y., Belyaev, A., Alexa, M., Turk, G., & Seidel, H. P. (2005). Multi-level partition of unity implicits. *ACM Transactions on Graphics*, *22*, 463–470. doi:10.1145/882262.882293

Oliensis, J. (1999). A multi-frame structure-from-motion algorithm under perspective projection. *International Journal of Computer Vision*, *34*(2–3), 163–192. doi:10.1023/A:1008139920864

Ong, S., & Raveendren, P. (2005). Image feature analysis by Hahn orthogonal moments. *Lecture Notes in Computer Science*, *3656*, 524–531. doi:10.1007/11559573_65

Oppenheim, A., & Schafer, R. (1989). *Discrete-time Signal Processing*. Upper Saddle River, NJ, USA: Prentice Hall.

Oram, D. (2001). Rectification for any epipolar geometry. In *Proceedings of the 12th British Machine Vision Conference (BMVC 2001)*, (pp. 653-662).

Ormrod, J. E. (2008). *Human learning* (5th ed.). Upper Saddle River, NJ: Prentice Hall.

Osher, S., & Fedkiw, R. P. (2001). *Level set methods: An overview and some recent results* (pp. 1–65). California, USA: IPAM GBM Tutorials.

Osher, S., & Rudin, L. I. (1990). Feature oriented image enhancement using shock filters. *SIAM Journal on Numerical Analysis*, *27*, 919–940. doi:10.1137/0727053

Osher, S., & Sethian, J. A. (1988). Fronts propagating with curvature dependent speed: Algorithms based on Hamilton-Jacobi formulations. *Journal of Computational Physics*, *79*, 12–49. doi:10.1016/0021-9991(88)90002-2

Pan, J. H., Huang, P. S., & Chiang, F. P. (2006). Color phase-shifting technique for three-dimensional shape measurement. *Optical Engineering (Redondo Beach, Calif.)*, *45*, 013602. doi:10.1117/1.2151160

Papadimitriou, D. V., & Dennis, T. J. (1996). Epipolar line estimation and rectification for stereo image pairs. *IEEE Transactions on Image Processing*, *5*(4), 672–676. doi:10.1109/83.491345

Paris, S., & Durand, F. (2009). A fast approximation of the bilateral filter using a signal processing approach. *International Journal of Computer Vision*, *81*(1), 24–52. doi:10.1007/s11263-007-0110-8

Park, J. Y., McInerney, T., Terzopoulos, D., & Kim, K. H. (2001). A non-selfintersecting deformable surface for complex boundary extraction from volumetric images. *Computers & Graphics*, *25*(3), 421–440. doi:10.1016/S0097-8493(01)00066-8

Paul, M. K. C., Wang, X., & McCallum, A. (2006). *Multiconditional learning for joint probability models with latent variables*. NIPS Workshop Advances Structured Learning Text and Speech Processing.

Pauly, M., Gross, M., & Kobbelt, L. P. (2002). Efficient simplification of point-sampled surfaces. In *Proceedings of the Conference on Visualization (VIS'02)*, (pp. 163-170).

Pegg, D. (2010*). Design issues with 3D maps and the need for 3D cartographic design principles.* Retrieved August 1, 2010, from http://lazarus.elte.hu/cet/academic/pegg.pdf

Penc, J., Klette, R., Vaudrey, T., & Morales, S. (2009). *Graph-cut and belief-propagation stereo on real-world image sequences.* MI Technical Report.

Perko, R., & Leonardis, A. (2007, December). On text driven focus of attention for object detection. In L. Paletta & E. Rome (Eds.), *Attention in Cognitive Systems. Theories and Systems from an Interdisciplinary Viewpoint (WAPCV 2007), LNAI 4840*, (pp. 216–233). Springer.

Permuter, H., & Franoos, J. (2000). Estimating the orientation of planar surfaces: Algorithms and bounds. *IEEE Transactions on Information Theory, 46*(5). doi:10.1109/18.857800

Perona, P. (1998). Orientation diffusions. *IEEE Transactions on Image Processing, 7*, 457–467. doi:10.1109/83.661195

Perona, P., & Malik, J. (1990). Scale space and edge detection using anisotropic diffusion. *IEEE Transactions on Pattern Analysis and Machine Intelligence, 12*, 629–639. doi:10.1109/34.56205

Petrov, M., Talapov, A., Robertson, T., Lebedev, A., Zhilyaev, A., & Polonskiy, L. (1998). Optical 3D digitizers: Bringing life to the virtual world. *IEEE Computer Graphics and Applications, 18*, 28–37. doi:10.1109/38.674969

Pettersson, R. (1993). *Visual information* (2nd ed.). New Jersey: Educational Technology Publications.

Pham, D. L., & Prince, J. L. (1999). Adaptive fuzzy segmentation of magnetic resonance images. *IEEE Transactions on Medical Imaging, 18*, 737–752. doi:10.1109/42.802752

Ping, Z., Ren, H., Zou, J., Sheng, Y., & Bo, W. (2005). Generic orthogonal moments: Jackobi-Fourier moments for invariant image description. *Pattern Recognition, 40*, 1245–1254. doi:10.1016/j.patcog.2006.07.016

Pollefeys, M., Koch, R., & Van Gool, L. (1999). A simple and efficient rectification method for general motion. In *Proceedings of the Seventh IEEE International Conference on Computer Vision*, Vol. 1, (pp. 496-501).

Pollefeys, M., Koch, R., Vergauwen, M., & Gool, L. V. (1998). Metric 3D surface reconstruction from uncalibrated image sequences. In *Lecture Notes in Computer Science 1506, 3D Structure from Multiple Images of Large-Scale Environments, European Workshop, SMILE'98* (p. 139-154).

Pollefeys, M., Koch, R., Vergauwen, M., & Van Gool, L. (1998). *Metric 3D surface reconstruction from uncalibrated image sequences. 3D Structure from Multiple Images of Large-Scale Environments, LNCS 1506* (pp. 139–154). Berlin, Germany: Springer.

Prabhakar, C. J., & Praveen Kumar, P. U. (2010). 3D surface reconstruction of underwater objects. *Abstract Proceedings of Indian Conference on Computer Vision, Graphics and Image Processing – 2010* (ICVGIP–2010), (pp. 4).

Prabhakar, C. J., & Praveen Kumar, P. U. (2010). Underwater image denoising using adaptive wavelet subband thresholding. In *Proceeding of the International Conference on Signal and Image Processing (ICSIP – 2010)*, (pp. 322-327).

Prados, E., & Faugeras, O. (2005). Shape from shading: A well-posed problem? In *Proceedings of the IEEE Conference on Computer Vision and Pattern Recognition (CVPR)*, San Diego, California, Vol. 2, (pp. 870–877).

Press, H., Teukolsky, S., Vetterling, T., & Flannery, B. (1992). *Numerical recipes in C: The art of scientific computing* (2nd ed.). Cambridge University Press.

Price, C. B. (1990). Image enhancement and analysis with reaction diffusion paradigm. *Proceedings of the Institution of Electrical Engineers, 137*, 136–145.

Proitte, T., & Luati, A. (2009). Low-pass filter design using locally weigthed polynomial regression and discrete spheroidal sequences. *MPRA Paper No. 15510*, (pp. 1 – 23).

Rajagopalan, S., & Robb, R. (2003). Image smoothing with Savitzky-Golay filters. In *Medical Imaging 2003: Visualization, Image-Guided Procedures, and Display*, Vol. 5029, May 2003, (pp. 773-781).

Rajan, J., Kannan, K., & Kaimal, M. R. (2008). An improved hybrid model for molecular image de-noising. *Journal of Mathematical Imaging and Vision, 31*, 73–79. doi:10.1007/s10851-008-0067-4

Reinhard, E., Ashikhmin, M., Gooch, B., & Shirley, P. (2001). Color transfer between images. *IEEE Computer Graphics and Applications*, *21*, 34–41. doi:10.1109/38.946629

Robert, L., Zeller, C., Faugeras, O., & Hebert, M. (1997). Applications of non-metric vision to some visually guided robotics tasks. In Aloimonos, Y. (Ed.), *Visual navigation: From biological systems to unmanned ground vehicles* (pp. 89–134).

Rogowitz, B., & Rushmeier, H. (2001). Are image quality metrics adequate to evaluate the quality of geometric objects? In Rogowitz, B. E., & Pappas, T. N. (Eds.), *SPIE on Human Vision and Electronic Imaging VI* (Vol. 4299, pp. 340–348). SPIE. doi:10.1117/12.429504

Romeny, B. ter H. (1994). *Geometry driven diffusion in computer vision*. Boston, MA: Kluwer.

Ross, K., & Laurie, S. J. (1980). *Markov random fields and their applications*. American Mathematical Society.

Rosten, E., & Drummond, T. (2005). Fusing points and lines for high performance tracking. *10th IEEE International Conference on Computer Vision*, Vol. 2, (pp. 1508-1515). Beijing, China: Springer

Rosten, E., & Drummond, T. (2006). *Machine learning for high speed corner detection*. 9th European Conference on Computer Vision. Springer.

Roth, G., & Whitehead, A. (2000). Using projective vision to find camera positions in an image sequence. In *Vision Interface Conference* (pp. 255-232).

Rothwell, C., Csurka, G., & Faugeras, O. (1995, April). *A comparison of projective reconstruction methods for pairs of views* (Tech. Rep. No. 2538). Unité de Recherche INRIA-Sophia Antipolis: Institut National de Recherche en Informatique et Automatique, INRIA.

Roy, A., Gale, N., & Hong, L. (2009). Fusion of Doppler radar and video information for automated traffic surveillance. In *Proceedings of the 12th International Conference on Information Fusion* (pp. 1989-1996), Seattle, WA, USA.

Roy, S., & Cox, I. J. (1998). A maximum-flow formulation of the n-camera stereo correspondence problem. In *Proceedings of the Sixth International Conference on Computer Vision*, (pp. 492-499).

Rudin, L. I., Osher, S., & Fatemi, E. (1992). Non linear total variation based noise removal algorithms. *Physica D. Nonlinear Phenomena*, *60*, 259–268. doi:10.1016/0167-2789(92)90242-F

Rusinkiewicz, S., & Levoy, M. (2001). Efficient variants of the ICP algorithm. In *Proceedings of the 3rd International Conference on 3D Digital Imaging and Modeling* (pp. 145- 152).

Rutkowski, W. S., & Rosenfeld, A. (1978). *A comparison of corner detection techniques for chain coded curves*. Technical Report 623, Maryland University.

Sabe, K., Fukuchi, M., Gutmann, J.-S., Ohashi, T., Kawamoto, K., & Yoshigahara, T. (2004). Obstacle avoidance and path planning for humanoid robots using stereo vision. In *International Conference on Robotics and Automation: Vol. 1* (pp. 592-597).

Saldner, H. O., & Huntley, J. M. (1997). Temporal phase unwrapping: application to surface profiling of discontinuous objects. *Applied Optics*, *36*, 2770–2775. doi:10.1364/AO.36.002770

Salinas, H., & Fernandez, D. C. (2007). Comparison of PDE-based nonlinear diffusion approaches for image enhancement and de-noising in optical coherence tomography. *IEEE Transactions on Medical Imaging*, *26*(6), 761–771. doi:10.1109/TMI.2006.887375

San Vicente, G., Buchart, C., Borro, D., & Celigüeta, J. T. (2009). Maxillofacial surgery simulation using a mass-spring model derived from continuum and the scaled displacement method. *International Journal of Computer Assisted Radiology and Surgery*, *4*, 89–98. doi:10.1007/s11548-008-0271-0

Savitzky, A., 7 Golay, M. (1964). Smoothing and differentiation of data by simplified least squares procedures. *Analytical Chemistry*, *36*(8), 1627–1639. doi:10.1021/ac60214a047

Saxena, A., Sun, M., & Ng, A. Y. (2007). Learning 3D scene structure from a single still image. In *ICCV Workshop on 3D Representation for Recognition (3dRR-07)*, (pp. 1-8).

Saxena, J. A., & Ng, A. Y. (2005). High speed obstacle avoidance using monocular vision and reinforcement learning. In *International Conference on Machine Learning (ICML)*, (pp. 713-717).

Saxena, A., Chung, S. H., & Ng, A. Y. (2005). *Learning depth from single monocular images. Neural Information Processing Systems.* NIPS.

Saxena, A., Chung, S. H., & Ng, A. Y. (2007). 3-D depth reconstruction from a single still image. [IJCV]. *International Journal of Computer Vision, 76*(1), 53–69. doi:10.1007/s11263-007-0071-y

Saxena, A., Driemeyer, J., Kearns, J., & Ng, A. Y. (2006). *Robotic grasping of novel objects using vision. Neural Information Processing Systems.* NIPS.

Saxena, A., Sun, M., & Ng, A. Y. (2009). Make3D: Learning 3D scene structure from a single still image. *IEEE Transactions on Pattern Analysis and Machine Intelligence, 30*(5), 824–840. doi:10.1109/TPAMI.2008.132

Scharstein, D., & Szeliski, R. (1998). Stereo matching with nonlinear diffusion. *International Journal of Computer Vision, 28*(2), 155–174. doi:10.1023/A:1008015117424

Scharstein, D., Szeliski, R., & Zabih, R. (2002). A taxonomy and evaluation of dense two-frame stereo correspondence algorithms. *International Journal of Computer Vision, 47*, 7–42. doi:10.1023/A:1014573219977

Schmit, J., & Creath, K. (1995). Extended averaging technique for derivation of error-compensating algorithms in phase-shifting interferometry. *Applied Optics, 34*, 3610–3619. doi:10.1364/AO.34.003610

Schroeder, W. J., Zarge, J. A., & Lorensen, W. E. (1992). Decimation of triangle meshes. In *Proceedings of the 19th Annual Conference on Computer Graphics and Interactive Techniques, SIGGRAPH '92* (pp. 65-70). New York, NY: ACM.

Scopigno, R., Cignoni, P., & Rocchini, C. (1998). Metro: Measuring error on simplified surfaces. *Computer Graphics Forum, 17*(2), 167–174. doi:10.1111/1467-8659.00236

Seah, M. P., Dench, W. A., Gale, B., & Groves, T. E. (1988). Towards a single recommended optimal convolutional smoothing algorithm for electron and other spectroscopies. *Journal of Physics. E, Scientific Instruments, 21*(4), 351–363. doi:10.1088/0022-3735/21/4/003

Sedgewick, R. (1988). *Algorithms.* Addison-Wesley.

Sedlazeck, A., Koser, K., & Koch, R. (2009). 3D reconstruction based on underwater video from ROV Keil 6000 considering underwater imaging conditions. *IEEE OCEANS'09-EUROPE*, (pp. 1-10).

Seymour, R. (2002). *Prosthetics and orthotics - Lower limb and spinal.* Lippincott Williams & Wilkins.

Shapiro, L., & Stockman, G. (2001). *Computer vision.* NJ: Prentice Hall.

Shen, T. F., & Vese, L. (2002). *Variational PDE models in image processing.* Joint Math Meeting, San Diego.

Shin, D., & Tjahjadi, T. (2005). 3D object reconstruction from multiple views in approximate circular motion. *Proceedings of IEE SMK UK-RI Chapter Conference on Applied Cybernetics* (pp. 70-75)

Skydan, O. A., Lalor, M. J., & Burton, D. R. (2002). Technique for phase measurement and surface reconstruction by use colored structured light. *Applied Optics, 41*, 6104–6117. doi:10.1364/AO.41.006104

Slabaugh, G., Culberston, B., Malzbender, T., & Schafer, R. (2001). A survey of volumetric scene reconstruction methods from photographs. In *Proceedings of the International Workshop on Graphics*, (pp. 81-100).

Smith, S. M., & Brady, J. M. (1997). SUSAN - A new approach to low level image processing. *International Journal of Computer Vision, 23*, 45–78. doi:10.1023/A:1007963824710

Snavely, N., Seitz, S. M., & Szeliski, R. (2006). Photo tourism: Exploring photo collections in 3D. In *SIGGRAPH Conference* (pp. 835-846).

Snavely, N., Seitz, S. M., & Szeliski, R. (2007). Modeling the world from Internet photo collections. *International Journal of Computer Vision, 80*(2), 189–210. doi:10.1007/s11263-007-0107-3

Soman, K. P., & Ramachandran, K. I. (2004). *Insight in to wavelets from theory to practice.* India: PHI.

Spanel, M. (2010). *Delaunay-based vector segmentation of volumetric medical images.* Unpublished PhD dissertation, Brno University of Technology, Czech Republic.

Spence, I. (1990). Visual psychophysics of simple graphical elements. *Journal of Experimental Psychology, 16*(4), 683–692.

Spence, I. (2004). The apparent and effective dimensionality of representations of objects (displays and controls). *Human Factors, 46*(4), 738–748. doi:10.1518/hfes.46.4.738.56809

Spence, I., & Krizel, P. (1994). Children's perception of proportion in graphs. *Child Development, 65*, 1193–1213. doi:10.2307/1131314

Spetsakis, M. E., & Aloimonos, J. Y. (1991). A multiframe approach to visual motion perception. *International Journal of Computer Vision, 6*(3), 245–255. doi:10.1007/BF00115698

Spiro, R. J., Coulson, R. L., Feltovich, P. J., & Anderson, D. (1988). Cognitive flexibility theory: Advanced knowledge acquisition in ill-structured domains. In V. Patel (Ed.), *Proceedings of the 10th Annual Conference of the Cognitive Science Society*. Hillsdale, NJ: Erlbaum.

Srivastava, R. (2011). A complex diffusion based nonlinear filter for speckle reduction from optical coherence tomography images. *International Conference on Communication, Computing & Security (ICCCS-2011), Rourkela, India*, (pp. 259-264). ACM Press. ISBN-978-1-4503-0464-1

Srivastava, R., & Gupta, J. R. P. (2010). A PDE-based nonlinear filter adapted to Rayleigh's speckle noise for de-speckling 2D ultrasound images. *International Conference on Contemporary Computing (IC3-2010), Communications in Computer and Information Science (CCIS), CCIS-94, India*, (pp. 1-12). Berlin, Germany: Springer-Verlag

Srivastava, R., Gupta, J. R. P., & Parthasarthy, H. (2009). Complex diffusion based speckle reduction from digital images. *IEEE International Conference on Methods and Models in Computer Science (ICM2CS-09)*, Delhi, India, (pp. 43-49).

Srivastava, R., Gupta, J. R. P., & Parthasarathy, H. (2009). Comparison of PDE based and other techniques for speckle reduction from digitally reconstructed holographic images. *Optics and Lasers in Engineering, 48*(5), 626–635. doi:10.1016/j.optlaseng.2009.09.012

Srivastava, R., Gupta, J. R. P., Parthasarathy, H., & Srivastava, S. (2011). An adaptive nonlinear PDE based speckle reduction technique for ultrasound images. *International Journal of Biomedical Engineering and Technology, 6*(3). doi:10.1504/IJBET.2011.041468

Stegmann, M. B. (2000). *Active appearance models: Theory, extensions and cases*. Master's thesis, Informatics and Mathematical Modelling, Technical University of Denmark.

Strecha, C., Hansen, W., Van Gool, L., & Thoennessen, U. (2007). *Multi-view stereo and lidar for outdoor scene modeling*. Photogrammetric Image Analysis.

Sutherland, I. E. (1974, September). Three-dimensional data input by tablet. *SIGGRAPH Computer Graphics, 8*, 86–86. Retrieved from http://doi.acm.org/10.1145/988026.988036

Su, W. H. (2007). Color-encoded fringe projection for 3D shape measurements. *Optics Express, 15*, 13167–13181. doi:10.1364/OE.15.013167

Su, W. H. (2008). Projected fringe profilometry using the area-encoded algorithm for spatially isolated and dynamic objects. *Optics Express, 16*, 2590–2596. doi:10.1364/OE.16.002590

Su, X., & Chen, W. (2001). Fourier transform profilometry: A review. *Optics and Lasers in Engineering, 35*, 263–284. doi:10.1016/S0143-8166(01)00023-9

Szeliski, R. (1993). Rapid octree construction from image sequences. *CVGIP: Image Understanding, 58*(1), 23–32. doi:10.1006/ciun.1993.1029

Szeliski, R., & Kang, S. B. (1994). Recovering 3D shape and motion from image streams using nonlinear least squares. *Journal of Visual Communication and Image Representation, 5*(1), 10–28. doi:10.1006/jvci.1994.1002

Takeda, M., Gu, Q., Kinoshita, M., Takai, H., & Takahashi, Y. (1997). Frequency-multiplex Fourier-transform profilometry: A single-shot three-dimensional shape measurement of objects with large height discontinuities and/or surface isolations. *Applied Optics, 36*, 5347–5354. doi:10.1364/AO.36.005347

Tankus, A., Sochen, N., & Yeshurun, Y. (2005, June). Shape-from shading under perspective projection. *International Journal of Computer Vision*, *63*(1), 21–43. doi:10.1007/s11263-005-4945-6

Terry, W. (1995). The challenge of 3D digitizing. *Computer Graphics World*, *18*(11), 21–25.

Thurston, J., & Brawn, J. (1992). The filtering characteristics of least-squares polynomial approximation for regional/residual separation. *Canadian Journal of Exploration Physics*, *28*(2), 71–80.

Tomasi, C., & Kanade, T. (1991). *Detection and tracking of point features*. Carnegie Mellon University Technical Report CMU-CS-91-132.

Tomasi, C., & Kanade, T. (1991). *Shape and motion from image streams: A factorization method – Part 3 detection and tracking of point features*. Technical Report CMU-CS-91-132, Computer Science Department, Carnegie Mellon University, USA.

Tomasi, C., & Manduchi, R. (1998). Bilateral filtering for gray and color images. In *ICCV '98: Proceedings of the Sixth International Conference on Computer Vision* (p. 839). Washington, DC: IEEE Computer Society.

Tomasi, C., & Kanade, T. (1992). Shape and motion from image streams under orthography: a factorization method. *International Journal of Computer Vision*, *9*(2), 137–154. doi:10.1007/BF00129684

Topiwala, P. N. (Ed.). (1998). *Wavelet image and video compression*. Kluwer Academic Publishers.

Tournois, J., Srinivasan, R., & Alliez, P. (2009). Perturbing slivers in 3D Delaunay meshes. In *Proceedings of the 18th International Meshing Roundtable* (pp. 157–173). Berlin, Germany: Springer.

Towers, C. E., Towers, D. P., & Jones, J. D. C. (2003). Optimum frequency selection in multifrequency interferometry. *Optics Letters*, *28*, 887–889. doi:10.1364/OL.28.000887

Towers, C. E., Towers, D. P., & Jones, J. D. C. (2005). Absolute fringe order calculation using optimised multifrequency selection in full-field profilometry. *Optics and Lasers in Engineering*, *43*, 788–800. doi:10.1016/j.optlaseng.2004.08.005

Trentacosta, J., & Kennedy, M. J. (Eds.). (1997). *Multicultural and gender equity in the mathematics classroom, the gift of diversity*. Reston, VA: National Council of Teachers of Mathematics.

Triggs, B., McLauchlan, P. F., Hartley, R. I., & Fitzgibbon, A. W. (1999, September). Bundle adjustment—A modern synthesis. *International Workshop on Vision Algorithms* (pp. 298–372).

Trucco, E., Petillot, Y. R., Tena Ruiz, I., Plakas, K., & Lane, D. M. (2000). Feature tracking in video and sonar subsea sequences with applications. *Computer Vision and Image Understanding*, *79*, 92–122. doi:10.1006/cviu.2000.0846

Trucco, E., & Verri, A. (1998). *Introductory techniques for 3-D computer vision*. Upper Saddle River, NJ: Prentice Hall PTR.

Tsai, R. Y. (1986). An efficient and accurate camera calibration technique for 3D-machine vision. In *Proceedings of the IEEE Conference on Computer Vision and Pattern recognition*. (pp. 364-374), Miami Beach, Florida.

Tufte, E. R. (1983). *The visual display of quantitative information*. Cheshire, CT: Graphics Press.

Turk, G. (1992). Re-tiling polygonal surfaces. In *Proceedings of the 19th Annual Conference on Computer Graphics and Interactive Techniques, SIGGRAPH '92* (pp. 55-64). New York, NY: ACM.

Udo Ahlvers, U. Z. (2005). *Inclusion of magnitude information for improved phase-based disparity estimation in stereoscopic image pairs*. Hamburg, Germany: Department of Signal Processing and Communications Helmut-Schmidt University.

USA Today. (2007). USA Today snapshot. *USA Today*. Retrieved July 2, 2008, from http://www.usatoday.com/news/snapshot.htm

Vanlanduit, S., Vanherzeele, J., Guillaume, P., Cauberghe, B., & Verboven, P. (2004). Fourier fringe processing by use of an interpolated Fourier-transform technique. *Applied Optics*, *43*, 5206–5213. doi:10.1364/AO.43.005206

Vella, J. (2008). *On teaching and learning: Putting the principles and practices of dialogue education into action*. San Francisco, CA: Jossey-Bass.

Verbee, E., & vanOosterom, P. J. (2010). *The Stin method: 3D-surface reconstruction by observation lines and Delaunay Tens.* Delft University of Technology, section GIS-technology. Retrieved August 1, 2010, from http://citeseerx.ist.psu.edu/viewdoc/download?doi=10.1.1.155.2671&rep=rep1&type=pdf

Vernon, D. (1991). *Machine vision.* Prentice-Hall.

Vincent, E., & Laganiere, R. (2001). Detecting planar homographies in an image pair. In *International Symposium on Image and Signal Processing and Analysis* (pp. 182-187).

Vivodtzev, F., Bonneau, G.-P., Linsen, L., Hamann, B., Joy, K. I., & Olshausen, B. A. (2003). Hierarchical isosurface segmentation based on discrete curvature. In *VISSYM'03: Proceedings of the Symposium on Data Visualisation 2003* (pp. 249–258). Aire-la-Ville, Switzerland: Eurographics Association.

Waechter, M., Riess, F., Schimmel, T., Wendt, U., & Peinke, J. (2004). Stochastic analysis of different rough surfaces. *The European Physical Journal B- Condensed Matter and Complex Systems, 41*(2), 259-277.

Wagner, K. V. (2008). *Gestalt laws of perceptual organization: Law of Pragnanz.* Retrieved September 28, 2008, from http://psychology.about.com/od/ sensationandperception/ss/gestaltlaws_3.htm

Wang, X., Klette, R., & Rosenhahn, B. (2005). Geometric and photometric correction of projected rectangular pictures. In B. McCane (Ed.), *International Conference on Image and Vision Computing 2005 (IVCNZ),* (pp. 223-228).

Wang, H., & Brady, M. (1995). Real-time corner detection algorithm for motion estimation. *Image and Vision Computing, 13,* 695–703. doi:10.1016/0262-8856(95)98864-P

Wang, J., Oliveira, M. M., Xie, H., & Kaufman, A. E. (2005). Surface reconstruction using oriented charges. *Computer Graphics International, 2005,* 122–128. doi:10.1109/CGI.2005.1500390

Wang, Z., Bovik, A. C., Sheikh, H. R., & Celli, E. P. S. (2004). Image quality assessment: From error visibility to structural similarity. *IEEE Transactions on Image Processing, 13*(4), 1–14. doi:10.1109/TIP.2003.819861

Wedel, A., Rabe, C., Vaudrey, T., Brox, T., Franke, U., & Cremers, D. (2008). Efficient dense scene flow from sparse or dense stereo data. [Springer-Verlag.]. *ECCV, 2008,* 739–751.

White, J. V. (1984). *Using charts and graphs: 1000 ideas for visual persuasion.* New York, NY: Bowker.

Williams, N., Luebke, D., Cohen, J. D., Kelley, M., & Schubert, B. (2003). Perceptually guided simplification of lit, textured meshes. In *Symposium on Interactive 3D Graphics* (pp. 113-121). ACM Press.

Williams, D. J., & Shah, M. A. (1992). Fast algorithm for active contours and curve estimation. *CVGIP: Image Understanding, 55,* 14–26. doi:10.1016/1049-9660(92)90003-L

Witkin, A. P. (1983). Scale space filtering. *International Joint Conference on Artificial Intelligence,* Germany, (pp. 1019-1023).

Wittrock, M. C. (1989). Generative processes of comprehension. *Educational Psychology, 24,* 345–376. doi:10.1207/s15326985ep2404_2

Wolf, P. R., & DeWitt, B. A. (2000). *Elements of photogrammetry (with applications in GIS)* (3rd ed.). McGraw-Hill Higher Education.

Wong, A. K. C., Niu, P. Y., & He, X. (2005). Fast acquisition of dense depth data by a new structured light scheme. *Computer Vision and Image Understanding, 98,* 398–422. doi:10.1016/j.cviu.2004.09.003

Wong, K., & Cipolla, R. (2001). Structure and motion from silhouettes. *Computer Vision, ICCV,* 217–222.

Worth, A. J. (1996). *Brain segmentation in MRI.* Retrieved November, 2010, from http://www.cma.mgh.harvard.edu/seg/

Wright, A. (1970). *Designing visual aid.* New York, NY: Van Nostrand Reinhold.

Wu, J., Hu, S., Tai, C., & Sun, J. (2001). An effective feature-preserving mesh simplification scheme based on face constriction. In *9th Pacific Conference on Computer Graphics and Applications* (pp. 12 - 21). IEEE Press.

Yang, G., Shu, H. C., Han, G., & Luo, L. (2006). Efficient Legendre moment computation for grey level images. *Pattern Recognition, 39*, 74–80. doi:10.1016/j.patcog.2005.08.008

Yap, P.-T., & Raveendren, P. (2003). Image analysis by Krawtchouk moments. *IEEE Transactions on Image Processing, 12*(11), 1367–1377. doi:10.1109/TIP.2003.818019

Yap, P.-T., & Raveendren, P. (2005). An efficient method for the computation of Legendre moments. *IEEE Transactions on Pattern Analysis and Machine Intelligence, 27*(12), 1996–2002. doi:10.1109/TPAMI.2005.232

You, Y. L., & Kaveh, M. (2000). Fourth order partial differential equations for noise removal. *IEEE Transactions on Image Processing, 9*, 1723–1730. doi:10.1109/83.869184

Yu, Y., & Acton, S. T. (2002). Speckle reducing anisotropic diffusion. *IEEE Transactions on Image Processing, 11*(11), 1260–1270. doi:10.1109/TIP.2002.804276

Yu, Y., & Chang, C. (2006). A new edge detection approach based on image context analysis. *Image and Vision Computing, 24*(10), 1090–1102. doi:10.1016/j.imavis.2006.03.006

Zhang, H. (2005). Automatic sensor platform positioning and 3-D target modeling from underwater stereo sequences. Ph.D. Thesis, Coral Gables, Florida.

Zhang, J. (1999). *Reconstruction of geometry from cardiac MR images*. Master's thesis. Johns Hopkins University.

Zhang, S. (2005). *High-resolution, real-time 3-D shape measurement*. PhD Dissertation, Stony Brook University.

Zhang, Y., Bajaj, C., & Sohn, B.-S. (2003). Adaptive and quality 3D meshing from imaging data. In *SM'03: Proceedings of the Eighth ACM Symposium on Solid Modeling and Applications* (pp. 286–291). New York, NY: ACM.

Zhang, Z. (1995). An automatic and robust algorithm for determining motion and structure from two perspective images. In *Lecture Notes in Computer Science 970, Computer Analysis of Images and Patterns CAIP '95, 6th International Conference* (pp. 174-181).

Zhang, Z. (1998). A new multistage approach to motion and structure estimation by gradually enforcing geometric constrains. In R. Chin & T. C. Pong (Eds.), *Third Asian Conference on Computer Vision* (Vol. II, p. 567-574). Hong Kong, China: Springer.

Zhang, Z. H., Towers, C. E., & Towers, D. P. (2008). Shape and colour measurement of colourful objects by fringe projection. In J. Schmit, K. Creath & C. E. Towers (Ed.), *The Conference of Interferometry XIV: Techniques and Analysis, Vol. 7063*. Doi:10.1117/12.794561

Zhang, H., Lalor, M. J., & Burton, D. R. (1999). Spatiotemporal phase unwrapping for the measurement of discontinuous objects in dynamic fringe-projection phase-shifting profilometry. *Applied Optics, 38*, 3534–3541. doi:10.1364/AO.38.003534

Zhang, L., Dugas-Phocion, G., Samson, J., & Seitz, S. M. (2001). Single view modeling of free-form scenes. *Computer Vision and Pattern Recognition, 1*, 990–997.

Zhang, L., Liu, L., Gotsman, C., & Huang, H. (2010). Mesh reconstruction by meshless denoising and parameterization. *Computers & Graphics, 34*, 198–208. doi:10.1016/j.cag.2010.03.006

Zhang, R., Tsai, P.-S., Cryer, J., & Shah, M. (1999, August). Shape from shading: A survey. *IEEE Transactions on Pattern Analysis and Machine Intelligence, 21*(8), 690–706. doi:10.1109/34.784284

Zhang, Z. (2000). A flexible new technique for camera calibration. *IEEE Transactions on Pattern Analysis and Machine Intelligence, 22*(11), 1330–1334. doi:10.1109/34.888718

Zhang, Z. H., Ma, H. Y., Zhang, S. X., Guo, T., Towers, C. E., & Towers, D. P. (2011). Simple calibration of a phase-based 3D imaging system based on uneven fringe projection. *Optics Letters, 36*(5), 627–629. doi:10.1364/OL.36.000627

Zhang, Z. H., Towers, C. E., & Towers, D. P. (2006). Time efficient color fringe projection system for 3D shape and color using optimum 3-frequency selection. *Optics Express, 14*, 6444–6455. doi:10.1364/OE.14.006444

Zhang, Z. H., Towers, C. E., & Towers, D. P. (2007). Uneven fringe projection for efficient calibration in high-resolution 3D shape metrology. *Applied Optics, 46*, 6113–6119. doi:10.1364/AO.46.006113

Zhang, Z. H., Towers, C. E., & Towers, D. P. (2010). Compensating lateral chromatic aberration of a color fringe projection system for shape metrology. *Optics and Lasers in Engineering, 48*(2), 159–165. doi:10.1016/j.optlaseng.2009.04.010

Zhou, J., & Li, B. (2006). Robust ground plane detection with normalized homography in monocular sequences from a robot platform. In *International Conference on Image Processing* (pp. 3017-3020).

Zhu, H., Shu, H., Liang, J., Luo, L., & Coatrieus, J.-L. (2007a). Image analysis by discrete orthogonal Racah moments. *Signal Processing, 87*, 687–708. doi:10.1016/j.sigpro.2006.07.007

Zitnick, C., & Kanade, K. (2000). A cooperative algorithm for stereo matching and occlusion detection. *IEEE Transactions on Pattern Analysis and Machine Intelligence, 22*(7), 675–684. doi:10.1109/34.865184

# About the Contributors

**Umesh C. Pati** is an Associate Professor in the Department of Electronics and Communication Engineering at National Institute of Technology, Rourkela, India. He received a B.E. in Electrical Engineering from Regional Engineering College (now National Institute of Technology), Rourkela and M.Tech. and Ph.D. in Electrical Engineering from Indian Institute of Technology, Kharagpur, India. His current research interests are in the areas of image processing, computer vision, signal processing, and instrumentation. He has published one book and more than 40 research papers in referred journals and conference proceedings. He has served as referee in different international journals and conferences. He is a member of IEEE.

\* \* \*

**Aiert Amundarain** received an undergraduate degree in Mechanical Engineering in 1998 and a PhD in Mechanical Engineering in 2003, both at the University of Navarra. In 1999, he joined the Applied Mechanics Department at CEIT. At present, he is a research scientist with the Computer Graphics and ITS & Simulators groups. His main research lines are computer graphics programming, GPU programming, simulator training and interaction techniques in virtual environments, mechanical behavior, and structure-property relationships. He has participated in 10 research projects and has supervised one doctoral thesis. Non-confidential results have lead to roughly 20 papers being published in international and national journals and conference proceedings and three technical documents with an ISBN number.

**Viswanath Avasarala** received the Ph.D. degree in Information Science and Technology from Pennsylvania State University in 2006. Dr. Avasarala has been with GE Global Research since 2006 serving as an information scientist at the Industrial Artificial Intelligence lab in Niskayuna, where he leads research and development in machine learning and Artificial Intelligence. For the past few years, Dr. Avasarala has been leading or participating in several GE-funded efforts to develop distributed machine-learning applications for massive datasets, using cloud-based platforms. As a part of this effort, Dr. Avasarala has led a multi-year GE research effort for using network-science based ideas to automatically detect and rank white-spaces based on patent correlation and citation graphs. Dr. Avasarala has authored over fifteen publications in international venues, including highly ranked journals and book chapters. He has also served as an organizing committee member for several IEEE computational intelligence conferences and serves as a reviewer for *IEEE SMC Journal* and *ACM Artificial Intelligence Journal*.

**Ukaiko Bitrus-Ojiambo** holds a Bachelor of Arts degree in Psychology (1999) from the United States International University, and a Master of Arts degree in Communication from the University of South Alabama (2001). Ukaiko began research and corporate communications editorial work in 2004, before engaging as an Adjunct Instructor. Her teaching and research areas include: mass media; intercultural, interpersonal, and small group communication; persuasion; public speaking; and business communication. Ukaiko received a Transformative Teaching Award in December 2010. Ukaiko is also involved in faculty development and training. Her career objective is to influence African higher education through practice, consultation, and publication. Her doctoral research interest is in African cultural and film analysis. She and her husband reside in Nairobi.

**Diego Borro** is (since 2003) a research staff member of the Simulation Unit (Applied Mechanics Department) at CEIT, and (since 2004) an Assistant Professor at TECNUN, the Technological Campus of the University of Navarra in San Sebastian, Spain. Actually, he is the responsible for the Bioengineering Group of the Simulation Unit of the department. He received his MS in Computer Science from the University of Basque Country (2000) and his PhD in Computer Science from the University of Navarra (2003). He was visiting scholar (2004) at Integrated Media Systems Center (IMSC) at University of Southern California (USC). His main research areas include collision detection, haptic rendering, computer vision, and augmented reality; everything focuses on industrial and medical applications. He is member of the Haptics Group and the Computer Graphics Group at CEIT. He has participated in 15 research projects, has already supervised 4 doctoral thesis (6 in progress), and he is author or co-author of about 10 papers in international journals and roughly 40 articles in international conferences. He is Member of IEEE, ACM, and Eurographics societies.

**Carlos Buchart** is a research staff member of the Simulation Unit (Applied Mechanics Department) at CEIT in San Sebastian, Spain (since January 2011).He received his MS in Computer Science from the University of Carabobo (2005) and his PhD in Computer Science from the University of Navarra (2010). His main research lines include surface reconstruction, volumetric visualization and GPU programming, focusing in the medical application and giving horizontal support to industrial projects. He is member of the Computer Graphics Group and the Bioengineering Group at CEIT. He is author or co-author of two international journal papers and about 10 international conferences contributions.

**Suhana Chikatla** is the Instructional Designer in the Department of e-Learning at Wallace State, Hanceville, USA. She also volunteers as the Honorary Director of Virtual Training at a refuge school in Thailand, Kaw Tha Blay Learning Center. Her duties include recruiting virtual teachers and teaching online via Skype technology. She was born in India. She received a B.S. in Computer Science, from Spicer Memorial College, in 1997 and then earned a M.A. in Secondary Education, from Andrews University, in 1999 along with a second M.A. in Sociology, from Tilak Maharashtra Vidyapeeth, in 2000. The burning desire of finding quality and alternative means of distance education drove her to earn a Ph.D. in Instructional Design and Development at the University of South Alabama, Mobile, which she completed in 2010. While working on her Doctorate she was awarded a graduate fellowship. Suhana is married to Royce Sutton of St. John's, Antigua.

**Rimon Elias** received his MCS and PhD degrees both in Computer Science from the University of Ottawa, Canada in 1999 and 2004, respectively. His main interests are computer vision, image processing, computer graphics, visualization, and Web technologies. He published one book, and several encyclopedia, journal, and conference papers. He taught at the University of Ottawa, Canada, for several years before joining the Faculty of Media Engineering and Technology at the German University in Cairo, Egypt. He is a senior member of IEEE and listed in Who's Who in the World and Who's Who in Science and Engineering.

**Phalguni Gupta** received the Doctoral degree from Indian Institute of Technology Kharagpur, India in 1986. Currently he is a Professor in the Department of Computer Science & Engineering, Indian Institute of Technology Kanpur, Kanpur, India. He works in the field of biometrics, data structures, sequential algorithms, parallel algorithms, and image processing. He is an author of 2 books and 13 book chapters. He has published more than 225 papers in international journals and international conferences. He is responsible for several research projects in the area of biometric systems, image processing, graph theory, and network flow. Prior to joining IITK in 1987, he worked in Space Applications Centre Ahmedabad, Indian Space Research Organization, India.

**P.S. Hiremath**, Professor, Department of P. G. Studies and Research in Computer Science, Gulbarga University, Gulbarga-585106, Karnataka, INDIA. He has obtained M.Sc. degree in 1973 and Ph.D. degree in 1978 in Applied Mathematics from Karnatak University, Dharwad. He had been in the Faculty of Mathematics and Computer Science of various Institutions in India, namely, National Institute of Technology, Surathkal (1977-79), Coimbatore Institute of Technology, Coimbatore (1979-80), National Institute of Technology, Tiruchinapalli (1980-86), Karnatak University, Dharwad (1986-1993) and has been presently working as Professor of Computer Science in Gulbarga University, Gulbarga (1993 onwards). His research areas of interest are computational fluid dynamics, optimization techniques, image processing, and pattern recognition. He has published 70 research papers in peer reviewed international journals.

**Sai Tejaswi Jonnalagadda** received his B. Tech degree in Computer Science from Kakatiya University, Hyderabad, India. He is currently a Software Engineer at Hetero Pharmacy, Hyderabad, India. Sai Tejaswi research interests are in the areas of pattern recognition and artificial intelligence. During his education, Sai Tejaswi has developed intelligent systems using decision-tree based classification and regression algorithms for use in multiple domains.

**Vandana Dixit Kaushik** is an Assistant Professor in the Department of Computer Science & Engineering, Harcourt Butler Technological Institute, Kanpur. She joined the department in 2003. She works in the field of image processing, database management systems, and biometrics. Most of her publications are available in the international conferences and journals. She submitted her Ph D thesis on 3D image processing algorithms to Gautam Buddh Technical University, Lucknow.

**Premysl Krsek** is an Associate Professor at Faculty of Information Technology, Brno University of Technology. Born 1969, he specializes in computer graphics, image and signal processing, human-machine interfaces, and applications. He received his M.Sc. degree from Faculty of Mechanical Engineering, Brno University of Technology in 3D in 1993. In 2001, he received Ph.D. degree from the same faculty in "Direct generation of FEM models from CT/MR data." Since 2008, he works as an Associate Professor (doc.) on the Faculty of Information technologies. His specialization is 3D reconstruction of human tissues from CT/MRI image diagnostic data and clinical applications of this technique (over 200 surgeries). Premysl Krsek is (co) author of over 25 conference papers, 3 book chapters, and several successful applications in human medicine.

**P U Praveen Kumar** received the B.Sc. degree in Computer Science and the M.Sc. degree in Computer Science from Kuvempu University, India, in 2006 and 2008, respectively. He is currently working toward the Ph.D. degree in Computer Science at Kuvempu University. His research interests include image processing, pattern recognition, computer vision, and combinatorial optimization.

**Nasrul Humaimi Mahmood** received his B.Sc. and M.Sc. degrees in Electrical and Electronic Engineering from Universiti Kebangsaan Malaysia (UKM) and Universiti Teknologi Malaysia (UTM) respectively. He obtained his Ph.D. degree in Engineering from the University of Warwick, United Kingdom. His research areas are three-dimensional (3D) object reconstruction from video sequences and from multiple views, biomedical image processing, medical electronics, and rehabilitation engineering. Since 1999, he is serving at the Faculty of Electrical Engineering, UTM. His current research interests include three-dimensional (3D) object reconstruction from video sequences and from multiple views, biomedical image processing, medical electronics, and rehabilitation engineering. Within the Faculty of Electrical Engineering at the Universiti Teknologi Malaysia, he teaches a number of courses related to his research and elementary to the electrical and electronics curriculum. Currently he is a Senior Lecturer at the Faculty of Electrical Engineering, Universiti Teknologi Malaysia, Skudai, Johor, Malaysia.

**S. Manikandan** is presently working as Scientist at Electronics and Radar Development Establishment, Defense Research and Development Organization, India. Earlier he was with Neurofocus Inc., as Senior Research Engineer. He has completed BE from Madras University, ME and PhD from CEG, Anna University, Chennai. His area of interests includes image and video processing, computer vision, and pattern recognition. He is a reviewer and Associate Editor for many leading image processing journals. He has chaired and delivered keynote addresses in many national and international conferences.

**S. Mohan** got his B.E in Computer Science and Engineering in 1998 from Bharathidasan University, Tamilnadu, India and M.Tech in Computer Cognition Technology in 2002 from University of Mysore, India. His PhD on Image Based Modelling and Rendering was also from University of Mysore in 2009. He is working as Professor and Head of Computer Science & Engg, Dr.NGP Institute of Technology (KMCH Group of institutions), Coimbatore, Tamilnadu since Apr 2011. Prior to that he worked in private universities like Amrita University and Karunya University. Also he worked as technical evangelist in Infosys Technologies, Mysore in Education & Research Department. His areas of research interest include computer vision, video analytics, and 3D computing.

**S. Murali** is the President of Maharaja Educational Trust, Mysore. He was working as Professor and Head-ISE department in PES college of Engg, Mandya. He got PhD from University of Mysore in 2002. His research interests include computer vision, document imaging, and pattern recognition.

**C. J. Prabhakar** is an Assistant Professor, Department of Studies in Computer Science, Kuvempu University, Karnataka, India. He has obtained M.Sc. degree in Mathematics from Kuvempu University in 1998, and the M.Tech. degree in Computer Science from University of Mysore in 2001. He has received the Ph.D. degree in Computer Science in the year 2009 from Department of Computer Science, Gulbarga University, India. His research interests include 3D reconstruction, stereo vision, and face recognition.

**Miloslav Richter** is an Assistant Professor at Faculty of Electrical Engineering and Communication, Brno University of Technology. Born 1968, he specializes in industrial applications of image processing and machine vision. He received his Ing. (M.Sc.) and Dr. (Ph.D) degrees from Brno University of Technology in 1991 and 2004, respectively, where he has wordked as Assistant Professor since 1993. Both works concern of machine vision. His current research interests include camera system calibration, 3D reconstruction, and visual-based traffic control – detection of red light violation, speed measurement, and traffic parameters detection. In these domains he participated in several successful industry applications.

**Michal Spanel** is an Assistant Professor at Faculty of Information Technology, Brno University of Technology. He received his M.Sc. degree in Computer Science and Engineering from the Brno University of Technology in 2003 and Ph.D. degree in Information Technology in 2011. Before joining the Faculty of Information Technology as an Assistant Lecturer and Researcher in 2006, he worked in industry (Virtual Reality Media s.r.o. and Hexagon Systems s.r.o.) in the field of flight simulation technologies. His research interests include medical image processing, computer vision and pattern recognition, 3D geometrical modeling and 3D meshing, and development of virtual collaborative environments for medicine. He (co)authored more than 15 conference papers and several software packages and applications in these areas.

**Rajeev Srivastava** was born in 1974 in Jaunpur, Uttar Pradesh, India. He received his B.E. degree in Computer Engineering from D.D.U. Gorakhpur University, Gorakhpur, Uttar Pradesh, India; & M.E. in Computer Technology and Applications and Ph.D. in Computer Engineering both from Delhi University, Delhi, India. He has about 13 years of teaching and research experience. Currently he is working as an Associate Professor in the Dept. of Computer Engineering, ITBHU, Varanasi, India since November 2007. Prior to joining ITBHU, he has been with NSIT, Delhi (Delhi University) from June 2001-November 2007 and GBPEC, Pauri, Uttarakhand, India from July 1998-June 2001. His research interests include image processing and computer algorithms. He has published around 30 research papers in international journals and conferences. He is listed in Marquis Who's Who in Science and Engineering-2011, USA; and "2000 Outstanding Intellectuals of the world-2010" by IBC, Cambridge. He has also been selected for the award of "Top 100 Educators of the World-2010," and "Man of the year award-2010," both by IBC, Cambridge. He is reviewer and member of editorial board of 02 international journals; member of technical program committee of 08 international conferences; and on the reviewer panel of Tata McGraw Hill and Oxford University Press, India. He has also received the research grant from the Ministry of HRD, Govt. of India, New Delhi, India for his project on "E-content development for the subject Digital Image Processing and Machine Vision."

379

**Sudheer Tumu** received his B. Tech. degree in Computer Science Engineering from Andhra University, Visakhapatnam, India in 2006. He is currently a Graduate student in Computer Science Department at University at Albany, State University of New York (SUNY). His research interests include computer vision, robotics, and machine learning. Since May 2010, Sudheer has been working as research intern at Industrial Artificial Intelligence (IAI) lab, GE Global Research, Niskayuna, USA, where he focused on developing probabilistic reasoning algorithms for monitoring clinical environments using uncertain evidence.

**Prasad Wadekar** received his B.E. degree in Computer Technology from Nagpur University, Maharashtra, India in 2005. He is currently working as a Software Engineer at Mahindra Satyam and Contractor at GE Energy. His research interests include computer vision, robotics, machine learning, and programming languages.

**Pavel Zemcik** is an Associate Professor and Vice-Dean of Faculty of Information Technology, Brno University of Technology. Born in 1965, he specializes in computer graphics, image and signal processing, human-machine interfaces, and applications. He received his Ing. (M.Sc.) and Dr. (Ph.D.) degrees from Brno University of Technology in 1989 and 1995, respectively, where he has worked as an Associate Professor (doc.) since 1999. He spent significant part of his professional life abroad, e.g. on an exchange at University of Bristol, UK, University of Surrey, UK, as a Researcher at Lappeenranta University of Technology, Finland, or as a visiting Professor at Penn State, Erie, Pa, USA. In 2002 he was appointed as a head of Department of Computer Graphics and Multimedia and in 2008 as a Vice-Dean for external relations. Pavel Zemcik is (co) author of over 15 journal papers, 50 conference papers, 3 book chapters, and several successful applications in industry and traffic.

**Zonghua Zhang** received the B.S., M.Sc and Ph.D degrees from Tianjin University, China, in 1992, 1998, and 2001, respectively. He is a Professor in the Department of Mechanical Engineering of Hebei University of Technology. He worked as a research fellow at School of Mechanical Engineering in University of Leeds, UK, from 2007 to 2009, research associate at Department of Mechanical Engineering in Heriot-Watt University, UK, from 2005 to 2007, Postdoctoral Researcher at BiomotionLab, first in Ruhr-University in Bochum, Germany and then in Queen's University, Canada, from 2003 to 2005. He acts as a reviewer for several leading international journals and conferences, and he is author of more than 60 papers, including four book chapters. His research interests include optical metrology, 3D imaging and modeling, human motion analysis, 3D biometrics, digital signal, and image processing.

# Index

3D acquisition systems 315
2D affine homography 342
3D broken objects 318
3D data 1-2, 21, 46, 149, 193, 283, 338, 349-350
2D latices 253
3D model acquisition 20, 46, 318
3D modeling 15-16, 28, 127, 159, 197-198, 206, 213, 313
3D object reconstruction 45, 160, 340, 350-351
3D object shape 1
3D orthonormal system 340
3D Point Clustering 287, 299, 301
3D scanned fragments 318
3D scanners 315
3D scene reconstruction 27, 179
3D shape calculation 269
3D surface reconstruction 24, 46, 86, 134, 159, 311, 338, 350-351

## A

AdaBoost 185, 196
Additive Noise 52-53, 62-66, 68, 72-73, 75-78, 80, 85, 89, 249
anisotropic moments 246, 257
Assimilation and Accommodation 159, 163-164

## B

Band Pass Filter 271
Bar Charts 149-150, 153, 163
Baseline 34, 45, 47, 119, 127, 170, 198, 257, 284-287, 307-308, 310-311, 313
Blackman window 270

## C

CAD/CAM technology 339
Calibration Matrix 6, 31, 36, 40-41, 47, 293
central limit theorem 71, 224
charts 137-155, 160, 162-164
Chebyshev polynomials 228-230
cleavage sites 314, 317-318, 323-330, 332-336
Cognitive Flexibility Theory 159, 162-163
Cognitive Load Theory 158, 163
Coherence Principle 139, 158, 163
Communication Theory or Principles 164
complementary part detection 314, 325, 336-337
Composite RGB Fringe Image 269, 280, 283
Computed Tomography (CT) 11
Computer-Aided Design (CAD) 338
Compute Unified Device Architecture (CUDA) 112
Conjugate Epipolar Lines 34, 47, 117, 125
Contiguity Principle 143, 151, 156, 158, 164
Contiguity Theory 158, 164
Corner Detection 174-176, 179-180
cyclic local approximation 254

## D

deformable models 16-17, 24, 27
Delaunay Triangulation (DT) 27
Depth Mapping 170, 180
DLP (Digital Light Processing) 265-266, 273, 283
Dual Channel Process 158, 164

## E

epipolar geometry 3-5, 7, 26-27, 29, 126, 133, 135, 171, 191, 295
Epipolar Line 5, 34-35, 37, 44, 47, 133, 170, 174, 296-297

Epipolar Plane 5, 34, 47, 170
Epipole 34, 36-37, 47, 173
Epistemological Beliefs 148-149, 163-164
Essential Matrix 37, 47
Exhaustive Search 176, 180
Extrinsic Parameters 6, 10, 32, 45-47, 116-118, 130

**F**

Fourier Transform 15, 51, 75, 123-124, 232, 255, 267-271, 274, 281-283
Fringe Projection 265-267, 272, 274-275, 277, 280-283, 338
Fundamental Matrix 7, 21, 29, 35-37, 40, 44-47, 118, 126, 130-131, 135, 171-173, 297-298

**G**

Galarkin methods 261
Gaussian distribution 62, 76, 89, 125, 224-225, 320
Gaussian noise 68, 123-125, 135, 224-225, 233-234
Gibbs error 243-245, 255, 257
Gram polynomial 231, 234-235, 257, 259-260
Gram-Schmidt orthogonalization process 230
Ground Plane Representation 287, 290

**H**

High Dynamic Range Imaging (HDRI) 165, 180
Homographic Transformation 45, 284, 308, 310-311, 313
Homography Matrix 38-39, 47, 204, 292-297, 308-309, 313
Homomorphic Filter 78, 84-85, 89

**I**

Ideal Plane 30, 41-42, 47
Ideal Point 47
Image Segmentation 14-16, 22, 24, 50, 55, 57-58, 92, 124, 190, 193, 196, 341
Intrinsic Parameters 6, 9, 31-32, 47, 116, 126-127, 342
iterative corresponding point (ICP) algorithm 343

**J**

JUDOCA 284, 288, 290, 308
Junction Detection 287-288, 305-306, 308
Junction Matching 287, 295

**L**

LCOS (Liquid Crystal On Silicon) 283
Line Chart 150, 155, 164
local approximation 253-254
Local Triangulations 104, 106, 113

**M**

Magnetic Resonance Imaging (MRI) 11, 62
Markov Random Field (MRF) 196, 198
Markov Random Fields (MRF) 310
Mean Square Error (MSE) 165, 180
medical imaging 2, 11, 15, 21-22, 24, 82, 88, 179, 263, 340
Modality Principle 156, 158-159, 164
Monocular Vision 194, 196-197, 213-214, 285, 313
multi-level extraction 286
multi-level granularity 337
Multimedia Principle 156, 158, 160, 164
multiviews reconstruction method 349
multiviews technique 349
myoelectric signals 340

**N**

Noise 8, 12, 15-17, 28, 41, 44-45, 49, 51-53, 56, 59-66, 68-80, 82, 85-89, 91-95, 100, 110, 122-125, 128-129, 135, 143, 148, 163-164, 174, 176, 200, 217, 223-225, 233-234, 240, 243, 246, 249-251, 267-268, 271-272, 310, 314, 319, 322, 329, 336
Normal Estimation 94, 100, 102, 113

**O**

Optical Axis 30, 33, 48, 340
Optical Center 30-31, 33-34, 36, 48, 184, 297, 304
Orthosis 340

**P**

Partial differential equation based filters 89
PDE-Based Filters 68, 85, 89
Perceptual Limitation Theory 164
Performance Metrics 53, 89
Perspective Image 197-199, 207, 211, 214, 291
Perspective Projection Matrix 30-31, 35-37, 42, 48, 118, 291
Phase Calculation 266, 270, 273-274, 277, 283

Phase Shifting 267, 283
Pictorial Charts 140, 164
Pie Charts 137, 147-149, 153-154, 164
Pixel 4, 6, 9, 27, 32, 45, 50, 57, 60-61, 65, 74-77, 118, 121, 124, 127-128, 169, 175, 185-188, 196, 214, 217, 219, 221, 267-268, 270-272, 274, 276, 280, 286, 297, 303-306
pixel coordinates 217, 219, 221, 303
Point Clustering 284, 287, 299, 301, 305-306, 313
Point Matching 7, 313
Points Projection 91, 107, 109, 113
polynomial regression 223, 225-227, 231, 251, 254, 263
Principal Point 6, 30, 32, 47-48, 116, 127, 340
Prior Misconceptions 148, 164
prosthetic designs 338

## R

Random Forest 187-188, 196
RANSAC 7-8, 21, 26-27, 36-37, 39, 131, 293-294, 297-298, 302, 308-309
region-level extraction 286
Restoration 49-53, 56-57, 61-64, 67, 77, 81-83, 87, 89, 135, 315
RGB channels 265, 268
Rotation Matrix 6, 32-34, 36, 41, 48, 116-118, 127, 293, 297, 318, 342
roughness detection descriptor 319
roughness factor 319-321, 337

## S

Savitzky-Golay smoothing 230, 232, 244, 253-256
shape from silhouette (SfS) 340
Shape Measurement 25, 265, 272, 281-283
Simultaneous Localization and Mapping (SLAM) 8
sinusoidal fringe 265-266, 268-270, 272-276, 279-281, 283

Speckle Noise 52-53, 59-62, 69-70, 74-78, 80, 82, 85, 87-89
Speckle Reduction 53, 75, 77-78, 80-86, 88-89
Spectral compactness 240, 242-243
stereo imaging 3-5, 7, 27, 133
Stereo Matching 27, 45, 118-119, 122, 127-128, 130-131, 133, 136, 168, 173-174, 179-180, 192, 194-195, 308, 311
Stereo Views 284, 310, 313
Stereovision 119-120, 122, 128, 132-133, 181-183, 186, 197, 214, 310, 312
stereo vision 3, 5, 26-27, 29, 34, 36, 114-116, 118, 122, 131-133, 136, 168, 172, 196-197, 310, 312
Structure from Motion (SFM) 115, 181, 196

## T

teleoperation 284
Three-Dimensional (3D) Charts 164
Tone Mapping 165-169, 179-180
turntable calibration 342
Two-Dimensional (2D) Charts 164

## V

Vandermonde matrix 226-227
Vanishing Point 198-201, 206-207, 212, 214
Visual Communication Perspective 155, 164
Visual Communication Theory 143, 148, 160, 163-164
Visual Fusion problem 286
volumetric scene reconstruction 134, 287, 311
Voxel 15, 115, 284, 287, 303-305, 307, 309, 312-313
Voxelization 287, 302, 304, 306, 309-310, 313

## W

Widely-Separated Stereo Views 284, 313
Wireframe 199, 206, 209, 213-214